Von Kontinuitäten und Brüchen: Ostrecht im Wandel der Zeiten

Festschrift für Friedrich-Christian Schroeder zum 75. Geburtstag

Herausgegeben von Herbert Küpper

PETER LANG
Frankfurt am Main · Berlin · Bern · Bruxelles · New York · Oxford · Wien

Bibliografische Information der Deutschen Nationalbibliothek
Die Deutsche Nationalbibliothek verzeichnet diese Publikation in der Deutschen Nationalbibliografie; detaillierte bibliografische Daten sind im Internet über http://dnb.d-nb.de abrufbar.

Umschlaggestaltung:
© Olaf Glöckler, Atelier Platen, Friedberg

Gedruckt auf alterungsbeständigem,
säurefreiem Papier.

ISBN 978-3-631-61995-7

www.peterlang.de

Sabine Leutheusser-Schnarrenberger
Bundesministerin der Justiz
Mitglied des Deutschen Bundestages

Vorwort für die Festschrift zum 75. Geburtstag von Prof. Dr. Dres. h.c. Friedrich-Christian Schroeder

Das Institut für Ostrecht München e. V. arbeitet seit 1973 unter der wissenschaftlichen Leitung von Friedrich-Christian Schroeder. Fast ebenso lange, nämlich seit 1977, ist innerhalb der Bundesregierung das Bundesministerium der Justiz für die Zusammenarbeit und Förderung des Instituts zuständig. Die Transformation der Rechtsordnungen der Staaten Mittel- und Osteuropas, der Aufbau rechtsstaatlicher Strukturen und die erfolgreiche Integration vieler Staaten in die Europäische Union waren und sind enorme politische Herausforderungen. Die Kooperation mit den Staaten Mittel- und Osteuropas ist deshalb auch für die deutsche Rechtswissenschaft eine wichtige Aufgabe. Das Institut für Ostrecht trägt mit seinem juristischen Sachverstand und seinen internationalen Kontakten dazu in vielfältiger Weise bei. Dies ist nicht zuletzt das Verdienst von Friedrich-Christian Schroeder.

Friedrich-Christian Schroeder wirkt seit vielen Jahren als Wissenschaftler und politischer Berater über die deutschen Grenzen hinweg. Er studierte Rechtswissenschaft und Osteuropakunde an der Universität Bonn, dem Osteuropa-Institut der FU Berlin und der Universität München. Der Promotion 1963 folgte 1968 die Habilitation in München mit der Lehrbefugnis für Strafrecht, Strafprozessrecht und Ostrecht. Alsbald erhielt er einen Ruf an die Universität Regensburg, der er bis zu seiner Emeritierung treu blieb. Prägend für seine wissenschaftliche Arbeit war die Verankerung sowohl im deutschen Recht, vor allem im Straf- und Strafprozessrecht, als auch im Ostrecht. Der Umfang seines publizistischen Werkes ist beeindruckend.

Unter der wissenschaftlichen Leitung von Friedrich-Christian Schroeder wurde das Institut für Ostrecht zu einem wichtigen Verfasser qualifizierter Gutachten für die deutsche Justiz und die öffentliche Verwaltung. Zugleich pflegte der Jubilar schon vor 1989 intensive Kontakte mit Kolleginnen und Kollegen über den Eisernen Vorhang hinweg und führte bei Veranstaltungen Juristinnen und Juristen aus Ost und West zusammen, als dies noch keineswegs selbstverständlich war. Manche seiner damaligen Gesprächskontakte haben in unseren Nachbarstaaten in Staat, Wissenschaft oder Wirtschaft inzwischen hohe Positionen inne. Nach dem Ende der SED-Diktatur nahm Friedrich-Christian Schroeder aktiv an ihrer wissenschaftlichen Aufarbeitung teil. Auch in der internationalen rechtlichen Zusammenarbeit mit den ehemals sozialistischen Staaten engagierte und engagiert er sich intensiv. Unter seiner Leitung wurde die im Institut für Ostrecht vorhandene Expertise zu einer wichtigen Stütze der deutschen Gesetzgebungsberatung in Osteuropa und darüber hinaus. 2009 führte er das Institut für Ostrecht in das „Bündnis für das deutsche Recht" und intensivierte so noch einmal die Zusammenarbeit auch mit dem Bundesministerium der Justiz.

Friedrich-Christian Schroeder wollte sich nie nur auf die Arbeit eines Rechtswissenschaftlers konzentrieren, und schon gar nicht begnügte er sich mit der Existenz im Elfenbeinturm der Wissenschaft. Seine Beiträge in der Frankfurter Allgemeinen Zeitung, seine Glossen und couragierten Stellungnahmen lesen sich mindestens mit so viel Gewinn wie seine wissenschaftlichen Werke.

Das Wirken von Friedrich-Christian Schroeder hat vielfache Anerkennung gefunden, zahlreiche Auszeichnungen im In- und Ausland sind ihm zu Teil geworden. Zu nennen sind etwa die Ehrendoktorwürden der Universitäten Wrocław (Breslau) und Huánuco sowie der Verdienstorden der Bundesrepublik Deutschland. Ich gratuliere Friedrich-Christian Schroeder zu seinem 75. Geburtstag und wünsche ihm noch viele Jahre fruchtbaren Schaffens im Dienst des Rechts und der grenzüberschreitenden rechtlichen Zusammenarbeit.

Sabine Leutheusser-Schnarrenberger, MdB

Bundesministerin der Justiz

Inhaltsverzeichnis

Zivil- und Zivilprozessrecht, Wirtschaftsrecht

Öffentliches Recht

Rechtswissenschaft in Ost und West

Straf- und Strafprozessrecht

Wergeld, Bloodwite, and the Emergence of Criminal Law

(Article 1 of the Short Redaction of the Russkaia Pravda)

Prof. Dr. Ferdinand Feldbrugge[*]

The immediate purpose of this paper is to establish the identity of the recipient of the sum of 40 *grivna*, to be paid in case of homicide, according to the first article of the early medieval Russian law code, the *Russkaia Pravda*. Whether the examination of the relevant minutiae of the law of medieval Russia will produce more than an answer to this question alone is something which will become clear in the course of our investigation. But before embarking on this endeavour I owe the benevolent reader a good bit of preliminary explanation. The confines of this paper do not permit such an introduction to be equipped with the appropriate arguments and footnotes; a general reference to the most important literature will have to suffice[1]. For the rest the reader must take the author's word for it[2].

I. Preliminary Explanation

The most eminent monument of early medieval Russian law is the *Russkaia Pravda* ('Russian Law', hereafter *RP*). It has come down to us in a great many

---

* Professor Emeritus für Osteuropäisches Recht der Universität Leiden.

1 The three-volume edition Pravda Russkaia by B.D. Grekov (ed.) of the USSR Academy of Sciences is still the standard modern publication, Moscow-Leningrad, 1940 (I), 1947 (II) and Moscow, 1963 (III); the second volume (quoted below as *Pravda Russkaia*, II) contains a comprehensive collection of excerpts and quotations from relevant Russian and foreign scholarly works, arranged as a commentary to both the *Short* and the *Expanded Pravda*. Other works of primary importance are the publication of the *RP* in the Pamiatniki Russkogo Prava, I, Moscow, 1952 (comments and modern Russian translations by *A.A. Zimin*), and in the series Rossiiskoe Zakonodatel'stvo X-XX vv., part I, Zakonodatel'stvo Drevnei Rusi (introduction and comments by *Ia.N. Shchapov* and *T.E. Novitskaia*), *A.A. Zimin's* monograph Pravda Russkaia, Moscow, 1999 (published posthumously; *A.A. Zimin* died in 1980), and *G. Baranowski*, Die Russkaja Pravda – ein mitteralterliches Rechtsdenkmal, Frankfurt a.M., 2005. The *Pamiatniki Russkogo Prava* will hereafter be quoted as *PRP*, the *Rossiiskoe Zakonodatel'stvo* as *RZ*.

2 The following 'preliminary explanation' is a very condensed version of the chapter on the *Russkaia Pravda* in my Law in Medieval Russia (Law in Eastern Europe, vol. 59), Leiden/Boston, 2009, 33-58.

copies, which can mainly be divided into two groups[3], a shorter text, known as the *Short Pravda*, and a much longer text, known as the *Expanded Pravda*. Most of the provisions of the *Short Pravda* are also found in the *Expanded Pravda*, but always in a somewhat different wording. All modern commentators agree that the *Short Pravda* predates the *Expanded Pravda*[4].

The *Short Pravda* consists of two main parts, the first 18 articles[5] form the so-called *Pravda of Iaroslav*, which is followed by a new preamble and arts. 19-41, known as the *Pravda of Iaroslav's Sons*[6]. The *Pravda of Iaroslav* is attributed to the Kievan grand prince *Iaroslav the Wise* (who ruled from 1016-1054) and is connected by most authors with inter-ethnic turmoil in Novgorod, where *Iaroslav* was the resident prince when his father *Vladimir*, grand prince of Kiev, died in 1015.

The *Pravda of Iaroslav* is not unlike some of the early Germanic laws, known as *leges barbarorum*; the *Lex Saxonum* of 802/803 offers the closest paallel. Such laws usually represent primarily an edited registration of customary law, occasioned by particular political circumstances. The background of *Iaroslav's Pravda* is supposed to be the violent disturbances which broke out between the population of Novgorod and members of *Iaroslav's druzhina*, his predominantly Viking companions and followers. These troubles had to be addressed urgently, as *Iaroslav* had suddenly become involved in the struggle for the succession to his father's throne in Kiev.

The first ten articles of *Iaroslav's Pravda* concern homicide and lesser forms of personal violence; the remaining eight articles are devoted to property disputes, three of them concerning slaves. There has been and still is some debate whether the *Pravda of Iaroslav* reflects ancient Slavic customary law or rather Germanic law. The question becomes moot if one accepts that these old-

---

3 A third text, known as the *Abridged Pravda* (*Sokrashchennaia Pravda*), can be disregarded in the context of this paper.

4 The final compilation of the *Short Pravda* is dated variously in the period between 1054 (death of *Iaroslav the Wise*) and 1136, with a date soon after 1054 being more likely; the final compilation of the *Expanded Pravda* at some time in the 12th century, with the *Short Pravda* serving as one of the sources. Cf. *A.A. Zimin*, Pravda Russkaia, 133-150. A divergent but well-argued position is occupied by *M.B. Sverdlov*, who regards the *Pravda of Iaroslav* and the *Pravda of Iaroslav's sons* as basically a single text; see *M.B. Sverdlov*, 'K istorii teksta Kratkoi redaktsii Russkoi Pravdy', Vspomogatel'nye Istoricheskie Distsipliny X, Leningrad, 1978, 135-158.

5 The division of the *RP* into articles, followed by all modern authors, is the one established by the USSR Academy of Sciences edition in three volumes.

6 Two separate provisions conclude the *Short Pravda*, art. 42 (the *pokon virnyi*, the law concerning the bloodwite collector) and art. 43 (the *urok mostnikov*, the bridge builders' statute).

est layers of Slavic and Germanic law shared common roots and were very similar[7].

II. Terminology: Wergeld and Bloodwite

Wergeld, a term well known in Old-Germanic law, will be used to refer to payment to be made by the offender and/or his kin to the relatives of the victim (in the case of homicide); the equivalent in Old-Russian is *golovnichestvo* ('head-money'), which occurs only once in the *RP* (in art. 5 of the *Expanded Pravda*)[8]. In both the *Short* and the *Expanded Pravda* the term of 'payment *za golovu*' ('for the head') is encountered several times; the *Expanded Pravda* also refers to the killer as the *golovnik.*

The standard amount of wergeld for the killing of a freeman in Old-Russian law was 40 *grivna*; lesser offences against the person resulted in payments of 12 or 3 *grivna* to the victim.

The fine due in cases of homicide or other offences against the person is called *vira*, a term used a number of times in the *Expanded Pravda*[9]. Both *G.Vernadsky* and *D.H. Kaiser* translate it as 'bloodwite', a practice which will be followed here. The bloodwite is a fine payable to the prince. In other sources, but not in the *RP*, *vira* confusingly occurs with the meaning of wergeld; several authors have sought the etymological origin of *vira* in the Germanic 'wergeld'.

III. Article 1 of the Short Pravda

Before getting into the central question of this paper, we must look at the text of art. 1 of the *Short Pravda*. The language of the *Pravda of Iaroslav* is unusually elliptic, which gives rise to varying translations. For the purpose of this paper I shall attempt a literal translation first[10].

---

7 I have discussed this question more extensively in the first chapter of my *Law in Medieval Russia, Law in Eastern Europe*, vol. 59, Leiden/Boston, 2009, esp. 5-18 ('The Indo-European Aspect'); an earlier and slightly different version of this text in F. Feldbrugge (ed.), *The Law's Beginnings*, Leiden/Boston, 2003, 258-268.

8 *Wer-* is of the same origin as in werewolf and has the meaning of 'man' (comp. Latin *vir*); 'wergeld' therefore means 'man-money'. *Vernadsky* has the highly unusual *bot* and *Kaiser* 'compensation', which is less precise than 'man-money'. On the complex terminology of private and public 'fines', see *K. v. Amira*, Grundriss des Germanischen Rechts, Strassburg, 1913 (3rd ed.), 243-246. The standard Latin term for wergeld is *compositio*.

9 In the *Short Pravda*, *virnoe* occurs in art. 20 and *vira* in art. 42 (the law on the payment of bloodwite).

10 The Old-Russian text, taken from the First Academic Copy, used in almost all editions and translations, is: *Ub'et' muzh' muzha, to m'stit' bratu brata, ili synovi ottsa, liubo ottsiu syna, ili bratochadu, liubo sestrinu synovi; ashche ne budet' kto m'stia, to 40 griven za golovu; ashche budet' rusin, liubo gridin, liubo kupchina, liubo iabetnik, liubo mechnik, ashche izgoi budet', libo slovenin, to 40 griven polozhiti za n'.*

> [If] a man kills a[nother] man, then [it is] for the brother to avenge [his] brother, or for the son [to avenge his] father or for the father [his] son, or for the son of the brother or for the son of the sister [to avenge] [their uncle, their cousin?]; if there will not be anybody to avenge [the person killed], then 40 *grivna* for the head; if [the person killed] will be a *Rusin*, or a guardsman, or a merchant, or a *iabetnik*, or a swordman, or if it will be an *izgoi*, or a *Slovenin*, then 40 *grivna* to pay for him.

A more easily understandable and freer translation, implying however a considerable amount of interpretation, would be:

> If a man kills a[nother] man, [the following relatives of the murdered man avenge him] the brother avenges the brother, or the son the father, or the father the son, or the son of the brother or the son of the sister [avenge their respective uncles]; if there is no one to avenge [the murdered man], then 40 *grivna* wergeld; be [the murdered man] a *Rusin*: a bodyguard, a merchant, a steward, or a sheriff, or rather an *izgoi* or a [Novgorodian] Slav, his wergeld is 40 *grivna*.

The original text and the literal translation raise many questions, some of which are answered implicitly in the second translation. Most of these questions can be left aside in this paper, but a few require some comment.

In accordance with the customs of those times, only men are mentioned as potential killers and victims. There are good reasons to assume that women were equally protected by the rule. In the *Expanded Pravda* (art. 16) the fine/bloodwite to be paid for killing a male slave was 5 *grivna*, and 6 *grivna* for a female slave.

The enumeration of persons mentioned in the last sentence of art. 1 suggests two main categories, *Rusini* (Rus' men, in *D.H. Kaiser's* translation), and local people – Novgorodians and *izgoi* ('outsiders'). The *Rusini* were in fact mostly Scandinavians, belonging to the prince's entourage[11], and then the four special categories which follow the *Rusini* in the text appear to be a specification of the term *Rusini*. The *izgoi* was a person who for some reason had ended up outside the normal structure of clan relationships.

IV. The Background of Art. 1

Most legal anthropologists and historians would nowadays accept that the general sequential pattern in the way early law dealt with homicide was: blood vengeance, wergeld (payment by the killer and/or his kin to the relatives of the person killed), payment of a fine to a ruler. As could be expected, the transition between these phases is usually gradual: wergeld might first emerge as an alter-

---

11 This used to be a touchy point in the Soviet era, but already *V.V. Mavrodin*, Ocherki istorii SSSR. Drevnerusskoe gosudarstvo, Moskva, 1956, 159, had argued that '*Rusin*' should not be understood as an ethnic term, but as a social category, and in this way the ethnic sensitivity was removed. In his posthumously published Obrazovanie drevnerusskogo gosudarstva (2nd ed.), Sankt-Petersburg, 2008, 482, the point is made more forcefully.

native option for blood vengeance; then it would ease out blood vengeance, culminating in the final prohibition of the latter; such a prohibition presupposes central power, a ruler, and then such power would start looking for ways to divert the payment of wergeld to its own coffers. This would ultimately result in the replacement of wergeld by a payment to the ruler (bloodwite). This pattern is easily observed in the law of pre-Kievan and Kievan Russia and then the question posed in the beginning of this paper could be rephrased as: Had the transition from wergeld to fine (bloodwite) already taken place before art. 1 of the *Short Pravda* was written down?

The understanding of art. 1 of the *Short Pravda* and particularly of the question to whom the 40 *grivna* are to be paid, depends first of all on reading the provision in the context of the entire *RP*, the Short as well as the *Expanded Pravda*. In the *Short Pravda* art. 1 is followed by a series of provisions (arts. 2-10) devoted to lesser offences against the person, prescribing payments of 12 or 3 *grivna*; arts. 1-5, 7, and 9-10 reappear in somewhat different wording in the *Expanded Pravda* (arts. 1, 29, 25, 23, 27, 28, 24, and 31). The second half of the *Short Pravda*, the *Pravda of Iaroslav's Sons*, begins with a series of provisions (arts. 19-27) dealing with the killing of various officials and servants of the prince.

An unbiased reading of these materials yields three major suggestions with regard to the question under consideration.

1. Arts. 1-10 of the Short Pravda concern wergeld and similar payments

These articles constitute a coherent set of rules characterized by uniformity of terminology, thematic consistence (homicide and lesser offences against the person), and structural similarity of the individual provisions. Art. 2, covering less serious injuries, explicitly mentions the victim as the recipient of the 3 *grivna* amount: 'then he is to take for the offence 3 *grivna*'. The formula 'for the offence so many *grivna*' also appears in arts. 4 and 7. 'Offence' in this case does not mean a violation of criminal law but 'insult' or 'injury' (*za obidu*). All this strongly suggests that the victim (or his relatives in the case of art. 1 – homicide) and not the prince receives the payment.

2. Arts. 19-27 of the Short Pravda concern bloodwite

These articles, as pointed out above, concern the killing of officials and servants of the prince. Similar to the block of provisions of arts. 1-10, they present a coherent set of identically structured rules. The potential victims indicated by the various provisions range from high officials (the *ognishchanin* in art. 19) to the lowest servants (the slave in art. 26). The rank of the victims is reflected in the amount to be paid for their killing: 80 *grivna* for the highest (i.e. twice the amount to be paid for an ordinary person), 12 or 5 *grivna* for persons of lower status.

Almost all commentators accept that arts. 19-27 concern the paying of bloodwite, i.e. the payment goes to the prince. A simple argument in favour of this view and based solely on the text is that surely the payment for killing the prince's slave can only be claimed by the prince himself and not by the slave's relatives; as the text does in no way (except in the amount of the payment) differentiate between the various servants of the prince, all payments for killing them are therefore payable to their master, the prince. At the same time, the relatives of higher ranking servants could presumably claim the wergeld from the killer. This is indirectly confirmed by art. 5 of the *Expanded Pravda* which prescribes the payment of bloodwite by the community (*verv'*) of which the killer is a member and then continues by directing the killer to pay the wergeld (*golovnichestvo*) as well as his share in the bloodwite.

3. Contradictory provisions of the Expanded Pravda

The first two articles of the *Expanded Pravda* throw new, but confusing light on the reading of art. 1 of the *Short Pravda.*

The second part of the *Short Pravda*, the *Pravda of Iaroslav's Sons*, had been preceded, as mentioned above, by a short preamble: 'The Pravda established for the Russian land, when Iziaslav, Vsevolod, Sviatoslav [Iaroslav's sons], Kosniachko Pereneg, Mikyfor the Kievan, and Chiudin Mikula met.' This preamble returns in slightly different wording and with an important addition in art. 2 of the *Expanded Pravda*: 'After Iaroslav, his sons came together again: Iziaslav, Sviatoslav, Vsevolod, and their men: Kosniach'ko Pereneg and Nikifor, and they abolished vengeance justice [*ubienie za golovu*, 'killing for the head'], but [ordered] buying off [vengeance] for money; and all else, as Iaroslav had decided, his sons also established likewise.'

While the preamble in the middle of the *Short Pravda* only referred to a meeting of the sons of *Iaroslav* (apparently resulting in the following arts. 19 ff.), the *Expanded Pravda* connected the meeting[12] specifically with the abolition of blood vengeance. The *Short Pravda* gives at least the impression that *Iaroslav* (in art. 1) had offered the alternative of paying wergeld instead of engaging in blood vengeance, and that his sons had introduced the paying of bloodwite for the killing of their officials and servants (arts. 19 ff.). Art. 2 of the *Expanded Pravda* seems to add that *Iaroslav's* sons, at the same time they were introducing bloodwite for those specific offences, abolished blood vengeance, leaving the payment of wergeld as the only option in the general case of homi-

12 Some authors have argued that the *Expanded Pravda*, which said that the princes came together *again*, was referring to a second meeting, in which blood vengeance was abolished. One cannot exclude this possibility, although I would side with the majority of authors who reject it.

cide[13]. The most obvious reading of the second part of the first sentence of art. 2 of the *Expanded Pravda* ('but [ordered] buying off for money') would be that the princes, forbidding the victim's relatives to engage in blood vengeance, allowed the killer to buy off his guilt towards the latter by paying the wergeld.

So far so good, but then art. 1 of the *Expanded Pravda* muddies the waters. It basically repeats art. 1 of the *Short Pravda*, but with at least one important addition:

> 'If a man kills a[nother] man, [the following relatives of the murdered man avenge him] the brother avenges the brother, or the father [the son] or the son [the father], or the son of the brother [his uncle] or the son of the brother [his cousin][14]; if there is no one to avenge [the murdered man], then 80 *grivna* is to be paid for the head, if [the person killed] is a man of the prince or the prince's overseer; if [the person killed] is a *Rusin* or a bodyguard, or a merchant, or a boyar's overseer, or a sheriff, or an *izgoi* or a [Novgorod] Slav, 40 *grivna* is to be paid for him.'

The first difficulty is that this provision allows blood vengeance, which is forbidden in the following provision. What is one to make of that? The second problem is that it seems to offer the same alternatives of blood vengeance and paying wergeld as had been offered by art. 1 of the *Short Pravda*, but that these alternatives also appear to apply to the prince's officials and servants, who apparently were subject to the special regime of bloodwite payment according to art. 19 ff. of the *Short Pravda*.

The first difficulty is solved by almost all commentators by assuming that the reference to blood vengeance in art. 1 of the *Expanded Pravda* was merely an historical relict; it could serve as an explanation of the new arrangements[15]. On the basis of art. 2 it would be hard to doubt that blood vengeance had been abolished during the reign of *Iaroslav's* sons (i.e. at least before 1076) and well before the final redaction of the *Expanded Pravda*.

The second difficulty can be solved easily if one accepts the theory that the various payments for killing and injuring, mentioned in the first part of the *Short Pravda* (the *Pravda of Iaroslav*), constituted fines, payable to the prince. Then the payment which was mentioned in art. 1 of the *Short Pravda* as a possible alternative for blood vengeance should be termed bloodwite, and wergeld would already have disappeared when the *Short Pravda* came into being. This theory is supported by a considerable number of scholars, although it does itself create a number of problems to which we shall return presently.

On the other hand, if one holds that at least during the reigns of *Iaroslav* (1016-1054) and his father *Vladimir* (978-1015) blood vengeance existed as well as payment of wergeld to the victim's kin as an alternative sanction for homi-

---

13 This reading is also suggested by *V. Sergeevich*, Lektsii i Izsledovaniiia po drevnei istorii russkago prava (4th ed.), Sankt-Petersburg, 1910, 393.

14 The translation of the terms *bratuchado* and *bratniu synovi* is much disputed.

15 *A.A. Zimin*, PRP I, 137; *Ia.N. Shchapov,* RZ I, 82; *Baranowski*, 339.

cide, then the second part of art. 1 of the *Expanded Pravda* remains contradictory. A possible solution is offered by considering more closely the undisputed historical character of art. 1. It was obviously inserted, when the *Expanded Pravda* was compiled in the course of the 12th century, in order to explain the historical background of art. 2, which itself referred to the abolition of blood vengeance, roughly a century ago. If one believes that blood vengeance and wergeld existed as legally recognized institutions during the 10th and at least a part of the 11th century and were abolished (blood vengeance) or eased out by the payment of bloodwite (in the case of wergeld) after the death of *Iaroslav*, then they were very much a thing of the past for the editors of the final compilation of the *Expanded Pravda*. In providing summary information on the more distant past development of their law on homicide, the editors lumped together older elements (art. 1) and newer elements (arts. 19 ff.) of the *Short Pravda* in art. 1 of the *Expanded Pravda*. The important distinction between wergeld and bloodwite was glossed over in this way. What mattered in the 12th century was that the prince became greatly interested in an elaborate system of fines (including bloodwite) for the most common crimes.

V. Vladimir and the Vira in 996

Support for this theory can be found in the Russian Primary Chronicle (*Nachal'naia Letopis'*) in several places. The treaties between the (still pagan) Russians (actually mostly Scandinavians) and the Byzantine emperors of 912 and 944 deal with inter-ethnic homicide in a similar (but not identical) manner: the right of the relatives of the victim to kill the killer is recognized, and if the killer has escaped, the relatives are entitled to take his property (or a certain part of it). The texts would certainly allow the reading that blood vengeance is the standard sanction and that the taking of property occurs only when the taking of the killer's life is excluded. Such a reading finds an echo in the text of art. 1 of the *Short Pravda* which contains the formula 'if there is no one to avenge [the person killed], then ...' (this formula is taken over in art. 1 of the *Expanded Pravda*).

Under the year 996 the Primary Chronicles recounts an episode which is of immediate interest to the question discussed in this paper.

> 'While Vladimir was thus dwelling in the fear of God, the number of bandits increased, and the bishops, calling to his attention the multiplication of robbers, inquired why he did not punish them. The prince answered that he feared the sin entailed. They replied that he was appointed of God for the chastisement of malefaction and for the practice of mercy toward the righteous, so that it was entirely fitting for him to punish a robber condignly, but only after due process of law [*no so ispytom*]. Vladimir accordingly abolished *vira* and set out to punish the brigands. The bishops and elders then suggested that as wars were frequent, the *vira* might be

properly spent for the purchase of arms and horses, to which Vladimir assented. Thus Vladimir lived according to the prescriptions of his father and grandfather'[16].

The passage, clearly reflecting an important point of transition in the development of the legal treatment of homicide, raises several questions which have been much debated by Russian historians[17]. For the sake of brevity I shall only give my own view here[18]. If *vira* is taken in the sense it has in the *RP* (a fine payable to the prince, a public punishment therefore), then its abolition and the introduction of public punishment are impossible to reconcile with the first part of the passage, which states repeatedly that *Vladimir* did *not* impose punishment before the bishops' intervention. Also, it is unlikely that a forceful ruler like *Vladimir* would give up an important source of income, only to re-introduce it a little while later, as a replacement of the punishment he had introduced in the meantime[19]. The second *vira* in the text is the bloodwite, the fine received by the prince. The first *vira* can only be the wergeld, due to the kin of the robbers' victims. This would agree with what is known about the chronological framework of the episode. At that time blood vengeance with the possible alternative of the payment of wergeld was the accepted way of dealing with homicide, in principle an affair between the offender and his victim (or rather his relatives) without the interference of central power. This explains why *Vladimir* was wary of upsetting the traditional order ('afraid to sin'). But the introduction of Christianity provided the catalyst in the strengthening of central power. The Church was opposed to blood vengeance and its support legitimized *Vladimir's* reform, which in fact diverted the money to be paid away from the victim's kin to the coffers of the prince. The essence of the 996 reform then would be the abolition of wergeld and its replacement by bloodwite.

---

16 The translation is taken from *S.H. Cross* and *O.P. Sherbowitz-Wetzor* (eds. & transl.), The Russian Primary Chronicle. Laurentian Text, Cambridge, MA, 1953 (3rd pr., 1973), 122, with the exception of *vira*, for which the translation 'wergild' is given, which would be totally confusing in the context of this paper.

17 See *V.O. Kliuchevskii*, Boiarskaia Duma, Moskva, 1902 (3rd ed.), 532-534 (Appendix II); *L.K. Goetz*, Das Russische Recht, I, Stuttgart, 1910, 193-211; *M.F. Vladimirskii-Budanov*, Russkaia Pravda [review of *L.K. Goetz*' Das Russische Recht], Universitetskie izvestiia, Kiev, 1911, no. 3, 1912, no. 10 (also in *Iu.S. Shemshuchenko* (ed.), Antolohiia ukrains'koi iuridychnoi dumky, T.2, Istoriia derzhavy i prava Ukrainy: Rus'ka Pravda, Kyiv, 2002, 139-154); *V. Sergeevich*, Lektsii, 394-395; *A.E. Presniakov*, Lektsii po russkoi istorii, T.I, Moskva, 1938, 202-203; *V.V. Mavrodin*, Ocherki istorii SSSR. Drevnerusskoe gosudarstvo, Moskva, 1956, 151; *A.A. Zimin*, Pravda Russkaia, 86-88.

18 A very similar view has been advanced by *E.D. Romanova*, 'Svobodnyi obshchinnik v Russkoi Pravde', Istoriia SSSR, 1961, no. 4, 76-90 (according to *Baranowski*, 171-172).

19 Most authors agree that capital punishment was not practiced in Kievan times and that the verb 'to punish' (*kazniti*) refers to some other form of punishment (most probably banishment, *potok*).

What remains is the problem of reconciling this reading with the view that blood vengeance and the alternative payment of wergeld was still the rule at the time of the *Pravda of Iaroslav*, a few decades later. A partial answer would be that *Vladimir's* innovation did not concern homicide in general, but only the special type of cases mentioned in the Chronicle, violence committed by outlaws. A more comprehensive answer would be that the reform process was not a matter of a single decision of the ruler, but rather a policy aimed at transforming a deeply ingrained tradition, still very much alive and officially recognized in the time of *Vladimir's* son *Iaroslav*.

If one starts from the theory that *vira* in this passage means bloodwite (a fine to be paid to the prince), which would imply that blood vengeance and wergeld were already a thing of the past in 996, the passage becomes absurd: the bishops asked the prince why he did not punish the robbers, when he was already exacting bloodwite from them, he then abolished blood vengeance (which did not exist anymore at that time) and bloodwite and started to punish the offenders, in some other manner apparently; then he re-introduced bloodwite.

VI. The 'Bloodwite'-Theories

As indicated at the beginning of this paper, an important section of the scholars who have written on the *RP*, about half of them, support the theory that the 40 *grivna* sum, mentioned in art. 1 of the *Short Pravda*, is due to the prince[20]. The reasons given for taking this view are very varied.

Among Soviet authors this view is dominant and based on a preconceived view of the politico-legal status of Kievan Russia. This was supposed to be a nascent or early feudal state with the institutional equipment assigned to it by historical materialism, including effective legislative powers[21]. The replacement, by the state, of blood vengeance by financial sanctions payable to the state was declared to be a general mechanism, of which art. 1 of the *Short Pravda* was a clear illustration, according to *S.V. Iushkov*[22]. Such payments were then termed *vira*, and this meant fine or bloodwite. As proof for this view the passage from the 996 entry in the Primary Chronicle, discussed above, is adduced by *S.V. Iushkov*[23]. Basically, the standard argument was circular: 'scientific' historical theory had established the proto-feudal character of Kievan Russia; active involvement of the state in legislation and revenue collection would be a neces-

20 See *Pravda Russkaia*, II, 27-32. *Baranowski*, op.cit., 169-173, discusses the same material, covering more recent authors as well.

21 *S.V. Iushkov*, the leading legal historian among the older generation of Soviet medievalists, declared in his Russkaia Pravda (Moskva, 1950, 246) that 'the basic current task of Soviet historians and legal historians is to overcome the views on the quite low level of legal development of the Eastern Slavs in the 9th-11th century.'

22 *Ibid.*, 248-249.

23 *Ibid.*, 249-250.

sary consequence – this was demonstrated and proved by the mention of *vira* – the payment mentioned in art. 1 of the *Short Pravda* was therefore *vira*, a payment to the prince.

Similar views, although devoid of the ideological prejudices, are sometimes encountered among prerevolutionary authors; without much argument, the Kievan state is regarded as a stable and coherent construct, which would imply a developed legislative and fiscal system[24]. The collection of revenue in the form of financial penal sanctions would be an obvious element of such a system. Several authors, however, put forward a more reasoned answer. *N.D. Ivanishev* wrote already in 1840 that the second part of art. 1 of the *Short Pravda* (concerning the payment replacing blood vengeance) would only become operational when there was nobody to avenge the person killed; the prince would then assume the handling of the case by imposing a fine of 40 *grivna*[25]. A similar but different position was occupied by *N. Lange* who argued that the victim's relatives could refrain from blood vengeance in exchange for a sum of money to be agreed with the killer. The interference of the prince (by imposing the 40 *grivna* fine) was limited to those cases where the absence of relatives, or another circumstance making blood vengeance impossible, would leave the killing unpunished[26].

In a review of *L.K. Goetz'* four-volume study on the *RP*[27], *K. Kadlec* interpreted art. 1 of the *Short Pravda* in such a way that the 40 *grivna* payment applied only when there was nobody to avenge the killing; if there was no avenger, argued *K. Kadlec*, to whom should the payment go, if not the prince? Similarly, the *izgoi*, mentioned at the end of the provision, is understood to be a person without any firm links in the community, and then only the prince would be a ready recipient of the payment for the killing of the former[28].

---

24 A typical example is *V.F. Vladimirskii-Budanov*, author of one of the leading pre-1917 textbooks on Russian legal history, in Obzor istorii russkogo prava (7th ed.), Kiev, 1915 (republished Rostov-na-Donu, 1995), 327 (337 in the 5th ed., quoted in *Pravda Russkaia*, II, and by *Baranowski*, 170).

25 *N.D. Ivanishev*, O plate za ubiistvom v drevnem russkom i drugikh slavianskikh zakonodatel'stvakh v sravnenii s gemanskoiu viroiu, Kiev, 1840, 92 (quoted from *Pravda Russkaia*, II, 28). The entire article was republished in *Iu.S. Shemshuchenko* (ed.), Antolohiia ukrains'koi iurydychnoi dumky, T.2 (Istoriia derzhavy i prava Ukrainy: Rus'ka Pravda), Kyiv, 2002, where the passage referred to is to be found on p. 41.

26 *N. Lange*, 'Issledovanie ob ugolovnom prave Russkoi Pravdy', Arkhiv istoricheskikh i prakticheskikh svedenii, otnosiashchikhsia do Rossii, kn. 1-3, 5-6, Sankt-Petersburg, 1859-1860 (quoted from *Pravda Russkaia*, II, 28; *Baranowski*, 169-170).

27 *L.K. Goetz*, 'Das Russische Recht', Zs. f. Vergl. Rechtsw., Bd. 24 (241-517), 26 (161-426), 28 (1-454), 31 (1-222), 1910-1913.

28 *K. Kadlec*, 'Neue Ansichten über die Russkaja Pravda', Archiv für Slavische Philologie, Bd. 36, 1916, 283-320 (quoted only by *Baranowski*, not in *Russkaia Pravda*, II).

Among the Soviet authors, *M.N. Tikhomirov*, one of the foremost authorities on the *RP*, made the intriguing proposal to divide up art. 1 differently. The usual reading involves a break in the middle: the first part mentions blood vengeance and the alternative of paying 40 *grivna*, the second part adds that the 40 *grivna* rule applies to members of different ethnic and social groups. *M.N. Tikhomirov* placed the break earlier: the 40 *grivna* alternative applied, in the form of bloodwite, in the case of killing the princely protégés (the *Rusini*: bodyguard, merchant, steward, sheriff); the last part of the article (concerning the *izgoi* and the *Slovenin*) was inserted in Novgorod in the course of the final redaction of the *Short Pravda* as a conciliatory gesture to the local population, which was granted thereby the same protection available to the prince's men[29].

The 'bloodwite'-theories understandably pay little or no attention to the question of some sort of compensation to the kin of the person killed. A few authors suggest that this matter would be left to the discretion of the parties involved and be covered by unwritten customary law.

A.A. Zimin, one of the most important medievalists of the Soviet era, occupied a position between the two main views. In the first part of art. 1 of the *Short Pravda* he saw, like many other authors, the reflection of ancient customary law, modernized to some extent in the available text. Blood vengeance was recognized, albeit in a more restricted form: only certain close relatives were entitled to practice it. If no avenger was available, a 40 *grivna* payment was due by the killer to the close kin of the person killed. The second part of art. 1 ('if the [person killed] is a *Rusin* ...') is connected by *A.A. Zimin* with the events in Novgorod in 1015-1016. The first group of persons mentioned in this text consisted of various members of the prince's retinue (the *druzhina*), and the Novgorod citizenry, which had suffered much from lawless violence of *Iaroslav's druzhina*, demanded to be more effectively protected. *Iaroslav*, forced by the external threat of his half-brother *Sviatopolk*, prince of Kiev, marching against him, to make peace with the men of Novgorod, assented to their demands. So far, *A.A. Zimin's* argument is supported by most commentators. He then argued that *Iaroslav* extended the same legal protection available to his *druzhina* to the Novgorod population (the indigenous 'Slovenes' and the 'outsiders', the *izgoi*). As there are good reasons to assume that the *Rusini* (the *druzhina* members) were protected at that moment against offences against their lives by the payment of bloodwite (to their master, the prince), it follows that similar protection had now been extended, in Zimin's view, to the Novgorod population.[30]

---

29 *M.N. Tikhomirov*, Posobie dlia izucheniia Russkoi Pravdy, Moskva, 1953, 75, and more extensively: Issledovanie o Russkoi Pravde, Moskva-Leningrad, 1941, 48-49, 74-75. A similar view had already been put forward by *B.A. Romanov* in *B.D. Grekov* (ed.), Pravda Russkaia. Uchebnoe posobie, Moskva/Leningrad, 1940, 37-38.

30 The point appears briefly in *A.A. Zimin*, PRP I, 85-86; he returned to it and explained his views at greater length in Pravda Russkaia, 89-92.

VII. The 'Wergeld'-Theories

Among the pre-revolutionary authors, holding that art. 1 of the *Short Pravda* referred to wergeld and not to bloodwite, several are worth mentioning for contributing new points to the debate.

A. Bogdanovskii was the first to emphasize that the payment of art. 1 was not meant to augment the prince's treasury, nor to compensate the family for the loss of a breadwinner, but to restore honour. He referred to the term *za obidu* ('for the insult', 'for the offence'), which is mentioned not in art. 1 but six times in the following articles of the *Pravda of Iaroslav*[31]. This point has been taken up by many later authors and is indeed of crucial importance for the understanding of the problem discussed in this paper.

V. Sergeevich understood the relationship between blood vengeance and the 40 *grivna* payment as a real alternative available to the victim's kin. He based this view on the consideration that if there was no possible avenger, there would also not be a possible recipient for the payment. In support of his argument he referred to a treaty between Smolensk and Riga which allowed the killing of an adulterer caught *in flagranti*, or, alternatively, if the culprit would not be killed, ordered the payment of 10 *grivna* of silver to the injured husband[32].

Most foreign authors have been inclined to regard the payment in art. 1 as wergeld, i.e. to the relatives of the victim[33]. *G. Vernadsky* only states the point in his edition of the *RP*, without offering any argument[34], but *D.H. Kaiser* deals with the question in more detail.[35] He places art. 1 in the context of the struggle of incipient princely power against vengeance justice; the innovative part of art. 1 would then be the offer of an alternative – composition or wergeld – for blood vengeance.

The entire question has not received much attention in modern Russian literature. At least one textbook accepts the wergeld theory[36].

---

31 *A. Bogdanovskii*, Razvitie poniatii o prestuplenii i nakazanii v russkom prave do Petra Velikogo, Moskva, 1857 (quoted from *Pravda Russkaia*, II, 28).

32 *V. Sergeevich*, Lektsii i Izsledovaniia, 393. The point is relevant, but not completely persuasive. The treaty is not really a contemporary of the *Short Pravda*, as *V. Sergeevich* put it, and the provision in question does not concern homicide. On the treaty, see the chapter on treaties in this work. Text in *PRP* II, 72-75.

33 *M. Szeftel* and *A. Eck* are the exception, although they only tentatively embrace the bloodwite theory; cf. *M. Szeftel* and *A. Eck*, Documents de droit public relatifs à la Russie médiévale, Bruxelles, 1963, 41.

34 *G. Vernadsky*, Medieval Russian Laws, New York, 1947, 14-15.

35 *D.H. Kaiser*, The Growth of the Law in Medieval Russia, Princeton, 1980, 63-65.

36 *V.K. Tsechoev*, Istoriia gosudarstva i prava Rossii s drevneishikh vremen do 1861 g., Rostov-na-Donu, 2000, 65. Another textbook, *I.A. Isaev*, Istoriia gosudarstva i prava Rossii, Moskva, 2006, 48, neatly avoids the dilemma.

VIII. Art. 1 in the Context of the Pravda of Iaroslav

The first half of the *Pravda of Iaroslav*, arts. 1-10, constitute a coherent whole, devoted to violence against the person. After homicide (art. 1) various forms of physical violence are mentioned. In some cases vengeance is expressly mentioned, in other cases it is alluded to. With the exception of art. 6 all other provisions contain monetary sanctions, ranging from 1 *grivna* to 40 *grivna*. The question asked with regard to art. 1 (who receives the 40 *grivna* payment?) is therefore equally valid for the following provisions and the answers found may help in finding an answer to the question regarding art. 1.

The most explicit pointers are provided by art. 2. This provision concerns the legal consequences of beating another person and primarily addresses the issue of evidence. If somebody has bleeding wounds or is blue with bruises, he does not need an eyewitness to substantiate his injury. If there are no visible signs of having been beaten, then an eyewitness is required, otherwise the alleged victim does not have a case. The provision then continues: 'If he is unable to avenge himself, then he is to take 3 *grivna* for the insult [*za obidu*] and the fee for the physician.' This rule is in perfect agreement with the wergeld theory: blood vengeance first, and a fixed payment to the victim as a subsidiary sanction[37].

Arts. 3-5 and 7-10 follow the model of the second part of art. 2, but in a more terse fashion and without reference to vengeance. Art. 8 is the shortest and simply states: 'And for the moustache 12 *grivna*, and for the beard 12 *grivna*.' In the context of the preceding provisions the meaning of this formula is unquestionably: 'And for cutting off somebody's moustache or beard the offender pays 12 *grivna*.'

The difference between the payments indicated in these various provisions suggests clearly that restoration of honour is the main consideration and not compensation of material or financial losses. Cutting off a finger warrants a payment of only 3 *grivna*, against 12 *grivna* for the beard or moustache; the 3 *grivna* payment of art. 2 (bleeding wounds and bruises) contrasts with the 12 *grivna* payment for the less serious (in our view) but more insulting offences of beating a person with a stick, the palm or the back of the hand, a cup or horn (art. 3) or the hilt of the sword (art. 4).

Art. 5, beating resulting in the loss of an arm or a hand, entails the same payment as homicide (40 grivna), presumably, according to several commenta-

---

37 Several supporters of the bloodwite theory (a.o. *N. Lange, S.V. Iushkov, M.B. Sverdlov, Baranowski*) regard the payment of art. 2 as bloodwite, apparently on the basis of the general consideration that all similar payments in the *Short Pravda* are to be considered as fines payable to the prince. In this case, however, the words of art. 2 completely contradict such a view. The most elaborate argument has been put forward by *M.B. Sverdlov* in Ot Zakona Russkogo k Russkoi Pravde, Moskva, 1988, 92.

tors, because it would cause a man to be defenceless. Art. 6, the foot having been struck, resulting in the victim becoming a cripple, is usually read as a continuation of art. 5; no payment is mentioned, instead the brief formula *chada smiriat'* is used. This can be translated as 'the children [including perhaps domestics] humble [the offender]', referring to their right to exercise appropriate vengeance against the offender or reach a settlement with him. Vengeance is implied in art. 3 where it is stated that if 'they do not catch him [the offender], then he is to pay'.

IX. Art. 1 of the Short Pravda in a Comparative Framework

Certain parallels between art. 1 of the *Short Pravda* and provisions of the *Expanded Pravda*, the early Russian treaties with Byzantium and later Russian laws (esp. the treaty between Smolens and Riga) have been indicated above. The manner of dealing with homicide as laid out in art. 1 of the *Short Pravda* may also be compared with the earliest legislative monuments of other Slavic peoples[38] and with the early laws of Germanic nations.

The Polish Law (*Polensche recht*), a 13th century registration (in medieval German) of Polish law, contains an extensive enumeration of offences against the person, most of which entail the payment of a fixed amount, related to the seriousness of the offence, to the victim, or, in case of homicide, to his relatives; additionally, the prince receives a fine in many cases[39].

Among the western Slavs, one of the earliest laws is the Statute of Vinodol, a small principality on the Adriatic coast, south of Rijeka. In this law, dating from 1288, there are quite a number of provisions which set fixed payments for various offences against the person. The law usually indicates the division of the payment between the two groups of the victim's close and more distant relatives; a small payment to the court or the prince is often also included[40].

Further south on the Dalmatian coast, just south of Split, the principality of Poljica (Politsa in Russian) survived as a semi-independent entity under

---

38 See also *Z.M. Chernilovskii*, 'Russkaia Pravda v svete drugikh slavianskikh sudebnikov', *G.V. Shvekov* (ed.), Drevniaia Rus': Problemy prava i pravovoi ideologii, Moskva, 1984, 3-35, esp. 27-30.

39 German text and Russian translation in *B.D. Grekov*, Izbrannye trudy, T.I, Moskva, 1957, 265-447 ('Pol'skaia Pravda. Opyt izucheniia obshchestvennogo i politicheskogo stroia Pol'shi XIII v. po Pol'skoi Pravde («Knige Prava»)'), at 425-427. Older Polish and German publications and studies are mentioned by *B.D. Grekov*; the code is also known in German as the Elbinger Rechtsbuch.

40 See *B.D. Grekov*, ibid., 31-107, 'Vinodol. Vinodol'skii Statut ob obshchestvennom i politicheskom stroe Vinodola', at 93-94. An early Russian edition of the Statute of Vinodol is *V.V. Iagich*, Zakon Vinodol'skii, Sankt-Petersburg, 1880. A more recent (incomplete) Russian text in *V.M. Koretskii* (ed.), Khrestomatiia pamiatnikov feodal'nogo gosudarstva i prava stran Evropy, Moskva, 1961, 916-926.

Venetian and then Austrian suzerainty until the time of Napoleon. Its various laws, going back to the 15th century, were united in a single statute in 1662. Among the most archaic elements of the law of Poljica was a certain amount of official recognition of the legality of blood vengeance. The fines imposed in cases of offences against persons (including homicide) were usually divided up in equal parts between the victim or his relatives and the court imposing the sentence[41].

On the territory of the present republics of Latvia and Estonia, in the old provinces of Livonia, Kurland and Estonia, the customary law of the various Baltic and Finnish peoples had been put down in writing, in German, in the course of the middle ages[42]. Together with a strong Germanic component, indigenous elements were also present and in this way these laws occupied a middle position between the *RP* and the Germanic tribal codes. The Livonian code dates from 1212, somewhat later during the same century a short code for Kurland was drafted. A new code was issued by the bishop of Livonia (Riga) during the first part of the 14th century, of which a number of redactions are available. At the end of the 14th century there was the Estonian code of the bishop of Ösel.

Most of these sources mention payments of fixed sums to the victim of an attack, or in case of homicide, to the relatives. In several cases the laws provide that two thirds of a fixed sum is to be paid to the relatives, and one third to the court or the authorities (the bishops of Riga, Tartu, or Ösel, or the Teutonic Order). Instead of the payment of a fixed sum (wergeld), the alternative of a negotiable settlement between the attacker and the victim's kin also appears in a few sources.

Many features encountered in the laws of the Slavic and Baltic peoples also appear in the laws of the various Germanic peoples. Among the continental Germanic nations, the wergeld and corresponding monetary sanctions for lesser injuries are generally to be paid to the victim or his kin. Art. 65 of the Salic law (507-511) explicitly directs that the *compositio* for the killing of the father is divided in equal parts between the children on the one hand and the close paternal and maternal relatives on the other; if there are no paternal or maternal relatives, their share belongs to the *fiscus*. In the Anglo-Saxon laws the state is more prominently involved in dealing with homicide and lesser personal offences and bloodwite is therefore more common. In the law of king *Ethelbert of Kent* (ca.

---

41 *B.D. Grekov*, *ibid.*, 111-263, Politsa. Opyt izucheniia obshchestvennykh otnoshenii v Politse XV-XVII vv.', at 244-245. Text of the Poljica Statute in *B.D. Grekov*, Politsa, opyt izucheniia obshchestvennykh otnoshenii v Politse XV-XVII vv., Moskva, 1951. Also (incomplete text) in *Koretskii*, op.cit., 928-945.

42 The most important texts, together with a Russian translation, were published by *E.L. Nazarova*: '«Livonskie Pravdy» kak istoricheskii istochnik', *V.T. Pashuto* (ed.), Drevneishie gosudarstva na territorii SSSR 1979 god, Moskva, 1980, 5-218. The basic publication is by *F.G. v. Bunge* in Beiträge zur Kunde der Liv-, Esth- und Curländischen Rechtsquellen, Riga/Dorpat, 1832.

600) the person killing a freeman pays 50 shillings to the king. The general development from blood vengeance to wergeld (composition) and then to bloodwite (a fine payable to the ruler) is extensively documented in the Germanic *leges barbarorum* such as the Salic law and has been described in detail in the vast literature on German legal history.

The same development may also be observed in the early laws of other Indo-European peoples, such as the Hittites, Greeks, and Celts. In the laws of Semitic peoples, such as the Code of Hammurabi or in the Old Testament (Deuteronomium), blood vengeance in a strictly retributive form ('an eye for an eye') is dominant, supplemented by the wide applicability of capital punishment. The predominance of the latter penalty reflects the strength of the central power of the state, a factor of only incipient importance in early Kievan Russia. In early medieval Georgia, the situation was more like that among the Indo-European peoples[43].

X. Returning to the Question

Reviewing all that has been said before, leads us back to the text of art. 1 of the *Short Pravda* and in particular to the words *ashche ne budet' kto m'stia* ('if there will not be anybody to avenge [the person killed]'). If these words would refer only to the absence of persons qualified by law to assume the role of the avenger, then the view that the following payments concern bloodwite (a fine to the prince) becomes hard to invalidate (because, as authors such as *N.D. Ivanishev* and *K. Kadlec* had argued, who else could be the recipient). But most authors regard the formula as referring also to persons who *could* act as avengers but preferred not to do so[44]. Then one could still understand the payments of art. 1 as referring to bloodwite.

In this connection the first part of art. 1 acquires renewed relevance. It lists the persons entitled to engage in blood vengeance. This enumeration is usually read, correctly in my view, as being exhaustive, and, in this sense, also an innovation[45]. Previously, the right to engage in blood vengeance belonged to a wider circle of relatives, defined as *blizhnye* ('kinsmen') in the Russian-Byzantine treaty of 944. The drafter of the pertinent part of art. 1 (*Iaroslav the Wise* presumably) restricted the exercise of this right to a narrower circle of close relatives.

The most likely reading of the words 'if there will not be anybody to avenge' is therefore: 'if among the persons mentioned in the first part of art. 1 nobody chooses to exercise the right to avenge, or if no such persons are avail-

43 See the chapter on 'Law's Beginnings and Early Law' in my Law in Medieval Russia, esp. 14-22, or *F. Feldbrugge* (ed.), *The Law's Beginnings*, 265-272 (as quoted in note 7).

44 See the summaries in *Baranowski*, 165-167.

45 *Ibid.*, 162-165.

able'. This reading does not offer a clear answer to the question posed in the beginning of this paper, although it fits more easily in the wergeld theory. If, as was obviously the case, the general tendency was towards a restriction of blood vengeance, then the possibility of accepting wergeld instead of engaging in a blood feud would constitute a more effective approach than handing the matter over entirely to the prince as the potential recipient of bloodwite.

There are other arguments as well, none of them conclusive by themselves.

Art. 1 of the *Short Pravda* should be read in the context of the entire first half of the *Short Pravda* (i.e. the *Pravda of Iaroslav*). Such a reading suggests that the various amounts payable by the person guilty of homicide and other personal injuries are intended primarily to restore the honour and status of the victim and his kin. Art. 2 explicitly identifies the victim as the recipient and the similar formulas of the following provisions allow a similar reading. I do not see any cogent reason to treat art. 1 separately. The treaty between Smolensk and Riga, referred to above, demonstrates beyond doubt that this reading of similar provisions was still current by the middle of the 13th century.

Secondly, placing *Iaroslav's Pravda* in the context of comparable Slavic and Germanic legislation, leads to the same conclusion.

Thirdly, as explained above, the important passus in the Primary Chronicle under the year 996 only makes sense if one accepts that payment of wergeld was already a current practice at that time.

Taken together, these arguments tilt the balance heavily in favour of the wergeld view in respect of art. 1 of the *Short Pravda*, even if they, taken separately, are not decisive. The arguments in favour of the bloodwite view are not in any way more conclusive; they rest ultimately on a particular conception of the early Kievan polity as an effective state with the appropriate paraphernalia of criminal sanctions, essentially a *petitio principii.*

XI. Concluding Remarks

Embracing the views outlined in the foregoing section leads to a few concluding remarks.

The process of state formation with the accompanying emergence of legislation is very well documented in Russia through the availability of the Primary Chronicle and the *Russkaia Pravda* in its subsequent chronological layers. The latter documents in particular reflect the transition from a society which was still dominated by tribal elements and customary law to a state-like organization with the first instruments to effectively promote its institutional interests. In our modern perception this could also be viewed as the emergence of the private-public law dichotomy. Public law at this stage was criminal law, the appropriation by the state of the regulation and sanction of socially unacceptable behaviour, an area previously left to the private activity of interested parties.

The different phases of the *RP* show how the 'state', or rather the prince and his administration, gradually penetrated into what had been the private sphere, by regulating and restricting blood feuds, providing alternative remedies, and then replacing the private actor altogether by claiming the exclusive right to deal with certain types of undesirable behaviour.

In this way an in-depth analysis of art. 1 of the *Short Pravda* offers not only a wide perspective on the nature of the Kievan Russian polity, but also on the broader topics of the origins of state and law.

In a predominantly tribal community such as pre-Kievan Russia, honour and status, and the concomitant practice of blood feuds and similar acts of inter-clan violence, served as constructive factors for social coherence. The transition to a more modern state of affairs was promoted by a number of other factors:

a. the weakening and dissolution of tribal coherence, caused by social and economic developments;
b. the emergence of the state which actively counteracted blood vengeance first by providing alternative remedies (wergeld) and then by negative sanctions (penalties/bloodwite);
c. the adoption of Christianity which disapproved of blood vengeance and legitimized the activity of the state;
d. the gradual transformation of popular conceptions and practices as a result of factors a., b., and c.

These considerations may also have some relevance for modern western societies which are frequently faced with violence caused by the presence of immigrants with divergent social and ethical views. This academic exercise could therefore even claim to have some practical use, a quality highly appreciated in these days.

Königin Absprache. Erzwungene oder konsensuelle Justiz in Russland und den postsowjetischen Republiken?

Prof. Stephen C. Thaman[*]

I. Einleitung

Am 09.06.2009 wurde die russische Strafprozessordnung ergänzt, um „Kooperationsvereinbarungen" einzuführen, wodurch der Angeklagte eine Abmachung mit der Staatsanwaltschaft schließen kann, um durch Mitarbeit mit den Strafverfolgungsbehörden eine Strafminderung oder sogar eine Einstellung des Verfahrens zu erwirken[1]. Diese Art Kronzeugeregelung ist die neuste Vorschrift in Russland, die eine Umgehung eines vollständigen Strafverfahrens mit seinen ganzen rechtsstaatlichen Garantien ermöglicht. Schon seit dem Inkrafttreten der neuen StPO-RU von 2001 gibt es die Möglichkeit, eine verfahrensbeendende Absprache (oder „Übereinstimmung mit der Anklage") zu schließen, wodurch der Angeklagte in Fällen mit einer Höchstfreitheitsstrafe von zehn Jahren eine Strafminderung von einem Drittel erlangen kann, wenn er darauf verzichtet, seine Schuld zu bestreiten[2].

Dieser triumphale Marsch der konsensuellen Verfahrensarten[3] geht nicht nur in Russland und den postsowjetischen Republiken voran, sondern zeigt sich überall in der Welt, sogar in Ländern wie Deutschland und Frankreich, wo der „Handel mit der Gerechtigkeit" traditionell am meisten angeprangert wurde. Das Fragwürdige an den Reformbestrebungen in den postsowjetischen Republiken liegt darin, dass dieser Teil der Welt erst vor etwa zwanzig Jahren anfing, ein rechtsstaatliches Strafverfahren mit ausgebauten Verteidigungsrechten zu gestalten, um mit der repressiven, politisch abhängigen und auf dem sog. „König der Beweismittel" – dem erzwungenen Schuldgeständnis[4] – basierenden sowjetischen Fließbandjustiz fertig zu werden. Dieser Reformtsunami wurde damals

---

* Kodirektor des Zentrums für Internationales Recht und Rechtsvergleichung, Saint Louis University.

1 Siehe Kapitel 40¹, §§ 317¹ et seq. Ugolowno-processual'nyj kodeks Rossijskoy Federacii, Prospekt-Moskau (2010) (hiernach StPO-RU).

2 Kapitel 40, §§ 314 et seq. StPO-RU.

3 *T. Weigend*, ZStW 104, 486, 493 (1992).

4 Für *Wyschinskij* und andere sowjetischen Inquisitoren waren Geständnisse immer die „Könige des Beweises" (*korelewo dokasatel'stwa*). *Thaman* (2008), S. 102.

zur Zeit der Gorbatschowschen *Glasnost*[5] durch enthüllungsjournalistische Horrorgeschichten über die Verurteilung und Hinrichtung von Unschuldigen ausgelöst, die, natürlich, alle ihre Schuld den Ermittlungsbeamten gestanden hatten[6].

Das 1991 verfasste Konzept der Justizreform hatte als Ziel, das inquisitorische, parteibonzenabhängige, mit einem Berufsrichter und zwei „nickenden" Volksschöffen ausgestattete Gericht durch ein auf dem adversarischen Verfahren basierendes Geschworenengericht zu ersetzen. Die Unschuldsvermutung und ein Schweigerecht wurden offiziell anerkannt und die Verteidigungsrechte sollten ausgebaut werden. Unabdingbar war eine unabhängige, den Partei- bzw. Verwaltungsorganen nicht mehr gehorsame Richterschaft, die von allen inquisitorischen Verfahrensbefugnissen befreit war, und die auch Kontrolle über die Grundrechtseingriffe der Ermittlungsorgane ausüben würde[7]. Freisprüche sollten endlich in einem System möglich sein, in dem alle Beteiligten über die extrem niedrige Qualität der Ermittlungstätigkeit übereinstimmten[8].

In den 1990er Jahren ging die Russische Republik ziemlich weit in ihrem reformgesetzgeberischen Bestreben voran. Die Verfassung von 1993 garantierte ein adversarisches Verfahren und ein Recht auf ein Geschworenengericht, dazu wurden auch die Unschuldsvermutung, das Schweigerecht und sogar ein Verbot der Verwertung von gesetzwidrig gesammelten Beweismitteln verfassungsmäßig verankert. Eine Reform der Richterschaft ging ebenfalls voran und die neuen konstitutionellen Prinzipien wurden in Form einer experimentellen Einführung der Geschworenengerichte in neun russischen Regionen auch eingeführt[9]. Diese Reformen fanden großen Anklang in den anderen aus dem Sowjetjoch befreiten Republiken, wo neue Verfassungen und Strafprozessordnungen das Strafverfahren ebenfalls adversarisch ausgestalten und die Verteidigungsrechte verstärken wollten[10]. Der Enthusiasmus für Geschworenengerichte, der am Anfang ziem-

---

5 Kritisch zur *Glasnost* *F.-C. Schroeder*, „74 Jahre Sowjetrecht", C.H. Beck: München (1992), S. 47.

6 *S.C. Thaman*, „The Resurrection of Trial by Jury in Russia", Stanford Journal of International Law, Bd. 31, 61 (1995), S. 68-69.

7 Ebenda, S. 72-74.

8 Über die Probleme bei der Überwindung der „fehlfreien" russisch-sowjetischen Justiz, *S.C. Thaman*, „Russland: Rückkehr der fehlfreien Justiz", in *D. Fischer* (Hrsg.), Transformation des Rechts in Ost und West. Festschrift für Prof. Dr. Herwig Roggemann zum 70. Geburtstag, S. 203-07 BWV: Berlin (2006).

9 *S.C. Thaman* (1995), S. 74-78.

10 Ich werde die folgenden Abkürzungen benutzen, wenn ich auf die StPO oder die Verfassung der 15 postsowjetischen Republiken hinweisen: Armenien (AR), Aserbaidschan (AS), Belarus (BE), Estland (ES), Georgien (GE), Kasachstan (KA), Kyrgysstan (KY), Lettland (LE), Litauen (LI), Moldawien (MO), Russland (RU), Tadschikistan (TA), Turkmenistan (TU), Ukraine (UK), und Usbekistan (US). Z.B. StPO-RU oder Verf.-BE.

lich verbreitet war, flaute jedoch ab und bis jetzt hat nur Georgien sich für die klassische Jury entschieden[11].

Diese notwendigen rechtsstaatlichen Reformen, die auf die Verstärkung des Rechts auf ein *fair trial* im Allgemeinen zielen, wurden allerdings wenig später durch einen entgegengesetzten Reformimpuls relativiert, d.h. durch die Einführung von vereinfachten, auf Schuldakzeptanz basierten Verfahrensweisen. Dass Russland und einige der postsowjetischen Republiken sich so schnell zu geständnisorientierten Verfahrensformen gewandt haben, bevor ihre grundlegenden Reformen Fuß gefasst und die Arbeitsweise der Ermittlungsbeamten und Richter sich geändert haben, ist beunruhigend.

Ich möchte zunächst kurz zur Funktion des Geständnisses in der Geschichte des Strafverfahrensrechts Stellung nehmen, bevor ich mich auf die Problematik der Flucht vor dem öffentlichen, adversarischen Verfahren durch die Verbreitung von *plea bargaining* in Russland und einigen anderen postsowjetischen Staaten konzentriere.

II. Geständnisse in den akkusatorischen und inquisitorischen Traditionen

Das Schuldgeständnis spielte eine ganz andere Rolle im alteuropäischen Gemeinrecht als später im kontinentaleuropäischen Inquisitionsverfahren. Im chthonischen Gemeinrecht Europas, wenn nicht der ganzen Welt, übte die Gemeinschaft Druck nicht nur auf den Straftäter und seine Sippschaft, sondern auch auf die Familie oder Sippschaft des Opfers aus, um den durch die Straftat ausgelösen sozialen Streit zu entschärfen und der Möglichkeit der Blutrache oder einer langandauernden Fehde entgegenzuwirken[12]. Diese Urverfahren, die oft durch die Ältesten oder die Weisen der Sippe geschlichtet wurden, zielten oft auch auf die Erlangung eines Geständnisses der Übeltat, weil das oft den Ärger der Betroffenen linderte, oder, metaphorisch (für uns!), die Luft vom Gestank des Delikts reinigte[13]. Das Ziel des Verfahrens war Ausgleich und Versöhnung,

---

11 Eine neue StPO trat Oktober 2010 in Kraft, die eine klassische Jury mit zwölf Geschworenen einschließt. Das 2007 in Kraft getretene kasachische Geschworenengericht ist eigentlich ein erweitertes Schöffengericht nach dem französischen Modell, in dem neun Laien mit zwei Berufsrichtern zusammensitzen. Zu den Schwurgerichtsreformen in den postsowjetischen Republiken, *S.C. Thaman*, „The Two Faces of Justice in the Post-Soviet Legal Sphere: Adversarial Procedure, Jury Trial, Plea-Bargaining and the Inquisitorial Legacy" in *J. Jackson* (Hrsg.), Crime, Procedure and Evidence in a Comparative and International Context: Essays in honour of Professor Mirjan Damaška, Hart: Oxford, Portland, OR (2008), S. 112-113.

12 *S.C. Thaman*, „A Typology of Consensual Criminal Procedures: An Historical and Comparative Perspective on the Theory and Practice of Avoiding the Full Criminal Trial", in *S.C. Thaman* (Hrsg.), World Plea Bargaining, Carolina Academic Press: Durham, N.C. (2010), S. 297-300.

13 Ebenda, S. 305.

nicht jedoch Strafe, und die Wiedergutmachung nahm üblicherweise die Form von festgesetzten Geldbeträgen oder Vieh an, das altdeutsche *wergeld* oder die altfranzösische *composition*[14]. Diese uralte akkusatorische Form des konsensuellen Ausgleichs ist offensichtlich das Modell für den modernen Täter-Opfer-Ausgleich, wenn man will die idealisierte Form des konsensuellen Versöhnungsverfahrens, das sich als Alternative zum konventionellen Strafverfahren anbietet[15].

Die andere, inquisitorische, Methode der Geständniserwirkung hatte ihren Ursprung wahrscheinlich in den Gottesurteilen, später aber ihren Höhepunkt in den auf Folter basierten Inquisitionsverfahren[16]. Wenn das Strafverfahren selbst eine schmerzhafte, ja peinliche Verdachtsstrafe war[17], wollte man dem ganzen System natürlich ausweichen und privat mit dem Opfer einen Ausgleich erlangen[18] oder, den prozessualen Zwängen nachgebend, ein Geständnis ablegen und jeweils die Namen und Aufenthaltsorte der Mittäter freigeben[19].

Die Folter wurde als Folge der Aufklärung offiziell abgeschafft und die Geständniserwirkung musste durch andere Verfahrensmechanismen verwirklicht werden. Die lange Untersuchungshaft in scheußlichen Kerkern wirkte hier hervorragend[20], auch konnte der inquisitorische Tatrichter natürlich versuchen, durch leichte Androhungen einer höheren bzw. Versprechen einer milderen Strafe, den hartnäckigen Angeklagten auch noch im Gericht der Hauptverhandlung zu einem Geständnis zu motivieren[21].

Obwohl das US-amerikanische *plea bargaining* eine lange Geschichte und seinen Ursprung scheinbar wie in Deutschland im frühen 19. Jahrhundert zur Erledigung von Bagatellkriminalität hat[22] – und vielleicht sogar, wie die herr-

---

14 Ebenda, S. 300.

15 Siehe *T. Weigend* (1992), S. 496; *C. Roxin*, FS Jauch (1990), S. 190, 195. Natürlich kennt das uralte *Russkaja Prawda* auch das *wergeld*, http://www.hrono.info/dokum/1000dok/pravda72.php.

16 Über die Folter als „judicialization of the ordeal" *R. Vogler*, A World View of Criminal Justice, Ashgate: Burlington, VT (2005), S. 25.

17 Sogar manchmal für den erfolglosen Ankläger. Siehe § 12 *Constitutio Criminalis Carolina*, bzw. *S.C. Thaman* (2010), S. 307.

18 In asiatischen Ländern wie Indien, aber besonders in den von dem Kofuzianismus beeinflussten Ländern Ostasiens (Korea, China, Vietnam), gilt es als Schande, überhaupt ins Gericht gerufen zu werden. *S.C. Thaman* (2010), S. 314-321.

19 Ebenda, S. 305-309. Hier findet man auch die Anfänge der heutigen Kooperationsverträge zwischen Angeklagten und Staatsanwalt.

20 Über die U-Haft als Verdachtsstrafe und „maskierte Folter" *L. Ferrajoli*, Diritto e ragione: Teoria del garantismo penale, Laterza: Rom (5. Aufl. 1998), S. 336, 562-566.

21 Für ein Beispiel eines vor der Entblößung der Absprachepraxis so ermunterten Geständnisses, BGHSt 14, 189, 190 (1960), mit Diskussion in *S.C. Thaman*, „Gerechtigkeit und Verfahrensvielfalt", FS *Klaus Röhl* (2003), S. 310-311.

22 *G. Fisher*, Plea Bargaining's Triumph, Stanford: Stanford, CA (2003), S. 64-81. Über die Ursprünge des Strafbefehls im Preußischen Mandatsvefahren *A. Vivell*, Die Strafbe-

schende Volksmeinung es glaubt, einen Auswuchs des amerikanischen akkusatorisch-adversarischen Verfahrens bildet[23] – kann man meines Erachtens das amerikanische *plea bargaining* nicht mehr als akkusatorisch-adversarisch bezeichnen. Die hohe Erfolgsquote in etwa 95% der Straffälle hat ihre Wurzeln in der immanenten Zwangsmäßigkeit der verfahrensmäßigen Situation des Angeklagten. Die Androhung von drakonischen Strafen, wie der Todesstrafe für Mord mit erschwerenden Umständen und der lebenslangen Freiheitstrafe für Rückfallsdiebe[24] – oder sogar bei Ersttätern im Bereich des Drogenhandels sowie hoher Mindestfreiheitsstrafen für andere Straftäter –, führt zu einer verheerenden Flucht vor der Gefahr eines Schuldspruchs vor einem Geschworenengericht zugunsten eines viel geringeren und mehr oder weniger sicheren Strafmaßes. Die Restauration der Todesstrafe und die galoppierende Inflation bei den angedrohten Freiheitsstrafen in den USA waren, ähnlich wie man jetzt in den postsowjetischen Ländern beobachtet, eine Reaktion auf die Revolution im Bereich der Gewährleistung eines fairen Verfahrens, die in den Sechziger Jahren des letzten Jahrhunderts durch die Entscheidungen des Obersten Gerichts der USA unter der Präsidentschaft von *E. Warren* stattgefunden hatte[25]. Die Vertragstheorie des USA-amerikanischen *plea bargaining*[26] kann unter solchen Zwangsumständen nicht mehr verteidigt werden. *Plea bargaining* in einem solchen System hat schwer zu verhüllende inquisitorische Wurzeln.

III. Die Fortdauer des Gebrauchs von Folter und anderen gesetzwidrigen Vernehmungsmethoden in den postsowjetischen Republiken

Es ist kein Geheimnis, dass der „König des Beweises“ in der Mehrzahl der postsowjetischen Republiken noch thront, und dass die Ermittlungsbeamten dieser Länder immer noch zu unmenschlicher bzw. erniedrigender Behandlung – wenn nicht gar Folter – greifen, um Geständnisse zu erzwingen[27]. In Russland schätzt man, dass gegen Art. 3 EMRK verstoßende Methoden bei ca. 50% aller Ange-

---

fehlsverfahren nach Eröffnung des Hauptverfahrens, Peter Lang: Frankfurt a.M. (2006), S. 26.

23 *M. Langer*, „From Legal Transplants to Legal Translations: The Globalization of Plea Bargaining and the Americanization Thesis in Criminal Procedure“, in *S.C. Thaman* (Hrsg.), World Plea Bargaining, S. 26.

24 In *Bordenkircher v. Hayes*, 434 USA 357 (1978) entschied das Oberste Gericht der USA, dass die vom Staatsanwalt angebotene Alternative, entweder einer fünfjährigen Freiheitsstrafe bei einem *guilty plea* oder lebenslänglich im Fall eines Juryschuldspruchs, nicht gegen das Gebot des *due process* der US-Verfassung verstößt.

25 *S.C. Thaman* (2010), S. 327-330.

26 Ebenda, S. 346-347.

27 Über den Gebrauch von Folter in allen postsowjetischen Republiken mit Literaturhinweisen *S.C. Thaman* (2008), S. 102.

klagten dazu gebraucht werden, und bei 80% derer, die sich weigern, ihre Schuld anfänglich zu gestehen[28].

Der Gebrauch von Folter und anderen Zwangsmethoden zur Geständniserzwingung hat schon zu Verurteilungen mancher postsowjetischer Republik wegen Verstoßes nicht nur gegen das Folterverbot des Art. 3 EMRK, sondern auch gelegentlich gegen das Gebot des fairen Verfahrens des Art. 6 EMRK (wegen der Verwertung von Geständnissen, die durch Zwang und ohne Verteidigerbeistand erlangt worden waren) geführt. Man findet solche Urteile des Öfteren gegen Russland[29], die Ukraine[30] und Moldawien[31], aber auch gegen Armenien[32]. Der EGMR hat auch indirekt auf die Folterpraktiken einiger nichteuropäischer postsowjetischer Republiken in Fällen hingewiesen, wo Beschwerdeführer sich gegen die Auslieferung an diese Länder gestämmt haben. In solchen Urteilen sind indirekt Usbekistan[33], Turkmenistan[34], Tadschikistan[35], Kasachstan[36] und

---

28 Zu den Foltertechniken gehören Prügeleien, Erstickung, Elektroschock und verschiedenartige Drohungen. *D. Lohman*, „Confessions at any cost: police torture in Russia", New York: Human Rights Watch (1999), S. 1, 21, 36.

29 Siehe u.a. *Antropov v. Russia*, no. 22107/03, §§ 25-30, 51, 67, ECHR 2009; *Dmitrachkov v. Russia*, no. 18825/02, §§ 7, 43-51, ECHR 2010; *Georgiy Bykov v. Russia*, no. 24271/03, §§ 8-12, 75-76, ECHR 2010; *Khadisov & Tsechoyev v. Russia*, §§ 110, 124-134, no. 21519/02, ECHR 2009; *Nadrosov v. Russia*, no. 9297/02, §§ 27-37, ECHR 2008; *Oleg Nikitin v. Russia*, no. 36410/02, §§ 5-7, 47-53, ECHR 2008; *Pavlenko v. Russia*, no. 42371/02, §§ 104-120, ECHR 2010; *Polonskiy v. Russia*, no. 30033/05, §§ 6-11, 118-125, ECHR 2009 (Art. 6 EMRK); *Sherstobitov v. Russia*, no. 16266/03, §§ 7-12, 75-81, ECHR 2010; *Aleksandr Sokolov v. Russia*, no. 20364/05, ECHR 2010.

30 Siehe u.a. *Bocharov v. Ukraine*, no. 21037/05, §§ 5, 11-13, 55-60, ECHR 2011; *Borotyuk v. Ukraine*, no. 33579/04, §§ 32, 84, ECHR 2010; *Dushka v. Ukraine*, no. 29175/04, §§ 40-54, ECHR 2011; *Kovalchuk v. Ukraine*, §§ 26, 55-70, no. 21958/05, ECHR 2010; *Lazarenko v. Ukraine*, no. 22313/04, §§ 11, 46-59, ECHR 2010 (Art. 6 EMRK); *Shabelnik v. Ukraine*, no. 16404/03, §§ 35, 59-60, ECHR 2009 (Art. 6 EMRK); *Suptel v. Ukraine*, no. 39188/04, §§ 8, 48-52, ECHR 2009.

31 Siehe u.a. *Buzilov v. Moldova*, no. 28653/05, §§ 7-9, 23-32, ECHR 2009; *Gurgurov v. Moldova*, no. 7045/08, §§ 7-23, 62, ECHR 2009; *Levinta v. Moldova*, no. 17332/03, §§ 8-14, 27-31, 60-92, 105-106, ECHR 2008 (Art. 6 EMRK); *Paduret v. Moldova*, no. 33134/03, §§ 9-16, 78-79, ECHR 2010; *Roşca v. Moldova*, no. 41704/02, §§ 8-21, 41-42, 76, ECHR 2009; *Vetrenko v. Moldova*, no. 36552/02, §§ 43, 58, ECHR 2010.

32 *Harutyunyan v. Armenia*, no. 36549/03, §§ 8-11, 66, ECHR 2007 (Art. 6 EMRK).

33 *Ismoilov & Others v. Russia*, no. 2947/06, ECHR 2008; *Sultanov v. Russia*, no. 15303/09, ECHR 2009; *Karimov v. Russia*, no. 54219/08, ECHR 2010; *Isakov v. Russia*, no. 14049/08, ECHR 2010; *Yuldashev v. Russia*, 1248/09, ECHR 2010; *Garayev v. Azerbaijan*, no. 53088/08, ECHR 2010; *Muminov v. Russia*, no. 42502/06, ECHR 2008.

34 *Soldatenko v. Ukraine*, no. 2440/07, ECHR 2008; *Kolesnik v. Russia*, no. 26876/08, ECHR 2010; *Khodzhayev v. Russia*, 52466/08, ECHR 2010; *Ryabkinin v. Russia*, no. 8320/04, ECHR 2008; *Garabayev v. Russia*, no. 38411/02, ECHR 2007.

35 *Gaforov v. Russia*, no. 25404/09, ECHR 2009; *Iskandarov v. Russia*, no. 17185/05, ECHR 2010; *Khaydirov v. Russia*, no. 21055/09, ECHR 2010.

Belarus[37] als Länder der Folter abgestempelt worden. Im Lichte dieser Wirklichkeit fragt man sich, ob die neuen Absprachevarianten in Russland, um die These von *J. H. Langbein* zu zitieren, als legaler Ersatz für die Folter dienen, um dieselben Schuldgeständnisse zu erwirken[38].

Russland hat auf dem Niveau des geschriebenen Rechts ehrlich und offen das Problem der erzwungenen Geständnisse anerkannt und bekämpft. Art. 51 Konst.-RU garantiert ein Schweigerecht, das 2001 in § 47(4)(3) StPO-RU implementiert wurde. Ein ähnliches Schweigerecht wird auch in den anderen postsowjetischen Republiken deklarativ geschützt[39]. Art. 50(2) Konst.-RU sieht auch vor, dass gesetz- bzw. verfassungswidrig gesammelte Beweismittel nicht verwertet werden dürfen und dieses Beweisverwertungsverbot wurde in § 75(1) StPO-RU verankert. In vielen anderen postsowjetischen Republiken wurden Beweisverwertungsverbote verabschiedet, die auch auf erzwungene Geständnisse angewandt werden können[40].

Bevor ein Beklagter in Russland vernommen werden kann, veranlassen §§ 173, 47(4)(3,8) StPO-RU den verhörenden Beamten, ihn über sein Schweigerecht bzw. sein Recht auf Verteidigerbeistand zu informieren; viele der postsowjetischen Republiken haben ähnliche *Miranda*-Rechte[41] verabschiedet[42]. Aber genauso wie bei der *Miranda*-Entscheidung darf ein Gefangener auf seine Rechte verzichten und sich vernehmen lassen. Der inhärente Zwang des Polizeigewahrsams führt oft zu einem Verzicht auf wichtige Verfassungsrechte. Russische Beschuldigte in der Untersuchungshaft verzichteten nicht nur oft auf ihre Schweigerechte, sondern verzichteten und verzichten immer noch auf ihr Recht auf ein Geschworenengericht, obwohl die Möglichkeit eines Freispruchs etwa zwanzig Mal größer ist als vor Berufsrichtern. Der russische Gesetzgeber ging aber weiter als die anderen Republiken und verbot mit § 75(2)(1) StPO-RU die Verwertung von zur Zeit der Hauptverhandlung nicht bestätigten Geständnissen,

---

36 *Baysakov & Others v. Ukraine*, no. 54131/08, ECHR 2010; *Kaboulov v. Ukraine*, no. 41015/04, ECHR 2009.

37 *Koktysh v. Ukraine*, no. 43707/07, ECHR 2009.

38 *J.H. Langbein*, „Torture and Plea Bargaining“, University of Chicago Law Review, Bd. 46, S. 3-22 (1978).

39 Art. 42(1), Konst.-AR; Art. 74 Konst.-AS; Art. 27(1) Konst.-BE; Art. 22(3) Konst-ES; Art. 42(8) Konst.-GE; Art. 77(3)(7) Konst.-KA; Art. 63, Abs. 1, Konst.-UK. Vgl. § 20(1) StPO-AR; § 20(1) StPO-AS; § 10(4) StPO-BE; § 73(1)(b) StPO-GE; § 12(2) StPO-KY; § 21 StPO-MO; § 25(1) StPO-TU; § 63, Abs. 1 StPO-UK.

40 Art. 42(2) Konst-AR; Art. 71(3) Konst.-AS; Art. 27(2) Konst-BE; Art. 42(7) Konst. GE; Art. 77(3, 9) Konst-KA; Art. 89(2) Konst-KY; Art.62(3) Konst.-UK.

41 In den USA wurden solche Warnungen zuerst in dem inzwischen legendär gewordenen Fall von *Miranda v. Arizona*, 382 USA 436 (1966), als verfassungsmäßig notwendig erklärt.

42 Siehe z.B. § 211(3) StPO-AR; § 90(7)(10), 232(4) StPO-AS; §§ 34, 75(2) StPO-ES; § 310(2,3) StPO-GE; §§ 114, 216(3), 217(2) StPO-KA; § 191(2) StPO-KY; §§ 150, 265(1) StPO-LE; §§ 64(2), 104(1) StPO-MO; § 255(3) StPO-TU.

wenn der angeblich Geständige ohne Verteidigerbeistand vernommen wurde. Diese Vorschrift entstand, um Beschuldigte gegen den Gebrauch von gesetzwidrigen Methoden des Vernehmens zu schützen[43].

Trotz dieser weitsichtigen rechtsstaatlichen Reform benutzen Ermittlungsbeamte sog. „Taschenanwälte" (*karmannij adwokat*), um diese Vorschrift zu umgehen. Sie sind von den Ermittlungsbeamten ernannte Pflichtverteidiger, die oft früher Polizisten, Ermittlungsbeamte oder Staatsanwälte waren und die ihre Mandanten ermuntern, bei der Vernehmung auszusagen oder schweigsam danebensitzen, während diese misshandelt werden[44]. Wenn ein Angeklagter versucht, die Verwertung eines durch Zwang erlangten Geständnisses zu verhindern, verlässt der Richter sich immer auf das Wort der Staatsanwaltschaft, dass ihre Untersuchung keine gesetzwidrigen Metoden festgestellt haben, um ein Beweisverbot abzulehnen[45]. Als Ergebnis der ständigen Rechtsprechung des russischen Obersten Gerichts darf weder der Angeklagte noch sein Verteidiger den Gebrauch von Folter oder anderen menschenrechtswidrigen Vernehmungstaktiken vor dem Geschworenengericht erwähnen, um die Glaubwürdigkeit des Geständnisses in Frage zu stellen. Das Oberste Gericht hat sehr viele Freisprüche des Geschworenengerichts wegen Verstoßes gegen diese Regel aufgehoben[46].

IV. Eine Analyse der vereinfachten konsensuellen Verfahrensformen in den postsowjetischen Republiken

1. Täter-Opfer-Ausgleich

Den im alten Gemeinrecht verwurzelten Täter-Opfer-Ausgleich gab es schon in den sowjetischen Strafprozessordnungen[47] und er ist immer noch populär in den postsowjetischen Ländern[48], wo man manchmal von einem „Recht auf Ausgleich mit dem Opfer" redet[49]. Er bildet oft die erste obligatorische Phase nach

43 *Thaman*, „The Nullification of the Russian Jury: Lessons for Jury-Inspired Reform in Eurasia and Beyond", Cornell International Law Journal, Bd. 40 (2007), S. 376.

44 Ebenda, S. 376-377.

45 Ebenda, S. 377. Das Gleiche geschieht in Kasachstan. Resultaty monitoringa sudebnych rasbiratel'stw w Respublike Kazachstan 2005-2006 g.g. otchet. OBSE/BDIPCh: Almaty (2007), S. 10.

46 *S.C. Thaman* (2007), S. 377-378.

47 § 5(6) StPO-RSFSR (1961).

48 Siehe § 36 StPO-AR; §§ 26(2), 29(1)(5), 30(1)(2) StPO-BE; §§ 536-538 StPO-LE; §§ 207, 420 StPO-LI; §§ 5(para.1)(3), 5.3 CCP-TA; §§ 532-86 CCP-US.

49 Z.B. § 66(1)(17) CCP-LA.

der Eröffnung einer Privatklage wegen Vergehen wie Tätlichkeiten, Vandalismus usw.[50].

Weil der Täter-Opfer-Ausgleich der Einwilligung des Geschädigten bedarf, meistens ohne Schuldurteil endet und nur bei Vergehen in Frage kommt, bei denen die Anordnung von U-Haft normalerweise keine Rolle spielt, ist er meines Erachtens rechtsstaatlich unbedenklich. Er gehört zur idealen Form des akkusatorischen Konsensualverfahrens und wird erfolgreich in manchen Republiken angewandt[51].

2. Strafbefehle

Meiner Kenntnis nach gibt es Strafbefehle nur in Estland und Litauen. In beiden Ländern darf der Staatsanwalt einen Strafbefehl nur beantragen, wenn keine Freiheitsstrafe in Frage kommt[52]. Die Entscheidung über den Antrag muss in Litauen binnen sieben, in Estland binnen zehn Tagen getroffen werden[53]. Während der Richter in Estland befugt ist, den Erlass eines Strafbefehls abzulehnen[54], ist das in Litauen nicht der Fall[55].

Trotz der Kritik, dass der Staatsanwalt durch den Strafbefehl die richterliche Rechtsprechungsrolle übernimmt[56], was besonders im Fall von Litauen zuzutreffend scheint, besteht nur eine geringe Gefahr, dass diese Verfahrensalternative koerzitiv missbraucht werden kann, da es sich hier lediglich um Vergehen und Geldstrafen handelt und die Angeklagten sich gewöhnlich nicht in U-Haft befinden, wenn ihnen die Strafbefehlsanträge zugesandt werden[57].

3. Guilty Pleas und andere Varianten der Schuldakzeptanz

Trotz der ideologischen Abneigung gegen Schuldvereinbarungen oder Kooperationsverträge auf dem europäischen Kontinent bin ich der Meinung, dass es sie fast immer gegeben hat. So war es mit *plea bargaining* in den USA und natür-

---

50 Z.B. § 84(para.5)(2) StPO-US; bei § 25 StPO-RU ist Täter-Opfer-Ausgleicht bei weniger- und mittelschwerer Strafdelikte anwendbar.

51 In Russland wurden z.B. 2008 1.124.000 Strafverfahren eröffnet, von denen 309.900 eingestellt wurden. 233.000 der Einstellungen waren Folge des Täter-Opfer-Ausgleichs, weniger als die 270.000 Einstellungen aus demselben Grund im Vorjahr; *S.C. Thaman* (2010), S. 338.

52 § 251(1) StPO-ES; § 425(1) StPO-LI.

53 §§ 427, 429 StPO-LI; § 254(6) StPO-ES.

54 § 253(3) StPO-ES.

55 § 427 StPO-LI.

56 *S.C. Thaman* (2010), S. 341.

57 In Estland und Litauen gibt es laut den Menschenrechtsberichten des US State Departement immer noch Berichte über den übermäßigen Gebrauch von U-Haft sowie über die Misshandlung von Gefangen, um Geständnisse zu erwirken. http://www.state.gov/g/drl/rls/hrrpt/2009/eur/136042.htm und http://www.state.gov/g/drl/rls/hrrpt/2009/eur/136029.htm.

lich auch mit Absprachen in Deutschland. Russische Rechts- und Staatsanwälte geben auch zu, dass es Kooperationsverträge mit der Polizei sogar zu Sowjetzeiten gab, durch die nach erfolgreicher Zusammenarbeit eine Strafanklage durch ein Ordnungswidrigkeitsverfahren ersetzt wurde[58].

In manchen europäischen Strafprozessordnungen des 19. Jahrhunderts wurde der Angeklagte am Anfang der Hauptverhandlung jeweils vor den Geschworenen gefragt, ob er seine Schuld gestehe. Eine Vorschrift der russichen StPO von 1864 erlaubte bei einem derartigen Schuldbekenntnis den sofortigen Übergang zu den Schlussplädoyers der Parteien, wenn die Richter, der Staatsanwalt, die Prozessbeteiligten und die Jury selbst nicht auf die Durchführung der Beweisaufnahme bestanden[59]. In der StPO Spaniens von 1882, die noch in Kraft ist, konnte der Angeklagte seine *conformidad* mit einer Anklage ausdrücken, solange die plädierte Freiheitsstrafe nicht mehr als sechs Jahre betrug[60].

Ähnliche Vorschriften findet man heute in einigen Republiken, die wie in Spanien nur bei weniger schweren Straftatbeständen anzuwenden sind[61]. In Kasachstan und Turkmenistan besteht dann die Beweisaufnahme nur in der Vernehmung des Angeklagten und des Geschädigten[62], während in Litauen nur der Angeklagte vernommen und die gesamte Akte des Ermittlungsverfahrens im Gericht verlesen wird[63]. Nach einem gerichtlichen Schuldgeständnis in Belarus geht man jedoch direkt zu den Schlussplädoyers über[64]. In Kasachstan üben Richter gelegentlich Druck auf den Angeklagten aus, seine Schuld zu gestehen, um die Hauptverhandlung schnell zum Abschluss zu bringen[65].

Sonst gab es erst mit der StPO Italiens von 1988 eine neue Wende zu konsensuellen Verfahrensformen, unter denen der Strafantrag oder *patteggiamento* am einflussreichsten war. Demzufolge konnte der Angeklagte seine

58 *S. Militsin*, „Sdelki o prisnanii viny: vosmozhen li rossijskij variant?“, Rossijskaja justitsia Bd. 12 (1999), S. 41-42.

59 §§ 680-682 Ustaw ugolownogo sudoproiswodstwa, 20. November 1864, http://www.gumer.info/bibliotek_Buks/History/Article/ust_ugprav.php.

60 *S.C. Thaman* (2010), S. 345.

61 Z.B. in Kasachstan und Turkmenistan, wo eine abgekürzte Beweisaufnahme bei geständigen Angeklagten möglich ist. § 363(1) StPO-KA; § 406(1), (2)(1) StPO-TU. In Litauen sind bei dem verkürzten Verfahren nur Schwerverbrechen ausgeschlossen, § 269(1) StPO-LI.

62 § 363(3) StPO-KA; § 406(2) StPO-TU.

63 §§ 269(1), 287(1) StPO-LI. Es gab dieses Modell auch in Estland, bis die StPO-ES von 2004 in Kraft trat. *M. Sillaots*, „Admission and Confession of Guilt in Settlement Proceedings under Estonian Criminal Procedure“, Juridica international, Bd. IX (2004), S.117-118.

64 § 326(1) StPO-BE. Eine ähnliche Vorschrift wurde in dem russischen Geschworenengerichtsgesetz von 1993 eingeführt, aber kaum benutzt. Sie gibt es nicht in der StPO-RU (2001). *S.C. Thaman* (1995), S. 103-104.

65 Für Beispiele des Drucks auf den Angeklagten, sich als schuldig in der Hauptverhandlung in Kasachstan zu erklären, siehe Rezultaty monitoringa, S. 9-10.

Straffälligkeit bis auf ein Drittel beschränken, wenn er zustimmte, ohne Hauptverhandlung bestraft zu werden. Am Anfang galt dieses Verfahren nur für Anklagen, in denen die Höchststrafe drei Jahre nicht überschritt, seit 2003 findet das Verfahren jedoch auch Anwendung, wenn die engültige Freiheitsstrafe nach einem Strafnachlass von einem Drittel fünf Jahre nicht übersteigt[66]. Das *patteggiamento* war das Modell für das 2001 eingeführte russische „Spezialverfahren für Entscheidung bei der Übereinstimmung des Angeklagten mit der Anklage[67]". In anderen postsowjetischen Republiken wurden Absprachen eingeführt, die aber mehr Ähnlichkeit mit dem amerikanischen *plea bargaining* aufweisen.

4. Kooperationsverträge

Bei den bundesamerikanischen Kooperationsverträgen hält die Staatsanwaltschaft die Zügel fest in der Hand. Nur wenn sie zustimmt, dass der Angeklagte ausreichend Hilfe geleistet hat, gibt es die Möglichkeit einer Abweichung von den strengen Strafzumessungsregeln (sog. *downward departure*), womöglich sogar bis unter die Mindeststrafe[68].

Schon 2004 gab es in der StPO Georgiens die Möglichkeit, einen Kooperationsvertrag besonders bei Schwerverbrechen und Korruptionsdelikten zu vereinbaren, der zu einem Straferlass bzw. einer Einstellung bei „außerordentlicher Hilfe" führen kann[69]. In Litauen kann das Ermittlungsverfahren eingestellt werden, wenn der Beschuldigte nach einem vollen Geständnis seiner Schuld bei der Ermittlung einer kriminellen Organisation mithilft. Falls sich der Beschuldigte danach jedoch weigert, im Verfahren gegen Dritte auszusagen, darf das Strafverfahren wieder aufgenommen werden[70].

In Lettland hat der Angeklagte ein „Kooperationsrecht", d.h. (1) ein Recht, einen vereinfachten Verfahrensmodus zu wählen, (2) ein Recht, den Verfahrenslauf zu beeinflussen und (3) ein Recht, die Straftaten Dritter aufzudecken[71]. Die Kooperation kann zu einer Einstellung aller – außer der schwersten Anklage-

66 *M. Langer* (2010), S. 63.

67 Ich habe selbst den ersten Entwurf des Kapitels über vereinfachte Verfahrensmoden geschrieben, in dem das *patteggiamento* vorgeschlagen wurde. *S.C. Thaman* (2010), S. 346.

68 Siehe § 5 K1.1 USA Sentencing Guidelines. Über dieses unbegrenzte Ermessen der Staatsanwaltschaft *G. Fisher*, S. 217-219.

69 §§ 679-1 StPO-GE (2004). Die Möglichkeit einer Einstellung als Folge der Kooperation bei der Verfolgung besonders schwerer Verbrechen in „außerordentlichen Fällen" findet man auch bei § 218(1) StPO-GE (2010).

70 § 210 StPO-LI.

71 §§ 22, 66(1)(2) StPO-LE. In Moldawien hat der Angeklagte ein Recht, die Anklage einzugestehen und eine Schuldvereinbarung mit der Staatsanwaltschaft zu treffen; er hat aber auch ein „Recht", die besondere Verfahrensforme zu wählen und mit dem Opfer einen Ausgleich zu verhandeln. §§ 64(2)(8,9,10,21) StPO-MO.

punkte – führen, solange die durch den Angeklagten aufklärte Straftat schwerwiegender war als seine eigene[72].

In den USA kennt der Kooperierende die endgültige Strafzumessung erst, nachdem die Staatsanwaltschaft die Adäquanz seiner Mitarbeit eingeschätzt hat. In Moldawien scheint der Richter das letzte Wort zu haben, ob der Angeklagte ausreichend bei der Strafverfolgung Dritter geholfen hatte[73].

In Russland gibt es viele strafrechtliche Vorschriften, die eine Befreiung von der Strafverantwortung ermöglichen, wenn ein Mittäter aktiv hilft, die Vollendung der Straftat zu verhindern oder eine vollendete Straftat aufzudecken[74]. Mit der Verabschiedung des neuen Kapitels der StPO-RU über Kooperationsvereinbarungen im Jahre 2009, dürfen jetzt Staatsanwaltschaft und Verteidigung legal die Bedingungen der Kooperation im Voraus aushandeln.

Laut dem neuen Gesetz stellt der Beschuldigte einen Antrag auf eine Kooperationsvereinbarung an den Ermittlungsbeamten vor dem Ende des Ermittlungsverfahrens. Wenn der Staatsanwalt mit dem Antrag übereinstimmt, lädt er den Verteidiger und den Ermittlungsbeamten ein, eine Vereinbarung zu schließen, in der Folgendes beschrieben wird: „die Taten, die der Beschuldigte/Angeklagte verspricht, auszuführen, um die in der vorgerichtlichen Kooperationsvereinbarung festgelegten Pflichten zu erfüllen[75]“. Wird der Beschuldigte am Schluss der Ermittlungen doch angeklagt, stellt der Staatsanwalt einen Antrag, das Spezialverfahren anzuwenden, der aus einer schriftlicher Erklärung der Hinlänglichkeit, Glaubwürdigkeit und Wichtigkeit der von dem Angeklagten geleisteten Hilfe zur Aufdeckung der Straftat, der durch die Straftat erlangten Gegenstände und zur Identifikation der Täter, einer Beschreibung der Straftaten, die dadurch aufgedeckt wurden sowie der Beschreibung der Gefahren für den Angeklagten und seine Familie und Freunde, die durch seine Mitarbeit verursacht wurden, besteht[76].

Der Antrag des Staatsanwalts wird vom Richter überprüft und kann akzeptiert werden, solange die Vereinbarung freiwillig zustande kam und die durch den Angeklagten vermittelte Information nicht ausschließlich mit seiner eigenen Verantwortung zu tun hatte[77]. Die Strafe darf nicht höher als die Hälfte der Höchststrafe sein und kann unterhalb der Mindeststrafe liegen. Die Strafe darf auch ausgesetzt werden. Die jetzt gesetzlich verankerte Kooperationsvereinba-

72 § 410(1,2) StPO-LE.

73 §§ 508-509 StPO-MO.

74 Es gibt eine allgemeine Vorschrift für nicht schwere Straftaten, aber auch besondere Vorschriften für besonders schwere Straftaten wie Terrorismus, Menschenhandel oder sogar Hochverrat. Siehe *S.C. Thaman*, „Russia“, in *K.J. Heller/M.D. Dubber* (Hrsg.), The Handbook of Comparative Criminal Law, Stanford Univ. Press: Stanford, CA (2010), S. 425-426.

75 § 317.3 StPO-RU.

76 § 317.5 StPO-RU.

77 § 317.6 StPO-RU.

rung wurde zum ersten Mal im Oktober 2009 in St. Petersburg angewandt, als ein Mitglied einer organisierten kriminellen Bande gegen den Bandenchef in einem Mordprozess aussagte[78].

5. Vereinbarung auf eine schriftliche Hauptverhandlung auf Basis der Ermittlungsakte

Neben dem *patteggiamento* wurde in der StPO Italiens von 1988 auch ein „abgekürztes Verfahren“ (*giudizio abbreviato*) eingeführt, das dem Angeklagten die Möglichkeit einräumt, sich einen Strafnachlass von einem Drittel zu sichern, indem er auf die öffentliche, mündliche, unmittelbare und adversarische Hauptverhandlung zugunsten einer schriftlichen „Hauptverhandlung“ auf Basis der Ermittlungsakte verzichtet. Anders als mit dem *patteggiamento* besteht diese Möglichkeit bei allen Strafverfolgungen, sogar wenn eine lebenslange Freiheitsstrafe verhängt werden könnte[79].

In Estland wurde ein ähnliches Verfahren mit einem Drittelstrafnachlass eingeführt, das in allen Fällen angewendet werden kann, solange keine lebenslange Freiheitsstrafe verhängt werden kann.

6. Strafrahmen der neuen konsensuellen Verfahrensformen

Die koerzitiven Möglichkeiten einer Absprache sind am Höchsten in Ländern wie den USA, in denen sogar Anklagen, die zu einem Todesurteil oder zu einer lebenslangen Freiheitsstrafe führen können, ohne Beschränkung den Verhandlungen des *plea bargaining* unterworfen sind. Unbeschränktes *plea bargaining* amerikanischen Stils findet sich auch in Lettland und Georgien[80]. In Moldawien werden nur die allerschwersten Straftaten aus dem Bereich des *plea bargaining* ausgeschlossen[81] und in Estland sind Verbrechen ausgeschlossen, für die eine Freiheitsstrafe von vier Jahren bis lebenslang möglich ist[82].

Normalerweise aber treffen die neuen Absprachenvarianten in Europa und Lateinamerika allerdings nur bei weniger schweren Straftatbeständen zu. Wie infolge des italienischen *patteggiamento*, ist die Höchststrafe auch in Russland merklich gestiegen. Bei der ersten Lesung des StPO-Entwurfs in der Staatsduma war das Spezialverfahren nur anzuwenden, wenn die Höchstfreiheitsstrafe nicht

---

78 Ebenda.

79 Statt lebenslang wird eine Freiheitsstrafe von 30 Jahren verhängt. §§ 438(1), 442(1-2) StPO Italien.

80 §§ 539-543 StPO-LE (2005); §§ 209-215 StPO-GE (2010). Eine Gesetzesänderung von 2004 hat das amerikanische *plea bargaining* schon in die alte StPO eingeführt. § 679 StPO-GE (2004), siehe *J.D. Reichelt*, „A Hobson’s Experiment: Plea Bargaining in the Republic of Georgia“, Journal of East European Law, Bd. 11 (2004), S. 159, 168.

81 § 504(2) StPO-MO.

82 § 239 StPO-ES.

mehr als drei Jahre betrug. In der endgültigen Fassung war sie auf fünf Jahre angehoben[83]. Mit der Ausweitung auf Freiheitsstrafen auf zehn Jahre kommen jetzt Absprachen auch bei einigen Straftatbeständen in Frage, die der Geschworenengerichtsbarkeit unterliegen[84].

7. Gesetzlicher Strafnachlass oder unbeschränktes Bargaining?

Obwohl die Bundesstrafzumessungsrichtlinien (*Federal Sentencing Guidelines*) in den USA einen Strafnachlass von einem Drittel bei einem *guilty plea* vorschlagen, liegt er mehr im Bereich von zwei Dritteln, was das System inhärent koerzitiv macht. In der Praxis der Gerichte des Vereinigten Königreichs ist ein Strafnachlass von einem Drittel auch informell anerkannt, obwohl nicht gesetzmäßig gefestigt[85].

Meines Erachtens wurde ein gesetzlich festgesetzer Strafnachlass für eine verfahrensbeendende Schuldvereinbarung zuerst mit der StPO Italiens 1988 eingeführt[86].

In Lettland, Estland, Moldawien und Georgien dürfen die Parteien anscheinend nicht nur über die zu verhängende Strafe, sondern auch über die Schuldqualifikation frei verhandeln. In den Vergleichsverfahren Estlands hat der Richter dagegen überhaupt keinen Einfluss auf das ausgehandelte Urteil. Wie bei einem Strafbefehl in Deutschland muss es etweder akzeptiert oder abgelehnt werden[87]. In Georgien kann der Richter Änderungen in dem *plea agreement* vorschlagen, die aber nur mit Zustimmung der Staatsanwaltschaft und der Verteidigung verwirklicht werden können[88].

8. Das Problem der richterlichen Kontrolle

Bei allen vereinfachten Verfahrensarten, die einer Hauptverhandlung ausweichen und direkt oder zumindest schneller zum Schluss gelangen, entsteht die Frage, auf welcher Basis die endgültige Urteilsfindung ruht und worin das Urteil überhaupt besteht. Schließlich muss man natürlich anlässlich der allgemeinen Abhängigkeit bzw. Korrumpiertheit der postsowjetischen Richterschaften auch fragen, ob sogar die Urteile, die nach einem vollen Ermittlungsverfahren durch Absprachen zustande kommen, rechtsstaatlichen Ansprüchen genügen.

---

83 *S.C. Thaman* (2010), S. 348-50.

84 *S.C. Thaman* (2007), S. 367-69.

85 Im Allgemeinen siehe *S.C. Thaman* (2010), S. 350-351.

86 § 316(7) StPO-RU. In Litauen darf der Richter auch die Strafe bis auf ein Drittel weniger als die Mindeststrafe setzen, § 440(1) StPO-LI.

87 §§ 245, 248 StPO-ES. „*The settlement includes an agreement as to the charges, the punishment and the amount, if any, of compensation or damages awarded to the aggrieved party or civil complainant.*“

88 § 213(5,6) StPO-GE.

In den USA spielt der Richter in manchen Bundesstaaten eine aktive Rolle bei dem Aushandeln der *plea bargains*, wie es eben der deutsche Richter bei der Verständigung gemäß § 257c STPO Deutschland tut. Die Bundesrechtsordnung und andere Staaten lehnen aber diese aktive Rolle ab, weil die Teilnahme des Richters als inhärent koerzitiv betrachtet wird[89]. Wir haben oben gesehen, dass der Richter in Georgien, Lettland, Estland und Moldawien gewisse Kontrollmöglichkeiten innehat, die Frage jedoch bleibt, ob ein Richter in diesen Ländern gegen die Staatsanwaltschaft eine angebotene prozessendende, mit angeblicher Übereinstimmung des Angeklagten erlangte Absprache im Dienste der Wahrheitsfindung ablehnen könnte und würde.

Meiner Kenntnis nach darf der Richter nie bei den vereinfachten Prozessformen auf Aktenbasis freisprechen, wie es mit dem spanischen *conformidad* und dem italienischen *patteggiamento* möglich ist[90]. Obwohl das russische Spezialverfahren wie das *patteggiamento* kein ausdrückliches Schuldgeständnis verlangt, sondern eine Übereinstimmung mit der Richtigkeit der Anklage, hat das Oberste Gericht Russlands erklärt, dass der Richter bei Zweifeln an der Schuld des Angeklagten den Fall in die normale Verfahrenslaufbahn zurückschicken sollte und nicht freisprechen darf[91].

Richter in den Ländern des anglo-amerikanischen Gemeinrechts müssen traditionell ihre Urteile weder nach einer vollen Hauptverhandlung noch nach einem *guilty plea* begründen. Der amerikanische Richter muss sich allenfalls nach einem *guilty plea* überzeugen, dass es eine „tatsächliche Grundlage“ (*factual basis*) der Schuld gibt, bevor er das Urteil fällt. Leider wird die Feststellung dieser „tatsächlichen Grundlage“ nicht sehr ernst genommen und lässt eine oberflächliche Erklärung der Staatsanwaltschaft genügen, dass sie hätte beweisen können, der Angeklagte habe die angeklagten kriminellen Handlungen ausgeführt[92].

Nach einer verfahrensendenden Vereinbarung in den meisten europäischen und lateinamerikanischen Ländern muss das endgültige Urteil entweder in der üblichen Weise begründet werden oder der Richter muss mindestens, wie in Italien, das Nichtvorhandensein von Schuldausschließungsgründen bzw. den be-

---

89 Siehe dazu *J. Turner*, „Judicial Participation in Plea Negotiations: A Comparative View“, 54 American Journal of Comparative Law, Bd. 54 (2006), *J. Comp. L.* (2006), S. 199-200, 258-259, die für eine aktive Rolle des Richters beim *plea bargaining* sowie bei deutschen Absprachen plädiert.

90 Die einzige Ausnahme wäre das estländische abgekürzte Verfahren auf Basis der Ermittlungsakte, das oben besprochen wurde. Über die Möglichkeit eines Freispruchs bei manchen prozessendenden Vereinbarungen siehe *S.C. Thaman* (2010), S. 367.

91 Postanowlenie No. 1 Plenuma Werchownogo Suda Rossijskoj Federazii (5. März 2004): „Nekotorye woprosy praktiki primenenija sudami ugolowno-prozessual’nychh norm pri osuschtschestwlenii prawosudija“, Bjulletin werchownogo suda rossijskoj federazii, No. 8 (24. August 2004).

92 *S.C. Thaman* (2010), S. 367-368.

gründeten Verdacht bestätigen[93]. Das Gleiche gilt mehr oder weniger auch für Moldawien und Lettland[94]. Bei Billigung einer Absprache in Estland bestätigt der Richter jedoch bloß die ausgehandelte Straftat, die Strafe und die zivilrechtliche Entschädigung[95]. Ähnlich läuft es in Russland bei dem Spezialverfahren, wo das Urteil nur eine Beschreibung der Straftat enthält, mit der der Angeklagte seine Übereinstimmung erklärt hatte. Das Gesetz lautet insoweit: „Eine Analyse der Beweismittel und ihre richterliche Würdigung wird im Urteil nicht ausgedrückt[96]". Es gibt auch weder Berufungs- noch Revisionsmöglichkeiten im Hinblick auf die Hinlänglichkeit der Beweismittel oder andere Verstöße gegen strafrechtliche bzw. strafverfahrensrechtliche Normen[97].

9. Häufigkeit des Gebrauchs von Absprachen

Im Jahre 2002 wurden 59.8% aller Strafverfahren in Estland durch ein „vereinfachtes Verfahren" erledigt, das zwischen 1996 und 2004 in Kraft war[98]. Das 2001 eingeführte Spezialverfahren in Russland wird auch jedes Jahr in zunehmendem Maße angewandt und hat wirklich Wurzeln geschlagen. So wurde es 2002 in nur 9% aller Fälle angewandt, in den folgenden zwei Jahren stieg der Prozentsatz jedoch bis auf 14,3% an. In den Friedensgerichten, wo nur Vergehen verhandelt werden, wurde das Spezialverfahren 2005 in 37,5% der Fälle, 2008 in 42,5% der Fälle und 2009 in 50,5% der Fälle angewandt. In den Bezirksgerichten (*rayonyj sud*) stieg der Prozentsatz von 30% (2005) bis 50% (2008) und auf 53% in der ersten Hälfte von 2010. In den oberen Gerichten für Schwerverbrechen, wo die Geschworenengerichten zuständig sein können, wuchs die Zahl der Absprachen von 2,4% (2004) auf 9% (2008) und erreichte fast 10% im Jahre 2009 und der ersten Hälfte von 2010[99]. Eine ähnliche Zunahme ist auch in Moldawien nachweisbar, wo der Prozentsatz der Absprachen 8.6% (2004) betrug, in den Folgejahren aber auf 35% (2005) und 49% (2006) anstieg[100].

In Russland wurden im Jahre 2006 54,5% aller Umweltstrafverfahren, 52,7% der Anklage wegen Verstößen gegen die Waffengesetze, 50,5% der Bestechungsdelikte, 44,7% der Anklagen wegen Veruntreuung oder Unterschlagung, 13,8% der Diebstähle und 42,2% der Betäubungsmittelfälle in den mittleren Bezirksgerichten erledigt, während die Zahlen in den Friedensgerichten bei 66,1% der Betäubungsmittelfälle, 62,3% der Umweltstrafsachen, 56,7% der

93 Ebenda, S. 368.
94 § 509 StPO-MO; § 543 StPO-LE.
95 § 249 StPO-ES.
96 § 316(8) StPO-RU.
97 §§ 317, 379(1) StPO-RU.
98 *M. Sillaots*, S.115-116.
99 *S.C. Thaman* (2010), S. 378. Für die erste Hälfte 2010 siehe http://www.cdep.ru/index.php?id=5&item=454, für 2009 siehe http://www.cdep.ru/index.php?id=5&item=302
100 *S.C. Thaman* (2010), S. 378.

Waffendelikte, 56,7% der Diebstähle und 55,1% der Veruntreuungsfälle liegen[101].

10. Zusammenfassung

Obwohl Strafrechtsdogmatiker immer noch behaupten, dass Absprachen jähe Verstöße gegen das Legalitätsprinzip, das Prinzip der materiellen Wahrheit, wenn nicht gar gegen die Unschuldsvermutung und andere Grundprinzipien des rechtstaatlichen Strafverfahrens sind[102], wurden sie jetzt weithin von den höchsten Gerichten Europas sowie Amerikas und sogar vom Europarat aus prozessökonomischen Gründen akzeptiert[103].

Die Kritik besteht jedoch in den westlichen Demokratien mit unabhängigen Richterschaften fort, wo der typische Drittelnachlass weithin nicht so koerzitiv ist wie das mit drakonischen Freiheitsstrafen unterstützte Angebot eines amerikanischen Staatsanwalts. *Ferrajoli* geht meines Erachtens am Weitesten, wenn er sagt, dass das *patteggiamento* und die anderen italienischen Spezialverfahren zu der „unausweichbaren Korrpution der Rechtsprechung, polizeistaatlicher Kontamination des Verfahrens und der Beweismittel und einem daraus entstehenden Verlust der politischen und äußeren Legitimation der richterlichen Gewalt führen[104]". Sie seien „die perverseste Innovation des neuen Regimes" und bedeuten eine Rückkehr zur „inquisitorischen Vernehmung des Angeklagten durch Polizei und Staatanwaltschaft[105]".

In der Tat hat *Ferrajoli* vielleicht dann recht, wenn der Richter durch seine Machtlosigkeit oder Abhängigkeit keine Kontrollfunktion ausübt oder – schlimmer – mit der Staatsanwaltschaft in einem gemeinsamen Komplott steht, um den Angeklagten zu überführen und ihm ein Geständnis abzupressen[106]. Der Staatsanwalt übernimmt effektiv die rechtsprecherische Funktion, indem er durch die Anklageentscheidung und die Entscheidung, mit einer Absprache oder einer Kooperationsvereinbarung übereinzustimmen, die Strafe (oder Straflosigkeit) bedingt.

Der Wahrheitsanspruch eines Strafverfahrens entsteht meines Erachtens nur aus zwei möglichen Quellen: entweder aus einem vollständigen, ausschöpfenden, professionellen und nicht einseitig auf die Erlangung eines Geständis zielenden Ermittlungsverfahren oder aus einer öffentlichen, mündlichen, unmittel-

---

101 Ebenda.

102 Siehe *S.C. Thaman* (2010), S. 371-376.

103 Council of Europe Comittee of Ministers Recommendation No. R. (87) 18, Concerning the Simplification of Criminal Justice I.A.6. (18. September 1987).

104 *L. Ferrajoli*, S. 625, 637, 773.

105 Ebenda.

106 Über die Angst, dass Ermittlungsbeamte *guilty pleas* genauso straflos erzwingen würden, wie sie Geständnisse erzwingen. *V. Machow/M. Peschkow*, „Sdelka o prisnanii winy", Rossijskaja justizija, Bd. 7 (1998), S. 17.

baren, adversarischen Hauptverhandlung vor einem unabhängigen Richter, in der dem Angeklagten kompetenter Verteidigerbeistand gewährleistet wird.

Bei 95% der Strafverfahren in den USA hat man weder das eine noch das andere. Die Polizeiermittlung in den USA ist meistens sehr schnell zu Ende und die Akteneinsicht seitens der Verteidigung ist, besonders in den Bundesgerichten, sehr begrenzt[107]. Eine tiefere Überprüfung der Glaubwürdigkeit der Beweise findet erst bei der Hauptverhandlung statt. In Russland hat man leider auch weder das eine noch das andere, wenn man auf eine öffentliche, adversarische Hauptverhandlung verzichtet und über die Schuld per Absprache entscheiden lässt. Die miserable Qualität des auf erzwungenen Geständnis- bzw. Zeugenaussagen aufgebauten Ermittlungsverfahrens gilt weder als Grundlage für eine Absprache noch für eine Hauptverhandlung. Das Beweisfundament löst sich auf, sobald der Angeklagte oder die Hauptzeugen ihre Aussagen zurücknehmen. Die relativ hohe Freispruchsrate bei den Geschworenengerichten ist auf diesen Mangel an glaubwürdigen Beweismitteln zurückzuführen: da es jedoch so wenige Prozesse vor der Jury gibt und der Löwenanteil der Freisprüche bei Schwerverbrechen vom Obersten Gericht aufgehoben werden, bleibt das Geschworenengericht höchstens eine schöne demokratische Dekoration[108].

Es ist längst bekannt, und ich wiederhole: Es gibt Freisprüche in Russland praktisch nur in den Geschworenengerichten, trotz des Mangels an glaubwürdigen Beweisen. Dasselbe gilt auch für andere postsowjetische Republiken[109]. Die Wende zu Absprachen heißt auch, dass ca. 50% der Verfahren jetzt ohne eine öffentliche Beweisaufnahme stattfinden, die normalerweise bei einer Hauptverhandlung zwingend ist[110]. Ob sich so viele Angeklagte freiwillig für eine Absprache entscheiden, weil die Erfolgsaussichten bei einer solchen Hauptverhandlung so gering sind oder weil sie unter Druck gesetzt werden, ist schwer zu entscheiden. Ob sie tatsächlich einen wesentlichen Strafnachlass bekommen, ist gleichfalls nicht sicher[111].

---

107 Zur *discovery* in den USA-Gerichten siehe *W.R. La Fave* et al., Criminal Procedure (5. Aufl. 2009), S. 952-975.

108 Ein Freispruch des neuen georgischen Geschworenengerichts wird sofort rechtskräftig werden wie in den USA, § 266(1) StPO-GE (2010). Es ist aber noch zu früh zu wissen, ob diese Institution sich da durchschlagen wird.

109 *S.C. Thaman* (2008), S. 108.

110 Obwohl Prozesse vor Geschworenengerichten und Berufsrichtern mehr und mehr hinter geschlossen Türen wegen sog. „Staatsgeheimnissen" stattfinden. Berühmte Beispiele sind der erste Prozess gegen *M. Chodorkowskij* und der Geschworenenprozess gegen einen einfachen *Wor w sakone* Wjatscheslaw Iwan'kow, oder „Japonschik". *S.C. Thaman* (2007), S. 378-379.

111 Für die Meinung, dass gestehende Angeklagte normalerweise längere Freiheitsstrafen büßen, als die, die schweigen und sich auf die Schwächen der Beweisgrundlage verlassen, siehe *V. Machow/M. Peschkow*, S. 17-18.

Letztlich muss hervorgehoben werden, dass die strafrechtliche Verfolgung in den postsowjetischen Ländern in vielen Fällen nicht wegen strafrechtlicher Politik durchgeführt wird. In Russland benutzen die Ermittlungsorgane und andere einflussreiche Beamte der Exekutive das Strafrecht, um sich zu bereichern oder politische Gegner aus dem Weg zu räumen. Die Strafverfolgung von *M. Chodorkowskij* ist beispielhaft. Aber sogar in weniger bekannten Fällen werden Strafverfolgungen gegen Geschäfte und Geschäftsleute eingeleitet, ohne jegliche Absicht, sie ins Gericht zu bringen. Der alleinige Zweck ist die Erpressung von Geld oder Eigentum von den Beschuldigten im Tausch gegen eine Einstellung des Verfahrens. In weniger als 40% der Ermittlungsverfahren wegen ökonomischer Straftaten kommt der Fall überhaupt vor Gericht und in nur 10-15% gibt es je ein Urteil – während der Prozentsatz auf 75-90% steigt für Vergewaltigung und Mord[112].

Meines Erachtens werden Absprachen und Kooperationsvereinbarungen in dieser korrupten Atmosphäre die Situation nur verschlechtern. Dafür kann man die erste Erfahrung von *plea bargaining* in Georgien als Beispiel nehmen. Nach der sog. „Rosenrevolution" hat die *Saakashvili*-Regierung Strafverfahren gegen oppositionelle „Oligarchen" wegen Korruptionsdelikten eingeleitet und sich bereichert, indem sie hohe Geldbeträge im Tausch gegen eine Einstellung verlangt hat. Eine Bedingung von solchen Absprachen war oft, dass Klagen wegen Folter oder anderen Misshandlungen während des Ermittlungsverfahrens zurückgenommen wurden[113].

Man kann voraussehen, dass die neuen Kooperationsvereinbarungen eine große Rolle in Russland spielen werden, soweit die *Putin*-Clique weiter versucht, wie bei *JUKOS* und *M. Chodorkowskij*, die erfolgreichsten Unternehmen durch *corporate raiding* unter ihre Gewalt zu bringen. Ein Beispiel war die Strafermittlung gegen *Jewroset*, die offensichtlich mit dem Ziel eingeleitet wurde, dieses sehr erfolgreiche Handy-Unternehmen in freundlichere, regierungsnähere Hände zu bringen. Die Aussagen eines kooperierenden Zeugen wurden aber von einem Geschworenengericht abgelehnt und alle Angeklagten wurden freigesprochen. Der Chef von *Jewroset*, *J. Tschitschwarkin*, hatte jedoch schon vor dem Prozess das Unternehmen verkauft und ist nach London ins Exil geflohen. Es gibt Gerüchte, dass der Staat eine zweite Anklage gegen ihn und seine Mitarbeiter vorbereitet, die von der Kooperation eines anderen ehemaligen An-

112 *W.W. Wolkow*, *E.L. Paneiazh*, *K.D. Titaew*, Proiswol'naja aktiwnost' prawoochranitel'nych organow w sfere bor'by s ekonomitscheskoj prestupnost'ju. Analis statistiki, Institut problemy prawoprimenenija. Europäische Universität: Sankt Petersburg (Januar 2010), S. 3, 21.

113 *J.D. Reichelt*, S.170-177, 180-181, 185.

gestellten abhängig ist – und die nicht in der Zuständigkeit der Geschworenengerichte liegen wird[114].

Literaturverzeichnis

Ferrajoli, L., Diritto e ragione: Teoria del garantismo penale: Laterza: Rom (5. Aufl. 1998).

Fisher, G., *Plea Bargaining's Triumph*, Stanford: Stanford, CA (2003).

La Fave, W.R. et al., *Criminal Procedure* (5. Aufl. 2009).

Langbein, J.H., „Torture and Plea Bargaining", *University of Chicago Law Review*, Bd. 46, (1978), S. 3-22.

Langer, M., „From Legal Transplants to Legal Translations: The Globalization of Plea Bargaining and the Americanization Thesis in Criminal Procedure", in S.C. Thaman (Hrsg.), *World Plea Bargaining*, S. 26.

Lohman, D., „Confessions at any cost: police torture in Russia", New York: Human Rights Watch (1999).

Machow, V./ Peschkow, M., „Sdelka o prisnanii winy", *Rossijskaja justizija.* Bd. 7 (1998), S. 17-19.

Militsin S., „Sdelki o prisnanii viny: wosmozhen li rossijskij wariant?", *Rossijskaja justitsia*, Bd. 12 (1999), S. 41-42.

Pomorski, S., „Modern Russian Criminal Procedure: The Adversarial Principle and Guilty Plea", *Criminal Law Forum*, Bd. 17, (2006) S. 129-148.

Reichelt, J.D., „A Hobson's Experiment: Plea Bargaining in the Republic of Georgia", *Journal of East European Law*, Bd. 11 (2004), S. 159-204.

Roxin, C., „Über die Reform des deutschen Strafprozessrechts", in B. Töpper (Hrsg.), *Wie würden Sie Entscheiden? Festschrift für Gerd Jauch zum 65. Geburtstag*, C.H. Beck: München (1990), S. 183-200.

Schumann, K.F., *Der Handel mit der Gerechtigkeit*, Suhrkamp: Frankfurt a.M. (1977).

Sillaots, M., „Admission and Confession of Guilt in Settlement Proceedings under Estonian Criminal Procedure", *Juridica international*, Bd. IX (2004), S. 116-124.

Thaman, S.C., „Gerechtigkeit und Verfahrensvielfalt", in S. Machura/S. Ulbrich (Hrsg.), *Recht-Gesellschaft-Kommunikation: Festschrift für Klaus F. Röhl*, Nomos: Baden-Baden (2003), S. 306-320.

114 *J. Yelena Schmaraewa*, Tschitschwarkinu sch'jut kontrabandu, Gaseta.ru, 14. Oktober 2010.

Thaman, S.C., „The Nullification of the Russian Jury: Lessons for Jury-Inspired Reform in Eurasia and Beyond“, *Cornell International Law Journal*, Bd. 40 (2007), S. 355-428 (Thaman 2007).

Thaman, S.C., „The Resurrection of Trial by Jury in Russia“, *Stanford Journal of International Law*, Bd. 31(1995), S. 61-274 (Thaman 1995).

Thaman, S.C., „Russia“, in K.J. Heller/M.D. Dubber (Hrsg.), *The Handbook of Comparative Criminal Law*, Stanford Univ. Press: Stanford, CA (2010), S. 414-454.

Thaman, S.C., „Russland: Rückkehr der fehlfreien Justiz“, in D. Fischer (Hrsg.), *Transformation des Rechts in Ost und West. Festschrift für Prof. Dr. Herwig Roggemann zum 70. Geburtstag*, BWV: Berlin (2006), S. 203-207.

Thaman, S.C., „The Two Faces of Justice in the Post-Soviet Legal Sphere: Adversarial Procedure, Jury Trial, Plea-Bargaining and the Inquisitorial Legacy“, in J. Jackson, et al. (Hrsg.), *Crime, Procedure and Evidence in a Comparative and International Context: Essays in honour of Professor Mirjan Damaška*, Hart: Oxford, Portland, OR (2008), S. 99-118 (Thaman 2008).

Thaman, S.C. (Hrsg.), World Plea Bargaining: Consensual Procedures and the Avoidance of the Full Criminal Trial, Carolina Academic Press: Durham, N.C. (2010).

Thaman, S.C., „A Typology of Consensual Criminal Procedures: An Historical and Comparative Perspective on the Theory and Practice of Avoiding the Full Criminal Trial“, in Thaman (Hrsg.), World Plea Bargaining, Carolina Academic Press: Durham, N.C. (2010), S. 297-396 (Thaman 2010).

Turner, J., „Judicial Participation in Plea Negotiations: A Comparative View“, American Journal of Comparative Law, Bd. 54 (2006), S. 199-267.

Vivell, A., Die Strafbefehlsverfahren nach Eröffnung des Hauptverfahrens. Peter Lang: Frankfurt a.M. (2006).

Vogler, R., A World View of Criminal Justice, Ashgate: Burlington, VT (2005).

Weigend, T., „Die Reform des Strafverfahrens. Europäische und deutsche Tendenzen und Probleme“, ZStW 104, 486 (1992).

Wolkow, W.W., Paneiazh, E.L., Titaew, K.D., Proiswol'naja aktiwnost' prawoochranitel'nych organow w sfere bor'by s ekonomitscheskoj prestupnost'ju. Analis statistiki, Institut problemy prawoprimenenija. Europäische Universität: Sankt Petersburg (Januar 2010).

Konstituzii stran SNG, Zheti Zharfy: Almaty (1999).

Resul'taty monitoringa sudebnych rasbiratel'stw v Republike Kasachstan 2005/2006 g.g. Ottschet: OBSE-BDIPCh: Almaty (2007).

Sbornik ugolowno-prozessual'nych kodeksow stran Zentral'noj Asii (Kasachstan, Kyrgysstan, Tadschikistan, Turkmenistan i Usbekistan), OBSE-BDIPCh: Almaty (2010).

Das zweite Strafurteil gegen die JUKOS-Manager Chodorkovskij und Lebedev

Prof. Dr. Otto Luchterhandt[*]

I. Das Urteil

Am 30.12.2010 endete mit der vollständigen Urteilsverkündung der zweite Strafprozess gegen *M. Chodorkovskij* und *P. Lebedev* vor dem Gericht des Moskauer Stadtbezirks Chamovniki, unweit des Kiewer Bahnhofs[1]. Richter *V. Danilkin* hatte die Verkündung am 27.12.2010 mit dem Schuldausspruch begonnen. Er schloss die Verlesung des 689 Seiten umfassenden Urteils am 30.12.2010 mit der Verkündung der Strafen ab. Die Angeklagten wurden – unter Berücksichtigung ihrer noch nicht abgebüßten Reststrafen aus dem ersten Strafprozess von 2005[2] – jeweils zu 14 Jahren Freiheitsentzug verurteilt, zu verbüßen in Besserungskolonien des allgemeinen Vollzugs[3]. Beide wurden folgender Taten für schuldig befunden:

1. Hätten die Angeklagten Unterschlagung und Veruntreuung in schweren Fällen begangen, d.h. in großem Umfang, unter Ausnutzung ihrer dienstlichen Stellung und als organisierte Gruppe fremdes, ihnen anvertrautes Vermögen, nämlich „Erdöl“, entwendet und sich dadurch angeeignet (Art. 160 Abs. 3 lit. a. und lit. b. [in der Fassung vom 13.06.1996] StGB Russlands (RF)), wofür das Gericht eine Strafe von acht Jahren Freiheitsentzug berechnete.

---

* Bis zu seiner Emeritierung Professor für Öffentliches Recht und Ostrecht und Direktor der Abteilung für Ostrechtsforschung der Universität Hamburg.

1 Zu den Vorgängen im Einzelnen siehe Nezavisimaja gazeta vom 28.12.2010, S. 1/3; Kommersant vom 28.12.2010, S. 1; *D. Heimann*: Chodorkowski erneut verurteilt, in: Neue Zürcher Zeitung (NZZ) vom 28.12.2010, S. 1; *dieselbe*: Erwartetes Ende eines politischen Prozesses, in: NZZ vom 29.12.2010, S. 4; *M. Ackeret*: Die Anklage triumphiert im Fall Chodorkowski, in: NZZ vom 31.12.2010, S. 3; siehe ferner die Berichte von *M. Ludwig* in der Frankfurter Allgemeinen Zeitung (FAZ) vom 28.12.2010, S. 2 („Urteil nach Plan“) sowie vom 29. und 30.12.2010, jeweils S. 1/2.

2 Zu ihm ausführlich *O. Luchterhandt*: Rechtsnihilismus in Aktion. Der Jukos-Chodorkovskij-Prozess in Moskau, in: Osteuropa 54. Jg. (2005), Nr. 7, S. 7-37 (17 ff.); zu den Anfängen des neuen Prozesses siehe *derselbe*: Der zweite Strafprozess gegen die Jukos-Chefs Michail Chodorkovskij und Platon Lebedev. Zwischenstand, in: WGO – MfOR 49. Jg. (2007), Heft 4, S. 242-248.

3 Der Text des Urteils wurde dem Verfasser freundlicherweise von *Prof. Dr. H.-H. Schröder* (SWP, Berlin) zur Verfügung gestellt. Der Text ist inzwischen zugänglich über http://khodorkovsky.ru/.

2. Hätten sie das „auf kriminellem Wege" (*prestupnym putem*) erlangte Erdöl mit Hilfe von diversen Finanzoperationen und sonstigen Rechtsgeschäften „legalisiert" und dadurch den Straftatbestand der „Geldwäsche", ebenfalls in schweren Fällen, erfüllt (Art. 174[1] Abs. 4 StGB RF [in der Fassung vom 07.04.2010]), wofür das Gericht eine Strafe von neun Jahren berechnete.

Die sich zu 17 Jahren Freiheitsentzug summierenden Strafen wurden aufgrund der Regelung des Art. 69 StGB über die Bildung von (reduzierten) Gesamtstrafen bei Verurteilung wegen mehrerer Straftaten auf 13 ½ Jahre verkürzt (Abs. 3). Die durch Art. 69 Abs. 5 eröffnete Möglichkeit, mit der erst teilweise verbüßten Strafe aus dem Urteil des Meščanskij Gerichts wiederum eine Gesamtstrafe zu bilden, führte zu der schließlich ausgeworfenen Strafe von 14 Jahren Freiheitsentzug[4]. Bei der Strafbemessung folgte das Gericht im Ergebnis den Anträgen der Staatsanwaltschaft in der Fassung ihres Schlussplädoyers vom 22.10.2010[5].

Es ist offensichtlich, dass die Bestrafung wegen Geldwäsche davon abhängt, ob die Angeklagten das Erdöl tatsächlich durch Unterschlagung (Art. 160 StGB) erlangt haben. Erweist sich der Vorwurf als unbegründet, dann bricht zwangsläufig auch der Vorwurf der Geldwäsche (Art. 174, 174[1] StGB) in sich zusammen. Die folgende Auseinandersetzung mit dem Urteil konzentriert sich deswegen auf die Frage, ob die Angeklagten tatsächlich ihnen anvertrautes Erdöl entwendet haben. Zuvor ist wenigstens knapp darzustellen, worum es in dem zweiten Strafprozess ging.

II. Der Sachverhalt im Überblick

Dem Urteil liegen Sachverhalte zugrunde, die bis in die 1990er Jahre zurückreichen. Sie werden hier primär aus der Sicht des Gerichts, aber natürlich – anders als im Urteil – unter Verzicht auf die bereits verurteilende Imprägnierung der Sprache referiert.

---

4 Siehe den Strafausspruch des Urteils, S. 687/ 688.

5 In ihrem Schlussplädoyer hatte Staatsanwalt V. Lachtin für beide Angeklagten 13 ½ Jahre für ihre im zweiten Prozess angeklagten Straftaten und – unter Berücksichtigung ihrer erst teilweise verbüßten Strafen aus dem Strafurteil von 2005 – eine Gesamtstrafe von 14 Jahren gefordert. Siehe: Schlussplädoyer des Staatsanwalts V. Lachtin, Text: http://khodorkovsky.ru/khamovnichesky_court/prosecution/2010/10/22/13730.html. In der ca. 900-seitigen Anklageschrift sind Strafanträge (noch) nicht enthalten. Die Anklageschrift war am 14.02.2007 vom stellvertretenden Generalstaatsanwalt V. Ja. Grin ausgefertigt worden und umfasst samt Anlagen auf 14 Aktenbände verteilte 3.460 Seiten. Siehe „Anklageschrift in der Strafsache No.18/432766-07", Text: http://khodorkovsky.ru/khamovnichesky_court/court_orders/2009/03/31/12333.html. Siehe auch die Verfügung der Untersuchungsbehörde vom 29.06.2008 über die Heranziehung M. Chodorkovskijs als Beschuldigter, Text: http://khodorkovsky.ru/media/2008.06.29..pdf.

In den Jahren 1995/1996 hatten *M. Chodorkovskij*, *P. Lebedev* und „andere Glieder der organisierten Gruppe[6]" mit Hilfe der von ihnen beherrschten Geschäftsbank „MENATEP" und durch von ihr kontrollierte Gesellschaften 33% des Aktienkapitals des im Eigentum Russlands befindlichen Erdölunternehmens JUKOS ersteigert und alsbald über geschäftliche Manipulationen ca. 90% des JUKOS-Aktienkapitals erworben. Kraft dieser beherrschenden Stellung hatten sie das Unternehmen dann zielstrebig zu einem hierarchisch strukturierten Konzern, bestehend aus der Offenen Aktiengesellschaft (OAO) NK[7] JUKOS als Muttergesellschaft und diversen, verschachtelten Tochtergesellschaften, umgestaltet. Der Erdölkonzern wurde von *M. Chodorkovskij*, in Verbindung vor allem mit *P. Lebedev*, über eine in Gibraltar eingetragene Holding, die „Group MENATEP Ltd", und weitere Off-Shore-Gesellschaften gesteuert. Mehrheitsaktionär des Konzerns war *M. Chodorkovskij*. Außerdem bekleideten beide Spitzenpositionen in den Führungsorganen des Konzerns und nahmen infolgedessen nicht nur als Großaktionäre maßgebende Managementfunktionen wahr.

Zu den JUKOS-Tochterunternehmen zählten auch die Erdölfördergesellschaften OAO Jugansneftegaz, OAO Samaraneftegaz und OAO Tomskneft´ VHK. Tomskneft´ war zunächst eine von zahlreichen Tochtergesellschaften der in Staatseigentum befindlichen „Vostočno-Sibirskaja Neftjannaja Kompanija" (VNK) gewesen, 1997/1998 im Zuge der Privatisierung der VNK aber ebenfalls von OAO NK JUKOS übernommen worden[8].

---

6 Sowohl in der Anklageschrift als auch im Urteil wird als Beleg für das taterschwerende und straferhöhende Merkmal der „organisierten Gruppe" i.S.d. Art. 160 sowie Art. 174 und 174[1] StGB durchgehend diese Formel gebraucht. Die Namen der anderen Gruppenmitglieder werden verschiedentlich genannt. Es handelt sich durchweg um Anteilseigner und Spitzenmanager von JUKOS.

7 *Neftjannaja kompanija* (NK) bedeutet Erdölgesellschaft.

8 *M. Chodorkovskij* und *P. Lebedev* war in der Anklageschrift vorgeworfen worden, sie hätten unrechtmäßig die VNK-Aktienmehrheit an sich gebracht. Ihrer Entgegnung, der damals erfolgte VNK-Aktientausch mit JUKOS-Aktien sei von der staatlichen Privatisierungsagentur GoskomImuščestvo genehmigt worden, außerdem zur Absicherung des Unternehmens (nur vorläufig) gegen die durchaus reale Gefahr einer kriminellen Übernahme des Unternehmens (*rejderstvo*) geschehen und die VNK-Aktien später (2001) vertragsgemäß zurückübertragen worden und schließlich dem Staat wegen des gestiegenen Aktienwertes kein Schaden entstanden, konnten die Staatsanwälte nichts entgegensetzen. Die Darstellung der Angeklagten wurde von *G. Gref*, der zur fraglichen Zeit Wirtschaftsminister war und heute Chef der SberBank Russlands ist, als Zeuge auf der ganzen Linie bestätigt. Siehe dazu die Prozess-Reportage in Novaja gazeta 2010, Nr. 66 (23.06.), S. 1-3 (*G. Gref*); Novaja gazeta 2009, Nr. 133 (30.11.), S. 12/13 (Zeuge *A. Tichonov*, VNK). Das Gericht hat über diesen Punkt der Anklage in der Sache nicht entschieden, sondern die Strafverfolgung des VNK-Komplexes (zu diesem im Urteil, S. 3; 73) wegen Ablauf der zehnjährigen Verjährungsfrist (Mai 2010) durch Beschluss vom 27.12.2010 eingestellt. Text des Beschlusses: http://khodorkovsky.ru/khamovnichesky_court/prosecution /2011/01/16/15808.html.

Ende Juli 1996 schloss die OAO NK JUKOS mit den Erdölfördergesellschaften OAO Jugansneftegaz und OAO Samaraneftegaz, im Oktober 1998 auch mit OAO Tomskneft´ VNK gleichlautende „Generalvereinbarungen“ (*general´nye soglašenija*) ab. Darin verpflichteten sich die Vertragsparteien dazu, die notwendigen organisatorischen Bedingungen dafür zu schaffen, dass das Erdöl durch den Abschluss von Kaufverträgen zwischen den Partnern „realisiert“ werden könne. Ferner wurde bestimmt, dass das Eigentumsrecht an dem von den Gesellschaften zu Tage geförderten Produkt auf die OAO NK JUKOS übergehen solle, und zwar an jedem konkreten Bohrloch (*skvažinna*) der Förderanlagen unmittelbar nach Austritt aus der Öffnung. Das Produkt wurde in der Vereinbarung als „Bohrlochflüssigkeit“ (*skvažinnaja židkost´*) bezeichnet. Sie ist selbst noch kein Erdöl, sondern ein Gemisch, das zu ca. 70% aus Wasser, Salz und sonstigen Stoffen und nur zu ca. 30% aus Erdöl besteht[9]. Von der Bohrlochflüssigkeit ist daher „Erdöl mit Warenqualität“ (*tovarnaja neft´*) zu unterscheiden. Es musste den schon zu UdSSR-Zeiten festgelegten Qualitätsstandards für Erdöl („*GOST-Neft´*“) entsprechen[10] und ist folglich das Ergebnis einer Aufbereitung, die erheblichen Einsatz technischer Mittel verlangt. Sie lag in den Händen der Fördergesellschaften.

Die Generalvereinbarungen waren Rahmenverträge zwischen der Konzernmutter – OAO NK JUKOS – und den drei erdölfördernden Tochtergesellschaften. Sie verfolgten das Ziel und schufen zugleich die Voraussetzung dafür, die Erdölrealisierung von der Förderung bis zur Veräußerung an die Abnehmer im In- und Ausland möglichst rationell sowie kosten- und steuersparend, also gewinnmaximierend, zu organisieren und abzuwickeln. Dementsprechend wurden die rechtlichen und administrativen Abläufe des Erdölgeschäfts im vertikal integrierten JUKOS-Konzern geordnet: Im Rahmen der Generalvereinbarung wurden zwischen den Vertragsparteien (Mutter- und jeweilige Tochtergesellschaft) regelmäßig Kaufverträge über die Lieferung bestimmter Mengen von Erdöl abgeschlossen. Der Aufkaufpreis wurde, auch das war Teil der Generalvereinbarung, von der Konzernmutter bestimmt. Seine Höhe schwankte: Er bewegte sich im prozessrelevanten Zeitraum, also zwischen 1998 und 2003, durchschnittlich zwischen 20% und 33% des Weltmarktpreises[11].

Das Erdöl wurde entsprechend den GOST-Bestimmungen mit Warenqualität von den Fördergesellschaften jeweils in das Pipelinenetz von Transneft´ einge-

---

9 Siehe die Reportage vom 267. Verhandlungstag des Prozesses in: Novaja gazeta 2010, Nr. 101 (13.09.), S. 14.

10 Zum Qualitätsstandard *GOST* siehe http://testrussia.ru/gost/neft/gost-11508-74-bitumy-neftyanye.-metody-opredeleniya-stsepleniya-bituma-s-mramorom-i-peskom.html. Inzwischen ist *GOST* durch das TU-Standardsystem abgelöste worden. Siehe http://elarum.com/info/standards/.

11 Siehe dazu die teilweise bis in die Monatsabrechnungen gehenden Übersichten der betreffenden Jahre in der Anklageschrift: S. 40 ff.; 58 ff.; 66 ff.; 76 ff.; 85 ff. Im Urteil werden die Kaufverträge ebenfalls bis 2003 erfasst, S. 14 ff.; 26 ff.; 47 ff.; 55ff.; 63 ff.

leitet, ein Unternehmen, das im Eigentum der Russischen Föderation steht, das Monopol am Öl- und Gasleitungssystem des Landes hält und der föderalen Regierung bzw. dem Energieministerium (MinĖnergo) untersteht. Die Einleitung des Erdöls geschah (und geschieht) an Mess- und Kontrollstellen des Transneft´-Netzes (*uzel učeta*). Einleitendes Unternehmen und eingeleitete Menge wurden dort sorgfältig vermerkt. Ebenso genau führt(e) darüber Buch die „Zentrale Dispatcherverwaltung für die Verteilung im Wärme- und Energiekomplex" von MinĖnergo[12].

Das weitere „Schicksal", das dem Erdöl innerhalb des Konzerns in rechtlicher Hinsicht zu Teil wurde, wurde von *M. Chodorkovskijs* und *P. Lebedevs* Strategie der Steuerminimierung bestimmt: Das Erdöl wurde an diverse Tochtergesellschaften veräußert, die ihren Firmensitz in sog. Geschlossenen Territorialen Verwaltungseinheiten (*Zakrytye Administrativnye Territorial´nye Obrazovanija – ZATO*) hatten. Es handelte sich um Städte, die zur Sowjetzeit wegen der dort betriebenen meist militärischen Forschungen und Versuche höchsten Geheimhaltungsstatus hatten und auf keiner Landkarte verzeichnet waren, nun aber ihren Status verloren und der Öffentlichkeit zugänglich waren. Um ihnen die Integration in marktwirtschaftliche Verhältnisse zu erleichtern und um Unternehmen einen Anreiz zu geben, sich dort niederzulassen, hatte der Gesetzgeber den ZATO beträchtliche Steuervergünstigungen eingeräumt[13]. OAO NK JUKOS erkannte die in den „Steueroasen" liegende Chance und gründete dort eine Reihe von Ölhandelsgesellschaften als Tochterunternehmen, die von den zuständigen ZATO-Behörden, nach Zustimmung auch des föderalen Finanzministeriums, registriert wurden. Die für JUKOS günstige Rechtslage der ZATO wurde erst Ende 2003, nach der Verhaftung *P. Lebedevs* und *M. Chodorkovskijs*, geändert.

Konzernintern wurden Kauf und Weiterverkauf des Erdöls zunächst von der Muttergesellschaft, ab 2000 von einer speziell für die Verwaltung der Ölfördergesellschaften zuständigen Tochtergesellschaft, der ZAO JUKOS RM[14], gesteuert. Sie steuerten auch den Abschluss der Kaufverträge über das Erdöl.

Von 1998–2000 sind von den drei Fördergesellschaften nach Feststellung des Urteils 147.189.184,248 Tonnen Erdöl, von 2001–2003 ca. 200.385.116 Tonnen geliefert worden, insgesamt also ca. 347,5 Mio. Tonnen Erdöl[15]. Das war die gesamte vom JUKOS-Konzern realisierte Erdölproduktion, und in dem-

---

12 Novaja gazeta 2010, Nr. 57 (31.05.), S. 3 (Zeugin der Verteidigung, *T. Lysova*, Chefreakteurin der Zeitung „Vedomosti").

13 Ausführlich *O. Luchterhandt*: Rechtsnihilismus in Aktion. Der Jukos-Chodorkovskij-Prozess in Moskau (Fn. 2).

14 „JUKOS Refining and Marketing" in der Rechtsform einer Geschlossenen Aktiengesellschaft (ZAO).

15 Urteil, S. 72, 73. Zu den Rechenfehlern der Anklagevertreter siehe Novaja gazeta 2010, Nr. 116 (18.10.), S. 14.

selben Umfange sollen *M. Chodorkovskij* und *P. Lebedev* den Tochtergesellschaften das Erdöl „entwendet" haben!

III. Zur Kritik: Das Urteil – ein Dokument des Rechtsnihilismus

Das Urteil ist zutiefst ungerecht. Es verstößt erstens massiv gegen justizielle Grundprinzipien des Rechtstaates (Art. 1 Verfassung Russlands). Zweitens ist es auch deswegen krass rechtswidrig, weil es die Angeklagten wegen Straftaten verurteilt, die sie nicht begangen haben und deren Tatbestandsvoraussetzungen, schon nach den eigenen Feststellungen des Gerichts, offensichtlich nicht erfüllt sind. Insgesamt zeichnen sich Prozessverlauf und Urteil durch ein erschreckendes Ausmaß von Missachtung nahezu sämtlicher Grundsätze eines *fair trial* aus.

1. Verstoß gegen das rechtsstaatliche Verbot *ne bis in idem*

Der geschilderte Sachverhalt ist wesentliche Grundlage der zweiten Verurteilung *M. Chodorkovskijs* und *P. Lebedevs*. Vergleicht man ihn mit dem Sachverhalt, welcher der Anklageschrift und dem Strafurteil des Meščanskij Rayongerichts von 2005 zugrundeliegt, dann springt die Übereinstimmung ins Auge: Es ging damals um dieselben Angeklagten, um die Rolle, die sie bei der Realisierung des von den JUKOS-Tochtergesellschaften geförderten Erdöls gespielt hatten und darüber hinaus um die strafrechtliche Bewertung der Abläufe im vertikal strukturierten JUKOS-Konzern insgesamt. Der Lebenssachverhalt, der *jetzt* von den Untersuchungsführern der Staatsanwaltschaft untersucht wurde und den Inhalt der Anklageschrift sowie die Grundlage der Verurteilung *M. Chodorkovskijs* und *P. Lebedevs* wegen der Straftat des Art. 160 StGB bildet, ist in vollem Umfang auch Gegenstand des ersten Prozesses und Strafurteils von 2005 gewesen.

Das ruft unweigerlich den klassischen Grundsatz des Rechtsstaates „Niemand darf zweimal wegen derselben Tat bestraft werden (*ne bis in idem*)" in Erinnerung! Er steht auch in der Verfassung Russlands (Art. 50 Abs. 1) und in Art. 6 Abs. 2 des Strafgesetzbuches: „Niemand darf für ein und dasselbe Verbrechen zweimal strafrechtlich zur Verantwortung gezogen werden." Unter Verbrechen versteht Art. 14 Abs. 1 StGB „eine gesellschaftlich gefährliche Handlung", die mit Strafe bedroht ist. Maßgebend ist also ein strafrechtlich relevanter Sachverhalt, den ein (staatliches) Gericht schon einmal untersucht und abgeurteilt hat. Art. 50 Abs. 1 der Verfassung verbietet, dass das mit einem solchen Sachverhalt verbundene Verhalten eines Täters nun mit Hilfe eines anderen Straftatbestands noch einmal bestraft wird. Der Grundsatz will verhindern, dass ein Mensch für ein bestimmtes strafwürdiges Verhalten immer von Neuem büßen muss. Mit der erfolgten Bestrafung ist seine Tat gesühnt und der Strafanspruch des Staates erschöpft und verbraucht. Der abgeurteilte Tatkomplex liefert dem Staat keine Legitimation mehr für eine weitere Bestrafung. Untersuchungsbeamte, Staatsanwälte und Richter *V. Danilkin* haben den Verfassungsgrundsatz, der auch ein strafprozessuales Grundrecht der Angeklagten ist, ignoriert und damit grob verletzt. Die Anklage hätte nicht erhoben, die Gerichtsverhandlung nicht eröffnet, die Verurteilung wegen Unterschlagung und Geldwäsche nicht erfolgen dürfen!

2. Das Urteil ist unbegründet: Die Verurteilten haben keine Unterschlagung begangen

Der Verurteilung *M. Chodorkovskijs* und *P. Lebedevs* stand nicht nur der Verfassungsgrundsatz *ne bis in idem* entgegen, sondern sie war auch deswegen unzulässig, weil das Erdöl gar nicht entwendet worden war, und zwar weder von ihnen noch von anderen Personen. Infolgedessen ist der Straftatbestand der Unterschlagung bzw. Veruntreuung i.S.v. Art. 160 StGB, der die Grundlage der Verurteilung bildet, gar nicht erfüllt!

a) Kein Diebstahl

Vorweg ist zu bemerken, dass nach den Feststellungen des Gerichts der Strafvorwurf des Diebstahls (russ.: *kraža*, Art. 158 StGB) nicht in Betracht kam. Denn *M. Chodorkovskij* und *P. Lebedev* hatten das Erdöl nicht für sich in eigene Kanäle abzweigen können; das wäre aus technischen Gründen, wegen der nicht zu umgehenden Realisierung des Erdöls über den Staatsmonopolisten Transneft´, also schon rein physisch, gar nicht möglich gewesen. Außerdem hätte das Gericht die Abzweigung des Erdöls dann als „Diebstahl" qualifizieren müssen. Es hat die Angeklagten aber wegen Unterschlagung und Veruntreuung verurteilt (Art. 160 StGB).

b) Kein fremdes, anvertrautes, vielmehr übereignetes Vermögen

Die Verurteilung und Bestrafung wegen Unterschlagung war ungerechtfertigt, weil die Erdölfördersellschaften OAO Jugansneftegaz, OAO Samaraneftegaz und OAO Tomskneft´ VHK das Erdöl *M. Chodorkovskij* und *P. Lebedev* nicht „anvertraut" haben. Hätte man ihnen das Erdöl anvertraut, dann wäre ihnen nur das Besitzrecht am Erdöl übertragen worden. Die Fördergesellschaften haben das Erdöl jedoch an JUKOS verkauft, es also übereignet. Die Übertragung des Eigentums am Erdöl schließt die Merkmale „fremdes Vermögen" und „anvertraut" im Tatbestand des Art. 160 StGB aber definitiv aus: entweder nur Besitz oder (volles) Eigentum!

aa) Eigentümer des Erdöls sind kraft der „Generalvereinbarungen" und der Kaufverträge außerdem nicht *M. Chodorkovskij* und *P. Lebedev* und die „anderen Glieder der organisierten Gruppe" als natürliche Personen geworden, sondern juristische Personen, nämlich – zunächst – die OAO NK JUKOS, ab 2000 die im JUKOS-Konzern mit dem Aufkauf des Erdöls betrauten Tochtergesellschaften (ZAO NK JUKOS RM usw.). Das hat, jedenfalls im Ansatz, auch das

Gericht eingeräumt. Es meint sich aber über die Klippe mit dem Argument hinwegsetzen zu können, die Generalvereinbarungen und die Kaufverträge seien wegen Verletzung des Aktienrechts und des Zivilrechts rechtswidrig, daher nicht zustande gekommen und das Erdöl folglich nicht wirksam übereignet worden.

bb) Aus der Sicht des *Aktienrechts* sind die betreffenden Verträge jedoch rechtswirksam zustande gekommen. Allerdings war die rechtliche Konstellation problematisch, weil *M. Chodorkovskij* und *P. Lebedev* als Hauptaktionäre der Verkäuferinnen, also der Erdölfördergesellschaften OAO Jugansneftegaz, OAO Samaraneftegaz und OAO Tomskneft´ VNK, auch die Käuferin des Erdöls, die OAO NK JUKOS, kontrollierten und deswegen an dem Zustandekommen des Geschäft stark interessiert waren. Zum Schutz der Minderheitsaktionäre bedurften die Verträge daher nicht nur der Zustimmung der Aktionärshauptversammlungen der Fördergesellschaften (Art. 83 Abs. 3 AktienG), sondern auch der Mehrheit ihrer „nichtinteressierten" Aktionäre (Abs. 4). Diese – qualifizierten – Zustimmungen sind nach den Feststellungen des Gerichts erteilt worden. Seine Ansicht, sie seien von den JUKOS-Managern durch Täuschung der Aktionäre erschlichen worden und deswegen unwirksam[16], findet im Aktiengesetz keine Stütze, denn die Fehlerhaftigkeit des Verfahrens führt nicht automatisch zur Unwirksamkeit der Zustimmung der Hauptversammlung und folglich auch nicht des Vertrags. Die zustande gekommenen Kaufverträge hätten vielmehr nur durch Klage beim Wirtschaftsgericht aufgehoben werden können (Art. 84 Abs. 1 AktienG). Solche Klagen sind aber nicht erhoben worden[17]!

cc) Aus der Sicht des *Zivilrechts* konnten die Generalvereinbarungen und die Kaufverträge über das Erdöl unter zwei Gesichtspunkten „nichtig" gewesen sein: erstens, wenn die Verträge „wissentlich (*zavedomo*) gegen die Grundlagen der Rechtsordnung und der Sittlichkeit gerichtet" waren (Art. 169 ZGB) oder wenn sie, zweitens, von den Partnern nur zum Schein, d.h. ohne ehrlichen Willen zur rechtlichen Bindung, geschlossen wurden (Art. 170 ZGB).

Das Urteil nennt Generalvereinbarungen und Kaufverträge nicht nur rechtswidrig, sondern wiederholt auch „fiktiv[18]" und scheint damit ihre Nichtigkeit zumindest andeuten zu wollen. Es bezieht sich aber an keiner Stelle ausdrücklich auf Art. 170 ZGB und liefert auch keine tragfähige juristische Begründung für die (angebliche) Fiktivität. Das möge die folgende, vom Urteil stereotyp wiederholte Passage illustrieren[19]: „Die betreffenden Verträge hatten fiktiven

16 Urteil, S. 164; 681 ff.

17 Sie hätten von den überstimmten Minderheitsaktionären innerhalb eines Jahres nach Bekanntwerden des Anfechtungsgrundes, also unter den gegebenen Umständen nach dem Ende der Hauptversammlung, erhoben werden müssen (Art. 179 Abs. 2 ZGB). *A. A. Kyrov.*: Kommentarij k federal´nomu zakonu „ob akcionernych obščestvach", Moskau 2007, S. 252.

18 Urteil, S. 12; 13; 14 f. und öfter. Die Passagen stimmen meist wörtlich mit der Anklageschrift überein. Siehe dort etwa S. 39.

19 Urteil, S. 12; 27.

Charakter, weil sie wissentlich falsche Angaben darüber enthielten, dass als Käufer des Erdöls die OAO NK JUKOS auftrete. Dabei war *Chodorkovskij, M. B., Lebedev, P. L.* und ihren Komplizen bestens bekannt, dass die OAO NK JUKOS faktisch (sic!) nicht der Käufer des Erdöls war, sondern die Produktion von den Erdöl fördernden Unternehmen unmittelbar an die russischen und ausländischen Verbraucher geliefert wurde. Außerdem waren die Angaben in den Verträgen darüber, dass die Partner Einigkeit über den Preis des Erdöls erzielt hätten, bewusst falsch. Faktisch (sic!) gab es eine solche Vereinbarung nicht, sondern der Preis für das Erdöl wurde von den Teilnehmern der von *Chodorkovskij, M. B., Lebedev, P. L.* und anderen Gliedern geführten organisierten Gruppe ohne irgendeine wirtschaftliche Notwendigkeit mit Vorbedacht gegenüber dem realen Marktpreis um ein Mehrfaches herabgesetzt."

dd) Die Passage des Urteils widerlegt die Behauptung der „Fiktion". Denn sie bestätigt, dass die Muttergesellschaft NK JUKOS Vertragspartnerin der Fördergesellschaften und damit Käuferin des Erdöls i.S.v. Art. 459 ff. ZGB war und dass ein Kaufpreis vereinbart war, der deutlich unter dem Marktpreis für Erdöl lag. Diese Vereinbarungen waren auch kein Schein, sondern von den Beteiligten unbedingt gewollt, weil von ihrer Ausführung nämlich die von *M. Chodorkovskij, P. Lebedev* und anderen entwickelte Strategie der Kostensenkung und der Gewinnmaximierung des Unternehmens entscheidend abhing. Das Urteil beschreibt diese von der Anklage und dem Gericht natürlich nicht akzeptierte, sondern für kriminell gehaltene juristische, gesellschaftsrechtliche und steuerrechtliche Strategie der „vertikal integrierten Struktur" des JUKOS-Konzerns[20] an vielen Stellen.

ee) Letztlich vermeidet das Gericht es im Übrigen, definitiv von „Scheinverträgen" zu sprechen. Es meint vielmehr, sie verstießen gegen Art. 179 ZGB[21]. Diese Bestimmung gibt einer Vertragspartei das Recht, einen Vertrag gerichtlich anzufechten, wenn sie durch Arglist dazu veranlasst wurde, in für sich äußerst nachteilige Vertragsbedingungen einzuwilligen. Selbst ein solcher „Knebelungsvertrag" (*kabal´naja sdelka*) ist aber nicht schon kraft Gesetzes unwirksam, sondern bedarf der Aufhebung durch Gericht (Abs. 1). Da entsprechende Entscheidungen nicht vorliegen, sind die Generalvereinbarungen und Kaufverträge gültig.

ff) Die im Urteil des Chamovniki-Gerichts aufgestellte Behauptung, die Erdölförder- bzw. Tochtergesellschaften des JUKOS-Konzerns seien Eigentümerinnen des Erdöls geblieben[22], wird folglich durch das Urteil selbst widerlegt, denn die vom Gericht für seine Behauptung ins Feld geführten Rechtsvorschriften begründen das Gegenteil: Weder nach dem AktienG (Art. 83, 84) noch nach dem ZGB (Art. 179) sind die Kaufverträge, selbst wenn sie rechtwidrig gewesen

20 Z.B. S. 6; 31.
21 Urteil, S. 12.
22 Urteil, S. 660.

sein sollten, nichtig, sondern bis zu ihrer Aufhebung durch das dafür zuständige Wirtschaftsgericht in vollem Umfang wirksam, und da die Fristen für ihre Anfechtung sogar schon zur Zeit des ersten Strafprozesses abgelaufen waren, blieben sie gültig. Das Chamovniki-Gericht durfte die Kaufverträge wegen dieses auch von ihm zu beachtenden juristischen Faktums nicht als ungültig behandeln.

Zu dieser Einschätzung der Rechtslage war bereits das Gericht des Meščanskij Rayons der Stadt Moskau im ersten Strafurteil gegen *M. Chodorkovskij* und *P. Lebedev* 2005 gelangt, und die Wirtschaftsgerichte hatten seine Position davor und danach in zahlreichen Entscheidungen geteilt. Nur deswegen hatten die beiden Angeklagten im ersten Prozess überhaupt wegen Steuerhinterziehung verurteilt werden können.

Das Chamovniki-Gericht hat im Ergebnis gleichwohl, wie sich in der weiteren Analyse des Urteils im Einzelnen zeigen wird, einen Eigentumswechsel des Erdöls von den JUKOS-Tochter- bzw. Fördergesellschaften auf die Muttergesellschaft OAO NK JUKOS verneint, um eine Verurteilung der beiden Angeklagten, nun wegen Unterschlagung des Erdöls als fremdes Eigentum, begründen und rechtfertigen zu können. Das hatte und hat allerdings den hohen Preis, dass sich die beiden Strafurteile im Kern widersprechen und sich daher wechselseitig ausschließen: Hat das Meščanskij Gericht Recht, dann hat das Chamovniki-Gericht zwangsläufig Unrecht und umgekehrt[23]. Man darf daher gespannt sein, wie das Stadtgericht Moskau als Kassationsinstanz[24] mit diesem Widerspruch umgehen wird, nachdem die Anwälte der Verurteilten Kassationsbeschwerden eingelegt haben[25]. In seiner Kassationsentscheidung zum ersten Strafprozess hatte es das Urteil des Meščanskij Gerichts bestätigt. Von politischer Seite wird das Stadtgericht massiv gedrängt werden, auch das konträre Urteil des Chamovniki-Gerichts abzusegnen. Gäbe es dem politischen Druck nach, würde es sich selbst ein öffentliches Zeugnis „juristischer Schizophrenie" ausstellen, kurz: Das Moskauer Stadtgericht befindet sich in der Klemme.

---

23 Dieser Widerspruch beherrschte von Anfang an die die JUKOS-Ermittlungen führende Untersuchungsgruppe des Generalstaatsanwalts Russlands unter ihrem Chef *S. Karimov*. Sie nahm diese juristische Schizophrenie in Kauf, um die von politischer Seite gewünschte weitere Verurteilung *M. Chodorkovskijs* und *P. Lebedevs* erreichen zu können. Dazu ausführlich *O. Luchterhandt*, Der zweite Strafprozess gegen die Jukos-Chefs Michail Chodorkovskij und Platon Lebedev (Fn. 2), S. 246 f.

24 Man sollte erwarten, dass den Verurteilten in zweiter Instanz ein Berufungsgericht als zweite Tatsacheninstanz zur Verfügung stehe, aber die Strafprozessordnung Russlands sieht gegen Urteile der Strafgerichte der ersten Instanz nur die Kassationsbeschwerde vor (Art. 354 Abs. 3 StPO). Eine Berufung ist nur gegen Entscheidungen der (untersten) „Friedensgerichte" eröffnet (Art. 356 Abs. 2 StPO).

25 *V. Kljuvgant*: My objazatel'no poidem v MosGorSud –takoj, kakoj on est', in: Novaja gazeta 2011, Nr. 1 (12.01.), S. 14; *A. Denisov*: Advokaty gotovy osporit' prigovor, in: Nezavisimaja gazeta vom 14.01.2011, S. 3.

c) Widerspruch des Strafurteils zur Rechtsprechung der Wirtschaftsgerichte und zu Russlands Rechtsstandpunkt im EGMR-Verfahren NK JUKOS ./. Russland

aa) Seinem krass rechtswidrigen Vorgehen hat Richter *V. Danilkin* dadurch die Krone aufgesetzt, dass er in seinem Urteil die seit 2004 ergangenen Entscheidungen von über 60 (!!) Wirtschaftsgerichten (!) Russlands, die die Kaufverträge für wirksam angesehen[26] und die OAO NK JUKOS dementsprechend als Eigentümerin des Erdöls behandelt haben, für irrelevant erklärt! Das geschieht mit so windigen Argumenten, dass es sich eigentlich erübrigt, sich mit ihnen auseinanderzusetzen. Da aber die Frage, ob die Tochtergesellschaften oder die Muttergesellschaft des JUKOS-Konzerns Eigentümerinnen des Erdöls waren, darüber entscheidet, ob die Angeklagten i.S.d. Art. 160 StGB „fremdes" Vermögen entwendet haben, muss zumindest kurz auf sie eingegangen werden.

Das Chamovniki-Gericht versucht, die in der Eigentumsfrage konträr von ihm abweichenden Positionen der Wirtschaftsgerichte durch drei Argumente zu neutralisieren:

Erstens hätten sich die Wirtschaftsgerichte mit der Eigentumsfrage gar nicht spezifisch befasst, sondern allein mit der Frage der Steuerhinterziehung durch manipulative Transaktionen im Schachtelkonzern JUKOS[27]. Dem ist entgegenzuhalten, dass die Wirtschaftsgerichte sehr wohl die Eigentumsverhältnisse geprüft haben und sie auch prüfen mussten, weil die Besteuerung nur an das von der OAO NK JUKOS legal als Eigentümerin veräußerte Erdöl anknüpfen konnte. Die Replik des Gerichts auf dieses Argument *M. Chodorkovskijs* geht darauf aus, diese schlichte Selbstverständlichkeit durch eine steuertechnische Formulierung und Verfremdung des Sachverhalts zu verschleiern[28]: „Objekte des Steuerverbrechens", so das Urteil, „sind die Beziehungen bei der Entrichtung von Steuerzahlungen an den Staatshaushalt. Grundlage der Berechnung der Steuersätze ist nicht das Vermögen, sondern das Abrechnungsquantum zwischen Einnahmen und Ausgaben." Dass (auch) ein „Abrechnungsquantum", wenn es aus der Realisierung von Diebesgut resultiert, vom Täter nicht zu versteuern ist, sondern als Teil der Beute vom Staat konfisziert wird, ignoriert das Urteil. Schlimmer noch: Es erweckt mit seiner Argumentation den Verdacht, als sei es gerechtfertigt, *M. Chodorkovskij* und *P. Lebedev* wegen der „Entwendung" (*chiščenie*) des gesamten vom JUKOS-Konzern zwischen 1998 und 2003 realisierten Erdöls zu bestrafen, gleichwohl aber auch JUKOS zur Zahlung einer Steuersumme in Höhe des gesamten vom Konzern in jenem Zeitraum erzielten

---

26 *M. Chodorkovskij* hatte in seinem Schlusswort von 61 wirtschaftsgerichtlichen Entscheidungen gesprochen, die seine Position stützten. Siehe Novaja gazeta 2010, Nr. 107 (27.09.), S. 14. Das Urteil greift die Zahl als Faktum auf: S. 660; vgl. auch S. 621, 622.

27 Urteil, S. 658.

28 Urteil, S. 659.

Gewinns aus der Realisierung eben jenes angeblich entwendeten Erdöls zu verurteilen!

Zweitens hätten die Wirtschaftsgerichte die Kaufverträge deswegen als wirksam behandelt, weil sie den entsprechenden Behauptungen der JUKOS-Manager auf den Leim gegangen seien und außerdem noch keine Kenntnis von dem „Mechanismus der Entwendung des Erdöls" gehabt hätten, über welche nun jedoch das Chamovniki-Gericht verfüge[29]. Die Replik grenzt an Täuschung, denn das Gericht stützt sich nicht auf im ersten Strafprozess unbekannte, neue Tatsachen. Der „Mechanismus" meint vielmehr nichts anderes als den Abschluss jener Generalvereinbarungen und Kaufverträge über das Erdöl, den das Chamovniki-Gericht jetzt nur anders bewertet, nämlich als Mittel der Angeklagten zur „Entwendung ihnen anvertrauten fremden Vermögens". Das geschieht, wie weiter unten näher dargelegt wird, unter völliger, grotesker Verdrehung des Straftatbestands der Unterschlagung (Art. 160 StGB).

Drittens hätten die Wirtschaftsgerichte im Blick auf die zu prüfende Steuerproblematik angenommen[30], dass OAO NK JUKOS nur „faktisches Eigentum" an dem Erdöl besessen habe. Wörtlich heißt es im Urteil[31]: „Durch die betreffende Entscheidung des Gerichts wird bestätigt, dass die OAO NK JUKOS faktisch die Rechte des Besitzes, der Nutzung und Verfügung in Bezug auf das Erdöl und die Erdölerzeugnisse hatte und nach ihrem Belieben in Bezug darauf beliebige Handlungen vornehmen konnte, darunter Veräußerung und Übergabe zur Verarbeitung über eine ganze Reihe von OAO NK JUKOS abhängiger Organisationen (...). Somit folgt aus den betreffenden Entscheidungen der Wirtschaftsgerichte, dass das Erdöl in das faktische Eigentum (*v faktičeskuju sobstvennost'*) der OAO NK JUKOS überging, sie juristisch aber nicht Eigentümerin des Erdöls war. In Wirklichkeit gehörte das Erdöl den das Öl fördernden Tochtergesellschaften."

Das Urteil macht hier den Versuch, seine Behauptung, OAO NK JUKOS sei nicht Eigentümerin des Erdöls gewesen, mit der gegenteiligen Rechtsprechung der Wirtschaftsgerichte zu harmonisieren. Es hat dazu den Begriff „faktisches Eigentum" erfunden[32] und ihn den Wirtschaftsgerichten untergeschoben, um dadurch den Eindruck zu erwecken, auch sie hätten OAO NK JUKOS nicht für die Eigentümerin des Erdöls gehalten. Tatsächlich sprechen die Wirtschaftsgerichte unter Hinweis auf Art. 209 ZGB aber immer nur von „Eigentum", und das ist juristisch auch völlig korrekt, denn eine Unterscheidung von „faktischem" und „rechtlichem" Eigentum kennt das russische Zivilrecht nicht[33]. Das Eigen-

29 Urteil, S. 621/622; 660/661.

30 Das Urteil bezieht sich direkt auf die Entscheidung des Wirtschaftsgerichts der Stadt Moskau vom 28.04.2005. Siehe S. 659 f.

31 Urteil, S. 660.

32 Siehe dazu die abenteuerliche Konstruktion des Urteils (S. 659 f.).

33 Siehe dazu Kap. 13-18 ZGB.

tumsrecht des ZGB ist, wie überall, ein Inbegriff von Rechten, ein Rechtsinstitut, dessen Kern die Rechte zu Besitz, Nutzung, Verfügung und Veräußerung bilden. Aus der eher beiläufigen Feststellung des Moskauer Wirtschaftsgerichts, dass derjenige, welcher „faktisch" die Rechte des Besitzes, der Nutzung, der Verfügung usw. habe und seine Rechte „faktisch" nutze, auch der (juristische) Eigentümer i.S.v. Art. 209 ZGB sei, macht das Chamovniki-Gericht „faktisches Eigentum" und suggeriert mit diesem sprachlichen Trick, dass es sich um eine eigene, selbstständige Erscheinungsform von Eigentum neben dem „juristischen Eigentum" handele. Einziger Sinn dieser aus Bösartigkeit geborenen, die Grenze zur Lächerlichkeit überschreitenden „zivilrechtlichen" Konstruktion des Urteils ist es, die OAO NK JUKOS nicht als Eigentümerin des Erdöls erscheinen zu lassen, weil andernfalls die Bestrafung *M. Chodorkovskijs* und *P. Lebedevs* wegen „Entwendung" (*chiščenie*) des Erdöls als ihnen angeblich anvertrautes fremdes Eigentum schon im Ansatz nicht zu rechtfertigen gewesen wäre und der Prozess mit einem Freispruch hätte enden müssen.

bb) Richter *V. Danilkin* hat Russland mit seinem Urteil außerdem noch um einen Treppenwitz bereichert. Denn das Chamovniki-Gericht setzt sich nicht nur in Widerspruch zu den Entscheidungen der Wirtschaftsgerichte, sondern auch zu dem offiziellen Standpunkt, den Russland in dem seit 2004 gegen sich laufenden Beschwerdeverfahren der OAO NK JUKOS vor dem Europäischen Gerichtshof für Menschenrechte (EGMR)[34] einnimmt. Dort verteidigt sich Russland gegen den Vorwurf, seine Behörden und Justiz hätten mit Hilfe ungerechtfertigter Steuerforderungen und einem manipulierten Insolvenzverfahren JUKOS damit zerschlagen und auf kaltem Wege verstaatlicht, dass die Steuernachforderungen auf das von JUKOS als Eigentümerin realisierte Erdöl rechtens gewesen seien[35]!

d) Auch bei Nichtigkeit der Kaufverträge keine Unterschlagung

M. Chodorkovskij und *P. Lebedev* hätten jedoch selbst dann nicht wegen Unterschlagung und Veruntreuung des Erdöls verurteilt werden dürfen, wenn man unterstellt, die Generalvereinbarungen und die Kaufverträge der OAO NK JUKOS mit den Tochter- bzw. Fördergesellschaften seien als Scheingeschäfte bereits kraft Gesetzes nichtig und daher unwirksam gewesen (Art. 170 ZGB), denn sie haben keine den Tatbestand der Unterschlagung oder Veruntreuung (Art. 160 StGB) erfüllenden Taten begangen. Zwar wäre das Erdöl dann weiter

---

34 Das Verfahren ist im März 2010 mit dem Beschluss des EGMR, in der Sache zu entscheiden, in seine entscheidende Phase eingetreten. Siehe dazu OAO NEFTYANAYA KOMPANIYA YUKOS v. RUSSIA, http://cmiskp.echr.coe.int/tkp197/view.asp.

35 Siehe dazu Nezavisimaja gazeta vom 05./06.03.2010, S. 1/2 (*G. Reznik*, Präsident der Moskauer Anwaltskammer: „Wenn der Staat anerkennt, dass es sich um kommerzielle Tätigkeit handelte, um Handel mit Erdöl, dass Steuern bezahlt wurden, dann kann von Diebstahl [sc. des Erdöls] nicht die Rede sein."); siehe ferner Novaja gazeta 2010, Nr. 23 (05.03.), S. 4; 2010, Nr. 24 (10.03.), S. 9; sowie zum Verfahren JUKOS Capital S.a.r.l. gegen RosNeft´ in Amsterdam Novaja gazeta 2009, Nr. 98 (07.09.), S. 13.

Eigentum der Fördergesellschaften geblieben[36] und daher für die Angeklagten „fremdes Vermögen" (*čužoe imuščestvo*) gewesen, aber die anderen Tatbestandsmerkmale des Art. 160 StGB treffen auf den Fall nicht zu: Weder ist das Erdöl *M. Chodorkovskij* und *P. Lebedev* „anvertraut" (*vvereno*) worden noch haben sie es den Fördergesellschaften „entwendet" (*chiščenie*).

aa) Das Erdöl wäre ihnen dann anvertraut worden, wenn sie durch ihre Dienststellung, durch Vertrag oder aufgrund eines speziellen Auftrags in den Besitz des Erdöls gekommen wären[37]. Der typische Fall ist die Übertragung des Besitzes durch einen Vertrag, sei es Miete, Pacht, Beförderung, Verwahrung, Leihe usw.[38]. Es kennzeichnet die Unterschlagung, dass die Erlangung des Besitzes mit dem Willen des Eigentümers und in rechtlich einwandfreier Weise geschieht[39]. Außerdem geht sie dem Vorgang der Entwendung voraus.

Keiner dieser üblichen Fälle von Besitzübertragung ist hier eingetreten. Es liegen nur nichtige Kaufverträge vor und die tatsächliche Einspeisung des Erdöls in das Transneft´-Netz. Auch wenn die Kaufverträge nichtig waren, sind sie im Prinzip doch gleichwohl auf Übereignung gerichtet; auf das Anvertrauen des Besitzes jedenfalls nicht. Wegen der anderen Willensrichtung der Vertragspartner können die fehlerhaften Kaufverträge nicht in Vorgänge der Anvertrauung des Erdölbesitzes umgedeutet werden. Zwar ist das Erdöl mit dem Willen der Fördergesellschaften in den Machtbereich der OAO NK JUKOS gelangt, aber der Straftatbestand des Art. 160 StGB schützt nicht den schieren Besitz, sondern stellt darauf ab, dass der Besitz dem Täter vom Eigentümer „anvertraut" wurde. Daran fehlt es hier offensichtlich, und zwar nicht zuletzt auch deswegen, weil die Vertragspartner von der Wirksamkeit der Kaufverträge und damit auch der Übereignung ausgingen.

Das vom Gesetzgeber durch Art. 160 StGB geschützte Rechtsgut ist das Vertrauen des Eigentümers darauf, dass sich diejenige Person, in deren Besitz und Obhut er seinen Vermögensgegenstand gegeben hat, ihn sich nicht aneignet.

---

36 Im russischen Zivilrecht gilt, anders als im deutschen, nicht das „Abstraktionsprinzip", d.h. die getrennte rechtliche Behandlung von schuldrechtlichem Kaufvertrag und sachenrechtlichem („dinglichen") Eigentumsübertragungsvertrag. Nach russischem Zivilrecht führt die Nichtigkeit des Kaufvertrags daher automatisch auch zur Nichtigkeit der Eigentumsübertragung. Die zwischen den Partnern bereits ausgetauschten Leistungen werden nach den Grundsätzen über die ungerechtfertigte Bereicherung rückabgewickelt (vgl. Art. 1102 ZGB).

37 *G. A. Kriger*: Kommentierung von Art. 160 StGB, in: *A. V. Naumov* (Red.): Kommentarij k ugolovnomu kodeksu Rossijskoj Federacii, Moskau 1996, S. 410-413 (411).

38 Punkt 24 Abs. 2 des Plenarbeschlusses des Obersten Gerichts Russlands vom 27.12.2007, Text: Bjulleten´ Verchovnogo Suda RF 2008, Nr. 2; http://www.supcourt.ru/vscourt_detale.php?id=5215.

39 *V. P. Verin* (Vizepräsident des Obersten Gerichts Russlands): Kommentierung von Art. 160 StGB, in: *V. M. Lebedev* (Red.): Kommentarij k ugolovnomu kodeksu Rossijskoj Federacii, Moskau 2001, S. 346/347.

Den Sinn bringt die zweite offizielle Bezeichnung des Artikels – „Veruntreuung“ – klar zum Ausdruck. Der Missbrauch des Vertrauens soll nicht nur zivilrechtliche, sondern auch strafrechtliche Konsequenzen haben.

bb) Indem nun aber das Chamovniki-Gericht die Übertragung des Erdöls unter den Umständen von „fiktiven“ Kaufverträgen mit dem Fall gleichgesetzt hat, dass dem Täter der Besitz an einem Vermögensgegenstand vertraglich „anvertraut“ wurde, hat es gegen das *Analogieverbot*, einen tragenden Grundsatz jedes rechtsstaatlichen Strafrechts, verstoßen. Es gilt auch in Russland; Art. 3 Abs. 2 StGB bestimmt: „Die Anwendung einer Strafvorschrift im Wege der Analogie ist unzulässig.“ Damit hat das Gericht zugleich noch einen weiteren Grundsatz rechtsstaatlicher, humaner Justiz verletzt, nämlich das klassische Prinzip *nullum crimen sine lege*, das Art. 54 Abs. 2 Satz 1 der Verfassung Russlands in folgender Formulierung verkündet: „Niemand darf wegen einer Handlung zur Verantwortung gezogen werden, die zum Zeitpunkt ihrer Begehung nicht als eine Rechtsverletzung anerkannt war.“ Das Analogieverbot ist ein Unterfall dieses Grundsatzes und genießt daher auch selbst Verfassungsrang[40]. Dessen Inhalt beschreibt *Ch. B. Šejnin* mit folgenden Worten[41]: „Die betrachtete Norm hat prinzipielle Bedeutung. Sie schließt vollständig die Möglichkeit aus, ein Strafgesetz analog anzuwenden, d.h. auf eine Handlung, die nicht im Gesetz bezeichnet ist, sondern nur diesem oder jenem Verbrechen ähnlich ist, was von der bis zur Verabschiedung des StGB der RSFSR von 1960 geltenden Strafgesetzgebung erlaubt war.“ Das aber ist hier geschehen: Dabei könnte die von Richter *V. Danilkin* vorgenommene Gleichsetzung des endgültigen (!) Besitzüberganges von Erdöl durch „fiktive Kaufverträge“ mit dem Fall des Art. 160 StGB, nämlich der Anvertrauung des Erdöls durch wirksame Verträge über eine zeitweilige (!) Besitzüberlassung, nicht einmal mehr mit einer Ähnlichkeit beider Fälle gerechtfertigt werden. Dafür sind ihre Situationen zu verschieden. Der Verstoß gegen das Analogieverbot ist daher offenkundig.

„Die kommentierte Vorschrift“, schreibt *Ch. B. Šejnin* hoffnungsvoll, „bildet eine Barriere auf dem Wege möglicher Verletzungen der Rechte und Freiheiten des Menschen und Bürgers und eine klare Rechtsbasis für die Rechtsschutzorgane und Gerichte, die es ihnen ermöglicht, Fehler bei der Entscheidung von Fragen der Verantwortung für Rechtsverletzungen zu vermeiden.“ Die Hoffnung des Autors, man sei gegen Rückfälle in sowjetische Strafrechtsprinzipien gesichert, hat Richter *V. Danilkin* gründlich enttäuscht. Wenn es politisch erwünscht oder „von oben“ befohlen ist, setzt sich, wie der Fall zeigt, ein Gericht skrupellos über das Analogieverbot hinweg.

---

40 *T. G. Morščakova*: Kommentierung zu Art. 54, in: *V. D. Zor'kin*, *L. V. Lazarev* (Red.): Kommentarij k Konstitucii Rossijskoj Federacii, Moskau 2009, S. 487-490 (488).

41 Kommentierung zu Art. 54, in: *L. V. Lazarev* (Red.): Kommentarij k Konstitucii Rossijskoj Federacii, 3-ee izdanie, Moskau 2009, S. 316-321 (319).

cc) Schließlich haben *M. Chodorkovskij* und *P. Lebedev* das Erdöl nicht „entwendet". Das Tatbestandsmerkmal bedeutet, dass der Täter von einem bestimmten Moment an den ihm vom Eigentümer anvertrauten, in seinem Besitz befindlichen Gegenstand für seine eigenen Zwecke benutzt und darüber wie ein Eigentümer verfügt. Es ist offensichtlich, dass der dem Urteil zugrundeliegende Sachverhalt keinerlei Möglichkeit eröffnet, die „fiktiven" Kaufverträge als einen Vorgang der „Entwendung" (*chiščenie*) zu deuten. Es fehlt dafür bereits die den Tatbestand der Unterschlagung kennzeichnende zeitliche Differenz und Aufeinanderfolge zwischen legaler Besitzübertragung und illegaler Aneignung. Zu Unrecht beruft sich das Chamovniki-Gericht bei seiner Begründung der „Entwendung" auf das Oberste Gericht Russlands[42]. Dieses hatte in seinem Plenarbeschluss vom 27.12.2007 über die Gerichtspraxis in Sachen Betrug, Unterschlagung und Veruntreuung zwar festgestellt, „dass die Entwendung von Vermögen, die im Wege gleichzeitiger Ersetzung durch einen weniger wertvollen Vermögensgegenstand erfolgt, als Entwendung im Umfang des weggenommenen Vermögenswertes qualifiziert wird"[43], das Oberste Gericht bezieht aber diese Passage ausdrücklich „auf die Feststellung des Umfanges und Ausmaßes", in welchem die Unterschlagung begangen wurde. Es meint damit Fälle, in denen der Täter einen ihm anvertrauten Vermögensgegenstand dadurch unterschlägt und sich aneignet, dass er ihn mit einem anderen, minderwertigen Gegenstand vertauscht. Der Plenarbeschluss lässt keinen Zweifel daran, dass der höherwertige Vermögensgegenstand dem Täter zunächst anvertraut worden sein muss. Angewendet auf den vorliegenden Fall würde das heißen, dass die Tochtergesellschaften das Erdöl durch einen entsprechenden Überlassungsvertrag der OAO NK JUKOS (nur) anvertrauen wollten und auch tatsächlich anvertraut haben mussten. Davon kann aber, wie schon ausführlich dargelegt wurde, keine Rede sein. Für den Vorgang einer „Entwendung" fehlt es offenkundig an entscheidenden Voraussetzungen. Gerade der Plenarbeschluss des Obersten Gerichts hätte dem Gericht klar machen müssen, wie abwegig es ist, den vorliegenden Fall als „Unterschlagung" zu deuten.

IV. Abschließende Bewertung

Das Urteil des Chamovniki-Gerichts hat zu Recht weltweit scharfe Kritik, Ablehnung und Verurteilung erfahren. Schon eine nur kurze Analyse wie diese zeigt eine erschreckende Fülle schwerer und schwerster Verletzungen tragender, von der Verfassung Russlands feierlich verkündeter Grundsätze des Strafrechts und des Rechtsstaates. Das zweite Strafurteil gegen *M. Chodorkovskij* und *P. Lebedev* übertrifft das erste bei weitem an Widersprüchlichkeit, Willkür und Bösartigkeit. Es ist ein weiteres, bestürzendes Dokument von Rechtsnihilismus

42 Urteil, S. 685: Punkt 25 des Plenarbeschlusses.

43 Text: Bjulleten´ Verchovnogo Suda RF 2008, Nr. 2; http://www.supcourt.ru/vscourt_detale.php?id=5215.

und auch von Zynismus der russischen Justiz, da es den willkürlichen Umgang mit dem Gesetz und die böswillige Verdrehung des Rechts kaum noch verschleiert.

Reformbemühungen im Strafvollzugs- und Untersuchungshaftrecht der Ukraine im Lichte europäischer Rechtsstandards

Dr. Stefan Hülshörster[*]

I. Vorbemerkungen

Der Jubilar hat sich vom Beginn seines wissenschaftlichen Wirkens an wie kaum ein anderer mit einer geradezu unüberschaubaren Vielzahl von Facetten nicht nur der Ostrechtswissenschaft befasst[1], deren Bezüge hier im Vordergrund stehen sollen. Die Ostrechtswissenschaft hat durch die Verwerfungen und Systembrüche, die durch den Zusammenbruch der Sowjetunion und die Entstehung und Festigung der Eigenstaatlichkeit der früheren Sowjetrepubliken und der anderen Ostblockstaaten geradezu eine Renaissance erlebt, wurde eine neue Perspektive, ein neues Betätigungsfeld[2]. Insofern weist der Titel dieser Festschrift in seiner Bipolarität von Brüchen und Kontinuitäten in die Richtung, die dieser Aufsatz zur Reform des Strafvollzugs- und des Untersuchungshaftrechts in der Ukraine aufgreifen will. Denn die gesamte Rechtsreform in den Staaten Mittel-, Südost- und Osteuropas ist geprägt von diesen Brüchen und Kontinuitäten. Die Rechtsreform ist dabei nur ein Teil der komplexen Systemtransformation[3]; die

---

* Der Autor ist Rechtsanwalt und Leiter des Projektbereichs Ukraine, Moldau und Belarus der Deutschen Stiftung für internationale rechtliche Zusammenarbeit e.V., Bonn. Dieser Aufsatz gibt die persönliche Meinung des Autors wieder.

1 *F.-C. Schroeder*, Recht und Rechtspflege in Russland nach dem Sozialismus, JOR 1995/1, S. 9-28; *ders.*, 74 Jahre Sowjetrecht, München 1992.

2 Die Staaten des ehemaligen Ostblocks waren (und sind es bis heute) bei der Reformierung des Rechtssystems und des Justizwesens auf die beratende Unterstützung der europäischen Nachbarländer angewiesen. Die in Deutschland an den Ostrechtsinstituten vorhandene ostrechtliche Expertise konnte in den deutschen und europäischen Beratungsprozess gewinnbringend eingebracht werden. Neue auch rechtsvergleichende Erkenntnisse bieten bis in die Gegenwart eine fruchtbare Grundlage für die Fortsetzung der Beratungen. Im Widerspruch hierzu steht damit die vermehrte Schließung bzw. Umwidmung einiger vor allem universitärer Ostrechtsinstitute und der hierdurch verursachte oder zumindest drohende Verlust gerade einer in rechtlicher und sprachlicher Hinsicht osteuropäisch ausgerichteten wissenschaftlichen Schwerpunktbildung, soweit eine solche nicht unter anderen Vorzeichen beibehalten wird.

3 Ausführlich hierzu bei *S. Hülshörster*, Recht im Umbruch, Frankfurt 2008, S. 21 f. m.w.N.; *C. Boulanger* (Hrsg.), Recht in der Transformation, Berlin 2002.

Rechtsberatung durch internationale Institutionen[4] hat sich an diesen Brüchen und Kontinuitäten zu orientieren, hat sie zu berücksichtigen und in ihre Konzeptionen und Strategien einfließen zu lassen, will sie nicht zur Erfolglosigkeit verdammt sein. Recht kann nicht einfach von einem in ein anderes Rechtssystem ohne Rücksicht auf die bestehenden rechtskulturellen[5] Traditionen übertragen werden[6]. Ansonsten werden nämlich Systembrüche erst provoziert, indem importiertes, fremdes Recht, das zwar im Empfängerstaat formell in Kraft getreten ist, nicht anerkannt, nicht gelebt, nicht befolgt und damit nicht rezipiert wird. Solch ein Recht wäre totes Recht, das keine Wirkung entfalten kann. Gerade dies ist der Ansatzpunkt für die Einflechtung und Nutzbarmachung der jahrzehntelangen Erkenntnisse der Ostrechtswissenschaft. Es ist daher nur selbstverständlich, dass *Professor Dr. Dres. h.c. Friedrich-Christian Schroeder* vor allem als Straf- und als Ostrechtler zu zahlreichen Fachberatungen verschiedener Institutionen, die im Zusammenhang mit der Rechtsreform in Osteuropa standen, hinzugezogen wurde.

Ein zentrales Anliegen der beratenden internationalen rechtlichen Zusammenarbeit ist – neben der wichtigen Rechtsangleichung und Harmonisierung im Zivil- und Wirtschaftsrecht – die Förderung des Rechtsstaats in den Partnerländern, also ein breiter angelegtes Petitum, das neben dem gesamten Justizbereich und dem Prozessrecht schon unter menschenrechtlichen Gesichtspunkten auch die Beratungen im Straf-, Strafprozess- und Strafvollzugsrecht erfassen muss. Die Reform und die Harmonisierung dieser Rechtsbereiche gehören „ohne Zweifel zu den zentralen Forderungen des Rechtsstaats“[7]. Da die Beratungen auf eine Gewährleistung, Verankerung und Implementierung europäischer Rechtsstandards auch in einem Europa außerhalb der politischen Grenzen der EU gerichtet sind, nimmt sich die Deutsche Stiftung für internationale rechtliche Zusammenarbeit e.V. (IRZ-Stiftung) als von der Bundesregierung mandatierte Beratungsinstitution daher dieses komplexen Themas in einem zumeist überaus schwierigen Beratungsumfeld an. In der Ukraine wurden und werden aktuell, wenngleich mit – durch die sich ständig ändernden politischen Rahmenbedin-

4 In Deutschland ist z.B. die vom Bundesministerium der Justiz gegründete und mandatierte Deutsche Stiftung für internationale rechtliche Zusammenarbeit e.V. mit der internationalen rechtlichen Zusammenarbeit befasst, siehe unter http://www.irz.de.

5 Ausführlich zur Rechtsgeschichte und zu rechtlichen Traditionen Osteuropas *H. Küpper,* Einführung in die Rechtsgeschichte Osteuropas, Frankfurt 2005, S. 1 ff., S. 667 ff.; zur Ukraine siehe *S. Hülshörster*, a.a.O. (Rn. 3), S. 39 ff.

6 *P. Legrand*, The Impossibility of Legal Transplants, in: Maastricht Journal of Comparative Law 1994, S. 111; siehe auch *R. Knieper*, Möglichkeiten und Grenzen der Verpflanzbarkeit von Recht, in: RabelsZ, Bd. 72: Rechtstransformation und Rechtsrezeption (2008), S. 88 f.; *ders.*, Juristische Zusammenarbeit: Universalität und Kontext, Wiesbaden 2004; *E. Stiefel*, Von der Berufung deutscher Juristen zum Aufbau des Rechts im Osten, JZ 94, S. 110.

7 So *R. Knieper* (Fn. 6 – Juristische Zusammenarbeit), S. 78.

gungen bedingt – wechselnder Intensität, zahlreiche Beratungen zur Reform der Gesetzgebung mit entsprechenden flankierenden oder folgenden Implementierungsmaßnahmen[8] durchgeführt[9], um die bisweilen labile Rechtsstaatlichkeit in der Ukraine[10] zu stärken.

Nachdem die IRZ-Stiftung das ukrainische Justizministerium, das Staatliche Strafvollzugsdepartment der Ukraine und die Rechtsstaatskommission beim Präsidenten der Ukraine unter Einbeziehung weiterer Partnerinstitutionen bereits längere Zeit auch zur Reform des Strafprozessrechts und des Strafvollzugsrechts beraten hatte[11], bat der Europarat die IRZ-Stiftung im Jahre 2007 darum, auch die bisher unter dem Dach des Europarates und von diesem selbst organisierten

---

8 Zur Implementierung neuen, reformierten, in Reformierung befindlichen oder sogar noch zu reformierenden Rechts gehören z.B. Maßnahmen der Aus- und Fortbildung aller juristischen Berufsgruppen, die Durchführung von berufsspezifischen Maßnahmen wie z.B. zur Relations- und Urteilstechnik, die Bekanntmachung des reformierten Rechts in Seminaren, Konferenzen, Vorlesungen mit entsprechender Anpassung der Lehrpläne an den Universitäten, die Erstellung und Veröffentlichung von fachspezifischem Informationsmaterial und dgl. mehr. Das Instrumentarium hierfür ist groß und man sollte damit auch alle Bereiche der Bevölkerung erreichen – hier stoßen die Beratungsinstitutionen aber bald an ihre Grenzen und die Umsetzung bestimmter Anliegen muss auch der Eigenverantwortlichkeit der Partnerländer überlassen bleiben.

9 In anderen Beratungsorganisationen wie z.B. der GTZ scheint dieser für die Achtung der Menschenrechte und die Förderung des Rechtsstaatsgedankens so wichtige Bereich des Straf-, des Strafprozess- und des Strafvollzugsrechts für die Beratung mehr oder weniger ausgeschlossen zu sein, siehe bei *R. Knieper* (Fn. 6 – Juristische Zusammenarbeit), S. 79. Die auch in Osteuropa tätigen US-amerikanischen Beratungsprogramme kümmern sich hingegen überaus intensiv und mit entsprechender finanzieller Unterfütterung um diesen Rechtsbereich.

10 Hierzu *A. Nußberger*, Die Ukraine – ein streitbarer Rechtsstaat, in: Ukraine-Analysen 76/2010, S. 2 f., siehe unter http://www.laender-analysen.de/ukraine/pdf/UkraineAnalysen76.pdf; *A. Nußberger/C. v. Gall*, Rechtsstaat ohne Masterplan. Recht und Gerichtswesen in der Ukraine, in: Osteuropa 2010/2-4, S. 89 f.; vgl. auch *F.-C. Schroeder*, Etablierung der Rechtsstaatlichkeit in der Ukraine, in: *Rill* (Hrsg.), Die Ukraine – Partner der EU, Argumente und Materialien zum Zeitgeschehen Nr. 61 (2008), S. 13 f., siehe unter http://www.hss.de/uploads/tx_ddceventsbrowser/AMZ61-Ukraine.pdf; *ders.*, Der Aufbau des Rechtsstaats in der Ukraine, in: Jahrbuch für Ostrecht Bd. 51 (2010, 1. Hb.), S. 97 f. sowie *O. Luchterhandt*, Der Kampf um das Regierungssystem der Ukraine – eine unendliche Geschichte, in: Ukraine-Analysen 80/2010, S. 2 f., siehe unter http://www.laender-analysen.de/ukraine/pdf/UkraineAnalysen80.pdf.

11 Als Experten wirkten an diesen Beratungen neben dem mit dieser Festschrift geehrten Jubilar u.a. auch der ehemalige Vizepräsident des BGH, *Prof. Dr. Jähnke*, OStA *Stange* und der ehemalige Staatssekretär der Berliner Senatsverwaltung für Justiz und jetzige deutsche Richter am Internationalen Gerichtshof für das ehemalige Jugoslawien *Flügge* (der die Ukraine bereits seit 1996 für den Europarat beraten hat und der maßgeblich in die Beratungen zum Untersuchungshaftrecht eingebunden war), der Abteilungsleiter des Berliner Justizsenats *Dr. Meinen* und viele Kollegen des Berliner Strafvollzugs mit, denen an dieser Stelle für ihre vielfältigen Einsätze gedankt wird.

Beratungen zum Strafvollzugs- und insbesondere auch zum Untersuchungshaftrecht der Ukraine im Sinne einer einheitlicheren Beratung[12] bilateral fortzuführen. Die U-Haft bildete dabei einen Schwerpunkt und wurde nach eingehender Analyse hinsichtlich der gesetzlichen Voraussetzungen ihrer Verhängung sowie hinsichtlich der Dauer und der Art ihrer Vollstreckung als ein sehr problematischer Bereich identifiziert. Grund hierfür war unter anderem das schwierige Verhältnis und die Kompetenzstreitigkeiten zwischen Justizministerium und Staatlichem Strafvollzugsdepartment und eine eher traditionell-konservativ geprägte Auffassung von einer Reform des Strafvollzugsrechts. Neben den genannten Institutionen waren an den Beratungen auch das Innenministerium, die Generalstaatsanwaltschaft, die Gerichte und die Strafverteidiger zu beteiligen – eine zwischenbehördliche Arbeitsgruppe wurde ins Leben gerufen. Ziel des ins Auge gefassten Beratungsvorhabens war die Erarbeitung konkreter Änderungsvorschläge zur Verbesserung der gesetzlichen Grundlagen des Strafvollzugsrechts, des Untersuchungshaftrechts und des Strafprozessrechts sowie zur Verbesserung der Vollzugsbedingungen in der Praxis.

II. Untersuchungshaftrecht im europäischen Vergleich

Besonderes Augenmerk wurde im Rahmen der Beratungen dem Untersuchungshaftrecht[13] gewidmet. Die Anordnung der U-Haft ist einer der massivsten Eingriffe des Staates in die Lebensverhältnisse und in die grundrechtlich geschützten Freiheiten des Bürgers. In erster Linie dient die U-Haft des Beschuldigten der Vorbereitung und Sicherung des durchzuführenden Strafverfahrens. Es wird ohne zugrundeliegendes rechtskräftiges Strafurteil bereits im Vorfeld des Strafverfahrens in die Freiheit des Bürgers eingegriffen. Dass dies nur unter besonders engen gesetzlichen Voraussetzungen[14] geschehen kann, bedarf im Grunde keiner besonderen Erwähnung, da einer der wichtigsten Bausteine des Rechtsstaatsprinzips – ausdrücklich in Art. 6 Abs. 2 EMRK normiert – die Unschuldsvermutung ist. Diese gebietet eine unvoreingenommene und möglichst wenig

---

12 Die aus Sicht des Europarates sinnvollerweise wohl nicht im Wege des Einsatzes von Experten aus verschiedenen Ländern geleistet werden konnte, sondern vorzugsweise bilateral und „aus einem Guss" erfolgen sollte.

13 Siehe m.w.N. G. Münchhalffen/N. Gatzweiler, Das Recht der Untersuchungshaft, München 2009; F. Dünkel, International vergleichende Strafvollzugsforschung, in: H.-J. Schneider (Hrsg.), Internationales Handbuch der Kriminologie, Bd. 2: Besondere Probleme der Kriminologie. Berlin 2009, S. 145-226 (siehe auch unter http://www.rsf.uni-greifwald.de/fileadmin/mediapool/lehrstuehle/duenkel/Duenkel_Intern_StVollzForsch_HBSchneider.pdf, S. 2 ff.).

14 *J. Meyer-Ladewig*, Europäische Menschenrechtskommission, Handkommentar 2. Aufl., Baden-Baden 2006, zu Art. 5 Buchst. c EMRK Rn. 12 f. (S. 86) und Rn. 34 f. (S. 94).

einschneidende Behandlung des Beschuldigten[15], sofern nicht eine konkrete Gefahr für die öffentlichen Interessen eine Beschränkung rechtfertigt. Die Vollzugsbedingungen der U-Haft sind entsprechend auszugestalten[16]. So gewährt nach Ansicht des Bundesverfassungsgerichts § 119 III StPO keine pauschale Blankovollmacht für Grundrechtseingriffe in der U-Haft, sondern setzt bei jeder Anordnung einer Haftbeschränkung eine genaue Verhältnismäßigkeitsprüfung voraus.

Die Ukraine hat die EMRK am 11. September 1997 ratifiziert und zudem den – für den normalen Vollzug und die U-Haft gleichermaßen geltenden – European Prison Rules (EPR) in ihrer Neufassung aus dem Jahr 2006[17] zugestimmt. Zudem sind die Empfehlungen des Europarates zur U-Haft[18] von 2006 zu beachten, die zu einer Beschränkung der Verhängung und zur Entwicklung von Alternativen zur U-Haft führen sollen. Auch wenn diese Empfehlungen für die Mitgliedstaaten des Europarates nicht verbindlich sind, so besteht doch ein faktischer Umsetzungsdruck, zumal das Ministerkomitee des Europarates eine Berichterstattung zum Stand der Umsetzung verlangen kann. So sind in den EPR zunächst einige Grundprinzipien postuliert und damit besonders hervorgehoben: Beachtung der Menschenrechte, Verhältnismäßigkeitsgrundsatz, Mittelknapp-

---

15 So z.B. BVerfG, Beschluss v. 10.01.2008 (2 BvR 1229/07) zum Nachtstromverbot in der U-Haft, kommentiert in NJW-Spezial 9/2008, S. 281.

16 Die deutschen Bundesländer haben nach der Föderalismusreform Anstrengungen unternommen, um das Recht der U-Haft über den teils für unzureichend, aber vom Bundesverfassungsgericht mit o.g. Beschluss (Fn. 15) für ausreichend erachteten § 119 StPO (geändert durch das sog. UHaftRÄndG, siehe BGBl. I 2009/2274, in Kraft seit 01.01.2010) hinaus einheitlich zu regeln, siehe beispielhaft das am 01.03.2010 in Kraft getretene Justizvollzugsgesetz NRW unter https://recht.nrw.de/lmi/owa/br_bes_text?anw_nr=2&gld_nr=4&ugl_nr=46&bes_id=13065&menu=1&sg=0&aufgehoben=N&keyword=UVollzG#det0.

17 Recommendation Rec(2006)2 of the Committee of Ministers to member states on the European Prison Rules vom 11.01.2006, siehe unter https://wcd.coe.int/ViewDoc.jsp?id=955747, in deutscher Sprache unter http://www.bmj.bund.de/files/-/2308/Europ%20Strafvollzugsgrundsaetze%202006.pdf. Siehe hierzu *F. Dünkel/C. Morgenstern/J. Zolondek:* Europäische Strafvollzugsgrundsätze verabschiedet! Siehe unter http://www.informationsplattform-strafvollzug.de/download/stvollz/20060811-Duenkel-EurStrfvoGrds.pdf. Auf Artt. 9 f. des Pakts über Bürgerliche und Politische Rechte der Vereinten Nationen soll an dieser Stelle nicht weiter eingegangen werden, siehe aber unter http://www.igfm.de/Internationaler-Pakt-ueber-buergerliche-und-politische-Rechte.143.0.html#content316. Auf Art. 5 EMRK und die Rechtsprechung des EGMR soll ebenfalls an dieser Stelle nicht gesondert eingegangen werden, zumal die o.g. Empfehlungen des Europarates auf der Rechtsprechung des EGMR beruhen.

18 Recommendation Rec(2006)13 of the Committee of Ministers to member states on the use of remand in custody, the conditions in which it takes place and the provision of safeguards against abuse vom 27.09.2006, siehe unter https://wcd.coe.int/ViewDoc.jsp?Ref=Rec%282006%2913&Language=lanEnglish&Ver=original&Site=COE&BackColorInternet=9999CC&BackColorIntranet=FFBB55&BackColorLogged=FFAC75.

heit keine Ausrede für mangelhafte Vollzugsbedingungen, Resozialisierung als Ziel, getrennte Unterbringung von jugendlichen Straftätern (unter 18 Jahre) bzw. Sicherstellung von Sonderregelungen für diesen Personenkreis. Es folgen zahlreiche Empfehlungen zu Haftbedingungen (z.B. Belegung, Tageslicht, sanitäre Anlagen, Trennung von Erwachsenen- und Untersuchungshaftvollzug bzw. von Erwachsenen und Heranwachsenden, Außenkontakte etc.). Neben den oben erwähnten Empfehlungen zur U-Haft enthält Abschnitt VII der EPR weitergehende Sonderempfehlungen (z.B. zusätzliche Außenkontakte soweit möglich etc.). Diese Empfehlungen sind also auch Maßstab für den ukrainischen Strafvollzug und die U-Haft und waren (und sind demgemäß) auch Maßstab für die von der IRZ-Stiftung durchgeführten Beratungen.

Als Grundlage für die anstehenden Beratungen diente neben den erwähnten Empfehlungen des Europarates und den von mehreren Experten erstellten Berichten[19] des Europarates zum Vollzugswesen in der Ukraine sowie den eigenen Analyse durch die beteiligten Experten auch eine rechtsvergleichende Studie[20] zur U-Haft in verschiedenen europäischen Staaten, die Fragen der Voraussetzung der Verhängung der U-Haft, des Verfahrens selbst, bestehender Alternativen und zur Ausgestaltung der Haft untersucht hat und mit der einheitliche europäische Standards dargestellt werden sollten.

Bezüglich der dem Beschuldigten vorgeworfenen Tat ist in den untersuchten europäischen Staaten regelmäßig ein begründeter oder dringender Tatverdacht[21] zur Verhaftung erforderlich, also ein höherer Grad eines Verdachts, wonach es mit großer Wahrscheinlichkeit zu einer Verurteilung kommen wird. Zudem müssen Haftgründe vorliegen[22]. Hinsichtlich der Dauer der U-Haft kommt es auf die konkreten Umstände des Einzelfalls an[23]. Die Haftdauer ist in den untersuchten Staaten ganz unterschiedlich geregelt: in den Niederlanden z.B. von zunächst zehn Tagen bis zu 30 Tagen (mit Verlängerungsmöglichkeiten von jeweils 30 Tagen); in Italien z.B. zunächst bis 18 Monate (danach Verlängerung bis zu

19 Siehe Fn. 40 und 41.

20 Nicht veröffentlichte Studie des Max-Planck-Instituts für Ausländisches und Internationales Strafrecht vom Januar 2008. Folgende Staaten wurden untersucht: Deutschland, England/Wales, Frankreich, Italien, Schweden, Niederlande, Polen, Bulgarien und Estland.

21 Art 5 Abs. 1 c EMRK spricht von hinreichendem Tatverdacht, was nach der Rechtsprechung des EGMR die Überzeugung eines objektiven Betrachters erfordert, nicht jedoch eine zur Anklageerhebung ausreichende Beweislage: MPI-Studie (s. Fn. 20), S. 5 mit Verweis auf diverse EGMR-Entscheidungen.

22 Vgl. §§ 112 Abs. 2 und 3 (in verfassungskonformer Auslegung, d.h. bei Fehlen jeglicher Fluchtgefahr greift dieser Haftgrund nicht), 112a StPO.

23 So hat der EGMR beispielsweise sehr unterschiedliche Haftlängen (z.B. eineinhalb Jahre: Sulaoja v. Estonia, Application No. 55939/00 v. 15.02.2005, vier Jahre und acht Monate: Vaccaro v. Italy, Application No. 41852/98 v. 16.11.2000) für konventionswidrig erklärt.

sechs Jahren möglich). Die Anordnung der U-Haft erfolgt in aller Regel durch einen Richter, hiergegen ist regelmäßig zumindest die Beschwerde eingeräumt. Überwiegend besteht das Recht auf einen Verteidiger unmittelbar mit Beginn der polizeilichen Ermittlungen bzw. der Festnahme[24]; Abweichungen gibt es im Einzelnen bei der Bestellung eines „öffentlichen" Verteidigers auf Kosten des Staates sowie bei Kontaktsperren[25] in bestimmten Einzelfällen. Auch Alternativen zur U-Haft sind regelmäßig durch einen Richter anzuordnen[26]. An Alternativen sind ganz überwiegend die Kaution[27], Reisebeschränkungen, Meldeweisungen, die Hinterlegung von Reisedokumenten und der Hausarrest (teils bei elektronischer Überwachung) vorgesehen. Daneben sind vereinzelt noch eine Sicherung der Opferansprüche[28], Drogentests[29], Rehabilitationsmaßnahmen[30], Kontaktverbote[31] und Bürgschaften[32] als Alternativen zu finden. Die Ausgestaltung der U-Haft wurde vor allem im Hinblick auf Kontaktmöglichkeiten (Besuche, Briefe, Pakete, Telefonate) zur Außenwelt, respektive etwaige Kontaktsperren (nur sehr eingeschränkt unter besonderen Bedingungen möglich), untersucht.

Da es speziell in diesem Bereich in der Ukraine bereits Aktivitäten der Direktion für Entwicklung und Zusammenarbeit (DEZA) des Eidgenössischen Departments für auswärtige Angelegenheiten zur Einrichtung von Modellgefängnissen gab[33], wurden die Beratungen koordiniert und teilweise auch unter Hinzuziehung der schweizerischen Fachleute durchgeführt. Das ukrainische Justizministerium hat es allerdings als vorrangig bezeichnet, die gesetzlichen Grundlagen für die Verhängung der U-Haft (vor allem zunächst bezüglich der Anordnung sowie der Haftdauer) so zu ändern, dass die Überbelegung in den Haftanstalten abgebaut werden könne. Denn es sei absehbar, dass die finanziellen Mittel nicht ausreichen würden, die allgemeine Haftsituation in allen Vollzugsanstalten durch die Verbesserung der baulichen Rahmenbedingungen alsbald entschärfen zu können.

---

24 Ausnahme z.B. Niederlande: erst bei Anordnung der Inhaftierung.

25 So kann z.B. in England/Wales der Kontakt mit dem Verteidiger für max. 36 Stunden im Zeitraum der polizeilichen Vernehmungen verweigert werden, wenn die Ermittlungen ansonsten erschwert würden.

26 In Schweden kann u.U. auch die Staatsanwaltschaft alternative Maßnahmen anordnen, die dann aber einer gerichtlichen Überprüfung zugänglich sind.

27 Ausnahme: Schweden.

28 Frankreich.

29 England/Wales und teils in den Niederlanden.

30 Frankreich; Italien: hinsichtlich einer psychiatrischen Unterbringung; Niederlande: im Rahmen allgemeiner Auflagen.

31 Ausnahme: Schweden, Polen und Estland.

32 So in den Niederlanden und in Polen.

33 Siehe unter www.swiss-cooperation.admin.ch/belarus//.../resource_de_160868.pdf (hier insb. S. 84 und S. 85) sowie unterwww.sdc.admin.ch/ressources/resource_de_99525.pdf.

Im Einzelnen sollten während der Beratungen mit der ukrainischen Arbeitsgruppe folgende Fragen beleuchtet werden, die als Leitfaden für die fachlichen Diskussionen dienen sollten:

- Rechtliche Voraussetzungen für Haftanordnungen (Tatverdacht, Haftgründe);
- Antrag Haftanordnung durch wen? Entscheidung durch wen?
- Rechtsmittel und Rechtsweg hiergegen;
- Fristen zur Überprüfung der Haftanordnungen;
- Höchstdauer der U-Haft;
- Bestimmungen für die Verteidigung (Bestellung, Zulassung, Finanzierung, Pflichtverteidigung bzw. *Legal Aid*, Kommunikation mit Beschuldigtem und Akteneinsichtnahme);
- Entscheidungen über konkrete Ausgestaltung der U-Haft;
- Entscheidungen über Kontakte (Besuche, Telekommunikation, Brief- u. Paketverkehr) bzw. Einschränkungen;
- Trennung von Untersuchungshäftlingen und Strafgefangenen; Trennung von Erwachsenen und Jugendlichen/Heranwachsenden;
- Rechtsmittel.

III. Situation in der Ukraine

Es ist offenkundig, dass in vielen Staaten der ehemaligen Sowjetunion die Zahl der Gefangenen schon fast „traditionell"[34] hoch ist[35]. Dies gilt auch für die Ukraine und betrifft sowohl den normalen Strafvollzug als auch die U-Haft. Etwa 0,4% der ukrainischen Bevölkerung (im Jahr 2010 etwa 46 Mio. Bürger) befanden sich Ende 2007 in Haft, eine im europäischen Vergleich recht hohe Zahl. Anfang 2010 lag die Zahl der Häftlinge in der Ukraine bei 344 pro 100.000 der Bevölkerung und damit noch bei gut 0,34%. Zum Vergleich: Ende November 2008 befanden sich nach Angaben des Statistischen Bundesamtes 75.200 Menschen in deutschen Gefängnissen, d.h. umgerechnet 91 Menschen auf 100.000 oder 0,091%, davon 16% in U-Haft. In der Ukraine gab es am 01.01.2010 allein 33 Untersuchungshaftanstalten mit über 38.000 Insassen bei steigender Tendenz

34 Zur strafrechtlichen Tradition vgl. beispielsweise bei *F.-C. Schroeder* (Fn. 1, 74 Jahre Sowietrecht), S. 11 und S. 15. Von repressiv-schützender Funktion (nicht nur) des Strafrechts mit einer erstaunlichen Härte des Strafensystems spricht *N. Reich*, in *Reich/Reichel*, Einführung in das sozialistische Recht, München 1975, S. 60 und *H.-C. Reichel*, a.a.O., S. 97, verweist auf die „konstruktive Rolle" des Strafrechts zur Unterstützung des Aufbaus des Sozialismus – Vorrang des Schutzes kollektiver Rechtsgüter vor dem Schutz persönlicher Rechtsgüter.

35 *F. Dünkel/C. Morgenstern/J. Zolondek* bezeichnen hohe Inhaftierungsraten allerdings als ein nicht nur osteuropäisches Problem, (Fn. 17), S. 2 m.w.N.; siehe auch *F. Dünkel* (Fn. 13), S. 5 f. („unterschiedliche Sanktionsstile und andersgeartete Kriminalpolitik" (S. 6), „Klima für liberale Strafvollzugs- und Strafrechtspolitik in MOE eher ungünstig" (S. 9)).

(2003 waren es noch ca. 32.000 Insassen). Die hohe Zahl an Häftlingen (sowohl im Strafvollzug als auch in U-Haft) resultiert in der Ukraine nicht zuletzt daraus, dass Alternativen[36] bzw. alternative Strafen nicht ausreichend gesetzlich geregelt sind und diese wenigen Alternativen trotz einer „Verordnung" des Plenums des Obersten Gerichts der Ukraine[37], die die Instanzgerichte besonders darauf hinweist, die U-Haft nur als *ultima ratio* anzuordnen, von den Gerichten bisher noch zu wenig angewandt wurden.

Naturgemäß waren also vor dem Hintergrund einer überschnellen Verhängung von Freiheitsstrafen (und der hiermit im Zusammenhang stehenden Vielzahl der U-Haftanordnungen[38]), bei Fehlen bzw. Nichtanwendung vorhandener Alternativen und der auch dadurch bedingten Überbelegung der Haftanstalten die Vollzugsbedingungen im normalen und im Untersuchungshaftvollzug stark verbesserungsbedürftig.

Zudem waren und sind die rechtlichen Regelungen für die Verhängung und Ausgestaltung der U-Haft wegen unklarer gesetzlicher Regelung[39] problematisch. Untersuchungen des Europarates aus den Jahren 1996[40] und 2003[41] zum Strafvollzugssystem in der Ukraine, die ein besonderes Augenmerk auch auf die U-Haft gerichtet haben, konnten etliche Defizite identifizieren. So wurde nahezu allen Anträgen der Staatsanwälte auf Anordnung der U-Haft durch die Gerichte stattgegeben[42]. Tatverdacht und besondere Untersuchungshaftgründe fehlten

---

36 Neben der in Art. 149 des ukrainischen Strafprozessgesetzes (UStPG) geregelten und durch einen Richter anzuordnenden U-Haft waren als Alternativen bisher nur noch ein Reiseverbot, die Übernahme einer Bürgschaft durch eine andere Person mit der Verantwortung, dass der Beschuldigte zu anberaumten Terminen erscheint, sowie eine Kaution vorgesehen.

37 Nr. 4 vom 25.04.2003 zur Anwendungspraxis der U-Haft.

38 Gemäß Art. 155 UStPG wird U-Haft angeordnet bei einem für das entsprechende Delikt vorgesehenen Strafrahmen von mehr als drei Jahren Freiheitsstrafe, in Ausnahmefällen auch darunter.

39 Artt. 148, 150 UStPG: Danach ist Voraussetzung für die Anordnung sog. vorbeugender Maßnahmen eine drohende Vereitelung der Ermittlungen, ein drohendes Nichterscheinen des Beschuldigten zu anberaumten Terminen oder eine drohende Fortsetzung der kriminellen Tätigkeit. Dabei sind auch die Schwere der vorgeworfenen Tat, das Alter und die Gesundheit, die Familienverhältnisse, das Vermögen und die Arbeitsverhältnisse sowie der Wohnort des Beschuldigten zu berücksichtigen.

40 Assessment of the Ukrainian Prison System, Report of Council of Europe Expert Missions to Ukraine in June and August 1996, UKR V.B. (97)1.

41 Reassessment of the Needs of the Ukrainian Prison System, Report of the Council of Europe Expert Mission to Ukraine in April 2003, SG/Ukraine (2003), 1 REV-).

42 Ähnlich für den Bereich der „Verwaltungsstraftaten" (zu denen z.B. Rowdytum gehört, für das das Gericht eine 15-tägige Haftstrafe verhängen kann): Hier trifft das Gericht die Entscheidung allein auf Grundlage der polizeilichen Akten, was fast in allen Fällen zur Haftanordnung führt, vgl. UN-Report on Arbitrary Detention (mission Ende 2008), Az. GE.07-14817 (E) 08107, S. 17.

bzw. waren nur rudimentär und unklar geregelt. Die Dauer der U-Haft[43] wurde regelmäßig über die gesetzlichen Fristen hinaus verlängert und führte – gerade wenn Anklage vor Gericht erhoben war – zu unverhältnismäßig langer Haftdauer. Aber auch die Ausgestaltung der U-Haft an sich war (und ist es wohl immer noch) stark verbesserungsbedürftig: Es bestehen nur sehr eingeschränkte Kontaktmöglichkeiten durch Brief- oder Paketpost, Besuche[44] etc., entsprechende erforderliche Genehmigungen wurden in der Praxis nur im Einzelfall erteilt; die bauliche Situation im Hinblick auf Überbelegung, Sanitäreinrichtungen, Sichtblenden und die Möglichkeiten, die Freistunden an der frischen Luft zu verbringen, ist bis heute desolat; jugendliche Untersuchungshäftlinge konnten aus Gründen der Disziplin mit maximal zwei Erwachsenen zusammengelegt werden.

Letztlich führt die hohe Zahl der verhängten Freiheitsstrafen (in der Ukraine etwa 25% aller Strafen) und der Untersuchungshaftanordnungen insgesamt zu unwürdigen Vollzugsverhältnissen, die wohl nicht im Einklang mit der EMRK und den EPR des Europarates stehen dürften.

IV. Beratungen und Vorschläge zur Änderung der gesetzlichen Grundlagen

Nach mehreren Fachgesprächen und Arbeitstreffen wurde von der für dieses Beratungsvorhaben gegründeten ukrainischen zwischenbehördlichen Arbeitsgruppe ein Katalog von 17 Vorschlägen ausgearbeitet, der in Teilen immer noch nachbesserungsbedürftig war und der von Expertenseite entsprechend kommentiert wurde. Neben eher allgemein gehaltenen Forderungen, das Strafprozess- und das Untersuchungshaftgesetz der Ukraine besser aufeinander abzustimmen und in Übereinstimmung mit Art. 6 EMRK die Durchführung von Ermittlungen und Hauptverfahren[45] in angemessener Frist sicherzustellen, um insbesondere die U-Haft nicht unnötig in die Länge zu ziehen, hatte man sich unter anderem darauf verständigt, das Institut des Ermittlungsrichters einzuführen[46], der für die

43 Gemäß Art. 156 UStPG zwei Monate, unter bestimmten Voraussetzungen auch bis 18 Monate – während des Ermittlungsverfahrens. Sobald die Ermittlungen abgeschlossen und Anklage erhoben ist, gelten diese zeitlichen Beschränkungen nicht mehr.

44 Gemäß Art. 161 UStPG kann Besuch zwar max. einmal pro Monat für eine bis vier Stunden genehmigt werden; nach den Feststellungen der Experten des Europarates bedeutete dies in der Praxis jedoch, dass ein Untersuchungsgefangener keine Außenkontakte hatte, solange er sich noch kein ganzes Jahr in U-Haft befand. Die Versagung einer Besuchserlaubnis war mithin die Regel.

45 Diesbezüglich wurde die Änderung des Art. 156 UStPG vorgeschlagen, wonach auch für das gerichtliche Hauptverfahren eine Haftfrist von sechs Monaten bis max. zwei Jahre gelten sollte (mit Ausnahme bei Androhung lebenslänglicher Freiheitsstrafe).

46 In diesem Punkt hat die Arbeitsgruppe wegen des sehr umfangreichen Regelungserfordernisses auf den parallelen Strafprozessgesetzentwurf der *Rule-of-Law*-Kommission

Anordnung der U-Haft bzw. für eine Entlassung aus dieser, die Anordnung alternativer Maßnahmen, die Genehmigung etwaiger mit Grundrechtseingriffen verbundener Ermittlungsmaßnahmen sowie die Einschränkung z.B. von Außenkontakten des Untersuchungsgefangenen u.a.m. zuständig sein sollte. Ferner sollten Verfahren nach Anklageerhebung nicht mehr an die Ermittlungsbehörden zur Durchführung weiterer für notwendig erachteter Ermittlungen zurückgegeben werden dürfen. Die U-Haft wurde in dem Vorschlagskatalog als *ultima ratio* bezeichnet und sollte grundsätzlich nur noch in Fällen eines gesetzlich vorgesehenen Strafrahmens von mehr als fünf Jahren für die dem Beschuldigten vorgeworfene Tat Anwendung finden. Nur in besonderen Fällen, z.B. bei wiederholter Tat, bei konkreter Wiederholungsgefahr bzw. bei Verstoß gegen verhängte Alternativmaßnahmen, sollte U-Haft auch bei einem darunter liegenden Strafrahmen angeordnet werden können. Vorgesehen war ferner eine gerichtliche Überprüfbarkeit der die U-Haft anordnenden Entscheidung bei Anhörung des Beschuldigten. Daneben wurde eine Reihe weiterer Alternativen zur U-Haft, wie z.B. der Hausarrest unter Aufsicht, ggf. mit „elektronischem Monitoring", ein Reiseverbot und ein Passeinzug sowie Kontaktsperren, Entzugsmaßnahmen u.a.m. vorgeschlagen. Allerdings wurde auch der fragwürdige Vorschlag einer teilweisen Entmündigung des Beschuldigten als Alternative zur U-Haft diskutiert und als „zu prüfen" aufgenommen, der aber wegen des erheblichen Grundrechtseingriffs und damit einhergehender Unverhältnismäßigkeit/Ungeeignetheit kaum tragfähig sein dürfte. Zur Sicherstellung einer angemessenen und unverzüglichen Verteidigung des Beschuldigten wurden Änderungen der Anwaltsgesetzgebung vorgeschlagen, wonach örtliche Anwälte verpflichtet werden sollten, sofortigen – auch im Rahmen staatlicher Kostenübernahme – Rechtsbeistand zu leisten. In diesem Zusammenhang wurde auch ein Vorschlag ausgearbeitet, wonach dem Verteidiger die Akten unmittelbar vorzulegen sind, die der Anordnung der U-Haft zugrunde gelegen haben. Zu den Haftbedingungen: Briefwechsel sollte nun i.d.R. unbeschränkt möglich sein, Einschränkungen sollten gesondert angeordnet werden müssen. Die Korrespondenz mit dem Verteidiger sollte nicht mehr kontrolliert werden. Angehörigenbesuche sollten zukünftig einmal im Monat (in Sonderfällen zweimal) für zwei bis vier Stunden möglich sein, Einschränkungen oder Verbote sind gesondert anzuordnen. Beaufsichtigte Telefonate sollten ermöglicht werden (einmal im Monat für 15 Minuten). Daneben sollte die tägliche Freistunde verlängert werden von einer auf zwei Stunden, die Gefangenen sollten neben Briefen auch Pakete und Päckchen ohne Einschränkungen empfangen dürfen und unter verbesserten Bedingungen einkaufen dürfen. Getrennte Unterbringung für Untersuchungsgefangene und Strafgefangene wurde ebenfalls gefordert, ebenso wollte man eine getrennte Unterbringung von Erwachsenen und Minderjährigen forcieren. Perspektivisch sollten die baulichen

---

verwiesen, der entsprechende Regelungsvorschläge enthielt, aber bisher nicht verabschiedet werden konnte.

Bedingungen verbessert werden und in Verbindung damit die Verbesserung der Gestaltungsmöglichkeiten der Freistunden.

V. Vorläufiges Zwischenergebnis

Nach den zum Teil überaus kontrovers geführten Fachgesprächen, bei denen auch um konkrete Formulierungen gerungen wurde, hat die Arbeitsgruppe aus diesem Katalog von 17 Vorschlägen bis Mitte 2009 erste Rohentwürfe für eine Änderung des Strafprozess[47]-, des Strafvollzugs- und des Untersuchungshaftgesetzes erarbeitet. Diese Rohentwürfe waren allerdings wenig ausgereift und in sich widersprüchlich[48], ebenso noch unklar und missverständlich formuliert. Teilweise waren Fragen und Anregungen, die in der Arbeitsgruppe diskutiert und in den Vorschlagskatalog aufgenommen worden waren, in den Entwürfen gar nicht mehr enthalten. Diese Entwürfe wurden wiederum diskutiert und überarbeitet.

In Art. 12 des Entwurfs für das Untersuchungshaftänderungsgesetz blieb es z.B. trotz des anderslautenden Forderungskatalogs dabei, dass der Untersuchungsgefangene Besuch nur nach schriftlicher Genehmigung des Ermittlungsorgans oder der Anstaltsleitung empfangen dürfe. Allerdings sollte ein Briefwechsel des Häftlings mit anderen Personen außerhalb der Anstalt unbegrenzt zulässig sein und die Korrespondenz mit dem Verteidiger sollte zudem ohne Kontrolle erfolgen können[49]. Die Dauer der Freistunde wurde im Entwurf verlängert von einer auf zwei Stunden, in besonderen Fällen von zwei auf bis zu drei Stunden. Einkäufe sollten unter verbesserten Bedingungen zugelassen, 15-minütige (bisher gar nicht vorgesehene) Telefonate der Untersuchungsgefangenen sollten nach entsprechender Genehmigung und unter Aufsicht ermöglicht

---

47 Der Fortgang der Arbeiten wurde allerdings ganz wesentlich dadurch erschwert, dass parallel von der Rechtsstaatskommission beim Präsidenten der Ukraine ein kompletter Neuentwurf eines Strafprozessgesetzes ausgearbeitet wurde. Zwar wurde die Kommission vom seinerzeitigen Justizminister geleitet, jedoch ließen sich die Arbeiten inhaltlich kaum koordinieren. Dies führte zu Verzögerungen durch strategische Überlegungen, wie die vorgeschlagenen Änderungen am besten durchgebracht werden könnten: entweder als Bestandteil des „Komplettentwurfs" der Rechtsstaatskommission oder als gesonderter Änderungsentwurf zu den geltenden Gesetzen. Die Arbeitsgruppe entschied sich seinerzeit in Bezug auf die meisten Forderungen für den zweiten Weg, weil man sich mit diesem Weg bessere und schnellere Realisierungschancen im Parlament versprach. Die bisherige Rechtsstaatskommission wurde nach dem Präsidenten- und Regierungswechsel in der Ukraine im Januar 2010 aufgelöst. Offenbar wird aber intern weiter an einer Änderung des Strafprozessgesetzes gearbeitet.

48 Z.B. parallele Regelung in Art. 51 des ukrainischen U-Haftgesetzänderungsentwurfs: in Nr. 3 „Verbot für Untersuchungshäftlinge, Besuch zu empfangen" und in Nr. 4 „Untersuchungshäftlinge sind berechtigt, monatlich kurze Besuche zu empfangen".

49 Diese Regelung ist bereits durch eine gesonderte Gesetzesänderung am 09.02.2010 in Kraft getreten.

werden[50]. Die für jeden Untersuchungsgefangenen in Ansatz zu bringende Haftfläche sollte von zweieinhalb auf drei qm[51] angehoben werden, in besonderen Fällen von viereinhalb auf bis zu fünf qm.

Weitere Änderungen wurden für das Strafprozessgesetz vorgesehen: So sollte fortan auch das Opfer einer Straftat bzw. dessen Vertreter über die Anordnung, Änderung oder Aufhebung der U-Haft (oder alternativer Maßnahmen) in Bezug auf den Verdächtigten informiert werden (Art. 49). Es sollten ferner – wie im Forderungskatalog enthalten und oben bereits erwähnt – mehr Alternativen zur U-Haft vorgesehen werden: Entzug des Reisepasses, Hausarrest unter Aufsicht und „elektronisches monitoring" (Art. 149). U-Haft wurde wie im Forderungskatalog auch in dem Gesetzentwurf als *ultima ratio* bezeichnet (Art. 155) und sollte demnach zukünftig nur noch dann verhängt werden, wenn das Gesetz für die Tat eine Freiheitsstrafe von mehr als fünf Jahren vorsieht. Eine solche Regelung würde die Justiz dazu zwingen, verstärkt Alternativen zur U-Haft anzuordnen. Sie würde im Übrigen nach Berechnungen des ukrainischen Justizministeriums zu einer Reduzierung der Belegung in den Untersuchungsgefängnissen von ca. 20% führen.

Ein weiteres Problem in der geltenden Strafprozessordnung waren und sind fehlende Fristen für die Durchführung der Strafverfahren – kombiniert mit fehlenden Fristen für die Dauer der U-Haft während der Hauptverhandlung führte dies in vielen Fällen zu einer überlangen Haftdauer von bereits angeklagten Häftlingen (zum Zeitpunkt der Beratungen machte diese Gruppe etwa 70% der Untersuchungshäftlinge aus). Hier wollte man nun gegensteuern und hat daher eine Änderung dergestalt vorgesehen, wonach die U-Haft während der Dauer des Gerichtsverfahrens sechs Monate und in besonderen Fällen zwei Jahre nicht überschreiten darf (Art. 156). Mit diesen Vorschlägen bewegte man sich im mit der o.g. Studie aufgezeigten Rahmen der untersuchten Staaten und im Rahmen der Empfehlungen des Europarates. Daneben wurde – ebenfalls zur Verfahrensbeschleunigung – auch im Änderungsentwurf vorgesehen, die Möglichkeit der Rückgabe des Verfahrens vom Gericht an die Staatsanwaltschaft zur Durchführung weiterer Ermittlungen zu streichen[52]. Sobald ein Fall bei Gericht angeklagt

---

50 Bereits am 16.02.2010 ist eine Änderung des ukrainischen Strafvollzugsgesetzes in Kraft getreten, wonach Gefangene im Strafvollzug (nicht U-Haft) ohne Beschränkung und unter Aufsicht telefonieren dürfen; die Regelung tritt allerdings aus technischen Gründen erst am 01.01.2012 in Kraft.

51 Zum Vergleich: In Deutschland sollen es sechs bis sieben qm für Strafgefangene sein, so das Bundesverfassungsgericht mit Beschluss vom 13.11.2007, Az. 2 BvR 2201/05 – für Untersuchungsgefangene dürfen es somit jedenfalls nicht weniger sein, zumal bei ihnen Möglichkeiten wie Freigang, Beurlaubung etc. ausgeschlossen sind. Im ukrainischen Strafvollzug (nicht U-Haft) wurde mit am 16.02.2010 in Kraft getretener Änderung die gesetzlich festgelegte Haftfläche von drei auf vier qm angehoben.

52 Eine solche Regelung war z.B. auch im oben erwähnten Entwurf eines Strafprozessgesetzes der Rechtsstaatskommission vorgesehen (Fn. 47). Man hat also zumindest ver-

ist, soll er auch dort bleiben. Eine weitere wichtige Änderung betraf die Akteneinsicht durch den Beschuldigten bzw. dessen Verteidiger: Die Staatsanwaltschaft wurde verpflichtet, auf Antrag Akteneinsicht zu gewähren, um die Einlegung von Rechtsmitteln gegen die Anordnung der U-Haft prüfen und vornehmen zu können (Art. 165).

Das Strafvollzugsgesetz[53] wurde zwischenzeitlich in mehreren Punkten geändert: Zulässigkeit von Telefonaten und Vergrößerung der Haftfläche[54] wurden bereits erwähnt. Der Kreis der Personen, die ohne besondere Erlaubnis Zutritt zu Vollzugsanstalten haben, wurde auf Mitglieder der Begnadigungskommission, den Justizminister, Mitglieder des Antifolterkomitees des Europarates und Mitglieder sog. Beobachterkommissionen erweitert, um die gesellschaftliche Kontrolldichte zu erhöhen. Es wurde ferner klargestellt, dass die Korrespondenz der Gefangenen mit dem EGMR nicht mehr kontrolliert wird.

Die Änderungsentwürfe konnten allerdings bis auf die genannten Änderungen des Strafvollzugsgesetzes aufgrund der veränderten (rechts-)politischen Rahmenbedingungen bisher nicht verabschiedet werden, mithin steht auch die Einführung des Instituts des Ermittlungsrichters noch aus. Die Reformbemühungen sollen aber fortgesetzt und auch in Zukunft beratend unterstützt werden. Die weiteren Entwicklungen bezüglich des Strafvollzugsrechts und insbesondere des Untersuchungshaftrechts sowie des Strafprozessrechts werden weiterhin beobachtet und analysiert werden, um zu gegebener Zeit weitere Beratungen anbieten und durchführen zu können. Man konnte allerdings im Zuge der bisher durchgeführten Beratungen auch den Eindruck gewinnen, dass die von der Arbeitsgruppe vorgeschlagenen und die wenigen letztlich schon in Kraft getretenen Änderungen derzeit das Maximum an Reformbereitschaft darstellen, zumal einige Vorschläge des ausgearbeiteten Katalogs nicht von allen Mitgliedern der Arbeitsgruppe mitgetragen wurden. Hinzu kommt, dass – selbst wenn der Wille zur Reformierung da ist – die technische Umsetzbarkeit den Änderungsvorhaben zumindest auf mittlere Sicht Grenzen setzt.

VI. Ausblick

Die Bemühungen auf ukrainischer Seite und sicherlich auch die durchgeführten Beratungen haben immerhin zu ersten Verbesserungen geführt, wenngleich europäische Standards noch nicht in jeder Hinsicht erreicht worden sind und auch der von der Arbeitsgruppe erstellte Forderungskatalog noch nicht gänzlich umgesetzt ist. Gerade der Bereich des Straf- und insbesondere des Strafvollzugs-

---

sucht, die betreffenden Vorschläge der Kommission mit den Arbeiten der Arbeitsgruppe in Einklang zu bringen und abzugleichen.

53 Allgemein hierzu siehe *M. Zaikina*, Länderbericht Ukraine, in: *F. Dünkel*, *J. Grzywa*, *P. Horsfield*, *I. Pruin* (Hrsg.), Juvenile Justice Systems in Europe: Current Situation and Reform Developments, Bd. 3, Mönchengladbach 2010, S. 1455 f., 1485.

54 Siehe Fn. 50 und 51.

rechts ist in der internationalen rechtlichen und beratenden Zusammenarbeit aufgrund des rechtshistorischen und rechtssoziologischen Hintergrundes überaus komplex und vielschichtig. Dabei muss der ukrainischen Seite zugestanden werden, dass gerade Fragen der Strafarten, eines zu verhängenden Strafrahmens sowie der Strafvollzug an sich für eine Reform besonders schwer zugänglich sind. Dies mag mit eher konservativen Mentalitäten und Rechtstraditionen gerade in sicherheitsrelevanten Bereichen[55] zusammenhängen, womit sich mit den hier offenkundig zutage tretenden Brüchen und Kontinuitäten der Kreis dieses Berichts schließt. Sicher hängen die Schwierigkeiten und die eher zögerliche Umsetzung der ausgearbeiteten Vorschläge auch mit den verbesserungsbedürftigen Vollzugsbedingungen zusammen – ohne immense technische und bauliche und damit finanzielle Anstrengungen bei chronischer Unterfinanzierung des Strafvollzuges durch den ukrainischen Staatshaushalt, wird man das überwiegend völlig veraltete und renovierungsbedürftige Vollzugssystem in der Ukraine kaum modernisieren und damit den Forderungen des Europarates nachkommen können, den Vollzug modernen Anforderungen entsprechend zu gestalten.

Es bleibt zudem zunächst abzuwarten, ob der Politikwechsel in der Ukraine Einfluss auf die Fortführbarkeit der Beratungen und des Reformvorhabens insgesamt haben wird. Der beschwerliche Weg zu einem modernen und rechtsstaatlichen, europäischen Standards entsprechenden Strafvollzug in der Ukraine ist jedenfalls noch nicht zu Ende gegangen, weitere Anstrengungen werden notwendig sein.

---

55 So konnte man sich beispielsweise nicht von dem praktizierten Ansatz lösen, die zu lebenslänglicher Haft verurteilten Strafgefangenen in gesonderten Haftanstalten unterzubringen (auch diese Frage wurde trotz des enger gefassten Themas der Beratungen behandelt, weil sie sich auch auf solche Personen erstreckt, bei denen das gegen sie verhängte Urteil „lebenslänglich“ noch nicht rechtskräftig geworden ist).

Entpolitisierung des Strafrechts in Polen

Prof. Dr. h.c. mult. Andrzej Zoll[*]

Der verehrte Jubilar ist einer von diesen deutschen Strafrechtslehrern, die schon in den 70er und 80er Jahren des 20. Jahrhunderts enge Kontakte zu der polnischen Strafrechtslehre pflegten. Ich kann mich noch sehr gut an den Krakauer Besuch von *Professor Dr. Dres. h.c. F.-C. Schroeder* in jenen Jahren erinnern. Solche Kontakte machten es uns, den Vertretern der Strafrechtslehre hinter dem eisernen Vorhang, möglich, mit der westlichen Wissenschaft in Verbindung zu bleiben. *Professor Dr. Dres. h.c. F.-C. Schroeder* ist ein hervorragender Kenner des durch das kommunistische System gestalteten Strafrechts[1]. Als ich 1991 an der Universität in Mainz Gastvorlesungen über den Übergang vom Totalitarismus zur Demokratie am Beispiel des Strafrechts hielt, waren mir die Arbeiten des werten Jubilars oft eine große Hilfe.

Will man von einer Entpolitisierung des Strafrechts sprechen, so kann man dabei an zwei sich zwar nicht ausschließende, dennoch deutlich voneinander zu unterscheidende Tendenzen denken.

Im ersteren Fall wird es um eine Politisierung des Strafrechts in diesem Sinne gehen, dass aus dieser Rechtsdisziplin ein Instrument zur Verteidigung eines nicht demokratischen politischen Systems gemacht wird. Das Strafrecht hat dann vor Verhaltensweisen zu schützen, die auf den Wandel des politischen Systems ausgerichtet sind und das Monopol der in einer Hand liegenden und nicht selten auch von außen unterstützten politischen Macht erschüttern wollen. Für ein diesem Zweck untergeordnetes Strafrecht sind Straftatbestände mit stark politischem Hintergrund zur Bestimmung von Verhaltensweisen kennzeichnend, die das Machtmonopol bzw. die dem antidemokratischen System zugrunde liegende ökonomische Basis (z.B. gesellschaftliches Eigentum) angreifen. Das Strafrecht in antidemokratischen Systemen zeichnet sich durch eine erhebliche Schwächung der Garantiefunktion des Strafrechts sowie dadurch aus, dass die Last der Feststellung, was eine Straftat bildet, auf die rechtsprechende Gewalt, d.h. auf Staatsanwälte und Richter übertragen wird, die in diesem System als Staatsfunktionäre gelten, die die Interessen des Staates und nicht die der Rechtmäßigkeit zu wahren haben.

Im zweiten Fall bedeutet die Politisierung des Strafrechts, dass dieses als ein Hilfsinstrument zur Machterlangung unter Befolgung von demokratischen Pro-

---

* Professor für Strafrecht an der Universität Krakau, ehemaliger Beauftragter für Bürgerrechte der Republik Polen.

1 Siehe *F.-C. Schroeder*, Das Strafrecht des realen Sozialismus. Eine Einführung am Beispiel der DDR, Opladen 1983.

zeduren und zur Aufrechterhaltung dieser Macht, ebenfalls ohne allzu weitgehende Verletzung dieser Prozeduren, betrachtet wird. Damit das Strafrecht diese instrumentale Rolle erfüllen kann, muss (oft über lange Zeit) die öffentliche Meinung beeinflusst und von einer notwendigen Verschärfung der Kriminalitätsbekämpfung überzeugt werden, damit man sich des Strafrechts zur Befriedigung der öffentlichen Erwartung bedienen und sich somit die Wählergunst sichern kann. Diese Richtung wird mittlerweile im Fachschrifttum als sog. „pönaler Populismus" bezeichnet[2].

Es steht außer Zweifel, dass das Strafrecht und die Strafpolitik in Polen vor der Wende von 1989 typisch für einen undemokratischen Staat mit ausgeprägten Merkmalen eines totalitären Staates waren. Es sei daran erinnert, dass das Strafrecht als Instrument zur Aufrechterhaltung der offen von der UdSSR unterstützten kommunistischen Macht in Polen in den Jahren 1944 mit unterschiedlicher Intensität missbraucht wurde. Es lassen sich einige Phasen unterscheiden. In der gemeinsam mit *Dr. E. Weigend* erstellten Studie[3] sind wir von vier Phasen ausgegangen: 1944-1948, 1949-1956, 1957-1981 und 1982-1989.

In der ersten Phase wurde das Strafrecht in hohem Maße zur physischen Eliminierung der in Polen sehr zahlreichen Gegner der kommunistischen Macht missbraucht. Diesem Zweck dienten die damaligen Dekrete der Exekutivgewalt, die im Rahmen der von ihr geregelten Materie zur Aufhebung des nach dem 2. Weltkrieg immer noch geltenden Strafgesetzbuches von 1932 führten.

Zu den wichtigsten gehörte das Dekret vom 31.08.1944 über die Strafzumessung für faschistisch-hitlersche Verbrecher, die der Tötung und Misshandlung von Angehörigen der Zivilbevölkerung und Kriegsgefangenen schuldig sind, sowie für Verräter des polnischen Volkes[4]. Dieses Dekret, in dem für den darin bestimmten Straftatbestand des Völkermordes und der Zusammenarbeit mit der deutschen Besatzungsmacht bei der Tötung von verfolgten Personen (Art. 1) einzig die Todesstrafe vorgesehen war, wurde nicht nur gegenüber Kriegsverbrechern, sondern auch gegenüber den gegen die deutsche Besatzungsmacht und Agenten der Sowjetunion kämpfenden Soldaten der Heimatarmee (Armia Krajowa) zur Anwendung gebracht. Während der Untersuchung wurde oft gefoltert, um ein Geständnis nicht begangener Verbrechen zu erzwingen und die Urteile waren auf gefälschtes Beweismaterial gestützt[5].

Ein Rechtsakt, der ausschließlich der Unschädlichmachung politischer Gegner und nicht selten als Grundlage für ihre physische Eliminierung diente, war das Dekret über die Verantwortung für die Septemberniederlage und die Faschi-

---

2 Siehe *J. Pratt*, Penal populism, London 2007.

3 *E. Weigend*, *A. Zoll* in: *A. Eser*, *J. Arnold*, Strafrecht in Reaktion auf Systemunrecht, Freiburg im Br. 2002, S. 41 ff.

4 Dz. U. 1944, Nr. 4, Pos. 16.

5 Siehe *A. Lityński*, Historia Prawa Polski Ludowej (Rechtsgeschichte von Volksrepublik Polen), Warszawa 2007, S. 116 u. 137.

sierung des Staatslebens vom 22.01.1946[6]. Mit diesem Dekret wurde entgegen dem im damals immer noch geltenden StGB von 1932 ausgedrückten *lex retro non agit*-Prinzip die Strafverantwortlichkeit für die ausschließlich vor dem Inkrafttreten dieses Dekrets begangenen Taten eingeführt, da es sich auf die vor dem 01.09.1939 erfolgten Ereignisse bezog.

In diesem Zusammenhang muss noch das Dekret vom 13.06.1945 über die im Stadium des Wiederaufbaus des polnischen Staates besonders gefährlichen Delikte[7], das sog. „kleine Strafgesetzbuch", erwähnt werden. Aufgrund dieses Dekrets wurden u.a. Taten gegen die Bodenreform und die Nationalisierung der Industrie sowie Taten verfolgt, die darauf ausgerichtet waren, durch Verbreitung von unwahren Informationen dem kommunistischen Staat Schaden zuzufügen – wie u.a. auch das Erzählen von politischen Witzen. Solche Taten waren mit der Freiheitsstrafe bis zu fünf Jahren bedroht. Das Dekret blieb bis zum 01.01.1970, d.h. bis zum Inkrafttreten des neuen Strafgesetzbuchs, in Kraft.

Von entscheidender Bedeutung für die Strenge der strafrechtlichen Repression und die Beschränkung von Prozessgarantien war das Dekret vom 16.12.1945 über das standrechtliche Verfahren[8]. Für die darin bezeichneten zahlreichen Straftatbestände, nicht nur politischen, sondern auch kriminellen Charakters (z.B. Diebstahl), konnte das Gericht ungeachtet der für die jeweilige Straftat im StGB vorgesehenen Strafdrohung die Todesstrafe verhängen. Gegen das standrechtliche Urteil war kein Rechtsmittel zulässig. Auch dieses Dekret galt – und wurde angewendet – bis zum Inkrafttreten des StGB von 1969.

In dieser Phase hegte die kommunistische Macht Misstrauen gegenüber den noch vor dem Krieg ausgebildeten Richtern. Durch das Dekret vom 16.11.1945 über die Entstehung und Zuständigkeit der Sonderkommission gegen Missbrauch und Wirtschaftsschädigung[9] wurde ein außergerichtliches Organ gegründet, dessen Mitglieder formal durch verschiedene Behörden berufen wurden und nicht unabhängig waren, d.h. jederzeit abberufen werden konnten. Die landesweit tätigen Sonderkommissionen ermittelten in Wirtschaftssachen und konnten die Beschuldigten für bis zu zwei Jahre in Arbeitslager einweisen sowie auf Vermögenseinziehung erkennen. Dem Beschuldigten stand kein Recht auf formale Verteidigung zu. Aufgrund dieses Dekrets haben Tausende Handwerker, Kaufleute, Kleinunternehmer und Großbauern (sog. Kulaken) ihre Freiheit und ihr Vermögens ohne gerichtliche Entscheidung verloren.

In der zweiten Phase, d.h. in den Jahren 1949-1956, hielt der politische Terror unter Ausnutzung des Strafrechts weiter an. Im Jahre 1952 saßen in Gefäng-

6 Dz. U. 1946, Nr. 5, Pos. 46.
7 Dz. U. 1946, Nr. 30, Pos. 192.
8 Dz. U. 1945, Nr. 53, Pos. 301.
9 Dz. U. 1945, Nr. 53, pos. 302.

nissen 49.500 politische Gefangene ein[10]. Der Schwerpunkt wurde in dieser Zeit zwar stärker auf den Schutz der zentral gesteuerten Wirtschaft und des gesellschaftlichen Eigentums/gemeinschaftlichen Vermögens verlegt, auf die Bekämpfung von wirklichen (oder sei es nur potenziellen) Gegnern des kommunistischen Systems mit Hilfe des Strafrechts wurde aber nicht verzichtet. Repressionen richteten sich in erster Linie gegen die katholische Kirche. Aufgrund des Dekrets vom 05.08.1949 über die Freiheit des Gewissens und die Konfession[11] wurden Geistliche wegen des mutmaßlichen Missbrauchs der Gewissens- und Religionsfreiheit zu staatsfeindlichen Zwecken strafverfolgt. Der entsprechende Tatbestand war mit Freiheitsstrafe bis zu 15 Jahren bedroht[12].

Eine totale Kontrolle der Gesellschaft durch den Sicherheitsapparat ermöglichte das Dekret vom 26.10.1949 über den Schutz des Staats- und Dienstgeheimnisses[13].

Ein für die zentral gesteuerte Wirtschaft in einem totalitären System typischer Rechtsakt war das Gesetz vom 19.04.1950 über die Sicherung der sozialistischen Arbeitsdisziplin[14]. Die unentschuldigte Arbeitsabwesenheit von einigen Tagen stellte eine Straftat dar, die mit einer gerichtlich zu verhängenden Strafe (25% Lohnkürzung samt Verbot der Auflösung des Arbeitsvertrags) bedroht war. Weitere Verletzungen der Arbeitsdisziplin waren mit Freiheitsentzug bis zu sechs Monaten bedroht[15].

Im Dekret vom 04.03.1953 über den erhöhten Schutz des gemeinschaftlichen Vermögens[16] wurde streng zwischen dem Schutz individuellen und persönlichen Eigentums und dem Schutz gemeinschaftlichen Vermögens/Eigentums unterschieden. Nach sowjetischem Vorbild wurde in den Tatbestand das Merkmal der Aneignung des gemeinschaftlichen Vermögens eingeführt, das neben dem Diebstahl auch andere Formen der ungerechtfertigten Vermögenszuwendung zum Nachteil des gesellschaftlichen Vermögens umfasste. Hat die Aneignung den Wirtschafts- bzw. Verteidigungsinteressen des Staates großen Schaden zugefügt, so konnte der Täter mit Freiheitsentzug von fünf Jahren bis lebenslänglich bestraft werden. Gegenüber den Tätern von Straftaten gegen gemeinschaftliches Vermögens konnte auf Antrag der Staatsanwaltschaft das standrechtliche Verfahren angewendet werden.

---

10 *A. Paczkowski*, Polacy pod obcą i własną przemocą (Polen unter fremder und eigener Gewalt), in: *S. Courtois*, *N. Werth*, *J.-L. Panne*, *A. Paczkowski*, *K. Bartosek*, *J.-L. Margolin* (Hrsg.), Czarna księga komunizmu. Zbrodnie, terror, prześladowania (Das Schwarzbuch des Kommunismus. Verbrechen, Terror, Verfolgung), Warszawa 1999, S. 357.

11 Dz. U. 1949, Nr. 45, Pos. 334.

12 Art. 8.

13 Dz. U. 1949, Nr. 55, Pos. 437.

14 Dz. U. 1950, Nr. 20, Pos. 168.

15 Art. 13.

16 Dz. U. 1953, Nr. 17, Pos. 68.

Das sog. Oktober-Tauwetter von 1956 brachte die Entlassung von vielen Inhaftierten und den verminderten Einsatz des Strafrechts im Rahmen der politischen Repression. Die Tauwetter-Periode hielt in Polen allerdings nicht lange an. In Bezug auf die Jahre 1957-1981 jedoch kann von einem politischen Terror mit Hilfe des Strafrechts grundsätzlich kaum mehr gesprochen werden.

Unter den für diese Zeit charakteristischen, das Strafrecht politisierenden Rechtsakten, ist das Gesetz zur Verschärfung der Strafbarkeit für Straftaten gegen das gesellschaftliche Vermögen zu nennen. Das Gesetz vom 21.01.1958 über den erhöhten Schutz des gemeinschaftlichen Vermögens vor Schäden aus Straftaten[17], sah für die Aneignung gemeinschaftlichen Vermögens die lebenslange Freiheitsstrafe und Einziehung des gesamten Vermögens vor. Bei Mittäterschaft wurde die Tat auf der Rechtsgrundlage bezüglich des Gesamtwertes des durch alle Mittäter angeeigneten Vermögens qualifiziert, was zur Verhängung von drastisch strengen Strafen gegenüber Personen führte, deren Rolle beim Diebstahl gemeinschaftlichen Vermögens nur nebenrangig war.

Zu erwähnen ist auch das Gesetz vom 23.05.1958 über die Verschärfung der Strafbarkeit für Hooliganismus[18]. Dieses Gesetz war ein Beispiel dafür, wie in die Strafgesetzgebung Voraussetzungen der Strafbarkeitsverschärfung eingeführt wurden, deren Feststellung dem freien Ermessen des erkennenden Gerichts allein überlassen wurde. Das Gesetz wurde zu politischen Zwecken missbraucht, z.B. gegen die öffentlich für Bürgerfreiheiten demonstrierenden Personen, wie es beispielsweise im März 1968 der Fall war.

In der besagten Zeit wurde vom Sejm ein neues StGB[19] verabschiedet, das am 01.01.1970 in Kraft trat. Insbesondere hinsichtlich der Strafbarkeitsgrundsätze knüpfte das neue StGB an seinen Vorgänger von 1932 an und trug diesbezüglich den in zivilisierten Ländern verbindlichen Kriterien Rechnung. Es ließ aber auch eine sehr strenge Strafpolitik zu und war eindeutig auf den Schutz des herrschenden politischen Systems ausgerichtet, indem es in dieser Hinsicht Merkmale eines totalitärstaatlichen StGB aufwies. Mit dem Inkrafttreten des StGB von 1969 wurden zahlreiche, seit der Zeit des politischen Terrors geltende Rechtsakte, aufgehoben, wie das Dekret über das standrechtliche Verfahren und über die im Stadium des Wiederaufbaus des polnischen Staates besonders gefährlichen Delikte.

In den 1970er Jahren nahm die Repressivität des Strafrechts erheblich zu. Betrug im Jahre 1970 die Länge der Freiheitsstrafe im Durchschnitt zehn Monate, so waren es 1979 bereits 27 Monate. Auch die Todesstrafe, die laut StGB von 1969 in absoluten Ausnahmefällen für schwerste Straftaten vorgesehen war, wurde in den 1970er Jahren häufiger zur Anwendung gebracht, als es in den

17 Dz. U. 1958, Nr. 4, Pos. 11.

18 Dz. U. 1958, Nr. 34. Pos. 152.

19 Gesetz vom 19.04.1969 (Dz. U. Nr. 13, Pos. 94).

1960er Jahren der Fall war[20]. In Strafanstalten saßen 1979 in Polen über 300 Personen pro 100.000 Einwohner ein, d.h. mindestens dreimal so viele wie in den meisten Ländern des demokratischen Europas. Unter den in den Gefängnissen herrschenden Bedingungen war an Resozialisierungsmaßnahmen überhaupt nicht zu denken.

Durch die Entstehung der Solidarność-Bewegung bekamen auch die Bemühungen um eine Entpolitisierung des Strafrechts und Rationalisierung der Strafpolitik neue Impulse.

Im Oktober 1980 forderten 80 polnische Strafrechtler den Justizminister zur Vorbereitung einer grundsätzlichen, vor allem auf die Einschränkung der Verurteilungen zum Freiheitsentzug wie auch auf die Verstärkung der Garantiefunktion des Strafrechts ausgerichteten Reform des Strafrechts auf. Das Justizministerium berief daraufhin den Ausschuss für die Reform des Strafrechts. Auch die um die Gewerkschaft Solidarność gruppierten Juristen bildeten eine Arbeitsgruppe, die u.a. einen Entwurf der Novellierung des Strafrechts erstellte. Beide Entwürfe wurden im August 1980 veröffentlicht, wobei sich herausstellte – was als ein recht charakteristisches Merkmal anzusehen war –, dass beide Papiere hinsichtlich der darin vorgeschlagenen Änderungen zum großen Teil übereinstimmend waren. Neben der Verstärkung der Garantiefunktion des Strafrechts strebten beide Entwürfe einen erheblichen Ausbau von alternativen Maßnahmen der Reaktion auf die Straftatbegehung, vor allem Bewährungsmittel, an.

Der erste Versuch einer politischen Reform in Polen ist bekanntlich gescheitert. Nach der Verhängung des Kriegsrechts am 13.12.1981[21] und dem Zusammenbruch der sozialen und politischen Reformen, kamen auch Arbeiten an der Strafrechtsreform zum Stillstand. Die Gesetzgebung dieser Zeit und die darauffolgenden Änderungen des StGB schlugen eine Gegenrichtung ein, indem die prozess- und materiellrechtlichen Garantien noch weiter geschwächt und die Voraussetzungen der Strafbarkeit erheblich verschärft wurden. Dies galt auch für die Todesstrafe, die nun wegen aller Straftaten verhängt werden konnte, die mit dem Freiheitsentzug von mehr als acht Jahren bedroht waren[22]. Von dieser Möglichkeit wurde allerdings unter dem Kriegsrecht kein Gebrauch gemacht und die drei Todesurteile wegen politischer Delikte ergingen in Abwesenheit der im Exil weilenden Personen. Es sei hier darauf hingewiesen, dass für die Strenge der Strafpolitik in den Jahren vor der politischen Wende 1989 nicht nur die

20 Siehe *A. Lityński*, Fn. 5, S. 157 f.

21 Der Kriegszustand wurde mit dem Dekret vom 13.12.1981 (Dz. U. 1981, Nr. 29, Pos. 154) eingeführt. Es ist unbestritten, dass die Verhängung des Kriegsrechts mit den Vorschriften der damals geltenden Verfassung unvereinbar war. Siehe dazu *J. Zakrzewska*, Ocena podstaw prawnych stanu wojennego (Bewertung der Rechtsgründe des Kriegszustands), Katowice 1990.

22 Siehe das Dekret vom 13.12.1981 über besondere Verfahrensarten bei Straftaten und Übertretungen während der Geltung des Kriegszustands (Dz. U. 1981, Nr. 29, Pos. 156).

Strafgesetzgebung allein verantwortlich war, sondern vielmehr auch die durch das politische Zentrum festgelegten Richtlinien der Strafpolitik, die vor allem in der Rechtsprechung des Obersten Gerichts ihren Niederschlag fanden.

Auch nach der Aufhebung des Kriegsrechts wurden zahlreiche, von einer radikalen Politisierung dieses Rechtszweiges zeugende Strafvorschriften in das damals geltende StGB aufgenommen, um z.B. Art. 282a zu nennen, der die „Vornahme von Handlungen zwecks Hervorrufung öffentlicher Unruhen oder Aufruhr“ sowie das „Organisieren oder Leiten einer entgegen den Rechtsvorschriften durchgeführten Protestaktion“ unter Strafe stellte. Aufgrund dieser Vorschrift wurden z.B. in den 1980er Jahren die Arbeiter einer Fabrik zu Freiheitsstrafen verurteilt, weil sie aus Protest gegen die Arbeits- und Lohnbedingungen weiß-rote Armbinden trugen.

Nach der politischen Wende von 1989 traten zwei Phänomene zutage. Von politischem Druck befreit, verhängten die Gerichte aufgrund der bislang geltenden Vorschriften nun auf der einen Seite erheblich mildere Strafen, sodass die Zahl der Inhaftierten in kurzer Zeit fast halbiert wurde. Auf der anderen Seite aber führte die Abschaffung des totalitären Staates zu einem rapiden Kriminalitätsanstieg, was jedoch zu erwarten war und unschwer zu verstehen und zu erklären ist. Im totalitären System schränkte die polizeistaatliche Kontrolle über die Gesellschaft zwangsläufig auch die Möglichkeiten kriminellen Treibens ein. Eine Demokratisierung des Lebens, Schutz der Bürgerfreiheiten, eingeschränkte Zuständigkeiten der Verfolgungsorgane, insbesondere bei Eingriffen in den Bereich der Bürgerfreiheiten und Bürgerrechte, sowie die grundlegende Umstrukturierung dieser Organe, die Öffnung der Grenzen und ein besserer Zugang zu Konsumgütern sind eine ausreichende Erklärung für diese Erscheinung. Der Kriminalitätsanstieg war der Preis, der für den politischen Wandel zu zahlen war. Kein StGB vermag dem vorzubeugen, es sei denn, man wünscht sich eine Rückkehr in die Zeit der totalen Versklavung der Bevölkerung. Bezeichnenderweise kam es zu diesem sprunghaften Anstieg der Kriminalität gerade unter diesem „nichtliberalen“ StGB von 1969, als an ein Moratorium für die Vollstreckung der Todesstrafe nicht einmal zu denken war. Weder die im StGB von 1969 vorgesehenen strengen Strafen noch die Androhung der Todesstrafe vermochten die zunehmende Kriminalität zu stoppen. 1990 wurden ca. 60% mehr Straftaten festgestellt als 1989. Dieser sprunghafte Anstieg war zwar eine einmalige Erscheinung, dennoch nahm die Kriminalität auch in den Folgejahren zu – wenn auch nicht mehr in diesem rasanten Tempo. Zwischen 1989 und 2000 stieg die Kriminalität in Polen um etwa 120% an, d.h. um mehr als das Doppelte. Eine Stabilisierung lässt sich um die Jahrhundertwende erkennen und seit 2001 registriert man in Polen eine stetige, wenn auch langsame Abnahme der festgestellten Kriminalität. Es ist hervorzuheben, dass die Kriminalität in Polen im Vergleich zu anderen europäischen Staaten nicht sonderlich hoch ist und im Verhältnis zur Einwohnerzahl mittleres Niveau erreicht. 2009 wurden in Polen

2907 Straftaten pro 100.000 Einwohner festgestellt – 2001 waren es 3597. Die Kriminalität nimmt auch im Bereich der Schwerstdelikte ab: 2001 wurden in Polen 1325 Tötungsfälle festgestellt, während es 2009 763 waren. Bei Vergewaltigungen waren es 2001 entsprechend 2339 Straftaten, 2009 noch 1530. Auch bei Straftaten gegen das Vermögen ist ein deutlicher Rückgang zu verzeichnen: 2001 wurde in 640.516, 2009 dagegen in 347.074 Fällen Diebstahl und Diebstahl mit Einbruch festgestellt. Zugleich stieg die Aufklärungsquote von 53,8% im Jahre 2001 auf 67,1 % im Jahre 2006 an[23].

Kurz nach der Wiedererlangung der Unabhängigkeit setzten in Polen Kodifizierungsarbeiten an einem neuen, den Anforderungen eines demokratischen Staates voll Rechnung tragenden StGB an. Es wurde am 06.06.1997 verabschiedet und trat am 01.09.1998 in Kraft[24]. Zu dieser Zeit gingen in Polen jene politischen Kräfte zur Offensive über, deren Tätigkeit im Bereich des Strafrechts ein nahezu musterhaftes Beispiel für die zweite Form einer Politisierung des Strafrechts im Sinne des Pönalpopulismus war.

Gleich nach der Verabschiedung des StGB wurden Versuche unternommen, das Inkrafttreten auf eine spätere Zeit zu verschieben und die Strafpolitik erheblich zu verschärfen. Es reicht in diesem Zusammenhang zu erwähnen, dass dem Sejm ein Entwurf der Abgeordneten aus dem politischen Umfeld der Kaczyński-Brüder vorgelegt wurde, in dem die Verhängung der Todesstrafe schon gegenüber 16-jährigen Tätern vorgesehen war und die Garantiefunktionen, insbesondere im Bereich des Rechts auf Verteidigung, auf ein Minimum reduziert wurden. Der Sejm lehnte diesen Entwurf nach der ersten Lesung ab. Schon damals aber startete die Partei der Kaczyński-Brüder[25] eine Kampagne gegen das StGB und machte es für den Kriminalitätsanstieg verantwortlich. Zu diesem Zweck bediente man sich der PiS-freundlichen Medien, darunter auch des öffentlich-rechtlichen Fernsehens, das in seinen täglichen Nachrichtenprogrammen drastische Beschreibungen begangener Straftaten sendete und bei der Bevölkerung ein stärkeres Gefühl der Bedrohung entstehen ließ, als dies durch das tatsächliche Kriminalitätsausmaß gerechtfertigt gewesen wäre. Es wurde zu einer politischen Konsolidierung zum Schutz der Sicherheit der Bürger aufgerufen, mit einem klaren Hinweis darauf, dass es den Befürwortern einer liberalen Strafpolitik daran gelegen war, Verbrecher und vor allem das korrupte Machtsystem zu schützen. Unter Zugriff auf raffinierte psycho-soziale Techniken gewann das Programm der Kaczyński-Partei breite Unterstützung in der Bevölkerung.

Im Jahre 2000 übernahm L. Kaczyński (der spätere Staatspräsident) das Justizministerium und zugleich das Amt des Generalstaatsanwalts. In kurzer Zeit

---

23 Alle Angaben der „*Statystyka Policyjna*“ (Polizeiliche Statistik) entnommen, http://www.statystyka.policja.pl.

24 Dz. U. 1997, Nr. 88, Pos. 553. *E. Weigend*, Das polnische Strafgesetzbuch (Kodeks karny), Deutsche Übersetzung und Einführung, Freiburg im Br. 1998.

25 „*Prawo i Sprawiedliwość*“ (Recht und Gerechtigkeit).

gelang es ihm die Strafpolitik zu verschärfen und innerhalb eines Jahres einen Anstieg der Inhaftiertenzahlen von 56.000 (142 pro 100.000 Einwohner) auf 79.000 (207 pro 100.000 Einwohner) zu bewirken. Erreicht wurde dieser Anstieg eigentlich ohne Änderungen der Gesetzgebung, vielmehr durch die unmittelbare Beeinflussung der vielfach handgesteuerten Staatsanwaltschaft sowie den auf die Gerichte durch die Politik der Anfechtung von Entscheidungen und Beantragung der Untersuchungshaft ausgeübten Druck. Es muss mit Bedauern festgestellt werden, dass dieser „Erfolg" von L. Kaczyński der Widerstandskraft der Gerichtsbarkeit gegen die von der Exekutivgewalt lancierte Strafpolitik nicht das beste Zeugnis ausstellt.

Während der Amtszeit von L. Kaczyński als Justizminister wurde der Entwurf einer umfassenden Novellierung – oder vielmehr der Entwurf eines neuen StGB – vorbereitet, denn es sollten nicht nur die StGB-Vorschriften in ihrem überwiegenden Teil, sondern darüber hinaus auch die theoretischen Grundlagen des StGB radikal geändert werden. L. Kaczyński gelang es, diese selbst im Vergleich zu dem aus der kommunistischen Ära stammenden StGB von 1969 die Strafbarkeit radikal verschärfende Novellierung durchzusetzen, die 2001 vom polnischen Parlament verabschiedet wurde. Für den Erfolg erwies sich die öffentliche Meinung als maßgebend, die aus den oben genannten Gründen einen kompromisslosen Kampf gegen die Kriminalität unterstützte. Die Parlamentarier, um die Wählergunst besorgt, wagten es nicht, sich den Einfällen der „Recht und Gerechtigkeit-Partei" zu widersetzen. Völlig ignoriert wurden die Stimmen der Vertreter der Strafrechtslehre, der Gerichtsbarkeit sowie des Gefängnisdienstes, denen das Absurde der Lösungen selbst wie auch die schädlichen Konsequenzen von derart verschärften Vorschriften für die Zukunft nicht verborgen blieben. Der damalige Staatspräsident, A. Kwaśniewski, zeigte sich seiner Aufgabe gewachsen und legte gegen das StGB-Novellierungsgesetz sein Veto ein, das abzulehnen der Sejm nicht in der Lage war.

Nach der Übernahme der Macht im Jahre 2005 durch die „Recht und Gerechtigkeit"-Partei und nach L. Kaczyńskis Amtsantritt als Staatspräsident, schien einer Änderung des seit 1997 geltenden StGB nichts mehr im Wege zu stehen. Der Justizminister Z. Ziobro ließ es sich nicht nehmen, in den Medien persönlich und bei jeder Gelegenheit den angeblichen Liberalismus des StGB anzuprangern und bewirkte einige geringe Änderungen in Richtung einer Verschärfung der Strafbarkeit, die aus der Sicht der Gesetzgebungsregeln der Homogenität des StGB schadeten. U.a. wurde im Jahre 2006 die nicht nur der polnischen Gesetzgebung aus der kommunistischen Zeit bekannte Figur des „hooliganischen Charakters der Tat" als Voraussetzung für die Verschärfung der Strafzumessung sowie die Anwendung des beschleunigten und vereinfachten Verfahrens eingeführt[26]. Im November 2006 wurde dem Sejm der Entwurf einer

26 Gesetz vom 16.11.2006 über die Änderung des Strafgesetzbuchs sowie einiger anderer Gesetze (Dz. U. 2006, Nr. 226, Pos. 1648).

Novellierung des StGB vorgelegt, der eine neu bearbeitete Fassung des 2001 von L. Kaczyński eingebrachten und vom Staatspräsidenten A. Kwaśniewski vetierten StGB-Entwurfs darstellte[27].

Das bisher geltende StGB sieht drei Arten von Freiheitsstrafen vor: Freiheitsentzug von einem Monat bis zu 15 Jahren, von 25 Jahren und die lebenslange Freiheitsstrafe. Der genannte Entwurf hob die beiden ersten Kategorien auf und führte an deren Stelle den Strafrahmen von einem Monat bis zu 25 Jahren ein. Die Folge wäre eine automatische Verschärfung der Strafandrohung für die meisten Verbrechen gewesen, die heute mit Freiheitsstrafe in Höhe von maximal 15 Jahren bedroht sind, aber auch erhöhte Grenzen des Strafmaßes bei Rückfall bzw. das erhöhte Gesamtstrafmaß bei der Realkonkurrenz (Tatmehrheit).

Der Entwurf sah die Verschärfung der gesetzlichen Strafandrohung vor, insbesondere durch die Anhebung des Strafmindestmaßes, häufig aber auch des Höchstmaßes bei über 50% der Straftatbestände. In der Praxis hätte dies zum Ausschluss der Möglichkeit geführt, gegenüber den Tätern Probationsmittel anzuwenden. Gem. Art. 66 des geltenden StGB kann die bedingte Verfahrenseinstellung für eine Probezeit mit bestimmten Auflagen gegenüber dem Täter einer Straftat angewendet werden, deren gesetzlich angedrohte Höchststrafe drei Jahre, und unter bestimmten Bedingungen fünf Jahre, nicht übersteigt. Die im Entwurf vorgesehenen Verschärfungen hätten in vielen Fällen die Anwendung dieses Rechtsinstituts unmöglich gemacht. Die Anhebung der gesetzlichen Strafandrohung sowie die Einführung einer sehr unbestimmten Kategorie des „hooliganischen Charakters einer Tat“ sollte auch die Anwendung der Strafaussetzung zur Bewährung erheblich einschränken. Aufgehoben wurde zudem die Möglichkeit der Aussetzung der Geldstrafe zur Bewährung sowie der Freiheitsbeschränkungsstrafe. Aus all dem geht eindeutig hervor, dass es den Begründern des Entwurfs daran gelegen war, aus der Freiheitsstrafe ein Hauptinstrument zur Bekämpfung der Kriminalität zu machen. In der Begründung wird direkt festgestellt, dass dem Entwurf die Richtlinie der Generalprävention zugrunde liege, im Sinne der Abschreckung von potenziellen Straftätern durch strenge Strafen.

Geplant war außerdem eine erhebliche Verschärfung der Strafrepression gegenüber jugendlichen Tätern. Das geltende StGB nimmt das 17. Lebensjahr als Strafbarkeitsgrenze an. Gegenüber Tätern von unter Strafandrohung verbotenen Taten, die das 17. Lebensjahr noch nicht vollendet haben, werden i.d.R. Besserungs- und Erziehungsmaßnahmen zur Anwendung gebracht. Nur wenn ein Jugendlicher nach Vollendung des 15. Lebensjahres einige im StGB bestimmte Verbrechen und schwerste Vergehen kriminellen Charakters begeht, kann das Gericht im Hinblick auf die Demoralisierung des Täters die im StGB vorgesehenen Strafbarkeitsgrundsätze anwenden. Allerdings unter der Voraussetzung, dass die verhängte Strafe ⅔ der gesetzlichen Höchststrafe nicht überschreiten

27 Siehe Sejm V kaden, Entwurf Nr. 1756, http://orka.sejm.gov.pl.

darf und das Gericht die Strafe außerordentlich mildern, d.h. eine Strafe unterhalb des Mindestmaßes oder eine mildere Strafe verhängen kann. Erheblich erweitert wurde im Entwurf der Katalog von Straftaten, für deren Begehung Jugendliche strafrechtlich belangt werden konnten sowie das niedriger festgesetzte Höchstmaß aufgehoben, was angesichts der oben erwähnten Verschärfung der gesetzlichen Strafandrohung die Grenzen der möglichen Repression erheblich erweitert hätte. Vorgesehen war auch die obligatorische Strafzumessung gegenüber Jugendlichen bei erneuter Begehung einer verbotenen Tat nach der vorherigen Anordnung der Besserungsmaßnahmen bzw. Verhängung einer Strafe. Die obligatorische Anwendung von Strafen gegenüber Jugendlichen ohne Rücksicht auf individuelle Resozialisierungsgründe scheint mit Art. 3 der Kinderrechtskonvention von 1989 unvereinbar zu sein.

Die oben nur exemplarisch dargestellten Änderungsversuche wurden vorgenommen, als in den polnischen Haftanstalten 91.000 Personen, d.h. 238 pro 100.000 Einwohner, untergebracht waren, während die Zahl der Plätze in den Strafanstalten unter Berücksichtigung der zulässigen internationalen Mindestnorm von $3m^2$ pro Person 71.000 betrug – und dies bereits nach der Umfunktionierung von Bibliotheken, Gemeinschaftsräumen, Korridoren oder gar Kapellen zu Wohnzellen. Die Überbelegung überschritt 28%, was in den Berichten des Menschenrechtskommissars des Europarats ständig gerügt wurde. Mehr noch, 45.000 rechtskräftige Verurteilungen zur Freiheitsstrafe konnten nicht vollstreckt werden. Bei der eingeschlagenen Richtung der Strafpolitik hätte die Kapazität der Strafanstalten verdoppelt werden müssen, was für den Staatsschatz eine enorme Belastung bedeutet hätte. Unter solchen Umständen die Strafpolitik verschärfen, längere Freiheitsstrafen verhängen und die Anwendung von Probationsmitteln einschränken zu wollen, muss als extrem unverantwortlich angesehen werden.

Im Juni und Juli 2007 fanden Konferenzen statt, an denen fast alle Strafrechtslehrer aus allen polnischen Universitäten und eine große Gruppe von Richtern und Staatsanwälten teilnahmen. Noch nie zuvor gab es in diesem Umfeld eine vergleichbare Einstimmigkeit. Wir alle waren entschieden gegen die von der Regierung vorgeschlagenen Änderungen im Strafrecht. Wir dürfen uns aber keinen Illusionen hingeben: Nicht unsere Überzeugung und nicht unsere Proteste waren es, die den Änderungen des StGB doch Einhalt zu gebieten vermochten – eine politische Krise führte zur vorzeitigen Auflösung des Parlaments und der fertige Novellierungsentwurf landete letztendlich im Papierkorb.

Die neue Regierung von D. Tusk setzte zur Reform des polnischen Justizsystems an. Als ein erster Schritt auf dem Weg zur Entpolitisierung des Strafrechts ist die Trennung der Ämter des Justizministers und des Generalstaatsanwalts anzusehen[28]. Dies soll die Staatsanwaltschaft vor eventuellen Versuchen

28 Gesetz vom 09.10.2009 über die Änderung des Gesetzes über die Staatsanwaltschaft sowie einiger anderer Gesetze (Dz. U. Nr. 178, Pos. 1375).

der Politiker schützen, auf laufende Strafverfahren Einfluss zu nehmen. Auch jetzt überhören die Politiker die Stimme der öffentlichen Meinung nicht und werden gegen sie keinerlei Schritte unternehmen wollen; selbst dann nicht, wenn dies aus strafpolitischer Sicht rational wäre. Als ein Beweis dafür kann der gescheiterte Versuch der Aufhebung der Vorschrift über den „hooliganischen Charakter der Tat" als verschärfender Umstand angeführt werden. Das vom Sejm verabschiedete einschlägige Gesetz lehnte der Senat in eben diesem Punkt ab und stellte mit seiner Änderung die aufgehobene Vorschrift wieder her. Der Sejm vermochte den einschlägigen Änderungsvorschlag des Senats nicht abzulehnen.

Es wird daraus ersichtlich, dass die Bemühungen um eine Entpolitisierung des Strafrechts mit dem Zusammenbruch totalitärer Systeme bei weitem nicht zu Ende sind. Auch in einem demokratischen Rechtsstaat wird das Strafrecht (wenn freilich auch in einer anderen Form) als ein Instrument zur Gewinnung von Wählerstimmen benutzt. Einer rationalen Strafpolitik ist dies alles andere als dienlich.

Die strafrechtliche Verantwortlichkeit der Richter und Staatsanwälte aus der Zeit des Unrechtsstaats in Polen

Prof. Dr. Witold Kulesza[*]

I. Nach Ansicht von *Prof. Dr. Dres. h.c. F.-C. Schroeder* stellen der Erlass unbestimmter Strafgesetze, die rückwirkende Anwendung von Strafgesetzen und schließlich auch eine völlig unhaltbare Subsumtion von Verhaltensweisen unter vorhandene Strafgesetze einen Verstoß gegen den Grundsatz *nulla poena sine lege stricta, scripta, praevia, certa* dar. Der Autor begründete seine Ansicht ausführlich auf der Basis der DDR-Rechtsprechung, indem er schreibt, dass sie ein reiches Anschauungsmaterial über die Verletzung des Grundsatzes *nulla poena sine lege* biete. Wichtig ist die Bemerkung des Autors: „Dabei ist zwischen der den Gesetzeswortlaut überschreitenden „Auslegung" des Gesetzes und der unzulässigen Subsumtion zu unterscheiden"[1]. Eine zusätzliche Begründung für die durchaus schlagkräftige Argumentation von *Prof. Dr. Dres. h.c. F.-C. Schroeder* können Unrechtsurteile, die durch polnische Gerichte während des totalitären Staates gefällt wurden, sein, sowie spätere Versuche, die Richter zur strafrechtlichen Verantwortlichkeit für die Übertretung der Richtergewalt zu ziehen. Deswegen erscheint es notwendig, die polnischen Erfahrungen mit der strafrechtlichen Aufarbeitung der Vergangenheit darzustellen; umso mehr, als es im polnischen StGB keine spezielle Vorschrift gibt, die die Tatbestandsmerkmale der Rechtsbeugung im engeren Sinne enthält.

II. Nach der Bekanntmachung der Machtübernahme durch das kommunistische *Polski Komitet Wyzwolenia Narodowego*[2] wurde im Sommer 1944 auf den Gebieten, die von der deutschen Besatzung befreit wurden, mit der Verhaftung derer begonnen, die die neue Staatsgewalt für politische Gegner hielt. Die Militärgerichte haben sie aufgrund des Erlasses des PKWN vom 30. Oktober 1944 über den Schutz des Staates zum Tode oder zu langjährigen Gefängnisstrafen verurteilt. Art. 1 lautete, dass jeder bestraft wird, „der an einer Vereinigung teilnimmt, die den Sturz der demokratischen Verfassung des Polnischen Staates zum Ziel hat oder dabei Hilfe leistet". Der Erlass stellte einen Akt des Sonderstrafrechts dar, das durch die kommunistischen Machthaber geschaffen wurde, weil man der Auffassung war, dass das damals geltende StGB von 1932 zu mil-

---

* Professor für Strafrecht an der Universität Łódź, Direktor der Hauptkommission zur Erforschung der Verbrechen am polnischen Volk.

1 *F.-C. Schroeder*, Der Bundesgerichtshof und der Grundsatz „*nulla poena sine lege*", NJW 1999, S. 89.

2 Polnisches Komitee der Nationalen Befreiung, kurz: „PKWN".

de und nicht ausreichend sei, um die Ziele der Staatsgewalt zu realisieren. Für eine „illegale Vereinigung" hielt man in erster Reihe die *Armia Krajowa*[3] sowie andere Organisationen, die gegen die deutschen Besatzer kämpften (mit Ausnahme der kommunistischen Volksarmee). Deren Mitglieder wurden unter Verletzung der Grundsätze des Prozessrechts und des materielles Rechts verurteilt, was diese Urteile als Justizverbrechen qualifizierte. Die Verhandlungen vor dem Gericht, das sich aus drei Richtern zusammensetzte, fanden geheim und ohne die Teilnahme eines Staatsanwalts und eines Verteidigers statt, man vernahm keine Zeugen und beschränkte sich auf die Erörterung des Anklageaktes, der durch Funktionäre des Militärsicherheitsdienstes vorbereitet und durch den Militärstaatsanwalt bestätigt wurde. Anfänglich wurden in vielen Fällen Handlungen bestraft, die vor der Bekanntmachung des Erlasses über den Schutz des Staates, der im Gesetzblatt vom 03. November 1944 mit Rechtskraft vom 15. August 1944 veröffentlicht wurde, stattgefunden hatten. Die Schuldsprüche, die aufgrund der Vorschriften dieses Erlasses gefällt wurden, umfassten in der Regel ca. 1-2 Seiten und begannen mit der Formulierung „Im Namen der Republik Polen". Im Urteil wurden der Name des Gerichts sowie die Nachnamen des Vorsitzenden, der zwei Beisitzer und des Protokollanten angegeben, wie auch die Personaldaten des Angeklagten sowie der Artikel des Erlasses, der die Grundlage für die Verurteilung bildete. Im Weiteren folgte die Formulierung, dass „im Verfahren festgestellt wurde (...)" und es folgte dann in einem oder zwei Sätzen die Beschreibung der Handlung, für die der Angeklagte verurteilt worden war. Die Urteile enthielten keine Begründung und endeten mit dem folgenden Satz: „Das Urteil ist endgültig und unterliegt keinem Rechtsbehelf". Das Verhalten, das die Grundlage für die Verurteilung war, wurde meist wie folgt formuliert: „Teilnahme an einer illegalen Organisation, deren Ziel im Sturz der demokratischen Verfassung des Polnischen Staates bestand" sowie „Kontakte mit anderen Mitgliedern der Organisation". Das Militärgericht Lublin hat aufgrund des Art. 1 des Erlasses über den Schutz des Staates u.a. folgende Personen zum Tode verurteilt:

- Einen Straßenbauingenieur dafür, dass er bis zum 30.10.1944 ein aktives Mitglied der Heimatarmee war, „dessen Teilnahme in der Aufbewahrung eines selbst verfassten illegalen Flugblattes bestand, mit einem Inhalt, der gegen das Polnische Komitee der Nationalen Befreiung und Veröffentlichungen dieser Organisation gerichtet war sowie wegen Kontakten mit anderen aktiven Mitgliedern der Heimatarmee" (Urteil vom 02. Dezember 1944)[4];

3 Heimatarmee, kurz: „AK".

4 Fotokopie des Urteils, veröffentlicht in: *Z. Leszczyńska*, Prokuratorzy i sędziowie lubelskich sądów wojskowych 1944-1955 (Staatsanwälte und Richter der Lubliner Militärgerichte 1944-1955), Lublin 2006, S. 197.

- Zwei Brüder, Beamte, dafür, dass sie „ (...) in der Zeit bis zum 31.08.1944 Mitglieder einer illegalen Organisation der Bauernbataillone gewesen waren, d.h. einer Organisation, die die Beseitigung der demokratischen Verfassung wollte, wobei ihre Tätigkeit in Kontakten mit Mitgliedern der illegalen Organisationen „*Boruta*“ und „*Wacław*“, (...) im Lesen und Tippen von Aufrufen gegen die Nichtanerkennung von Obersten Staatsorganen und für die Ablehnung ihrer Anordnungen bestand (...)“ (Urteil vom 10. November 1944)[5];
- Einen Juristen, ein rang-ältester Assistent an der Katholischen Universität Lublin, dafür, dass „... er in der Zeit (...) bis zum 25.10.1944 zur Organisation der Heimatarmee gehörte, wobei seine Tätigkeit in Kontakten mit anderen Mitgliedern dieser Organisation und im Verfassen eines Aufrufes mit dem Titel „*Polska Sprawiedliwa*“ (Gerechtes Polen) mit einem Inhalt, der die Anfechtung der Autorität der höchsten Gewalt des Demokratischen Polens – Polnisches Komitee der Nationalen Befreiung – bezweckte und gegen die UdSRR gerichtet war, (...)“ (Urteil vom 30. Dezember 1944)[6].

Es ist zu unterstreichen, dass alle Urteile eindeutig gegen das Rückwirkungsverbot verstießen, das als grundlegender Rechtsgrundsatz in Art. 1 des damals geltenden StGB von 1932 enthalten war und die verhängte Strafe ein Akt reiner richterlicher Willkür war.

Zu weiteren Todesstrafen wurden durch das Gericht nach derselben Strafvorschrift u.a. folgende Personen verurteilt:

- Ein Elektrotechniker, Artillerie-Oberstleutnant, der gestanden hatte, dass er „(...) bis zum 19.10.1944 zur Heimatarmee gehörte und daran aktiv teilgenommen hatte, indem er Kontakte mit anderen Mitgliedern der Heimatarmee gepflegt hatte“ (Urteil vom 02. Dezember 1944)[7];
- Ein Wohnungsbesitzer für das Verstecken eines aktiven Mitglieds der Organisation, deren Ziel der Umsturz der demokratischen Staatsverfassung war (...), in der Wohnung „(...) von den ersten Tagen des Monats Oktober bis zum 09.11.1944“ (Urteil vom 02. Dezember 1944)[8];
- Eine Stenotypistin, die „(...) von Mitte September bis zum 02.11.1944 die Organisationszeitung der Heimatarmee „*Wiadomości codzienne lubelskie*“ (Lubliner Tagesnachrichten) und einmalig die Wochenschrift „*Brandfackel*“ getippt hatte“ (Urteil vom 13. Dezember 1944)[9] .

Nach Art. 6 des Erlasses über den Schutz des Staates wurde ein Landwirt, der in der Zeit der deutschen Besatzung, wie man dem Urteil entnehmen kann, „(...) in den Jahren 1943/1944 in der Partisanenabteilung an Aktionen der Bahn- und

5 Fotokopie des Urteils, veröffentlicht in: *Z. Leszczyńska*, Fn. 4, S. 181.
6 Fotokopie des Urteils, veröffentlicht in: *Z. Leszczyńska*, Fn. 4, S. 209.
7 Fotokopie des Urteils, veröffentlicht in: *Z. Leszczyńska*, Fn. 4, S. 191.
8 Fotokopie des Urteils, veröffentlicht in: *Z. Leszczyńska*, Fn. 4, S. 188.
9 Fotokopie des Urteils, veröffentlicht in: *Z. Leszczyńska*, Fn. 4, S. 203.

Telefonsabotage teilgenommen hatte“, dafür verurteilt, dass er am 04.11.1944 während des Krieges ohne rechtskräftige Genehmigung der Behörden in seiner Wohnung in Krasnystaw einen Zweiröhren-Rundfunkempfänger der Marke „*Philips*“ hatte und ihn öffentlich in Anwesenheit vieler Personen benutzte. Im Todesurteil für den Besitz eines Rundfunkgerätes schrieben die Richter: „Der Angeklagte, der jedoch die Tat nicht leugnete und dem Gericht die Umstände der Sache ehrlich darstellte, rechtfertigte sein Verhalten damit, dass er die Anordnung über die Rückgabe des Rundfunkgerätes nicht verstanden habe, und dies wegen seiner Leichtsinnigkeit getan habe, was er jetzt sehr bereue. Trotzdem stellt seine Tat das im Art. 6 des Erlasses über den Schutz des Staates vorgesehene Verbrechen dar“. Man sollte darauf aufmerksam machen, dass die Strafvorschrift des Erlasses über den Schutz des Staates, die unter der Androhung des Todes den Besitz eines Rundfunkgerätes verbot, im Gesetzblatt am 03. November 1944 veröffentlicht wurde, dessen Inhalt dem Angeklagten bereits am nächsten Tag sicherlich nicht bekannt sein konnte, was für die Richter jedoch keine Bedeutung hatte.

Es wurden auch die Personen verurteilt, die von dem Rundfunkgerät wussten. Die Richter ließen jedoch die Tatsache außer Acht, dass die Personen, die wegen der Unterlassung der Denunziation verurteilt wurden, vor der Bekanntmachung des Erlasses gar nicht wussten, dass die Staatsgewalt, unter Androhung von Strafe, die Denunziation anderer Personen von ihnen zwingend verlangte[10].

Wie ein Spott klingen die in den Urteilen enthaltenen Erklärungen, dass die drakonischen Strafen für sämtliche Äußerungen, die als Verbrechen angesehen wurden, im Namen einer Staatsgewalt gefällt wurden, die „die demokratische Richtung und Entwicklung der Verfassung vertritt“[11].

Die kommunistischen Machthaber schufen damals ein Sonderstrafrecht, indem sie Erlasse verabschiedeten, was dazu beigetrug, dass das damals geltende StGB aus dem Jahre 1932 (das bis Ende 1969 galt) und die Grundsätze des Strafrechts, auf die sich das StGB stützte, durch die Gerichte verletzt und in den Hintergrund geschoben wurden. In der Einführung des Handbuchs zum Strafrecht Volkspolens, das durch das Justizministerium im Jahre 1950 erstmals her-

---

10 Im Urteil des Militärgerichts in Lublin vom 05. November 1944 wurde eine Hausfrau zu zehn Jahren Gefängnis verurteilt, weil sie die Staatsgewalt nicht darüber benachrichtigt hatte, dass in ihrem Haus zwei Männer vom 11.-13. September 1944 Radiomitteilungen aus London empfangen hatten, während die Pflicht der Denunziation sieben Wochen später durch Art. 11 des Erlasses über den Schutz des Staates auferlegt wurde.

11 In Bezug darauf, dass die neue Staatsgewalt in Polen „eine demokratische Richtung und Verfassung repräsentiert“, verurteilte das Militäramtsgericht Warschau am 22.01.1945 aufgrund Art. 1 des Erlasses über den Schutz des Staates ein Mitglied der Redaktion „der illegalen Zeitschrift „Alarm“, die durch die illegale Vereinigung AK herausgegeben wird“ sowie den Journalisten, der „in den Tagen vom 10. November bis zum 22. November 1944 „politische Artikel“ in diesem Schreiben verfasst hatte“, zum Tode. Das Urteil wurde nicht veröffentlicht.

ausgegebenen wurde, stand direkt: „(...) die Strafgesetzgebung aus der Vorkriegszeit, die bis heute gilt, gehört zu den Institutionen und Normen, zu denen man mit Recht meinte, dass sie wie lange „Schwänze“ sind, die die Volksdemokratien aus der früheren Zeit hinter sich her schleppen und die die Entwicklung des sozialistischen Aufbaus hemmen“[12]. Über das neue Strafrecht, dessen Hauptteil der Erlass vom 13. Juni 1946 über Verbrechen ausmachte, die in der Zeit des Wiederaufbaus des Staates äußerst gefährlich waren (auch kleines StGB genannt), wurde direkt gesagt: „(...) die Staatsgewalt hat den Staatsanwälten und Richtern neue Strafvorschriften geliefert, die so formuliert wurden, dass sie eine weitreichende Freiheit hinsichtlich der Anklage und Verurteilung derjenigen zulassen, die sie als Klassenfeinde anerkannten, die Staatsanwälte und Richter handelten aber auch in Eigeninitiative, indem sie die strengste Strafe verhängten[13]“. Sowohl Staatsanwälte als auch Richter wurden in Eigeninitiative tätig durch die Beugung des ohnehin schon „elastischen“ neuen Strafrechts, was zur Verurteilung zum Tode u.a. wegen Sabotage im Fall kleiner Diebstähle oder auch zur Gefängnisstrafe allein schon für Witze über die sozialistische Verfassung oder ihre Prominenten führte[14].

Das Recht wurde gebeugt, indem der Begriff „Staatsgeheimnis“ alle Grenzen überschreitend ausgedehnt wurde. Für die Enthüllung eines solchen Geheimnisses wurde ein Militärstaatsanwalt zum Tode verurteilt, der in seiner eigenen Wohnung zu einem Bekannten gesagt hatte, dass Ende 1947 die Zahl der Verurteilten durch die Militärgerichte 72.000 betrug, darunter vor allem zivile

---

12 *I. Andrejew, L. Lernell, J. Sawicki*: „Prawo karne Polski Ludowej“ (das Strafrecht Volkspolens), Warschau 1950, S. 5.

13 *Z. Kliszko* (Stellvertretender Justizminister): W pięciolecie wymiaru sprawiedliwości (Zum fünften Jahrestag der Justiz), [in:] Reforma procedury karnej (Reform der Strafprozedur), Hrsg.: Ministerstwa Sprawiedliwości (Justizministerium), Warschau 1949, S. 18 f.

14 Die Vorschrift des Art. 22 des kleinen Strafgesetzbuches besagte: „Wer falsche Informationen, die dem Interesse des Polnischen Staates einen wesentlichen Schaden zufügen, oder das Ansehen seiner wichtigsten Organe vermindern könnten, verbreitet, unterliegt der Gefängnisstrafe von bis zu fünf Jahren (...)“. Zu vier Jahren Gefängnisstrafe wurde ein Unteroffizier der Bürgermiliz verurteilt, der am 26.12.1946 die Hochzeitsgäste zum Lachen gebracht hatte, weil er sagte, dass er in Warschau war und gesehen hat, dass der Verkehr durch die Miliz und den Sicherheitsdienst ganz aufgehalten wurde und einer der Funktionäre ihm gesagt hatte, dass „der Marschall der Polnischen Armee gerade hier Rad fahren lernt“. *M. Żukowski*: „Szeptana propaganda“ (Geflüsterte Propaganda) in der Rechtsprechung des Militär-Amtsgerichts in Köslin in Jahren 1950 – 1955 [in:] *W. Kulesza, A. Rzepliński* (Hrsg.), Przestępstwa sędziów i prokuratorów w Polsce lat 1944-1956 (Verbrechen der Richter und Staatsanwälte in Polen in Jahren 1944-1956), Warschau 2001, S. 310.

Personen, wobei 3.000 Personen mit dem Tode bestraft wurden; auch habe er Anschriften der Militärstaatsanwaltschaften „enthüllt"[15].

Die Richter, die die drakonischen Strafen verhängten, beugten sowohl das materielle Recht und verletzten zudem auch die Grundsätze des Prozessrechts, letzteres aufgrund der Tatsache, dass sie das Schuldbekenntnis des Angeklagten für einen ausreichenden Beweis hielten. Das Bekenntnis wurde regelmäßig aufgrund von Folter während der Strafverfolgung erzwungen. Foltermaßnahmen wurden vor allem in Ermittlungen gegen Klassenfeinde angewendet. Auf die Beschwerden der Angeklagten, die während der Gerichtsverhandlungen berichteten, dass sie gefoltert wurden, reagierten die Richter überhaupt nicht oder hielten sie für eine Beleidigung der Strafverfolgungsorgane. Durch die Rechtsbeugung seitens der Staatsanwälte und Richter wurde auch der einfache Bürger im Alltag gequält, zum Beispiel weil er essbares Fett „bestimmungswidrig" gekauft hatte, um die auf dem Markt fehlende Seife herzustellen[16]. Ihm wurde vorgeworfen, er habe Lebensmittel des täglichen Bedarfs gekauft, in einer Anzahl, die „den normalen Bedarf überstieg", auch wenn dies ohne die Absicht eines Spekulationsgewinns erfolgte[17].

III. Die Zeit von 1944-1955, die man auch als Zeit des stalinistischen Gerichtsterrors bezeichnen kann, endete im Jahre 1956 mit dem Versuch der Festlegung der Verantwortlichkeit der Richter und der Bestimmung einer strafrechtlichen Grundlage für diese Verantwortlichkeit. Im polnischen StGB von 1932 gab es – wie bereits erwähnt – keine eigene Straftat der „Rechtsbeugung" und die Grundlage für die strafrechtliche Verantwortlichkeit der Richter und Staatsanwälte wurde in Art. 286 § 1 bestimmt: „Ein Beamter, der seine Machtbefugnis überschritten oder seine Pflicht nicht erfüllt hat, der zum Schaden eines öffentlichen oder privaten Interesses gehandelt hat, unterliegt einer Gefängnisstrafe bis zu fünf Jahren". Absicht der Kodifizierungskommission, die das Projekt dieses Gesetzbuches vorbereitete, war es, dass die so formulierte Vorschrift die vielen unterschiedlichen Straftaten im Amt erfassen sollte, die in den drei Strafgesetzbüchern der Teilungsmächte beschrieben wurden, welche in Polen nach der Wiedergewinnung der Unabhängigkeit im Jahre 1918 galten. Nach der Begründung des Projekts des Gesetzbuches sollte der Inhalt des Art. 286 eine Synthese darstellen und gleichzeitig die ganze Breite von strafbaren Verhaltensweisen der Beamten umfassen, die getrennt in den Strafvorschriften des deutschen StGB

15 Urteil des Oberstes Militärgerichts vom 25. Mai 1949. Der Staatspräsident wandelte zur Begnadigung am 11. Juli 1949 die Todesstrafe in lebenslange Gefängnisstrafe um.

16 Urteil des Obersten Gerichts vom 14.-17. Oktober 1950. Nowe Prawo 1951, Nr. 11, S. 34.

17 Beschluss des Obersten Gerichts vom 14. März 1950, Demokratyczny Przegląd Prawniczy 1950, Nr. 4, S. 43.

von 1871 beschrieben wurden[18], in dem russischen StGB von 1903[19] sowie im österreichischen Strafgesetz von 1852, darunter – worauf besonders hingewiesen wurde – „die richterliche Ungerechtigkeit“[20]. Im Kommentar zu dieser Vorschrift wurde darüber hinaus darauf hingewiesen, dass ein Staatsanwalt das dort beschriebene Verbrechen begeht, der gegen eine andere Person die Verfolgung aufnimmt oder Anklage erhebt, obwohl er von ihrer Unschuld wusste[21]. Die Ungerechtigkeit des Richters als ein strafbares Verhalten wurde jedoch in Art. 286 § 1 StGB, in dem das Amtsdelikt sehr allgemein beschrieben wurde, verwässert, und seine Merkmale als umfassende Rechtsbeugung wurden in der Doktrin nicht kommentiert. Aufgrund dieser Vorschrift wurde damals kein Prozess gegen einen Richter oder Staatsanwalt durchgeführt.

Auf die Überschreitung der Befugnisse der Richter und die Nichterfüllung der Pflichten als Rechtsgrundlage ihrer strafrechtlichen Verantwortlichkeit wurde nach der Zeit des Stalinismus in Polen in dem Bericht einer staatlichen Sonderkommission hingewiesen, die im Jahre 1957 die durch das Höchste Militärgericht, insbesondere in den Jahren 1952-1953, gefällten Urteile prüfte. Die Richter dieses Gerichts hatten in Scheinprozessen u.a. 37 Militäroffiziere zum

---

18 Im Kommentar zum § 336 (Rechtsbeugung) des StGB, das auf westlichen Gebieten des Polnischen Staates galt, wurde geschrieben, dass diese Strafvorschrift sich nicht nur auf gerichtliche Sachen, sondern auf alle Sachen, in denen zwei Parteien auftreten, die gegensätzliche Interessen haben (darunter in Sachen, in denen eine Partei der Staat ist), bezieht. *J. Kałużniacki, R. A. Leżański*, Kodeks karny obowiązujący na Ziemiach Zachodnich Rzeczypospolitej Polskiej (Strafgesetzbuch, das auf dem Westlichem Gebiet der Republik Polen galt), Warschau – Posen, 1925, S. 336.

19 Die Vorschrift des Art. 675 des russischen StGB von 1903 wies eine Ähnlichkeit mit § 336 des deutschen StGB auf, weil sie besagte, dass „der Richter oder ein anderer Beamter, der zur Entscheidung von zivilen Straf- oder Disziplinarsachen bevollmächtigt wurde, oder ein Schiedsrichter, der sich eines unfairen Urteils bewusst schuldig gemacht hat, mit einer Gefängnisstrafe von einem bis sechs Jahren bestraft wird.“ Im Kommentar wurde unterstrichen, dass die Bedingung für die Verantwortlichkeit des Richters sein Vorsatz ist, der darin besteht, dass das von ihm gefällte Urteil „grundlos ist und es deswegen mit Schaden für die Gerechtigkeit gefällt wurde.“ Es wurde auch betont, dass der Vorsatz sowohl eine direkte Absicht als auch *dolus eventualis* umfasst. Es wurde darüber hinaus darauf hingedeutet, dass ein ungerechtes Urteil ein Urteil ist, bei dem der Richter ein Gesetz verdreht hat, d.h. er hat es fehlerhaft interpretiert oder er hat unwahre Tatsachen für wahr gehalten und hat eine Entscheidung entgegen der Gerechtigkeit getroffen. *W. Makowski*: Kodeks karny obowiązujący tymczasowo w Rzeczypospolitej Polskiej na ziemiach b. zaboru rosyjskiego (Strafgesetzbuch, das auf dem ehem. russischen Besatzungsgebiet in der Republik Polen vorläufig galt), B. III, Warschau 1922, S. 507-508.

20 Komisja Kodyfikacyjna Rzeczypospolitej Polskiej (Kodifizierungskommission der Republik Polens), Projekt Kodeksu Karnego (Entwurf des Strafgesetzbuches). Erläuterung des Besonderen Teils, Warschau 1930, S. 247-248.

21 *J. Makarewicz*, Kodeks karny z komentarzem (Strafgesetzbuch mit Kommentar), Lemberg 1938, S. 648 f.

Tode verurteilt, die ohne Beweise angeklagt und beschuldigt wurden, dass sie „Organe der Macht beseitigen wollten und die Änderung der Staatsverfassung beabsichtigten", was einige von ihnen nach vielen Monaten schrecklicher Folter während der Strafverfolgung zugaben[22]. Im Bericht der Sonderkommission wurden die Namen von vier Richtern genannt, die Todesurteile fällten, die zur sog. „eisernen Richtergruppen, die im Fällen von Todesurteilen zuverlässig waren", gehörten. Die Kommission forderte, sie für die Überschreitung ihrer Befugnisse und die Nichterfüllung ihrer Pflichten vor Gericht zu stellen, wie auch für die auf diese Art und Weise begangenen Justizmorde. Die Richter erklärten vor der Kommission, dass sie sich des Unrechts der gefällten Urteile nicht bewusst waren[23]. Die Kommission hielt jedoch eine solche Begründung nicht für glaubwürdig, da die Richter „(...) sich des verbrecherischen Charakters ihres Verhaltens bewusst sein mussten". Die Forderung einer Einleitung von Strafverfahren wegen der Gerichtsmorde wurde jedoch nicht erfüllt und es wurde kein Strafprozess gegen stalinistische Militärrichter durchgeführt.

IV. Nach dem sozialen und politischen Umbruch in Polen drängte die Frage nach der strafrechtlichen Verantwortlichkeit dieser Richter im Jahre 1993 zurück in die öffentliche Diskussion aufgrund des Erscheinens eines Buches, das die Dokumentation eines Prozesses von 1952 enthält, in dem der General *A. Fieldorf*, ein Held (Deckname „*Nil*") im Kampf mit dem deutschen Besatzern während des 2. Weltkriegs, ohne Beweise zum Tode verurteilt wurde[24]. In der absurden Anklageschrift stand, dass *A. Fieldorf* als Chef der Leitung einer Division der Heimatarmee in der Zeit von 1943-1945 „Befehle zur Beseitigung sowjetischer Partisanenkommandos und Untergrund- und Unabhängigkeitsgruppierungen sowie von Bürgern jüdischer Staatsangehörigkeit gegeben habe". Der Vorsitzenden des Gerichts, der Richterin *Maria G.*, die den Angeklagten als „Nazi-Verbrecher" verurteilte, wurde vorgeworfen, dass sie in dieser Sache bei der Verhängung des Todesurteils mit vollem Unrechtsbewusstsein handelte. Eine Gerichtsverhandlung fand jedoch nicht statt, weil das Verfahren im Jahre 1998 wegen des Todes der Angeklagten eingestellt wurde[25].

---

22 *J. Poksiński*, „My, sędziowie, nie od Boga ..." (Wir, Richter, nicht vom Gott ...), Warschau 1996, S. 273.

23 Einer der Richter führte zu seiner Verteidigung aus: „Ich bin der Meinung mit dem ganzen Gefühl der parteilichen und richterlichen Verantwortlichkeit, dass die Urteile in den Fälle von mir so getroffen wurden, wie es mir mein Gewissen und meine Verpflichtung dem Vaterland und der Partei gegenüber aufgegeben hat und es ist mir nie in den Sinn gekommen, dass es in den Fällen irgendwelche Zweifel in Bezug auf die Schuld der Angeklagten gegeben hat". Zit. nach *J. Poksiński*, Fn. 22, S. 115.

24 *M. Fieldorf*, *L. Zachuta*, Generał „Nil" August Emil Fieldorf. Fakty, dokumenty, relacje (General „Nil" August Emil Fieldorf. Tatsachen, Unterlagen, Berichte), Warschau 1993.

25 Näheres: *W. Kulesza*, Sądowe karanie jako przypadek sądowej zbrodni – przeszłość z perspektywy współczesności (Gerichtliches Strafen als ein Fall der richterlichen Untat –

Mit einer systematischen Analyse rechtswidriger Urteile, die in Polen zur Zeit der kommunistischen Macht gefällt wurden, begann man im Jahre 1998 zur Vorbereitung der Anklage gegen noch lebende Richter und Staatsanwälte. Ausgangspunkt der Vorbereitungsverfahren war die Erläuterung des Begriffs des Gerichtsverbrechens, d.h. des Urteils, das unter Überschreitung der richterlichen Macht gefällt wurde und das eine Repression der staatlichen Gewalt darstellte, und dadurch die Menschenrechte verletzte. Der Begriff wurde durch den Hinweis auf sechs Fallgruppen präzisiert, in denen die Richter Unrecht begangen hatten[26].

Die erste Fallgruppe umfasst Urteile, die unter Verstoß gegen den Grundsatz *lex retro non agit* gefällt wurden, also aufgrund eines rückwirkend geltenden Gesetzes. Beispiele sind u.a. Urteile aufgrund des Erlasses vom 28. Juni 1946 über die Verantwortung für die Septemberniederlage und die Faschistisierung des staatlichen Lebens, der besagte, dass die staatlichen Beamten dafür bestraft werden, dass sie in der Zeit zwischen dem 1. und 2. Weltkrieg „den Wehrgeist der polnischen Gesellschaft geschwächt hatten“[27].

Die zweite Fallgruppe enthält Urteile, in denen die Richter sich einer allgemein formulierten Vorschrift bedient hatten und sich ein Verbrechen selbst „schufen“. Andere Beispiele sind die Todesurteile für „Spionage-Verbrechen“ für diejenigen, die „(...) zum Nachteil des polnischen Staates handelnd Informationen gesammelt hatten, die ein Staatsgeheimnis darstellten“. Die allgemeine Formulierung des Art. 90 des Militär-StGB vom 23. September 1944 erfasste als „Spione“ auch diejenigen strafrechtlich, die keinerlei Verbindung mit einem fremden Geheimdienst eingegangen waren.

Die dritte Gruppe umfasst Urteile, in denen die Richter, obwohl sie in dem Urteil das strafbare Verhalten deutlich beschrieben, den semantischen Inhalt der Vorschrift überschritten, um den Angeklagten zur Vergeltung der Verletzung

---

Vergangenheit aus der Perspektive der Gegenwart), [in:] Aktualne problemy prawa karnego kryminologii i penitencjarystyki. Księga ofiarowana Profesorowi Stefanowi Lelentalowi w 45 roku pracy naukowej i dydaktycznej. (Aktuelle Probleme des Strafrechts der Kriminologie und des Strafvollzugssystems. Das Buch, das Professor Stefan Lelental zum 45. Jahrestag der wissenschaftlichen und didaktischen Arbeit geschenkt wurde), Łódź 2004, S. 171 ff.

26 *W. Kulesza*, Odpowiedzialność karna sędziów i prokuratorów za zbrodnię sądową (Die Strafrechtliche Verantwortlichkeit der Richter und Staatsanwälte für ein gerichtliches Verbrechen) [in:] *W. Kulesza, A. Rzepliński* (Hrsg.), Fn. 14, S. 510-513.

27 Für „die Faschistisierung des staatlichen Lebens und die Abschwächung der Wehrkraftzersetzung“ haben die Gerichte die Handlungen der staatlichen Beamten gegen die kommunistische Partei gehalten, wobei man feststellte, dass die Staatsmacht in den Jahren 1920-1939 in Polen „faschistische Gewalt“ ausübte. So im Urteil des Woiwodschaftsgerichts Warschau vom 06. November 1952, in dem ein Funktionär der politischen Polizei zum Tode verurteilt wurde. *M. R. Bombicki*, Zbrodnie prawa, Wyroki Sądów Wojskowych w latach 1944-1954 (Verbrechen des Rechts, Urteile der Militärgerichte in den Jahren 1944-1954), S. 53 ff.

der totalitären Macht zu verurteilen. Eines der Beispiele ist die Verurteilung eines Angeklagten für das Herunterreißen der roten Fahne von einem Schulgebäude. Für die Richter war die rote Fahne ein „Verfassungssymbol" i.S.d. Art. 125 des kleinen StGB, obwohl die Strafvorschrift solche Fahnen nicht schützte, sondern nur die polnische Staatsfahne, also die weiß-rote Fahne.

Die vierte Fallgruppe bilden Urteile, die die Richter für Taten, die Verbrechen sind, fällten, in denen sie aber drakonische Strafen verhängten, die allen Richtlinien der Strafzumessung und dem elementaren Gerechtigkeitsgefühl widersprachen. Zahlreiche Beispiele für diese Gruppe liefern Verurteilungen zum Tode oder zu langjähriger Gefängnisstrafe, die aufgrund des Erlasses über den Schutz des Staates, des Militär-StGB und des kleinen StGB gefällt wurden.

Die fünfte Fallgruppe enthält Urteile, durch die Personen verurteilt wurden, denen kein Recht auf Verteidigung gewährt wurde und die während der Strafverfolgung gefoltert wurden. Körperliche und psychische Folter durch Funktionäre der Sicherheitsorgane gegenüber den Verhafteten war tagtägliche Praxis. Dies wussten sowohl Richter als auch Staatsanwälte.

Die sechste Fallgruppe, in denen Richter gerichtliche Verbrechen begangen hatten, sind Urteile, die ohne Beweise oder aufgrund gefälschter Beweise, die während der Strafverfolgung hergestellt wurden, und die durch Richter nicht überprüft wurden, gefällt wurden. Beispiele dafür liefern sowohl geplante Schauprozesse gegen die „Verschwörer gegen die Staatsverfassung" als auch Prozesse, in denen die einzigen Beweise der Anklage die Aussagen von Personen waren, die bereits früher in denselben Sachen zum Tode verurteilt wurden.

V. Von mehr als einigen Dutzend strafrechtlicher Vorverfahren, die der Sache nach wegen Gerichtsverbrechen eingeleitet wurden, endeten nur einige mit einem abschließenden Gerichtsurteil. Hier einige Beispiele:

1. Das Urteil des Militärbezirksgerichts in Posen vom 11. Dezember 2000 beendete den Prozess gegen den ehemaligen Militärstaatsanwalts *Wacław K.*, der der Tat angeklagt wurde, im Jahre 1946 die Todesstrafe für eine 17-jährige Krankenpflegerin aus einer Partisanengruppe, die mit dem kommunistischen Widerstand gekämpft hatte, zu verlangen[28]. In der Anklage gegen den Staatsanwalt wurde unterstrichen, dass er trotz des schwachen Beweismaterials das Gericht aufhetzte, die Todesstrafe zu verhängen. Die Vorwürfe gegen die Krankenpflegerin betrafen völlig unverhältnismäßige Taten. Die Strafbarkeit der Tat des Staatsanwalts wurde rechtlich gestützt auf die Vorschrift über die Strafbarkeit der Anstiftung zu Straftaten und aus der Vorschrift, die die Merkmale der Tötung eines Menschen enthält (Art. 26 und 225 § 1 StGB von 1932). Der angeklagte Staatsanwalt sagte vor Gericht aus, dass nicht er die Todesstrafe für die Krankenpflegerin verlangt hätte und erklärte, dass er am Prozess gegen die Krankenpflegerin nicht teilgenommen hätte und lediglich zum Ende der Verhandlung die Anweisung seines Vorgesetzten ausgeführt habe, indem er den An-

28 Das Urteil wurde nicht veröffentlicht.

trag auf die Strafzumessung verlesen habe, er habe aber das Wort „streng" vergessen. Die Erklärung stand mit dem Protokoll der damaligen Verhandlung im Widerspruch. Aus dem Protokoll folgte, dass *Wacław K.* im Gerichtssaal während der gesamten Verhandlung anwesend war und dass er die Todesstrafe für die Angeklagte verlangt hatte. Das Gericht sprach jedoch den ehemaligen Staatsanwalt frei, weil es seine Erklärung für glaubwürdig hielt und stellte gleichzeitig fest, dass das Protokoll der Verhandlung nicht glaubwürdig sei. Zwar habe der Protokollant als Zeuge ausgesagt, dass das Protokoll ordnungsgemäß geführt wurde und den tatsächlichen Lauf der Verhandlung wiedergegeben habe, doch meinte das Gericht, dass der Zeuge die Umstände des Prozesses vergessen haben konnte. Das Gericht wies auch darauf hin, dass der damalige Vorsitzende des Militärgerichts an Prozessen, in denen 46 Personen zur Todesstrafe verurteilt wurden, teilgenommen habe, und dass er den Inhalt des Protokolls der Gerichtsverhandlung gegen die Krankenpflegerin aus Gleichgültigkeit nicht zur Kenntnis nahm[29]. In der Begründung des Freispruchs des ehemaligen Staatsanwalts wurde ausgeführt, dass man in dieser Sache die Erwägungen, ob die Besetzung des Gerichts das Justizverbrechen begangen habe, indem es die 17-jährige Krankenpflegerin zum Tode verurteilt hat (das Urteil wurde vollstreckt), „für gegenstandslos halten müsse".

2. Im Beschluss des Militärbezirksgerichts Posen vom 19. Juli 2002 über die Einstellung des Strafverfahrens gegen den Beisitzer und den Staatsanwalt in einer gerichtlichen Verhandlung wurde darauf hingewiesen, dass ihr Fehler in der Beurteilung der Beweise keine strafrechtliche Verantwortlichkeit für das drakonische Urteil nach sich ziehen würde, weil ihr Verhalten nicht rechtswidrig gewesen sei[30]. Nach dem Urteil, das durch das Militärgericht im Jahre 1949 gefällt wurde, waren zwei Schrott-Sammler für das Verbrechen der Sabotage (Art. 3 kleines StGB) verurteilt worden, die einen Teil einer nicht von ihnen zerstörten deutschen Lokomotive gestohlen hatten und an der Schrottannahmestelle verkaufen wollten. Den Diebstahl hielt der Staatsanwalt für Sabotage, d.h. für die Vernichtung eines öffentlichen Verkehrsmittels, und forderte die Verurteilung der beiden Angeklagten zum Tode, was in Bezug auf einen der beiden „Saboteure" auch realisiert wurde (das Urteil wurde vollstreckt). Dem zweiten Saboteur maß das Gericht eine Strafe von 15 Jahren Gefängnis zu. Die Zumessung von solchen Strafen wäre ohne Rechtsbeugung unmöglich gewesen. Diese bestand in der Feststellung, dass Diebstahl oder Plünderei mit dem Verbrechen der Sabotage gleichzusetzen seien. Das, was der Staatsanwalt und die Richter hier getan hatten, war die Überschreitung ihrer Befugnis und in der Folge eine Straftat gegen das Leben des ersten Verurteilten und der rechtswidrigen Freiheitsbe-

29 Das Vorverfahren in der Sache des Vorsitzenden des Gerichts und des Beisitzers, die die Krankenpflegerin verurteilt haben, wurde im Jahre 1990 wegen des Todes der Verdächtigen eingestellt.

30 Der Beschluss wurde nicht veröffentlicht.

raubung gegenüber dem Zweiten von ihnen. Die Einstellung des Strafverfahrens gegen diese Juristen wurde damit begründet, dass beide ihren Funktionen gemäß das damals geltende Recht angewandt hatten und aufgrund der eigenen, wenn auch fehlerhaften Einschätzung das Verhalten der Angeklagten als Sabotage interpretiert hatten, sodass sie eine so strenge Strafe verdient hätten. Die Beschwerde der Anklagebehörde bezüglich des Beschlusses über die Einstellung des Verfahrens wurde durch das Oberste Gericht am 20. September 2002 abgelehnt und zusätzlich damit begründet, dass der Militärstaatsanwalt die Todesstrafe für Saboteure auf Veranlassung seines Vorgesetzten verlangt hatte[31]. Die Anweisung wurde durch das Oberste Gericht für einen Militärbefehl gehalten, der bedingungslos erfüllt werden musste, ein Ungehorsam hiergegen hätte den untergeordneten Staatsanwalt durch eine disziplinäre oder strafrechtliche Verantwortlichkeit gefährdet. Nach damals geltendem Recht trug ausschließlich derjenige die Verantwortung, der den Befehl erteilt hatte[32]. Die Argumente für die Begründung der Einstellung des Verfahrens gegenüber dem Staatsanwalt gingen jedoch nicht aus seinen Aussagen hervor und die durch das Gericht ganz außer Acht gelassen wurden. Der Staatsanwalt sagte nämlich, dass er die Todesstrafe für angebliche Saboteure auf Befehl seines Vorgesetzten, jedoch entgegen seiner eigenen Überzeugung verlangt habe und gab zu, dass wenn er es nicht getan hätte, er durch seinen Vorgesetzten „angeschnauzt" worden wäre und Berufung hätte einlegen müssen. Die Worte des Staatsanwalts zeugen demnach davon, dass er von den mangelnden faktischen und rechtlichen Grundlagen für die Anklage der Schrott-Sammler wegen des Sabotage-Verbrechens gewusst hatte und deswegen ist die Behauptung des Gerichts unverständlich, dass sein Verhalten aus „einer berechtigten fehlerhaften Beurteilung folgte". Die Erwägung, ob der ihm drohende Tadel seitens des Vorgesetzten einen Notstand herbeiführte, in dem er die Todesstrafe für die angeklagten Saboteure forderte, war unbegründet. Im Fall des angeklagten Richter ist ferner anzumerken, dass in der Begründung des Einstellungsbeschlusses die Frage ausgelassen wurde, ob die Zumessung so strenger Strafen, wie sie der Richter im Falle eines kleinen Diebstahls verhängte, berechtigt war, indem er den Diebstahl als Straftatbestand der Sabotage wertete. Generell ist zu bemerken, dass das Oberste Gericht sich im Falle dieses Urteils auf die Beweisführung konzentrierte, dass weder der Staatsanwalt noch der Richter eine Verantwortung dafür tragen, welche Rollen sie im Strafprozess spielten. Die Frage nach der Höhe der Strafe, die angesichts der begangenen Taten ganz unverhältnismäßig war, wurde nicht erwogen.

3. Durch eine tiefgründige und eingehende Argumentation zeichnet sich bisher lediglich ein Urteil aus, das einen Richter verurteilte; ein Urteil, welches am

31 Der Beschluss wurde nicht veröffentlicht.

32 Die Einstellungen von NS-Verfahren durch deutsche Gerichte wegen Befehlsnotstandes weisen hier eindeutig eine Parallelität auf. *D. Schenk*, Hitlers Mann in Danzig. Gauleiter Forster und die NS-Verbrechen in Danzig-Westpreußen, Bonn 2000, S. 170-172.

18. April 2003 durch das *Wojskowy Sąd Garnizonowy* (Garnisongericht) in Warschau gefällt wurde[33]. In diesem Urteil bestätigte das Gericht die Schuld des *Tadeusz N.* und stellte fest, dass er im Jahre 1950 als Vorsitzender Richter seine Befugnisse verletzte, als er einen Beamten des Hafenvorstands in Stettin, *Marian T.*, wegen der Vorbereitung einer gewaltsamen Änderung der Staatsverfassung und der Verbreitung von falschen Informationen, die für den Staat schädlich waren, zu einer rechtswidrigen Freiheitsstrafe verurteilte. Für den Richter machte sich der angeklagte Beamte durch folgende Bemerkungen strafbar, die er in Anwesenheit einiger Mitarbeiter während einiger Monate des Jahres 1950 machte:

- „In polnischen Zeitungen sind Lügen zu lesen, als ob die Amerikaner den Krieg in Korea begonnen haben, obwohl man allgemein weiß, dass der Krieg durch koreanische Kommunisten provoziert wurde";
- „Jetzt ist es in Polen so wie in Russland und man darf aus einer Stadt in eine andere nicht ohne Passierschein reisen";
- „Es wird unnötig so viel Geld für rote Lappen ausgegeben" [über die staatliche Feier am Jahrestag der Bekanntmachung über die Machtübernahme durch das kommunistische Polnisches Komitee der Nationalen Befreiung, 22. Juli 1944];
- „Er ist nur gebürtiger Pole, aber alle seine frühen Jahre hat er in Russland verbracht (...) sein Lebenslauf wurde entsprechend überarbeitet" [über den polnischen Marschall *Rokossowski*];
- „Bei uns in Polen werden sowjetische Verhältnisse eingeführt und die Leute haben Angst, miteinander zu sprechen".

In der Begründung des Urteils wegen der „Vorbereitung der gewaltsamen Änderung der Staatsverfassung" (Art. 87 des Militär-StGB) schrieb der Richter, dass solche Aussagen „(...) zum Ziel haben, Aufruhr zu schüren und das Misstrauen der Gesellschaft in die jetzige Verfassung zu erwecken, damit man die Verfassung einfacher stürzen kann". Für eine getrennte Straftat hielt der Richter die Aufbewahrung eines Blatt Papiers und das Vorlesen seines Inhalts gegenüber Kollegen im Jahre 1950. *Marian T.* hatte nämlich aus einer Zeitung aus der Vorkriegszeit eine Katastrophen-Prophezeiung abgeschrieben. Die Zeugen sagten vor Gericht aus, dass in dieser Prophezeiung von „solchem Quatsch" die Rede war, wie: „Der Osten wird in den Westen übergehen, Polen wird bei Moskau liegen, es wird weder Sonne noch Mond geben." Der Inhalt dieser Prophezeiung wurde durch das Gericht sehr ernst genommen aufgrund dessen, dass sie falsche Informationen enthielt und ihr Vorlesen „bezweckte, die Überzeugung zu erwecken, dass die gegenwärtige polnische Verfassung instabil sei", was als eine getrennte Straftat i.S.d. Art. 23 § 1 des kleinen StGB gewertet wurde.

33 Das Urteil wurde nicht veröffentlicht.

Der der Überschreitung seiner Befugnis angeklagte Richter behauptete, er habe das Urteil im Fall *Marian T.* aufgrund der damals geltenden Gesetzgebung gefällt und sehe sein Verhalten als Vorsitzender Richter lediglich als einen gewöhnlichen gerichtlichen Irrtum bei der Interpretation der Vorschriften an. Weiter fuhr er fort, dass er sich bei der Auslegung der Vorschriften nach den Anweisungen des Obersten Militärgerichts gerichtet habe, die während der Besprechungen in seinem Gericht vorgelesen worden waren. Er gab darüber hinaus zu, dass er sich als Richter vor Repressionen des Sicherheitsapparates nicht fürchtete und die Verurteilung von *Marian T.* zu sechs Jahren Gefängnis seiner eigenen Überzeugung entsprach, die er im Urteil ausdrücken konnte.

Der rechtlichen Beurteilung der Tat des Richters ging eine Reflexion des Gerichts über die Bedeutung der *Radbruchschen* Formel über die Bestimmung der Verantwortlichkeit der Juristen für die zur Zeit des Dritten Reichs und der DDR begangenen Verbrechen voran. Die Zusammenfassung dieses Teils der Erwägungen wurde durch das Gericht folgendermaßen formuliert: „Der Auffassung des Angeklagten, dass jedes Recht, das durch staatliche Gewalt geschaffen wurde, auch wenn es den grundlegenden Werten widerspricht, die Taten der Staatsfunktionäre rechtfertigt, kann man nicht zustimmen". Im Weiteren behauptete das Gericht, dass nach der Überwindung des kommunistischen Totalitarismus in Polen das Primat des natürlichen Rechts und der objektiven Gerechtigkeit über das kommunistische positive Recht gestellt wurde. Im Hauptteil der Begründung wies das Gericht darauf hin, dass der angeklagte Richter das Urteil unter Verstoß gegen das damals geltende Recht gefällt habe, indem er einen Akt größter Willkür sowohl bei der Interpretation dieses Rechts als auch in der Beurteilung der Beweise ausgeübt habe. Die Machtüberschreitung durch den Richter bestand darin, dass er sich auf die Vorschrift des Art. 87 des Militär-StGB stützte, der von der Strafbarkeit der Vorbereitung einer „gewaltsamen" Änderung der staatlichen Verfassung handelte und der verurteilte *Marian T.* keinerlei Absicht hatte, einen gewaltsamen Staatsstreich durchzuführen. Der Richter schrieb dem Angeklagten einen realen Vorsatz zu, obwohl die kommunistische Verfassungswirklichkeit durch das Militär, die Miliz, die Sicherheitsorgane und die in Polen stationierte Rote Armee geschützt wurde. Die zweite angewandte Vorschrift – Art. 23 § 1 des kleinen StGB – stellte die Verbreitung und das Verfassen „falscher Nachrichten" unter Strafe. Die Prophezeiung aus der Vorkriegszeitung konnte indes eine solche Nachricht nicht sein, denn man kann an eine Prophezeiung glauben, dass sie in der Zukunft in Erfüllung geht, oder man kann nicht an sie glauben. Das Gericht unterstrich, dass selbst in der Zeit des Stalinismus der Glaube an Prophezeiungen nicht verboten gewesen sei. Die Machtüberschreitung durch den Richter bestand auch darin, dass er für die Begründung der Verurteilung von *Marian T.* in der Anklageschrift dessen Aussagen angeführt hatte, die die Zeugen in der Verhandlung nicht bestätigten. Der Richter schrieb trotzdem, dass die Worte des Angeklagten gegenüber Mitarbeitern wie „das im Land herrschende Elend" und „die Unterordnung von Ländern der Volksdemokratien durch die Sowjetunion" aus seiner Sicht Unrechtshandlungen darstellten.

In der Beurteilung des Verhaltens des stalinistischen Richter stellte das Gericht fest, dass die Verurteilung des *Marian T.* für die gemachten Aussagen sogar mit dem damals geltenden totalitären Recht nicht übereinstimmte, das der Repression von politischen Gegnern diente. Deswegen stellte das Gericht fest, dass „der Angeklagte als Vorsitzender Richter seine Rechte vorsätzlich missbraucht und einer unschuldige Person ihre Freiheit genommen hat". Mit einem solchen Verhalten machte er sich nach damals geltendem Recht schuldig, weil der Tatbestand der Strafbarkeit der Machtüberschreitung durch einen Staatsfunktionär (Art. 286 § 1 StGB) sowie die rechtswidrige Freiheitsentziehung (Art. 248 § 2 StGB von 1932) erfüllt war. Für diese Straftat verhängte das Gericht gegen den angeklagten Richter eine Freiheitsstrafe von zwei Jahren ohne Bewährung und betonte, dass der Richter auch gegenwärtig sein Verhältnis zu dem von ihm bestraften Menschen nicht verändert habe, da er vor dem Gericht aussagte, dass er den „verbissenen Verfassungsgegner" im Jahre 1950 zu Recht verurteilt habe.

Der verurteilte Richter legte gegen das Urteil Berufung ein, in der er den Vorwurf erhob, dass man grundlos angenommen habe, dass er sich der Rechtswidrigkeit seines Verhaltens als Richter bewusst gewesen sei und dass er für die Machtüberschreitung und die Freiheitsberaubung eines Menschen ohne Grund verurteilt worden sei.

Das Militär-Bezirksgericht in Warschau hob am 18. April 2003 das Urteil auf und stellte das Strafverfahren gegen den Richter *Tadeusz N.* ein, weil es festgestellte, dass dem ehemaligen Richter eine formale Richterimmunität zustehen würde, die das Gericht der ersten Instanz nicht berücksichtigt hatte[34]. Im erstinstanzlichen Urteil gegen den ehemaligen Militärrichter wurde festgestellt, dass nach gegenwärtiger Rechtslage nach dem Gesetz über die Verfassung der Militärgerichte vom 21. August 1997 die Einwilligung des Disziplinargerichts, den angeklagten Richter zur Verantwortlichkeit zu ziehen, nicht erforderlich sei, weil er schon lange nicht mehr Richter sei. Das Gericht zweiter Instanz stellte jedoch fest, dass das gegenwärtige Recht auch den ehemaligen Richter schützt, der in stalinistischer Zeit Urteile fällte und schloss aus, ihn ohne vorangehende Einwilligung des Disziplinargerichts vor Gericht zu stellen. Das Fehlen dieser Einwilligung wurde durch das Berufungsgericht für ein absolutes Prozesshindernis gehalten, das ein Strafverfahren auch gegen eine Person, die nur in der

34 Im polnischen Recht bedeutet die formale Immunität der Richter und Staatsanwälte, dass die vorherige Einwilligung des Disziplinargerichts notwendig ist, um gegen sie ein Strafverfahren einzuleiten. Das Fehlen einer solchen Einwilligung ist ein formales Hindernis für die Einleitung des Strafverfahrens.

Vergangenheit die Stellung eines Richters inne hatte und ihr mittlerweile entsagt oder sie aus anderen Gründen verloren hat, unmöglich machte.

VI.Die Rückkehr zur stalinistischen Ideologie der Rechtsanwendung erfolgte in Polen nach der Einführung des Kriegszustands in der Nacht vom 12. auf den 13.12.1981. Die Richter begingen in dieser Zeit viele Justizverbrechen, die Gegenstand eines Ermittlungsverfahrens zwanzig Jahre später wurden. Die Disziplinargerichte willigten jedoch nicht ein, Richter, die nach der Einführung des Kriegszustands in Polen Mitglieder der Gewerkschaft „Solidarität“ unter Verletzung des Rückwirkungsverbots verurteilten, zur Verantwortlichkeit zu ziehen. Die Rechtswidrigkeit des richterlichen Verhaltens bestand darin, dass sie Angeklagte aufgrund der Organisation von Streiks und Protestaktionen an diesem Tage – d.h. am 13.12.1981 –, die davor nicht verboten waren, verurteilten. Ein solches Verhalten wurden durch den Erlass über die Einführung des Kriegszustands, der im Gesetzblatt mit dem Datum des folgenden Tages, d.h. des 14.12.1981 veröffentlicht wurden, zu Straftaten erklärt. Das Gesetzblatt, das diesen Erlass enthielt, wurde erst vom 17.-18.12.10981 gedruckt, und vom 19.-23.12.1981 verschickt. Die Richter bezogen sich bei der Verurteilung der Organisation der Proteste in den ersten Stunden des Kriegszustands auf eine Vorschrift des Erlasses, die besagte, dass der Erlass „am Tag seiner Bekanntmachung mit Rechtskraft seit dem Tag seines Beschlusses in Kraft tritt“. Die Richter zogen diese Formulierung heran, um Urteile zu fällen, deren Inhalt gegen das Rückwirkungsverbot, das in Art. 1 des damals geltenden StGB von 1969 enthalten ist, verstieß. In Disziplinarverfahren, die nach dem Gesetz vom 03. Dezember 1998 geführt wurden[35], in denen den Richtern vorgeworfen wurde, dass Juristen während des Kriegszustands die richterliche Unabhängigkeit verraten hätten, behaupteten diese gemeinsam, dass ihnen die Rechtswidrigkeit ihrer Urteile nicht bewusst gewesen sei und sie überzeugt gewesen waren, dass „der Richter das geltende Recht anzuwenden hat, egal wie es lautet[36]“.

Eines der Beispiele für solche Urteile, die dem Grundsatz *lex retro non agit* verletzten, war die standrechtliche Verurteilung von *Andrzej S.* und *Jerzy K.*, die die Gewerkschaft „*Solidarność*“ in Łódź leiteten, durch das Woiwodschaftsgericht Łódź am 30.12.1981. Sie wurden dafür verurteilt, dass sie die Protestaktion am 13.12.1981 von 7 – 14 Uhr in Łódź im Sitz der Gewerkschaft organisiert und persönlich durchgeführt und zum Generalstreik aufgerufen hatten. Beide Angeklagten wurden zu einer Freiheitsstrafe von vier Jahren und sechs Monaten

35 Gesetz vom 03. Dezember 1998 über die Disziplinarverantwortlichkeit der Richter, die in den Jahren 1944-1989 die richterliche Unabhängigkeit verraten haben.

36 *A. Strzembosz, M. Stanowska*, Sędziowie warszawscy w czasie próby 1981-1988 (Warschauer Richter in der Probezeit 1981-1988), Warschau 2005, S. 277. Keiner von den ca. 50 Richtern, die vor dem Disziplinargericht standen, wurde wegen des Verrats der richterlichen Unabhängigkeit mit einer Disziplinarmaßnahme bestraft. Op. cit. S. 273-274.

verurteilt. Das Oberste Gericht erhöhte im Urteil vom 01. März 1982 die Strafen auf sechs Jahre[37].

Eines der Disziplinargerichte, das den Antrag des Staatsanwalts auf Erteilung der Zustimmung dazu erhielt, einen Richter wegen seiner Urteile aus der Zeit des Kriegszustands zur Verantwortlichkeit zu ziehen, wandte sich im Jahre 2007 an das Oberste Gericht mit der Rechtsfrage von wesentlicher Bedeutung: „Ist es selbstverständlich, dass die Richter davon befreit waren, das Datum, das im Gesetzblatt angegeben wurde (14. Dezember 1981), zu respektieren“ und hatten sie die Pflicht, die retroaktiven Strafvorschriften des Erlasses über den Kriegszustand anzuwenden[38]?

Die Antwort, die das Oberste Gericht im Beschluss vom 20. Dezember 2007 gab, soll angeführt werden, weil sie in die Sammlung der Rechtsgrundsätze aufgenommen wurde. Sie besagte, dass „(...) die Gerichte, die in Strafverfahren über Unrechtstaten aufgrund des Erlasses des Staatsrats vom 12. Dezember 1981 über den Kriegszustand urteilten, (...) von der Pflicht zur Anwendung der retroaktiven Strafvorschriften im Gesetzrang nicht befreit waren“. Diese Feststellung bedeutet, dass die Richter den Umfang ihrer Macht nicht überschritten, indem sie für Taten verurteilten, die vorher nicht strafbar waren und die am 13.12.1981, d.h. vor der Veröffentlichung des Erlasses, begangen wurden. Die These bedeutete also, dass auch die Juristen, die das oben genannte Urteil fällten, nicht zur strafrechtlichen Verantwortlichkeit gezogen werden durften. Zur Begründung seiner Auffassung bezog sich das Oberste Gericht auf Folgendes:

In der damals geltenden Verfassung der Polnischen Volksrepublik vom 1952 war der Grundsatz *lex retro non agit* nicht enthalten;

Es existierte kein rechtlicher Mechanismus, der es ermöglichte, die Übereinstimmung der Vorschriften von Gesetzrang mit der Verfassung zu überprüfen[39].

---

37 *J. Kochanowski*, *T. de Virion*, Glosse zum Urteil vom 01.03.1982, V KRN 50/82, „Państwo i Prawo“ 1982 Nr. 9, S. 151.

38 Prawo o ustroju sądów powszechnych (Das Recht über die Verfassung der ordentlichen Gerichte) vom 27. Juli 2001 besagt in Art. 80 § 2 b, dass das Disziplinargericht den „offensichtlichen unbegründeten“ Antrag, einen Richter zur Strafverantwortlichkeit zu ziehen, ohne inhaltliche Prüfung verweigern kann. Für einen so völlig unbegründeten Antrag hielt das Disziplinargericht den Antrag bezüglich eines Richters im Ruhestand, der im Kriegszustand zwei Organisatoren der Proteststreiks in den Tagen vom 13.-14.12.1981 festnehmen ließ. Die Staatsanwaltschaft, die den Richter zur strafrechtlichen Verantwortlichkeit ziehen wollte, begründete den Antrag damit, dass das Organisieren des Protests damals keine Unrechtstat gewesen sei. Deswegen habe der Richter seine Berechtigungen überschritten, als er die Protestierenden als Täter betrachtete und ihnen ihre Freiheit raubte. Das Disziplinargericht wandte sich an das Oberste Gericht mit der Rechtsfrage, ob ein solcher Antrag des Staatsanwalts offensichtlich unbegründet sei.

39 Zu bemerken ist die weitgehende Ähnlichkeit dieses Gedankengangs mit der folgenden Argumentation im Urteil des Landgerichts Nürnberg vom 04. März 1968 bezüglich der Verurteilungen nach dem Blutschutzgesetz während des Nationalsozialismus: „Seiner-

Das zweite Argument lautete: „Es fehlte eine Regelung, die die Stellung des Internationalen Pakts der bürgerlichen und politischen Rechte im System der Gesetze des Staates festlegte“, der durch die Polnische Volksrepublik am 03.03.1977 ratifiziert worden war und dessen Art. 15 bestimmt, dass der Grundsatz *lex retro non agit* auch im Fall der Einführung eines Ausnahmezustands nicht aufgehoben werden darf. Da es in der damals geltenden Verfassung keine Bestimmung mit dem Inhalt gab, dass international Verträge in der innerstaatlichen Rechtsordnung eine unmittelbar geltende Rechtskraft haben, stellte das Oberste Gericht fest, dass die retroaktiv wirkenden Strafvorschriften des Erlasses über den Kriegszustand nicht gegen die Rechtsordnung, die in der Polnischen Volksrepublik herrschte, verstießen[40]. Der Beschluss des Obersten Gerichts bedeutet, dass die Richter während des Kriegszustands verpflichtet waren, aufgrund des Gesetzesunrechts zu urteilen und die Eintragung dieses Beschlusses in die Sammlung der Rechtsgrundsätze verlieh diesem Unrecht höchsten Rang. Mit anderen Worten: Das Gesetzesunrecht aus der Zeit des totalitären Staates wurde in der Gegenwart in die Sammlung der Rechtsgrundsätze eingetragen mit einer Formel, die es unmöglich macht, Richter und Staatsanwälte, die während der vorgenannten Zeiten des Unrechtsregimes in Polen handelten, zur Verantwortlichkeit zu ziehen[41]. Auch die stalinistischen Richter, die drakonische Strafen u.a. für kleine Vergehen zumaßen, können sich zu ihrer Verteidigung

---

zeit hatten die Gerichte jedoch keine Möglichkeit, sich der Anwendung dieses Gesetzes zu entziehen. Die Gerichte waren damals weder berechtigt noch verpflichtet, die anzuwendenden Gesetze unter dem Gesichtspunkt nachzuprüfen, ob sie mit der Verfassung und den Grundgeboten der Sittlichkeit in Einklang stünden. Die in der Weimarer Republik durch die Rechtsprechung entwickelte Befugnis der Gerichte zur Nachprüfung von Gesetzen auf ihre Verfassungsmäßigkeit, war zur Zeit der nationalsozialistischen Gewaltherrschaft als unvereinbar mit der heutigen Staatsauffasung abgelehnt und bei Gesetzen aus dieser Zeit auch nicht praktiziert worden.“ Zit. nach *J. Friedrich*, Freispruch für die Nazi-Justiz. Die Urteile gegen NS-Richter seit 1948. Eine Dokumentation, Berlin 1998, S. 361.

40 Einem anderen Gedankengang folgten die Rechtsprechung des BGH und die Doktrin nach der Wiedervereinigung bezüglich des rechtlichen Beitritts der DDR zum Internationalen Pakt über bürgerliche und politische Rechte im Jahre 1976. Man stellte Folgendes fest: „Durch die Ratifizierung war die DDR an diesen Pakt gebunden; die Berufung auf innerstaatliche Rechtsvorschriften, d.h. die Nichtumsetzung in DDR-Recht, konnte die DDR nicht von ihren völkerrechtlichen Verpflichtungen entbinden.“ *A. Eser, J. Arnold* (Hrsg.), Strafrecht in Reaktion auf Systemunrecht, Freiburg im Breisgau 2000, S. 137, wo man sich auf die frühere Publikation von *F.-C. Schroeder* bezog.

41 Auf dieselbe Grundlage stützte sich die Aussage einer der Marinerichter, der sich in der Nazi-Zeit an Todesurteilen beteiligte: „Was damals rechtens war, kann heute nicht Unrecht sein“. Zit. nach *M. Sagenschneider*, 50 Klassiker Prozesse, Hildesheim 2005, S. 198. Nach *W. Stadler* ging auch die österreichische Nachkriegsjustiz „(...) vom Grundsatz aus, dass das, was von 1938 bis 1945 Recht war, nach 1945 nicht Unrecht sein konnte“, „...Juristisch bin ich nicht zu fassen“, Berlin 2007, S. 291.

darauf berufen, dass es in der Verfassung weder ein Verbot für die Zumessung unverhältnismäßig strenger Strafen noch ein Verbot einer den Wortlaut überschreitenden Auslegung des Gesetzes gab. Auf dasselbe Argument können sich Richter berufen, die in der Zeit des Kriegszustands urteilten, in der eine Rückkehr zu den „Auslegungs"-Methoden der stalinistischen Zeit stattfand. Seit Ende 1981 verurteilten Richter wiederholt für solche Verhaltensweisen, wie

- den Ausspruch von Parolen: „Ein Russisches Bündnis ist für uns unnötig" sowie „die Krähe [poln.: *„Wrona"* – populäre Bezeichnung der *Wojskowa Rady Ocalenia Narodowego* (nach den ersten Buchstaben), deutsch: „Höchste Behörde des Kriegszustands"] wird den Adler nicht überwinden"[42];
- die Bearbeitung einer Abhandlung über die Einführung des Kriegszustands durch einen wissenschaftlichen Mitarbeiter[43];
- das Vorlesen eines privaten Briefes von einer internierten Person während des Kriegszustands in einer Privatwohnung in Anwesenheit einiger Personen, dessen Fragment „falsche Nachrichten" enthielt"[44].

Infolge des Beschlusses des Obersten Gerichts vom 20. Dezember 2007 unterließ es die Staatsanwaltschaft, neue Anträge bezüglich der Richter aus der Zeit des Kriegszustands an die Disziplinargerichte zu stellen. Die Situation hat sich gewissermaßen dank dem Urteil des Verfassungsgerichts vom 27. Oktober 2010 geändert, in dem festgestellt wurde, dass Art. 80 § 2 b des Rechts über die Verfassung der ordentlichen Gerichte aus dem Jahre 2001, der die Grundlage dafür lieferte, den Antrag für „offensichtlich grundlos" zu halten und ihn ohne Prüfung abzulehnen, gegen Art. 2 der Verfassung aus dem Jahre 1997 verstößt[45]. Dies bedeutet, dass die Disziplinargerichte verpflichtet sind, eine inhaltliche Analyse des Antrags des Staatsanwalts auf Einwilligung, einen Richter zur strafrechtlichen Verantwortlichkeit zu ziehen, durchzuführen. Dies bedeutet selbstverständlich nicht, dass das Disziplinargericht nach der Durchführung eines Verfahrens in einer konkreten Sache eine solche Einwilligung erteilen wird. In der Begründung seines Urteils stellte das Verfassungsgericht fest, dass die richterli-

42 Die erste Aufschrift wurde als Straftat des Aufrufs zu Taten gegen die Bündnis-Einheit mit der Sowjetunion angesehen, die zweite wurde als Beleidigung eines grundlegenden Organs der Volksrepublik Polen gehalten, obwohl der *Wojskowa Rada Ocalenia Narodowego* im rechtlichen Sinne kein grundlegendes Staatsorgan war. Der Staatsanwalt forderte für einen der Autoren der Aufschriften die Strafe von dreieinhalb Jahren Gefängnis, das Gericht verhängte gegen ihn eine Strafe von einem Jahr und drei Monaten Gefängnis. *A. Strzembosz, M. Zdanowska*, Fn. 36, S. 107.

43 Der Staatsanwalt forderte für den Autor vier Jahre Freiheitsstrafe, das Gericht verhängte gegen ihn zwei Jahre Freiheitsstrafe. *A. Strzembosz, M. Stanowska*, Fn. 36, S. 99.

44 Urteil des Obersten Gerichts vom 17. Dezember 1982. Rechtsprechung des Obersten Gerichts. Straf- und Militärkammer, 1983, Nr. 6 Pos. 48.

45 Art. 2 der Verfassung lautet: „Die Republik Polen ist ein demokratischer Rechtsstaat, der die Grundsätze der sozialen Gerechtigkeit verwirklicht".

che Immunität nicht als Gruppenprivileg für die Befreiung von strafrechtlicher Verantwortlichkeit gesehen werden kann, weil sie eine Garantie der Unabhängigkeit darstellt und jeden Richter individuell schützt. Des Weiteren machte der Gerichtshof darauf aufmerksam, dass die Ablehnung der Aufhebung der Immunität zur Befreiung des Richters von strafrechtlicher Verantwortlichkeit sicherlich ein schwerer Missbrauch dieser Institution wäre. Aus diesem Grund soll das Disziplinargericht einwilligen, gegen einen Richter strafrechtlich zu ermitteln, wenn ein angemessen begründeter Vorwurf besteht, dass er eine Straftat begangen hat. Obwohl der Verfassungsgerichtshof Gerichtsurteile nicht inhaltlich untersucht, sondern nur die Verfassungsmäßigkeit des Rechts einschätzt, auf dessen Grundlage die Urteile gefällt wurden, äußerte er sich doch zum Beschluss des Obersten Gerichts vom 20. Dezember 2007. Der Verfassungsgerichtshof stellte fest, dass der Beschluss, der die Richter des Kriegszustands zur Anwendung des rückwirkendes Strafgesetzes verpflichtete, die Gerichte der unteren Instanz und andere Staatsorgane auf eine Weise gebunden habe, was einen „*chilling effect*“ verursachen könne. Der Beschluss könne die Strafverfolgungsorgane entmutigen, den Versuch zu unternehmen, die Richter zur Strafverantwortlichkeit zu ziehen, die aufgrund der rückwirkenden Vorschriften des Erlasses über den Kriegszustand verurteilten[46].

VII. Zusammenfassend ist festzustellen, dass die Forderung, Richter zur strafrechtlichen Verantwortlichkeit zu ziehen, im Jahre 1957 – also nach dem Ende des Stalinismus – formuliert und dann einige Jahre nach der Wiedergewinnung der vollständigen Souveränität Polens im Jahre 1990 wiederholt wurde. Die Richter und Staatsanwälte, die der totalitären Macht dienten, wirkten an rechtswidrigen Verurteilungen zum Tode oder an hohen Gefängnisstrafen nicht nur tatsächlicher oder angeblicher politischer Gegner, sondern auch der einfachen Bürger mit. Diese Richter und Staatsanwälte verwirklichten mit ihrem Verhalten die Tatbestandsmerkmale der Überschreitung ihrer Befugnisse und der Nichterfüllung ihrer Pflichten und handelten dadurch zum Nachteil des öffentlichen oder privaten Interesses. Die Unrechtsurteile erfüllen gleichzeitig die Tatbestandsmerkmale der Tötung oder der Freiheitsberaubung gegenüber den verurteilten Menschen. Bei der strafrechtlichen Qualifikation der richterlichen Verhaltensformen kam es also zu einer Realkonkurrenz der Rechtsnormen. Das Verhalten der Staatsanwälte, die drakonische Strafen forderten, entsprach einer strafbaren Anstiftung der Richter, rechtswidrige Urteile zu fällen. Im Schrifttum wurden sechs Fallgruppen unterschieden, in denen die Unrechtstaten der Macht-

---

46 Es ist zu bemerken, dass die freisprechenden Urteile für NS-Justizverbrecher, die durch BRD-Gerichte gefällt wurden, zur Reflexion über das Verhalten der Staatsanwälte führten: „Unter diesen Umständen erscheint nicht verwunderlich, dass die Staatsanwaltschaften in ähnlichen Fällen es meist nicht einmal zur Anklage kommen ließen. Sie stellten die Verfahren ein.“ *J. Weber*, *M. Piazolo*, Justiz im Zwielicht, München 1998, S. 79.

überschreitung durch einen Richter stattfanden. Dies beschreibt die Grundlage für seine strafrechtliche Verantwortlichkeit für die Begehung einer Straftat gegen das Leben und die Freiheit der verurteilten Person. In den Straf- und Disziplinarverfahren, die gegen Richter geführt wurden, bezogen sie sich auf ihre Überzeugung, dass sie verpflichtet waren, damals geltendes Recht anzuwenden. Eine solche Ansicht wurde auch durch das Oberste Gericht im Beschluss vom 20. Dezember 2007 zum Ausdruck gebracht, der in die Sammlung der Rechtsgrundsätze eingetragen wurde und in dem es um Richter geht, die rückwirkende Strafvorschriften des Erlasses über den Kriegszustand vom 13. Dezember 1981 anwandten. Die Führung eines Strafverfahrens gegen einen Richter oder einen Staatsanwalt ist nur dann zulässig, wenn das Disziplinargericht einwilligt, sie strafrechtlich zur Verantwortung zu ziehen (formale Immunität). In der Regel verweigerten die Disziplinargerichte eine solche Einwilligung, was in der Hauptsache dazu führte, dass obwohl die Richter des totalitären Staates tausende von Urteilen fällten, die Justizverbrechen waren, gegenwärtig nur vereinzelt Strafprozesse gegen Richter und Staatsanwälte aus der Zeit des Unrechts stattfinden. Keines dieser Strafverfahren endete mit einer rechtskräftigen Verurteilung weder eines angeklagten Richters noch eines Staatsanwalts.

„Stadionverbote“ im polnischen Strafrecht

Prof. Dr. Dr. h.c. Andrzej J. Szwarc[*]

Mit der vorliegenden Bearbeitung möchte ich mich bei *Prof. Dr. Dres. h.c. F.-C. Schroeder* für die langjährige Bekanntschaft und das Wohlwollen bedanken, das ich von ihm erfahren habe.

Die Themenwahl für die vorliegende Bearbeitung hängt damit zusammen, dass die Problematik des Sportrechts auch von Herrn *Prof. Dr. Dres. h.c. F.-C. Schroeder* aufgenommen wurde, wovon die mit *H. Kauffmann* herausgegebene Monographie „Sport und Recht“ (Berlin 1972) Zeugnis ablegt.

I. Einführung

„Stadionverbot“ ist eine Begriffskonvention[1], ein Begriff, der unterschiedliche Bedeutungen erfährt. Sog. Stadionverbote können unterschiedlichen Rang, unterschiedliche Gestalt und unterschiedliche rechtliche Bedeutung aufweisen, unterschiedliche Orte betreffen sowie durch unterschiedliche Subjekte gegenüber unterschiedlichen Adressaten aus unterschiedlichen Gründen verhängt werden. Im Allgemeinen bedeutet dieser Begriff ein Verbot der Organisation einer Sportveranstaltung an einem bestimmten Objekt oder Verbot der Teilnahme an einer Veranstaltung (bzw. mehreren Veranstaltungen) von bestimmten Personen.

Obwohl der Begriff das Wort „Stadion“ beinhaltet, geht es um Sportveranstaltungen an allen Objekten, an denen Sportveranstaltungen stattfinden können. Obwohl solche Verbote am häufigsten für Stadien verhängt werden, können sie (solche Fälle sind ebenfalls bekannt) Sportveranstaltungen an anderen Objekten wie Fußballfeldern, Regattabahnen, Hallen, Schauspiel- oder Sporthäusern bzw. ähnliche Orte betreffen. Manchmal umfasst das Verbot auch das Verbleiben an einem bestimmten Ort des Sportobjekts.

Das Verhängen von Stadionverboten kann unterschiedliche Ursachen haben. Dazu zählen der schlechte technische Zustand des Objekts oder des Geländes, die Wetterbedingungen, unterschiedliche mit dem Sport verbundene Geschehnisse (z.B. die Nichterfüllung von bestimmten Bedingungen durch einen Sportverein) oder andere Ursachen, wie z.B. angeordnete Staatstrauer. Am häufigsten werden Stadionverbote in Verbindung mit Hooliganausschreitungen unter Zuschauern von Sportveranstaltungen verhängt[2].

---

* Inhaber des Lehrstuhls für Strafrecht der Universität Posen.

1 Dazu *W. Wróbel*, in: *M. Melezini* (Hrsg.), System prawa karnego. 6. Band, Kary i środki karne. Poddanie sprawcy próbie (Das System des Strafrechts, Strafen und Strafmaßnahmen. Bewährungsmaßnahmen), Warszawa 2010, S. 558.

2 Zu Hooliganausschreitungen oder Stadionkriminalität in der polnischen Literatur vgl. z.B. *P. Chlebowicz*, Chuligaństwo stadionowe. Studium kryminologiczne (Das Stadion-

Stadionverbote werden gegen unterschiedliche Subjekte verhängt. Zu den Adressaten von Stadionverboten können der Veranstalter eines Sportevents, der Eigentümer des Objekts oder der Objektverwalter zählen. Ihnen wird aufgrund eines solchen Verbots die Organisation und Durchführung einer oder mehrerer bestimmter Sportveranstaltungen untersagt. Das Verbot kann auch einen bestimmten Sportverein oder seine Mitglieder betreffen. Zudem kann das Verbot auch auf natürliche Personen, eine bestimmte Person oder bestimmte Personengruppe (wie z.B. die Gruppe der Fans eines Sportvereins) angewandt werden. Es ist durchaus möglich, dass wegen eines an natürliche Personen gerichteten generellen Stadionverbots eine Sportveranstaltung ohne Zuschauer stattfindet.

Stadionverbote können von unterschiedlichen Subjekten stammen. Dazu zählen Verwaltungsorgane, Sportorganisationsorgane (z.B. eine internationale Sportföderation, ein nationaler Sportverband oder Sportverein), Eigentümer von Sportobjekten, Verwalter solcher Objekte oder Veranstalter eines Sportevents bzw. Gerichte, die ein solches Verbot als Strafe oder als eine andere rechtlich vorgesehene Maßnahme verhängen. Dieser Differenzierung unterliegen entsprechend die Form, der Rang und die rechtliche Erheblichkeit eines solchen Verbots. Das Verbot kann entweder ein Verwaltungsakt, ein Urteil eines ordentlichen Gerichts (darunter insbesondere eines Strafgerichts) oder auch ein Akt ohne einen solchen Rang sein, was insbesondere bei Verboten von Sportverbänden vorkommt.

---

rowdytum. Kriminologische Studie), Warszawa 2009; *ders.*, Międzynarodowe uregulowania tzw. przestępczości stadionowej (Internationale Regelungen der Stadionkriminalität), „Państwo i Prawo“, 2009, Nr. 8, S. 98-105; *G. Gozdór*, Bezpieczeństwo imprez masowych. Komentarz (Die Sicherheit von Massenveranstaltungen. Kommentar), Warszawa 2008; *T. Sahaj*, Fani futbolowi. Historyczno-społeczne studium zjawiska kibicowania (Fussballfans. Eine historisch-gesellschaftliche Studie des Phänomens), Poznań 2007; *S. Wanat*, Socjologia zachowań chuligańskich w sporcie (Soziologie von rowdyhafen Verhalten), „Sport Wyczynowy“, 1993, Nr. 1-2, S. 16; *S. Wanat/A. Gorący*, Psychologiczne uwarunkowania zachowań chuligańskich na imprezach sportowych (Psychologische Gegebenheiten von rowdyhaften Verhalten), „Roczniki Naukowe AWF“, Band XXXVI, Warszawa 1997. In der Literatur anderer Länder vgl. z.B. *T. Andersson*, Swedish Football Hooliganism. 1900-1939 (Schwedisches Fußballrowdytum 1900-1939), „Soccer and Society“, 2001, Vol. 2, Nr. 1; *G. Armstrong*, Football Hooligans: Knowing the Score (Fußballrowdys: Bestandaufnahme), Berg, Oxford and New York 1998; *G. Armstrong/R. Giulianotti*, Fear and Loathing in World Football (Angst und Schrecken im Weltfußball), Oxford 2001; *R. Ingham* (Hrsg.), Football Hooliganism: The Wider Context (Fußballrowdytum im weiteren Kontext), London 1978; *E. Dunning*, Towards a Sociological Understanding of Football Hooliganism as a World Phenomenon (Soziologisches Verständnis vom Fußballrowdytum als Weltphänomen), „European Journal on Criminal Policy and Research“, 2000, Band 8, Nr. 2; *K. van Limbergen/C. Colaers/L. Walgrave*, The Societal and Psycho-Sociological Background of Football Hooliganism (Psychosoziologischer Hintergrund vom Fußballrowdytum), Current Psychology, Spring 1989.

II. Stadionverbote in Polen

Angelehnt an die Praxis in anderen Ländern, funktionieren Stadionverbote – in der oben beschriebenen unterschiedlichen Form – auch in Polen[3]. Im weiteren Verlauf dieses Beitrags wird insbesondere auf die im Strafrecht vorgesehenen Stadionverbote eingegangen, also solche, die im Zusammenhang mit der Verantwortlichkeit für das Begehen einer unter Strafandrohung verbotenen Tat vollstreckt werden[4].

Neben den anderen Formen von Stadionverboten gebührt der sog. Sportvereinssperre Aufmerksamkeit, die durch die Veranstalter von Fußballspielen verhängt werden, sowie den Verboten, die im Wege des Verwaltungsakts durch Verwaltungsbehörden ausgesprochen werden. Die Rechtsgrundlage für diese Verbote bilden insbesondere die Vorschriften des Gesetzes vom 20. März 2009 über die Sicherheit von Massenveranstaltungen[5].

Das Gesetz findet – mit wenigen Ausnahmen[6] – nur auf solche Veranstaltungen Anwendung, die den Charakter einer Massenveranstaltung haben und betrifft somit auch Sportveranstaltungen[7]. Das Gesetz regelt Verhaltensgrundsätze, deren Einhaltung für die Gewährleistung der Sicherheit von Massenveran-

---

3 In diesem Beitrag wurden nur aktuell in Polen geltende Rechtsregelungen berücksichtigt. Zu früheren Regelungen zu Stadionverboten vgl. z.B. *G. Gozdór*, op. cit.; *A. Janisławski/B. Kwiatkowski*, Analiza krytyczna ustawy z dnia 20 marca 2009 r. o bezpieczeństwie imprez masowych (Kritische Analyse des Gesetzes vom 20. März 2009 über die Sicherheit von Massenveranstaltungen), „Czasopismo Prawa Karnego i Nauk Penalnych", 2010, Nr. 1, S. 59-85; *R. A. Stefański*, Środek karny zakazu wstępu na imprezy masowe w świetle projektu noweli do kodeksu karnego (Die Strafmaßnahme des Zutrittsverbots zu Massenveranstaltungen im Lichte des Änderungsentwurfs zum Strafgesetzbuch), „Wojskowy Przegląd Prawniczy", 2007, Nr. 3, S. 48-59; *ders.*, Środek karny zakazu wstępu na imprezę masową (Die Strafmaßnahme des Zutrittsverbots zu Massenveranstaltungen), „Prokuratura i Prawo", 2010, Nr. 1-2, S. 271-288; *W. Wróbel*, in: *M. Melezini*, op. cit., S. 558; *P. Suski*, Zgromadzenia i imprezy masowe (Versammlungen und Massenveranstaltungen), Warszawa 2010, S. 291-293; *W. Zalewski*, in: *M. Królikowski*, *R. Zawłocki* (Hrsg.), Kodeks karny. Część ogólna. Band II. Komentarz do artykułów 32-116 (Strafgesetzbuch, Allgemeiner Teil, Kommentierung der Art. 32-116), Warszawa 2010, S. 120-121.

4 Zu Stadionverboten in anderen Ländern vgl. z.B. *G. Gozdór*, op. cit., S. 257; *M. Tarnawski/A. Tarnawski*, Bezpieczeństwo imprez masowych – uwagi na tle ustawy z 22.8.1997 r. (Die Sicherheit von Massenveranstaltungen – Bemerkungen zum Gesetz vom 22.08.1997), „Ruch Prawniczy, Ekonomiczny i Socjologiczny", 1998, Nr. 3-4, S. 98-99; *W. Zalewski*, in: *M. Królikowski*, *R. Zawłocki* (Hrsg.), op. cit., S. 121-122.

5 Dz. U. 2009, Nr. 62, Pos. 504. Dies wurde früher durch das Gesetz vom 22. August 1997 über die Sicherheit von Massenveranstaltung geregelt (Dz. U. 2005, Nr. 108, Pos. 909 mit späteren Änderungen).

6 Art. 2 des Gesetzes.

7 Die Begriffe „Massenveranstaltung" und „Sportmassenveranstaltung" sowie andere im Gesetz verwendete Begriffe sind in Art. 3 des Gesetzes definiert.

staltungen notwendig sind, die Anforderungen an die Sicherheit solcher Veranstaltungen, die Grundsätze und das Verfahren der Vergabe von Genehmigungen für die Durchführung solcher Veranstaltungen, die Grundsätze der Speicherung und Verarbeitung von Informationen bezüglich der Sicherheit von Massenveranstaltungen und die Grundsätze der Verantwortlichkeit der Veranstalter für Schäden, die infolge der Organisation von Massenveranstaltungen entstanden sind. Das Gesetz beinhaltet auch Strafvorschriften, die eine strafrechtliche Verantwortlichkeit für (als Straftaten oder Übertretungen aufgefasste) Taten vorsehen, die die Sicherheit von Massenveranstaltungen beeinträchtigen oder gefährden.

Zu den im Zusammenhang mit Stadionverboten im Gesetz geregelten Rechtsinstrumenten zur Gewährleistung der Sicherheit bei Massenveranstaltungen zählen u.a.:

1) Die Anwendung des Stadionverbots in Form einer sog. Sportvereinssperre, die durch einen Fußballspielveranstalter verhängt wird[8]. Es besteht im Teilnahmeverbot an Massenveranstaltungen, die durch den Fußballspielveranstalter durchgeführt werden. Das Verbot wird gegen Personen verhängt, die die für das Objekt oder Gelände vorgesehene Ordnung oder die Ordnung einer Massenveranstaltung missachtet haben. Das Verbot kann für die Dauer von bis zu zwei Jahren verhängt werden;
2) das Verkaufsverbot von Eintrittskarten oder anderen Dokumenten, die zur Teilnahme am Fußballspiel oder einer Massenveranstaltung berechtigen, an eine Person, gegen die eine Entscheidung ergangen ist, die ihr den Zutritt zur Massenveranstaltung verbietet oder sie zum Fernbleiben von Orten verpflichtet, an denen Massenveranstaltungen durchgeführt werden. Dies betrifft auch eine Person, gegen die eine Sportvereinssperre oder ein ausländisches Verbot (d.h. ein durch berechtigte Subjekte anderer Staaten auferlegtes und dem Hauptkommandanten der Polizei bekanntes Stadionverbot) verhängt wurde[9];
3) die Zutritts- und Aufenthaltsverweigerung für eine Massenveranstaltung für die im Gesetz erwähnten Personen, insbesondere wenn gegen sie eine Sportvereinssperre oder ein ausländisches Verbot verhängt wurde[10];
4) die Zulässigkeit des Eintritts zum Fußballspiel für minderjährige Personen unter 13 Jahren nur in Begleitung einer volljährigen Person[11];
5) das Verbot der Organisation einer Massenveranstaltung ohne Genehmigung[12]. Das Gesetz bestimmt zur Erteilung einer solchen Genehmigung zu-

8 Art. 14 des Gesetzes.

9 Art. 15 i.V.m. Art. 3 Punkt 17 des Gesetzes.

10 Art. 10 des Gesetzes.

11 Art. 16 des Gesetzes.

12 Das Organisieren einer Massenveranstaltung ohne erforderliche Genehmigung oder Nichterfolgung der in der Genehmigung genannten Voraussetzungen oder Durchführung einer solchen Veranstaltung gegen ein erlassenes Verbot ist nach Art. 58 Abs. 1 des Gesetzes eine Straftat, die mit Geldstrafe nicht unter 240 Tagessätzen, mit der Strafe

ständige Verwaltungsorgane[13], das Verfahren zur Beantragung einer solchen Genehmigung, die Voraussetzungen für die Genehmigungserteilung und Grundsätze ihres Erlasses bzw. ihrer Verweigerung[14]. Bestimmt sind des Weiteren Regeln zur Unterbrechung einer Massenveranstaltung[15] und zur Untersagung einer Massenveranstaltung trotz einer früheren Genehmigung[16]. Alle genannten Entscheidungen haben Verwaltungsaktcharakter[17];

6) ein durch den *Woiwoden* im Wege des Verwaltungsakts erteiltes Verbot der Durchführung einer Massenveranstaltung mit Beteiligung von Zuschauern sowie ein zeitlich (un-)bestimmtes Verbot der Durchführung von Massenveranstaltungen in einer Woiwodschaft oder einem Teil der Woiwodschaft[18].

Im weiteren Verlauf des Beitrags wird lediglich auf die im Strafrecht vorgesehenen Stadionverbote (also solche, die in Zusammenhang mit der Verantwortlichkeit für das Begehen einer unter Strafandrohung verbotenen Tat vollstreckt werden) eingegangen[19].

Im polnischen Strafrecht kann das Stadionverbot sowohl bei unter Strafandrohung verbotenen Handlungen, die Straftaten sind, als auch bei Taten, die Übertretungen sind, verhängt werden. Bei Straftaten kann ein solches Verbot in manchen Fällen auf der Grundlage von bestimmten im StGB[20] vorgesehenen Vorschriften, in anderen Fällen auf der Grundlage des Gesetzes über die Sicherheit von Massenveranstaltungen verhängt werden. Im StGB ist die Verhängung des Stadionverbots entweder als Straf- oder Bewährungsmaßnahme (bei einer zur Bewährung ausgesetzten Strafe) oder als eine Maßregel der Sicherung vorgesehen. Bei Taten, die Übertretungen sind, kann das Stadionverbot – unter Berücksichtigung des Übertretungsgesetzes[21] – auf Grundlage des Gesetzes über die Sicherheit von Massenveranstaltungen für die dort bezeichneten Übertretun-

---

der Freiheitsbeschränkung oder mit Freiheitsstrafe von sechs Monaten bis zu acht Jahren bedroht ist.

13 Art. 24 Abs. 1 i.V.m. Art. 3 Punkt 18 des Gesetzes.

14 Art. 25-30 des Gesetzes.

15 Art. 31 Abs. 4 des Gesetzes.

16 Art. 32 des Gesetzes.

17 Art. 29 Abs. 5 des Gesetzes.

18 Art. 34 des Gesetzes.

19 Unberücksichtigt bleiben in diesem Beitrag Probleme mit Stadionverboten, die andere Rechtsgebiete betreffen, wie z.B. das Verwaltungsrecht, das Verwaltungsverfahrensrecht oder das Zivilrecht; vgl. dazu *J. Fritzweiler/B. Pfister/Th. Summerer*, Praxishandbuch Sportrecht, München 1998, S. 268; *B. Pfister/U. Steiner*, Sportrecht von A-Z. Vereine und Verbände, Sportanlagen, Arbeitsrecht und Besteuerung, Unfallhaftung, Sponsoring, Gerichtsbarkeit, München 1995.

20 Gesetz vom 06. Juni 1997 – Strafgesetzbuch (Dz. U. 1997, Nr. 88, Pos. 553 mit späteren Änderungen).

21 Gesetz vom 20. Mai 1971 – Übertretungsgesetz (Dz. U.1971, Nr. 12, Pos. 114 mit späteren Änderungen).

gen verhängt werden. Bei Minderjährigen, die aufgrund ihres Alters nicht zur strafrechtlichen Verantwortlichkeit gezogen werden können, kann das Stadionverbot auf Grundlage des Gesetzes vom 26. Oktober 1982 über das Verfahren in Minderjährigensachen[22] verhängt werden.

Aufgrund der notwendigen Einschränkungen dieses Beitrags werden die oben genannten Möglichkeiten der Verhängung von Stadionverboten in Umrissen, jedoch ohne eine detailliertere Vertiefung dargestellt.

III. Stadionverbot als Maßnahme bei Straftaten

1. Stadionverbot als Maßnahme im StGB

a) Stadionverbot als Strafmaßnahme

Als „Strafmaßnahme" werden im StGB Maßnahmen bezeichnet, die früher im polnischen Strafrecht und im Strafrecht anderer Länder als Nebenstrafe bezeichnet wurden. Aus den Strafmaßnahmen in Art. 39 StGB kann das Stadionverbot als eine von zwei folgenden Strafmaßnahmen verhängt werden:

1) Die Pflicht zum Fernbleiben von bestimmten Milieus oder Orten, das Verbot der Kontaktaufnahme mit bestimmten Personen, das Verbot der Annäherung an bestimmte Personen oder das Verbot des Verlassens eines bestimmten Aufenthaltsortes ohne gerichtliche Zustimmung (Art. 39 Punkt 2b sowie Art. 41a § 1 StGB);
2) das Verbot des Zutritts zu Massenveranstaltungen (Art. 39 Punkt 2c sowie Art. 41b StGB).

Die erste dieser Maßnahmen ist so allgemein gefasst, dass im Rahmen der „Pflicht zum Fernbleiben von bestimmten Milieus oder Orten" auch das Verbot des Aufenthalts auf dem Gelände eines Sportobjekts während einer Sportveranstaltung verhängt werden kann. Die Möglichkeit einer fakultativen Verhängung dieser Maßnahme ist nämlich u.a. bei der „Verurteilung aufgrund einer vorsätzlichen Gewalttat" (Art. 41a § 1 StGB) gegeben und das Stadionrowdytum kommt häufig in Form solcher Taten vor[23]. Die zweite der Maßnahmen ist – wie ihr Name schon verdeutlicht – ein Stadionverbot und betrifft Massenveranstaltungen nicht nur sportlicher Natur. Ihre fakultative oder (wenn gesetzlich vorgeschrieben) obligatorische Anwendung ist breiter als die Maßnahme nach Art. 39 Punkt 2b und Art. 41a § 1 StGB, nämlich jeweils dann, „wenn das Verhalten des Täters beim Begehen von Straftaten darauf deutet, dass seine Teilnahme an Massenveranstaltungen wesentliche geschützte Rechtsgüter gefährdet" (Art. 41b § 1 StGB).

---

22 Dz. U. 1982, Nr. 35, Pos. 228 mit späteren Änderungen.

23 Dazu *W. Zalewski*, in: *M. Królikowski*, *R. Zawłocki* (Hrsg.), op. cit., S. 117.

Soll das Verbot in Form der ersten Maßnahme ergehen, kann es mit Meldepflichten bei der Polizei oder einem anderen angewiesenen Organ in bestimmten Zeitabständen verbunden werden (Art. 41a § 1 StGB). Dagegen ist die zweite Maßnahme stets mit der Pflicht zum persönlichen Erscheinen während der Dauer der Massenveranstaltung bei der Polizei oder an einem anderen Ort verbunden, der von dem für den Aufenthaltsort des Verurteilten örtlich zuständigen Bezirkskommandanten der Polizei bestimmt wird. Das Verbot, das in Form der ersten Maßnahme ergeht, kann auch ein Fußballspiel der polnischen Nationalmannschaft und eines polnischen Sportvereins außerhalb der Grenzen der Republik Polen betreffen (Art. 41b § 4 StGB).

Bei beiden Maßnahmen wird das Verbot in Jahren verhängt. Bei der ersten Maßnahme von einem bis zu 15 Jahren, bei der zweiten Maßnahme von zwei bis zu sechs Jahren (Art. 43 § 1 StGB). Bei beiden Maßnahmen kann das Verbot auch neben einer Strafe bzw. auch ohne ihre Verhängung (dies ist möglich in Fällen des Absehens von der Strafe nach Art. 59 § 1, Art. 61 § 1 und 2 sowie nach Art. 60 § 7 StGB oder in Fällen der Verurteilung ohne ein Strafverfahren nach Art. 343 der Strafprozessordnung[24]) ergehen.

b) Das Stadionverbot als Bewährungsmaßnahme bei einer zur Bewährung ausgesetzten Strafvollstreckung

Im Falle einer zur Bewährung ausgesetzten Vollstreckung von Freiheitsstrafen bis zu zwei Jahren, Strafen der Freiheitsbeschränkung und Geldstrafen (Art. 69-76 StGB), kann das Stadionverbot in einer der zwei möglichen Formen verhängt werden:

1) Das Stadionverbot wird neben einer zur Bewährung ausgesetzten Strafvollstreckung als Strafmaßnahme (in einer der zwei unter Punkt III. 1. des Beitrages beschriebenen Formen) verhängt;
2) ein Gericht, das die zur Bewährung ausgesetzte Strafvollstreckung verhängt, kann als Verpflichtung oder Verbot (aus Art. 72 StGB) dem Verurteilten die Teilnahme an Sportveranstaltungen verbieten. Dies ermöglicht die Verpflichtung „zu einem anderen Verhalten während der Probezeit, soweit es einer erneuten Straftatbegehung vorbeugen kann“ (vorgesehen in Art. 72 § 1 Punkt 8 StGB).

Im ersten der beiden o.g. Fälle ist das Stadionverbot in Wirklichkeit keine Bewährungsmaßnahme, sondern eine Strafmaßnahme, die neben der Strafe verhängt wird, obwohl die Strafe (bei einer erfolgreichen Probezeit) nicht vollstreckt wird, weil sie zur Bewährung ausgesetzt wurde. Das Stadionverbot ist erst im zweiten Fall eine Bewährungsmaßnahme. Dennoch kann das Missachten des verhängten Verbots in beiden Fällen die Grundlage für die fakultative An-

24 Das Gesetz vom 06. Juni 1997 – Die Strafprozessordnung (Dz. U. 1997, Nr. 88, Pos. 555 mit späteren Änderungen).

ordnung der Vollstreckung der zur Bewährung ausgesetzten Strafe sein (Art. 75 § 2 StGB).

c) Das Stadionverbot als Maßnahme der Sicherung

Begeht der Täter eine unter Strafandrohung verbotene Tat in einem Zustand der Schuldunfähigkeit (Art. 31 § 1 StGB), begeht er keine Straftat und kann deswegen nicht bestraft werden. Das StGB sieht aber bei solchen Personen die Möglichkeit der Anwendung von Maßnahmen der Sicherung vor. Als Maßnahmen der Sicherung können auch solche Maßnahmen angewandt werden, die bei Tätern, die zur strafrechtlichen Verantwortlichkeit gezogen werden können, als Strafmaßnahmen verhängt werden (Art. 99 StGB). Dies betrifft u.a. auch solche Maßnahmen, die das Stadionverbot betreffen (wovon bereits unter III. 1. a) berichtet wurde). Abgesehen vom Zustand der Schuldunfähigkeit setzt ihre Anwendung als Maßnahme der Sicherung die Feststellung voraus, dass dies „zum Schutz der Rechtsordnung“ notwendig ist.

Im Gegensatz zu Fällen, in denen diese Maßnahmen als Strafmaßnahmen verhängt werden, ist ihre Anordnung als Maßnahme der Sicherung unbefristet. Das Gericht hebt das Verbot auf, wenn die Voraussetzungen seiner Verhängung weggefallen sind (Art. 99 § 2 StGB).

2. Das Stadionverbot als Maßnahme im Gesetz über die Sicherheit von Massenveranstaltungen

Als Grundlage für die Verhängung des Stadionverbots bei Straftätern kann auch das Gesetz über die Sicherheit von Massenveranstaltungen (Art. 66-68 des Gesetzes) herangezogen werden. Im Vergleich mit den oben geschilderten Voraussetzungen für die Verhängung eines solchen Verbots nach dem StGB, ist die Anordnung des Stadionverbots bei Straftätern auf Grundlage des Gesetzes über die Sicherheit von Massenveranstaltungen ein wenig anders geregelt.

Vor allem ist diese Maßnahme nach dem kommentierten Gesetz nur bei bestimmten, im Gesetz erfassten Straftaten (Art. 66 des Gesetzes) vorgesehen. Dazu zählen folgende Straftaten:

1) Das Hineinbringen oder der Besitz von Waffen, pyrotechnischen Erzeugnissen, brandgefährlichen Materialien oder anderen gefährlichen Gegenständen oder Sprengstoffen (Art. 59 Abs. 1 des Gesetzes; für diese Straftat wurde eine Geldstrafe nicht unter 180 Tagessätzen, eine Strafe der Freiheitsbeschränkung oder Freiheitsstrafe von drei Monaten bis zu fünf Jahren vorgesehen);
2) das Eindringen während einer Massenveranstaltung, darunter eines Fußballspiels, auf das Gelände, wo die Sportveranstaltung stattfindet, oder das Nichtverlassen eines solchen Ortes trotz der Aufforderung einer berechtigten Person (Art. 60 Abs. 1 des Gesetzes; für diese Straftat wurde eine Geldstrafe nicht unter 180 Tagessätzen, eine Strafe der Freiheitsbeschränkung oder Freiheitsstrafe von bis zu drei Jahren vorgesehen);

3) das Werfen von Gegenständen, die Leben, Gesundheit oder Sicherheit von Personen gefährden könnten, die sich auf dem Gelände oder im Objekt, wo die Massenveranstaltung stattfindet, aufhalten oder eine Beeinträchtigung einer solchen Veranstaltung in einer anderen, genauso gefährlichen Weise (Art. 60 Abs. 2 des Gesetzes; für diese Straftat wurde eine Geldstrafe nicht unter 120 Tagessätzen, eine Strafe der Freiheitsbeschränkung oder Freiheitsstrafe von bis zu zwei Jahren vorgesehen);
4) die Beeinträchtigung der körperlichen Unversehrtheit eines Mitglieds des Ordnungs- oder Informationsdienstes (Art. 60 Abs. 3 des Gesetzes; für diese Straftat wurde eine Geldstrafe nicht unter 120 Tagessätzen, eine Strafe der Freiheitsbeschränkung oder Freiheitsstrafe von bis zu zwei Jahren vorgesehen);

Das gesetzliche Strafmaß für die in den Punkten 2)-4) beschriebenen Straftaten wird verschärft, wenn:

1) Der Täter bei solchen Taten ein Bekleidungselement oder einen Gegenstand zur Verdeckung des Gesichts zwecks Erschwerung seiner Wiedererkennung verwendet (Art. 60 Abs. 4 des Gesetzes; für diese Straftaten wurde eine Geldstrafe nicht unter 240 Tagessätzen, eine Strafe der Freiheitsbeschränkung oder Freiheitsstrafe von drei Monaten bis zu fünf Jahren vorgesehen);
2) ein bereits für solche Taten bestrafter Täter innerhalb von zwei Jahren seit der letzten Bestrafung oder Verurteilung eine ähnliche vorsätzliche Übertretung oder Straftat begeht (Art. 62 des Gesetzes; in einem solchen Fall kann das Gericht eine Strafe bis zu der um die Hälfte erhöhten gesetzlich angedrohten Höchststrafe verhängen).

Die Verhängung der kommentierten Maßnahme auf der Grundlage des Gesetzes über die Sicherheit von Massenveranstaltungen ist auch für die oben beschriebenen Straftaten vorgesehen, wenn sie während eines Fußballspiels der polnischen Nationalmannschaft sowie einem polnischen Sportverein außerhalb der Grenzen der Republik Polen begangen werden.

In allen im Gesetz über die Sicherheit von Massenveranstaltungen vorgesehenen Fällen ist die Verhängung dieser Maßnahme obligatorisch (Art. 66 des Gesetzes).

Schließlich wurde diese Maßnahme, obwohl sie im Gesetz über die Sicherheit von Massenveranstaltungen wie im StGB als „Verbot des Eintritts zu einer Massenveranstaltung“ beschrieben ist, nicht als Strafmaßnahme bezeichnet (Art. 66 des Gesetzes). Trotzdem ist anerkannt, dass sie in solchen Fällen den Charakter einer Strafmaßnahme hat, weswegen auch in solchen Fällen das StGB entsprechende Anwendung findet. Dies bedeutet insbesondere, dass im Falle der Verhängung dieser Maßnahme auf der Grundlage des Gesetzes über die Sicherheit von Massenveranstaltungen:

1) Sie für die Zeit von zwei bis zu sechs Jahren verhängt wird (Art. 43 § 1 StGB);
2) die Maßnahme obligatorisch mit der Pflicht verbunden ist, persönlich während der Massenveranstaltungsdauer bei der Polizei oder an einem anderen Ort zu erscheinen, der von dem für den Aufenthaltsort des Verurteilten örtlich zuständigen Bezirks-, Kreis- oder Stadtkommandanten der Polizei bestimmt wird (Art. 41b § 4 StGB);
3) das Verbot neben einer Strafe bzw. ohne ihre gleichzeitige Vollstreckung verhängt wird, was – wie bereits erwähnt – entweder im Falle der Aussetzung der Verhängung der Strafe (nach Art. 59 § 1, Art. 61 § 1 und 2 sowie in Art. 60 § 7 StGB) oder der Verurteilung ohne Durchführung eines Hauptverfahrens (nach Art. 343 der Strafprozessordnung) möglich ist.

IV. Das Stadionverbot als eine Maßnahme, die bei Übertretungen vorgesehen ist

Ähnlich wie das StGB sieht auch das Übertretungsgesetz die Verhängung von Strafmaßnahmen nach Art. 28 bei Übertretungen vor. Zu den unmittelbar erwähnten Maßnahmen zählt keine Maßnahme, in deren Form ein Stadionverbot verhängt werden könnte. Die Aufzählung ist jedoch nicht abschließend. Nach Art. 28 Punkt 5 des Übertretungsgesetzes zählen zu den für Übertretungen verhängten Maßnahmen auch „andere gesetzlich vorgesehene Strafmaßnahmen", also auch Strafmaßnahmen, die in einem anderen Gesetz als dem Übertretungsgesetz vorgesehen wurden.

Obwohl das Verhängen des Stadionverbots als Strafmaßnahme also nicht unmittelbar in das Übertretungsgesetz aufgenommen wurde, ist seine Verhängung auch bei Übertretungen möglich, denn sie wurde im Gesetz über die Sicherheit von Massenveranstaltungen vorgesehen (Art. 65 Abs. 2-4 des Gesetzes). Dieses Gesetz ordnet eine obligatorische Verhängung des Zutrittsverbots zu Massenveranstaltungen für die Dauer von zwei bis sechs Jahren an, wenn jemand für eine bestimmte, in Verbindung mit einer Massenveranstaltung (darunter auch einem Fußballspiel) begangene und im Übertretungsgesetz und dem Gesetz über die Sicherheit von Massenveranstaltungen genannte Übertretung bestraft wurde. Zu solchen Übertretungen aus dem Übertretungsgesetz zählen: das Nichtverlassen einer Ansammlung (Art. 50), die Störung der Ordnung (Art. 51), ein Aufruf zu einer Straftat, Gewalt oder die Billigung einer Straftat (Art. 52a), die Zerstörung fremder Sachen (Art. 124) und die Erschwerung der Nutzung von öffentlich genutzten Anlagen (Art. 143). Zu Übertretungen aus dem Gesetz über die Sicherheit von Massenveranstaltungen zählen: die Nichtbefolgung von Ordnungsanweisungen (Art. 54 Abs. 1), der Aufenthalt an Orten, die für die Zuschauer nicht vorgesehen sind (Art. 54 Abs. 2), die Nichtbefolgung von Anweisungen der Polizei oder der Militärpolizei (Art. 55) sowie das Hineinbringen oder der Besitz von alkoholischen Getränken während einer Massenveranstaltung (Art. 56).

Die genannte Maßnahme ist obligatorisch mit der Pflicht verbunden, persönlich während der Dauer der Massenveranstaltung bei der Polizei oder an einem anderen Ort, der vom für den Aufenthaltsort des Verurteilten örtlich zuständigen Bezirks-, Kreis- oder Stadtkommandanten der Polizei bestimmt wird, zu erscheinen (Art. 65 Abs. 3 des Gesetzes).

Sowohl im Falle der Verhängung von Stadionverboten bei Übertretungen nach dem Übertretungsgesetz als auch bei Übertretungen nach dem Gesetz über die Sicherheit von Massenveranstaltungen, erfolgt die Vollstreckung der Rechtsfolgen für solche Taten, z.B. auch die Verhängung von Stadionverboten, nach den im Übertretungsgesetz für die Übertretung vorgesehenen Regeln. Nach Art. 48 des Übertretungsgesetzes sind die Vorschriften des Allgemeinen Teils des Übertretungsgesetzes auch auf Übertretungen aus anderen Gesetzen anwendbar, soweit diese Gesetze keine abweichenden Vorschriften beinhalten.

V. Das Stadionverbot als Maßnahme bei Minderjährigen

Begeht ein Minderjähriger eine unter Strafandrohung verbotene Tat, kann er aufgrund des Alters nicht zur strafrechtlichen Verantwortlichkeit gezogen werden. Die in Polen geltende Altersgrenze im Zeitpunkt der Tatbegehung beträgt 17 Jahre (Art. 10 § 1 StGB). In bestimmten Fällen kann auch ein Täter zur strafrechtlichen Verantwortlichkeit gezogen werden, der im Zeitpunkt der Tatbegehung das 15. Lebensjahr vollendet hat[25]. Bei einem Minderjährigen, der nicht zur strafrechtlichen Verantwortlichkeit gezogen werden kann, ist also die Verhängung eines Stadionverbots in den oben genannten Formen nicht möglich.

Ein Minderjähriger, der nicht zur strafrechtlichen Verantwortlichkeit gezogen werden kann, unterliegt jedoch der besonderen Verantwortlichkeit für Jugendliche, die in Polen im Gesetz über das Verfahren in Minderjährigensachen geregelt ist. Dieses Gesetz sieht bei Minderjährigen die Anwendung von Maßnahmen der Erziehung oder Besserung in Form ihrer Unterbringung in einer Besserungsanstalt vor (Art. 5 und 6 des Gesetzes). Unter den Erziehungsmaßnahmen ist das Stadionverbot nicht *expressis verbis* aufgezählt. Ein solches Verbot kann aber als Erziehungsmaßnahme nach Art. 6 Punkt 2 des Gesetzes – „die Verpflichtung zu einem bestimmten Verhalten insbesondere (...) zum Fernbleiben von bestimmten Milieus oder Orten (...)"– verhängt werden[26].

---

25 Die Fälle sind in Art. 10 § 2 StGB und in Art. 13 und 94 des Gesetzes über Verfahren in Minderjährigensachen bestimmt.

26 Dazu ausführlich *P. Górecki/St. Stachowiak*, Ustawa o postępowaniu w sprawach nieletnich. Komentarz (Das Gesetz über Verfahren in Minderjährigensachen, Kommentar), 4. Aufl., Warszawa 2007, S. 36 f.

VI. Die Nichtbefolgung eines durch ein Gericht verhängten Stadionverbots

Die Wirksamkeit eines durch ein Gericht verhängten Stadionverbots ist durch zwei Rechtsinstrumente gewährleistet. Das erste Instrument ist im Gesetz über die Sicherheit von Massenveranstaltungen enthalten. Es hat die Form eines Verkaufsverbots von Eintrittskarten oder anderen Dokumenten, die zum Aufenthalt bei Fußballspielen oder anderen Massenveranstaltungen berechtigen, und es betrifft Personen, gegen die ein Verbot des Zutritts zu Massenveranstaltungen und ein Aufenthaltsverbot für Orte, an denen Massenveranstaltungen durchgeführt werden, erteilt wurde. Das zweite Instrument ist die im StGB vorgesehene strafrechtliche Verantwortlichkeit für die Nichtbefolgung eines solchen Verbots. Die Missachtung eines Stadionverbots, das durch ein Gericht verhängt wurde, ist in Polen eine Straftat nach Art. 244 oder eventuell 244a StGB.

Nach Art. 244 StGB droht einer Person, die ein nach Art. 39 Punkt 2b und Art. 41a § 1 StGB („Verpflichtung zum Fernbleiben von bestimmten Milieus oder Orten") verhängtes Stadionverbot missachtet hat, eine Freiheitsstrafe von bis zu drei Jahren.

Nach Art. 244a StGB droht einer Person, die ein nach Art. 39 Punkt 2c und 41b StGB verhängtes Stadionverbot (verhängt als Zutrittsverbot zu Massenveranstaltungen) nicht befolgt, eine Geldstrafe, eine Strafe der Freiheitsbeschränkung oder eine Freiheitsstrafe von bis zu zwei Jahren. Eine strafrechtliche Verantwortlichkeit aus dieser Vorschrift droht nicht nur bei Missachtung des Stadionverbots, sondern auch bei der Nichtbefolgung der Pflicht, persönlich während der Massenveranstaltungsdauer bei der Polizei oder an einem anderen Ort, der vom für den Aufenthaltsort des Verurteilten örtlich zuständigen Bezirks-, Kreis- oder Stadtkommandanten der Polizei bestimmt wird, zu erscheinen (Art. 65 Abs. 3 des Gesetzes).

Auf Grundlage der genannten Vorschriften sind die dort bestimmten Verhaltensweisen nicht nur dann strafbar, wenn das Stadionverbot nach Art. 39 Punkt 2b und Art. 41a StGB als Strafmaßnahme neben einer vollstreckbaren Strafe verhängt wurde, sondern auch dann, wenn die verhängte Strafe zur Bewährung ausgesetzt wurde und wenn nach Art. 72 § 1 Punkt 8 StGB das Stadionverbot als Bewährungsmaßnahme („Verpflichtung zu einem anderen angebrachten Verhalten während der Probezeit") verhängt wurde.

Bei Nichtbefolgung des Stadionverbots können auch folgende Personen zur strafrechtlichen Verantwortlichkeit nach Art. 244 oder 244a StGB gezogen werden:

1) Eine Person, bei der ein solches Verbot nach Art. 6 Punkt 2 des Gesetzes über das Verfahren in Minderjährigensachen als Erziehungsmaßnahme in Form der „Verpflichtung zu einem bestimmten Verhalten insbesondere (...) zum Fernbleiben von bestimmten Milieus oder Orten (...)" für die Tat, auf-

grund derer die Person aus Altersgründen nicht zur strafrechtlichen Verantwortlichkeit gezogen wurde, verhängt wurde;

2) eine Person, bei der ein solches Verbot durch ein Gericht nach Art. 99 StGB als Maßnahme der Sicherung für eine im Zustand der Schuldunfähigkeit begangene Tat verhängt wurde.

Beide oben genannte Personenkategorien werden für die Missachtung des Stadionverbots nur dann zur strafrechtlichen Verantwortlichkeit herangezogen, wenn die Nichtbefolgung des Verbots zu einem Zeitpunkt geschah, zu dem ihre altersmäßige oder schuldfähigkeitsbedingte strafrechtliche Verantwortlichkeit zulässig war.

Das tschechische Strafrecht am Wendepunkt des Jahrtausends

*Prof. Dr. Vladimír Kratochvíl**

I. Einführung

Mit der Person von *Prof. Dr. Dres. h.c. Friedrich-Christian Schroeder* verbinden sich nicht nur meine fachlichen und professionellen, sondern auch viele persönliche Erinnerungen. Gleich nach der „Samtenen Revolution" im November 1989 (besser gesagt seit Beginn der 1990er Jahre) kam er als einer der Ersten mit einer kleinen Gruppe Studenten der Universität Regensburg an die Juristische Fakultät in Brünn, die damals schon wieder den Namen *Masarykova* Universität trug, und reagierte damit auf unseren ersten Kontakt im Jahre 1988 im polnischen Karpacz[1]. Die Besuche haben sich noch mehrmals wiederholt[2] und wurden gerne erwidert, z.B. als ich Gast des Jubilars in den Jahren 1992 und 2001 in Regensburg war.

Ich muss zugeben, dass diese persönlichen und vor allem fachbezogenen Kontakte zu *Prof. Dr. Dres. h.c. Schroeder* für mich zweifelsfrei eine große Bereicherung darstellen. Den folgenden Beitrag verstehe ich deshalb als einen symbolischen Dank für unsere fruchtbare Zusammenarbeit sowie Erfahrungsaustausch.

II. Überblick über die Reformen des tschechischen Strafrechts in den 1990er Jahren des XX. Jahrhunderts[3]

Die Anfänge dieser Periode habe ich schon in meinen früheren Publikationen beschrieben[4]. Zu diesem Zeitpunkt waren das Suchen nach und die Bestimmung

---

* Inhaber des Lehrstuhls für Strafrecht an der Universität Brünn.

1 Damals fand das internationale Symposium der Universität Wroclaw statt, 23.05.1988. Bei dieser Gelegenheit hat mir der Jubilar seine Publikation: *Schroeder*, Das Strafrecht des realen Sozialismus. Eine Einführung am Beispiel der DDR. Opladen: Westdeutscher Verlag, 1983, überreicht.

2 Zuletzt war *Prof. Dr. Dres. h.c. F.-C. Schroeder* im Jahre 2004 in Brünn: Veranstaltung am Lehrstuhl für Strafrecht der Juristischen Fakultät der Masaryk-Universität zu Brünn am 19.11.2004, „Der aktuelle Stand und die Perspektiven der Entwicklung des Strafprozessrechts in Deutschland und in der Tschechischen Republik".

3 Eine erste Bearbeitung des tschechoslowakischen Strafrechts in deutscher Sprache stammt, soviel ich weiß, aus der Feder von *H. Weber*, Grundriss des tschechoslowakischen Strafrechts. Verlag der Gebrüder Stiepel Ges.m.b.H, Reichenberg 1929.

der Grundaspekte der Reform typisch. Zu solchen gehörten und gehören auch heute noch die Grundeigenschaften der Ausrichtung sowie die Phasen der Strafrechtsreform im Bereich des materiellen und prozessualen[5] Strafrechts.

Im Folgenden behandle ich konkrete Fragen und ausgewählte Probleme dieser Reform, unter besonderer Berücksichtigung des materiellen Strafrechts, das eines meiner Forschungsschwerpunkte ist.

Die verschiedenen Phasen der Reform haben inhaltliche (materielle), formelle und zeitliche Aspekte. Während der Reformarbeiten wurde von einer bestimmten Kombination der inhaltlichen (materiellen) Kontinuität und Diskontinuität der strafrechtlichen Entwicklung und der daran anknüpfenden strafrechtlichen Gesetzgebung ausgegangen.

D.h. Kontinuität überall dort, wo man an positive Momente der bisherigen strafrechtlichen Regelung sowie der strafrechtlichen Konzeptionen seit 1918 bis Ende der 1980er Jahre anknüpfen konnte und die inhaltliche Diskontinuität in all jenen Fällen, in denen die bisherige strafrechtliche Regelung oder die Reformprojekte wegen ausschließlicher Ideologisierung oder auch nur aus rein juristischen Gründen (vom legislativ-technischen Gesichtspunkt her gesehen) unbrauchbar wurden. Außer der erwähnten Entideologisierung hat die Reform die Ziele der Entkriminalisierung, Depönalisierung sowie Differenzierung der strafrechtlichen Verantwortlichkeit verfolgt. Die angeführten Grundsätze charakterisieren den bisherigen Verlauf der Reform und ihre inhaltlichen Aspekte. Sie werden zweifellos auch in der Zukunft maßgeblich sein.

Die Charakteristika der Reform beziehen sich nicht nur auf das materielle Strafrecht, man kann sie analog und adäquat auch auf das Strafprozessrecht beziehen. Für dieses Strafrechtsgebiet stehen die Vereinfachung und die Beschleunigung des Prozesses im Vordergrund[6].

---

4 *Kratochvíl*, Gegenwärtiger Zustand und Perspektiven der Strafrechtsreform in der ČSFR (ausgewählte Probleme). In *Hungr*, *Smaus* (Hrsg.), Normativität und Realität des Rechts. Intensiver Lehrgang im Rahmen von TEMPUS in Brno vom 15.–22.03.1992. Brno 1993, MU, AUBI, No 121, S. 44 ff. *Kratochvíl*, Aktuelle Entwicklungen im tschechischen Strafrecht. In: Strafrechtliche Probleme der Gegenwart. 28. Strafrechtliches Seminar 2000. Ottenstein. Wien: Bundesministerium für Justiz, 2000, S. 75 ff.; *Kratochvíl/Šámal*, Tschechisches Strafrecht am Wendepunkt des Jahrtausendes. In *Csaba*, *Csongor* (Hrsg.), Emlékkönyv. Vargha László Egyetemi Tanár. Születésének 90. Évfordulójára. Pécs: Studia Iuridica Auctoritate Universitatis Pécs Publicata, No 132, 2003, S. 213 – 226. Siehe auch *Kratochvíl* et al., Kurs trestního práva. Trestní právo hmotné. Obecná část (Kurs des Strafrechts. Materielles Strafrecht. Allgemeiner Teil), 1. Aufl., C. H. Beck, Prag 2009, S. 139–140.

5 *Růžička*, Aktuální stav rekodifikace trestního práva procesního v České republice. Státní zastupitelství (Der aktuelle Stand der Rekodifikation des Strafprozessrechts in der Tschechischen Republik) 2008, Jahrgang 6, Nr. 7–8, S. 6.

6 *Kratochvíl/Šámal*, Tschechisches Strafrecht am Wendepunkt des Jahrtausendes. In *Csaba*, *Csongor* (Hrsg.), Emlékkönyv. Vargha László Egyetemi Tanár. Születésének 90. Évfordulójára. Pécs: Studia Iuridica Auctoritate Universitatis Pécs Publicata

Demgegenüber steht die ausschließliche formelle Kontinuität, die den ununterbrochenen Prozess der Rechtsentwicklung und die Rechtssicherheit garantieren muss. Unter dem zeitlichen Aspekt der strafrechtlichen Reform sind die Phasen ihres bisherigen und beabsichtigten Verlaufs zu verstehen.

Der ersten Phase lag und liegt noch immer die Notwendigkeit augenblicklicher Veränderungen in beiden Strafrechtsgebieten zugrunde, und zwar wegen der neuen, sich stets ändernden politischen, ökonomischen und sozialen Bedingungen. Die zweite Phase hingegen sollte den Bedarf an langfristigen, perspektivischen, auf die Schaffung eines demokratischen Rechtsstaates orientierten Änderungen berücksichtigen[7].

Vom legislativen und in diesem Sinne auch formellen Gesichtspunkt entsprechen der ersten Phase zahlreiche Novellen strafrechtlicher Vorschriften. Für die zweite Phase sind Neufassungen des materiellen und prozessualen Strafrechts typisch. Für diese Reformentwicklung ist signifikant, dass beide Phasen grundsätzlich parallel verlaufen. Das ist sehr anspruchsvoll, nicht nur gesetzgebungstechnisch, sondern auch für die im Strafverfahren tätigen Organe. Abgesehen davon wird dadurch ebenso die Lehre des Strafrechts an den Universitäten relativ kompliziert[8].

In diesem Umfeld und unter diesen Bedingungen ist die tschechoslowakische und später tschechische Strafrechtsreform verlaufen. Seit Ende der 1990er Jahre arbeitet die derzeitige Rekodifizierungskommission des Justizministeriums durchgehend an den Projekten der beiden Gesetzbücher (StGB und StPO). Ein Produkt der Reformbemühung wurde bislang leider nur das neue StGB, keinesfalls jedoch die StPO, die sich weiterhin erst im Vorbereitungsstadium des Gesetzgebungsprozesses befindet[9].

Was die konkreten Fragen bzw. ausgewählten Schlüsselprobleme dieser Reform betrifft, waren für die Ausgangspunkte der Reform z.B. das Wissen über die Kriminalität, die Erkenntnisse über die Effektivität oder Ineffektivität des bisherigen Strafrechts, eine neue tschechische Konzeption der Strafpolitik (Kriminalpolitik), die verfassungsrechtlichen Vorgaben der Reform u.a. sehr wichtig[10].

No 132, 2003, S. 213–214. Siehe auch *Schroeder*, Das Strafrecht des realen Sozialismus. Eine Einführung am Beispiel der DDR. Opladen, Westdeutscher Verlag, 1983, S. 53 ff.; *Gratzl*, Die Reform der tschechischen Strafprozessordnung nach 1989. Frankfurt a.M., Peter Lang Europäischer Verlag der Wissenschaften, Studien des Instituts für Ostrecht München, Band 41, 2002.

7 *Kratochvíl/Šámal*, a.a.O, S. 214.

8 *Kratochvíl/Šámal*, a.a.O, S. 214–215.

9 Die Slowakische Strafrechtsreform war insoweit erfolgreicher, als dass beide Gesetzbücher parallel verabschiedet werden konnten. Dazu StGB, Gesetz Nr. 300/2005 Z.z. und StPO, Gesetz Nr. 301/2005 Z.z.

10 Näher siehe *Kratochvíl*, Gegenwärtiger Zustand und Perspektiven der Strafrechtsreform in der ČSFR (ausgewählte Probleme). In *Hungr*, *Smaus* (Hrsg.), Normativität und

Unter besonderer Berücksichtigung des materiellen Strafrechts geht es unter anderem um die Auffassung der Straftat, der Strafe und um weitere Probleme, nicht nur des Allgemeinen Teils, sondern auch des Besonderen Teils des Strafgesetzbuchs.

Wie ein roter Faden zieht sich durch die Reform des materiellen Strafrechts die Frage, ob anstelle der bisherigen materiellen Auffassung der Straftat die formelle Auffassung der Straftat[11] zu Grunde gelegt werden soll oder ob die monistische Auffassung der Strafsanktionen der zweispurigen Auffassung vorzuziehen sei. Im Bereich des materiellen Strafrechts stand die Frage der neuen Systematik des StGB im Vordergrund[12].

Seit Ende der 1990er Jahre werden bei der Reform des materiellen Strafrechts insbesondere die nachfolgenden Ziele verfolgt:

- Einen umfassenden Schutz der Bürger- und Menschenrechte und Freiheiten sowie von weiteren durch die Verfassung und die Liste der Grundrechte und Freiheiten (LGF) garantierten Rechte zu gewährleisten,
- die strafrechtliche Verantwortlichkeit von natürlichen Personen zu differenzieren und zu individualisieren sowie die Rechtsfolgen dieser Verantwortlichkeit zu konkretisieren,
  - unter genau festgelegten Bedingungen die strafrechtliche Verantwortlichkeit von juristischen Personen zu verankern,
  - die gesamte Philosophie der Verhängung von Sanktionen zu ändern, insbesondere die Hierarchie der Sanktionen so zu verschieben, dass die Freiheitsstrafe als *ultima ratio* verstanden werden kann und zusätzlich dabei die individuellen Aspekte der Strafverhängung zu betonen, damit der Täter durch die Anwendung von alternativen Sanktionen zur Besserung motiviert wird,

Realität des Rechts. Intensiver Lehrgang im Rahmen von TEMPUS in Brno vom 15.-22.03.1992. Brno 1993, MU, AUBI, No 121, S. 46 ff. Weiter siehe z.B.: Trestní politika, kriminalita a kriminologie – zkušenosti a nové výzvy. Konference u příležitosti 50. výročí existence Institutu pro kriminologii a sociální prevenci (Strafpolitik, Kriminalpolitik und Kriminologie – Erfahrungen und neue Herausforderungen. Konferenz zur Gelegenheit des 50. Jahrestags der Existenz des Institutes für Kriminologie und der Sozialvorbeugung), Praha 16.–17.09.2010; http://www.kriminologie.cz.

11 Es geht um die Straftat nur als Grund der strafrechtlichen Verantwortlichkeit, also um die Frage der Schuld des Täters, keinesfalls um die Straftat als ein Kriterium der Ahndung von Strafen.

12 Das frühere Herangehen des Gesetzgebers (StGB Nr. 140/1961 Sb.) „kopiert" in dieser Richtung die sog. „biblische" Auffassung, wie z.B. die Systematik des Besonderen Teils des deutschen Strafgesetzbuchs. *De lege ferenda* setzte man voraus, wie z.B. in Österreich, dass der Strafschutz der individuellen Interessen dem Schutz von kollektiven Interessen vorhergehen muss. Das steht auch im Einklang mit der Auffassung der Liste der Grundrechte und Freiheiten (Nr. 2/1993 Sb.), weiter auch „LGF" genannt, die sich auf das naturrechtliche Konzept stützt.

- eine komplexe rechtliche Regelung des Jugendschutzes durch Verknüpfung des Jugendstrafrechts mit Normen aus anderen relevanten Bereichen der Rechtsordnung zu erreichen, und nicht zuletzt,
- ein vergleichbares Niveau mit modernen europäischen Standards des Strafrechts zu erzielen[13].

Im Einklang damit stehen auch die zu berücksichtigenden strafrechtlichen Grundsätze:

- Legalitätsprinzip des Strafrechts (*nullum crimen, nulla poena sine lege*, Art. 39 LGF),
- Subsidiaritätsprinzip des Strafrechts (Strafrecht als *ultima ratio*),
- Retroaktivitätsverbot (*nullum crimen, nulla poena sine lege praevia*, Art. 40 Abs. 6 LGF),
- individuelle strafrechtliche Verantwortlichkeit von natürlichen Personen, die eine kollektive Verantwortlichkeit ausschließt, die strafrechtliche Verantwortlichkeit von juristischen Personen unter den im StGB angeführten Bedingungen jedoch zulässt,
- Verschuldensprinzip (*nullum crimen sine culpa, „culpa"* hier i.S.d. Verschuldens),
- Angemessenheitsprinzip von Strafen, d.h. die Auferlegung, Vollstreckung und der Vollzug der Strafen berücksichtigt das Verhältnis zwischen der Schwere der Straftat und der Person (Persönlichkeit) des Täters[14].

Erwähnte Ziele und Grundsätze der strafrechtlichen Reform sind in ihrer Geltung selbstverständlich auch in der Zukunft zu berücksichtigen.

Bezüglich der Reform des formellen Strafrechts, also des Strafprozessrechts, spielt derzeit die große Novelle der StPO (Nr. 265/2001 Sb.; Sb. = Gesetzblatt der ČR) eine Schlüsselrolle. Diese große Novelle der StPO gab damals den Startschuss auch für die Rekodifizierung des Strafprozessrechts. Ein Problem ergab sich jedoch im Parlament, das im Mai 2000 die große Novelle der StPO verworfen hatte, weil z.B. die Einführung des kontradiktorischen Prozesses in der Hauptverhandlung zu umfangreich und grundsätzlich war[15]. Der überarbeitete Entwurf dieser Novelle ist dann im Parlament im Sommer 2001 ohne Probleme durchgegangen.

Als untrennbarer Bestandteil der tschechischen Strafrechtsreform ist auch das Jugendgerichtsgesetz (JGG) Nr. 218/2003 Sb. zu betrachten, das am 1. Januar 2004 in Kraft getreten ist. Diese Regelungen verkörpern teilweise einen

13 Siehe mehr *Kratochvíl/Šámal*, Tschechisches Strafrecht am Wendepunkt des Jahrtausends. In *Csaba, Csongor* (Hrsg.), Emlékkönyv. Vargha László Egyetemi Tanár. Születésének 90. Évfordulójára. Pécs: Studia Iuridica Auctoritate Universitatis, Pécs Publicata No 132, 2003, S. 217.

14 *Kratochvíl/Šámal*, a.a.O., S. 218.

15 *Kratochvíl/Šámal*, a.a.O., S. 215.

Rückgriff auf die Zwischenkriegsjahre, d.h. zum JGG Nr. 48/1931 Sb. Im neuen JGG geht es aber um die Anwendung moderner Philosophien[16] nicht nur auf dem Gebiet der Grundlagen der strafrechtlichen Verantwortlichkeit der Jugendlichen, sondern auch im Bereich der Strafsanktionen.

Die Frage der Strafbarkeit juristischer Personen wurde bis zur Gegenwart nicht gelöst. Im Jahre 2004 wurde ein selbstständiger Gesetzentwurf im Parlament abgelehnt, sogar bereits in der ersten Lesung. Seither ist dieses Thema politisch sehr brisant. Gegenwärtig wird insbesondere eine Alternative zur Lösung dieser Frage diskutiert, die sich an die deutsche Regelung anlehnt. Die setzt jedoch eine umfangreiche Reform der Verwaltungsregelungen in der Tschechischen Republik voraus, da eine solche Regelung *de lege lata* nicht zu erreichen ist.

Aufgrund der aktuellen politischen Entwicklung im Jahre 2010 ist jedoch nicht ausgeschlossen, dass die neue Regierung den abgelehnten Gesetzentwurf aus dem Jahre 2004 wieder aufgreift[17].

III. Das tschechische Strafrecht in der ersten Dekade des XXI. Jahrhunderts

Das materielle Strafrecht verkörpert in der Phase der Novellen einen Prozess der „Europäisierung".

Offenkundig hängt dies mit der Mitgliedschaft der Tschechischen Republik in der Europäischen Union (seit 01.05.2004) zusammen. Große Bedeutung hat in diesem Zusammenhang das Änderungsgesetz des StGB Nr. 537/2004 Sb. Es regelt die Möglichkeit der Übergabe eines Bürgers der Tschechischen Republik an einen anderen Mitgliedsstaat der EU, allerdings ausschließlich aufgrund des europäischen Haftbefehls.

Für die geplante Neufassung des materiellen Strafrechts ist der bereits in Paragraphen gefasste Entwurf des neuen StGB aus dem Jahre 2004 und zugleich der vorgelegte Entwurf des Gesetzes über die strafrechtliche Verantwortlichkeit von juristischen Personen typisch[18].

---

16 *Válková*, Základy trestní odpovědnosti ... mladistvých (Die Grundlagen der strafrechtlichen Verantwortlichkeit ... von Jugendlichen). Právní následky provinění mladistvých ... (Die Rechtsfolgen der Verstöße von Jugendlichen), in *Kratochvíl* et al., Kurs trestního práva. Trestní právo hmotné. Obecná část (Kurs des Strafrechts. Materielles Strafrecht. Allgemeiner Teil), 1. Aufl., C. H. Beck, Prag 2009, S. 414 ff., 565 ff.

17 Siehe: http://www.vlada.cz/cz/media-centrum/dulezite-dokumenty/koalicni-smlouva-74245/, 28.09.2010.

18 Zu dieser spezifischen Frage siehe näher z.B. *Šámal*, Die strafrechtliche Verantwortlichkeit von juristischen Personen de lege lata und de lege ferenda in der Tschechischen Republik. In *Kratochvíl*, *Löff* (Hrsg.), Wirtschaftsstrafrecht und die Strafbarkeit juristischer Personen, Masaryks Universität zu Brünn 2003, AUBI, Nr. 272, S. 104 ff. Relativ aktuell dann: *Záhora*, *Kert* (Hrsg.), *Höpfel*, *Mathern* (Gutachter), Trestná zodpovednosť právnických osôb (Die strafrechtliche Verantwortlichkeit von juristischen Personen),

Auch das Strafprozessrecht durchläuft im Rahmen der Novellen einen Prozess der „Europäisierung".

Die Novelle der StPO Nr. 539/2004 Sb. regelt, ausgehend von der zuständigen Rahmenentscheidung des Rates der EU und in Anknüpfung an das geänderte materielle Strafrecht, die prozessualen Voraussetzungen und Bedingungen der Entscheidung über den europäischen Haftbefehl.

Im Jahr 2004 genehmigte dann die Regierung das Sachvorhaben zur Ausarbeitung einer neuen StPO.

Die Parlamentswahlen im Jahre 2006 haben den Reformprozess ein wenig verlangsamt, die Reform des materiellen Strafrechts ist jedoch zu diesem Zeitpunkt bereits fast abgeschlossen. Nach mehr als zehn Jahren Reformbemühungen wurde das neue StGB 2009 gebilligt und trat als Gesetz Nr. 40/2009 Sb. zum 1. Januar 2010 in Kraft.

Obwohl ein Gesetz, und insbesondere ein Gesetzbuch, ein Symbol der rechtlichen Stabilität sein sollte, wurde das neue StGB schon im Verlauf des *vacatio legis* novelliert (Gesetz Nr. 306/2009 Sb.). Es bleibt nur zu hoffen, dass diese „neue Tradition" sehr schnell wieder ausstirbt.

Die Reform des Strafprozessrechts erlebt dagegen auch jetzt den Zustand einer permanenten „Agonie" und kann die Phase des bloßen Sachvorhabens nicht überwinden. Das bedeutet, dass der Reformprozess der StPO im Jahre 2010 wieder an seinem Anfang steht. Immerhin besteht gegenwärtig der paragraphierte Entwurf des Allgemeinen Teils der neuen StPO (2009) und dazu ein neues Sachvorhaben der Regierung (2010).

Im weiteren Text werden daher nur ausgewählte wichtige Änderungen näher dargestellt, die die neue Kodifikation des materiellen Strafrechts aufweist. In erster Linie betrifft es den Bereich der Grundlagen der strafrechtlichen Verantwortlichkeit.

Die erste Neuregelung betrifft den zeitlichen Wirkungskreis des StGB. Gemäß § 2 Abs. 1 und 4 StGB ist der Zeitpunkt der Begehung der Straftat nur an die Handlung, keinesfalls jedoch an die Folgen der Tat, also nicht an die Vollendung der Straftat geknüpft. Dies bedeutet, dass aus Gründen der Prävention[19] die Strafbarkeit der vollendeten Tat nach dem zum Zeitpunkt der Handlung geltenden StGB beurteilt werden muss, also ohne die Berücksichtigung des StGB, das beim Eintritt der Tatfolgen inzwischen in Kraft getreten ist. Ich fürchte aber, dass es sehr schwer sein wird, zwischen Vollendung und Versuch zu differenzie-

Tagungsband zur Internationalen Konferenz am 12. November 2009, 1. Aufl., Bratislava 2009, EUROKÓDEX, s. r. o.

19 Siehe: http://www.psp.cz/sqw/text/tiskt.sqw?o=5&ct=410&ct1=0, 21.07.2010.

ren. Auf der anderen Seite beginnt jedoch die Verjährung der Strafbarkeit ab dem Zeitpunkt der Vollendung der Straftat[20].

Eine ähnliche Einstellung des tschechischen Gesetzgebers ist bei der Strafbarkeit der Teilnahme erkennbar. Gemäß § 4 Abs. 4 StGB ist im Fall der Beteiligung an der Auslands(straf)tat keine Bedingung für die Anwendung des StGB, dass die Hauptstraftat im Ausland strafbar wurde. Nach dem Begründungsbericht handelt es sich bei § 4 Abs. 4 StGB um eine Modifikation des Akzessorietätsgrundsatzes (§ 24 StGB), sodass der „Versuch" des Hauptdelikts im Ausland ausreicht[21].

Neben dem Legalitätsgrundsatz (§ 12 Abs. 1 StGB) regelt dieses Gesetzbuch ausdrücklich auch den Subsidiaritätsgrundsatz, als Ausdruck des *Ultima-ratio*-Prinzips (§ 12 Abs. 2 StGB)[22]. Das hängt sehr eng mit der Lösung der erwähnten Frage zusammen, ob die formelle oder die materielle Auffassung der Straftat angewendet wird. I.V.m. § 13 Abs. 1 StGB (formelle Definition der Straftat)[23] stellen diese Bestimmungen eine sog. Kombinierte Auffassung der Straftat dar. Konkret gesagt handelt es sich um die formell-materielle Auffassung der Straftat, um einen Grund der strafrechtlichen Verantwortlichkeit[24]. An erster Stelle steht in diesem Sinn der formelle Begriff der Straftat (§ 13 Abs. 1 StGB) und als ein materieller Korrektiv dieser reinen Form wirkt das Subsidiaritätsprinzip (§ 12 Abs. 2 StGB), das auf die „gesellschaftliche Schädlichkeit" der Tat abstellt. Nach dem tschechischen Kommentar zum StGB handelt es sich dabei um ein Zurückkehren zum Begriff der „materiellen Rechtswidrigkeit" der Tat[25].

---

20 Die Inspiration des tschechischen Gesetzgebers seitens des deutschen gültigen StGB (weiter auch „dStGB") § 2 Abs. 1, § 8 dStGB ist offensichtlich. Siehe dazu S/S – Eser Rn. 1.

21 Siehe: http://www.psp.cz/sqw/text/tiskt.sqw?o=5&ct=410&ct1=0, 21.07.2010; auch an dieser Stelle ist der Einfluss des deutschen Strafrechts, § 9 Abs. 2 dStGB, spürbar.

22 Diese Bestimmung lautet: „Strafrechtliche Verantwortlichkeit und die damit verbundenen strafrechtlichen Folgen sind nur in den gesellschaftlich schädlichen Fällen anwendbar, in denen die Anwendung anderer Normen nicht ausreicht."

23 Diese Bestimmung lautet: „Die Straftat ist eine rechtswidrige Tat, wenn das Strafgesetz sie als strafbar bezeichnet und sie die Merkmale aufweist, die in diesem Gesetz aufgeführt sind."

24 Siehe näher *Kratochvíl* et al., Kurs trestního práva. Trestní právo hmotné (Kurs des Strafrechts. Materielles Strafrecht. Allgemeiner Teil), 1. Aufl., C. H. Beck, Prag 2009, S. 37, 154–155. Ganz aktuell siehe *Pokorný*, Ústavněprávní aspekty přijetí formální koncepce trestného činu (Verfassungsrechtliche Aspekte des Empfangs der formellen Auffassung der Straftat), Právník 2010, Nr. 1, S. 1–22.

25 *Šámal* et al., Trestní zákoník I. § 1 bis § 139, Komentář. 1. Aufl., C. H. Beck, Prag 2009, S. 102 und der dort aufgeführte Verweis auf das deutsche Strafgesetzbuch, 38. Aufl., C. H. Beck, München 2002, S. 18. Über den formalen Verbrechensbegriff, zum Unterschied zu einem materialen Verbrechensbegriff spricht auch S/S – Eser § 12 Rn. 21.

Während der tschechische und auch ein wenig der deutsche Zugang zur Auffassung der Straftat nicht rein formell ist, bieten die österreichischen Strafrechtsregelungen eine interessante Lösung an.

Der ehemalige § 42 österreichisches StGB (weiter auch „öStGB") sprach von der mangelnden Strafwürdigkeit der Tat[26], was eine bestimmte Analogie zur tschechischen Regelung im §§ 12 Abs. 2, 13 Abs. 1 StGB darstellte. Im § 191 Abs. 1 öStPO, der als „Ersatz[27]" für § 42 a.F. öStGB angesehen werden kann, wurde die Verfahrenseinstellung wegen Geringfügigkeit der Tat eingeführt, die sich auf den Grundsatz *minima non curat praetor* (also keine Opportunität?) stützt[28]. Die österreichische Regelung behält also als Grund der strafrechtlichen Verantwortlichkeit eine rein formelle Auffassung der Straftat bei und beseitigt die entstehende Härte über die Anwendung – *in concreto* – im Strafprozess.

Die bisherige nominale Monopartition von Straftaten, d.h. Existenz nur der einzigen Kategorie der Straftat, ersetzt § 14 StGB durch eine Dichotomie in Form von Vergehen und Verbrechen.

Vergehen sind alle fahrlässigen und diejenigen vorsätzlichen Straftaten, die mit einer Freiheitsstrafe von bis zu fünf Jahre bedroht sind.

Verbrechen sind sodann alle Straftaten, die nach dem Strafgesetz keine Vergehen sind; besondere schwere Verbrechen sind die vorsätzlichen Straftaten, die mit einer Freiheitsstrafe von mindestens zehn Jahren bedroht sind.

Nach dem Begründungsbericht[29] drückt und differenziert die Dichotomie die Schwere der Straftaten aus. In diesem Sinne hat der tschechische Gesetzgeber die Kategorie der Verbrechen etwas enger definiert, als es im § 12 dStGB der Fall ist. Die tschechische Strafrechtsregelung der Dichotomie ist daher näher an der österreichischen Regelung angesiedelt (§ 17 öStGB). Diese Auffassung halte ich wegen des Subsidiaritätsgrundsatzes des Strafrechts i.S.d. *ultima ratio* für passender. Die Kategorisierung von Straftaten eröffnet mehr Raum für alternative Strafen (z.B. *community services*) und für größere Differenzierungen der Sanktionen.

Die erwähnte Dichotomie gilt aber nicht bei Jugendlichen. Die von Jugendlichen begangene Straftat wird als „schuldhafte rechtswidrige Handlung" (*provinění*) bezeichnet[30].

---

26 Siehe mehr bei *Zipf*, Die mangelnde Strafwürdigkeit der Tat (§ 42 öStGB), Universitätsverlag, Salzburg 1975.

27 *Schweighofer*, Die neue Strafprozessordnung, WUV, Wien 2008, S. 30.

28 *Schweighofer*, a.a.O., S. 356.

29 Siehe: http://www.psp.cz/sqw/text/tiskt.sqw?o=5&ct=410&ct1=0, 21.07.2010. Auch an dieser Stelle ist der Einfluss des deutschen Strafrechts sichtbar. Siehe näher S/S – Eser § 12 Rn. 1.

30 Vgl. schon historisch z.B. *Miřička/Scholz*, O trestním soudnictví nad mládeží (Über die strafrechtliche Gerichtsbarkeit der Jugend), Der tschechoslowakische Kompass, Prag 1932, S. 13, 19–20.

Eine relativ grundlegende Änderung beinhaltet § 15 Abs. 1 Buchst. b), Abs. 2 StGB, bezüglich des Verschuldens in der Form des Vorsatzes, der demnach neben dem Einverständnis des Täters auch die Inkaufnahme der Folgen i.S.d. § 5 Abs. 1 öStGB (Eventualvorsatz) beinhaltet[31]. Die Inkaufnahme des Täters umfasst nicht nur den positiven Willen, sondern auch den niedrigeren Grad dieses Willens. Die Inkaufnahme liegt an der Grenze zwischen „Nichtwollen“ (Fahrlässigkeit) und „Einverständnis“ (Dolus), etwas näher an dem Einverständnis. Es ist daher möglich, eine solche Inkaufnahme unter den *dolus eventualis* zu subsumieren, was zu einer Verschärfung der Strafbarkeit führt.

In gleicher Weise unterlag auch die Fahrlässigkeit einer wichtigen Modifikation. Die Regelungen des § 16 Abs. 2 StGB definieren die grobe Fahrlässigkeit. Diese Form des Verschuldens besteht darin, dass der Täter die erforderliche Sorgfalt (Vorsicht) in qualifizierter Form außer Acht lässt, was auf seine offensichtliche Rücksichtslosigkeit hindeutet. Diese gesetzliche Definition bedeutet aber nicht *culpa lata dolus est*.

Es handelt sich nicht um eine dritte Form des fahrlässigen Verschuldens. Die grobe Fahrlässigkeit stellt nur die höhere Intensität der bewussten oder unbewussten Fahrlässigkeit dar. Als Tatbestandsmerkmal wird diese Form der Fahrlässigkeit nur selten verwendet, ein Beispiel findet sich im § 224 StGB (Herbeiführung der Insolvenz). Sie soll die Ausweitung der Strafrepressionen zu verhindern helfen. Es geht darum zu verhindern, dass im Zusammenhang mit den Straftatbeständen des Wirtschaftsstrafrechts eine übermäßige Kriminalisierung eintritt.

Die Abwesenheit der positiven Regelung des Irrtums im Strafrecht hat häufig in der Praxis verschiedene Probleme bei der Anwendung des früheren Strafgesetzes bereitet. Die im Strafverfahren tätigen Organe haben die Stütze über die Bestimmungen des Verschuldens gesucht. Die neuen gesetzlichen Regelungen führen daher den Tatirrtum und den Verbotsirrtum ein[32]. Die neuen Regelungen befinden sich im Einklang mit den bisherigen Straftheorien über den Irrtum.

An erster Stelle ist der Irrtum über Tatumstände/Tatirrtum (§ 18 StGB) zu nennen, weiterhin steht nun auch der Verbotsirrtum/Rechtsirrtum (§ 19 StGB) zur Verfügung.

---

31 Zur Abfindungstheorie, Billigungstheorie siehe näher z.B. *H. Fuchs*, Österreichisches Strafrecht. Allgemeiner Teil I., 7. Aufl., Springer Verlag, Wien 2008, S. 128 ff.

32 So der Begründungsbericht: http://www.psp.cz/sqw/text/tiskt.sqw?o=5&ct=410&ct1=0, 21.07.2010; auch an dieser Stelle ist der Einfluss des deutschen Strafrechts nicht zu übersehen. Siehe auch S/S – Cramer/Sternberg-Lieben, § 16, § 17 Rn. 1. Ebenfalls hat auch das öStGB ein Vorbild für uns dargestellt; §§ 8, 9 öStGB, siehe näher *H. Fuchs*, a.a.O., S. 125 ff., 242–243.

Als Tatirrtum gilt der Irrtum über die normativen Tatbestandsmerkmale[33]. Diese Bezeichnung entspricht Rechtsbegriffen, Rechtsinstituten oder Rechtsverhältnissen, die in anderen Rechtsgebieten definiert sind, z.B. „fremde Sache", „Steuer" u.ä. In diesem Zusammenhang ist wichtig zu wissen, dass das StGB sich nicht auf diese Definitionen beruft. Es hat die normativen Tatbestandsmerkmale sozusagen nur „ausgeliehen".

Weitere Bedeutung hat in diesem Kontext der Rechtsirrtum. Vor allem für die Strafpraxis existiert hier aber ein Risiko des Verwechselns des Irrtums über die normativen Tatbestandsmerkmale mit dem Rechtsirrtum und umgekehrt. Den negativen Rechtsirrtum definiert das StGB so:

> „Wer bei der Begehung der Straftat nicht erkennt, dass seine Tat rechtswidrig ist, handelt nicht schuldhaft, wenn ihm der Irrtum nicht vorzuwerfen ist."

Im Interesse der Rechtssicherheit definiert man auch den vermeidbaren Rechtsirrtum:

> „Ein Rechtsirrtum ist vermeidbar, wenn der Täter seiner Pflicht nachkommt, entsprechende sich aus einem Gesetz oder aus einer anderen allgemeinverbindlichen Norm, aus einer amtlichen Entscheidung, aus einem Vertrag oder einem Beschäftigungsverhältnis, aus seiner Position oder Funktion ergebende Pflichten zu kennen oder wenn die Rechtswidrigkeit der Handlung für den Täter leicht erkennbar war."

Liegt ein vermeidbarer Irrtum vor, so ist der Täter für die betreffende vorsätzliche oder fahrlässige Straftat verantwortlich. Der vorwerfbare Rechtsirrtum kann aber einen mildernden Umstand darstellen (§ 41 Buchst. h) StGB) oder einen Grund für eine Strafzumessung unterhalb der unteren Grenze des Strafrahmens (§ 58 Abs. 6 StGB).

Nach dem Begründungsbericht betrifft diese Regelung des Rechtsirrtums die Rechtswidrigkeit als Merkmal der Straftat i.S.d. § 13 Abs. 1 StGB, einschließlich der außerstrafrechtlichen Rechtsnormen, auf die sich das StGB beruft. Bezüglich der Definition der Tatbestandsmerkmale im StGB gilt in diesem Zusammenhang weiter der klassische Grundsatz *ignorantia iuris nocet* (*neminem excusat*).

Das neue StGB legt für die Strafbarkeit der Vorbereitung aufgrund des Subsidiaritätsgrundsatzes (Strafrecht als *ultima ratio*) eine Doppelbeschränkung auf.

Die erste Stufe besteht darin, dass das StGB die Vorbereitung nur im Verhältnis zu den besonders wichtigen Verbrechen kriminalisiert. Die zweite Stufe bedeutet, dass diese Strafbarkeit im Besonderen Teil des StGB ausdrücklich unter Strafe gestellt sein muss (§ 20 Abs. 1 StGB; z.B. Mord gemäß § 140 Abs. 4 StGB).

---

33 Vgl. *Kratochvíl*, Negative error in law concerning non-claimed and claimed non-penal element of the body of a crime (national and European law aspects). Legal studies and practice journal, Nr. 3/2008, S. 297–304.

Infolgedessen existieren Straftatbestände bei Verbrechen, bei denen die Vorbereitung nicht strafbar ist; so z.B. § 144 StGB – Vorbereitung der Hilfeleistung zum Selbstmord – diese Straflosigkeit gilt sogar für den qualifizierten Fall im Abs. 3 (gegen ein Kind unter 15 Jahren), obwohl es sich hier um ein besonders schweres Verbrechen handelt.

Dagegen unterliegt die Strafbarkeit des Versuchs (§ 21 StGB) keinen ähnlichen Beschränkungen wie die Vorbereitung. Das bedeutet, dass der Versuch, im Unterschied zu den deutschen Regelungen (§ 23 dStGB), auch bei Vergehen generell strafbar ist.

Das tschechische StGB definiert den Versuch sehr ähnlich wie das deutsche oder das österreichische StGB (§ 15 Abs. 2 öStGB). Der untaugliche Versuch ist im § 46 Abs. 2 StGB im Zusammenhang mit dem Absehen von der Bestrafung, vergleichbar mit § 23 Abs. 3 dStGB und § 15 Abs. 3 öStGB, definiert. Diese Konstruktion des § 46 Abs. 2 StGB gilt auch für die Vorbereitung.

Der Rücktritt vom Versuch, aber auch von der Vorbereitung, ist im tschechischen Recht im Grunde ähnlich konstruiert wie im § 24 dStGB oder § 16 öStGB.

Das neue tschechische StGB setzt weiterhin einerseits die traditionelle direkte (unmittelbare) Täterschaft voraus (§ 22 Abs. 1 StGB), regelt aber andererseits auch die indirekte (mittelbare) Täterschaft (§ 22 Abs. 2 StGB); vergleichbar mit § 25 Abs. 1 dStGB[34].

Die neue Legaldefinition der mittelbaren Täterschaft im § 22 Abs. 2 StGB bekräftigt im Unterschied zu den bisherigen Regelungen die Legalität des Strafrechts und die Rechtssicherheit. Sie trägt so auch besser zur Differenzierung zwischen dieser Form der Täterschaft einerseits und der Beteiligung (Teilnahme) andererseits bei.

Die Mittäterschaft definiert das neue StGB im § 23 wie eine vorsätzliche Begehung der Straftat durch eine gemeinsame Handlung von zwei oder mehreren Personen (vgl. § 25 Abs. 2 dStGB). Nach dem Begründungsbericht[35] des Gesetzesentwurfs präzisiert die neue Regelung diesen Begriff im Interesse einer besseren Unterscheidbarkeit der Mittäterschaft und der Beteiligung (Teilnahme), vor allem der Beihilfe. Die tschechische Strafrechtspraxis interpretierte das Institut der Mittäterschaft bislang sehr weit. Infolgedessen wurde unter diesen Begriff auch die Beteiligung, vor allem gerade die Beihilfe verstanden, was im Widerspruch zum Prinzip des Strafrechts als *ultima ratio*, aber auch im Widerspruch zum Analogieverbot *in malam partem* stand.

Die Beteiligung/Teilnahme gemäß § 24 StGB (Organisator, Anstifter und Gehilfe) beruht nach wie vor auf dem Akzessorietätsgrundsatz. Im Vergleich zum § 29 dStGB, wo es sich um eine sog. limitierte Akzessorietät[36] handelt, ver-

---

34 S/S – Cramer/Heine, § 25 Rn. 7.

35 Dazu: http://www.psp.cz/sqw/text/tiskt.sqw?o=5&ct=410&ct1=0, 21.07.2010.

36 S/S – Cramer/Heine, § 25 Rn. 23.

steht die tschechische Rechtsregelung im neuen StGB die Akzessorietät in dem Sinne, dass die Hauptstraftat mindestens das Stadium eines Versuchs erreicht haben muss.

Im Unterschied zu den deutschen Regelungen (§ 19 dStGB, 14 Jahre) hat das tschechische StGB im § 25 die Altersgrenze der strafrechtlichen Verantwortung auf 15 Jahre festgelegt[37].

Das bisherige Strafgesetz (Nr. 140/1961 Sb.) hat die Gründe der Zurechnungsunfähigkeit/Schuldunfähigkeit relativ eng bestimmt, d.h. den Begriff der seelischen Störung. Ganz anders ist die Problematik nunmehr durch § 26 i.V.m. § 123 StGB geregelt. Vor allem geht die Legaldefinition der seelischen Störung nunmehr weiter, und zwar nach dem Vorbild des § 20 dStGB. Auch der tschechische Gesetzgeber hat so auf die neuesten medizinischen Erkenntnisse reagiert.

Im Grunde gilt dasselbe auch für die verminderte Schuldfähigkeit gemäß § 27 StGB, die an die Regelungen des § 21 dStGB angelehnt ist.

Die Kehrseite der Grundlagen der strafrechtlichen Verantwortlichkeit stellen die die Rechtswidrigkeit ausschließenden Umstände und das Erlöschen der strafrechtlichen Verantwortlichkeit dar.

Das neue StGB ordnet in die erste Gruppe den Notstand (§ 28 StGB), die Notwehr (§ 29 StGB), die Einwilligung des Opfers (§ 30 StGB), das erlaubte Risiko (§ 31 StGB) und die berechtigte Anwendung einer Waffe (§ 32 StGB) ein.

In die zweite Gruppe fallen tätige Reue (§ 33 StGB) und die Verjährung der strafrechtlichen Verantwortlichkeit (§ 34 StGB).

Im Unterschied zum früheren StGB stärken die neuen Bestimmungen den Legalitätsgrundsatz und die Rechtssicherheit, indem sie die Einwilligung des Opfers und das erlaubte Risiko ausdrücklich regeln.

In diesem Zusammenhang ist es erforderlich hervorzuheben, dass im Begründungsbericht ausdrücklich aufgeführt ist[38], dass die Aufzählung der die Rechtswidrigkeit ausschließenden Umstände nicht abschließend ist.

Im Hinblick darauf, dass die Auffassung der die Rechtswidrigkeit der Tat ausschließenden Umstände im deutschen und im tschechischen Recht sehr unterschiedlich sind, wäre eine Gegenüberstellung im Rahmen dieses Beitrags ein wenig zu umfangreich[39].

---

37 Diese Frage stellt in den tschechischen Bedingungen einen legislativen „*Evergreen*" dar. Der ursprüngliche Vorschlag des StGB sah nämlich die Grenze von 14 Jahren vor. Letztendlich wurde die Altersgrenze durch die Novelle Nr. 306/2009 Sb. wieder auf 15 Jahre angehoben, so wie sie im StGB Nr. 140/1961 Sb. bereits enthalten war.

38 Näher dazu: http://www.psp.cz/sqw/text/tiskt.sqw?o=5&ct=410&ct1=0, 21.07.2010.

39 Aus der tschechischen Literatur vgl. z.B. *Kuchta*, Nutná obrana (Notwehr), Masarykova Universität zu Brünn, Brünn 1999, AUBI, No 26, S. 32 ff.

Zum Schluss sollen noch ein paar Bemerkungen über die im Strafgesetzbuch enthaltenen Strafsanktionen folgen.

Die neue Philosophie[40] der Auferlegung von Strafen geht vom Entpönalisierungsgrundsatz aus, mit dem sich besonders die alternativen Strafen im Einklang befinden. Andererseits wird aber betont, dass bei der besonders schwerwiegenden Kriminalität die Repression ihre berechtigte Bedeutung hat. In diesem Kontext ist es notwendig, die Relativität des Gegensatzes zwischen der Repression und Prävention hervorzuheben, die schon historisch an *Franz von Liszt* erinnert[41].

Das neue tschechische StGB enthält daher neue Grundsätze der Bestrafung. Diese sind z.B. die Angemessenheit der Strafsanktionen (§§ 38 Abs. 1, 39 StGB), der Subsidiaritätsgrundsatz (§ 38 Abs. 2 StGB) oder die humanitären Aspekte der Strafe (§ 37 Abs. 2 StGB). Schließlich wird ein spezieller Grundsatz des Schutzes der Opferinteressen (§ 38 Abs. 3 StGB) definiert.

IV. Fazit

Dieser kurze Umriss der Entwicklung des tschechischen Strafrechts am Wendepunkt des Jahrtausends zeigt, dass beide strafrechtlichen Bereiche schwere Zeiten hinter sich haben.

In erster Linie ist es das materielle Strafrecht, das eine relativ komplizierte Reformperiode durchschreiten musste.

Keine leichtere Entwicklung wartet auch auf das Strafprozessrecht, vor allem nach den Wahlen im Jahre 2010, die zu anderen politischen Kräfteverhältnissen geführt haben als denen, unter denen das StGB verabschiedet wurde.

Es bleibt daher nur zu hoffen, dass die zukünftigen legislativen Bemühungen um die neue StPO erfolgreich fortgeführt werden, damit die tschechische Strafrechtsreform bald relativ erfolgreich abgeschlossen werden kann.

Sehr wichtig ist in diesem Zusammenhang das Wort „relativ“, denn die Reform des Straf- und Strafprozessrechts kann, nicht nur in der Tschechischen Republik, nie als vollkommen abgeschlossen betrachtet werden.

---

40 So der Begründungsbericht: http://www.psp.cz/sqw/text/tiskt.sqw?o=5&ct=410&ct1=0, 21.07.2010.

41 *H. Ostendorf*, Von der Rache zur Zweckstrafe. 100 Jahre Marburger Programm von Franz von Liszt (Der Zweckgedanke im Strafrecht), neu herausgegeben und erläutert von *Prof. Dr. H. Ostendorf*, Universität Hamburg, Alfred Metzner Verlag, Frankfurt a.M. 1982.

Die Entwicklung des ungarischen Strafrechts seit dem EU-Beitritt

Prof. Dr. Herbert Küpper[*]

I. Einführung

Wer die ungarische Rechtsentwicklung beobachtet, dem fallen sofort spektakuläre Vorkommnisse wie die drastische Verkleinerung des Parlaments, das Scheitern der Neukodifizierung des bürgerlichen Rechts oder die völkerrechtlich und politisch bedenkliche Ferneinbürgerung für die magyarischen Minderheiten in den Nachbarländern auf. Im Vergleich dazu erscheint die Entwicklung im Straf- und Strafprozessrecht unauffällig, auch wenn sie weder uninteressant noch unwichtig ist. Zudem unterliegen das materielle Strafrecht, das Strafverfahren und die rechtliche Zusammenarbeit in Strafsachen andauernd Fortentwicklungen durch Gesetzgebung und Rechtsprechung, sodass man keinesfalls von einer Stagnation sprechen kann.

Das materielle Strafrecht ist nach wie vor in einem aus sozialistischer Zeit stammenden Gesetzbuch niedergelegt, nämlich dem Gesetz 1978:I[1]. Dass in einem derart alten Gesetz nicht nur die Wende, sondern auch der EU-Beitritt immer wieder Anpassungsbedarf erzeugt, liegt auf der Hand. Allerdings gehen manche der Änderungen auf heimische Anlässe zurück, z.B. die Bekämpfung des zunehmenden Rechtsextremismus. Auf lange Sicht ist ein neues StGB geplant, aber bis dies so weit ist, muss das vorhandene permanent an neue Entwicklungen angepasst werden. Im Strafprozessrecht ist der Erlass eines postsozialistischen Kodex in Gestalt des Gesetzes 1998:XIX[2] bereits gelungen, wenngleich sich das Inkrafttreten um mehrere Jahre bis zum 01.07.2003 verzögert hat, u.a. um den vollständigen Wiederaufbau der vierten Gerichtsebene abzuwarten[3].

In der Folge werden einige Entwicklungen seit dem EU-Beitritt, dem für Recht und Rechtskultur wichtigsten Ereignis seit der Wende 1989/90, dargestellt. Hierbei wird zwischen völkerrechtlich veranlassten, mit der EU-

---

* Wissenschaftl. Referent und Geschäftsführer des IOR, Honorarprofessor der Andrássy Universität Budapest.

1 Gesetz 1978:IV über das Strafgesetzbuch v. 31.12.1978, Magyar Közlöny (Gesetzblatt, in der Folge: MK) 1978 Nr. 92.

2 Gesetz 1998:XIX über das Strafverfahren v. 23.03.1998, MK 1998 Nr. 23.

3 Die Wiedererrichtung der Tafelgerichte, die dem deutschen OLG entsprechen, begann 1997 und zog sich bis 2003 hin: *H. Küpper/B. Tildi*, Ungarn: Die Eröffnung der ersten Tafelgerichte, JOR 45 (2004) 269-279; *H. Küpper*, Justizreform in Ungarn, forost-Arbeitspapier 23, München 2004, S. 19.

Mitgliedschaft zusammenhängenden und autonomen Entwicklungen unterschieden. Berücksichtigt sind Ereignisse bis einschließlich Juni 2010.

II. Völkerrechtlich veranlasste Entwicklungen

1. Völkerstrafrecht

Seit dem EU-Beitritt unterzeichnete Ungarn mehrere völkerrechtliche Verträge mit strafrechtlichem Inhalt. Die meisten erforderten keine Maßnahmen im nationalen Recht, weil dieses bereits vor Unterzeichnung vertragskonform war. Hierzu gehören das Protokoll v. 24.02.1988 zum Abkommen über die Bekämpfung von Straftaten gegen die Sicherheit der Zivilluftfahrt[4], das Europaratabkommen über Computerkriminalität[5], die UN-Abkommen gegen Korruption[6] und grenzüberschreitende Kriminalität[7], die Anti-Doping-Konvention[8] oder die Fakultativprotokolle über Kinderprostitution und -pornografie zur Kinderrechte-Charta[9].

In einigen Fällen hingegen musste das heimische Strafrecht an neue völkerrechtliche Pflichten angepasst werden. Das wohl wichtigste Gesetz in diesem Bereich war Gesetz 2005:XXX über die Änderung einiger Rechtsvorschriften über die Verkündung einzelner völkerrechtlicher Verträge sowie des Gesetzes 1978:IV über das Strafgesetzbuch v. 13.05.2005[10]. Es verkündete das Einheitsübereinkommen über Suchtstoffe v. 30.03.1961 einschließlich Protokoll v. 25.03.1972 und das Übereinkommen über psychotrope Stoffe v. 21.02.1971 neu und novellierte zugleich das Drogenstrafrecht i.S.d. völkerrechtlichen Vorgaben. Das Europaratabkommen über Geldwäsche v. 16.05.2005 erforderte die Erweiterung der Befugnisse der Kontrollbehörden, was das Ratifikationsgesetz selbst bewirkte[11].

Den Empfehlungen der GRECO-Gruppe des Europarats und der Antikorruptions-Arbeitsgruppe der OECD in Bezug auf eine Verschärfung und Präzisie-

4 Ratifiziert durch Gesetz 2004:XXXVII v. 04.05.2004, MK 2004 Nr. 62.

5 Gesetz 2004:LXXIX v. 15.09.2004, MK 2004 Nr. 129.

6 Gesetz 2005:CXXXIV v. 06.12.2005, MK 2005 Nr. 156; von der Umsetzung des fakultativen Art. 20 sieht Ungarn ab, weil – so die Begründung zur Regierungsvorlage zum Ratifikationsgesetz – die Pönalisierung einer ungerechtfertigten Bereicherung von Beamten gegen die Grundsätze des ungarischen Strafrechts verstoße.

7 Gesetze 2006:CI (Abkommen), 2006:CII (Menschenhandel-Protokoll) und 2006:CIII (Menschenschmuggel-Protokoll) v. 06.12.2006, MK 2006 Nr. 149.

8 Ratifiziert durch RegVO 99/2007. (V. 8.) Korm. v. 08.05.2007, MK 2007 Nr. 56; die sportrechtlichen Sanktionen in der Zuständigkeit der Sportverbände regeln §§ 15-20 RegVO 55/2004. (III. 31.) Korm. v. 31.03.2004, MK 2004 Nr. 39.

9 Gesetz 2009:CLXI v. 30.12.2009, MK 2009 Nr. 196.

10 MK 2005 Nr. 64.

11 Gesetz 2008:LXIII v. 07.11.2008, MK 2008 Nr. 158.

rung der Strafbarkeit juristischer Personen, kam Ungarn durch die Novellierung des einschlägigen Sondergesetzes nach[12].

Einige völkerrechtliche Abkommen machten terminologische Änderungen im Strafrecht nötig. Anfang 2007 passte eine StGB-Novelle[13] den Sprachgebrauch der Nukleardelikte (§§ 264-264/A StGB) an das UN-Abkommen über die Bekämpfung nuklearterroristischer Handlungen v. 13.04.2005 an. Zudem änderte eine weitere Strafrechtsnovelle 2007[14] den Kriegsbegriff i.S.d. von Ungarn bereits seit langem unterzeichneten Genfer Konventionen ab.

Im Militärstrafrecht wurden 2004 die einschlägigen Regeln in Übereinstimmung mit der Abschaffung der Wehrpflicht und dem zunehmenden Einsatz ungarischer Soldaten bei humanitären oder friedenserhaltenden Einsätzen im Ausland gebracht[15].

Auch die Verfahrensstellung konsularischer Vertreter beschäftigte die Rechtsprechung. § 238 Abs. 2 StPO besagt, dass ihnen im Falle ausländischer Angeklagter die Teilnahme am Verfahren zu ermöglichen ist. Aus völkerrechtlichen Gründen legt die Rechtsprechung dies so aus, dass dem Konsul nicht nur Zugang zu gewähren sei, sondern er auch von Amts wegen geladen werden müsse. Die Verletzung dieses Ladegebots wirke allerdings wegen der geringen Rechte des Konsuls als Streithelfer in den seltensten Fällen zu Lasten des Angeklagten und könne somit nur ausnahmsweise ein Rechtsmittel begründen[16].

2. Internationale Zusammenarbeit

Im Berichtszeitraum ratifizierte Ungarn das Übereinkommen über die Vorrechte und Immunitäten des Internationalen Strafgerichtshofs v. 09.09.2002[17], ohne dass dies Änderungen der nationalen Gesetzgebung nötig machte. Dasselbe gilt für die zahlreichen bilateralen Abkommen über die Zusammenarbeit bei der Kriminalitätsbekämpfung.

Die internationale Rechtshilfe in Strafsachen wurde 2007 in vielen Bereichen neu geregelt[18]. Ein Schwerpunkt der Änderungen war die Anerkennung des ausländischen Urteils als Voraussetzung der Vollstreckung in Ungarn. Im Hin-

---

12 Gesetz 2008:XXVI über die Änderung des Gesetzes 2001:CIV über die strafrechtlichen Maßnahmen, die gegenüber juristischen Personen angewandt werden können, v. 10.6.2008, MK 2008 Nr. 86. Zur Strafbarkeit juristischer Personen s.u. Punkt IV.1.

13 Gesetz 2007:XXVII v. 20.04.2007, MK 2007 Nr. 50.

14 § 3 Gesetz 2007:CLXII v. 21.12.2007, MK 2007 Nr. 180.

15 StGB-Änderungsgesetz 2004:CXXXI v. 25.12.2004, MK 2004 Nr. 200.

16 Tafelgericht Szeged, Bírósági Határozatok (amtl. Entscheidungssammlung, in der Folge: BH) 2005 Nr. 278.

17 Gesetz 2006:XXXI v. 23.02.2006, MK 2006 Nr. 21.

18 Gesetz 2007:XIII über die Änderung des Gesetzes 1996:XXXVIII über die internationale Rechtshilfe in Strafsachen und des Gesetzes 2003:CXXX über die Zusammenarbeit in Strafsachen mit den Mitgliedstaaten der Europäischen Union v. 28.03.2007, MK 2007 Nr. 36.

blick auf den ungarischen *ordre public* als negative Anerkennungsvoraussetzung braucht sich das ausländische Strafurteil nicht mehr positiv „in Übereinstimmung mit dem ungarischen Recht“ zu befinden, sondern muss nur negativ „nicht im Gegensatz zur ungarischen Rechtsordnung“ stehen[19]. Auch die Übernahme zur Strafvollstreckung in Ungarn und die Übergabe zur Strafvollstreckung im Ausland wurden in vielen Details neu formuliert.

Bei der Vollstreckung eines ausländischen Strafurteils stellt sich in der Praxis die Frage des Haftgrades, denn in Ungarn wird die Freiheitsstrafe entweder im Zuchthaus (*fegyház*), im Gefängnis (*börtön*) oder in der Arrestanstalt (*fogház*) verbüßt; das Strafgericht ordnet den Haftgrad nach §§ 42-44 StGB an. Nach einem Grundsatzurteil des Obersten Gerichts[20] ist die Freiheitsstrafe im Gefängnis zu verbüßen, falls ein ausländisches Urteil, wie das streitgegenständliche italienische, keinen Haftgrad kennt oder nennt, und zwar auch dann, wenn das ungarische Recht für die Straftat Zuchthaus vorsieht. Den Rückgriff auf das ungarische Recht erlaubt das Gesetz über internationale Rechtshilfe in Strafsachen[21] nur, wenn das Urteil mit ungarischem Recht nicht vereinbar ist. Ein abweichender oder fehlender Haftgrad bewirkt aber noch keine Unvereinbarkeit.

Anders als beim Haftgrad, wo ungarisches Recht in Gänze außer Betracht bleibt, entschied das Oberste Gericht im Rechtseinheitlichkeitsbeschluss[22] in Strafsachen 1/2010. (II. 26.) BJE[23] im Hinblick auf die Haftaussetzung auf Bewährung. Bei einem ausländischen Strafurteil, das die Aussetzung eines Teils der Strafe zur Bewährung vorsieht, greift das Oberste Gericht auf ungarisches Recht zurück. Die Länge der Bewährungsfrist müsse an § 48 StGB gemessen werden, und wenn das ausländische Urteil eine kürzere Dauer der Aussetzung vorsieht, gelte diese; anderenfalls sei die längere ausländische Frist auf die Frist zu verkürzen, die als sog. bedingte Freilassung nach § 48 StGB im Falle eines vergleichbaren inländischen Urteils gelten würde. Dass hier anders als beim Haftgrad auf heimisches Recht zurückgegriffen wird, begründet das Oberste Gericht damit, dass das ungarische Recht die Bewährung i.S.d. ausländischen Ur-

19 Damit könnte z.B. ein ausländisches Urteil, das auf Führerscheinentzug wegen einer nicht mit dem Straßenverkehr zusammenhängenden Tat vollstreckt werden: Da Ungarn den Führerscheinentzug auf Verkehrsstraftaten beschränkt (s.u. Punkt IV.6.), befindet sich ein derartiges Urteil nicht „in Übereinstimmung mit dem ungarischen Recht“, aber es steht jedenfalls dann nicht „im Gegensatz zur ungarischen Rechtsordnung“, wenn man die Beschränkung der Strafart Führerscheinentzug nicht als Teil des ungarischen *ordre public* betrachtet.

20 BH 2006 Nr. 395.

21 Nachgewiesen in Fn. 18.

22 Rechtseinheitlichkeitsbeschlüsse sind seit 1997 wieder in der Verfassung verankerte quasinormative Auslegungsbeschlüsse, die das Oberste Gericht außerhalb eines konkreten Rechtsfalls erlässt, um eine divergierende untergerichtliche Rechtspraxis zu vereinheitlichen; sie sind für Gerichte verbindlich.

23 MK 2010 Nr. 27.

teils nicht kenne, weshalb derartige Anordnungen in fremden Urteilen in das nächste ungarische Institut umgeformt werden müssen, d.h. in die bedingte Freilassung. Worin der genaue Unterschied zwischen bedingter Freilassung und Bewährung liegt, ließ das Oberste Gericht allerdings offen. Bei der Umformung in die bedingte Freilassung dürfen ungarische Gerichte aber nicht strenger vorgehen, als das materielle ungarische Recht zulässt. Anlass für den Rechtseinheitlichkeitsbeschluss waren abweichende Urteile des Hauptstädtischen Gerichts zur Bewährungsfrist in österreichischen Strafurteilen.

III. Entwicklungen im Zusammenhang mit Ungarns EU-Mitgliedschaft

1. Nationale Vorschriften

Die EU-Mitgliedschaft Ungarns hat Auswirkungen auf das materielle Strafrecht und die Zusammenarbeit mit den anderen EU-Staaten. Im Strafrecht hatten wesentliche Änderungen bereits vor dem Beitritt stattgefunden, v.a. bei der Erweiterung bestimmter nationaler Schutzgüter um ihr europarechtliches Pendant. Diese Bestimmungen waren meist „Vorratsgesetze", d.h. sie waren bereits einige Zeit vor dem Beitritt erlassen worden, traten aber erst 2004 – einige 2005 zusammen mit der Ratifizierung des EU-Abkommens über strafrechtliche Zusammenarbeit v. 29.05.2000[24] – in Kraft. Hierzu gehören z.B. die Förderung rechtswidrigen Aufenthalts (§ 214/A StGB), die Erstreckung der Justizdelikte auf Taten gegen die europäische Justiz und die der anderen EU-Staaten (§§ 228/B, 244 Abs. 5, 249/B) sowie der Amtsdelikte auf bestimmte in Ungarn tätige EU-Beamte (§ 275 Abs. 2).

Auch nach dem Beitritt machte das Gemeinschaftsrecht bisweilen die Schaffung neuer Straftatbestände notwendig, z.B. bei den Drogenausgangsstoffen[25]. Seit 2007 enthalten §§ 283/A, 286/A Abs. 3 StGB die notwendigen Regelungen[26]. Ebenfalls 2007 wurde die Strafbarkeit von Kinderpornografie entsprechend den Vorgaben des Rahmenbeschlusses in § 204 StGB verankert[27]. Die Pönalisierung der Holocaustleugnung 2010 wird wegen ihres engen Zusammenhangs mit dem Kampf gegen Rechts in Punkt IV.2. behandelt.

---

24 In Ungarn ratifiziert durch Gesetz 2005:CXVI v. 28.10.2005, MK 2005 Nr. 143.

25 Einschlägig sind die VOen (EG) Nr. 273/2004 des Europäischen Parlaments und des Rates v. 11.02.2004 betreffend Drogenausgangsstoffe und (EG) Nr. 111/2005 des Rates v. 22.12.2004 zur Festlegung von Vorschriften für die Überwachung des Handels mit Drogenaustauschstoffen zwischen der Gemeinschaft und Drittländern.

26 Eingefügt durch die StGB-Novelle v. Dezember 2007 (Fn. 14).

27 Rahmenbeschluss 2004/68/JI des Rates v. 22.12.2003 zur Bekämpfung der sexuellen Ausbeutung von Kindern und der Kinderpornografie, umgesetzt durch die StGB-Novelle v. April 2007 (Fn. 13).

Ein wichtiges Feld gemeinschaftsrechtlicher Einflussnahme auf das nationale Strafrecht ist der immer stärker miteinander verwobene Bereich von Terrorismus, Geldwäsche und organisierter Kriminalität. Die Geldwäsche-Richtlinie[28] wurde in ihren administrativen Bereichen durch ein gesondertes Gesetz umgesetzt[29], während die flankierenden strafrechtlichen Maßnahmen zuvor bereits durch Präzisierungen in den einschlägigen Tatbeständen der §§ 303-303/C StGB geschaffen worden waren[30]. Die Verletzung gemeinschaftsrechtlicher Außenwirtschaftsverbote stellte die StGB-Novelle 2005 unter Strafe[31], während die Anpassung des Missbrauchs von Rüstungsgütern an gemeinschaftsrechtliche Handelsverbote durch die StGB-Novelle v. 20.04.2007 erfolgte[32].

Teilweise begründete die Regierung auch die Einführung des Straftatbestands der Belästigung (*zaklatás*, nach dt. Diktion: Nachstellung[33]) in § 176/A durch die StGB-Novelle vom Dezember 2007[34] mit europarechtlichen Vorgaben. Strafbar ist die beständige unerwünschte Kontaktaufnahme; richtet sich diese gegen frühere Partner oder gegen Schutzbefohlene, ist dies ein qualifizierter Fall. Strafbar ist zudem die Bedrohung mit Straftaten.

Nicht nur der Gesetzgeber reagiert auf EU-bedingte Veränderungen, sondern auch die Rechtsprechung. Die parallelen Schutzvorschriften zugunsten inländischer und europäischer öffentlicher Rechtsgüter führen dazu, dass ein Tatsachenirrtum über den Inhaber des geschützten Rechtsguts unbeachtlich ist, wie das Oberste Gericht erstmals 2008 entschied: Wenn der Täter einen Subventionsbetrug begeht, spielt es keine Rolle, ob er richtig einschätzt, ob die angestrebten Zahlungen Gelder des ungarischen Staates (dann § 288 StGB) oder der EG (dann § 314 StGB) sind. Da beide Subventionsgeber gleich geschützt sind und bei der Subventionsvergabe zudem häufig ineinandergreifen, braucht der Täter keine genaue und schon gar keine korrekte Vorstellung davon zu haben, wessen Töpfe er schädigt[35]. Auch sind Waren aus anderen EU-Ländern seit dem

---

28 RL 2005/60/EG des Europäischen Parlaments und des Rates v. 26.10.2005 zur Verhinderung der Nutzung des Finanzsystems zum Zwecke der Geldwäsche und der Terrorismusfinanzierung.

29 Gesetz 2007:CXXXVI über die Vorbeugung und Verhinderung von Geldwäsche und Terrorismusfinanzierung v. 28.11.2007, MK 2007 Nr. 162.

30 StGB-Novelle 2007 (Fn. 13); nur § 303/B wurde erst durch das Geldwäschegesetz selbst (Fn. 29) in das StGB eingefügt.

31 § 261/A StGB i.d.F. des Gesetzes 2005:XCI v. 15.07.2005, MK 2005 Nr. 100.

32 § 263/B StGB i.d.F. des Gesetzes 2007:XXVII (Fn. 13); gemeinschaftsrechtlicher Bezugsrahmen ist die VO (EG) Nr. 1236/2005 des Rates v. 27.06.2005 betreffend den Handel mit bestimmten Gütern, die zur Vollstreckung der Todesstrafe, zu Folter oder zu anderer grausamer, unmenschlicher oder erniedrigender Behandlung oder Strafe verwendet werden könnten.

33 So in § 238 dt. StGB; außerhalb des Gesetzestexts ist meist von Stalking die Rede.

34 Siehe Fn. 14.

35 BH 2009 Nr. 169.

Beitritt keine Zollwaren und somit kein geeigneter Gegenstand für Zollstraftaten wie Schmuggelei mehr. Die Rechtsprechung verurteilt in solchen Fällen allerdings weiterhin wegen Urkundsdelikten[36].

Mehr noch als bei den Straftatbeständen wirkt sich der EU-Beitritt im Sanktionensystem aus. Die Nebenstrafe des Verbots der Teilnahme an öffentlichen Angelegenheiten (§§ 53-54 StGB) muss seit 2004 differenzieren, ob ein EU-Bürger oder ein Drittausländer betroffen ist. Die Rechtsprechung weitet den Anwendungsbereich dieser Nebenstrafe bei EU-Bürgern aus und trägt damit der Tatsache Rechnung, dass EU-Bürger in sehr viel weiterem Maße als Drittausländer an öffentlichen Angelegenheiten teilnehmen dürfen. Dem privilegierten Status von EU-Bürgern entspricht daher eine erweiterte Sanktionsmöglichkeit[37].

Heikel ist die Ausweisung als Nebenstrafe, weil EU-Bürger über ein gemeinschaftsrechtliches Aufenthaltsrecht verfügen. Den Ausgleich schafft seit 2007 § 61 Abs. 6 StGB dergestalt, dass aufenthaltsberechtigte Ausländer nur ausgewiesen werden können, wenn sie eine Tat begangen haben, die mit fünf oder mehr Jahren Freiheitsstrafe bedroht ist. Das Oberste Gericht entschied 2008, dass es hierbei auf den oberen Strafrahmen ankommt[38]. Deshalb konnte die Ausweisung als Nebenstrafe gegen einen rumänischen Staatsbürger verhängt wurde, der wegen geschäftsmäßigen Menschenschmuggels gemäß § 218 Abs. 3 Buchst. c) StGB zu vier Jahren und zwei Monaten verurteilt worden war. Die Obergrenze für dieses Delikt liegt bei acht Jahren und somit über der Fünf-Jahres-Schwelle in § 61 Abs. 6 StGB.

2. Zusammenarbeit in Strafsachen

Im Bereich der justiziellen Zusammenarbeit war nicht so sehr der Beitritt das entscheidende Ereignis, sondern die Ratifikation des EU-Abkommens über strafrechtliche Zusammenarbeit v. 29.05.2000 einschließlich des Zusatzprotokolls von 2001 durch Gesetz 2005:CXVI[39]. Es setzte das in Teilen als Vorratsgesetz erlassene Gesetz 2003:CXXX über die strafrechtliche Zusammenarbeit mit den Mitgliedstaaten der Europäischen Union v. 29.12.2003 (EU-StrZusG)[40] vollends in Kraft. Das Durchführungsabkommen zu dem EU-Abkommen und seinem Protokoll v. 19.12.2003, das u.a. die Erweiterung der justiziellen Zusammenarbeit auf Island und Norwegen beinhaltete, ratifizierte Ungarn durch Gesetz 2007:LXV v. 20.06.2007[41].

36 Erstmals Komitatsgericht Hajdú-Bihar, BH 2005 Nr. 6.

37 Grundlegend die Entscheidung des Tafelgerichts Szeged, BH 2008 Nr. 111, unter ausdrücklicher Aufgabe der Vor-Beitritts-Rechtsprechung in BH 2001 Nr. 205.

38 BH 2009 Nr. 196.

39 Siehe Fn. 24.

40 MK 2003 Nr. 58.

41 MK 207 Nr. 77.

Das bereits in Punkt II.2. erwähnte Gesetz über die internationale Rechtshilfe in Strafsachen[42] brachte auch für die Zusammenarbeit mit EU-Staaten einige Änderungen, v.a. um den Rahmenbeschluss über die gegenseitige Anerkennung von Geldstrafen und -bußen[43] umzusetzen. Das ermöglicht die Vollstreckung ausländischer Geldsanktionen in Ungarn ebenso wie das Eintreiben ungarischer Geldstrafen und -bußen in anderen Mitgliedstaaten. In Ungarn sind die örtlichen Gerichte für die Vollstreckung der ausländischen Strafen zuständig, und in ungarischen Verfahren kann sich das Gericht, das die Geldstrafe verhängt, unmittelbar an das ausländische Vollstreckungsgericht wenden.

Vergleichsweise wenig Grundsatzprobleme bereitete Ungarn der Europäische Haftbefehl. Seine Rechtsgrundlagen finden sich in §§ 25-33 EU-StrZusG[44]. Verfassungsrechtliche Probleme traten nicht auf und auch die verfassungs- und andere rechtliche Literatur widmete dem Haftbefehl wenig Aufmerksamkeit. Lediglich die Ratifizierung des Auslieferungsabkommens der EU mit Island und Norwegen wurde durch das Verfassungsgericht für vorübergehend verfassungswidrig qualifiziert, da das Inkrafttreten der bereits verabschiedeten verfassungsrechtlichen Anpassungen an das Inkrafttreten des Vertrags von Lissabon geknüpft war; da sich dies sehr verzögerte, war das Auslieferungsabkommen zum Zeitpunkt der beabsichtigten Ratifizierung noch nicht von der Verfassung gedeckt[45].

Der Rechtsprechung oblag es, den Europäischen Haftbefehl in das innerstaatliche Rechtssystem einzubauen. In einem Grundsatzurteil klärte das Oberste Gericht das Verhältnis zwischen StPO und EU-StrZusG in dem Sinne, dass letzteres eine *lex specialis* darstellt. Deshalb kann weder für die Auslieferungs- und Auslieferungsverweigerungsgründe noch für die Anordnung der Abschiebehaft auf die allgemeinen Vorschriften der StPO zurückgegriffen werden[46]. Dementsprechend ist auch das Verfahren der Auslieferung eine Sondermaterie, die nicht allgemeinem Verfahrensrecht unterliegt. Das bedeutet nach der höchstrichterlichen Rechtsprechung, dass bei einem Auslieferungsbegehren eines EU-Staats ungarische Behörden nur prüfen dürfen, ob die in Auslieferungshaft genommene und dem Haftrichter vorgeführte Person mit der im europäischen Haftbefehl ausgeschriebenen identisch ist. Weiter gehende Beweisaufnahmen sind unstatthaft. Ergibt die Prüfung der Personenidentität, dass der Inhaftierte nicht die gesuchte Person ist, hat das Gericht den staatsanwaltlichen Antrag auf Ausliefe-

42 Siehe Fn. 18.

43 Rahmenbeschluss 2005/214/JI des Rates v. 24.02.2005.

44 Die heutige Fassung wurde eingefügt durch Gesetz 2007:CV über die Zusammenarbeit und den Informationsaustausch im Rahmen des Schengener Durchführungsabkommens v. 11.07.2007, MK 2007 Nr. 93.

45 Verfassungsgerichtsurteil 32/2008. (III. 12.) AB v. 12.03.2008, Az Alkotmánybíróság határozatai (offizielle Entscheidungssammlung, in der Folge: ABH) 2008, 325.

46 BH 2010 Nr. 37.

rungshaft, nicht aber – wie von dem in europäischen Haftsachen landesweit zuständigen Hauptstädtischen Gericht praktiziert – den Haftbefehl zurückzuweisen. Der Haftbefehl bleibt bestehen und die ungarischen Behörden haben nach der tatsächlich ausgeschriebenen Person zu suchen. Rechtsmittel gegen den Auslieferungsbeschluss des Hauptstädtischen Gerichts sind nur bei vereinfachten Auslieferungsverfahren – welches u.a. die Zustimmung des Betroffenen voraussetzt – ausgeschlossen; im Übrigen ist die Berufung zum Hauptstädtischen Tafelgericht zulässig[47].

Schließlich sind Urteile im Zusammenhang mit dem Europäischen Haftbefehl und der Auslieferung in EU-Staaten nicht revisionsfähig, weil sie nicht in den abschließenden Katalog revisibler Rechtsverletzungen in § 416 StPO aufgenommen wurden[48].

IV. Autonome Entwicklungen

Die Hauptakteure bei der autonomen Fortentwicklung des Straf- und Strafprozessrechts waren naturgemäß der Gesetzgeber, der insbesondere 2007 mehrere große Novellen zum StGB erließ sowie die Rechtsprechung, v.a. das Oberste Gericht.

Eine wichtige Rolle kam auch dem Verfassungsgericht zu, das in manchen Entscheidungen bestehende Regelungen für verfassungskonform erklärte, in nicht wenigen Fällen allerdings auch verfassungswidrige Vorschriften aufhob. Spektakulär war eine Entscheidung von Ende 2004, in der das Verfassungsgericht die Entkriminalisierung des Besitzes minimaler Mengen leichter Drogen mit dem Argument für verfassungswidrig erklärte, das soziale Grundrecht auf möglichst gute Gesundheit in § 70/D Verf. verpflichte den Staat dazu, den Einzelnen zur Not gegen seinen Willen zu gesundem Verhalten zu zwingen, und zwar auch und gerade mit der *ultima ratio* des Strafrechts[49]. Berichterstatter war der Strafrechtler *Á. Erdei*, was die strafrechtsfreundliche Tendenz erklären mag. Im Übrigen ist ein solcher Rückfall in die Ideologie des paternalistischen Zwangsbeglückungsstaats vereinzelt geblieben[50]. Akzeptabler ist die Entscheidung, dass der Gesetzgeber kein verfassungswidriges Unterlassen begangen hat, weil er das Verfassungsgebot der „strengen Bestrafung jedweder Art nachteiliger Unterscheidung“[51] nicht durch einen eigenen Straftatbestand „Nachteilige

47 Oberstes Gericht, BH 2009 Nr. 268.

48 Oberstes Gericht, BH 2010 Nr. 87.

49 VerfG 54/2004. (XII. 13.) AB v. 13.12.2004, ABH 2004, 690.

50 Kritik kam v.a. von Verfassungsrechtlern, kaum aber von Strafrechtlern: *T. Győrfi*, Üzenet az elefántcsonttoronyból: az Alkotmánybíróság droghatározata, Fundamentum 2005/1, S. 73-85; *M. Lévai*, Paternalizmus és jogbizonytalanság, Fundamentum 2005/1, S. 86-98.

51 § 70/A Abs. 2 Verf.: „(2) Das Gesetz bestraft streng jedwede nachteilige Unterscheidung zwischen Menschen […]“.

Unterscheidung“ umgesetzt hat. Nach Ansicht des Verfassungsgerichts enthält das StGB derart viele Delikte, die den Einzelnen vor Diskriminierung schützen, dass damit der Verfassungsauftrag erfüllt ist[52].

Hinzuweisen ist in diesem Zusammenhang auch auf das Volk. Seit etwa 2007 nimmt die Zahl direktdemokratischer Initiativen sehr zu. Einige davon betreffen den hier betrachteten Bereich und zielen fast alle auf die Ausweitung der Strafbarkeit oder die Verschärfung von Sanktionen. Alle Begehren müssen vorab vom Landeswahlausschuss auf ihre Verfassungs- und Gesetzmäßigkeit geprüft werden. Auf verfassungsrechtliche Bedenken stieß die Initiative, Vermögensdelikte mit äußerst geringem Schaden von Ordnungsdelikten zu Straftaten hochzustufen; der Landeswahlausschuss sah das Verhältnismäßigkeitsgebot als verletzt an[53]. An dem formellen Erfordernis einer eindeutigen Frage scheiterte das Begehren, eine *Third-shot*-Regel mit obligatorischer lebenslanger Freiheitsstrafe bei der dritten Verurteilung im Bereich der mittleren und schweren Kriminalität einzuführen[54], sowie ein offensichtlich nicht ernst gemeintes Bündel von Initiativen zur Pönalisierung der Leugnung der nationalsozialisitschen und/oder der kommunistischen Verbrechen, des Holodomor, der chinesischen Hungersnot 1958/61 und des Massakers vom Tienanmen[55]. Vermutlich sollte diese Initiative den kurz vor seiner Einführung stehenden Tatbestand der Holocaustleugnung durch Inflationierung geschützter „Wahrheiten“ diskreditieren. In früheren Jahren häufigere, aber inhaltlich unzulässige Initiativen zur Wiedereinführung der Todesstrafe wurden seit dem EU-Beitritt nicht wiederholt. Für zulässig erachtet wurden Begehren, die Strafmündigkeitsgrenze von 14 auf 12[56] oder gar auf 10[57] Jahre abzusenken, die Holocaust-Leugnung in das StGB auf-

52 VerfG 41/2007. (VI. 20.) AB, ABH 2007, 551.

53 Beschluss des Landeswahlausschusses 167/2009. (V. 20.) OVB v. 20.05.2009, MK 2009 Nr. 69, bestätigt durch VerfG 87/2010. (VI. 2.) AB v. 02.06.2010.

54 Beschluss des Landeswahlausschusses 168/2009. (V. 20.) OVB v. 20.05.2009, MK 2009 Nr. 69, bestätigt durch Verfassungsgerichtsurteil 83/2010. (V. 20.) AB v. 20.05.2010, MK 2010 Nr. 83.

55 Beschlüsse des Landeswahlausschusses 254/2010. (III. 31.) OVB bis 257/2010. (III. 31.) OVB, alle v. 31.03.2010, MK 2010 Nr. 47.

56 Beschluss des Landeswahlausschusses 230/2008. (VII. 16.) OVB v. 16.07.2008, MK 2008 Nr. 105. Initiator war die rechtsradikale Jobbik-Bewegung.

57 Beschluss des Landeswahlausschusses 275/2008. (IX. 26.) OVB v. 26.09.2008, MK 2008 Nr. 139. Initiator war eine anonyme Privatperson. Hierzu *M. Herczog*, Nincsenek csodák! A gyermekkori bűnelkövetés megelőzéséről és kezeléséről, Fundamentum 2008/2, S. 79-88; *L. Korinek*, „Cseszszopók, akikben megnő az értelem“. A gyermekek büntethetőségéről, Fundamentum 2008/2, S. 69-78.

zunehmen[58] und die Zahlung und Entgegennahme des im Gesundheitssektor allgegenwärtigen „Dankgeldes“ zu einem Straftatbestand zu machen[59].

Nicht auf eine Verschärfung zielte die Initiative, eine sechsköpfige Geschworenenbank zur Entscheidung über Schuld und Unschuld in der ersten Instanz einzuführen[60]. Allerdings sind auch die zulässigen Verfahren von den Initiatoren nicht so weit weiterverfolgt worden, dass auch nur in einem Fall die zum Erfolg notwendige Unterschriftenzahl gesammelt wurde.

1. Strafbarkeit juristischer Personen

Bereits 2001 wurde ein Gesetz über die Strafbarkeit juristischer Personen erlassen, das zum EU-Beitritt in Kraft trat[61] – mit der unzutreffenden Begründung, dass hiermit Rechtsangleichungspflichten erfüllt würden[62]. Auch nach dem Beitritt kam die Praxis zu diesem Gesetz praktisch nicht in Gang, weil materielle und Verfahrensvorschriften schlecht aufeinander abgestimmt waren und die Staatsanwaltschaften lieber auf dem bekannten Terrain der Verfolgung natürlicher Personen blieben[63].

Das soll eine Novelle von 2008 ändern[64]. Sie behält den Grundsatz bei, dass die juristische Person sich selbst– in Ermangelung einer eigenständigen Strafrechtssubjektivität[65] – nicht strafbar macht, sondern für das strafgerichtlich festgestellte Verhalten der für sie handelnden Personen sanktioniert wird. Zahlreiche Präzisierungen sollen nunmehr für eine bessere Zuordnung und Verfolgbarkeit von Taten im Innenbereich der juristischen Person sorgen und Empfehlungen v.a. der GRECO-Gruppe und der OECD umsetzen. Zudem öffnet die Novelle die Revision in Verfahren gegen juristische Personen. Auch wenn die Praxis

---

58 Beschluss des Landeswahlausschusses 297/2007. (VIII. 23.) OVB v. 23.08.2007, MK 2007 Nr. 113.

59 Beschluss des Landeswahlausschusses 306/2007. (VIII. 23.) OVB v. 23.08.2007, MK 2007 Nr. 113. Zur Praxis des Dankgeldes siehe *H. Küpper*, Ungarn: Auf dem Weg zum gläsernen Beamten, in F.-C. Schroeder, H. Küpper (Hrsg.), Korruptionsbekämpfung in Osteuropa, forost Arbeitspapier Nr. 46, München 2008, S. 375-539 (376-377).

60 Zulässig gemäß Verfassungsgerichtsurteil 40/2006. (IX. 27.) AB, ABH 2006, 510, unzulässig, weil gegen die Verfassungsgarantie des Berufsrichters verstoßend, gemäß Verfassungsgerichtsurteil 30/2007. (V. 24.) AB, ABH 2007, 362.

61 Gesetz 2001:CIV über die strafrechtlichen Maßnahmen, die gegenüber juristischen Personen angewandt werden können, v. 24.12.2001, MK 2001 Nr. 153.

62 So die Regierungsbegründung zum Gesetzentwurf.

63 *M. Bodor*, A jogi személlyel szemben alkalmazható büntetőjogi intézkedések, Gazdaság és Jog 5/2004, S. 3-8; *B. Busch*, A jogi személy büntetőjogi felelőssége, in FS *I. Békés*, Budapest 2000, S. 97-114; *Z. Kiss*, A jogi személyek büntetőjogi felelőssége, Cég és Jog 2002/4-5, S. 2-6; *H. Küpper* in *F.-C. Schroeder, H. Küpper* (Fn. 59), S. 407-408.

64 Siehe Fn. 12.

65 So die offizielle Begründung zu der Regierungsvorlage des Gesetzes 2001:CIV.

nach wie vor spärlich ist, so steigt langsam die Zahl der Verfahren gegen juristische Personen[66].

2. Bekämpfung des politischen Extremismus

Ein Dauerelement der Strafrechtsentwicklung ist die Bekämpfung des politischen Extremismus, der in Ungarn vornehmlich von rechts kommt und immer aggressiver auftritt. Seit vielen Jahren bildet die Bestrafung von verbaler Aggressivität, der sog. *gyűlöletbeszéd* (Hassrede) – das Ungarische hat den englischen Begriff der *hate speech* wörtlich übersetzt – ein zentrales Thema der verfassungs- und strafrechtlichen Diskussion[67]. Es gibt mit Ausnahme des neuen BGB kaum ein anderes Thema, zu dem derart viele juristische Beiträge erscheinen.

Die Entwicklung findet aber nicht nur in der Wissenschaft statt, sondern auch in Gesetzgebung und Rechtsprechung. Allerdings wurde die am 08.12.2003 beschlossene Neufassung des § 269 StGB, die die „Hetze gegen eine Gemeinschaft“ schon beim „Aufreizen“ (*izgat*) statt wie bisher erst beim „Aufhetzen“ (*uszít*) unter Strafe stellen sowie auch schon den Aufruf hierzu pönalisieren wollte, im Wege der präventiven Normenkontrolle vom Verfassungsgericht wegen unverhältnismäßiger Beschränkung der Meinungsfreiheit (§ 61 Verf.) für verfassungswidrig erklärt[68]. Die Rechtsprechung „verwässerte“ das Potenzial des § 269 StGB noch weiter, indem sie die „Hetze gegen eine Gemeinschaft“ als konkretes und nicht abstraktes Gefährdungsdelikt interpretierte[69]. Infolgedessen muss dem Täter die konkrete Gefahr nachgewiesen werden, dass wegen seiner hetzenden Äußerung Gewalt gegen nationale, ethnische, rassische oder religiöse Gemeinschaften droht; im vorliegenden Fall wurde dies bei einem Zeitungsartikel, in dem ein calvinistischer Geistlicher dazu aufgerufen hatte, die „Scharen galizischer Dahergelaufener“[70] aus Ungarn zu vertreiben, verneint. Die Verurteilungszahlen nach § 269 StGB sind äußerst gering[71], trotz der allgegenwärtigen „Hassrede“ in den einschlägigen Medien.

Die Rede- und Meinungsfreiheit setzte sich auch gegen den geplanten Straftatbestand der Schmähung der ungarischen Nation oder einzelner Gruppen – u.a.

---

66 *Z. Fantoly*, A jogi személyek büntetőjogi felelőssége, Budapest 2008; *Z. A. Nagy*, A jogi személy büntetőjogi felelősségét megállapító törvényről, Jura 1/2009, S. 94-100.

67 Den aktuellen Diskussionsstand fassen *G. Bárándy*, A gyűlöletbeszéd Magyarországon, Budapest 2010 und *Á. Ujvári*, Büntetőjogi eszközök a közösségek elleni verbális támadásokkal szemben – ítélkezési problémák, jogalkotói válaszok, Magyar Jog 2010, S. 282-286, zusammen.

68 VerfG 18/2004. (V. 25.) AB v. 25.04.2004, ABH 2004, 303.

69 Hauptstädtisches Tafelgericht, BH 2005 Nr. 46.

70 Damit sind für jeden ungarischen Leser unmissverständlich die Juden gemeint.

71 Központi Statisztikai Hivatal (Zentrales Statistikamt; Hrsg.), Az ismertté vált bűncselekmények és elkövetőik Magyarországon, Miskolc 2008, http://portal.ksh.hu/pls/ksh/docs/hun/xftp/idoszaki/regiok/orsz/ismertbun.pdf, S. 44.

auch durch Körperbewegungen; damit sollte der Hitlergruß pönalisiert werden – durch. Der geplante § 181/A StGB wurde im Wege der präventiven Normenkontrolle für verfassungswidrig erklärt, weil die mit Rede- und Meinungsfreiheit konkurrierenden Rechtsgüter nur vage umschrieben seien und der Entwurf zudem bereits ihre abstrakte Gefährdung zur Straftat mache, was unverhältnismäßig sei[72].

Um die Bekämpfung nationalsozialistischer Propaganda zu intensivieren und das sinkende Ansehen Ungarns im Ausland wiederherzustellen, wurde ein § 269/C mit der amtlichen Überschrift „Öffentliches Leugnen des Holocaust" eingefügt[73]. Dies ist insofern eine autonome und keine gemeinschaftsrechtlich veranlasste Entwicklung, als weder das Gesetz noch die Regierungsbegründung Bezug auf Europarecht nehmen. Nunmehr wird mit bis zu drei Jahren Freiheitsentzug bestraft, wer „öffentlich die Würde der Opfer des Holocaust dadurch verletzt, dass er die Tatsache des Holocaust leugnet, in Zweifel zieht oder als unbedeutend darstellt". Bemerkenswert ist, dass die Strafvorschrift selbst das geschützte Rechtsgut – die Würde der Holocaustopfer – nennt. Allerdings ist der Gesetzgeber insofern inkonsequent, als er den neuen Tatbestand nicht bei den „Straftaten gegen die Freiheit und die Menschenwürde" (§§ 174-183/A StGB) regelt, sondern in örtlicher Nähe zu den politischen Delikten wie der erwähnten „Hetze gegen eine Gemeinschaft", der „Verletzung von Nationalsymbolen" und dem „Gebrauch von Symbolen der Willkürherrschaft" (§§ 269-269/B) im Unterkapitel der „Straftaten gegen die öffentliche Ruhe"[74]. Die erste Strafrechtsnovelle der im April 2010 mit Zweidrittelmehrheit gewählten nationalkonservativen Regierung weitete § 269/C StGB auf das „Öffentliche Leugnen der Verbrechen der nationalsozialistischen und kommunistischen Systeme" aus[75].

Ebenfalls dem Kampf gegen Rechts dient eine zweite Novelle[76], die in dem neu geschaffenen § 212/A die Teilnahme an einer gerichtlich aufgelösten Vereinigung unter Strafe stellt. Das richtet sich aktuell gegen die „Ungarische Garde" (*Magyar Gárda*), eine rechtsradikale paramilitärische, uniformierte und bewaffnete Vereinigung, die sich v.a. durch Gewalt und Einschüchterungen gegen Zigeuner hervortut. In einem mehrjährigen, über drei Instanzen gehenden Prozess,

---

72 VerfG 95/2008. (VII. 3.) AB, ABH 2008, 782.

73 StGB-Novelle 2010:XXXVI v. 11.03.2010, MK 2010 Nr. 34; hierzu *G. Bárándy*, A holokauszt tagadása. Mi lett volna, ha ... és vajon lesz-e valami?, Magyar Jog 2009, S. 735-745.

74 Hierzu *Á. Balogh*, Büntetőjog II. Különös Rész, Budapest, Pécs 2005, S. 319-329; *E. Belovics/G. Molnár/P. Sinku*, Büntetőjog. Különös rész, 8. Aufl., Budapest 2009, S. 387-392; *F. Nagy* (Hrsg.), A magyar büntetőjog különös része, Budapest 2009, S. 426-433.

75 StGB Novelle 2010:LVI v. 23.06.2010, MK 2010 Nr. 107.

76 StGB-Novelle 2010:XXXV v. 11.03.2010, MK 2010 Nr. 34.

wurde sie rechtskräftig aufgelöst[77]. Bereits nach dem erstinstanzlichen Auflösungsurteil verkündeten ihre Anführer, nicht nur Rechtsmittel einlegen, sondern auch die gerichtliche Auflösung ignorieren zu wollen. Daraufhin wurde Mitte 2009 die Fortführung einer aufgelösten Vereinigung und die Teilnahme an deren Tätigkeit zu bußgeldbewehrten Ordnungswidrigkeiten gemacht[78]. In zeitlicher Nähe zu dem letztinstanzlichen Auflösungsurteil und im Hinblick auf die öffentliche Ankündigung, die Garde fortzuführen, wurde der Tatbestand zur Straftat hochgestuft.

Der strafrechtliche Kampf gegen den politischen Extremismus richtet sich nicht nur gegen Rechts, sondern auch gegen Links, wobei diese Aktivitäten weniger eine akute Bedrohung abwehren, als vielmehr der Abrechnung mit dem alten Regime dienen[79]. *Sedes materiae* ist der „Gebrauch von Symbolen der Willkürherrschaft" (§ 269/B StGB), der seit 1993 strafbar ist. Wegen dieser Straftat verurteilte das Hauptstädtische Gericht im Juni 2008 den Vizepräsidenten einer linken Splitterpartei, der einen roten Stern an der Kleidung getragen hatte, zu einer Geldstrafe. Das Gericht ließ sich auch nicht davon beirren, dass wegen dieser Strafvorschrift ein Verfahren beim EGMR anhängig war und das Urteil kurz bevorstand[80].

Einen Monat später erging das erwartete Straßburger Urteil, das in der Sache Vajnai ./. Ungarn die Pönalisierung des Tragens des roten Sterns für konventionswidrig erklärte. Zwar stehe die Redefreiheit einer Beschränkung der Werbung für totalitäre Ideologien nicht entgegen, der rote Stern aber sei kein totalitäres Symbol, da zahlreiche legale Parteien in Europa ihn verwenden. Auch aus den Erfahrungen der jüngeren ungarischen Geschichte, wo der rote Stern für eine Diktatur gestanden habe, ergebe sich keine andere Wertung, da diese fast zwei Jahrzehnte zurückliege[81].

Nach einem Urteil des Obersten Gerichts von 2009 erfüllt den Tatbestand des § 269/B nicht, wer die Symbole verwendet, um vor eben diesen Ideologien zu warnen, und sie in einem eindeutig negativen Kontext verwendet. Diese an sich erfreuliche teleologische Auslegung wird allerdings durch eine unerfreuli-

77 In letzter Instanz in dem Urteil des Obersten Gerichts BH 2010 Nr. 126; hierzu *H. Küpper*, A Legfelsőbb Bíróság ítélete a Magyar Gárda feloszlatása ügyében, Jogesetek Magyarázata 2010/2, S. 17-24.

78 RegVO 146/2009. (VII. 14.) Korm. über die Änderung der RegVO 218/1999. (XII. 28.) Korm. über einzelne Ordnungswidrigkeiten, MK 2009 Nr. 97 (Teilnahme); RegVO 253/2009. (XI. 18.) Korm. über die Änderung der RegVO 218/1999. (XII. 28.) Korm. über einzelne Ordnungswidrigkeiten, MK 2009 Nr. 162 (Fortführung).

79 Näher hierzu Punkt IV.5.

80 Népszabadság, 10.06.2008.

81 Urteil v. 08.07.2008, 33629/06; hierzu *H. Küpper*, Länderbericht Ungarn, in *F.-C. Schroeder*, *H. Küpper* (Hrsg.), Die rechtliche Aufarbeitung der kommunistischen Vergangenheit in Europa, Studien des Instituts für Ostrecht München Bd. 63, Frankfurt/M. 2010, S. 271-322 (316-318).

che dogmatische Konstruktion untermauert: In einem solchen Fall fehle es an der „Sozialgefährlichkeit", die gemäß § 10 Abs. 2 StGB immer noch zu den Voraussetzungen der Strafbarkeit gehört[82].

3. Wirtschaftsstrafrecht

Ein zentraler Bereich der Entwicklung war das Wirtschaftsstrafrecht[83]. Soweit Entwicklungen durch völker- und europarechtliche Vorgaben angestoßen wurde, wird darüber in Punkten II.1. und III.1. berichtet. Darüber hinaus weist dieser Bereich auch autonome Elemente auf.

So stellte die StGB-Novelle von 2005[84] die „wettbewerbsbeschränkende Abrede in öffentlichen Beschaffungs- und Konzessionsverfahren" (§ 296/B) unter Strafe und erweiterte die Strafbarkeit des Insiderhandels in § 299/A, indem sie die Beschränkung auf Wertpapiere aufhob[85]. Die StGB-Novelle vom April 2007[86] erweiterte und präzisierte u.a. die Konkursdelikte, die Nichtabführung von Sozialversicherungsbeiträgen und die Verletzung geistiger und gewerblicher Schutzrechte.

Auch die Rechtsprechung trug zur Verschärfung des Wirtschaftsstrafrechts bei. So subsumierte das Oberste Gericht vorgetäuschte Grundstücksverträge unter den Tatbestand der Fälschung einer öffentlichen Urkunde in § 274 Abs. 1 Buchst. c) StGB, wenn der nicht dem Willen der Parteien entsprechende Vertrag zu Eintragungen im Grundbuch führt. Hintergrund ist die Praxis, durch Strohmänner die Erwerbsverbote für Ackerboden zu umgehen; da dies unmittelbar nur schwer strafrechtlich erfasst werden kann, nutzt die Rechtsprechung den Umweg über die Beurkundungsdelikte[87].

Das Wirtschaftsstrafrecht war auch ein Schwerpunkt der strafrechtsbezogenen Verfassungsrechtsprechung. Keine Verletzung der Unternehmensfreiheit in § 9 Abs. 2 Verf. stellt demnach die Strafbarkeit der Herstellung und des Vertriebs von Produkten mangelhafter Qualität sowie der Verbrauchertäuschung (§§ 292-294, 296/A StGB) dar. Da privatrechtliche Rechtsfolgen gegen diese Handlungen keinen ausreichenden Schutz böten, sei eine Pönalisierung nicht unverhältnismäßig[88]. Auch die Strafbarkeit der Unterlassung von Meldepflichten

---

82 BH 2009 Nr. 131. Zur Sozialgefährlichkeit im heutigen Strafrecht siehe *Á. Balogh/L. Kőhalmi*, Büntetőjog I. Általános Rész, 2. Aufl., Budapest Pécs 2007, S. 32-33; sehr kritisch *A. Jakab/M. Hollán*, Die dogmatische Hinterlassenschaft des Sozialismus im heutigen Recht: das Beispiel Ungarn, JOR 46 (2005) 11-40 (34-39).

83 Umfassend *I. Gál*, Gazdasági büntetőjog közgazdászoknak, Budapest 2007.

84 Siehe Fn. 31.

85 Eine pessimistische Bilanz der Praxis zieht *Á. Kaszás*, Elvi elszántság, gyakorlati tehetetlenség: a bennfentes kereskedelem elleni küzdelem első másfél évtizede, Magyar Jog 2008, S. 96-103.

86 Siehe Fn. 13.

87 BH 2008 Nr. 10.

88 VerfG 334/B/2004 v. 31.03.2006, ABH 2006, 1573.

bei Geldwäsche gemäß § 303/B StGB verstößt nicht gegen die Verfassung. Zwar ist die Strafnorm v.a. durch Verweise sehr kompliziert formuliert, aber in diesem Fall ist dies auch aus Sicht der gesteigerten Anforderungen an die Normenklarheit im Strafrecht unbedenklich, weil sich nur bestimmte Bankangestellte strafbar machen können, von denen entsprechende Kenntnisse erwartet werden können[89].

4. Hinwendung zu den Opfern

Auch in Ungarn hat die allgemeine Tendenz weg vom reinen Täterstrafrecht und hin zu einer größeren Berücksichtigung der Opfer Fuß gefasst.

Ein wichtiger Punkt war die Einführung des Täter-Opfer-Ausgleichs, für den Ende 2006 ein Mediationsverfahren eingerichtet wurde[90]. Kurz zuvor hatte bereits eine StPO-Novelle[91] die Brücke im Strafprozessrecht durch Einbettung der Mediation in das Verfahren in § 221/A StPO und im materiellen Strafrecht durch Neufassung der tätigen Reue in § 36 StGB geschlagen. Danach kann bei bestimmten Straftaten gegen individuelle Rechtsgüter von Strafe abgesehen oder die Strafe gemildert werden, wenn der Täter bis zur Anklageerhebung gesteht und im Rahmen der Mediation den Schaden des Opfers wiedergutmacht (*jóvâteszi*). § 36 StGB wurde durch die StGB-Novelle von 2009[92] präzisiert und der Erfolg der Mediation stärker als bisher von der Annahme durch den Geschädigten abhängig gemacht.

Dieselbe Novelle stärkte die Position des Opfers auch dadurch, dass bei der Notwehr das Verhältnismäßigkeitsgebot abgeschwächt wurde (§§ 29, 29/A StGB)[93].

Seit der Neuregelung der Opferentschädigung aus öffentlichen Kassen 2005[94] stehen dem bedürftigen Tatopfer in bescheidenem Ausmaß soziale Ansprüche zu, falls der Täter nicht ermittelt oder wegen z.B. Verjährung oder Schuldunfähigkeit nicht verurteilt werden kann. Deutlich großzügiger ist die staatliche Opferversorgung, wenn das Tatopfer seine Ansprüche gegen den Täter

---

89 VerfG 673/B/2004 v. 20.06.2006, ABH 2006, 1604.

90 Gesetz 2006:CXXIII über die Vermittlertätigkeit in Strafsachen v. 21.12.2006, MK 2006 Nr. 159; hierzu *B. Fellegi*, Út a megbékéléshez. A helyreallító igazságszolgáltatás intézményesülése Magyarországon, Budapest 2009; *I. Görgényi*, Kárjóvátétel a büntetőjogban, mediáció a büntetőügyekben, Budapest 2006.

91 Gesetz 2006:LI v. 03.03.2006, MK 2006 Nr. 26.

92 Gesetz 2009:LXXX v. 10.07.2009, MK 2009 Nr. 96. Kritisch zu diesem Teil der Novelle *Z. Schweighardt*, Kritikai kérdések a helyreállító igazságszolgáltatás elméletével összefüggésben, Magyar Jog 2009, S. 361-373.

93 Zur für das sich wehrende Opfer recht strengen alten Rechtslage siehe *Á. Balogh/ L. Kőhalmi* (Fn. 82), S. 128-142.

94 Gesetz 2005:CXXXV über die Hilfe für Opfer von Straftaten und die staatliche Schadenslinderung v. 06.12.2005, MK 2005 Nr. 56.

nicht durchsetzen kann, weil dieser wegen seiner Zusammenarbeit mit den Strafverfolgungsbehörden vor Strafe geschützt wird (Kronzeuge)[95].

5. Strafrechtliche Vergangenheitsbewältigung

Einen schweren Rückschlag erlitt die strafrechtliche Aufarbeitung des kommunistischen Unrechts durch den EGMR. Diese ist in Ungarn ohnehin nicht einfach, weil das heute noch strafwürdige staatliche Unrecht in den wilden Erschießungen während und unmittelbar nach dem Aufstand 1956, d.h. sehr weit zurück liegt. Bereits Mitte der 1990er Jahre nahm das Verfassungsgericht in insgesamt vier Verjährungsurteilen ausgewogen Stellung und bejahte die heutige Verfolgungsmöglichkeit nur für bereits seinerzeit völkerrechtlich verjährungsfrei gestellte Straftaten, d.h. Kriegsverbrechen und Verbrechen gegen die Menschlichkeit[96].

In einem der wenigen überhaupt durchgeführten Strafverfahren hatte sich der so verurteilte Täter nach Straßburg gewandt, und der EGMR sah wenig überzeugend in der Verurteilung wegen Verbrechen gegen die Menschlichkeit eine gemäß Art. 7 EMRK verbotene rückwirkende Rechtsanwendung[97]. Problematisch ist v.a., dass der EGMR eigene Sachverhaltsermittlungen an die Stelle der Feststellungen der ungarischen Gerichte stellte. Anders als im Fall Kononov[98] hatte der EGMR im Fall Korbely allerdings keine Gelegenheit, sein Fehlurteil durch die Große Kammer zu revidieren, da diese bereits die Ausgangsentscheidung erlassen hatte.

Ganz ließ sich die ungarische Rechtsprechung hiervon nicht entmutigen. 2009 erging eine weitere Verurteilung gegen einen Täter von1956, der während des Aufstands mehrere, wohl unbewaffnete Demonstranten erschossen hatte. Unter Berücksichtigung der EGMR-Rechtsprechung ging das Oberste Gericht stärker als in früheren Urteilen auf das Ineinanderwirken des seinerzeit geltenden ungarischen Strafrechts und des einschlägigen Völkervertragsrechts ein, um so dem Vorwurf rückwirkender Rechtsanwendung zu begegnen[99].

---

95 § 67 Abs. 2 Gesetz 1994:XXXIV über die Polizei v. 20.04.1994, MK 1994 Nr. 41.

96 Dazu *G. Brunner/G. Halmai*, Länderbericht Ungarn, in *G. Brunner* (Hrsg.), Juristische Bewältigung des kommunistischen Unrechts in Osteuropa und Deutschland, Berlin 1995, S. 9-40 (25-30); *H. Küpper* (Fn. 81), 304-308.

97 Korbely ./. Ungarn, 19.09.2008, 9174/02. Kritisch zu dieser EGMR-Rechtsprechung *F.-C. Schroeder/H. Küpper*, Europäischer Menschenrechtsgerichtshof: Der EGMR und die Bestrafung stalinistischer Verbrechen. Dokumentation der Urteile Kononov ./. Lettland und Korbely ./. Ungarn mit einer Einführung, JOR 50 (2009) 213-266; *F.-C. Schroeder*, Neues Urteil des EGMR in der Sache Kononov ./. Lettland, JOR 51 (2010), 341-381.

98 Kononov ./. Lettland, 17.05.2010, 36376/04.

99 BH 2009 Nr. 321.

6. Sanktionen

Im Recht der Tatfolgen sind zahlreiche Entwicklungen zu verzeichnen. In einigen Fällen entwickelte der Gesetzgeber die bestehenden Rechtsgrundlagen fort. Die bereits erwähnte StGB-Novelle von 2005[100] stellte die Ausweisung in § 61 StGB auf eine rechtsstaatlichere Grundlage, indem die Ausweisungsgründe von Generalklauseln auf Kataloge und Mindeststrafschwellen umgestellt wurden. Zudem wurde die Ausweisung dauerhaft im Land lebender Ausländer nochmals erschwert. Die Rechtsprechung ist bei dieser Strafart ohnehin zurückhaltend, wenn familiäre Beziehungen oder inländische Unterhaltsansprüche darunter leiden könnten[101].

Umfassende Strafschärfungen bei schwerer und Gewaltkriminalität sieht die StGB-Novelle 2009[102] vor. Eine stärkere Ausdifferenzierung bei Rückfalltätern erlaubte es dem Gesetzgeber, gerade bei rückfälligen Gewalttätern die Strafandrohungen drastisch zu verschärfen (§ 97/A StGB), ohne allerdings die bisweilen geforderte *Third-shot*-Regel einzuführen[103]. Berufs- und Fahrverbot sowie Ausweisungen wurden von Neben- zu Hauptstrafen angehoben, die Bindung des Fahrverbots an Verkehrsdelikte ist allerdings geblieben. Zudem hob die Novelle im BT manche Strafobergrenzen an und kodifizierte in § 20 Abs. 2 StGB den richterrechtlich bereits anerkannten mittelbaren Täter. Die Strafrechtsnovelle vom Juni 2010 verschärfte diese Regeln noch einmal, insbesondere für Täter von Gewaltdelikten gegen Personen[104].

Wichtiger noch als die Gesetzgebung ist im Bereich der Tatfolgen die Rechtsprechung. Ein nicht geringer Teil der jährlich ca. 3-5 Rechtseinheitlichkeitsentscheidungen in Strafsachen betreffen die Sanktionen.

Einen Schwerpunkt höchstrichterlicher Rechtsprechung bildet die Einziehung des aus oder im Zusammenhang mit der Tat erworbenen Vermögens gemäß § 77/B Abs. 1 Buchst. a) StGB[105] bei Drogendelikten. Rechtseinheitlichkeitsentscheidung 1/2008. BJE[106] befürwortet die weite Auslegung i.S.d. Einziehung des gesamten „mit der Verwertung des Rauschgifts“ zusammenhängenden Vermögenszuwachses und nicht nur des Veräußerungsgewinns. Dieselbe Tendenz zeigt Rechtseinheitlichkeitsentscheidung 2/2008. BJE[107]. Danach kann

---

100 Siehe Fn. 31.

101 Oberstes Gericht, BH 2007 Nr. 211, unter ausdrücklicher Berufung auf die EMRK.

102 Siehe Fn. 92.

103 Zum Diskussionsstand *A. Borbíró*, „Three Strikes and you're out“ Magyarországon – kriminálpolitikai racionalitás vagy szimbolikus jogalkotás?, Acta Facultatis Budapestinensis 2008, S. 165-181.

104 StGB-Novelle 2010:LVI (Fn. 75).

105 Umfassend hierzu *M. Hollán*, Vagyonelkobozás. Bűncselekményekből származó vagyon elvonása, Budapest 2008.

106 MK 2008 Nr. 36.

107 MK 2008 Nr. 78.

Vermögen schon dann eingezogen werden, wenn die Ermittlungen sich noch gegen Unbekannt richten, falls die allgemeinen Voraussetzungen der Sequestrierung in § 159 StPO vorliegen, d.h. die Gefahr besteht, dass ohne die Maßnahme das Vermögen dem Zugriff des Staats und der Geschädigten entzogen wird. Der Vermögenszuwachs ist brutto zu berechnen, d.h.er umfasst alle Vermögensvorteile aus dem Drogenbesitz. Die Investitionen wie z.B. der Kaufpreis und die Aufbewahrungs- und Veräußerungskosten für die Drogen können hiervon nicht abgezogen werden[108].

Von der Vermögenseinziehung ausgenommen sind gemäß der Stellungnahme Nr. 69 des Kollegiums für Strafsachen am Obersten Gericht[109] Gegenstände, an denen der Geschädigte einen zivilrechtlichen Anspruch hat. Da der Zweck der Maßnahme der Vermögenseinziehung in der Abschöpfung des Verbrechensgewinns liegt, kann sie sich nicht auf dem Geschädigten zustehende Werte beziehen. Grundsätzlich haben Opferansprüche sogar einen gewissen Vorrang, denn der abzuschöpfende Vermögenszuwachs berechnet sich unter Abzug der dem Opfer zustehenden Gegenstände und Leistungen.

Rechtseinheitlichkeitsentscheidung 2/2006. BJE[110] hatte die 1998 novellierte Gesamtstrafe in § 92 StGB zum Gegenstand. Ausgehend von deren Zweck, Nachteile des Täters auszugleichen, wenn mehrere seiner Straftaten in getrennten statt in einem Verfahren abgeurteilt werden, präzisierte das Oberste Gericht die Voraussetzungen der obligatorischen Gesamtstrafenbildung: mehrere zeitige, noch nicht vollständig verbüßte Taten, die alle vor dem ersten rechtskräftigen Urteil begangen wurden.

Schließlich fanden die Haftbedingungen für Behinderte keine Gnade vor dem EGMR. In der Sache Engel ./. Ungarn[111] sah das Straßburger Gericht eine erniedrigende Behandlung i.S.v. Art. 3 EMRK dadurch verwirklicht, dass der an den Rollstuhl gefesselte Beschwerdeführer für zahlreiche tägliche Verrichtungen (z.B. Körperpflege, Toilette) auf die Hilfe seiner Mithäftlinge verwiesen wurde und Transporte in Handschellen antreten musste, was ihm Verletzungen verursachte. Deshalb sprach der EGMR dem Beschwerdeführer den vollen geforderten Schmerzensgeldbetrag von 12.000,- € zu.

7. Strafverfahren

Die umfangreichen Entwicklungen im Strafprozessrecht[112] können aus Platzgründen nicht alle dargestellt werden. Daher seien nur zwei besonders wichtige

108 Tafelgericht Szeged, BH 2009 Nr. 1.

109 BH 2008 Heft 11.

110 MK 2006 Nr. 53.

111 Urteil v. 20.05.2010, 46857/06.

112 Hierzu umfassend in Deutsch *A. Széchényi*, Das neue ungarische Strafprozessrecht im Spannungsverhältnis zwischen Rechtsstaatsprinzip, Verfahrensökonomie und Effizienz, Studien des Instituts für Ostrecht München Bd. 48, Frankfurt/M. 2003.

Fragen hervorgehoben: die gesetzliche Anklage und die Beweismittel. Zudem sind, ausgehend von der Rechtsprechung des EGMR und des Verfassungsgerichts, Waffengleichheit und Fairness im Strafprozess immer wieder durch einzelne Regelungen verletzt, ohne dass sich hieraus jedoch ein systematischer Missstand ableiten lässt.

Der Grundsatz der gesetzlichen Anklage in § 2 StPO wurde durch die Novelle 2006[113] neu gefasst. Gemäß § 2 Abs. 1 StPO ist Voraussetzung eines jeden Verfahrens die gesetzliche Anklage (*törvényes vád*), die in Abs. 2 wie folgt definiert wird: „Gesetzlich ist die Anklage, falls der zur Anklageerhebung Berechtigte in seinem Antrag an das Gericht wegen einer genau umschriebenen, gegen das Strafgesetz verstoßenden Handlung einer bestimmten Person, die Durchführung des gerichtlichen Verfahrens beantragt". Hierüber kann das Gericht im Verfahren nicht hinausgehen. Diese Bindewirkung wirft in der Praxis immer wieder erhebliche Zweifelsfragen auf. Klar ist, dass die Anklage rechtsfehlerhaft und das Verfahren einzustellen ist, wenn die Anklageschrift den Tathergang nicht ausreichend identifizierbar beschreibt, sodass rechtliche Folgerungen nicht gezogen werden können[114]. Andererseits ist der Anklagegrundsatz nicht verletzt, wenn Staatsanwaltschaft und Gericht die Tat rechtlich abweichend bewerten. In einem Fall hatte die Staatsanwaltschaft wegen Untreue angeklagt, das Gericht aber wegen Betrugs verurteilt, was zulässig ist[115].

Es kommt v.a. auf die von der Staatsanwaltschaft dargelegten realen Vorgänge an. Das bedeutet auch, dass der Antrag des Staatsanwalts, bestimmte Handlungsteile rechtlich nicht zu bewerten, das Gericht an einer Bestrafung hindert[116]. Hingegen können in der Anklageschrift nicht enthaltene Teile eines Tatkomplexes in Handlungseinheit mit den angeklagten Handlungen ohne Verletzung der gesetzlichen Anklage in das Verfahren einbezogen und ggf. bestraft werden[117]. Dies präzisierte das Oberste Gericht später dahingehend, dass Erkenntnisse, die aus der Beweisaufnahme zur angeklagten Tat geschöpft werden, zur Ausdehnung des Prozessgegenstands herangezogen werden dürfen[118]. Ist die Tat aber gar nicht in der Anklageschrift enthalten, darf sie nicht zum Verfahrensgegenstand gemacht werden. Ein solcher Fall lag in einem wegen zahlreicher Urheberrechtsverletzungen eingeleiteten Verfahren vor: Als im Prozess weitere Fälle offenbart wurden, bedeutete deren Einbeziehung eine Verletzung des Anklagegrundsatzes[119].

---

113 Siehe Fn. 91. Zur Anklage vor der Novelle *C. Fenyvesi* u.a., Új magyar büntetőeljárás, Budapest, Pécs 2004, S. 132-136; *T. Király*, Büntetőeljárási jog, 2. Aufl., Budapest 2001, S. 352-366.

114 Oberstes Gericht, BH 2009 Nr. 267.

115 Oberstes Gericht, BH 2006 Nr. 278.

116 Tafelgericht Pécs, BH 2006 Nr. 281.

117 Oberstes Gericht, BH 2009 Nr. 5.

118 Oberstes Gericht, BH 2010 Nr. 114, BH 2010 Nr. 174.

119 Oberstes Gericht, BH 2009 Nr. 6.

Die verfassungsrechtliche Übertragung der Anklage auf die Staatsanwaltschaft (§ 51 Verf.) führt dazu, dass Vorschriften in der StPO verfassungswidrig sind, die die Staatsanwaltschaft von der Anwesenheitspflicht in der mündlichen Verhandlung freistellen[120]. Vor diesem Verfassungsgerichtsurteil fanden nach Angaben des Generalanwalts über ein Drittel aller Verfahren ohne Staatsanwalt statt.

Im Beweismittelrecht gab es Entwicklungen sowohl im Ermittlungs- als auch im Hauptverfahren. Im Ermittlungsverfahren war die geheime Datensammlung ein Problempunkt. Nachdem die StPO-Novelle 2006[121] die der Polizei[122] und Staatsanwaltschaft gemäß §§ 201-202 StPO erlaubten geheimen Ermittlungen – wenn auch unter Richtervorbehalt – recht weit gefasst hatte, hob das Verfassungsgericht die meisten dieser Befugnisse alsbald als übermäßige Beeinträchtigung der Privatsphäre als Teil der in § 54 Verf. geschützten Menschenwürde sowie der informationellen Selbstbestimmung (§ 59 Verf.) auf; lediglich in Bezug auf Schwerkriminalität hatten die Vorschriften Bestand[123]. §§ 201-202 StPO wurden daraufhin unter Beachtung der Vorgaben des Verfassungsgerichts durch ein StPO-Änderungsgesetz Ende 2007 neu gefasst[124].

Keine Bedenken hatte das Verfassungsgericht hingegen beim verdeckten Ermittler und dessen weitreichender Straffreiheit. Da der Staat das Strafmonopol und der Geschädigte keinen subjektiven Anspruch auf Bestrafung habe, besitze der Staat ein gewisses, beim verdeckten Ermittler nicht überschrittenes Ermessen, ob er bestimmte Personen aus Gründen des öffentlichen Interesses von der Bestrafung ausnehme. Zur wirksamen Bekämpfung der organisierten Kriminalität seien verdeckte Ermittler, die selbst gewisse Straftaten begehen dürfen, geeignet und angemessen. Wegen dieses vernünftigen Grundes scheidet auch eine verfassungswidrige Ungleichbehandlung zwischen Ermittlern und anderen Straftätern aus[125].

Der Beginn einer zuvor angekündigten Durchsuchung einer Rechtsanwaltskanzlei, obwohl die Rechtsanwältin zu dem Termin noch nicht anwesend war,

---

120 VerfG 72/2009. (VII. 10.) AB, ABH 2009, 715.

121 Siehe Fn. 91.

122 Die Polizei als Ermittlungsbehörde ist geregelt in der VO des Ministers für Justiz und Öffentliche Ordnung 3/2008. (I. 16.) IRM über die Befugnisse und örtlichen Zuständigkeiten der Ermittlungsbehörden der Polizei v. 16.01.2008, MK 2008 Nr. 6. Ausdrücklich keine hoheitlichen Befugnisse haben die 2006 eingeführten Bürgermilizen: Gesetz 2006:LII über die Bürgermiliz v. 03.03.2006, MK 2006 Nr. 26.

123 VerfG 2/2007. (I. 24.) AB v. 24.01.2007, ABH 2007, 65. Zur geheimen Datensammlung siehe *T. Jakucs*, A büntetőeljárási törvény magyarázata, 2 Bde, Budapest 2003, Bd. 1, S. 400-405.

124 Gesetz 2007:CLXXXIII v. 29.12.2007, MK 2007 Nr. 186.

125 VerfG 135/B/2006. AB v. 21.05.2007, ABH 2007, 1942. Die Rechtsgrundlagen des verdeckten Ermittlers sind §§ 67/A, 175 Abs. 2, 192 Abs. 2-3 Polizeigesetz (s.o. Fn. 95).

wurde vom EGMR als Verletzung der Unverletzlichkeit von Privaträumen (Art. 8 EMRK) gewertet; dieses Vorgehen ist auch aus Sicht der StPO bedenklich[126].

Im Hauptverfahren geben die Beweisverbote immer wieder Anlass zur höchstrichterlichen Rechtsfortbildung. § 78 Abs. 4 StPO verbietet die Verwertung von „aus solchen Beweismitteln stammenden Tatsachen, die das Gericht, der Staatsanwalt oder die Ermittlungsbehörde im Wege einer Straftat, auf andere verbotene Weise oder unter wesentlicher Beschränkung der Verfahrensrechte der Teilnehmer erlangt hat“. Obwohl der Wortlaut für ein weitgehendes Verwertungsverbot zu sprechen scheint, lehnt das Oberste Gericht eine strenge *Forbidden-fruit*-Doktrin ab. So erfolgt die Gewinnung einer Aussage, die ein Beteiligter vor einem nicht vorschriftsmäßig besetzten Gericht macht, nicht „auf andere verbotene Weise“[127]. Zudem ist die Verletzung beweisrechtlicher Vorschriften regelmäßig eine bloß relative und keine absolute Verletzung von Verfahrensrecht und damit nur eingeschränkt revisionsfähig[128]. Eine dogmatische oder rechtspolitische Begründung gibt das Oberste Gericht nicht.

V. Offene Fragen

Hier sollen nur einige der wichtigsten Probleme erwähnt werden. Die wohl bedeutendste offene Flanke ist der schlechte Zustand des StGB. Dieses ist vor und v.a. nach der Wende unzählige Male novelliert worden, z.T. in grundlegenden Bereichen. Dadurch ist es zu einem Flickenteppich geworden und enthält v.a. im Allgemeinen Teil widersprüchliche Wertungen. Hier kann nur der Erlass eines vollständig neuen StGB aus einem Guss Abhilfe schaffen. Dieser ist langfristig vorgesehen. Zu diesem Zweck bestand ab 2003 als Forum der rechtspolitischen Diskussionen die Zeitschrift *Büntetőjogi Kodifikáció* (Strafrechtliche Kodifikation)[129].

Im materiellen Recht ist als weiteres Problem die fast vollständige Nichtanwendung der Vorschriften über die Strafbarkeit juristischer Personen zu erwähnen. Unabhängig davon, ob man dies für sinnvoll hält oder nicht: Solange nach geltendem Recht auch juristische Personen sanktioniert werden können, ist es für die Rechtsstaatlichkeit und das Vertrauen in die Strafrechtspflege ein schweres Manko, wenn die Justiz hiervor zurückschreckt, weil sie Angst vor unbekanntem Terrain hat.

Die Rechtsprechung in Strafsachen trifft noch ein weiterer Vorwurf: den der mangelnden Konstitutionalisierung. Straf- und noch mehr Strafprozessrecht unterliegen starken verfassungsrechtlichen Einflüssen, was sich u.a. an der regen

126 Turán ./. Ungarn, 06.07.2010, 33068/05.

127 BH 2008 Nr. 237.

128 BH 2008 Nr. 264.

129 Parallel dazu gab es bis zum Abschluss der Kodifikationsarbeiten am BGB 2008 die Zeitschrift *Polgári Jogi Kodifikáció* (Bürgerlich-rechtliche Kodifikation).

Spruchtätigkeit des Verfassungsgerichts zu straf- und strafverfahrensrechtlichen Vorschriften zeigt. Das vollziehen die Strafgerichte nicht ausreichend nach. In den Köpfen vieler Richter ist noch die „Arbeitsteilung" verankert, dass das Verfassungsrecht Sache der Verfassungsrichter sei und der ordentliche Richter sich auf StGB und StPO beschränken könne. Selbst beim Obersten Gericht nimmt die Berücksichtigung verfassungsrechtlicher Einflüsse auf das einfache Recht erst allmählich zu; bei den Untergerichten ist diese Denkweise noch kaum angekommen[130].

Im Strafverfahren ist das größte Manko nach wie vor die zu lange Prozessdauer. Ungarn wird vom EGMR kontinuierlich wegen der Verletzung des Konventionsrechts auf zügige Gerichtsverfahren verurteilt. Dies betrifft zwar in den meisten Fällen Zivil- und Verwaltungsprozesse, aber auch Strafverfahren bieten immer wieder Anlass zur Verurteilung[131]. Die Beschleunigungsnovelle 2009[132] schafft möglicherweise eine erste Abhilfe, löst das Problem aber noch nicht.

---

130 *M. Bencze*, Díszítőelem, álcázháló vagy tartóoszlop? A büntetőbírói gyakorlat és az alkotmány, Fundamentum 2007/3, S. 5-21; *M. Hollán*, Az alkotmánybíróság határozatainak hivatkozása a büntetőbíróságok döntéseiben, Fundamentum 2008/3, S. 81-92.

131 So im Fall Medgyes und Rusz ./. Ungarn, 08.06.2010, 14308/07: Das Strafverfahren hatte sich vom 27.05.1992 (Eröffnung der Ermittlungen) bis zum 29.06.2006 (Freispruch in zweiter Instanz) hingezogen. Dass dies eine Verletzung von Art. 6 Abs. 1 EMRK darstellt, wurde auch von Ungarn nicht bestritten. Auch die Verletzung von Art. 5 Abs. 3 EMRK wurde in manchen Straßburger Urteilen gerügt, z.B. in Maglódi ./. Ungarn, 09.11.2004, 30103/02.

132 StPO-Änderungsgesetz 2009:LXXXIII v. 14.07.2009, MK 2009 Nr. 97.

Die Angst vor den Gefährdungsdelikten im Straßenverkehr

Wie in Südosteuropa die Angst vor der Pönalisierung von Gefährdungsdelikten im Straßenverkehr die Angst vor konkreten Lebensgefährdungen überwiegt

Prof. Dr. Damjan Korošec[*]

I. Einführend über den Erfolg im (Straßenverkehrs-)Strafrecht

Es gehört wohl zu den Grundlagen der Strafrechtstheorie, dass es innerhalb der Tatbestandsmäßigkeit als Element des mehrteiligen Verbrechensbegriffs zwei Formen des Erfolgs – oder, wie es seit jeher im slowenischen Strafrecht heißt: der verbotenen Folgen (der tatbestandsmäßigen Handlung) – gibt: die Verletzung und die Gefährdung des Strafrechtsguts. Deshalb unterscheiden wir auch traditionell Verletzungs- und Gefährdungsdelikte. Die neue Erscheinung der Besitzdelikte, die unter offensichtlichem Einfluss des Europäischen Strafrechts und der Politik im Sexualstrafrecht bei kinderpornographischen Schriften entstanden ist, ändert dabei im Grunde nicht viel. Im Rahmen der hier interessierenden Verkehrsdelikte reicht ihre bloße Erwähnung aus.

Vor allem aus rechtsvergleichender Sicht gibt es interessante Kulturen bzw. Tätigkeitsgebiete innerhalb einzelner Gesellschaften, die sich der Logik der Gefährdungsdelikte zu entziehen scheinen. Sie scheinen es geschafft haben, eine Art undurchdringliche Immunität bezüglich der Gefährdungsstrafbarkeit aufzubauen und aufrechtzuerhalten. Das gilt vor allem für den Straßenverkehr, wie er im Strafrecht vor allem vieler ost- und südosteuropäischer Staaten behandelt wird.

Wegen der Natur und der gesellschaftlichen Aufgaben des Strafrechts, insbesondere des Grundsatzes der Begrenztheit der Repression (Strafrecht als *ultima ratio*), fällt es nicht besonders schwer, das quantitative Verhältnis zwischen Verletzungs- und Gefährdungsdelikten auf der präskriptiven, gesetzgeberischen Ebene zu ermitteln: Man stellt sofort die ausgeprägte Vorherrschaft der Verletzungsdelikte fest. Die systematische Zurückhaltung des Gesetzgebers wie auch

* Ordentlicher Professor am Lehrstuhl für Strafrecht der Juristischen Fakultät der Universität Ljubljana.

der Anwender des Strafrechts als desjenigen Rechts, das für die Sicherstellung von Sicherheit und Ordnung in der Gesellschaft die zumindest im Vergleich mit Disziplinarvergehen und Ordnungswidrigkeiten schwersten Formen der Repression verwendet, ist eine zivilisatorische Errungenschaft. Sie muss sich unter anderem auch darin zeigen, dass sich das Strafrecht in erster Linie den gefährlichsten Eingriffen in Strafrechtsgüter widmet. Das sind in diesem Kontext die Verletzungen und nicht die Gefährdungen. Natürlich kann und soll man bei allen, ganz besonders aber bei indisponiblen sowie abstrakteren Strafrechtsgütern darüber diskutieren, was das Wesen dieser Güter ausmacht, und damit verbunden, ob sie durch bestimmte Handlungseingriffe (auch unterlassender Art![1]) gefährdet oder bereits verletzt werden. Solche Überlegungen sind verfassungsrechtlich, kriminalpolitisch und strafrechtssystematisch wichtig, ganz besonders in Staaten, die Erfahrungen mit totalitären politischen Systemen und massiven Menschenrechtsverletzungen machen mussten. Vertiefte Analysen von Strafrechtsgütern liegen in Slowenien zwar vor, vor allem bei politischen Delikten und Sexualdelikten, sie sind aber nach wie vor eher selten und werden sogar immer seltener, wie sich anlässlich der Verabschiedung des neuen Strafgesetzbuchs in Slowenien 2008 gezeigt hat. Aber an der Grundprämisse bezüglich der Rolle des Erfolgs (der verbotenen Folgen) ändert das nichts. Im Strafrecht bleiben Rechtsgutverletzungen von zentraler Bedeutung, während demgegenüber Rechtsgutgefährdungen eine komplementäre Erscheinung sind[2].

Das moderne Strafrecht pönalisiert Gefährdungen – und das sei bei der Einführung in einen Rechtsvergleich besonders zu betonen – allgemein als logische Folge des Grundsatzes der Begrenztheit der Repression in zweifacher Hinsicht prinzipiell nur ausnahmsweise: Eine Gefährdungsstrafbarkeit besteht erstens nur dann, wenn zum Schutz des Rechtsguts außerstrafrechtliche Eingriffe nicht mehr genügen und zweitens nur dann, wenn die Natur des Rechtsguts oder die Natur der Handlung wegen qualitativer oder quantitativer Besonderheiten neben dem Schutz vor Verletzungen auch den Schutz vor Gefährdungen als einer Vorstufe von Verletzung verlangen. Die Logik dabei ist ähnlich der, die wir aus der Dogmatik des *iter criminis* kennen, in erster Linie beim Versuch. Vereinfacht gesagt: Das moderne Strafrecht schützt nur Rechtsgüter, die es gemäß einer ver-

1 Über Strafrechtsgutsverletzungen und die sogenannten punktuellen Gefährdungen sowohl bei unechten als auch bei echten Unterlassungsdelikten siehe z.B. das in Slowenien seit langem zentrale Lehrbuch des materiellen Strafrechts von *L. Bavcon, A. Šelih, D. Korošec, V. Jakulin, K. Filipčič*: Kazensko pravo, splošni del [Strafrecht, Allgemeiner Teil], Ljubljana: Uradni list RS, 2003, S. 155–170.

2 Hierzu z.B. *C. Roxin*: Strafrecht – Allgemeiner Teil, Bd. I, München: C.H. Beck, 2006, S. 34–40. Speziell zum slowenischen Strafrecht siehe *M. Ambrož*: Spremembe slovenske materialne kazenske zakonodaje in argument primerjalnega prava [Änderungen des slowenischen Strafrechts und das Argument des Rechtsvergleichs], *Dnevi slovenskih pravnikov 2008 od 16. do 18. oktobra, Portorož* (Podjetje in delo 2008 (34); 6/7), S. 1420–1426.

fassungsrechtlichen Stufenleiter zu den wichtigsten oder zumindest zu den gefährdetsten zählt, nicht nur gegen Verletzungen sondern auch noch gegen Gefährdungen (Gefährdungsstrafbarkeit). Die Tatsache, dass ein Gut auch gegen Gefährdungen geschützt wird, zeugt angesichts des Grundsatzes der Beschränktheit der Repression von der besonderen Bedeutung des geschützten Strafrechtsguts.

In modernen liberalen Strafrechtssystemen zählen zu den genannten wichtigsten Gütern, die zusätzlich durch Gefährdungsdelikte geschützt werden, vor allem das Menschenleben und die elementare körperliche Unversehrtheit des Menschen. Auch in den ost- und südosteuropäischen Staaten hat der lange überdimensionierte, hypertrophe Schutz des Staates und seiner Machtstrukturen stark nachgelassen, sodass das Menschenleben und die Autonomie des Einzelnen mit ihren vielen persönlichen Rechtsgütern strafrechtlich in den Vordergrund rücken konnten. Interessanterweise unterscheiden sich die einzelnen nationalen Strafrechtssysteme gerade bei der Konkretisierung des Schutzes des Lebens und der elementaren körperlichen Unversehrtheit des Menschen im Straßenverkehr nach wie vor stark voneinander. Hierfür lassen sich allerdings selbst nach vertieften Studien nur schwer Argumente in der Doktrin der tatbestandsmäßigen Handlung, des Erfolgs oder der Schuld und erst recht nicht in tiefergreifenden Rechtsgutsdiskussionen oder in anderen Teilgebieten des materiellen und prozessualen (besonders des Beweis-)Strafrechts finden.

In diesem Beitrag sollen als Teil der Diskussion zum Ostrecht am Beispiel von Staaten, die aus der ehemaligen Sozialistischen Föderativen Republik Jugoslawien entstanden sind, einige vielleicht im Rest Europas nicht bekannte Besonderheiten des Verkehrsstrafrechts und vor allem des strafrechtlichen Schutzes „des Menschen auf der Straße“ aufgezeigt werden. Der EU-Mitgliedstaat Slowenien wird hierbei wegen seiner zahlreichen Strafrechtsreformen in den letzten Jahren besonders im Vordergrund stehen.

II. Das Festhalten an (schweren) Verletzungsfolgen im traditionellen Verkehrsstrafrecht Sloweniens

Die Strafrechtstheorie sowohl im Westen als auch im Osten unterscheidet traditionell zwei Grundtypen der Gefährdungsfolgen der Tat: zum einen konkrete und zum anderen abstrakte Gefährdungen als Erfolg. Die Theoretiker heben als Grundunterschied den Grad der Gefahr hervor, dass die Gefährdung in eine Verletzung des Strafrechtsguts umschlägt. Bei konkreten Gefährdungsdelikten besteht eine unmittelbare große Gefahr in diese Richtung, bei abstrakten bloß eine mittelbare, entfernte, hypothetische. In dieser Frage ähneln sich rechtsvergleichend alle Strafrechtssysteme traditionell sehr und das ehemalige sozialistische Jugoslawien einschließlich seiner Teilrepublik Slowenien bildete keine Ausnahme.

Bei der Konkretisierung dieser Ausgangspunkte in der Gesetzgebung des Besonderen Teils des StGB und auch bei der doktrinären Auslegung und Begründung einzelner Gefährdungsdelikte, scheint jedoch gerade Slowenien beim Schutz von Menschenleben speziell im Straßenverkehr seit langem wesentlich restriktiver zu verfahren als viele westliche Staaten. Bei abstrakten Gefährdungen erreicht diese Zurückhaltung das Ausmaß einer völligen – angesichts des Fehlens relevanter wissenschaftlicher Abhandlungen geradezu tabuartigen – Ablehnung. Die Figur der abstrakten Gefährdung wird von der slowenischen Strafrechtsdogmatik zumindest im Verkehrsstrafrecht traditionell argumentationslos, d.h. im Vergleich mit anderen Staaten radikal ignoriert[3].

Bei einer rückblickenden Analyse sind wissenschaftliche, insbesondere strafrechtsdogmatische Antworten darauf schwer zu finden. Dennoch soll hier eine gewisse Spekulation gewagt werden. Es scheint, dass das slowenische Strafrecht in großem Maße unter dem Einfluss historischer Erfahrungen steht, die Jugoslawien und auch die slowenische Nation mit politischen Missbräuchen und andauernden massiven potenziellen Missbräuchen und Fehlanwendungen von Strafrecht, besonders bezüglich des Konzepts der abstrakten Gefährdung bestimmter indisponibler Strafrechtsgüter, machen mussten. Das scheint die Hauptursache zu sein, dass hierzulande, wie auch in allen anderen Nachfolgestaaten Jugoslawiens, die Subsidiarität der Gefährdungsdelikte und ganz besonders der abstrakten Gefährdungsdelikte als sehr wichtig empfunden wird und dass man versucht, im Strafrecht an der Verletzungslogik entschiedener festzuhalten als anderswo. Straßenverkehrsdelikte sind dabei keine Ausnahme, obwohl man nicht leugnen kann, dass auf diesem speziellen Gebiet das Strafrecht zumindest im Vergleich mit anderen Deliktgruppen, allen voran den Straftaten gegen den Staat und die Amtspflichten, historisch im sogenannten vordemokratischen Slowenien kaum aktuell oder potenziell gebeugt und missbraucht wurde. Diese Aussage schließt natürlich grobe Fehlanwendungen und Strafrechtsdilettantismus jeder Art und Stufe im Straßenverkehr nicht aus, denn diese sind historisch ohne jeden Zweifel erwiesen. Als sehr wichtige Ursache für die beschriebene scharf ablehnende Haltung gegenüber der Gefährdung besonders im Straßenverkehrsrecht sind noch besondere technische Beweisschwierigkeiten zu erkennen. Damit einher geht die in der slowenischen Strafrechtstheorie stark betonte Gefahr der arbiträren und somit diskriminierenden repressiven Verfolgung seitens der Polizei und der Staatsanwaltschaft.

Anstatt nach Lösungen zu suchen, wie Gefährdungsdelikte rechtskonform in das Verkehrsstrafrecht Sloweniens integriert werden können, und zu versuchen, aus einschlägigen ausländischen Erfahrungen zu lernen, ging die amtliche Kri-

---

3 Dazu *L. Bavcon* et al. (Fn. 1), S. 182 und besonders 183, wo das Institut der abstrakten Gefährdung zwar kurz behandelt wird. In der Lehre und vor allem auch im Besonderen Teil der geltenden Gesetzgebung sucht man allerdings weitestgehend vergebens nach ihm.

minalpolitik mit starker Unterstützung der in Slowenien ungewöhnlich einflussreichen Kriminologie servil von angeblichen Besonderheiten der slowenischen (Trink- und Fahr-)Kultur aus. Sie betonte überall und somit auch im Straßenverkehrsrecht die Gefahren der Repression (und konnte zu diesem Zweck die in der zweiten Hälfte des 20. Jahrhunderts verständlicherweise noch tief in den Knochen sitzende Angst der Bürger vor Strafrechtsmissbrauch ausnützen), minimierte damit innerhalb des Strafrechts mit kriminalpolitisch eher zweifelhaften Langzeitwirkungen sozusagen alle Probleme der Gefährdung von Menschenleben als dem verfassungsrechtlich wohl wichtigsten Rechtsgut überhaupt und baute, die Repressionsbegrenzung im Straßenverkehr als allerwichtigstes politisches Ziel vor Augen, sowohl politisch geschickt auf die allgemeine Abneigung der Repressionsapparate im Land gegenüber Neuerungen, als auch gleichzeitig auf die große und politisch nicht zu unterschätzende Bedeutung des damals sich schnell verbreitenden Pkw für den Durchschnittsbürger. So entstand unter tatkräftiger Mitwirkung der slowenischen Kriminalpolitik und angesichts der auf diesem Spezialgebiet eher passiven einheimischen (vergleichenden) Strafrechtstheorie, die lange in jeder Hinsicht als selbstverständlich empfundene und bis heute politisch nur mit allergrößter Mühe abzumildernde amtliche slowenische Abneigung gegenüber Gefährdungstatbeständen im Straßenverkehrsstrafrecht, insbesondere zur Pönalisierung der Trunkenheitsfahrt.

Hier wollen wir nun das kriminalpolitische und historische Terrain verlassen und uns wieder – für das slowenische Verkehrsstrafrecht eher untypisch – der Strafrechtsdogmatik und der Rechtsvergleichung zuwenden. Im Allgemeinen Teil des StGB stehen in Slowenien die Dinge bezüglich des Erfolgs (der verbotenen Tatfolgen) und seiner prinzipiellen Strafbarkeit zumindest in der Theorie seit jeher recht einfach: Das sogenannte Straßenverkehrsstrafrecht bzw. das Recht der tatbestandsmäßigen Handlungen, die zum Erfolg (zu verbotenen Folgen) im Straßenverkehr oder in Verbindung mit ihm führen können, ist Teil des Strafrechts. Als solches ist es grundsätzlich offen für alle Formen des Erfolgs (der verbotenen Folgen) und das sind Verletzungen und Gefährdungen. Die slowenische Strafrechtsdogmatik befasst sich jedenfalls seit der Abschaffung des in der Theorie stark kritisierten Instituts der geringen Bedeutung der Tat, das als gesetzlich geregeltes Institut des AT teilweise auch für solche Zwecke in Frage kam[4], nicht mit besonderen Tatbestandsausschließungsgründen oder Rechtfertigungsgründen speziell in Richtung des erlaubten Risikos. Auch in der Rechtspraxis sucht man vergebens nach ihnen. Die Tatsache, dass mit dem Straßenverkehr ein gewisses Maß an technisch und menschlich unbeherrschbaren Gefahren für wichtige Strafrechtsgüter verbunden ist, beziehungsweise die Tatsache, dass

4 Über dieses rechtsvergleichend hochinteressante Institut des materiellen Strafrechts eingehender *D. Korošec*: Das materialrechtliche Institut der Geringfügigkeit der Tat im slowenischen Strafrecht, Zeitschrift für die gesamte Strafrechtswissenschaft 2003 (115) 3, S. 126–136 (742–752).

gerade deswegen im Strafrecht leichte, typischerweise abstrakte, aber auch einige konkrete Gefährdungen von Strafrechtsgütern einschließlich der wichtigsten und allen voran des menschlichen Lebens potentiell nicht tatbestandsmäßig oder zumindest nicht rechtswidrig zu sein scheinen, können an dieser axiomatischen Offenheit nichts ändern. Dasselbe muss auch für angeblich typische Erkenntnis- und Beweisprobleme gelten, die bei Straßenverkehrsdelikten ohne konkrete Verletzungsfolgen wie einer (schweren) Körperverletzung auftreten.

Jahrzehntelang gab es in Slowenien im geltenden Strafrecht[5], das traditionell kein Nebenstrafrecht kennt, unmissverständlich nur einen einzigen allgemeinen Straßenverkehrstatbestand im engeren Sinne: Art. 325 StGB 1994. Sein Titel war „Fahrlässige Verursachung eines Verkehrsunfalls“[6]. Er lautete:

> Art 325. (1) Der Verkehrsteilnehmer, der durch die Verletzung von Vorschriften über die Sicherheit im Straßenverkehr aus Fahrlässigkeit einen Verkehrsunfall verursacht, in dem eine Person schwer körperlich verletzt wird [...].
>
> (2) Wenn die Tat aus dem vorigen Absatz den Tod einer oder mehrerer Personen zur Folge hat [...].

Eine noch so schwerwiegende konkrete Gefährdung noch so vieler Menschenleben genügt auf der Tatbestandsebene nicht einmal bei umfangreichsten Ketten gröbster Verstöße gegen die Straßenverkehrsordnung, z.B. bei einem schwer betrunkenen Pkw-Fahrer, dem wegen einer tödlichen Verkehrsstraftat der Führerschein bereits rechtskräftig entzogen und bis zum Tatzeitpunkt nicht zurückgegeben worden war, der als Geisterfahrer auf einer stark befahrenen Autobahn unterwegs war und dabei Hunderte konkreter Menschenleben stark gefährdete. Auch durch Wetten motivierte Autorennen von typischerweise jugendlichen Fahrern auf öffentlichen Straßen und die so verursachten Verkehrsunfälle, einschließlich der Verletzung von an dem Rennen unbeteiligten Personen, bleiben tatbestandslos, solange niemand eine schwere (!) Körperverletzung erleidet. Auf der anderen Seite bleibt es für das StGB 1994 auf der Tatbestandsebene ohne Bedeutung, mit welcher Schuld der Beteiligte im Verkehr die Vorschriften über die Sicherheit im Straßenverkehr bricht. Es wird nur die Schuld in Form von Fahrlässigkeit[7] bezüglich des Verkehrsunfalls festgelegt. Auch genügt es für die

---

5 Auch nach der Unabhängigkeit galt bis 2008 ein Strafrecht, das mit dem früheren jugoslawisch-slowenischen Strafrecht praktisch identisch war: StGB von 1994, Ul RS (Gesetzblatt Sloweniens) Nr. 63/94, 70/94, 23/99, 40/04, 95/04. Einen informativen Überblick über dieses Strafrecht bieten z.B. *D. Korošec*: Das materielle Strafrecht Sloweniens, Jahrbuch für Ostrecht 42 (2001), S. 111–129, und *D. Korošec/M. Ambrož*: Das Slowenische Strafrecht zum Zeitpunkt des Beitritts Sloweniens zur EU (am 01. Mai 2004), Zeitschrift für die gesamte Strafrechtswissenschaft 2006 (118) 2, S. 51–73 (489-511).

6 Im Original: »Povzročitev prometne nesreče iz malomarnosti«. Alle Übersetzungen aus dem slowenischen Original in dieser Darstellung stammen vom Verfasser.

7 In Slowenien werden der Vorsatz und die Fahrlässigkeit nach wie vor als zwei Erscheinungsformen der Schuld gesehen und so selbstverständlich systematisch in der Schuld

Tatbestandsmäßigkeit, wenn der am Verkehr teilnehmende Täter selbst als Einziger schwer körperlich verletzt wurde, da der Straftatbestand nicht auf „einem Anderen“ als Opfer besteht, sondern sich mit „einer Person“ begnügt. Auf jeden Fall gilt allgemein die (in solchen Fällen typischerweise zufällige) schwere Körperverletzung in Art. 325 Abs. 1 StGB 1994 als objektive Bedingung der Strafbarkeit, die nach slowenischem Recht im Grunde außerhalb der Tatbestandsmäßigkeit steht und sich so den Regeln der Schuld entzieht[8]. Der Tod in Abs. 2 ist eine schwerere „überfahrlässige“, also tatbestandsmäßige und zweifellos nach allgemeinen Regeln schuldhafte Folge des an die objektive Bedingung der Strafbarkeit gebundenen fahrlässigen Grunddelikts. Diese zweifache Stellung, einmal der Körperverletzung und einmal des Todes der(selben) Opferperson, ist zumindest aus der Sicht der Dogmatik des allgemeinen Verbrechensbegriffs problematisch.

Allgemeine Delikte gegen die öffentliche Sicherheit, wie z.B. die „Verursachung einer allgemeinen Gefahr“ gemäß Art. 317 StGB 1994, kommen in solchen Fällen nicht einmal subsidiär in Frage, da nach der historischen, vor allem aber nach der allgemein anerkannten teleologischen Auslegung des Strafrechts seit jeher gilt, dass die schwere Körperverletzung im Straftatbestand der dargestellten fahrlässigen Verursachung eines Verkehrsunfalls eine objektive Bedingung der Strafbarkeit und deswegen auf eine besondere Weise speziell gegenüber den allgemeinen Gefährdungsdelikten ist. Wegen der bloßen Existenz solcher speziellen Delikte für Straßenverkehrsgefährdungen, die mit objektiven Bedingungen der Strafbarkeit an schwere Formen von Verletzungen gebunden sind und so funktional zu Verletzungsdelikten werden, bleiben im Straßenverkehr die Türen zu den allgemeinen Gefährdungsdelikten fest verschlossen[9]. Dies galt seit jeher als zwingend logisch und als systematisch unproblematisch. Was nicht bedeuten soll, dass einzelne Theoretiker nicht schon seit längerem massive Wertungsprobleme und dogmatische Paradoxien sahen und vor allem mit rechtsvergleichenden Argumenten eine Umstrukturierung des slowenischen

als Element des allgemeinen Verbrechensbegriffs behandelt. Siehe z.B. *M. Ambrož*: Kaznivo dejanje in njegove vrednostne prvine [Die Straftat und ihre normativen Elemente], Ljubljana: Inštitut za kriminologijo pri Pravni fakulteti, 2007, S. 156–157.

8 Dazu siehe *L. Bavcon, A. Šelih, D. Korošec, M. Ambrož, K. Filipčič*: Kazensko pravo, splošni del [Strafrecht, Allgemeiner Teil] Ljubljana: Uradni list RS, 2009, S. 185, 187-189.

9 Allgemein über die Natur und die kriminalpolitischen Funktionen besonderer Straßenverkehrsdelikte mit objektiven Bedingungen der Strafbarkeit siehe z.B. *L. Bavcon*: O zamislih za kazenskopravno reagiranje zoper nedisciplino v cestnem prometu [Gedanken zum strafrechtlichen Reagieren gegen die Disziplinlosigkeit im Straßenverkehr], Inštitut za javno upravo: Izobraževanje in usposabljanje v javni upravi, 2004, S. 293-301; *L. Bavcon* et al.: Uveljavljanje novih institutov kazenskega materialnega in procesnega prava [Die Durchsetzung neuer Institute des materiellen und prozessualen Strafrechts], Ljubljana: Uradni list RS, 2000.

Straßenverkehrsrechts forderten, besonders bei massenhaften Gefährdungen durch einen Beteiligten im Verkehr, bei wiederholten Gefährdungen, wie sie durch betrunkene Fahrer typisch sind, bei mehrfachen gleichzeitigen Ordnungswidrigkeiten im Straßenverkehr mit konkreten Lebensgefährdungen, ganz besonders bei vorsätzlichen Verletzungen der Straßenverkehrsordnung durch illegale Autorennen auf öffentlichen Straßen sowie durch Wetten und Fahren im Straßenverkehr aus ähnlichen Motiven[10]. Es wurden in den letzten Jahren sogar vermehrt Stimmen laut, dass in vielen Rechtssystemen, wie z.B. im deutschen oder im finnischen, unvergleichbar engmaschigere Strafbestimmungen und zahlreiche Gefährdungsstraftatbestände im Straßenverkehr am Werk sind, insbesondere fahruntüchtige Personen unter der Wirkung psychotropischer Substanzen als Gefährdungstäter. Man begann zu zweifeln, ob in Slowenien statistische, verfassungsrechtliche oder ernstzunehmende kulturelle Gründe für diese kriminalpolitischen Unterschiede bestehen. Mit anderen Worten: Neben strafrechtlicher wurde auch kriminalpolitische Kritik an den bestehenden traditionellen Lösungen laut.

III. Das Festhalten an (schweren) Verletzungsfolgen im neuen Straßenverkehrsstrafrecht Sloweniens

Slowenien war der erste Nachfolgestaat Jugoslawiens, der nach dem Zerfall des gemeinsamen Staates Anfang der 1990er Jahre eine eigene neue Strafgesetzgebung erließ. Das bereits zitierte StGB 1994 wurde als erstes Strafgesetzbuch des selbstständigen Sloweniens im September 1994 verabschiedet[11] und trat am 01.01.1995 in Kraft. Kleinere Änderungen und Ergänzungen folgten 1999[12], die nächsten und letzten Änderungen dieses Gesetzbuchs fanden im Jahre 2004 statt[13]. Keine der Novellen ist auf dem Gebiet des Straßenverkehrsstrafrechts von spezifischer Bedeutung.

Das slowenische Parlament verabschiedete, für die große Mehrheit der einheimischen Strafrechtstheoretiker, aber auch für die Strafrechtspraxis zumindest aus strafrechtlich theoretischer Sicht eher überraschend, vor allem aber nach einer nur wenige Monate dauernden, fast zur Gänze vor der (Fach-)Öffentlichkeit geheim gehaltenen Vorbereitungsphase, ein neues StGB, das in Slowenien so-

---

10 So vor allem *D. Korošec*: Sodobna dogmatika kazenskega prava cestnega prometa [Gegenwärtige Dogmatik des Straßenverkehrsstrafrechts], Javna uprava 2008 (44) 1, S. 77-99. Der Autor vergleicht kritisch das alte und neue slowenische Straßenverkehrsrecht mit dem deutschen Strafrecht. Siehe auch *V. Jakulin*: Analiza kaznivega dejanja »Povzročitve prometne nesreče iz malomarnosti« [Analyse des Straftatbestandes »Verursachung eines Verkehrsunfalls aus Fahrlässigkeit«], Inštitut za javno upravo: Izobraževanje in usposabljanje v javni upravi, 2004, S. 313–322.

11 Ul RS Nr. 63/94.

12 Ul RS Nr. 23/99.

13 Ul RS Nr. 40/04.

genannte StGB-1[14], das kurz nach seinem Erlass am 1.09.2008 in Kraft trat. Neben der Neunummerierung der Artikel änderte es sowohl den AT als auch den BT recht umfassend. Das neue Gesetzbuch wird allgemein als Versuch der Eingliederung verschiedener internationaler Konventionen in das nationale Strafrecht verstanden. Zweifellos spielte bei der hastigen Änderung des slowenischen Strafrechts in den letzten Jahren auch der offensichtliche politische Wunsch nach einem demonstrativen Bruch mit dem als kommunistisch empfundenen alten Strafrecht eine wichtige Rolle.

Entsprechend der slowenischen Tradition bleiben auch im StGB-1 alle Straftatbestände innerhalb des StGB, was bedeutet, dass auf Nebenstrafrecht auch weiterhin verzichtet wird. Nur auf dem Gebiet des internationalen Strafrechts im Zusammenhang mit dem Römischen Statut, das im BT des StGB-1 integriert ist, diskutiert die slowenische Strafrechtstheorie neuerdings lebhaft, ob es kriminalpolitisch und rechtsystematisch nicht vernünftiger wäre, hier – und ausschließlich hier – ein Nebenstrafrecht zuzulassen. Das Strafprozessrecht wurde bei weitem nicht so tiefgreifend geändert; es wurde überhaupt noch nicht systematisch novelliert.

Im Besonderen Teil des StGB-1 war eine der größten und wegen ihrer konkreten Ausführung gleichzeitig überraschendsten Neuerungen, die Umgestaltung der Straßenverkehrsdelikte. Der Gesetzgeber beließ den Straftatbestand der Verursachung eines Verkehrsunfalls aus Fahrlässigkeit samt Titel unverändert. Diese Tat ist nun in Art. 323 StGB-1 geregelt, weiterhin gebunden an eine schwere Körperverletzung als objektive Bedingung der Strafbarkeit und belastet mit allen dogmatischen und kriminalpolitischen Problemen, die diesem Delikt schon früher anhafteten. Neu hinzu kam allerdings der Straftatbestand der sogenannten „Rücksichtslosen Fahrt im Straßenverkehr" („Predrzna vožnja v cestnem prometu"), der als kumulativ-alternatives Gefährdungsdelikt in Art. 324 StGB-1 wie folgt formuliert ist:

> Art. 324. (1) Ein Fahrer eines Motorfahrzeugs, der mit rücksichtsloser Fahrt im Straßenverkehr das Leben oder den Körper der Mitreisenden oder anderer anwesender Beteiligter im Straßenverkehr dadurch gefährdet, dass er die auf einer Straße, in einer Ortschaft, in einer Fußgängerzone, in einer verkehrsberuhigten Zone oder in einer Zone mit begrenzter Geschwindigkeit erlaubte Geschwindigkeit mehr als einmal überschreitet, oder unter Einfluss von Alkohol mit mehr als 1.10 Gramm Alkohol pro Kilogramm Blut oder mit mehr als 0,52 Milligramm Alkohol pro Liter ausgeatmeter Luft, oder unter Einfluss von Drogen, psychoaktiver Pharmaka oder anderer psychoaktiver Substanzen fährt und dabei
> - andere Fahrzeuge entgegen den Vorschriften über die Sicherheit im Straßenverkehr überholt,
> - Vorschriften über die Vorfahrt nicht berücksichtigt,
> - mit zu geringem Sicherheitsabstand fährt,

14 Ul RS Nr. 55/08, 66/08, 39/09.

- auf einer Straße mit zwei oder mehreren gekennzeichneten Fahrspuren für die Fahrt in eine Richtung auf der Fahrspur fährt, die der Fahrt in die andere Richtung bestimmt ist,
- mit einer anderen Verletzung von Vorschriften über die Sicherheit im Straßenverkehr eine gefährliche Situation verursacht, wegen der sich ein Verkehrsunfall ereignen könnte, den jedoch andere Beteiligte im Straßenverkehr durch rechtzeitiges Handeln vermeiden konnten, [...].

(2) Wenn die Tat aus dem ersten Absatz einen Verkehrsunfall mit schwerer Körperverletzung einer oder mehrerer Personen zur Folge hat [...].

(3) Wenn die Tat aus dem ersten Absatz dieses Artikels einen Verkehrsunfall mit dem Tod einer oder mehrerer Personen zur Folge hat [...].

Das slowenische Straßenverkehrsrecht wird gerade jetzt, während dieser Überblick zu Ehren des geschätzten Jubilars, *Professor Dr. Dres. h.c. F.-C. Schroeder*, fertig gestellt wird, großen Neugestaltungen unterworfen. Aufgrund der erhältlichen Informationen werden diese Novellierungen aber weder ein Nebenstrafrecht auf dem Gebiet des Straßenverkehrsrechts anstreben noch ernsthaft in dieses Gebiet des StGB eingreifen. So muss man davon ausgehen, dass das geschilderte Straßenverkehrsstrafrecht in Slowenien noch einige Zeit auf dem vorhandenen Stand bleiben wird.

Das 2008 in Kraft getretene neue Straßenverkehrsstrafrecht ist wahrhaft ein Unikum und muss überraschen. Der Gesetzgeber ging bei seiner Verabschiedung offensichtlich von dem Bedürfnis aus, das Straßenverkehrsrecht zu verschärfen, und hatte dabei wohl zumindest schemenhaft ein Bewusstsein von den kriminalpolitischen und vielleicht sogar auch den dogmatischen Spannungen, die aus dem traditionellen slowenischen Beharren auf der Verletzungsfolge und zusätzlich noch auf der objektiven Bedingung der Strafbarkeit herstammen. Es sieht danach aus, als ob der Gesetzgeber die Unterschiede zwischen dem slowenischen und dem – in der Vorlage des StGB-1 ausdrücklich genannten[15] – deutschen Straßenverkehrsstrafrecht abbauen wollte. Das traditionelle slowenische System entpuppt sich im Vergleich mit z.B. dem deutschen und einigen anderen tatsächlich als wenig an der Gefahr der Handlung und sehr an ihrer Verletzungsfolge orientiert, obwohl Verletzungsfolgen in Rahmen des Verkehrs naturgemäß mehr oder weniger zufällig (aleatorisch) entstehen, wo also die Schuld des Täters typischerweise keine Schlüsselrolle spielen kann. In diesem Sinne erschien das Bestreben des slowenischen Gesetzgebers im Rahmen der großen Neugestaltung des Strafrechts, die er im Jahre 2008 so überraschend wagte, zumindest aus der Sicht der Dogmatik des materiellen Strafrechts und der Rechtsvergleichung vernünftig.

Der Gesetzgeber spricht in der Begründung von einer Gesetzesänderung nach deutschem Vorbild, begründet jedoch gleichzeitig nicht die zahlreichen

15 Abschnitt „Zu Artikel 324 (Rücksichtslose Fahrt im Straßenverkehr)“ der Begründung der Vorlage des StGB, veröffentlicht 2007 als Parlamentsdrucksache (Publikation ohne Seitennummerierung).

Unterschiede, die er zum deutschen Verkehrsstrafrecht gelassen hat: Er erklärt nicht, warum er bei der Verabschiedung des StGB-1 nicht bereit war, entschlossener das Konzept eines ausführlichen Katalogs der erfahrungsgemäß gefährlichsten Ordnungswidrigkeiten im Straßenverkehr mit Gefährdungsfolge nach deutschem Vorbild zu übernehmen, insbesondere die Pönalisierung der abstrakt gefährdenden Trunkenheitsfahrt nach § 316 des deutschen StGB. Er begründet ebenfalls nicht die zahlreichen nicht einfachen Interaktionen zwischen dem überkommenen Verletzungsstraftatbestand in Art. 323 StGB-1 und dem neuen Straftatbestand der konkreten Gefährdung in Art. 324 StGB-1. Vergebens sucht man z.B. nach einer Erklärung, warum sich der Straftatbestand der Verursachung eines Verkehrsunfalls aus Fahrlässigkeit in Art. 323 StGB-1 weiterhin mit irgendeiner körperlich schwer verletzten Person begnügt und auf diese Weise auch den Täter des Verkehrsdelikts einschließt, der neue Straftatbestand mit dem Titel „Rücksichtslose Fahrt im Straßenverkehr" nach Art. 324 StGB-1 aber viel wählerischer die Gefahr für das Leben oder den Körper der Mitreisenden oder anderer anwesender Beteiligter im Straßenverkehr fordert, also den Täter selbst bereits auf der Tatbestandsebene ausschließt. Auch einige aus jeder Hinsicht ungewöhnliche Häufungen von Tatbestandsmerkmalen (Deliktkumulationen) in der alternativ disponierten Strafandrohung des Art. 324-1 StGB werden in der Gesetzesbegründung kaum oder gar nicht diskutiert. Der slowenische Gesetzgeber geht nicht auf kriminalpolitische, rechtssystematische und andere eventuelle Nachteile des deutschen Rechts, das er ausdrücklich als Vorbild nennt, und anderer engmaschiger Verkehrsstrafrechtssysteme ein und lässt so bei der Novellierung des Strafrechts von 2008 breiten Raum für Spekulationen. Man darf den Schluss wagen, dass er politisch vulgären Respekt besonders vor unter psychotropen Substanzen stehenden fahruntüchtigen Personen – immerhin eine wichtige Wählergruppe – als Gefährdungstätern zeigte und dass dies nicht nur der Hauptgrund, sondern der einzige Grund dafür war, dass er keinen ernsthaften Schritt in Richtung Pönalisierung der abstrakten Gefährdung nach deutschem Muster wagte.

Und wie funktioniert nun das neue Straßenverkehrsrecht in der Praxis? Slowenische Staatsanwälte und Strafrichter sind mit dem neuen Art. 324 StGB-1 nun zwar im Vergleich sehr zurückhaltend, aber dennoch auch für konkrete Gefährdungen im Straßenverkehr strafrechtlich bewaffnet, was einflussreiche Theoretiker als eine unnötige Verschärfung der staatlichen Repression in Slowenien bezeichnen. Nach vorliegenden Berichten sind sie aber kaum bereit, diese Normen auch anzuwenden. Alles deutet darauf hin, dass es sich dabei um die kulturelle Trägheit von Institutionen handelt, also das Fehlen der Bereitschaft, sich mit ernsthaften kriminalpolitischen oder gar theoretischen Argumenten zu dem Thema auseinanderzusetzen oder ihre Strafverfolgungspolitik dem Wert des Menschenlebens als ultimativ geschütztem Rechtsgut sowie der in Slowenien nach wie vor beunruhigenden Todes- und Körperverletzungsstatistik rational anzupassen.

Theoretisch stören vor allem die im Vergleich zu anderen Rechtsordnungen bizarren Häufungen der verlangten Straßenverkehrsordnungswidrigkeiten und das moralisch sonderbare Beharren auf konkreten Gefährdungen auch bei volltrunkenen professionellen Fahrern. In Slowenien müssen wir auch nach dem Inkrafttreten des StGB-1 z.B. einem Geisterfahrer auf der Autobahn strafrechtlich auch dann eine schwere Betrunkenheit nachweisen, wenn er als Folge eines verabredeten Rennens oder einer Wette in die verbotene Richtung gerast ist! In solchen Fällen, die auf unseren Straßen leider nicht nur theoretische Konstrukte sind[16], kommt nach der Grundform der Strafandrohung in Art. 324 Abs. I StGB-1 höchstens noch die Überschreitung der erlaubten Geschwindigkeit „für mehr als einmal" in Frage, was freilich bei der Fahrt in die verbotene Richtung auf der Autobahn eine wertmäßig absurde, nicht zuletzt aber auch mathematisch unmögliche oder zumindest unsinnige Bedingung ist. Bei diesen kumulativen Tatbestandsmerkmalen bleibt zu hoffen, dass die erlaubte Geschwindigkeit auf Autobahnen in verbotener Richtung Null bleibt, einmal mehr als Null müsste auch weiterhin Null bleiben. Deswegen halte ich solche Normenkumulationen für logisch redundant. Solche Häufungen von Bedingungen im Straßenverkehrsstrafrecht können weiterhin leicht als Beweis für die zynische Beziehung der slowenischen Gesellschaft zum Leben wirken.

Das Spielen des Gesetzgebers mit den Opfern fahrlässiger Verkehrsdelikte in Art. 323 StGB-1 und der „Rücksichtslosen Fahrt im Straßenverkehr" nach Art. 324 StGB-1 auf der Tatbestandsebene, ist aus der Sicht der Rechtsgutdogmatik und vor allem der strafrechtlichen Lehre von der Einwilligung des Opfers unverantwortlich.

In dieser kurzen Darstellung möchte ich jedoch besonders betonen, dass die Kritik an dem neuen Straßenverkehrsstrafrecht in Slowenien in ihrer Mehrheit wieder nicht strafrechtsdogmatisch, sondern kriminalpolitisch und auf die Abschaffung des Gefährdungsdeliktes gerichtet ist. Man findet in den Medien und auch in den juristischen Fachdiskussionen Argumente, die sich auf den Grundsatz der Begrenztheit der Repression i.S.v. „Verlangen von moralischer und ethischer Rechtfertigung eines jeden repressiven Eingriffs in die Freiheiten und Rechte des Menschen auf der gesetzgeberischen und der praktischen Ebene"[17] berufen, auf die übermäßige Belastung slowenischer Gerichte mit Strafsachen von geringer Bedeutung, auf angeblich unüberwindbare typische Beweisschwierigkeiten bei Gefährdungsdelikten im Strafrecht und die damit verbundene „die Rechtssicherheit zersetzende und somit verfassungswidrige" unklare Abgren-

---

16 So die Berichte z.B. in der Tageszeitung Dnevnik vom 23.10.2009, S. 1 (sic!), unter dem vielsagenden Titel „Komische Strafen für die Gefährdung von Menschenleben durch Geisterfahrer" (Autor *M. Terzić*); vertiefend in derselben Zeitung auf S. 28.

17 Nach *L. Bavcon* et al. (Fn. 8), S. 119.

zung zwischen Ordnungswidrigkeiten und Straftaten im Straßenverkehr, auf die sogenannte „feuchte Gesellschaft“ Sloweniens mit ihrer großen politischen Toleranz gegenüber dem Alkoholkonsum und den damit einhergehenden Gefährdungen im Straßenverkehr als schon fast einem nationalen Naturphänomen, das hingenommen werden muss wie Naturkatastrophen. Man erstrebt die Begrenzung des Straßenverkehrsrechts auf Verletzungen oder zumindest auf kumulativ definierte konkrete Gefährdungen im dargestellten Sinne. Strafrechtsdogmatische Zweifel an diesen Behauptungen und Argumenten werden typisch als lebensfremd und politisch nicht durchsetzbar abgetan oder sogar als kriminalpolitisch totalitär abgestempelt.

Bei allem Respekt gegenüber dem Grundsatz der Begrenztheit der Repression erscheint mir persönlich all dies strafrechtlich, aber auch kriminalpolitisch stark befremdlich. Es ist nicht so sehr die zwingende Folge des Grundsatzes der Begrenztheit der Repression, sondern die Folge anderer Begrenztheiten bei dem Verständnis des Strafrechts als Wissenschaft und in der Rechtspraxis. Selbstverständlich ist der Grundsatz der Begrenztheit der Repression einer der wichtigsten Grundsätze des Strafrechts. Seine Bedeutung für eine ausgeglichene, erfolgreiche Kriminalpolitik kann nicht stark genug betont werden. Aber pauschal verwendet und rechtsvergleichend so krampfhaft originell wie im neuen Straßenverkehrsrecht Sloweniens, scheint er für das Strafrecht und sein Ansehen in der Gesellschaft kontraproduktiv zu sein. Er wirkt dann eher als Maske für Desinteresse an der Strafrechtswissenschaft, für die Unbeholfenheit in der Rechtsvergleichung und für groben strafrechtsdogmatischen Dilettantismus.

Videoüberwachungs- und andere technische Anlagen und Mechanismen, die sich auch in Slowenien wegen ihrer weiten Verbreitung und Genauigkeit als einfache Quellen von Beweisen geradezu aufdrängen, haben in den letzten Jahren zweifellos entscheidende Neuerungen auch in die beweisrechtliche Dimension der Gefährdungsdelikte gebracht und müssten eigentlich als solche auch materiell-rechtliche Bremsen bei der Pönalisierung schwerster Gefährdungen von Menschenleben auf den Straßen enthemmen.

IV. Schlussbetrachtung

Neue rechtsvergleichende und allgemeine dogmatische Erkenntnisse auf dem Gebiet des materiellen Strafrechts und Strafprozessrechts, hunderte von hochauflösenden Überwachungskameras in Straßentunneln, auf Viadukten, Brücken und neuerdings bereits auf jeder größeren Straßenkreuzung, verschiedene moderne Geschwindigkeitsmessungstechnologien und nicht zuletzt auch politischer Anstand, der den Respekt vor dem Menschenleben auch auf den Straßen bitter nötig hat, all das fordert eine ernsthaftere, wesentlich vertieftere und systematischere wissenschaftliche Auseinandersetzung des slowenischen Strafrechts mit Gefährdungen von Menschenleben im Straßenverkehr. Ein Recht, nach dem Wettrennen in verbotener Richtung auf Autobahnen bloß als Ordnungswidrigkeiten zu ahnden sind, d.h. innerhalb einer Kategorie von strafbaren Handlungen, in die wir auch ein fahrlässiges Überschreiten der erlaubten Parkdauer auf Parkplätzen oder Urinieren in der Öffentlichkeit einordnen, das den Weg zur strafrechtlichen Reaktion aber trotz sehr konkreter Lebensgefährdungen verschlossen hält (StGB 1994, Art. 323 StGB-1) oder ihn durch wertmäßig schwer ergründbares Häufen von Ordnungswidrigkeiten mit der Trunkenheitsfahrt oder schweren Geschwindigkeitsübertretungen (Art. 324 StGB-1) erschwert, zeigt sich als Recht mit schweren dogmatischen und wertungsmäßigen Fehlern. Die Politik und insbesondere die Kriminalpolitik, die das Ahnden der in dieser Darstellung behandelten schweren Gefährdungshandlungen auch mit Strafrecht erschweren, wenn auch unter Berufung auf den guten alten Grundsatz der Begrenztheit der Repression, wecken ernsthafte Zweifel, auch wenn das Prinzip, auf das sie sich berufen, über alle Zweifel erhaben ist.

Wie auch immer man das Phänomen Ostrecht definiert, es spielte und spielt weiterhin eine wichtige Rolle als spezialisierte Rechtsvergleichung, die – vielleicht noch ganz besonders im strafrechtlichen Segment – zwingend auf umfangreichen speziellen historischen, kulturellen und (kriminal-)politischen Kenntnissen dieser in vielerlei Hinsicht immer noch besonderen Region aufbaut. Es würde mich sehr freuen, wenn diese Darstellung des historischen und des geltenden Straßenverkehrsstrafrechts in Slowenien, das nach bekannten Informationen zumindest im langjährigem Verharren auf Verletzungen als wesentlicher Folge aller Straßenverkehrsdelikte für die gesamte südosteuropäische Region repräsentativ ist, sich als nützlich für zukünftige ostrechtliche Arbeiten erweisen kann. Wenn der geschätzte Jubilar, *Professor Dr. Dres. h.c. F.-C. Schroeder*, noch sehr lange eine wichtige Rolle bei solchen Analysen spielen wird, würde mich dies umso mehr freuen.

Einige aktuelle Entwicklungen bei der strafrechtlichen Korruptionsbekämpfung in Rumänien

*Axel Bormann**

I. Rückblick und politische Rahmenbedingungen

Mit dem Beginn der Verhandlungen zum Beitritt in die Europäische Union im Jahre 2000 gerieten Ausmaß und schleppender Verlauf der Bekämpfung der Korruption in Rumänien in den Fokus der europäischen Institutionen, die nachhaltige Fortschritte in diesem Bereich als Beitrittsvoraussetzung verlangten. Neben der Korruptionsprävention war eine zentrale Forderung der Europäischen Kommission, die in die Fortschrittsberichte zum Stand des Beitrittsprozesses immer wieder von Neuem aufgenommen wurde, die nach einer effizienten Strafverfolgung von Korruptionsdelikten. Rumänien reagierte hierauf mit einer Reihe gesetzgeberischer Maßnahmen. Diese umfassten Änderungen des materiellen Strafrechts und des Strafprozessrechts, aber auch institutionelle Reformen. So wurde 2002 eine Sonderstaatsanwaltschaft zur Bekämpfung der Korruption (*Parchetul general anticorupție*) mit erweiterten Kompetenzen geschaffen, da die allgemeine Staatsanwaltschaft offenbar mit den Aufgaben zur strafrechtlichen Verfolgung der Korruption, die sich aus den zahlreichen speziellen Gesetzen und den allgemeinen Strafvorschriften ergaben, überfordert war[1]. Erfolge, insbesondere bei der Bekämpfung der „Großkorruption“[2], ließen allerdings weiter auf sich warten. Erst mit der Präsidentschaft von *T. Băsescu*[3], der die allumfassende Korruption als ernste Gefahr für die EU-Integration erkannte und seinen Wahlkampf entscheidend auf diesem Gesichtspunkt aufbaute, kam es zur Ausarbeitung einer nationalen Strategie zur Bekämpfung der Korruption, die

---

* Wissenschaftl. Referent für rumänisches und moldowisches Recht am IOR.

1 Zudem stand die allgemeine Staatsanwaltschaft zu diesem Zeitpunkt noch unter nachhaltigem politischen Einfluss (insbesondere aus Regierung und Justizministerium), sodass unliebsame Ermittlungen entweder von vornherein unterblieben oder auf politischen Wunsch verschleppt oder eingestellt wurden.

2 Dieser Begriff wird in Rumänien in erster Linie in Abgrenzung zur Klein- oder Alltagskorruption definiert und umfasst üblicherweise Korruptionsfälle größeren Ausmaßes und/oder mit Beteiligten aus führenden wirtschaftlichen, administrativen oder politischen Funktionen.

3 *T. Băsescu* ist seit 2004 Präsident und wurde Mitte 2006 aufgrund eines Misstrauensvotums des Parlaments vorübergehend von seinem Amt suspendiert, jedoch per Volksabstimmung mit deutlicher Mehrheit wieder in seine Funktion eingesetzt. 2009 wurde er mit einem recht knappen Ergebnis wiedergewählt.

u.a. eine tatsächlich unabhängige Korruptionsbehörde sowie einige damit zusammenhängende Reformen in der Justiz vorsah. Unter der auch bald international anerkannten Justizministerin *M. Macovei* wurde diese Strategie schließlich weitgehend umgesetzt, was bei der Europäischen Kommission den Eindruck erweckte, Rumänien sei nun auf dem richtigen Weg. Wie sehr hier jedoch lediglich Politik mit Blick auf den Beitrittstermin gemacht wurde, zeigt insbesondere die mangelnde Nachhaltigkeit der Maßnahmen. Schon wenige Wochen nach dem Beitritt zerbrach die Regierungskoalition aus *T. Băsescus* Demokratischer Partei und der Liberal-Demokratischen Partei von Ministerpräsident *C. Popescu-Tăriceanu*. Letzterer versuchte sich wechselnde Mehrheiten mithilfe der Parteien diverser Polituntemehmer zu sichern, wobei er regelmäßig von der Sozial-Demokratischen Partei als Nachfolgepartei der Kommunistischen Partei Rumäniens gestützt wurde. Sowohl gegen *C. Popescu-Tăriceanu* selbst als auch gegen Personal seiner Partei sowie seiner Koalitionspartner wurde zu diesem Zeitpunkt bereits durch die Antikorruptionsbehörde ermittelt; einige der Ermittlungen standen kurz vor der Anklageerhebung. Man entschloss sich daher, die Notbremse zu ziehen und den weiteren Fortgang der Ermittlungen zu unterminieren. So wurde *M. Macovei* schon drei Monate nach dem Beitritt durch den unerfahrenen 30-jährigen *T. Chiuariu* ersetzt, der sich in erster Linie durch besondere Treue zu seinem Mentor und damaligen Regierungschef *C. Popescu-Tăriceanu* auszeichnete und überwiegend unglücklich agierte[4].

Nach dem EU-Beitritt zum Jahresbeginn 2007 entstand zudem, auch mit Blick auf einige gesetzgeberische Vorhaben, der Eindruck, die zuvor erreichten Fortschritte sollten rückabgewickelt werden. Hierzu trugen Projekte bei wie die Entkriminalisierung des Bankbetrugs oder die Absicht, die Höchstdauer für strafrechtliche Ermittlungen drastisch zu kürzen[5].

Nachdem die Parlamentswahl von 2008 und die Präsidentschaftswahl von November 2009[6] die politischen Verhältnisse weitgehend konserviert haben, ergibt sich weiterhin ein bipolares Bild: auf der einen Seite die vom gegenwärti-

4 Eine seiner ersten Amtshandlungen war der dilettantisch unternommene Versuch, einen der führenden Staatsanwälte der Antikorruptionsbehörde unter dem Vorwurf „mangelnder Effizienz“ seines Amtes zu entheben. Ein positiv zu bewertendes Zeichen ist zweifellos, dass dieser Versuch nicht erfolgreich verlief, da neben der Öffentlichkeit auch viele Richter und Staatsanwälte gegen die geplante Absetzung protestierten und sich insbesondere auch der Oberste Rat der Magistrate als Selbstverwaltungsorgan der Richter und Staatsanwälte eindeutig positionierte.

5 Diese Vorhaben sah auch die Europäische Kommission mit wachsender Sorge; vgl. Fortschrittsbericht der Kommission über Rumänien im Rahmen des Kooperations- und Kontrollverfahrens. Der zweite Bericht vom 14.02.2008 befasste sich in seinem ersten Teil schwerpunktmäßig mit der Erreichung der mit Rumänien vereinbarten Zielvorgaben und kam hier wieder zu sehr gemischten Ergebnissen; siehe unter http://eur-lex.europa.eu/LexUriServ/LexUriServ.do?uri=COM:2008:0062:REV1:DE:PDF.

6 Aus diesen ging wiederum *T. Băsescu* als Wahlsieger hervor.

gen Staatspräsidenten *T. Băsescu* überwiegend unterstützte Koalitionsregierung unter Ministerpräsident *E. Boc* und seiner Demokratisch-Liberalen Partei, auf der anderen Seite die PSD als Nachfolgepartei der kommunistischen Partei Rumäniens mit ihren Verbündeten. Letztere hat, gerade mit Blick auf ihre jahrelange führende Regierungsbeteiligung, insbesondere auch während der „heißen Phase" der Privatisierung sowie wegen der tiefen Verstrickung großer Teile ihres Personals in Korruption[7] kein Interesse an einer Stärkung rechtsstaatlicher Elemente. Inwieweit es dabei Staatspräsident *T. Băsescu*, wie von ihm reklamiert, um die „Reform der politischen Klasse in Rumänien" oder doch eher um die Ausschaltung rivalisierender politischer Kräfte geht, kann wohl kaum eindeutig beantwortet werden. Erkennbar steht *T. Băsescu* jenen marktradikalen Kräften nahe, die sich seit längerem bemühen, die teilweise noch aus der kommunistischen Staatspartei und dem Geheimdienst Securitate stammenden alten Seilschaften zu zerschlagen; ein wichtiges Motiv bilden dabei zweifellos auch wirtschaftliche Interessen. Jedoch spricht gegenwärtig für die Position von *T. Băsescu*, dass er das modernere und besser mit der Mitgliedschaft in der EU zu vereinbarende Politikkonzept vertritt.

II. Vorgaben im Rahmen des Kooperations- und Kontrollverfahrens

Der Beitritt Rumäniens und Bulgariens zur EU erfolgte schließlich trotz zahlreicher zum Beitrittszeitpunkt noch bestehender schwerwiegender Defizite. Die Europäische Kommission initiierte deshalb ein sog. Kooperations- und Kontrollverfahren, in dessen Rahmen die Fortschritte der beiden Länder in wichtigen Kerngebieten anhand halbjährlicher Berichte geprüft und bewertet wurden und das zunächst im Rahmen von Schutzklauseln auch die Anwendung begrenzter Sanktionen im Falle mangelhafter Fortschritte vorsah. Die Vorgaben der Europäischen Kommission im Rahmen des Kooperations- und Kontrollverfahrens beziehen sich mit Blick auf die Korruptionsbekämpfung im Wesentlichen auf vier Bereiche. An erster Stelle stehen die Fortsetzung und Vollendung der Justizreform. Hier hat das Land in den letzten Jahren einige Leistungen erbracht und erhebliche Umstrukturierungen erreicht. Diese bezogen sich in erster Linie auf die Herauslösung der Justiz aus der Exekutive und die Schaffung der Voraussetzungen für eine tatsächlich unabhängige Funktionswahrnehmung. Ein wesentliches und mittlerweile schwierig zu lösendes Problem ergibt sich aus der personellen Besetzung vieler, gerade auch höherer Richter- und Staatsanwaltsstellen, durch Personen, die durch ihre Vergangenheit im staatssozialistischen

---

7 Ein großer Teil der von der Antikorruptionsbehörde eingeleiteten Strafverfahren gegen Politiker richtet sich gegen Mitglieder der Sozial-Demokratischen (Partei als Nachfolgepartei der Kommunistischen Partei Rumäniens. Diese betreffen u.a. auch den langjährigen Regierungschef *A. Năstase*, der mittlerweile als einer der korruptesten Politiker Rumäniens angesehen wird.

System belastet sind. Versuche, dies zumindest für leitende Richterstellen zu ändern, scheiterten bereits 2005 am Widerstand des Verfassungsgerichtshofs[8]. 2010 hat das rumänische Parlament das sog. „Kleine Reformgesetz[9]“ erlassen, das Maßnahmen zur Beschleunigung der Gerichtsverfahren sowie zur Umsetzung weiterer Reformvorhaben enthält. Einige der wesentlichen gesetzgeberischen Maßnahmen werden nachfolgend näher behandelt.

Eine weitere Vorgabe der Kommission war die Einrichtung einer arbeitsfähigen und effizienten Integritätsbehörde, die die Integrität von Volksvertretern und höheren Beamten der Zentral- und Kommunalverwaltungen sicherstellen soll. Insbesondere sollte die Behörde deren Vermögensverhältnisse prüfen und möglichen Interessenkonflikten nachgehen. Die Rechtsgrundlagen für diese Behörde wurden im zweiten Quartal 2007 geschaffen[10], zeugten in ihrer konkreten Ausgestaltung jedoch deutlich vom Widerwillen der damaligen Regierungskoalition, eine wirklich effiziente Arbeit der Behörde zu ermöglichen. Wichtige Kritikpunkte waren hier die mangelnde Sicherung der Unabhängigkeit der Behörde und ihrer Mitarbeiter sowie die fehlende Wirksamkeit ihrer Befugnisse. Auf massiven Druck der Kommission wurde das Gesetz per Dringlichkeitsverordnung zwar nachfolgend in Teilen geändert, jedoch bezogen sich die Änderungen bei weitem nicht auf alle Kritikpunkte der Kommission. Im September 2010 trat allerdings eine Novelle[11] des Gesetzes in Kraft, die nun die wesentlichen Kritikpunkte der Kommission aufgriff. Einige wichtige Änderungen werden nachfolgend ebenfalls näher behandelt.

Die dritte Vorgabe der Kommission bezog sich direkt auf die Bekämpfung der Korruption auf höchster Ebene. Mit Blick auf die Vergangenheit muss man feststellen, dass sowohl zahlreiche laufende Verfahren als auch die bisher erfolgten Verurteilungen wegen Korruptionsstraftaten ganz überwiegend nicht der

8 Entscheidung Nr. 375/2005, 591/2005, M. Of. Nr. 591/2005, Gesetz Nr. 247/2005 über die Reform im Bereich des Eigentums und der Justiz sowie einige damit zusammenhängende Maßnahmen, M. Of. Nr. 653/2005. Siehe zum Gesetz und der Entscheidung des Verfassungsgerichtshofs auch *A. Bormann*, JOR Bd. 47/1, S. 69 f. Die Entscheidung des Verfassungsgerichts erfolgte im Rahmen eines von Abgeordneten beider Parlamentskammern beantragten Normenkontrollverfahrens schon vor Verabschiedung des Gesetzes; dieses wurde schließlich in einer stark modifizierten Form erlassen. Inhaltlich mag die Entscheidung auch damit zusammenhängen, dass bei strikter Anwendung der vom Gesetzgeber vorgesehenen Kriterien für die Besetzung leitender Richterstellen lediglich einer der entscheidenden Richter des Verfassungsgerichtshofs diese vollständig erfüllt hätte; allerdings war eine Anwendung der geplanten Regelungen auf die Richter des Verfassungsgerichtshofs zu keinem Zeitpunkt vorgesehen.

9 Gesetz Nr. 202/2010 über einige Maßnahmen zur Beschleunigung der Gerichtsverfahren, M. Of. Nr. 714/2010.

10 Gesetz Nr. 144/2007, M. Of. Nr. 359/2007, schon drei Tage nach dem Inkrafttreten geändert durch die Dringlichkeitsverordnung der Regierung Nr. 49/2007, M. Of. Nr. 375/2007.

11 Gesetz Nr. 144/2007, M. Of. Nr. 359/2007.

„höchsten Ebene" zuzuordnen sind; noch bis Anfang 2006 fehlten derartige Verurteilungen ganz, selbst Ermittlungsverfahren waren selten. Erst auf massiven Druck der Kommission und des Europäischen Parlaments kam es zum verstärkten Vorgehen der Antikorruptionsbehörde und der Gerichte gegen einflussreiche Personen des öffentlichen Lebens[12], Ende 2006 liefen Ermittlungsverfahren gegen zahlreiche höhere Vertreter der politischen Elite, davon allein gegen 73 Mitglieder der beiden Parlamentskammern. Soweit hier jedoch schon Verurteilungen erfolgten, was angesichts der langen Verfahrenszeiten die Ausnahme ist, fielen schon die erstinstanzlichen Urteile sehr milde und keineswegs, wie von der Kommission verlangt, „abschreckend" aus. Darüber hinaus ist zu beobachten, dass die gegen diese Personen ergangenen Urteile vielfach von übergeordneten Gerichten wieder aufgehoben oder die Verfahren insgesamt verschleppt werden. So ist eine Verfahrensdauer von drei bis vier Jahren keine Seltenheit. Gerade diese Aufhebungen wurden von der Kommission in den Fortschrittsberichten immer wieder kritisiert. Erst 2010 wurde das Gesetz über den Verfassungsgerichtshof dahingehend geändert, dass die Erhebung der Einrede der Verfassungswidrigkeit[13] nicht mehr zu einer Suspendierung des gesamten Strafverfahrens führen kann; auf die Änderung wird weiter unten näher eingegangen.

Die vierte Vorgabe schließlich war die Bekämpfung der Korruption in den Kommunalverwaltungen. Hier waren zumindest im institutionellen Bereich einige Fortschritte zu verzeichnen, die jedoch ganz überwiegend in die Amtszeit der Justizministerin *M. Macovei* fallen. Diese beziehen sich u.a. auf die Einrichtung einer Telefonnummer zur unbürokratischen Meldung von Verdachtsfällen, verschiedene Kampagnen zur Aufklärung der Behördenmitarbeiter über die Rechtsfolgen von Verstößen gegen die geltenden Antikorruptionsvorschriften sowie die Einrichtung des Nationalen Zentrums für Integrität[14].

III. Rechtsrahmen mit Blick auf die Strafverfolgung

Ein Blick auf den aktuellen Rechtsrahmen der Korruptionsbekämpfung zeigt, dass es sich hier nicht um ein eigenständiges normatives Feld, sondern eine Querschnittsmaterie handelt, deren Rechtsnormen über eine Vielzahl von Geset-

---

12 Prominente Beispiele sind hier der ehemalige Regierungschef *A. Năstase* und der Bürgermeister von Cluj-Napoca (Klausenburg), *E. Boc*.

13 Der Rechtbehelf ist in verfahrensrechtlicher Hinsicht mit dem Verfahren der konkreten Normenkontrolle vergleichbar.

14 Das Nationale Zentrum für Integrität ist nicht mit der Nationalen Integritätsbehörde zu verwechseln, die auf der Grundlage des Gesetzes über die Gründung, Organisation und Arbeitsweise der Integritätsbehörde (Gesetz Nr. 144/2007, M. Of. Nr. 359/2007) errichtet wurde. Während es sich bei Letzterer um eine staatliche Behörde handelt, die in erster Linie Ermittlungsarbeit leisten soll, handelt es sich bei dem Nationalen Zentrum um ein unabhängiges paritätisch besetztes Beratungsgremium, das zusammen mit Vertretern der Zivilgesellschaft betrieben wird.

zen verstreut sind. Ein einheitliches Gesetz zur Korruptionsbekämpfung fehlt, jedoch gibt es eine Reihe von Gesetzen, deren hauptsächlicher Zweck in der Bekämpfung der Korruption liegt. Korruptes Verhalten wird in den einzelnen Gesetzen jeweils anlass- und zweckbezogen definiert. Die rumänische Verfassung befasst sich nicht direkt mit dem Thema der Korruptionsbekämpfung, formuliert jedoch einige Grundsätze, die für diesen Bereich von entscheidender Bedeutung sind. Hierzu zählt zunächst die Definition Rumäniens als Rechtsstaat. Dieser verpflichtet die Gewalten zum gesetzeskonformen Handeln und schließt bei seiner strikten Befolgung korruptes Verhalten weitgehend aus. Weitere bedeutende Verfassungsregelungen betreffen etwa die Rechtsweggarantie, insbesondere auch gegen staatliche Handlungen, die Regelungen zur Gewährleistung einer unabhängigen und dem Recht verpflichteten Justiz sowie das Recht auf Zugang zu staatlichen Informationen. Schließlich stehen auch die Vorschriften der Verfassung über Inkompatibilitäten bei der Besetzung öffentlicher Ämter in engem Zusammenhang mit der Vermeidung von Interessenkonflikten als Voraussetzung korrupten Verhaltens.

Mit Blick auf die Strafverfolgung hat Rumänien, anders als einige andere der neuen Mitgliedstaaten, bereits im Jahr 2000 ein Antikorruptionsgesetz erlassen. Das Gesetz über die Vermeidung, Aufdeckung und Bestrafung von Korruptionstaten[15] wurde nachfolgend mehrfach geändert und, nachdem es zunächst nur auf die im StGB geregelten Korruptionsstraftatbestände verwies, um weitere Straftatbestände erweitert. Eine umfassende Änderung erfolgte 2003[16]. Während das Gesetz zum Zeitpunkt seines Erlasses und in den ersten Jahren seiner Geltung als Ausdruck eines folgenlosen gesetzgeberischen Aktionismus bewertet werden kann, der praktisch keinerlei Resultate im Hinblick auf die rechtspraktische Verfolgung von Korruption zeigte, entwickelte es sich seit 2004 zu einem wichtigen Instrument, insbesondere bei der strafrechtlichen Verfolgung der Korruption. Das Antikorruptionsgesetz stellt vor allem hinsichtlich der strafrechtlichen Sanktionierung der Korruption in Rumänien gegenwärtig eine der Kernregelungen dar. Das Gesetz enthält keine eigene Definition des Begriffs „Korruption“. Aus dem Inhalt der Regelungen geht jedoch hervor, dass der Begriff in einem erweiterten Sinne verstanden wird und über die klassische Amtsträgerkorruption deutlich hinausgeht.

Auch das StGB enthält eine Reihe von Vorschriften, die für die Korruptionsbekämpfung von Bedeutung sind: Das rumänische Recht kennt inzwischen eine ganze Reihe von Strafvorschriften, die Handlungen unter Strafe stellen, die dem Begriff der Korruption unterfallen. Dabei sind die betreffenden Bestimmungen sowohl im StGB als auch in anderen Rechtsvorschriften, wie etwa dem Antikorruptionsgesetz, zu finden. Insgesamt ist das Rechtsgebiet von einer tendenziellen Ausweitung der Strafbarkeit gekennzeichnet. Dabei wurden sowohl

15 Gesetz Nr. 78/2000, M. Of. Nr. 219/2000, zuletzt geändert durch Gesetz Nr. 69/2007.

16 Durch Gesetz Nr. 161/2003.

neue Tatbestände in das im StGB kodifizierte Kernstrafrecht aufgenommen als auch weitere Strafvorschriften in neuen Spezialgesetzen verabschiedet. Generell ist dabei jedoch vielfach festzustellen, dass die in den Spezialgesetzen geregelten Strafvorschriften auf die Straftatbestände im StGB verweisen, indem sie etwa neue Spezialtatbestände oder Qualifikationen zu diesen schaffen oder womöglich ohnehin schon erfasste Handlungen noch einmal genauer spezifizieren.

Nach dem derzeit gültigen StGB ist sowohl die Bestechung als auch die Bestechlichkeit strafbar[17]. Die Bestechlichkeit stellt zunächst ein Spezialdelikt dar, das nur ein öffentlicher Amtsträger begehen kann. Der Tatbestand ist insgesamt weit gefasst. So braucht kein tatsächlicher vermögenswerter Vorteil gewährt zu werden, vielmehr reicht das Versprechen eines solchen durch einen Dritten, ohne dass der Amtsträger dieses Versprechen zurückweist. Auch reicht etwa die bloße Verzögerung einer Amtshandlung unter Wirksamwerden der Einflussnahme des Dritten aus. Der Strafrahmen ist mit drei bis zwölf Jahren recht weit gefasst. Eine Qualifikation stellt zudem die Bestechlichkeit eines solchen Amtsträgers dar, der eine Kontrollfunktion ausübt. Dieses Merkmal bezieht sich zum einen auf Führungspersonal und zum anderen auf Bedienstete von Behörden oder Behördenabteilungen, deren besondere Aufgabe gerade in der Prüfung der Rechtmäßigkeit des Verwaltungshandelns liegt[18]. Hier reicht der Strafrahmen bis zu 15 Jahren. Neben der Bestechlichkeit ist zudem die Bestechung strafbar[19]. Auch hier ist das Versprechen bzw. das Anbieten eines vermögenswerten Vorteils der eigentlichen Gewährung eines solchen gleichgestellt. Der Strafrahmen ist mit einer Spanne von sechs Monaten bis fünf Jahren deutlich knapper gestaltet als der der Bestechlichkeit. In zwei Fällen, in denen eine Tat als Bestechung zu qualifizieren wäre, scheidet eine Strafbarkeit dennoch aus[20]. Dies ist zunächst dann der Fall, wenn der Bestechende vom Amtsträger in jeglicher Weise zu der Bestechungshandlung genötigt wurde. Im Interesse der Rechtspflege entfällt eine Strafbarkeit auch dann, wenn sich der Bestechende den Behörden offenbart; dies jedoch nur dann, wenn die Offenlegung der Handlung erfolgt, bevor die Behörden von sich aus Ermittlungen in der Angelegenheit anstellen. In den beiden genannten Fällen greift zudem eine Ausnahme von der grundsätzlichen Regel, nach der der bei der Bestechung eingesetzte vermögenswerte Vorteil vom Staat eingezogen wird[21]. Neben der Bestechlichkeit ist auch die Vorteilsnahme strafbar, der Strafrahmen reicht hier, wie bei der Bestechung, von sechs Mona-

17 Art. 254 und 255 rum. StGB.

18 Hierunter fallen neben den die Aufgaben der inneren Revision ausübenden organisatorischen Einheiten der Behörden auch Behörden mit besonderen Aufgaben, wie etwa der Rechnungshof oder die Antikorruptionsstaatsanwaltschaft.

19 Art. 255 rum. StGB.

20 Art. 255 Abs. 2 und 3 rum. StGB.

21 Art. 255 Abs. 4 rum. StGB.

ten bis zu fünf Jahren[22]. Anders als bei der Bestechlichkeit ist es hier jedoch Voraussetzung, dass dem Amtsträger tatsächlich ein vermögenswerter Vorteil zufließt. Als weiterer Straftatbestand ist die Einflussnahme auf Amtshandlungen unter Strafe gestellt. Der Straftatbestand ist analog zu dem der Bestechlichkeit aufgebaut, erfasst jedoch Personen, die Einfluss auf einen Amtsträger bei der Ausübung einer Amtshandlung ausüben oder behaupten, solchen auszuüben und sich dafür vermögenswerte Vorteile gewähren oder versprechen lassen. Der Strafrahmen reicht hier von zwei bis zu zehn Jahren. Erst durch eine Änderung des StGB im Sommer 2006 wurde der Tatbestand der strafbaren Interessenkollision in das Strafgesetzbuch aufgenommen[23]. Danach wird ein Amtsträger bestraft, der im Zuge der Ausübung seiner Funktion eine Amtshandlung ausführt bzw. an der Ausführung einer derartigen Handlung teilnimmt, durch die, direkt oder indirekt, ihm selbst, seinem Ehepartner, Verwandten bis zum zweiten Grad oder einer anderen Person, mit der der Amtsträger innerhalb der letzten fünf Jahre in einem geschäftlichen oder Arbeitsverhältnis stand oder von dem er innerhalb dieses Zeitraumes eine Dienstleistung oder einen sonstigen Vorteil jeglicher Art erhalten hat, ein materieller Vorteil zufließt. Der Strafrahmen reicht in diesem Fall von sechs Monaten bis zu fünf Jahren. Akte der Gesetzgebung sind jedoch von der Strafbarkeit nach der Vorschrift ausgeschlossen. Mit Blick auf das geplante Inkrafttreten des neuen StGB zu Beginn des Jahres 2012[24] ist zudem mit einer Reihe von Änderungen auch hinsichtlich der Straftatbestände zu rechnen, die für die Korruptionsbekämpfung besonders relevant sind.

Der Kontrolle von Finanzströmen und der Aufdeckung von Transaktionen, die in Zusammenhang mit strafrechtlich relevantem Verhalten auftreten, dienen in erster Linie die gesetzlichen Vorschriften zur Verhinderung und Aufdeckung der Geldwäsche sowie die mit deren Umsetzung betrauten Institutionen. Grundsätzlich erfasst der Begriff der Geldwäsche alle Handlungen, die zur Rückführung von aus Straftaten stammenden Einnahmen in den regulären und legalen Finanzkreislauf dienen. Damit geht der Anwendungsbereich der betreffenden Vorschriften deutlich über den Bereich der Korruption hinaus, erfasst diesen aber gleichwohl mit, soweit es sich um strafbares Verhalten handelt. Zentrales Gesetz in diesem Bereich ist das Gesetz Nr. 656/2002[25] über die Vermeidung und Bestrafung der Geldwäsche sowie zur Einführung einiger Maßnahmen zur Vermeidung und Bekämpfung der Finanzierung von terroristischen Akten (Geldwäschegesetz). Das Gesetz verlangt u.a., dass Notare, Banken und Mitar-

22 Art. 256 rum. StGB.

23 Art. 253^1 rum. StGB, eingeführt durch Gesetz Nr. 278/2006 über die Änderung und Ergänzung des StGB.

24 Veröffentlicht in M. Of. Nr. 510/2009. Derzeit steht noch die Verabschiedung des Einführungsgesetzes aus, das nach den diesbezüglichen Regelungen des neuen StGB seit einiger Zeit überfällig ist.

25 M. Of. Nr. 904/2002.

beiter von anderen Finanzdienstleistern sämtliche Geldtransfers melden, die den Betrag von 10.000,- € (bzw. dessen Äquivalent in Lei) übersteigen. Daneben definiert das Gesetz auch spezielle Straftatbestände um den Begriff der Geldwäsche. Zur Umsetzung des Gesetzes wurde mit dem Nationalbüro für die Vermeidung und Bekämpfung der Geldwäsche eine besondere Behörde geschaffen. Anders als das Antikorruptionsgesetz, das seit der umfassenden Änderung von 2007 unverändert Bestand hat, wurde das Geldwäschegesetz bisher mindestens einmal jährlich geändert, wobei die letzten Änderungen erst zum 01.01.2011[26] in Kraft traten.

IV. Besonderheiten des institutionellen Rahmens

Eine gewisse Besonderheit in institutioneller Sicht stellt die Tatsache dar, dass in Rumänien eine Sonderstaatsanwaltschaft besteht, die sich ausschließlich mit der Verfolgung von Korruptionsstraftaten mittlerer und großer Bedeutung sowie unmittelbar damit zusammenhängender Delikte befasst. Die Institution wurde durch eine Dringlichkeitsanordnung der Regierung von 2002 mit dem erklärten Ziel ins Leben gerufen[27], insbesondere die Bekämpfung der Großkorruption bei dieser Behörde zu konzentrieren und die allgemeine Staatsanwaltschaft in diesem Bereich zu entlasten. Während der ersten Jahre des Bestehens der Einrichtung ließen jedoch ihre Erfolge zu wünschen übrig. Wie weiter oben angemerkt, kam es gerade im Bereich der Großkorruption kaum zur Eröffnung von Strafverfahren, geschweige denn zu Verurteilungen. Die der Institution zugrunde liegenden Rechtsvorschriften wurden nachfolgend in rascher Folge Änderungen unterzogen. Dies geschah nicht in erster Linie, um deren Effizienz zu steigern, sondern eher in dem Bemühen, durch die ständige Befassung mit dem Thema den Eindruck zu erwecken, man sei an einer erfolgreichen Entwicklung der Behörde interessiert. Erst im unmittelbaren zeitlichen Vorfeld des Beitritts Rumäniens zur EU konnte die Behörde unter der zu dieser Zeit amtierenden Justizministerin *M. Macovei* erste Erfolge vorweisen, die sich in zahlreichen Ermittlungsverfahren gegen hochrangige Vertreter des politischen und wirtschaftlichen Lebens Rumäniens ausdrückten. Nach dem Beitritt ging die Regierung jedoch ohne größere Verzögerung daran, die in der Amtszeit von *M. Macovei* durchgeführten Reformen rückabzuwickeln und die Behörde in ihrer Arbeit zu behindern. Nachdem die Behörde, die dem Obersten Kassations- und Gerichtshof zugeordnet ist, zunächst gleichgeordnet neben der allgemeinen Staatsanwaltschaft bestand und Rumänien damit zeitweise über zwei Generalstaatsanwälte verfügte, wurde die Behörde nachfolgend zu einer autonomen Abteilung der allgemeinen Staatsanwaltschaft umgestaltet und der leitende Staatsanwalt war nun dem

26 Zuletzt durch die Dringlichkeitsverordnung Nr. 26/2010 betreffend die Kreditinstitute, die Angemessenheit von deren Kapitalausstattung und andere Normativakte, M. Of. Nr. 208/2010.

27 Dringlichkeitsanordnung der Regierung Nr. 43/2002, M. Of. Nr. 244/2002.

ersten Stellvertreter des (allgemeinen) Generalstaatsanwalts gleichgestellt. Diese Änderung wurde auch durch eine neue Behördenbezeichnung verdeutlicht, die nunmehr „Nationale Generaldirektion für Korruptionsbekämpfung" (*Direcția Națională de Anticorupție – DNA*) lautet.

V. Aktuelle Reformen

Eine Analyse der Gesetzgebung im Jahr 2010 mit Blick auf für die Korruptionsbekämpfung besonders relevante Projekte zeigt, dass im letzten Jahr eine Reihe von Gesetzesänderungen in Kraft trat, die sich insbesondere auf die Strafverfolgung von Korruptionsdelikten positiv auswirken dürfte. Diese betreffen sowohl prozessuale Änderungen als auch den institutionellen Bereich und werden nachfolgend überblicksartig dargestellt.

1. Erfolge der Antikorruptionsbehörde

Nachdem es die Antikorruptionsbehörde zunächst sehr schwer hatte, Erfolge in der Form von erfolgreichen Ermittlungsverfahren zu erzielen, die letztlich auch zu Verurteilungen führten, werden der Behörde im aktuellen Fortschrittsbericht im Kooperations- und Kontrollverfahren[28] deutliche Fortschritte und Erfolge bescheinigt. Insbesondere betont der Bericht, dass auch die Verfolgung der Korruption auf hoher Ebene Fortschritte macht und gute Ergebnisse erzielt. So wurde im zweiten Halbjahr 2010 gegen ein Mitglied des Europäischen Parlaments, drei frühere Minister, zwei Staatssekretäre und mehrere Richter und Staatsanwälte Anklage erhoben. Ebenso hat die Anzahl der Verurteilungen zugenommen, bei denen auch mehrjährige Gefängnisstrafen verhängt wurden. Sollte sich diese Entwicklung verstetigen, käme die rumänische Justiz damit endlich der von der Kommission schon seit mehreren Jahren erhobenen Forderung nach abschreckenden Urteilen in Korruptionsverfahren nach. Auch würde dann deutlich, dass selbst ein hohes politisches oder sonstiges öffentliches Amt nicht mehr in jedem Fall faktische Immunität gegenüber der Strafverfolgung wegen der Begehung von Korruptionsstraftaten verleiht.

2. „Kleines Reformgesetz"

Das Gesetz betreffend einige Maßnahmen zur Beschleunigung der Gerichtsverfahren[29], das zum 25. November 2010 in Kraft trat, regelt eine ganze Anzahl unterschiedlicher Maßnahmen, die sowohl der Beschleunigung der Zivil- als auch der Strafverfahren dienen sollen, aber auch spezielle Verfahren, wie etwa das familiengerichtliche Verfahren, betreffen. Daneben werden einige strukturelle Reformen bei den Justizinstitutionen angeordnet. Kleinere Änderungen betreffen

28 Im Internet unter http://ec.europa.eu/dgs/secretariat_general/cvm/index_de.htm.

29 Gesetz Nr. 202/2010, M. Of. Nr. 714/2010.

das Gesetz über die Gerichtsvollzieher und das Gesetz über das Verwaltungsstreitverfahren und weitere Gesetze.

Eine wesentliche Änderung für die Strafverfolgung betrifft die Einführung des Opportunitätsprinzips in das staatsanwaltliche Ermittlungsverfahren. Damit verfügt die rumänische Staatsanwaltschaft nun über ein Instrument, das es ihr deutlich einfacher macht, die Ermittlungen in solchen Fällen nicht weiter zu betreiben, in denen etwa die schlechte Beweislage dies nahe legt. Eine weitere Erleichterung stellt die neue Regelung dar, nach der in weniger gravierenden Fällen von Seiten der Staatsanwaltschaft kein eigener Ermittlungsbericht mehr verfasst werden muss, sondern der betreffende polizeiliche Ermittlungsbericht übernommen werden kann. Neben einigen weiteren Maßnahmen zur Vereinfachung des strafgerichtlichen Verfahrens führt die Reform auch die bisher nicht geregelte Möglichkeit eines Schuldanerkenntnisses ein. Gerade die letztgenannte Änderung dürfte sich positiv auf die Länge vieler Gerichtsverfahren auswirken.

Schließlich stellen die vom Reformgesetz geregelten Maßnahmen zur Straffung des Revisionsverfahrens im Strafprozess einen wichtigen Schritt dar, um den erheblichen Zeitbedarf für diesen Verfahrensabschnitt zu verringern und auf diese Weise zukünftig schneller zu rechtskräftigen Verurteilungen zu kommen. Trotz der Änderungen für das Revisionsverfahren soll dessen Rolle als wichtigstes Instrument der Rechtsvereinheitlichung in Rumänien erhalten bleiben.

3. Änderungen des Gesetzes über den Verfassungsgerichtshof

Eine weitere wichtige Änderung aus dem Jahr 2010 betrifft das Gesetz über den Verfassungsgerichtshof[30] sowie eine entsprechende Änderung der rumänischen StPO. Macht der Beklagte im Strafverfahren die Verfassungswidrigkeit einer für das Verfahren relevanten Strafvorschrift, Regelung der Strafprozessordnung oder anderweitig maßgeblichen gesetzlichen Regelung geltend, so ist das Gericht grundsätzlich verpflichtet, diese Frage dem Verfassungsgerichtshof im Rahmen eines Verfahrens zur konkreten Normenkontrolle vorzulegen, soweit der Antrag nicht offensichtlich missbräuchlich ist, weil die Rechtsfrage durch den Verfassungsgerichtshof bereits entschieden wurde. Nach der bisher geltenden Rechtslage führte ein zulässiger Antrag zwingend zu einer Suspendierung des Verfahrens und weiteren Auswirkungen, wie etwa der Überprüfung des weiteren Fortbestehens eventueller Haftgründe. Durch die Vielzahl derartiger Anträge verlängerten sich in den letzten Jahren die Verfahrenslaufzeiten vor dem Verfassungsgerichtshof erheblich. Zusammen mit der Möglichkeit, immer wieder von neuem einen entsprechenden Antrag bei Gericht zu stellen, führte dies zu einer durch den Beklagten nahezu beliebig zu gestaltenden Verfahrensverzö-

30 Gesetz Nr. 47/1992 betreffend die Organisation und Funktionsweise des Verfassungsgerichtshofs, M. Of. Nr. 101/1992.

gerung, die das Ergehen rechtskräftiger Urteile in vielen Fällen nicht unerheblich verzögerte. Zahlreiche der unter starker öffentlicher Anteilnahme ablaufenden Verfahren in Korruptionsstrafsachen waren von diesem Problem in besonderer Weise betroffen. Durch die Änderung des Gesetzes über den Verfassungsgerichtshof sowie der StPO wurden die betreffenden Vorschriften ersatzlos gestrichen[31].

4. Reformiertes Gesetz über die Integritätsbehörde

Bereits 1996[32] hat das rumänische Parlament ein Gesetz verabschiedet, das Abgeordnete, Richter, Amtsträger und bestimmte Führungspersonen von Wirtschaftssubjekten (hier insbesondere Unternehmen mit staatlicher Beteiligung) zur Deklaration ihrer Vermögensverhältnisse verpflichtete[33]. Die genannten Erklärungspflichten führen für die Amtsträger regelmäßig zu der Notwendigkeit, Details ihres Privatlebens offen zu legen. Bei der Ausgestaltung der genannten Pflichten ist daher zwischen dem öffentlichen Interesse an einer effizienten und frei von sachfremden Interessen arbeitenden Verwaltung und dem Schutz der Persönlichkeitssphäre des Amtsträgers abzuwägen. Aufgrund seiner besonderen Beziehung zum Staat als Teil der öffentlichen Verwaltung werden hier die Pflichten des Amtsträgers in der Regel deutlich weiter gehen, als dies bei Nichtamtsträgern der Fall ist[34]. Mit dieser Thematik hat sich wiederholt auch der rumänische Verfassungsgerichtshof auseinander gesetzt, die Verfassungsmäßigkeit der vorliegenden Regelungen jedoch jeweils bestätigt[35].

Praktisch waren die genannten Erklärungspflichten jedoch viele Jahre ohne echte Relevanz, da es insbesondere an einer Institution zu ihrer Durchsetzung fehlte, was immer wieder auf Kritik der Europäischen Kommission stieß. Nach langer politischer Diskussion verabschiedete das Parlament schließlich im Mai

---

31 Durch Gesetz Nr. 177/2010 zur Änderung und Ergänzung des Gesetzes 47/1992 über die Organisation und Funktionsweise des Verfassungsgerichtshofes, der Zivilprozessordnung und der Strafprozessordnung, M. of. Nr. 672/2010

32 Gesetz Nr. 115/1996 über die Erklärung und Kontrolle des Vermögens von Abgeordneten, Richtern, Amtsträgern und bestimmten Führungspersonen, M. Of. Nr. 263/1996, nachfolgend Vermögenserklärungsgesetz.

33 Zu den Einzelheiten der Umsetzung dieser gesetzgeberischen Vorgabe siehe weiter unten.

34 Dies ist auch in Rumänien mittlerweile weitgehend unumstritten. So ist etwa ein Projekt zur Einführung eines Gesetzes (bekannt als *„legea ilicitului“*), das sämtliche Bürger verpflichten sollte, die Herkunft ihres Vermögens aus legalen Quellen zu belegen und, soweit dies für Teile des Vermögens nicht möglich war, diese als illegal anzusehen und einzuziehen, letztlich immer wieder an schwerwiegenden verfassungsrechtlichen Bedenken gescheitert. Zuletzt in das Parlament eingebracht wurde ein derartiger Vorschlag von der Konservativen Partei (*Partidul Conservator*) im Juni 2005; vgl. Artikel in der Tageszeitung Adevarul vom 03.06.2005.

35 Zuletzt in der Entscheidung Nr. 312/2007 vom 16.05.2007.

2007 das Gesetz über die Integritätsbehörde. Die im Gesetzestitel genannte Behörde wurde durch das Gesetz neu geschaffen[36]. Ihre Funktion liegt in erster Linie darin, die von gewählten Volksvertretern und öffentlichen Beschäftigten jährlich abzugebenden Vermögenserklärungen auf deren Richtigkeit zu prüfen. Dabei soll insbesondere in einem allgemeinen Überprüfungsverfahren untersucht werden, ob sich das Vermögen der betroffenen Personen während der Ausübung ihrer öffentlichen Funktion in einer Weise verändert hat, die einen Interessenkonflikt oder sonstige Inkompatibilitätsgründe für die Ausübung dieser öffentlichen Funktion nahe legen. Einem weiter gehenden Kontrollverfahren sollen dann nicht sämtliche Vermögenserklärungen unterzogen werden, sondern lediglich solche, bei denen das Überprüfungsverfahren einen ersten Verdacht ergeben hat. Darüber hinaus erfolgt ein Kontrollverfahren auch auf Antrag jedweder natürlichen oder juristischen Person, der ausreichende Hinweise zur Begründung des Verdachts von Unregelmäßigkeiten liefert. Die Hinweisgeber bzw. Antragsteller haben dabei den jeweiligen Verdachtsfall konkret zu bezeichnen und mit Hinweisen zu belegen, die eine Rechtsverletzung nahe legen; ebenso sind die Anträge zu datieren und zu unterzeichnen, sodass eine anonyme Anzeigenerstattung zunächst ausgeschlossen ist. Soweit die Ermittlungen der Behörde ergeben, dass eine erhebliche Differenz zwischen den während der öffentlichen Tätigkeit gezahlten öffentlichen und den genehmigten anderen Bezügen auf der einen und der tatsächlichen Vermögensentwicklung auf der anderen Seite besteht, wird zunächst geprüft, ob die Vermögenszuflüsse auf rechtmäßige Weise erzielt wurden. Soweit dies nicht der Fall ist, werden weitere Ermittlungsbehörden (Finanzverwaltung, Staatsanwaltschaft) von dem Verdachtsfall in Kenntnis gesetzt. Die Behörde hat bei ihrer Tätigkeit umfassende Ermittlungsbefugnisse, insbesondere das Recht, von anderen Behörden oder privaten Personen die Herausgabe von Dokumenten zu verlangen, die im Zusammenhang mit den Ermittlungen stehen. Das Gesetz regelt weiterhin, wer zur Angabe einer Vermögenserklärung verpflichtet ist sowie welche Rechtsfolgen bei einer Verletzung von Vorschriften des Gesetzes eintreten. Anders als zunächst in der Diskussion, hält das Gesetz insgesamt bei der Vermögensüberprüfung an der Vermutung eines rechtmäßigen Vermögenserwerbs fest, Rechtsverstöße sind durch die Ermittlungsbehörden nachzuweisen. Schon wenige Tage nach dem Inkrafttreten der ersten Fassung wurde das Gesetz allerdings in zahlreichen Punkten geändert[37], nachdem sich die Kommission hinsichtlich der Erstfassung sehr kritisch geäußert hatte. Dabei ergaben sich inhaltlich einige Verbesserungen, die jedoch nicht ausreichend waren, um ein zuverlässiges Funktionieren der Behörde zu gewährleisten. Die Defizite der Institution blieben somit auch in den nachfolgenden Jahren Gegenstand der ständigen Kritik vonseiten der EU.

---

36 Zu den Einzelheiten vgl. im nächsten Abschnitt.

37 Dringlichkeitsverordnung der Regierung Nr. 49/2007, M. Of. Nr. 375/2007.

Nach mehreren zwischenzeitlichen Gesetzesänderungen, die an den grundlegenden Defiziten der Integritätsbehörde sowie dem von ihr beaufsichtigten und kontrollierten Verfahren wenig änderten, verabschiedete das Parlament erst Mitte 2010 eine grundlegend überarbeitete Version des Gesetzes[38]. Diese greift auf der einen Seite die Kritik der Kommission auf und führt etwa die Möglichkeit der Einziehung unrechtmäßig erlangten Vermögens wieder ein. Eingeführt werden zudem einige neue Pflichten der zur Offenlegung ihrer Vermögensverhältnisse verpflichteten Personen. So müssen Amtsträger künftig Einkünfte aus öffentlichen oder nichtöffentlichen finanzierten Aufträgen angeben, von denen sie direkt oder indirekt profitieren. Weitere Änderungen betreffen etwa die Anhebung der spezifischen Verjährungsfrist von einem auf drei Jahre, die Einschränkung einiger bisheriger Strafausschließungsgründe sowie eine begrenzende Präzisierung der bisher notorischen Berichtigungsmöglichkeiten bei Abgabe einer falschen Erklärung. Auf der anderen Seite gewährleistet die Neufassung aber auch in stärkerem Maße den Schutz der Persönlichkeitsrechte der Erklärungspflichtigen, indem zwischen der Erklärung, die gegenüber der Behörde abzugeben ist, auf der einen und der für die Publikation bestimmten Erklärung auf der anderen Seite differenziert wird.

Inwieweit die genannten und die weiteren Änderungen hinsichtlich der Pflicht zur Abgabe einer Vermögenserklärung sowie der behördlichen Kontrolle der Richtigkeit dieser Erklärungen zu einer höheren Effizienz dieses Instrumentes bezüglich der Prävention und Verfolgung von Korruption in Rumänien führen, bleibt abzuwarten. Ein fragwürdiges Signal waren insoweit sicher die massiven Kürzungen im Haushalt der Integritätsbehörde im Zuge der allgemeinen Bemühungen zur Konsolidierung des Staatshaushaltes im Dezember 2010.

38 Gesetz Nr. 176/2010 betreffend die Integrität bei der Ausübung öffentlicher Ämter und Wahlfunktionen, die Änderung und Ergänzung des Gesetzes Nr. 144/2007 über die Gründung, Organisation und Funktionsweise der Nationalen Behörde für Integrität sowie zur Änderung und Ergänzung weiterer Rechtsakte, M. Of. Nr. 621/2010.

Zivil- und Zivilprozessrecht, Wirtschaftsrecht

Über Medvedevs Reform des russischen Zivilgesetzbuchs

Prof. Dr. Alexander Trunk[*]

I. Einführung

Die Russische Föderation verfügt mit dem in vier Stufen erlassenen Zivilgesetzbuch (Teil 1 von 1994, Teil 2 von 1996, Teil 3 von 2001, Teil 4 von 2006[1]; nachfolgend: ZGB) bereits über eine moderne, in vieler Hinsicht internationale Entwicklungstendenzen aufnehmende Kodifikation des Zivilrechts[2]. Für den außenstehenden Betrachter erscheint es daher vielleicht überraschend, dass in Russland bereits jetzt eine breit angelegte Reform des ZGB vorbereitet wird und sogar kurz vor dem Abschluss steht.

In seinem *Ukaz* Nr. 1108 vom 18. Juli 2008[3] gab Präsident *Medvedev* eine grundlegende Reform des ZGB in Auftrag[4], die folgende Ziele benannte:

a) die weitere Entwicklung der grundlegenden Prinzipien des russischen Zivilrechts;
b) die Kodifikation zum ZGB ergangener Rechtsprechung;
c) die Annäherung von Bestimmungen des ZGB an entsprechende Regelungen der Europäischen Union;
d) die Nutzung neuester Erfahrungen europäischer Länder bei der Modernisierung ihrer Zivilrechtskodifikationen auch für das russische Recht;
e) die Stützung der Einheitlichkeit zivilrechtlicher Regelungen in den Mitgliedstaaten der GUS;
f) die Sicherung der Stabilität der Zivilrechtsgesetzgebung in Russland.

Eine Rechtfertigung der geplanten Reform liegt sicher im zeitgebundenen, kompromisshaften oder auch rechtstechnisch unvollkommenen Charakter vieler Be-

---

* Direktor des Instituts für Osteuropäisches Recht der Christian-Albrechts Universität zu Kiel.

1 Der Text ist (mit Nachweis späterer Änderungen) beispielsweise in den kommerziellen Datenbanken Garant (www.garant.ru), Kodeks (www.kodeks.ru) oder Konsultant Pljus (www.consultant.ru) zugänglich.

2 *Solotych*, Das Zivilgesetzbuch der Russischen Föderation – Erster Teil, 2. Aufl. (1997), S. 15 ff.

3 http://www.rg.ru/2008/07/23/kodeks-dok.html.

4 Organisationstechnisch enthält der *Ukaz* die Annahme eines entsprechenden Vorschlags des Rats für Kodifikation und Vervollkommnung der Zivilgesetzgebung beim Präsidenten der Russischen Föderation, eines im Jahr 1999 gegründeten Beratungsgremiums unter der Leitung des Präsidialberaters für Rechtsfragen, *V. Jakovlev*. Zur Person von *V. Jakovlev* siehe http://ru.wikipedia.org/.

stimmungen des ZGB. Man geht aber wohl nicht fehl in der Annahme, dass das persönliche Interesse von Präsident *Medvedev* – ehemals Dozent am Lehrstuhl für Zivilrecht der Juristischen Fakultät der Staatlichen Universität St. Petersburg[5] – an Recht im Allgemeinen und an Zivilrecht im Besonderen diesem Vorhaben den entscheidenden Impuls gab[6].

Auf der Grundlage des Erlasses vom 18. Juli 2008 erarbeitete der Rat für Kodifikation und Vervollkommnung der Zivilgesetzgebung beim Präsidenten der Russischen Föderation gemeinsam mit dem Forschungszentrum für Privatrecht beim Präsidenten der Russischen Föderation eine Konzeption zur Entwicklung des russischen Zivilrechts, die am 07.10.2009 vom Rat verabschiedet wurde[7]. Der Text der Konzeption ist, gemeinsam mit vorbereitenden Entwürfen zu einzelnen Abschnitten der Konzeption, auf der Webseite des Forschungszentrums für Privatrecht und der Russischen Schule für Privatrecht („Portal des russischen Privatrechts", http://www.privlaw.ru/) zugänglich[8]. Die Konzeption und ihre vorbereitenden Entwürfe sind für die Interpretation der geplanten Neuregelungen von grundlegender Bedeutung, da sie die Vorstellungen des historischen Gesetzgebers zum Ausdruck bringen. Die Konzeption enthält im Wesentlichen eine (überarbeitete) Zusammenstellung der in den Vorentwürfen erarbeiteten Vorschläge mit knapper Begründung. Die vorbereitenden Entwürfe gehen inhaltlich über den Text der Konzeption hinaus, indem sie ausführlich auch die bestehende Rechtslage analysieren, aus der sich der Reformbedarf ableitet.

Die Konzeption ist in eine Einleitung und sieben weitere Abschnitte gegliedert, die den sieben Hauptbereichen der Reform (und dazu eingerichteten Arbeitsgruppen[9]) entsprechen: ZGB-AT, Juristische Personen, Sachenrecht, Schuldrecht-AT, Wertpapiere und Finanzgeschäfte, Geistiges Eigentum, Inter-

---

5 http://www.medvedev65.ru/; http://www.ladno.ru/person/medvedev/bio/.

6 Stimmen, die sich für eine grundlegende Reform des ZGB aussprachen, gab es bereits seit einiger Zeit, so schreibt etwa *A. Makovskij*, einer der einflussreichsten Gestalter des russischen Zivilrechts und treibende Kraft auch der bevorstehenden Reform, er habe bereits im Jahr 2000 öffentlich zu einer grundlegenden Überarbeitung des ZGB aufgerufen, siehe *ders.*, O kodifikatskii grazhdanskogo prava (2010), S. 57.

7 Der Text ist u.a. verfügbar bei http://www.privlaw.ru/index.php?section_id=83 sowie http://rozhkova-ma.narod.ru/resh071009.pdf.

8 http://www.privlaw.ru/index.php?section_id=24.

9 http://www.privlaw.ru/index.php?section_id=100. Führende Mitglieder der Arbeitsgruppen waren bereits an der Ausarbeitung des geltenden ZGB beteiligt (*A. Makovskij*, *V. Jakovlev*, *E. Suchanov* u.a.). Die Arbeitsgruppe Allgemeiner Teil des ZGB wurde von *V. Jakovlev* geleitet, die Arbeitsgruppe Juristische Personen von *E. Suchanov*, die Arbeitsgruppe Sachenrecht von *A. Ivanov* (Vorsitzender des Obersten Arbitragegerichts), die Arbeitsgruppe Schuldrecht Allgemeiner Teil von *V. Vitrjanskij*, die Arbeitsgruppe Wertpapiere von *S. Sarbash*, die Arbeitsgruppe Internationales Privatrecht von *I.Zykin* und die Arbeitsgruppe Geistiges Eigentum von *E. Pavlova*. Die Mitglieder des Rats für Kodifikation der Zivilgesetzgebung werden unter http://www.privlaw.ru /index.php?section_id=21 angegeben (abgefragt am 18.03.2011).

nationales Privatrecht. Dieser Aufbau löst sich etwas von der Struktur des ZGB, da er die Gebiete des Wertpapierrechts und des Gesellschaftsrechts, die im ZGB in den Allgemeinen Teil eingeordnet sind, zu Recht eigenständig behandelt und das Internationale Privatrecht aus der nur gesetzeshistorisch erklärbaren Umklammerung zwischen Erbrecht (ZGB Teil 3 Abschnitt 5) und Geistigem Eigentum (ZGB Teil 4) löst und an das Ende der Konzeption stellt. Die Systematik der Konzeption könnte insofern als Anregung für eine künftige neue Redaktion des ZGB dienen, welche mit der geplanten Reform nicht angestrebt wird[10]. Die die Reform leitenden Überlegungen werden in der Einleitung der Konzeption, mit Bezugnahmen auf den Präsidialerlass vom 18. Juli 2008, zusammengefasst[11]: Das ZGB, insbesondere dessen Erster Teil von 1994, sei zu einer Zeit entstanden, in der der wirtschaftliche und rechtliche Transformationsprozess noch in vieler Hinsicht unerprobt und ungefestigt gewesen sei; daraus erklärten sich viele Unvollkommenheiten des geltenden ZGB und der dieses ergänzenden Gesetze. Inzwischen habe sich eine reiche Rechtsprechung zum ZGB entwickelt, die in die geplante Reform einfließen solle. Zugleich habe die Erfahrung der letzten Jahre eine Vielzahl von Rechtsverletzungen deutlich werden lassen, auf die mit den Mitteln des geltenden Rechts nicht immer adäquat reagiert werden konnte. Die Reform wolle die systematische Stimmigkeit und Ausgewogenheit des ZGB verbessern, z.B. durch Verbesserung der Struktur der Regelungen zum Sachenrecht. Sie wolle des Weiteren die ethische Ausrichtung des Zivilrechts stärken, z.B. durch Einführung des Prinzips von Treu und Glauben und eine Stärkung des Haftungsrechts. Sie wolle zum Dritten auf die zwischenzeitliche Entwicklung im Bereich der Technologie und Wirtschaft reagieren, beispielsweise durch Überarbeitung der Regelungen zum Geistigen Eigentum und des Gesellschaftsrechts. Dies diene auch der Verbesserung der systematischen Stimmigkeit des russischen Zivilrechts, etwa indem als Folge der geplanten ZGB-Reform überflüssige Sonderregelungen in Nebengesetzen aufgehoben werden könnten. Man wolle dabei auch internationale Erfahrungen, etwa von Unidroit oder der EU, nutzen. Ein viertes Ziel sei die bessere Austarierung privater und öffentlicher Elemente des Zivilrechts, mit einer Grundtendenz zur Reduktion öffentlich-rechtlicher Regelungsmechanismen im ZGB. Ein weiteres übergreifendes Ziel sei schließlich die Sicherung der Stabilität des Zivilrechtsverkehrs, etwa durch Verbesserung der Technik der Normsetzung (Klarheit von Normen), die Streichung überflüssiger Rechtsinstitute und die Einführung von Übergangsvorschriften mit ausreichender Anpassungszeit.

Auf der Grundlage der Konzeption erarbeiteten der Rat für Kodifikation und das Forschungszentrum für Privatrecht sodann vier Gesetzentwürfe zur Änderung des ZGB (nachfolgend: ZGB-E)[12]. Sie betreffen die Allgemeinen Bestim-

10 Konzeption S. 2.

11 Konzeption, S. 3 ff.

12 Die Texte sind u.a. verfügbar unter http://www.privlaw.ru/index.php?section_id=100.

mungen des ZGB (ZGB Teil 1 Abschnitt 1), das Sachenrecht (ZGB Teil 1 Abschnitt 2), den Allgemeinen Teil des Schuldrechts (ZGB Teil 1 Abschnitt 3), das Internationale Privatrecht (ZGB Teil 3 Abschnitt 6) sowie das Recht des Geistigen Eigentums (ZGB Teil 4 Abschnitt 7). Noch in Vorbereitung befindet sich wohl – wenn man die Konzeption vom 07.10.2009 vergleichend heranzieht – ein weiterer Gesetzesentwurf, der sich mit Teilbereichen des Besonderen Schuldrechts (ZGB Teil 2 Abschnitt 4) – Finanzgeschäften – befassen soll. Nicht Gegenstand der Überarbeitung sind bislang das Besondere Schuldrecht außerhalb der Finanzgeschäfte[13] und das Erbrecht (ZGB Teil 3 Abschnitt 5[14]).

Im Folgenden soll versucht werden, einen Überblick über zentrale Inhalte der geplanten ZGB-Reform zu geben[15]. Dabei soll aus Raumgründen der Akzent auf die geplanten Neuregelungen im Allgemeinen Teil des Zivilrechts und im Allgemeinen Teil des Schuldrechts gelegt werden. Die Änderungen im Bereich des Gesellschaftsrechts, das nach der Systematik des russischen ZGB auch im Allgemeinen Teil verortet ist, im Sachenrecht sowie im Internationalen Privatrecht, werden nur kurz angesprochen. Ausgeklammert werden das Besondere Schuldrecht, da insoweit noch kein Gesetzesvorschlag vorliegt, sowie die spezielle Materie des Geistigen Eigentums. Maßstab für die folgenden Ausführungen soll sein, inwieweit die vorgeschlagenen Änderungen den Zielvorgaben des Präsidialerlasses vom 18. Juli 2008 entsprechen und ob die Änderungen aus rechtsvergleichender (europäischer) Sicht zu einer inhaltlichen Verbesserung des ZGB führen.

II. Grundstrukturen des ZGB

Die äußere, „pandektistische“ Gliederung des ZGB in sieben Abschnitte (Allgemeine Bestimmungen – Sachenrecht – Allgemeiner Teil des Schuldrechts – Besonderer Teil des Schuldrechts – Erbrecht – Internationales Privatrecht – Geistiges Eigentum[16]) sowie darunter gestellte Unterabschnitte und durchlau-

13 Sowie einiger weniger Verträge, die einen besonders engen Zusammenhang zum Rechtsgebiet des Geistigen Eigentums aufweisen (Anlage 1 und 2 zum Entwurf zur Reform von Teil 4 des ZGB).

14 Die Konzeption spricht den Grund für die Ausklammerung dieser beiden Rechtsgebiete nicht an. Es liegt aber in der Logik der Reform, nach einiger Zeit auch das Besondere Schuldrecht – mit seinen z.T. ausgeuferten besonderen Vertragstypen, die mit dem Allgemeinen Schuldrecht nur unvollkommen abgestimmt sind – und das z.T. lückenhafte Erbrecht einer grundlegenden Überarbeitung zu unterziehen.

15 Die geplante Reform wird in der russischen Fachöffentlichkeit inzwischen intensiv diskutiert, siehe etwa das Interview mit *V. Jakovlev* vom 30.03.2010, http://www.garant.ru/action/conference/236915/, das Interview mit *M. Sazonova* (Präsidentin der Russischen Notarkammer) vom 17.11.2010, http://www.rg.ru/2010/11/17/sazonova-site.html, sowie zahlreiche Beiträge in Fachzeitschriften.

16 Die Pandektentradition gliedert nach Allgemeinem Teil, Sachenrecht, Schuldrecht, Erbrecht und Familienrecht, siehe http://de.wikipedia.org/wiki/Privatrecht; vgl. auch *Butler*,

fende Kapitel wird durch die Reform nicht tangiert, obgleich die Abschnittsüberschriften z.T. verändert und vor allem die Inhalte zahlreicher Kapitel grundlegend umgestaltet werden[17]. Unverändert bleibt auch das Grundkonzept einer monistischen, allgemeines Bürgerliches Recht und Handelsrecht umfassenden Kodifikation[18]. Erhalten und partiell sogar verstärkt[19] wird ferner die allgemeine Verwandtschaft des russischen ZGB mit den Zivilrechtskodifikationen des deutschen Rechtskreises[20] im Hinblick auf grundlegende dogmatische Institute und Konstruktionen (Rechtsgeschäftslehre, Systematik des Sachenrechts, Gesellschaftsrechts, Schuldrechts und Erbrechts). Daneben finden sich im ZGB – wie bisher – Anleihen aus anderen Rechtskreisen und Einflüsse internationaler Konventionen. Diese Elemente werden durch die geplante Reform aber nicht in spezifischer Weise verstärkt. Anders steht es mit der Beziehung zwischen dem russischen Zivilrecht und dem Privatrecht der EU. Der Präsidialerlass vom 18. Juli 2008 erklärt die Annäherung des russischen Zivilrechts an das Recht der EU ausdrücklich zu einem Ziel der Reform. Die Konzeption zur Reform des russischen Zivilrechts und die vorliegenden Gesetzesvorschläge folgen dieser Aufforderung aber nur mit Zurückhaltung. In Teilbereichen, etwa im Gesellschaftsrecht oder im Internationalen Privatrecht, ist die Annäherung an europäische Regelungen deutlich sichtbar, eine systematische Ausrichtung etwa auf die *Principles of European Contract Law* (*PECL*)[21] oder den *Draft Common Frame of Reference* (*DCFR*)[22] wird aber durch die Reform nicht angestrebt. Das russische ZGB enthält auch weiterhin viele Spezifika der russischen bzw. sowjeti-

---

Russian Law (1999), S. 338; insofern ist das russische ZGB eine freie Variante des Pandektenmodells. Das russische Familienrecht bleibt wie bisher weitgehend sondergesetzlich geregelt (Familiengesetzbuch von 1995).

17 Die Aufteilung des ZGB in drei Teile ist durch die Entstehungsgeschichte bedingt, sie hat neben der sachlichen Gliederung des gesamten ZGB in sieben Abschnitte keine eigenständige Bedeutung.

18 In der russischen Literatur wie auch auf der Ebene der GUS wird gelegentlich die Frage einer verselbstständigten Kodifikation des Handelsrechts, vielleicht sogar darüber hinausgehend, des Wirtschaftsrechts, aufgeworfen, siehe etwa das Projekt eines Handelsgesetzbuchs für die Mitgliedstaaten der GUS, http://www.iacis.ru/html/?id=66&nid=26; vgl. auch *A. Ivanov*, Kommercheskoe pravo Rossii: vchera, segodnja, zavtra, http://www.arbitr.ru/_upimg/581A588F31BFFDEA52284A6C5D2E4BA6_z-1_Ivanov.pdf.

19 Z.B. durch den künftigen Verzicht auf die Unterscheidung von „offenen" und „geschlossenen" Aktiengesellschaften oder durch die stärkere Ausformung des Besitzes im Sachenrecht.

20 Zur Rechtskreislehre und insbesondere zum sog. deutschen Rechtskreis siehe *Zweigert/Kötz*, Einführung in die Rechtsvergleichung, 3. Aufl. (1996), S. 62 ff., 130 ff.; siehe auch *Glenn*, in: *Reimann/Zimmermann* (Hrsg.), The Oxford Handbook of Comparative Law (2008), S. 421 ff.

21 http://www.jus.uio.no/lm/eu.contract.principles.parts.1.to.3.2002/.

22 http://webh01.ua.ac.be/storme/2009_02_DCFR_OutlineEdition.pdf.

schen Rechtstradition und versteht sich als Kodifikation zur Gestaltung des Übergangs vom sowjetischen zu einem demokratisch-marktwirtschaftlich geprägten Gesellschaftssystem. Die Reform lässt beispielsweise das Nebeneinander des ZGB und – häufig rechtsgebietübergreifenden – Spezialgesetzbüchern unberührt[23] und ändert auch nichts an der offenen Formulierung vom beanspruchten, aber nicht sanktionierten Vorrang des ZGB vor zivilrechtlichen Vorschriften in anderen Gesetzen (Art. 3 Pkt. 2 Abs. 2 ZGB). Vor diesem Hintergrund sind auch die Vorschriften des ZGB zu verstehen, die beispielsweise – in Anlehnung an entsprechende Regelungen der russischen Verfassung vom 12.12.1993 – die Gleichheit der Parteien des Rechtsverkehrs, die Unberührbarkeit des Eigentums, die Unzulässigkeit von „Einmischungen" in private Angelegenheiten (vgl. Art. 1 Pkt. 1 ZGB) und die Freiheit des Waren-, Dienstleistungs- und Kapitalverkehrs innerhalb der Russischen Föderation (Art. 1 Pkt. 3 ZGB) postulieren. Die Reform reduziert aber die Zahl „öffentlich-rechtlicher" Regelungen bzw. Regelungsteile im ZGB und stärkt damit die klassische, auf den Ausgleich der Interessen von Privatpersonen ausgerichtete Funktion des ZGB[24].

III. Allgemeiner Teil des ZGB

Die „Allgemeinen Bestimmungen" des russischen ZGB (ZGB Teil 1 Abschnitt 1) umfassen Unterabschnitte über die Zivilgesetzgebung und deren Anwendung, allgemeine Regeln über die Entstehung und Durchsetzung von Rechten und Pflichten des Zivilrechts (Unterabschnitt 1), über die Personen des Zivilrechtsverkehrs (Unterabschnitt 2), über Objekte des Rechtsverkehrs (Unterabschnitt 3), über Rechtsgeschäfte (Unterabschnitt 4) sowie über Fristen und Verjährung (Unterabschnitt 4). Unterabschnitt 2 enthält im Wesentlichen das gesamte Gesellschaftsrecht und soll gesondert angesprochen werden[25].

1. Zivilgesetzgebung und Rechte

Unterabschnitt 1 der Allgemeinen Bestimmungen, gewissermaßen der Allgemeine Teil des Allgemeinen Teils, wird im Wesentlichen um drei Regelungen unterschiedlichen Charakters ergänzt: Die Einführung des Prinzips von Treu und Glauben (Art. 1 Pkt. 4 ZGB-E) hat fundamentale Bedeutung für das russische Zivilrecht und darüber hinaus für das das russische Recht insgesamt. Die Klarstellung, dass auch das Gesellschaftsrecht dem Zivilrecht zuzurechnen ist (Art. 2 Pkt. 1 ZGB-E), ist die Reaktion des Gesetzgebers auf eine sachlich wenig überzeugende einschränkende Auslegung des ZGB durch Teile der russischen

---

23 Eine Änderung dieses Ansatzes hätte wohl auch Verfassungsänderungen erfordert, da die Gesetzgebungskompetenz für das Zivilrecht anders geregelt ist als für einige Rechtsbereiche, in denen Spezialkodizes bestehen (z.B. Bodenrecht).

24 Konzeption S. 7 f.

25 Siehe unten V.1.

Rechtslehre und Rechtsprechung. Die neue, sehr ausführliche Vorschrift über die staatliche Registrierung von Rechten an Vermögen (Art. 8/I ZGB-E), fasst in übergreifender Form Regelungen des materiellen und formellen Registerrechts zusammen.

a) Treu und Glauben

Die wohl zentrale Neuregelung im Allgemeinen Teil des ZGB ist die gesetzliche Verankerung des Prinzips von Treu und Glauben in Art. 1 Pkt. 4 ZGB-E. Begründet wird dies in der Konzeption mit den in der russischen Rechtspraxis der vergangenen Jahre aufgetretenen zahlreichen und verschiedenartigen Fällen von Rechtsmissbrauch oder diesem nahe stehenden Handeln. Die ausdrückliche Anerkennung des Prinzips von Treu und Glauben im Gesetz solle dazu beitragen, die moralischen Grundlagen des Rechtsverkehrs zu festigen[26]. Es mag überraschen, dass der Grundsatz von Treu und Glauben bislang nicht als allgemeines Prinzip des russischen (Zivil-)Rechtsverkehrs anerkannt ist. Dies hängt wohl damit zusammen, dass im sowjetischen Recht der Akzent auf andere Generalklauseln gesetzt wurde (z.B. Art. 5 ZGB 1964: Unzulässigkeit der Rechtsausübung im Widerspruch zu den Grundsätzen einer sozialistischen Gesellschaft beim Aufbau des Kommunismus, etc.) und dass der Gesetzgeber der Auffassung sein mochte, die wichtigsten Fallgruppen von Verstößen gegen Treu und Glauben durch spezielle Regelungen erfassen zu können. Bereits der Entwurf zum ZGB (Erster Teil) von 1994 hatte die Aufnahme des Prinzips von Treu und Glauben vorgesehen; im weiteren Gesetzgebungsverfahren war die entsprechende Regelung aber gestrichen worden, um die Rechtssicherheit nicht zu beeinträchtigen[27]. Die russische Rechtsprechung hat zwar das in Art. 10 Pkt. 1 ZGB niedergelegte Verbot des Rechtsmissbrauchs z.T. extensiv interpretiert, sodass es scheinen könnte, als ginge das Prinzip von Treu und Glauben im Verbot des Rechtsmissbrauchs auf[28]. Diese Rechtsprechung stand aber ihrerseits unter Kritik, nicht zuletzt auch wegen der uneinheitlichen Handhabung dieser Regelung. Sollte der Grundsatz (das Gebot) von Treu und Glauben im Rahmen der bevorstehenden Reform ausdrücklich in das ZGB aufgenommen werden, wäre dies ein fundamentaler positiver Beitrag zur Weiterentwicklung des russischen Zivilrechts. Zugleich wäre dies eine Bekräftigung der Zugehörigkeit zur europäischen Rechtsgemeinschaft, denn der Grundsatz von Treu und Glauben ist im europäischen Raum – und darüber hinaus – als zentrales Prinzip des Zivilrechts allgemein anerkannt (siehe etwa Art. III – I:103 DCFR, Art. 1:201 PECL, Art. 1.7 *Unidroit Principles of International Commercial Contracts*). Um der wie bei anderen Generalklauseln gegebenen Gefahr einer Überdehnung oder

---

26 Konzeption, S. 5.

27 *Makovskij*, O kodifikazii grazhdanskogo prava (2010), S. 51.

28 Dazu näher *Trunk*, Treuepflichten von Gesellschaftern im russischen Recht?, FS Kreutz (2010), S. 881 (882 ff.).

möglicherweise ihrerseits missbräuchlichen Anwendung des Grundsatzes von Treu und Glauben zu begegnen, bedarf es einer genaueren dogmatischen Strukturierung dieses Prinzips und der Herausbildung von Fallgruppen. Ansätze hierzu finden sich sowohl im Vorentwurf zur Konzeption zu den Allgemeinen Bestimmungen des ZGB als auch in der Konzeption selbst, wo darauf hingewiesen wird, dass das Prinzip von Treu und Glauben in allen Stadien des Rechtsverkehrs, sowohl bei der Entstehung als auch bei der Verwirklichung von Rechten und Pflichten, zur Anwendung kommen könne[29]. Von Bedeutung wäre auch der Hinweis, dass sich aus Treu und Glauben nicht nur eine Beschränkung der Rechtsausübung (wie grundsätzlich bei Art. 10 Pkt. 1 ZGB) ableiten lässt, sondern dass Treu und Glauben auch zur Begründung von Rechten oder Verpflichtungen führen kann. Auch der russische Reformgesetzgeber sieht den Bedarf nach einer Strukturierung des Grundsatzes von Treu und Glauben und führt ihn daher in einer Reihe weiterer Vorschriften ein, etwa in Art. 10 Pkt. 1 ZGB-E. Die Konzeption verweist zusätzlich darauf, dass einige weitere Neuregelungen, z.B. die geplante gesetzliche Verankerung der Haftung aus *culpa in contrahendo*, sich auch als Konkretisierung von Treu und Glauben verstehen lassen[30].

b) Gesellschaftsrecht als Teil des Zivilrechts

Eine etwas eigenartige, nur vor dem Hintergrund der russischen Diskussion verständliche Ergänzung soll nach dem Gesetzesvorschlag in Art. 2 Pkt. 1 ZGB eingefügt werden. Art. 2 ZGB bestimmt den Begriff zivilrechtlicher Beziehungen und damit mittelbar zugleich den Anwendungsbereich des ZGB und anderer zivilrechtlicher Rechtsvorschriften. Gemäß Art. 2 Pkt. 1 Abs. 1 ZGB, der Kernregelung von Art. 2 ZGB, regelt das Zivilrecht „die rechtliche Stellung der Teilnehmer des Zivilrechtsverkehrs". Art. 2 Pkt. 1 Abs. 1 ZGB bleibt bei dieser Formulierung aber nicht stehen, sondern fügt additiv in gleichgeordneter Aufstellung konkretere Teilkategorien des Zivilrechts hinzu: „die Grundlagen der Entstehung und das Verfahren der Verwirklichung des Eigentumsrechts und anderer dinglicher Rechte, der Rechte auf die Ergebnisse geistiger Tätigkeit (...), vertragliche und andere Verpflichtungen sowie andere vermögensbezogene und persönliche nicht vermögensbezogene Beziehungen (...)". Nicht ausdrücklich aufgeführt waren in dieser Aufstellung bislang Rechtsbeziehungen auf dem Gebiet des Gesellschaftsrechts. Daraus wurde von Teilen der russischen Rechtslehre und Rechtsprechung abgeleitet, gesellschaftsrechtliche Beziehungen seien nicht Bestandteil des Zivilrechts, und das ZGB finde auf sie keine Anwendung[31]. Der Gesetzgeber will nun durch eine entsprechende Ergänzung des Art. 2 Pkt. 1 ZGB ausdrücklich klarstellen, dass auch gesellschaftsrechtliche Rechtsbezie-

29 Konzeption, S. 10; Vorentwurf Konzeption Allgemeiner Teil, S. 4.
30 Konzeption, S. 5.
31 Vorentwurf Konzeption Allgemeiner Teil, S. 3.

hungen dem Zivilrecht zuzurechnen sind, sodass das ZGB auf sie Anwendung findet.

c) Bräuche des Rechtsverkehrs

Eine besondere Vorschrift widmete das ZGB bislang den Handelsbräuchen (Art. 5 ZGB). Der Reformgesetzgeber will den Anwendungsbereich von Art. 5 jetzt auf Gebräuche außerhalb des Handelsverkehrs (Verkehrssitten) ausweiten[32]. Die Kommentarliteratur zu Art. 5 ZGB hatte bisher Verkehrssitten nur insoweit Bedeutung zugemessen, als sie in speziellen Vorschriften (z.B. Art. 19 Pkt. 1 ZGB für das Namensrecht, Art. 221 ZGB für das Sammeln wilder Beeren, etc.) für maßgeblich erklärt wurden[33]. Art. 5 ZGB wird jetzt zu einer allgemeinen Regelung, die tendenziell weitreichende Auswirkungen haben kann, da – wie bisher – Kenntnis oder Kennenmüssen der Teilnehmer des Rechtsverkehrs von den betreffenden Gebräuchen nicht gefordert wird. Als Schutz gegenüber unerwarteten Gebräuchen steht, abgesehen von gesetzlichen Vorschriften oder abweichenden vertraglichen Regelungen, letztlich nur das Erfordernis, dass die Bräuche „weit verbreitet" und „gefestigt" sein müssen.

d) Allgemeine Regelung über Register für Rechte an Vermögen

In den Unterabschnitt über Entstehung und Durchsetzung von Rechten, soll durch die Reform eine allgemeine Vorschrift über (konstitutive) staatliche Register von Rechten an Vermögen eingeführt werden (Art. 8/I ZGB-E). Modell für die Vorschrift ist das im Gesetz über die staatliche Registrierung von Rechten an Immobilien und darauf bezügliche Rechtsgeschäfte[34] geregelte Immobilienregister (russisches Grundbuch). Art. 8/I ZGB-E erstreckt seine Geltung aber auch auf Register über Rechte an beweglichem Vermögen, z.B. auf Rechte des Geistigen Eigentums[35]. Die Vorschrift ist überaus umfangreich und fällt damit aus dem Rahmen der anderen Bestimmungen dieses Abschnitts. Sie enthält sowohl Regelungen des formellen als auch des materiellen Registerrechts. Nicht Gegenstand von Art. 8/I ZGB-E ist das Unternehmensregister (Handelsregister). Durch Art. 8/I ZGB soll wohl die Bedeutung des Registerrechts für den Zivil-

---

32 Nicht ganz ideal erscheint die Stellung dieser Vorschrift zwischen der Regelung zur intertemporalen Rechtsanwendung (Art. 4 ZGB) und zur analogen Rechtsanwendung (Art. 6 ZGB).Überzeugender wäre eine Einordnung nach Art. 3 ZGB, der die (staatlichen) Rechtsnormen auf dem Gebiet des Zivilrechts betrifft.

33 *Rovnyj*, in: *Sergeev* (Hrsg.), Kommentar zum ZGB der RF, Teil 1 (2010), Art. 5 Anm. 1.

34 Gesetz vom 21.07.1997 mit späteren Änderungen, zugänglich unter http://base.consultant.ru/cons/cgi/online.cgi?req=doc;base=LAW;n=108974;fld=134;dst=4294967295;from=71478-0ю.

35 Art. 164 Pkt. 2 ZGB sieht bereits jetzt die Möglichkeit der Einrichtung von Registern an Mobilien vor. Die Grundsätze des Registerrechts sind aber bislang im ZGB nicht einheitlich bzw. nur rudimentär geregelt.

rechtsverkehr unterstrichen und zugleich eine inhaltliche Überarbeitung des Registerrechts eingeleitet werden. In Abkehr vom bisherigen Ansatz des russischen Registerrechts sollen künftig nur noch Rechte an Vermögen[36], nicht mehr Rechtsgeschäfte eintragungsfähig sein[37]. Für Rechtsgeschäfte, die sich auf eintragungspflichtige Rechte beziehen, wird nunmehr grundsätzlich die notarielle Form vorgeschrieben (Art. 8/I Pkt. 2 Abs. 2 ZGB-E). Dies wird die Funktion des Notariats in Russland stärken, insbesondere im Immobilienverkehr[38]. Art. 8/I ZGB-E trifft auch einige Grundaussagen über den guten Glauben des Registers. In allgemeiner Form wird dem Register „Vertrauenswirkung" (*dostovernost'*) zugeschrieben (Art. 8/I Pkt. 1 Abs. 2 ZGB-E)[39] und Art. 8/I Pkt. 5 Abs. 2 ZGB-E konkretisiert, eine Person, die die Unrichtigkeit der Registereintragung kenne oder kennen müsse, könne sich nicht auf das Register berufen. Viele Einzelfragen des Gutglaubensschutzes bleiben jedoch offen und sind durch die Rechtsprechung zu klären.

2. Objekte des Rechtsverkehrs

Der Unterabschnitt des ZGB über Objekte (Gegenstände) des Zivilrechtsverkehrs (Unterabschnitt 3, Kap. 6–8) soll durch die Reform einige wesentliche Präzisierungen und Ergänzungen erhalten. Insbesondere ist das Wertpapierrecht (Kap. 7) grundlegend neu gestaltet worden[40].

Im Rahmen der Allgemeinen Bestimmungen dieses Unterabschnitts werden zunächst der Begriff des Geldes und der Wertpapiere genauer gefasst. Gemäß Art. 128 Abs. 1 ZGB-E findet der Sachbegriff grundsätzlich nur auf Bargeld und verkörperte Wertpapiere Anwendung. Auf Buchgeld und unverkörperte Wertpapiere sollen die Vorschriften des Schuldrechts (nicht des Sachenrechts) angewandt werden, soweit sich nicht aus Rechtsvorschriften oder dem Wesen des Objekts etwas anderes ergibt (Art. 182 Abs. 2 ZGB-E).

Gestrichen wird die bisherige Qualifikation von Schiffen, Flugzeugen und Weltraumobjekten als Immobilien (Art. 130 Pkt. 1 Abs. 2 ZGB). Stattdessen wird eine flexiblere Vorschrift eingeführt, nach der auf solche Gegenstände die Vorschriften über Immobilien angewandt werden sollen, wenn gesetzlich nichts anderes bestimmt ist oder sich aus dem Wesen des Gegenstands ergibt. Eben-

---

36 Art. 8/I ZGB-E lässt offen, ob nur einzelne Vermögensgegenstände oder auch Vermögensgesamtheiten (z.B. ein Unternehmen) Gegenstand von dinglichen Rechten sein können.

37 Vorentwurf Konzeption Allgemeiner Teil, S. 11, 15.

38 Bislang bedürfen Immobiliengeschäfte nach russischem Recht nur ausnahmsweise der notariellen Beurkundung, siehe dazu *Sergeev*, in: *ders*. (Hrsg.), Kommentar zum ZGB der RF, Teil 1 (2010), Art. 163 Anm. 4. Zur Bewertung des Reformentwurfs, insbesondere von Art. 8/I ZGB-E aus der Sicht des Notariats, siehe *Sazonova*, http://www.rg.ru/2010/11/17/sazonova-site.html.

39 Vorentwurf Konzeption Allgemeiner Teil S. 12, 13.

40 Siehe hierzu unten V.2.

falls gestrichen wird die bisherige Qualifikation eines „Unternehmens“ als Immobilie (Art. 132 Pkt. 1 Abs. 2 ZGB). Als Grund hierfür wird in der Konzeption angegeben, die bisherige Qualifikation als Immobilie habe sich in der Praxis nicht bewährt, u.a. deshalb, weil die Grenzen der Zugehörigkeit von Einzelgegenständen zu einem Unternehmen und die sich daraus ergebenden rechtlichen Konsequenzen in vieler Hinsicht unklar gewesen seien[41]. Stattdessen werden jetzt in Art. 132 Pkt. 2–4 ZGB-E zentrale Fragen, die sich auf Rechtsgeschäfte über das Unternehmen als Ganzes beziehen, direkt geregelt (Rechtsübergang nach allgemeinen Regeln, notarielle Beurkundungspflicht, Publikation). Als neues Immobilienobjekt wird der sog. Einheitliche Immobilienkomplex eingeführt (Art. 130 Pkt. 2 ZGB-E), der eine einheitliche Verfügung über technische Gesamtheiten wie Versorgungsleitungen, Verkehrslinien u.ä. ermöglichen soll. Auch Grundstücke mit unvollendeten Bauten werden als Einheit bestimmt (Art. 130 Pkt. 2 Abs. 2 ZGB-E).

3. Rechtsgeschäfte

Eine grundlegende, viele Einzelvorschriften erfassende Überarbeitung erfährt der Unterabschnitt des ZGB über Rechtsgeschäfte (Abschnitt 1 Unterabschnitt 4, Kap. 9–11). Liest man die vorgeschlagenen Änderungen, so gewinnt man beinahe den Eindruck, als hätten die Verfasser des Reformentwurfs das russische ZGB im Schwerpunkt mit dem deutschen BGB abgeglichen. Die vorgeschlagenen Änderungen verstärken die ohnehin ausgeprägten Strukturähnlichkeiten beider Rechtsordnungen in diesem Bereich noch weiter, auch wenn die Lösungen im Detail und bei einigen dogmatischen Grundansätzen divergieren.

Ein Unterschied zwischen dem deutschen und dem russischen Recht betrifft zunächst den Begriff des Rechtsgeschäfts[42]. Das ZGB setzt bisher – und auch künftig – den Begriff des mehrseitigen Rechtsgeschäfts mit Verträgen gleich (siehe Art. 154 Pkt. 1 ZGB). Daraus ergab sich bislang eine Regelungslücke für Beschlüsse von Personenmehrheiten (die im deutschen Recht als differenziert zu behandelnder Sonderfall von Rechtsgeschäften betrachtet werden[43]). Der Reformentwurf will nun ein besonderes, speziell den „Beschlüssen von Versammlungen“ gewidmetes Kapitel 9/I (Art. 181/I – 181/5 ZGB-E) einführen. Beschlüsse werden danach nicht als eine Unterart von Rechtsgeschäften, sondern als eine besondere Art von Rechtsakten neben Rechtsgeschäften verstanden.

41 Konzeption S. 14.

42 Der Begriff des Rechtsgeschäfts (*sdelka*) wurde bereits im 19. Jahrhunderts aus der deutschen Dogmatik in das russische Recht übernommen und fand in die sowjetischen Zivilrechtskodifikationen Eingang. Eine komplementäre Ergänzung durch den Begriff der Willenserklärung verwendet das ZGB nicht, obwohl der Begriff der Willenserklärung in der russischen Dogmatik durchaus Verwendung findet, siehe etwa *Mozolin/Masljajev*, Grazhdanskoe pravo, chast' pervaja (2005), S. 258.

43 *Palandt-Ellenberger*, BGB, 70. Aufl. (2011), Überbl. Vor § 104 Rz. 12.

Damit finden die Vorschriften über Rechtsgeschäfte auf Beschlüsse grundsätzlich keine Anwendung, soweit nicht im Einzelfall gesetzlich etwas anderes bestimmt ist oder sich zum Beispiel durch Analogie begründen lässt. Bemerkenswert an der vorgeschlagenen Regelung ist insbesondere, dass sie übergreifende Geltung für alle Beschlüsse beansprucht, auch im Gesellschaftsrecht und im Insolvenzrecht. Es liegt nahe, dass sich hieraus Friktionen mit den jeweiligen Spezialregelungen, z.B. des Insolvenzrechts, ergeben können. Der Begriff der geschäftsähnlichen Handlung[44] wird im ZGB bislang nicht verwendet und ist auch in der russischen Dogmatik nicht eingebürgert. Es ist daher bemerkenswert, dass der russische Gesetzgeber jetzt mit einer neuen Vorschrift (Art. 165/I ZGB-E) den Zugang von „juristisch bedeutsamen Mitteilungen" ausdrücklich regelt, auch wenn diese nicht die Begriffsmerkmale eines Rechtsgeschäfts erfüllen. Damit wird der Sache nach auch im russischen Recht der Begriff der rechtsgeschäftsähnlichen Handlung anerkannt.

Nicht näher ausgestaltet waren im russischen ZGB bisher die Arten, Voraussetzungen und Wirkungen einer Zustimmung Dritter zu einem Rechtsgeschäft. Art. 157/I ZGB-E füllt diese Lücke mit einer Regelung, deren Grundstruktur an §§ 182–185 BGB angelehnt erscheint. Anders als im deutschen Recht fehlt aber beispielsweise eine Aussage darüber, ob eine nachträgliche Zustimmung (Genehmigung) auf den Zeitpunkt der Vornahme des Rechtsgeschäfts zurückwirkt.

Die Vorschriften über die Form von Rechtsgeschäften (Art. 158–165 ZGB[45]) bleiben weitgehend unverändert. Für den internationalen Rechtsverkehr mit russischen Partnern ist es aber von Bedeutung, dass das bisherige zwingende Schriftformerfordernis für Außenwirtschaftsverträge (Art. 162 Pkt. 3 ZGB) gestrichen werden soll. Die Konzeption begründet dies damit, die bisherige Formvorschrift habe ihren Ursprung in einem aus der sowjetischen Epoche stammenden Misstrauen gegenüber Verträgen mit internationalen Partnern, das heute nicht mehr gerechtfertigt sei[46].

Sehr weitgehende Eingriffe erfahren demgegenüber die Vorschriften über die Unwirksamkeit von Rechtsgeschäften (Art. 166–181 ZGB). Aus der Vielzahl von Einzeländerungen können hier nur einige herausgehoben werden. Mehrere Änderungen stärken die Rechte der Parteien des Rechtsgeschäfts bei der Geltendmachung der Nichtigkeit oder Anfechtung von Rechtsgeschäften, etwa indem die Anfechtung oder die Geltendmachung der Nichtigkeit durch Dritte

---

44 *Palandt-Ellenberger*, BGB, 70. Aufl. (2011), Überbl. Vor § 104 Rz. 6 ff.

45 Art. 164 ZGB regelt die staatliche Registrierung von Rechtsgeschäften; diese Vorschrift wird nach der Einführung von Art. 8/I ZGB nunmehr wesentlich gekürzt. Trotz der systematischen Stellung des Art. 164 im Kontext der Formvorschriften wird in der russischen Literatur wohl überwiegend die Auffassung vertreten, das Erfordernis der Registereintragung sei kein Formerfordernis, sondern ein materielles Wirksamkeitserfordernis des Rechtsgeschäfts; siehe *Sergeev*, in: *ders.* (Hrsg.), Kommentar zum ZGB der RF (2010), Art. 164 Anm. 1.

46 Konzeption, S. 15; siehe auch Vorentwurf Konzeption Allgmeiner Teil, S. 46.

sowie die Befugnis des Gerichts zur Entscheidung von Amts wegen beschränkt – allerdings nicht vollständig beseitigt – werden (siehe etwa Art. 166 Pkt. 2–4 ZGB-E). Beseitigt wird ferner die Einziehung des bei bestimmten unwirksamen Rechtsgeschäften (z.B. bei bestimmten Formen von Sittenwidrigkeit) Geleisteten durch den Staat (siehe Art. 169 ZGB-E, Art. 179 Pkt. 4 ZGB-E). Eingeschränkt wird ferner die Unwirksamkeit von Rechtsgeschäften wegen Gesetzesverstoßes (Art. 168 ZGB-E). Die derzeitige Fassung war von den Gerichten sehr extensiv verstanden worden und hatte zu Missbräuchen Anlass gegeben[47]. Der klareren Trennung des Zivilrechts vom Öffentlichen Recht dient die Streichung der Regelung, nach der ein Rechtsgeschäft anfechtbar war, wenn einer Partei die öffentlich-rechtliche Lizenz zu einer entsprechenden Tätigkeit fehlte (siehe Art. 173 ZGB-E). Nicht ungefährlich ist eine neu vorgeschlagene Vorschrift, nach der das Fehlen der erforderlichen Zustimmung eines Dritten, eines Organs einer juristischen Person oder einer Behörde (!) das Rechtsgeschäft anfechtbar macht (Art. 173/I ZGB-E). Ob ein solches Zustimmungserfordernis vorliegt, ist häufig nicht beiden Parteien eines Rechtsgeschäfts in gleicher Weise erkennbar und könnte von einer Seite missbräuchlich benutzt werden. Allerdings kann nach der neuen Regelung des Art. 167 Pkt. 4 ZGB-E das Gericht in solchen und anderen Fällen u.U. auf den Ausspruch der Unwirksamkeit verzichten. Neu ist auch eine Vorschrift über die Unwirksamkeit von Rechtsgeschäften, die gegen ein (gesetzliches, behördliches oder anderes) Verfügungsverbot oder eine Verfügungsbeschränkung verstoßen (Art. 174/I ZGB-E). Die Vorschrift nennt als Anwendungsbeispiele ausdrücklich den vollstreckungsrechtlichen Arrest sowie Verfügungsbeschränkungen des Insolvenzrechts. Aus rechtsvergleichender Sicht interessant ist schließlich die Neugestaltung der Vorschrift über die Irrtumsanfechtung (Art. 178 ZGB-E). Durch eine Liste von Regelbeispielen (Art. 178 Pkt. 2 ZGB-E) versucht der russische Gesetzgeber, den Gerichten und dem Rechtsverkehr die Anwendung der abstrakten Irrtumsregelung zu erleichtern.

Einige wesentliche Änderungen erfährt auch das Stellvertretungsrecht (ZGB Kap. 10). Hervorzuheben ist vor allem die flexiblere Gestaltung der Rechtsfolgen eines Vertragschlusses durch Vertreter ohne Vertretungsmacht. Wie bisher bleibt es grundsätzlich dabei, dass der Vertrag im Fall fehlender Genehmigung durch den Vertretenen als zwischen dem Vertreter und der anderen Partei abgeschlossen gilt (so bereits derzeit Art. 183 Pkt. 1 ZGB). Art. 183 Pkt. 1 Abs. 2 ZGB-E räumt der anderen Vertragspartei in diesem Fall aber das Recht ein, sich von diesem Vertrag zu lösen. Die Vollmacht bleibt auch weiterhin der Schriftform unterworfen (Art. 185 Pkt. 1 ZGB)[48], die bisherige zeitliche Beschränkung

47 Konzeption S. 19, Vorentwurf Konzeption Allgemeiner Teil, S. 84 ff.

48 Gleichwohl sieht Art. 182 Pkt. 1 Abs. 2 ZGB, dass sich die Vertretungsmacht auch aus den Umständen ergeben kann; eine vertiefte Diskussion über Duldungs- und An-

auf höchstens drei Jahre soll aber künftig entfallen (Art. 186 Pkt. 1 ZGB-E). Um den in der Praxis häufig aufgetretenen Fälschungen von Vollmachtsdokumenten entgegenzuwirken, sollen künftig Personen, denen gegenüber eine Vollmacht verwendet wird, generell eine notarielle Beurkundung der Vollmacht verlangen dürfen (Art. 185/I Abs. 2 ZGB).

4. Verjährung

Die Vorschriften des ZGB über Fristen und Verjährung (Unterabschnitt 5) werden durch die geplante Reform vergleichsweise wenig berührt. Teilweise handelt es sich um redaktionelle Änderungen, vier sachliche Änderungen haben aber größere Tragweite. Zum einen will der Gesetzgeber die Effizienz der Verjährungsvorschriften dadurch erweitern, dass nach Eintritt der Verjährung einseitige Durchsetzungsmaßnahmen des Gläubigers für unzulässig erklärt werden (Art. 199 Pkt. 3 ZGB-E). Zum Zweiten wird die Durchführung eines alternativen Streitbeilegungsverfahrens (Mediation, administratives Vorverfahren, u.ä.[49]) als neuer Hemmungsgrund aufgenommen (Art. 202 Pkt. 3 ZGB-E). Zum Dritten wird die Auswirkung eines gerichtlichen Verfahrens zur Durchsetzung der Forderung neu geregelt (Art. 204 ZGB-E). Nach der geplanten Neufassung scheint eine Klageerhebung nur noch zur Hemmung, nicht mehr zur Unterbrechung der Verjährung zu führen. Eine vierte, nicht unwichtige Neuerung ist die Beseitigung der Unverjährbarkeit von Vindikationsansprüchen (bislang Art. 208 4. Spiegelstrich ZGB). Dies kann beispielsweise dazu führen, dass rechtswidrige Privatisierungsmaßnahmen der 1990er Jahre nunmehr endgültig unangreifbar werden[50].

IV. Allgemeiner Teil des Schuldrechts

Das Schuldrecht macht – gemeinsam mit dem Sachenrecht – den Kern des privaten Wirtschaftsrechts aus. Die im Allgemeinen Teil des russischen ZGB geregelten Rechtsgeschäfte sind überwiegend solche des Schuldrechts. Die bevorstehende Reform konzentriert sich vorläufig auf den im Ersten Teil des ZGB kompakt geregelten Allgemeinen Teil des Schuldrechts (ZGB Teil 1 Abschnitt 3). Das weit verzweigte Besondere Schuldrecht in Teil 2 des ZGB soll in dieser Stufe der Reform nur partiell reformiert werden[51]. Das russische Schuldrecht ist in seiner Grundstruktur und vielen Einzelregelungen dem deutschen Recht sehr ähnlich. Es weist aber auch eine Reihe von Besonderheiten auf, etwa

---

scheinsvollmacht ist in der russischen Rechtslehre oder Rechtsprechung bislang nicht erkennbar.

49 Die Konzeption (S. 25) nennt als weiteres Beispiel auch „Verhandlungen"; diese erscheinen aber im Text des Gesetzesentwurfs nicht mehr ausdrücklich.

50 Dies korrespondiert mit einer leichten Änderung von Art. 181 ZGB, der Sonderregelung über die Verjährung von Ansprüchen aus der Nichtigkeit von Rechtsgeschäften.

51 Siehe Fn. 14.

die Regelung des Pfandrechts im Rahmen des Schuldrechts, das Fehlen einer allgemeinen Regelung über das Schadensrecht[52], die Aufteilung des Leistungsstörungsrechts primär nach der Zielrichtung von Rechtsbehelfen, der Verzicht auf eine geschlossene Regelung des Rücktrittsrechts, die vergleichsweise geringe Akzentuierung von Besonderheiten des gegenseitigen Vertrags und die häufige Überlagerung des Allgemeinen Schuldrechts durch das Besondere Schuldrecht, insbesondere das Recht einzelner Vertragstypen. Keine dieser Besonderheiten wird durch die geplante Reform berührt; insofern kann man die Reform als konservativ bezeichnen. Gleichwohl sind die vorgeschlagenen Änderungen etwa ebenso umfangreich wie im Bereich des Allgemeinen Teils des ZGB. Insbesondere die Regelung über das Pfandrecht (Art. 334 ff. ZGB) soll durch die Reform praktisch vollständig neu geschrieben werden. Auch die übrigen Reformvorschläge bringen einige sehr tiefgreifende Neuerungen, etwa die Einführung der Haftung für *culpa in contrahendo* (Art. 434/I ZGB-E). Die folgenden Ausführungen müssen sich auf die Darstellung einiger besonders wesentlicher Änderungen beschränken.

1. Inhalt und Erfüllung von Schuldverhältnissen

Anders als das deutsche Recht enthält das russische ZGB in Art. 307 eine generalisierende Beschreibung des Inhalts und der Entstehungsgründe von Schuldverhältnissen. Man mag diese und ähnliche Vorschriften des ZGB als lehrbuchhaft und eigentlich überflüssig betrachten[53], sie erfüllen aber in der immer noch andauernden Systemtransformation den Zweck, den – nicht immer juristisch ausgebildeten – Rechtsanwendern die Bedeutung der Regelung verständlich zu machen. Problematisch werden derartige Beschreibungsregelungen, wenn sie, wie in Russland verbreitet, wörtlich ausgelegt werden und daraus weitreichende, nicht immer zwingende Folgerungen gezogen werden. So wird bisher beispielsweise das Bereicherungsrecht in Art. 307 ZGB nicht ausdrücklich angesprochen. Der Reformgesetzgeber sieht sich deshalb veranlasst, diese „Lücke“ durch eine entsprechende Erweiterung des Art. 307 ZGB zu füllen. Auch Rechtsbeziehungen auf dem Gebiet des Gesellschaftsrechts sind in Art. 307 ZGB nicht eigens aufgeführt. Wohl mit Rücksicht auf die verbreitete Auffassung, nach der das Gesellschaftsrecht nicht dem Zivilrecht zuzurechnen sei[54], schafft der Reformgesetzgeber insoweit eine besondere Vorschrift (Art. 307/I Pkt. 3 ZGB-E), nach der die Vorschriften des Schuldrechts auf gesellschaftsrechtliche Rechtsbeziehungen (und auch auf das Bereicherungsrecht) nur insoweit anzuwenden seien, als sich aus dem Wesen der betreffenden Beziehungen nichts anderes ergebe.

52 Mit Ausnahme der rudimentären Vorschrift des Art. 15 ZGB im Allgemeinen Teil des ZGB.

53 *Solotych*, Das Zivilgesetzbuch der Russischen Föderation – Erster Teil , 2. Aufl. (1997), S. 19.

54 Siehe Fn. 31.

a) Erfüllung allgemein

Die allgemeinen Vorschriften über die Erfüllung von Rechtsgeschäften (ZGB Kap.22) werden durch die Reform im Wesentlichen nur technisch verfeinert. Aus deutscher Sicht ungewöhnlich ist eine vorgeschlagene Differenzierung des Erfüllungsortes (Art. 316 ZGB-E) für Ansprüche auf Zahlung von Bargeld (Wohnsitz des Gläubigers) und Buchgeld (Sitz der Bank des Gläubigers). Auch die Tilgungsreihenfolge bei Zahlungen auf Geldschulden und andere gleichartige Forderungen soll künftig unterschiedlich geregelt werden (Art. 319 ZGB und Art. 319/I ZGB-E).

b) Sicherung der Erfüllung

Das russische ZGB regelt im Rahmen des Allgemeinen Schuldrechts auch verschiedene Arten der Forderungssicherung (ZGB Kap.23), insbesondere Vertragsstrafe, Pfandrecht, Bürgschaft und Garantie.

aa) Pfandrecht

Für das Pfandrecht folgt aus dieser gesetzessystematischen Einordnung ein seit langen Jahren geführter Streit, ob das Pfandrecht ein dingliches Recht, ein obligatorisches Recht oder ein gemischtes Rechtsinstitut sei[55]. Die bevorstehende Reform lässt diese Frage weiter offen. Der Abschnitt über das Pfandrecht (Kap.23 § 3 ZGB) soll aber vollständig umgestaltet und wesentlich erweitert werden (Art. 334–358/20 ZGB). Die Grundstruktur des (vertraglichen) Pfandrechts als Konsensualgeschäft – Faustpfand nur als Gestaltungsvariante – bleibt unverändert. Zahlreiche bislang streitige Einzelfragen werden jetzt aber ausdrücklich geregelt, z.B. die Möglichkeit des gutgläubigen Erwerbs eines Pfandrechts (Art. 334 Pkt. 4 ZGB-E)[56] und das Erlöschen des Pfandrechts im Fall eines gutgläubigen lastenfreien Erwerbs der Pfandsache (Art. 352 Pkt. 1 Ziff. 2 ZGB-E). Ausführlich geregelt werden auch zahlreiche Spezialkonstellationen, z.B. das Pfandrecht an Rechten (Art. 358/I ff. ZGB-E), an Ausschließlichkeitsrechten (Art. 358/16 ZGB-E), an Aktionärsrechten (Art. 358/17 ZGB-E), an Wertpapieren (Art. 358/18–20 ZGB-E). Auffallend ist die Vielzahl von Vorschriften über die Verwertung des Pfandrechts (Art. 348–351 ZGB-E) oder über den Schutz des Pfandrechts bei Zwangsvollstreckung in den Pfandgegenstand (Art. 354 ZGB-E). Das ZGB greift mit diesen Regelungen in klassische Themenbereiche des Zwangsvollstreckungsrechts hinüber.

---

55 Hierzu etwa *Lassen*, Die Hypothek nach russischem Recht als Kreditsicherungsmittel (2007), S. 67 ff.

56 Zum geltenden Rechtszustand hierzu vgl. *Marschhausen*, Das russische Pfandrecht in der neuen Gesetzgebung und Rechtsprechung (1999), S. 84 ff.

bb) Garantie

Als weiteres Kreditsicherungsinstrument sieht die geltende Fassung des ZGB Bankgarantien vor (Art. 368–369 ZGB). Durch die Reform soll der Anwendungsbereich der Art. 368 ff. auf selbstständige Garantieverträge allgemein erweitert werden. Zugleich werden aufgrund der Erfahrungen aus der russischen Rechtsprechungspraxis die Selbstständigkeit der Verpflichtung des Garanten gestärkt (Art. 370 ZGB)[57] und der notwendige Inhalt der Garantie gesetzlich festgelegt (siehe Art. 368 Pkt. 4 ZGB). Die Neuregelung nimmt dabei insbesondere auch Elemente des UNCITRAL-Übereinkommens über unabhängige Garantien und *Stand-by Letters of Credit* von 1995[58] auf[59].

2. Personenwechsel im Schuldverhältnis

Nach Einschätzung der Verfasser des Reformprojekts entsprechen die Vorschriften des geltenden ZGB über Personenwechsel im Schuldverhältnis – Zession und Schuldübernahme – (ZGB Kap.24) nicht den Erfordernissen des mittlerweile entwickelten Wirtschaftsverkehrs in Russland, insbesondere nicht dem Bedarf, Forderungen als Mittel der Kreditsicherung einzusetzen[60]. Der Entwurf sucht diesem Bedürfnis durch eine stärkere Ausdifferenzierung der Vorschriften über die Forderungszession (z.T. Unterscheidung nach Geld- und anderen Forderungen, Zession im Privatverkehr und im unternehmerischen Verkehr) sowie durch die Lockerung einiger Beschränkungen (z.B. Ermöglichung der Abtretung künftiger Forderungen, Art. 388/I ZGB-E) zu entsprechen. Wesentlich erweitert werden ferner die Bestimmungen über die Schuldübernahme (Art. 391 ff. ZGB-E) und auch die Vertragsübernahme wird nunmehr ausdrücklich anerkannt (Art. 393/III ZGB-E).

3. Haftung für Pflichtverletzungen

Das russische ZGB fasst die Regelungen über Leistungsstörungen in Schuldverhältnissen nicht einem einheitlich gestalteten Abschnitt zusammen, sondern verteilt sie auf getrennte Unterabschnitte, insbesondere über Schadensersatz für Pflichtverletzungen (Kap. 25), Beendigung der Verpflichtung (Kap. 26), Änderung und Auflösung von Verträgen (Kap. 29) und zahlreiche Einzelvorschriften des Besonderen Schuldrechts.

Die Vorschriften über den Schadensersatz für Pflichtverletzungen werden nach Auffassung der Entwurfsverfasser in der Praxis zu selten angewandt. Dies beruhe vor allem auf der mangelhaften Ausgestaltung der Bestimmungen über

57 Vorentwurf Konzeption Schuldrecht Allgmeiner Teil, S. 40.

58 http://www.uncitral.org/uncitral/en/uncitral_texts/payments/1995Convention_guarantees_credit.html.

59 Konzeption, S. 91.

60 Vorentwurf Konzeption Schuldrecht Allgemeiner Teil, S. 50.

den Umfang des zu ersetzenden Schadens[61]. Der Reformentwurf schlägt deshalb eine Reihe von Neuregelungen insbesondere zum Umfang des Schadensersatzes vor (Art. 393, 393/I ZGB-E). Auch hier greift der Entwurf teilweise in das Zivilprozessrecht hinüber, etwa wenn in Art. 393 Pkt. 5 ZGB-E formuliert wird, „das Gericht könne einen Anspruch auf Schadensersatz wegen Pflichtverletzungen nicht allein deshalb abweisen, weil der Umfang des Schadens nicht mit vernünftiger Sicherheit feststehe". Vielmehr „habe das Gericht in diesem Fall den Schaden unter Berücksichtigung aller Umstände des Falles festzustellen". Man mag sich fragen, ob eine solche Regelung nicht besser in die Prozessgesetze passen würde oder überhaupt einer gesetzlichen Verankerung bedarf.

4. Allgemeine Bestimmungen über den Vertrag

Spektakulärer sind die im Reformprojekt vorgeschlagenen Änderungen im Bereich des (allgemeinen) Schuldvertragsrechts (ZGB Kap. 27). Zwar wird hierzu in der Konzeption ausgeführt, diese Vorschriften hätten sich gut bewährt und bedürften nur weniger Änderungen[62], gleichwohl empfehlen die Verfasser des Entwurfs hier einige Änderungen, die erhebliche wirtschaftliche Auswirkungen haben dürften.

Zunächst wird die starre Regelung des Art. 426 Pkt. 2 ZGB über den sog. öffentlichen Vertrag (an die Öffentlichkeit gerichtetes Angebot unternehmerischer Leistungen) gelockert, nach welcher der Preis der Leistungen für alle Verbraucher gleich zu sein hat. Nach der vorgeschlagenen neuen Fassung muss der Preis nur noch für Verbraucher entsprechender Kategorien gleich sein. Es bleibt abzuwarten, ob die Rechtsprechung die Bildung von Kategorien von Verbrauchern einer rechtlichen Überprüfung unterziehen wird (z.B. höhere Preise für ausländische Kunden).

Eine zweite, noch wesentlich weiterreichende Änderung betrifft Verträge mit Verwendung allgemeiner Geschäftsbedingungen (Art. 428 ZGB). Anders als bisher soll die AGB-Kontrolle künftig auch im unternehmerischen Verkehr gelten (Aufhebung der bisherigen Fassung von Art. 428 Pkt. 2 ZGB).

Eine dritte Neuerung ist die Einführung der Haftung für Verschulden beim Vertragsschluss (*culpa in contrahendo*) in das russische Recht. Der Reformentwurf enthält hierzu zwei Vorschriften: Art. 431/II ZGB-E begründet eine Haftung für Täuschungshandlungen bei Vertragsverhandlungen und Art. 434/I ZGB-E statuiert eine Haftpflicht für treuwidrigen Abbruch von Vertragsverhandlungen. Einzelheiten, wie z.B. die Haftung Dritter für Täuschungshandlungen bei Art. 431/II ZGB-E oder die Frage, ob sich aus Art. 434/I ZGB-E unter Umständen ein Anspruch auf Vertragsschluss ergeben kann, werden von der Rechtsprechung zu klären sein.

61 Konzeption, S. 97.

62 Vorentwurf Konzeption Schuldrecht Allgemeiner Teil, S. 78 f.

V. Weitere Rechtsgebiete

Um das Bild der geplanten Reform abzurunden, sollen abschließend noch die vorgeschlagenen Änderungen im Gesellschaftsrecht, Wertpapierrecht, Sachenrecht sowie im Internationalen Privatrecht kurz umrissen werden.

1. Gesellschaftsrecht

Das Gesellschaftsrecht[63] ist im russischen ZGB, wenn man von der isolierten Regelung der einfachen Gesellschaft[64] im Zweiten Buch absieht, im Allgemeinen Teil des Ersten Buches unter der Überschrift „Juristische Personen" (Unterabschnitt 2, Kap.4) geregelt. Die Bestimmungen des ZGB über GmbHs (Art. 87 ff. ZGB) und Aktiengesellschaften (Art. 96 ff. ZGB) werden durch das GmbH-Gesetz von 1998[65] und das Aktiengesetz von 1995[66] ergänzt, die teilweise mit den Bestimmungen des ZGB wortidentisch sind. Darüber hinaus wurde im Laufe der letzten Jahre eine Vielzahl weiterer Nebengesetze auf dem Gebiet des Gesellschaftsrechts und der – ebenfalls im ZGB geregelten – nichtkommerziellen Organisationen erlassen. Ein der sowjetischen Tradition entstammendes Spezifikum des russischen Gesellschaftsrechts ist u.a. der Erhalt einer besonderen Gesellschaftsform für staatliche[67] Unternehmen, des sog. staatlichen Einheitsunternehmens.

Die Reform unterzieht das russische Gesellschaftsrecht (teilweise auch das Handelsrecht[68]) einer umfassenden Überarbeitung, insbesondere im Bereich des Kapitalgesellschaftsrechts. Der „Allgemeine Teil" des Gesellschaftsrechts (genauer: des Rechts juristischer Personen) soll erweitert werden. Damit verbunden ist die Aufnahme einer zusätzlichen Ordnungskategorie, die nach „korporativen" und „unitären" juristischen Personen unterscheidet (Art. 65/I ZGB-E)[69]. Die das

---

63 Dem russischen Recht fehlt ein spezifischer Ausdruck für das Gesellschaftsrecht als Gesamtheit; meist wird der vom U.S.-amerikanischen „*corporate law*" abgeleitete Begriff „*korporativnoe pravo*" verwendet, der allerdings – anders als das amerikanische Pendant – auch das Personengesellschaftsrecht einschließen soll; siehe etwa *Shishkina* (Hrsg.), Korporativnoe pravo (2007), S. 3 ff. Ein anderer verbreiteter Begriff ist derjenige des „Rechts der Juristischen Personen" (so auch ZGB Kap.4), der über Gesellschaften hinaus (zu denen nach russischem Recht auch die Personenhandelsgesellschaften gehören) auch weitere juristische Personen umfasst, z.B. Stiftungen, „Einrichtungen" und gesellschaftliche/religiöse Organisationen.

64 Art. 1041–1056 ZGB.

65 http://base.garant.ru/12109720/.

66 http://base.garant.ru/10105712/.

67 Der Begriff „staatlich" wird hier im weiteren Sinne verstanden und schließt etwa auch kommunale Unternehmen ein.

68 Geplant ist beispielsweise die Einführung öffentlichen Glaubens für das russische Unternehmensregister, Art. 50/I ZGB-E. Dies wäre für das russische Handelsrecht geradezu revolutionär.

69 Konzeption, S. 29.

russische Gesellschaftsrecht durchaus auch prägende Unterscheidung zwischen Personengesellschaften (*tovarishchestva*) und Kapitalgesellschaften (*obshchestva*) wird durch die Reform eher in den Hintergrund gespielt. Für das Aktienrecht ist von besonderer Bedeutung, dass die bisherige Unterscheidung zwischen geschlossenen und offenen Aktiengesellschaften aufgehoben werden soll. Künftig wird es grundsätzlich nur noch einen Typ von Aktiengesellschaften geben. Als neue Variante der Aktiengesellschaft wird aber die „öffentliche" Aktiengesellschaft eingeführt, deren Aktien am Wertpapiermarkt gehandelt werden (Art. 97 ZGB-E). Verschiedene vorgeschlagene neue Einzelregelungen werden auch mit der Absicht begründet, das russische Gesellschaftsrecht dem Gesellschaftsrecht der EU anzunähern[70]. Begleitend wird eine Zusammenfassung des Aktienrechts und des GmbH-Rechts in einem Gesetz über Wirtschaftsgesellschaften und darüber hinaus eine Bereinigung der Gesamtheit der gesellschaftsrechtlichen Nebengesetze in Aussicht gestellt[71].

2. Wertpapierrecht

Der Unterabschnitt des ZGB über Wertpapiere (ZGB Kap.7) wird durch die Reform grundlegend umgestaltet, stärker systematisiert und erweitert. Er gliedert sich künftig in Allgemeine Bestimmungen (Art. 142–143 ZGB-E) sowie Teilabschnitte über verkörperte und unverkörperte Wertpapiere (Art. 143/I–149/5 ZGB-E). Ein besonderes Anliegen ist es den Verfassern, bisher auf einzelne Wertpapiere bezogene Vorschriften, die häufig in Spezialgesetzen enthalten sind, nach Möglichkeit in verallgemeinerter Form in das ZGB zu übernehmen[72].

3. Sachenrecht

Eine tiefgreifende Überarbeitung ist auch für das Sachenrecht geplant, das in Abschnitt 2 des ZGBs und zahlreichen flankierenden Gesetzen (z.B. im Bodengesetzbuch von 2001[73]) geregelt ist. U.a. soll die Systematik des sachenrechtlichen Abschnitts grundlegend neu geordnet werden. An die Spitze soll – ähnlich wie im deutschen BGB – eine ausführliche Regelung des Besitzes gestellt werden (Kap. 13 und 14). Daran sollen sich allgemeine Bestimmungen über Sachenrechte anschließen (Kap. 15 und 16). Der dritte und umfangreichste Unterabschnitt soll dem Eigentum als wichtigstem Sachenrecht gewidmet sein (Kap. 17-19). Den Abschluss bildet ein Abschnitt über andere (beschränkte) Sachenrechte (Kap. 20–20/7). Aus den zahlreichen vorgeschlagenen Änderungen soll hier nur auf die Reduktion der aus der sowjetischen Epoche stammenden besonderen Verwaltungsrechte an Staatsvermögen hingewiesen werden. Das sog. Recht der wirtschaftlichen Führung (Art. 294, 295 ZGB) soll beseitigt wer-

70 Konzeption, S. 39, 42 (geplante Erhöhung des Mindestkapitals).

71 Konzeption, S. 27, 38.

72 Konzeption, S. 109.

73 http://base.garant.ru/12124624/.

den, das Recht der operativen Leitung (Art. 296 ZGB) bleibt jedoch erhalten und wird ausführlicher geregelt (Kap.20/7 ZGB-E).

4. Internationales Privatrecht

Die für das Internationale Privatrecht (ZGB Teil 3 Abschnitt 6) vorgesehenen Änderungen sind vielleicht weniger spektakulär als die Änderungen des materiellen Rechts, aber gleichwohl praktisch sehr bedeutsam. Zwei Vorschriften des Allgemeinen Teils des Internationalen Privatrechts, die in der russischen Rechtsprechung z.T. äußerst extensiv ausgelegt worden waren, um russisches Recht entgegen den allgemeinen kollisionsrechtlichen Regeln zur Anwendung zu bringen (Art. 1192 ZGB: international zwingende Vorschriften, Art. 1193 ZGB: *ordre public*)[74] sollen präziser – d.h. enger – gefasst werden. Im Besonderen Teil des Internationalen Privatrechts sollen das Internationale Vertragsrecht und das Internationale Deliktsrecht der neueren Entwicklung des Europäischen Kollisionsrechts (sog. Rom I-Verordnung von 2008 über internationales Vertragsrecht[75] und Rom II-Verordnung von 2007 über Internationales Deliktsrecht u.a.[76]) angepasst werden[77]. Hinzu kommen einige Verfeinerungen insbesondere im Bereich des Internationalen Gesellschafts- und Sachenrechts.

VI. Zusammenfassende Bewertung

Die geplante Reform des ZGB beruht auf einer soliden Analyse von Stärken und Schwächen der geltenden Fassung des ZGB wie auch des derzeitigen russischen Zivilrechts im Ganzen. Der Analyse der Schwächen der derzeitigen Fassung – Unstimmigkeiten, Lücken, technisch unvollkommene Regelungen – kann aus rechtsvergleichender Sicht voll zugestimmt werden, und auch die vorgeschlagenen Änderungen erscheinen ganz überwiegend sachgerecht und überzeugend. Besondere Hochachtung verdient das Bemühen der Verfasser der Reform um eine Verbesserung der systematischen Struktur vieler Teilbereiche, insbesondere des Wertpapierrechts und des Sachenrechts. Die vorgeschlagenen Änderungen im Allgemeinen Teil des ZGB sowie im Schuldrecht betreffen weniger die Grundstruktur dieser Teile, enthalten aber eine Vielzahl z.T. fundamentaler Neuerungen (z.B. die Einführung des Prinzips von Treu und Glauben). In der Grundtendenz lässt sich eine gewisse Abschwächung der „öffentlich-rechtlichen" Komponenten des ZGB erkennen, ebenso wie eine vorsichtige weitere Reduktion von Erbstücken der sowjetischen Tradition (z.B. Beseitigung von Anfallsrechten an den Staat bei bestimmten unwirksamen Rechtsgeschäften, Beseitigung des Rechts der wirtschaftlichen Führung). Über die dogmatische Überzeugungskraft einzelner Elemente der Reform mag man streiten (z.B. über die

74 Vorentwurf Konzeption Internationales Privatrecht, S. 2 f.

75 http:/www.dejure.org/gesetze/Rom-II-VO.

76 http:/www.dejure.org/gesetze/Rom-II-VO.

77 Keine vollständige Übernahme der beiden Verordnungen, aber Annäherung.

angeblich grundlegende Bedeutung der Unterscheidung von „korporativen“ und „nichtkorporativen“ juristischen Personen[78]). Vergleicht man die Reformvorschläge mit Strukturelementen oder Einzelkomponenten des ZGB, die durch die Reform nicht geändert werden sollen, so zeigt sich, dass die Reform einen Mittelkurs steuert: Einige Vorschläge können, jedenfalls aus der Perspektive des geltenden Rechts, als kühne Neuerungen bezeichnet werden (z.B. die Einführung des Prinzips von Treu und Glauben und die grundlegende Umgestaltung der Regelungssystematik des Sachenrechts). Andere Aspekte, etwa die geplanten Reformen im Bereich des allgemeinen Schuldrechts, sind eher Detailarbeit auf der Grundlage des Bestehenden. Im Gesamteindruck ist die geplante Reform ein deutlicher Schritt nach vorne, eine Verbesserung des geltenden geschriebenen Rechts. Manche Neuerungen hätten sich wohl auch durch die Rechtsprechung entwickeln lassen. Zu einer Zeit, zu der sich die russische Rechtsprechung aber noch selbst in einem Transformationsprozess befindet, ist aber wohl die Notwendigkeit klarer Signale des Gesetzgebers unbestritten. Aus deutscher Sicht ist es bemerkenswert, dass die geplante Reform zu einer weiteren Annäherung an das BGB führt. Demgegenüber sind Elemente europäischer Rechtsangleichung in den Reformentwürfen eher vereinzelt. Eine durchgehende Orientierung der Reform etwa am *Draft Common Frame of Reference* (*DCFR*)[79] war aber wohl auch nicht zu erwarten. Es wäre jedoch eine lohnende Aufgabe, einen Dialog der russischen und europäischen Rechtswissenschaft über weitere Entwicklungsplanungen des Zivilrechts zu beginnen[80]. Bei allen positiven Elementen der bevorstehenden Reform sollte nicht vergessen werden, dass die Herausforderungen an die weitere Entwicklung des russischen Rechtssystems heute vor allem auf der Ebene der Rechtsanwendung liegen. Gute Gesetze sind hierfür eine Voraussetzung, aber gefordert ist auch systematische Arbeit zur Verbesserung der Qualität des Justizsystems, der juristischen Ausbildung und der gesellschaftlichen Rahmenbedingungen.

78 Konzeption, S. 29.

79 http://webh01.ua.ac.be/storme/2009_02_DCFR_OutlineEdition.pdf.

80 Einen Rahmen hierfür könnten beispielsweise die zwischen der EU und Russland sowie zwischen Russland und Deutschland vereinbarten sog. Modernisierungspartnerschaften geben. Zur juristischen Komponente der deutsch-russischen Modernisierungspartnerschaft siehe die Rede von Außenminister Westerwelle vor der Vereinigung Russischer Juristen am 01.11.2010 in Moskau, http://www.auswaertiges-amt.de/DE/Infoservice/Presse/Reden/2010/101101-BM-Russ-Juristenvereinigung.html (deutsch-russische Partnerschaft); zu der europäisch-russischen Modernisierungspartnerschaft siehe http://www.consilium.europa.eu/showFocus.aspx?lang=EN&focusID=485.

Organe des Staates als juristische Personen im russischen Recht

Anmerkungen aus deutscher Sicht

Prof. Dr. Burkhard Breig[*]

Mit dem Erlass des ersten Teils des Zivilgesetzbuchs der Russischen Föderation im Jahr 1994[1] (im Folgenden: „ZGB“) wurde unter anderem eine neue gesetzliche Grundlage für das System der Rechtssubjekte des Privatrechts geschaffen. Das neue Gesellschaftsrecht sollte einen Teil der Rahmenbedingungen für die entstehende Marktwirtschaft bilden. Das Bestreben des Gesetzgebers, bereits im ersten Teil des ZGB für die weitere Rechtsentwicklung grundlegende Strukturen vorzuprägen[2], zeigt sich am Gesellschaftsrecht besonders deutlich.

Für eine nach Zahl und Bedeutung umfangreiche Gruppe von Teilnehmern des Rechtsverkehrs sind jedoch bis heute der privatrechtliche Status und die rechtliche Ausgestaltung der Teilnahme am Privatrechtsverkehr unsicher und in vielen Fragen strittig: Viele Behörden und sonstige in die Staatsverwaltung eingebundene Stellen der Russischen Föderation, der Subjekte der Russischen Föderation, die die bundesstaatlichen Teilstaaten der Russischen Föderation bilden, und der kommunalen Körperschaften werden in ihren Organisationsstatuten als juristische Personen bezeichnet. Meist wird dabei weder in dem Organisationsstatut noch in einer anderen Norm die Rechtsform genauer bezeichnet.

Eine Regelung des Rechts solcher Organe des Staates, die juristische Personen ohne näher spezifizierte Rechtsform sind, ist im Gesetz nicht zu finden. Dennoch liegt es auf der Hand, dass nicht alle Vorschriften über juristische Personen auf die Organe des Staates anwendbar sind. Kaum vorstellbar erscheint etwa die Eröffnung eines Insolvenzverfahrens über ein föderales Ministerium (Art. 61 Pkt. 4, 65 ZGB) oder dessen Umwandlung in eine Aktiengesellschaft (Art. 57 ZGB).

---

* Prof. am Osteuropa-Institut der FU Berlin, Abteilung für Recht Osteuropas.

1 Graždanskij kodeks Rossijskoj Federacii (čast' pervaja) [Zivilgesetzbuch der Russischen Föderation (erster Teil)] vom 30. November 1994 Nr. 51-FZ, Sobranie zakonodatel'stva Rossijskoj Federacii (Gesetzessammlung der Russischen Föderation, im Folgenden: „SZ RF“) 2004, Nr. 32, Pos. 3301; Einführungsgesetz: Föderales Gesetz vom 30. November 1994 Nr. 52-FZ, SZ RF 2004, Nr. 32, Pos. 3302.

2 Dazu etwa *Solotych, S.:* Einführung, in: *dies.:* Das Zivilgesetzbuch der Russischen Föderation – Erster Teil – Textübersetzung mit Einführung, 1. Aufl. Baden-Baden 1996, S. 15, 28 f.

Staatliche und kommunale Organe, die in ihren Gründungsdokumenten als juristische Personen bezeichnet sind, sind z.B. föderale Ministerien[3], Agenturen[4] und Dienste[5] sowie vielfach auch deren Untergliederungen, die Rechnungskammer der Russischen Föderation[6] und die Zentrale Wahlkommission der Russischen Föderation[7]. Keine juristischen Personen sind dagegen der Präsident, die Staatsduma und die Regierung der Russischen Föderation, wohl aber die Präsidialverwaltung[8] und der Apparat der Staatsduma[9]. Dagegen bestimmt das Orga-

---

3 Als Beispiele genannt seien Pkt. 13 des Statuts des Ministeriums für auswärtige Angelegenheiten, bestätigt durch Ukaz des Präsidenten der Russischen Föderation vom 11. Juli 2004 Nr. 865 „Voprosy Ministerstva inostrannych del Rossijskoj Federacii" (Fragen betreffend das Ministerium für Auswärtige Angelegenheiten der Russischen Föderation"), SZ RF 2004, Nr. 28, Pos. 2880; Pkt. 13 des Statuts des Verteidigungsministeriums der Russischen Föderation, bestätigt durch Ukaz vom 16. August 2004 Nr. 1082 „Voprosy Ministerstvo oborony Rossijskoj Federacii" (Fragen betreffend das Verteidigungsministerium der Russischen Föderation), SZ RF 2004, Nr. 34, Pos. 3538; Pkt. 12 des Statut des Ministeriums für Bildung und Wissenschaft der Russischen Föderation, bestätigt durch Verordnung der Regierung der Russischen Föderation vom 15. Mai 2010 Nr. 337 „O Ministerstve obrazovanija i nauki Rossijskoj Federacii" (Über das Ministerium für Bildung und Wissenschaft der Russischen Föderation), SZ RF 2010, Nr. 21, Pos. 2603.

4 So z.B. Pkt. 12 des Statuts der Föderalen Agentur für Angelegenheiten der Gemeinschaft Unabhängiger Staaten und der im Ausland lebenden Landsleute und für internationale humanitäre Zusammenarbeit, bestätigt durch Erlass des Präsidenten der Russischen Föderation vom 6. September 2008 Nr. 1315 „O nekotorych voprosach gosudarstvennogo upravlenija v oblasti meždunarodnogo sotrudničestva" (Über einige Fragen der staatlichen Verwaltung im Bereich der internationalen Zusammenarbeit), SZ RF 2008, Nr. 37, Pos. 4181.

5 So z.B. Pkt. 11 des Statuts des Föderalen Dienstes für geistiges Eigentum, Patente und Marken, bestätigt durch Verordnung der Regierung der Russischen Föderation vom 16. Juni 2004 Nr. 299 „Ob utverždenii Položenija o Federal'noj službe po intellektual'noj sobstvennosti, patentam i tovarnym znakam" (Über die Bestätigung des Statuts des Föderalen Dienstes für geistiges Eigentum, Patente und Marken), SZ RF 2004, Nr. 26, Pos. 2668.

6 Art. 1 Abs. 3 des föderalen Gesetzes vom 11. Januar 1995 Nr. 4-FZ „O Sčetnoj palate Rossijskoj Federacii" (Über die Rechnungskammer der Russischen Föderation), SZ RF 1995, Nr. 3, Pos. 167.

7 Art. 21 Pkt. 2 des föderalen Gesetzes vom 12. Juni 2002 Nr. 67-FZ „Ob osnovnych garantijach izbiratel'nych prav i prava na učastie v referendume graždan Rossijskoj Federacii" (Über grundlegende Garantien der auf Wahlen bezogenen Rechte und des Rechts auf Teilnahme an einer Volksabstimmung der Bürger der Russischen Föderation), SZ RF 2002, Nr. 24, Pos. 2253.

8 Pkt. 17 des Statuts der Präsidialverwaltung, bestätigt durch Ukaz vom 06. April 2004 Nr. 490 „Ob utverždenii Položenija ob Administracii Prezidenta Rossijskoj Federacii" (Über die Bestätigung des Statuts der Administration des Präsidenten der Russischen Föderation), SZ RF 2004, Nr. 15, Pos. 1395.

nisationsstatut des Apparats der Regierung der Russischen Föderation[10] zwar, dass dieser eigene Stempel, Siegel sowie einen eigenen Briefkopf besitzt (Pkt. 27), legt jedoch nicht fest, dass der Apparat der Regierung eine juristische Person sei. Kraft Anordnung durch föderales Gesetz sind auch bestimmte Organe der Subjekte der Russischen Föderation juristische Personen, so z.B. die Wahlkommissionen der Subjekte der Russischen Föderation[11] sowie das gesetzgebende Organ und das oberste Organ der Exekutive eines jeden Subjekts der Russischen Föderation[12]. Weitere regionale Stellen werden durch Rechtsvorschriften der Subjekte der Russischen Föderation und der kommunalen Körperschaften zu juristischen Personen erklärt.

Im Folgenden sollen einige Rechtsfragen angesprochen werden, die sich nach geltendem Recht für die Organe des Staates stellen, die nach ihren Organisationsstatuten juristische Personen unbenannter Rechtsform sind (III.). Zuvor werden die Verwendung des Begriffs des Organs des Staates (I.) und das System der Subjekte des Zivilrechts (II.) dargestellt. Abschließend wird ein Blick auf die bevorstehende Reformierung des Zivilgesetzbuchs und seine Auswirkungen auf die rechtliche Lage der staatlichen Organe im Zivilrecht geworfen werden (IV.).

---

9 Abschnitt I Pkt. 1 S. 2 des Statuts des Apparats der Staatsduma der Russischen Föderation, bestätigt durch Verfügung des Vorsitzenden der Staatsduma der Russischen Föderation vom 16. Februar 2004 Nr. 18r-1, SZ RF 2004, nicht offiziell bekanntgemacht; zugänglich auf der Internet-Seite der Staatsduma der Russischen Föderation unter http://www.duma.gov.ru/index.jsp?t=apparat/polozhenie/pApparat.html (abgerufen am 23. Januar 2011).

10 Statut über den Apparat der Regierung der Russischen Föderation, bestätigt durch Verordnung der Regierung der Russischen Föderation vom 1. Juni 2004 Nr. 260 „O Reglamente Pravitel'stva Rossijskoj Federacii i Položenii ob Apparate Pravitel'stva Rossijkoj Federacii“ (Über die Geschäftsordnung der Regierung der Russischen Föderation und das Statut über den Apparat der Regierung der Russischen Föderation), SZ RF 2004, Nr. 23, Pos. 2313.

11 Art. 23 Pkt. 2 des föderalen Gesetzes vom 12. Juni 2002 Nr. 67-FZ (Fundstelle s.o. Fn. 7).

12 Art. 4 Pkt. 7 und Art. 20 Pkt. 4 des föderalen Gesetzes vom 06. Oktober 1999 Nr. 184-FZ „Ob obščich principach organizacii zakonodatel'nych (predstavitel'nych) i ispolnitel'nych organov gosudarstvennoj vlasti sub''ektov Rossijskoj Federacii“ (Über allgemeine Grundsätze der Organisation der gesetzgebenden Organe (Vertretungsorgane) und der ausführenden Organe der Staatsgewalt der Subjekte der Russischen Föderation), SZ RF 1999, Nr. 42, Pos. 5005.

I. Organe des Staates, staatliche Organe und Organe der Staatsgewalt im russischen Recht

1. Verfassungsrecht

Nach einer gängigen Formel sind Organe der Staatsgewalt (*organy gosudarstvennoj vlasti*) besondere Organisationen, die über eine hinreichend genau bestimmte Organisationsstruktur verfügen (oder, wie im Fall des Präsidenten der Russischen Föderation oder der Leiter der Verwaltung der Subjekte der Russischen Föderation, Einzelpersonen), die damit betraut sind, hoheitliche Befugnisse mit Außenwirkung wahrzunehmen, und denen die erforderlichen materiellen Mittel zur Verfügung gestellt sind[13]. Neben den Organen der Staatsgewalt gibt es weitere organisatorische Einheiten, bei denen nicht alle Merkmale eines Organs der Staatsgewalt vorliegen und die dennoch „staatliche Organe" (*gosudarstvennye organy*) sind. Dazu gehören z.B. Stellen ohne die Befugnis, verbindliche Regelungen mit Außenwirkung gegenüber Bürgern und ihren (nichtstaatlichen) Vereinigungen zu treffen[14]. Der Staatsapparat (*gosudarstvennyj apparat*) wird gebildet durch die Gesamtheit der Organe der Staatsgewalt und der sonstigen staatlichen Organe[15].

Der Begriff der staatlichen Organe, oft auch bezeichnet als Organe des Staates (*organy gosudarstva*), umfasst alle im Bereich der Staatsverwaltung tätigen organisatorischen Einheiten. Staatliche Organe können dabei nicht nur ein rechtlich unselbständiger Teil der Staatsgewalt sein, sondern es gibt staatliche Organe, die selbst Träger eigener Rechte und Pflichten sein können[16].

2. Zivilrecht

Das ZGB verwendet sowohl den Begriff des Organs der Staatsgewalt als auch den des staatlichen Organs. Gemäß Art. 125 ZGB kann der Staat durch Organe der Staatsgewalt und (sonstige) staatliche Organe im Rechtsverkehr handeln. Hierbei handeln Organe der Staatsgewalt aufgrund ihrer ihnen durch ihre Organisationsakte zugewiesenen Befugnisse, während staatliche Organe, die keine Organe der Staatsgewalt sind, nur aufgrund einer besonderen Ermächtigung für den Staat handeln können (Art. 125 Pkt. 1 und 3 ZGB).

---

13 *Ščekočichin, P.G.,* in: Kokotov, A.N. / Kukuškin, M.I. (Hrsg.): Konstitucionnoe pravo Rossii (Das Verfassungsrecht Russlands), 3. Auflage Moskau 2008, Kap. 19 § 1 (S. 329).

14 Zu dieser Unterscheidung s. etwa den Beschluss des Verfassungsgerichts der Russischen Föderation vom 29. Mai 1997 Nr. 55-O, SZ RF 1997, Nr. 22 Pos. 2664.

15 Zu diesen Begriffen: *Ščekočichin, P.G.* (Fn. 13), S. 329; andere Autoren setzen die Begriffe des Organs der Staatsgewalt und des staatlichen Organs anscheinend gleich, so z.B. *Zinov'ev, A.V.:* Konstitucionnoe pravo Rossii (Das Verfassungsrecht Russlands), St. Petersburg 2010, Kap. 8 § 2 (S. 322).

16 *Ščekočichin, P.G.* (Fn. 13), S. 329.

Punktuell finden sich in der zivilrechtlichen Gesetzgebung Vorschriften, die darauf hindeuten, dass Organe des Staates Rechtssubjekte sein können. Ein Hinweis auf die Möglichkeit der Teilnahme von Organen des Staates am Privatrechtsverkehr findet sich in Art. 66 Pkt. 4 Abs. 3 ZGB, nach dem staatliche Organe und Organe der örtlichen Selbstverwaltung sich weder an Wirtschafts(kapital)gesellschaften (*chozjastvennye obščestva*) noch als Kommanditisten an Kommanditgesellschaften beteiligen dürfen[17], sofern durch Gesetz nichts anderes bestimmt ist. Diese Vorschrift setzt also voraus, dass es rechtsfähige Organe des Staates und der örtlichen Selbstverwaltung gibt.

In dieselbe Richtung deutet Art. 268 Pkt. 1 ZGB nach seiner Anpassung an den später ergangenen Art. 20 Pkt. 1 BodenGB[18]. Nach diesen Vorschriften kann das Recht der ständigen (unbefristeteten) Nutzung eines staatlichen oder kommunalen Grundstücks einer staatlichen oder kommunalen Einrichtung, einem Fiskusunternehmen, einem Organ der Staatsgewalt oder einem Organ der örtlichen Selbstverwaltung zugeteilt werden. Damit werden Organe der Staatsgewalt und der örtlichen Selbstverwaltung als Rechtsträger behandelt.

Im Jahr 2006 wurde in das Gesetz über nichtkommerzielle Organisationen[19] eine Vorschrift eingefügt, nach der dieses Gesetz unter anderem nicht auf Organe der Staatsgewalt, sonstige Organe des Staates und Organe der örtlichen Selbstverwaltung anzuwenden ist (Art. 1 Pkt. 5)[20].

Nach dem ZGB sind es damit Organe der Staatsgewalt und – bei besonderer Bevollmächtigung – auch andere staatliche Organe, durch die der Staat als Rechtssubjekt im Rechtsverkehr auftreten kann. Darüber hinaus kommt im ZGB – ebenso wie im Verfassungsrecht – zum Ausdruck, dass staatliche Organe auch als Rechtsträger am Rechtsverkehr beteiligt sein können.

---

17 Die Beteiligung als unbeschränkt haftender Gesellschafter an Personengesellschaften ist bereits nach Art. 66 Pkt. 4 Abs. 1 ZGB ausgeschlossen.

18 Bodengesetzbuch der Russischen Föderation vom 25. Oktober 2001 Nr. 136-FZ, SZ RF 2001, Nr. 44, Pos. 4147.

19 Föderales Gesetz vom 21. Januar 1996 Nr. 7-FZ „O nekommerčeskich organizacijach" (Über nichtkommerzielle Organisationen), SZ RF 1996, Nr. 3, Pos. 145.

20 Eingefügt durch Föderales Gesetz vom 10. Januar 2006 Nr. 10-FZ Nr. 18-FZ „O vnesenii izmenenij v nekotorye zakonodatel'nye akty Rossijskoj Federacii" (Über die Änderung einiger Akte der Gesetzgebung der Russischen Föderation), SZ RF 2006, Nr. 3, Pos. 282; die Regelung wurde nochmals geändert durch Föderales Gesetz vom 08. Mai 2010 Nr. 83-FZ „O vnesenii izmenenij v otdel'nye zakonodatel'nye akty Rossijskoj Federacii v svjazi s soveršenstvovaniem pravovogo položenija gosudarstvennych (municipal'nych) učreždenij" (Über die Änderung einzelner Gesetzgebungsakte der Russischen Föderation im Zusammenhang mit der Vervollkommnung der rechtlichen Situation der staatlichen (kommunalen) Einrichtungen), SZ RF 2010, Nr. 19, Pos. 2291.

II. Subjekte des Privatrechts

Gemäß Art. 2 Pkt. 1 Abs. 2 ZGB können an bürgerlich-rechtlichen Rechtsverhältnissen natürliche und juristische Personen sowie die Russische Föderation, die Subjekte der Russischen Föderation und die kommunalen Körperschaften (*municipal'nye obrazovnaija*) beteiligt sein[21].

1. Der Staat und die kommunalen Körperschaften als Privatrechtssubjekte

Der russische Staat ist kein einheitliches Rechtssubjekt, sondern das ZGB behandelt neben der Russischen Föderation auch die Subjekte der Russischen Föderation, die in der russischen Literatur auch zusammenfassend staatliche Körperschaften (*gosudarstvennye obrazovanija*) genannt werden, als eigene Rechtssubjekte. Rechtssubjekte sind ferner die kommunalen Körperschaften, die neben dem Staat existieren. Kommunale Körperschaften und staatliche Körperschaften werden gemeinsam auch öffentlich-rechtliche Körperschaften (*publično-pravovye obrazovanija*) genannt. Die öffentlich-rechtlichen Körperschaften sind Rechtssubjekte *sui generis*[22]. Ihrer Teilnahme am Privatrechtsverkehr ist, wie bereits im russischen Zivilgesetzbuch von 1964[23] (im Folgenden: „ZGB 1964"), ein eigenes Kapitel des ZGB gewidmet.

Die staatlichen und die kommunalen Körperschaften nehmen gleichberechtigt mit natürlichen und juristischen Personen am bürgerlich-rechtlichen Rechtsverkehr teil (Art. 124 Pkt. 1 ZGB). Auf sie finden die Regelungen über die Teilnahme juristischer Personen am Rechtsverkehr Anwendung, soweit sich nicht aus dem Gesetz oder aus den Besonderheiten des jeweiligen Rechtssubjekts et-

---

21 Dazu s. nur *Egorov, N.D.*, in: Sergeev, A.P. / Tolstoj, Ju.K. (Hrsg.): Graždanskoe pravo (Bürgerliches Recht), Band 1, 6. Auflage, Moskau 2002, S. 98 f.

22 Anders noch das russische Recht vor der Revolution: *Šeršenevič, G.F.:* Učebnik russkogo graždanskogo prava (Lehrbuch des russischen Bürgerlichen Rechts), Neudruck nach der Ausgabe von 1907, Moskau 1995, S. 91; *Mejer, D.I.:* Russkoe graždanskoe pravo (Russisches Bürgerliches Recht), Neudruck nach der 8. Auflage 1902, Moskau 1997, Bd. 1, S. 135 f.; s. auch Art. 13 Abs. 1 Nr. 1) des Entwurfs des Bürgerlichen Gesetzbuchs des Russischen Imperiums von 1910, veröffentlicht in: Graždanskoe uloženie. Kniga 1. Položenija obščie: proekt Vysočajše učreždennoj Redakcionnoj komissii po sostavleniju Graždanskogo uloženija (Bürgerliches Gesetzbuch. Buch 1. Allgemeine Vorschriften: Entwurf des durch den Zaren eingesetzten Redaktionsausschusses zur Schaffung eines Bürgerlichen Gesetzbuchs), Hrsg.: A.L. Saatčian; wissenschaftliche Redaktion: I.M. Tjutrjumov, Neudruck Moskau 2007 (Originalausgabe: St. Petersburg 1910).

23 Zivilgesetzbuch der Russischen Sozialistischen Föderativen Sowjetrepublik, bestätigt durch Gesetz der RSFSR vom 11. Juni 1964 „Ob utverždenii Graždanskogo kodeksa RSFSR" (Über die Bestätigung des Zivilgesetzbuchs der RSFSR), Vedomosti Verchovnogo Soveta RSFSR (Mitteilungsblatt des Obersten Sowjet der RSFSR) 1964, Nr. 24, Pos. 406.

was anderes ergibt (Art. 124 Pkt. 2 ZGB). Sie sind damit grundsätzlich juristischen Personen gleichgestellt.

Das Handeln im Rechtsverkehr erfolgt nach Art. 125 Pkt. 1 und 3 ZGB durch staatliche Organe (insbesondere die Organe der Staatsgewalt) bzw. die Organe der örtlichen Selbstverwaltung.

Die Haftungsmasse, mit der die öffentlich-rechtlichen Körperschaften für ihre Verbindlichkeiten einstehen, beschreibt Art. 126 Pkt. 1 ZGB. Jede öffentlich-rechtliche Körperschaft haftet danach mit dem in ihrem Eigentum stehenden Vermögen, soweit an ihm nicht bereits juristischen Personen das Recht der operativen Verwaltung oder der Bewirtschaftung eingeräumt wurde (sog. nicht verteiltes Vermögen[24]). Von der Haftungsmasse ausgenommen ist solches Vermögen, das nur öffentlich-rechtlichen Körperschaften gehören kann.

Nach Art. 126 Pkt. 2 ZGB haftet eine durch eine öffentlich-rechtliche Körperschaft geschaffene juristische Person nicht für die Verbindlichkeiten der betreffenden Körperschaft. Gem. Art. 126 Pkt. 3 ZGB haftet umgekehrt die Körperschaft ebenfalls nicht für die Verbindlichkeiten der durch sie geschaffenen juristischen Personen, außer wenn eine Haftung durch Gesetz vorgesehen ist. Solche Ausnahmen regelt das ZGB für staatliche und kommunale Fiskusunternehmen (*kazënnye predprijatija*) (Art. 115 Pkt. 5 ZGB) und für Fiskuseinrichtungen (*kazënnye učreždenija*) (Art. 120 Pkt. 2 Abs. 4 S. 2 ZGB in der ab 01. Januar 2011 geltenden Fassung)[25].

2. Juristische Personen

Organisationen, die nicht zu den öffentlich-rechtlichen Körperschaften gehören, können nach dem ZGB allein als juristische Person rechtsfähig sein.

Der erste Teil des ZGB enthält grundlegende Vorschriften über die juristischen Personen (Kapitel 4 des ZGB). Dem Aufbau des ZGB 1964 folgend[26] wird die Regelung eingeleitet durch einen allgemeinen Teil des Rechts der juristischen Personen. Danach folgen grundlegende Regelungen über wichtige Rechtsformen juristischer Personen.

Zwischen juristischen Personen des öffentlichen Rechts und juristischen Personen des Privatrechts unterscheidet das ZGB nicht[27]. Es regelt jedoch einige Rechtsformen für durch öffentlich-rechtliche Körperschaften geschaffene juristische Personen, insbesondere die staatlichen und kommunalen Einheitsunter-

---

24 *Suchanov, E.A.:* Ob otvetstvennosti gosudarstva po graždansko-pravovym objazatel'stvam (Über die Haftung des Staates aufgrund bürgerlich-rechtlicher Verbindlichkeiten), Vestnik VAS RF 2001, Nr. 3 (zit. nach der Datenbank Consultant Plus).

25 Die neue Fassung wurde geschaffen durch Föderales Gesetz vom 08. Mai 2010 Nr. 83-FZ (s.o. Fn. 20).

26 Kap. 2 Ziffer 2 (Art. 23-40) des ZGB 1964.

27 Dazu *Solotych, S.* (Fn. 2), S. 30.

nehmen (Art. 113-115 ZGB) sowie staatliche und kommunale Einrichtungen (Art. 120 Pkt. 2 Abs. 1 Alt. 2 ZGB in der ab 1. Januar 2011 geltenden Fassung).

Art. 50 Pkt. 1 ZGB unterteilt die juristischen Personen in kommerzielle und nichtkommerzielle Organisationen. Kommerzielle Organisationen sind solche, deren grundlegendes Ziel die Erzielung von Gewinn ist (Art. 50 Pkt. 1 Alt. 1 ZGB). Nichtkommerzielle Organisationen sind solche, deren grundlegendes Ziel nicht die Erzielung von Gewinn ist und die etwaigen erzielten Gewinn nicht an ihre Teilnehmer ausschütten (Art. 50 Pkt. 1 Alt. 2 ZGB). Diese Aufteilung ist abschließend, d.h. jede juristische Person gehört einer der beiden Klassen an[28]. Die Unterteilung wird allein anhand des Kriteriums der Gewinnerzielungs*absicht* vorgenommen und – trotz Art. 50 Pkt. 1 Alt. 2 ZGB – ohne Rücksicht darauf, ob ein etwaiger Gewinn ausgeschüttet wird[29].

Der Kreis der zulässigen Rechtsformen kommerzieller Organisationen (*kommerčeskie organizacii*) ist gemäß der Intention des Gesetzgebers (Art. 50 Pkt. 2 ZGB) im ZGB abschließend festgelegt[30]. Für nichtkommerzielle Organisationen können dagegen durch Gesetz auch im ZGB nicht vorgesehene Rechtsformen geschaffen werden – eine Möglichkeit, von der der Gesetzgeber in der Folge extensiven Gebrauch gemacht hat.

Einheitsunternehmen sind kommerzielle Organisationen; diese Rechtsform kommt daher für Organe des Staates nicht in Frage, denn die Gewinnerzielung ist in keinem Fall das grundlegende Ziel von Organen des Staates. Als Rechtsform für Organe des Staates kommen daher nur nichtkommerzielle Organisationen in Betracht.

3. Die Einrichtung i.S.v. Art. 120 ZGB

Unter den im ZGB genannten Rechtsformen kommt am ehesten die Einrichtung nach Art. 120 ZGB für staatliche Organe in Frage. Weitere Rechtsformen, die das Gesetz über nichtkommerzielle Organisationen zur Verfügung stellt, sind hier nicht zu betrachten, da dieses Gesetz für Organe des Staates nicht gilt (s.o. I. 2.).

Gemäß Art. 120 Pkt. 1 Abs. 1 ZGB ist eine Einrichtung eine nichtkommerzielle Organisation, die durch den Eigentümer zur Wahrnehmung von nichtkommerziellen Funktionen im Bereich der Verwaltung, des Sozialwesens oder

---

28 *Suchanov, E.A.*, in: ders. (Hrsg.): Graždanskoe pravo v 4-x tomach (Bürgerliches Recht in vier Bänden), Band 1, 3. Auflage, Moskau 2004, S. 227.

29 Dies entspricht, soweit ersichtlich, der einhelligen Auffassung in der Literatur. So z.B. implizit *Levšina, T.L. / Rachmilovič, V.A.*, in: Sadikov, O.N. (Hrsg.): Kommentarij k Graždanskomu kodeksu Rossijskoj Federacii časti pervoj (postatejnyj) (Nach Artikeln geordneter Kommentar zum ersten Teil des Zivilgesetzbuchs der Russischen Föderation), 3. Aufl., Moskau 2005, Art. 48, Anm. 1, die davon sprechen, nichtkommerziellen Organisationen sei es verboten, Gewinn auszuschütten.

30 Hierfür statt vieler *Suchanov, E.A.* (Fn. 28), S. 225.

der Kultur oder in sonstigen Bereichen geschaffen wurde. Die Einrichtung kann nicht Eigentümerin von Vermögen sein, sondern sie hat an dem ihr durch den Gründer / Eigentümer zugewiesenen Vermögen das Recht der operativen Verwaltung nach Art. 296 ZGB (Art. 120 Pkt. 1 Abs. 2 ZGB). Das Eigentum an dem Vermögen verbleibt beim Gründer der Einrichtung, der daher im Gesetz im Verhältnis zur Einrichtung als der Eigentümer bezeichnet wird. Dies war für das der Einrichtung vom Gründer zugewiesene Vermögen von Anfang an im Gesetz ausdrücklich geregelt, traf jedoch nach herrschender Meinung auch für Vermögen, das die Einrichtung durch eigene Tätigkeit später hinzuerwarb, zu. Mittlerweile trifft Art. 120 Pkt. 1 Abs. 2 ZGB eine klarstellende ausdrückliche Regelung.

Gründer – bzw. nach der Wortwahl des Art. 120 ZGB: Eigentümer – einer Einrichtung können öffentlich-rechtliche Körperschaften, aber auch natürliche oder juristische Personen sein (Art. 120 Pkt. 2 Abs. 1 ZGB). Von natürlichen und juristischen Personen gegründete Einrichtungen heißen private Einrichtungen; von kommunalen oder staatlichen Körperschaften gegründete Einrichtungen heißen kommunale bzw. staatliche Körperschaften (Art. 120 Pkt. 2 Abs. 1 ZGB n.F.).

Nach Art. 120 Pkt. 2 S. 2 ZGB in der vor Einführung der autonomen Einrichtung geltenden Fassung haftete eine Einrichtung ihren Gläubigern nur mit den ihr zur Verfügung stehenden Geldmitteln[31]. Das erhebliche Risiko, das darin für die Gläubiger lag, wurde dadurch abgemildert, dass der Eigentümer des Vermögens der Einrichtung für deren Verbindlichkeiten subsidiär haftete, wenn das Geld der Einrichtung zur Befriedigung der Gläubiger nicht ausreichte (Art. 120 Pkt. 2 S. 2 ZGB a.F.).

Bei staatlichen und kommunalen Einrichtungen unterscheidet das Gesetz mittlerweile zwischen autonomen Einrichtungen (*avtonomnye učreždenija*), Haushaltseinrichtungen (*bjudžetnye učreždenija*) und Fiskuseinrichtungen (*kazënnye učreždenija*) (Art. 120 Pkt. 2 Abs. 2 ZGB). Die Unterscheidung zwischen autonomer und Haushaltseinrichtung wurde 2006 eingeführt[32]. Die zusätzliche Rechtsform der Fiskuseinrichtung wurde mit Wirkung zum 01. Januar 2011 eingeführt. Nach der ab 01. Januar 2011 geltenden Gesetzesfassung haftet der Eigentümer nicht für Verbindlichkeiten der durch ihn gegründeten autonomen Einrichtungen und Haushaltseinrichtungen, sondern nur noch für Verbindlichkeiten der Fiskuseinrichtungen subsidiär.

---

31 Dazu Informationsbrief des Obersten Arbitragegerichts der Russischen Föderation vom 14. Juli 1999 Nr. 45 „Ob obraščenii vzyskanija na imuščestvo učreždenija“, Vestnik VAS RF 1999, Nr. 11 (zit. nach der Datenbank Consultant Plus).

32 Föderales Gesetz vom 03. November 2006 Nr. 174-FZ „Ob avtonomnych učreždenijach“ (Über autonome Einrichtungen), SZ RF 2006, Nr. 45, Pos. 4626.

III. Einzelne Fragen im Zusammenhang mit Organen des Staates als juristische Personen

Im Folgenden sollen anhand bisher ergangener gerichtlicher Praxis und der Diskussion in der Literatur einige rechtliche Fragen im Zusammenhang mit der Teilnahme der staatlichen Organe, die als juristische Personen mit unbestimmter Rechtsform gegründet wurden, am Zivilrechtsverkehr angesprochen werden.

1. Wirksame Gründung

Folge der Errichtung eines Organs der staatlichen Gewalt in der Form einer Einrichtung im Sinne des Art. 120 ZGB ist, dass es unter seinem eigenen Namen im Rechtsverkehr auftreten kann und daraus selbst berechtigt und verpflichtet wird[33]. Eine juristische Person erlangt ihre Rechtsfähigkeit im Augenblick ihres Entstehens (Art. 49 Pkt. 3 Abs. 1 ZGB). Sie entsteht am Tag ihrer Eintragung im einheitlichen staatlichen Register der juristischen Personen (Art. 51 Pkt. 2 ZGB). Verfahrensmäßige Voraussetzung für die Eintragung einer juristischen Person ist die Vorlage von Unterlagen über den Gründungsbeschluss und des Gründungsdokuments (Art. 12 lit. c) des Gesetzes über die Registrierung juristischer Personen[34]). Schließlich können sich aus der Definition der juristischen Person in Art. 48 ZGB weitere Anforderungen an das Entstehen einer Einrichtung gem. Art. 120 ZGB ergeben.

a) Gründungsdokument. Nennung der Rechtsform

Über das Verfahren der Gründung einer Einrichtung und die notwendigen Schritte dazu enthält Art. 120 ZGB keine Regelungen. Damit sind die allgemeinen Vorschriften der Art. 48 ff. ZGB anwendbar. Gründungsdokument einer juristischen Person können gemäß Art. 52 Pkt. 1 ZGB eine Satzung (*ustav*) und ein Gründungsvertrag (*učreditel'nyj dogovor*) sein. Ist nur ein einziger Gründer vorhanden, so heißt das Gründungsdokument Satzung (Art. 52 Pkt. 1 Abs. 2 ZGB). In der Praxis werden jedoch Status und Struktur staatlicher Organe typischerweise durch ein Statut (*položenie*), nicht durch eine Satzung (*ustav*) bestimmt[35]. Dies soll indes einer wirksamen Gründung nicht entgegenstehen[36].

---

33 *Suchanov* (Fn. 28), S. 380; *Ivanov, A.A.*, in: Sergeev / Tolstoj (Fn. 21), S. 228 f.

34 Föderales Gesetz vom 08. August 2001 Nr. 129-FZ „O gosudarstvennoj registracii juridičeskich lic i individual'nych predprinimatelej" (Über die staatliche Registrierung der juristischen Personen und Einzelunternehmer), SZ RF 2001, Nr. 33 (Teilband 1), Pos. 3431.

35 Dazu s. nur die in Fn. 3 bis 12 angeführten Beispiele.

36 *Kozlova, N.V.*, in: Suchanov, E.A. (Hrsg.): Rossijskoe graždanskoe pravo. Učebnik v dvuch tomach (Russisches Bürgerliches Recht. Lehrbuch in zwei Bänden), Bd. 1, Moskau 2010, S. 280; *Suchanov, E.A.*, in: ders. (Hrsg.): Naučno-praktičeskij kommentarij k časti pervoj Graždanskogo kodeksa Rossijskoj Federacii dlja predprinimatelej (Wissenschaftlich-praktischer Kommentar zum ersten Teil des Zivilge-

In dem Gründungsdokument muss die Rechtsform der juristischen Person angegeben werden, wie sich aus Art. 52 Pkt. 2 S. 1 in Verbindung mit Art. 54 Pkt. 1 S. 1 ZGB ergibt. Typischerweise enthalten die Gründungsdokumente von Organen des Staates jedoch keinen Hinweis auf die Rechtsform.

b) Registrierung

Gemäß Art. 51 Pkt. 2 ZGB entsteht eine juristische Person (erst) in dem Augenblick ihrer staatlichen Registrierung. Die Registrierung erfolgt gem. Art. 2 des Gesetzes über die Registrierung juristischer Personen im einheitlichen staatlichen Register der juristischen Personen[37]. Für die Registrierung zuständig ist der Föderale Steuerdienst (*Federal'naja nalogovaja služba*), Art. 2 Gesetzes über die Registrierung juristischer Personen i.V.m. Pkt. 1 (Abs. 2), 5.3.1, 5.5.6 des Statuts des Föderalen Steuerdienstes[38]. Oft werden Organe des Staates, die juristische Personen sind, in der Tat staatlich registriert. Unabhängig davon wird in der Literatur die Meinung vertreten, dass für staatliche Organe bzw. Organe der staatlichen Gewalt eine Eintragung für die Entstehung nicht konstitutiv sei[39]. Dies entspricht offensichtlich der Verwaltungspraxis. So ist in den Methodischen Erläuterungen zur Registrierung juristischer Personen[40], die der Föderale Steuerdienst 2004 bestätigt hat, ausgeführt, dass Organe der Staatsgewalt unab-

---

setzbuchs der Russischen Föderation), 2. Aufl., Moskau 1999, S. 213; *Čirkin, V.E.*: Neobchodimo li ponjatie juridičeskogo lica publičnogo prava? (Ist der Begriff der juristischen Person des öffentlichen Rechts erforderlich?), Gosudarstvo i pravo (Staat und Recht) 2006, Nr. 5, S. 22 (26).

37 Dazu *Suchanov, E.A.*, in: ders. (Hrsg.): Rossijskoe graždankoe pravo. Učebnik v dvuch tomach (Russisches Bürgerliches Recht. Lehrbuch in zwei Bänden), Band 1, Moskau 2010, S. 197 f.

38 Statut des Steuerdienstes der Russischen Föderation, bestätigt durch Verordnung der Regierung der Russischen Föderation vom 30. September 2004 Nr. 506 „Ob utverždenii Položenija o Federal'noj nalogovoj službe" (Über die Bestätigung des Statuts des Föderalen Steuerdienstes), SZ RF 2004, Nr. 40, Pos. 3961.

39 So wohl *Čirkin, V.E.* (Fn. 36), S. 26; möglicherweise auch *Majfat, A.V. / Mironov, I.B.*, in: Krašeninnikov, P.V. (Hrsg.): Unitarnye predprijatija, učreždenija. Pravo chozjajstvennogo vedenija i pravo operativnogo upravlenija. Postatejnyj kommentarij k stat'jam 113-115, 120 i glave 19 Graždanskogo kodeksa Rossijskoj Federacii (Einheitsunternehmen, Einrichtungen. Recht der Bewirtschaftung und Recht der operativen Verwaltung. Nach Artikeln geordneter Kommentar zu den Artikeln 113-115 und 120 und zu Kapitel 19 des Zivilgesetzbuchs der Russischen Föderation), Moskau 2010, Anm. 5 zu Art. 120 (S. 40).

40 Anlage 1 zur Anweisung (*prikaz*) des Föderalen Steuerdienstes der Russischen Föderation vom 01. November 2004 Nr. SAĖ-3-09/16@ „O Metodičeskich raz''asnenijach po zapolneniju form dokumentov, ispol'zuemych pri gosudarstvennoj registracii juridičeskogo lica i individual'nogo predprinimatelja" (Über Methodische Erläuterungen zum Ausfüllen der bei der staatlichen Registrierung von juristischen Personen und Einzelunternehmern erforderlichen Formulare), Rossijskaja gazeta vom 29. Dezember 2004.

hängig von einer staatlichen Registrierung bereits mit der Verabschiedung des staatlichen Rechtsakts über die Gründung entstehen (Pkt. 4.10 der Erläuterungen).

c) Weitere Merkmale?

Fraglich ist, ob es Fälle gibt, in denen ein als juristische Person staatlich registriertes bzw. durch Verabschiedung eines staatlichen Rechtsakts als juristische Person geschaffenes staatliches Organ dennoch nicht als juristische Person entstanden ist, etwa weil es nicht die Begriffsmerkmale einer juristischen Person nach Art. 48 Pkt. 1 Abs. 1 ZGB erfüllt. Dies würde erhebliche Rechtsunsicherheit mit sich bringen.

Art. 48 Pkt. 1 Abs. 1 ZGB lautet:

> „Eine juristische Person ist eine Organisation, der das Eigentum, die Bewirtschaftung oder die operative Verwaltung an abgesondertem Vermögen zusteht, die für ihre Verbindlichkeiten mit diesem Vermögen haftet und die im eigenen Namen vermögensmäßige und persönliche nichtvermögensmäßige Rechte erwerben und ausüben sowie Verpflichtungen eingehen kann und vor Gericht Klägerin und Beklagte sein kann“.

Diese Vorschrift wird in der russischen Literatur üblicherweise als Definition der juristischen Person bezeichnet. Eine Legaldefinition, aus der sich ersehen ließe, ob eine bestimmte Organisation eine juristische Person ist, liefert die Vorschrift freilich gerade nicht. Sie umschreibt vielmehr – nach Art vieler „Definitionen“ in der russischen Gesetzgebung – das Phänomen der juristischen Person typologisch, indem sie charakteristische Merkmale der juristischen Person nennt. Die in Art. 48 Pkt. 1 Abs. 1 ZGB genannten Merkmale müssen jedoch nicht immer vollständig erfüllt sein, damit eine juristische Person vorliegt. Andererseits müssen zu ihnen andere Merkmale hinzutreten, damit eine juristische Person tatsächlich zur Entstehung gelangt: Das in Art. 48 Pkt. 1 Abs. 1 ZGB genannte Merkmal der Haftung für die eigenen Verbindlichkeiten mit dem gesamten eigenen Vermögen („diesem Vermögen“) ist gerade für Fiskuseinrichtungen durchbrochen, die nur mit einem Teil ihres Vermögens für die eigenen Verbindlichkeiten haften. Umgekehrt gelangt eine juristische Person erst durch Registrierung zur Entstehung, obwohl dieses Merkmal in Art. 48 Pkt. 1 ZGB nicht erwähnt ist.

In der Rechtsprechung wird ferner die in Art. 48 Pkt. 1 Abs. 2 ZGB statuierte Pflicht juristischer Personen, eine selbständige Bilanz oder einen selbständigen Haushaltsplan zu führen, mitunter als Begriffsmerkmal der juristischen Person behandelt. So wurde eine Hausverwaltung einer regionalen militärischen Einheit, für die ein Statut aus dem Jahr 1981[41] galt, aus dem Grund nicht als ju-

---

41 Položenie o domoupravlenijach, obščežitijach i gostinicach Ministerstva oborony (Statut über Hausverwaltungen, Wohnheime und Gästehäuser des Verteidigungsministeriums), bestätigt durch Anordnung Nr. 45 vom 24. März 1981 des für Bauwesen und Un-

ristische Person anerkannt, weil sie nicht über eine eigenständige Bilanz oder einen eigenständigen Haushaltsplan verfügte[42].

Damit scheint es möglich, dass trotz Eintragung eines staatlichen Organs als juristische Person im einheitlichen staatlichen Register im Einzelfall bestritten werden kann, dass das Organ als juristische Person wirksam entstanden ist.

d) Zwischenergebnis

Die allgemeinen Vorschriften über die Gründung von juristischen Personen werden also in der Praxis auf staatliche Organe, die in ihren Gründungsdokumenten als juristische Personen bezeichnet werden, ohne dass die Rechtsform benannt ist, nur mit deutlichen Einschränkungen angewandt[43].

2. Rechtsfähigkeit staatlicher Organe. Schuld und Haftung staatlicher Organe und des Staates

a) Sachlich beschränkte (spezielle) Rechtsfähigkeit der staatlichen Organe

Einrichtungen im Sinne von Art. 120 ZGB verfügen – anders als juristische Personen der meisten anderen Rechtsformen – nur über eine spezielle Rechtsfähigkeit, d.h. sie können nur solche Rechtsgeschäfte vornehmen, die in ihren Gründungsdokumenten vorgesehen sind[44]. Diese Vorschrift findet nach herrschender Auffassung direkt oder analog auf staatliche Organe Anwendung, die juristische Personen mit unbenannter Rechtsform sind.

Nach Art. 15 Pkt. 3 FG über den Schutz des Wettbewerbs[45] sind staatlichen Organen und Organen der örtlichen Selbstverwaltung auf Gewinnerzielung gerichtete Tätigkeiten grundsätzlich verboten, können aber durch Rechtsvorschrif-

---

terbringung der Streitkräfte zuständigen Stellvertreters des Verteidigungsministers der UdSSR, zit. nach Urteil des Föderalen Arbitragegerichts des Uralgebiets vom 02. August 2007 (Fundstelle s. sogleich Fn. 42).

42 Urteil des Föderalen Arbitragegerichts des Uralgebiets vom 02. August 2007 Nr. F09-6048/07-S5, Verfahrens-Nummer: A47-6170/2006; das Urteil wurde bestätigt durch Beschluss des Obersten Arbitragegerichts der Russischen Föderation vom 07. Dezember 2007 Nr. 15885/07, beide Entscheidungen sind verfügbar unter http://kad.arbitr.ru/ (abgerufen 12. Februar 2011). Die Argumentation der Entscheidungen ist allerdings insofern in dem hier interessierenden Punkt unklar, als bereits gemäß dem Statut von 1981 nur Hausverwaltungen, die über eine eigene Bilanz verfügten, juristische Personen waren. Damit kam es auf Art. 48 Pkt. 1 Abs. 2 ZGB hier wohl nicht an.

43 So auch die Bewertung bei *Kantor, N.:* Celi i principy sozdanija juridičeskich lic publično-pravovymi obrazovanijami (Ziele und Grundsätze der Gründung juristischer Personen durch öffentlich-rechtliche Körperschaften), ChiP 2004, Nr. 5, S. 53, 62.

44 *Kozlova, N.V. / Suchanov, E.A.*, in: *Suchanov E.A.* (Fn. 28), S. 368.

45 Föderales Gesetz vom 26. Juli 2006 „O zaščite konkurencii" (Über den Schutz des Wettbewerbs), SZ RF 2006, Nr. 31 (Teilband 1), Pos. 3434.

ten zugelassen werden[46]. Dieses Verbot hat nach gängiger Auffassung ebenfalls eine Beschränkung der Rechtsfähigkeit zur Folge.

b) Wirkung von außerhalb der Rechtsfähigkeit vorgenommenen Rechtsgeschäften

Nimmt eine juristische Person mit spezieller Rechtsfähigkeit ein Rechtsgeschäft vor, auf das sich ihre Rechtsfähigkeit nach ihrem Gründungsdokument und dem Gesetz nicht erstreckt (sog. *Ultra-vires*-Geschäft), so liegt ein Rechtsgeschäft vor, das nicht den Anforderungen des Gesetzes oder sonstiger Rechtsakte entspricht. Gesetzeswidrige Rechtsgeschäfte sind nach Art. 168 ZGB grundsätzlich nichtig. Zum Schutz des Rechtsverkehrs gilt jedoch für *ultra vires* geschlossene Rechtsgeschäfte juristischer Personen mit spezieller Rechtsfähigkeit eine Sondervorschrift: Art. 173 ZGB sieht – in bewusster Abkehr von der Rechtslage nach dem ZGB 1964 – im Interesse des Verkehrsschutzes vor, dass ein *ultra vires* oder ohne eine erforderliche staatliche Genehmigung vorgenommenes Rechtsgeschäft grundsätzlich wirksam ist, jedoch durch Gericht auf Antrag der juristischen Person, ihrer Organe oder der für ihre Beaufsichtigung zuständigen staatlichen Stellen für unwirksam erklärt werden kann, wenn die andere Partei wusste, dass das Rechtsgeschäft ungesetzlich war oder wenn sich dies ihr hätte aufdrängen müssen.

c) Rechtsgeschäftliches Handeln staatlicher Organe im eigenen Namen und im Namen des Staates

Organe des Staates, die juristische Personen sind, können im Rechtsverkehr sowohl im eigenen Namen als auch für den Staat auftreten. Dies ist Folge ihrer Rechtsfähigkeit. Selbstverständlich steht es aber nicht im Belieben der staatlichen Organe, im eigenen Namen oder im Namen der staatlichen Körperschaft, deren Organe sie sind, zu handeln, sondern sie haben bei der Erfüllung staatlicher Aufgaben grundsätzlich für den Staat zu handeln[47]. In der Literatur kritisiert wurde z.B. die Begebung einer „Eisenbahn-Anleihe“[48] in den 1990er Jah-

---

46 So – zur Vorgängervorschrift Art. 7 Pkt. 3 WettbewerbsG 1991 (Gesetz der RSFSR vom 22. März 1991 Nr. 948-1 „O konkurencii i ograničenii monopolističeskoj dejatel'nosti na tovarnych rynkach“ (Über den Wettbewerb und die Begrenzung monopolistischer Betätigung auf Warenmärkten), Vedomosti SND i VS RSFSR 1991, Nr. 16, Pos. 499) – *Kantor, N.:* ChiP 2004, Nr. 5, S. 53, 62.

47 *Suchanov, E.A.* (Fn. 36), S. 290 f.

48 Dazu s. die Verordnung der Regierung der Russischen Föderation vom 17. Juli 1996 Nr. 868 „O železnodorožnom zajme“ (Über die Eisenbahn-Anleihe), SZ RF 1996, Nr. 31, Pos. 3732; Statut „O železnodorožnom zajme MPS Rossii“ (Über die Eisenbahnanleihe des Ministeriums für Transportwege Russlands), bestätigt durch das Ministerium für Transportwege Russlands am 29. August 1996 (registriert beim Justizministerium der Russischen Föderation am 02. Oktober 1996 unter Nr. 1172), Bjulleten' normativnych aktov federal'nych organov ispolnitel'noj vlasti („BNA“) 1996, Nr. 8;

ren durch das Ministerium für Transportwege der Russischen Föderation, obwohl dieses weder seinem Statut nach zur Ausgabe von Anleihen im eigenen Namen befugt war, noch über Haushaltsmittel zur Rückzahlung der Anleihe verfügte[49].

Das rechtliche Können geht aber anscheinend weiter als das rechtliche Dürfen. Letztlich wird durch Auslegung zu ermitteln sein, ob ein Organ im Einzelfall im eigenen Namen oder im Namen der öffentlichen Körperschaft, deren Organ es ist, handelt.

d) Staat und staatliche Organe als Schuldner deliktischer Ansprüche

Nach Art. 1069 ZGB richtet sich der Amtshaftungsanspruch wegen rechtswidriger Handlungen der staatlichen Organe und der Organe der kommunalen Selbstverwaltung gegen den Fiskus der Russischen Föderation, der Subjekte der Russischen Föderation oder der kommunalen Körperschaften, je nachdem, welcher öffentlich-rechtlichen Körperschaft das Organ zugeordnet ist.

Zur Zahlung verurteilt wird jeweils das zuständige staatliche Organ „auf Kosten" des Fiskus der entsprechenden staatlichen Körperschaft (Art. 1071 ZGB). Ist das zuständige Organ im Urteilstenor nicht richtig angegeben, so kann das Urteil angefochten werden. Ein Beispiel (Streit um einen Anspruch auf Entschädigung wegen Strafverfolgung eines Unschuldigen nach Art. 1070 ZGB) findet sich in einem Beschluss des Obersten Gerichts der Russischen Föderation (Gerichtskollegium für Strafsachen) von 2008[50]. Das Instanzgericht und das Kassationskollegium des Obersten Gerichts hatten die Verwaltung des föderalen Staatsschatzes im Gebiet Novosibirsk (*Upravlenie Federal'nogo kaznačejstva po Novosibirskoj oblasti*), eines Subjekts der Russischen Föderation, zum Schadensersatz „auf Kosten" der Staatskasse der Russischen Föderation verurteilt. Dieses Urteil hob das Gerichtskollegium für Strafsachen im Aufsichtsverfahren auf und verurteilte stattdessen das Finanzministerium der Russischen Föderation zum Schadensersatz auf Kosten der Staatskasse der Russischen Föderation[51].

Amtshaftungsansprüche sind Ansprüche wegen schädigender Handlungen staatlicher Organe im Zusammenhang mit der Ausübung staatlicher Befugnis-

---

dazu der Brief der Zentralbank der Russischen Föderation vom 15. Dezember 1996 Nr. 375 „Ob operacijach kreditnych organizacij s obligacijami železnodorožnogo zajma" (Über Geschäfte von Kreditinstituten mit Stücken der Eisenbahnanleihe), Vestnik Banka Rossii vom 24. Dezember 1996.

49 Dazu s. die diesbezügliche Kritik bei *Suchanov* (Fn. 28), S. 380.

50 Beschluss des Gerichtskollegiums für Strafsachen des Obersten Gerichts der Russischen Föderation vom 03. Dezember 2008, Az. 67-D08/35, zugänglich unter http://docs.cntd.ru/document/902134697 (abgerufen am 12. März 2011).

51 Kritisch zu dieser wenig gläubigerfreundlichen Praxis äußert sich *Ivanov, A.A.*, in: Sergeev / Tolstoj (Fn. 21), S. 229 f.

se[52]. Sofern ein staatliches Organ nicht durch hoheitliches Handeln, sondern auf sonstige Weise andere schädigt, haftet es nicht aus Amtshaftung nach Art. 1069-1071 ZGB, sondern aufgrund allgemeinen Deliktsrechts nach Art. 1064 ff. ZGB auf Schadensersatz. In diesem Fall kann das staatliche Organ, sofern es rechtsfähig ist, selbst Schuldner des Anspruchs sein. Als Beispiel wird etwa ein Verkehrsunfall angeführt, der durch ein Auto eines staatlichen Organs verursacht worden ist[53]. Im Ergebnis können in derartigen Fällen Geschädigte schlechter gestellt sein, als wenn der Staat haftet, da sie das Risiko tragen, dass das entsprechende staatliche Organ vermögenslos ist, und damit auf eine subsidiäre Haftung des Staates angewiesen sind.

e) Status des Vermögens der staatlichen Organe und subsidiäre Gründerhaftung

Gemäß Art. 120 Pkt. 1 Abs. 2 ZGB a.F. hat eine Einrichtung an dem ihr zugewiesenen Vermögen das Recht der operativen Verwaltung gemäß Art. 296 ZGB. Das Eigentum verbleibt bei dem Gründer der Einrichtung, der daher im ZGB im Verhältnis zur Einrichtung als Eigentümer bezeichnet wird. In der ursprünglichen Fassung des ZGB konnte die Einrichtung das ihr vom Eigentümer zugewiesene Vermögen im Rahmen der geltenden Rechtsvorschriften gemäß den Aufgaben der Einrichtung besitzen und nutzen und mit Zustimmung des Eigentümers über dieses Vermögen verfügen (Art. 296 Pkt. 1 ZGB). Sie haftete für ihre Verbindlichkeiten (nur) mit den ihr zur Verfügung stehenden Geldmitteln, nicht mit sonstigem Vermögen. Dafür haftete der Eigentümer für die Verbindlichkeiten der Einrichtung unbeschränkt subsidiär (Art. 120 ZGB)[54].

Art. 298 Pkt. 2 ZGB a.F. bestimmte, dass Einkünfte, die eine Einrichtung im Rahmen ihrer durch ihre Gründungsdokumente gestatteten Tätigkeit erzielte, und Vermögen, das die Einrichtung für solche Einkünfte erwarb, in die „selbständige Verfügung" der Einrichtung gelangten und in einer gesonderten Bilanz zu erfassen waren. Umstritten war, ob eine Einrichtung über solches Vermögen selbständig verfügen konnte[55]. Art. 298 ZGB n.F. differenziert nach der Art der Einrichtung:

---

52 Auslegungsanweisung des Obersten Arbitragegerichts der Russischen Föderation vom 22. Juni 2006 Nr. 23 „O nekotorych voprosach primenenija arbitražnymi sudami norm Bjudžetnogo kodeksa Rossijskoj Federacii" (Über einige Fragen der Anwendung von Vorschriften des Haushaltsgesetzbuchs der Russischen Föderation durch die Arbitragegerichte), Vestnik Vysšego Arbitražnogo Suda Rossijskoj Federacii (Mitteilungsblatt des Obersten Arbitragegerichts der Russischen Föderation) 2006, Nr. 8, S. 58-67.

53 *Suchanov, E.A.* (Fn. 24).

54 *Suchanov, E.A.*, in: ders. (Hrsg.): Naučno-praktičeskij kommentarij k časti pervoj Graždanskogo kodeksa Rossijskoj Federacii dlja predprinimatelej (Wissenschaftlich-praktischer Kommentar zum ersten Teil des Zivilgesetzbuchs der Russischen Föderation), 2. Aufl., Moskau 1999, S. 213.

55 Dazu s. etwa *Tolstoj, Ju.K.*, in: Sergeev / Tolstoj (Fn. 21), S. 489 f.

- Eine autonome Einrichtung kann über die ihr durch den Eigentümer zugeteilten Immobilien und besonders wertvollen beweglichen Vermögensgegenstände nur mit Zustimmung des Eigentümers verfügen. Über sonstiges Vermögen, insbesondere über die Einkünfte aus eigener erlaubter Tätigkeit kann sie selbständig verfügen. Einkünfte aus eigener erlaubter Tätigkeit gelangen zur freien Verfügung an die autonome Einrichtung (Art. 298 Pkt. 2 ZGB). Autonome Einrichtungen haften für ihre Verbindlichkeiten mit dem gesamten ihnen zum Recht der operativen Verwaltung zugewiesenen und später hinzuerworbenen Vermögen; ausgenommen davon sind Immobilien und besonders wertvolle bewegliche Gegenstände. Der Staat trägt keine subsidiäre Haftung.
- Für eine Haushaltseinrichtung gilt dasselbe wie für eine autonome Einrichtung, jedoch kann sie auch über Immobilien, die ihr nicht vom Eigentümer zugeteilt wurden, nicht verfügen (Art. 298 Pkt. 3 ZGB).
- Fiskuseinrichtungen können ohne Zustimmung des Eigentümers nicht über Vermögen verfügen. Einkünfte aus eigener erlaubter Tätigkeit gelangen in den Haushalt des Eigentümers (Art. 298 Pkt. 4 ZGB; diese Vorschrift tritt jedoch erst zum 01. Januar 2012 in Kraft: Art. 33 Pkt. 7 des Änderungsgesetzes vom 08. Mai 2010[56]). Fiskuseinrichtungen haften für ihre Verbindlichkeiten allein mit dem ihnen zur Verfügung stehenden Geld. Der Staat haftet subsidiär.

Auch wenn der Staat Eigentümer des gesamten den staatlichen Einrichtungen zugewiesenen und von diesen durch eigene Tätigkeit erworbenen Vermögens ist, ist dieses Vermögen gemäß Art. 126 Pkt. 1 ZGB dem Zugriff der Gläubiger des Staates entzogen. Nach dieser Vorschrift haften die Russische Föderation, die Subjekte der Russischen Föderation und die kommunalen Körperschaften für ihre Verbindlichkeiten mit dem gesamten in ihrem Eigentum stehenden Vermögen, mit Ausnahme desjenigen Vermögens, das zum Recht der Bewirtschaftung oder zum Recht der operativen Verwaltung den durch diese Körperschaften geschaffenen juristischen Personen zugewiesen ist[57].

Art. 126 Pkt. 2 ZGB regelt zusätzlich, dass die durch die Russische Föderation, die Subjekte der Russischen Föderation und die kommunalen Körperschaften geschaffenen juristischen Personen nicht für Verbindlichkeiten dieser staatlichen bzw. kommunalen Körperschaften haften.

Als Ergebnis dieser Regelung ist insbesondere das Vermögen, das den staatlichen Einrichtungen zugewiesen ist – und erst recht das Vermögen, das staatli-

---

56 Fundstelle des Änderungsgesetzes s.o. Fn. 20.

57 Zu dieser Vorschrift s. z.B. *Ruzakova, O.A.*, in: Kraševinnikov, P.V. (Hrsg.): Publično-pravovye obrazovanija v častnom prave. Postatejnyj kommentarij glavy 5 Graždanskogo kodeksa Rossijskoj Federacii (Öffentlich-rechtliche Körperschaften im Privatrecht. Nach Artikeln geordneter Kommentar zu Kapitel 5 des Zivilgesetzbuchs der Russischen Föderation), Moskau 2010, Anm. zu Art. 126 ZGB.

che Einrichtungen aufgrund eigener Tätigkeit hinzuerwerben – dem Zugriff der Gläubiger der Russischen Föderation entzogen, während die staatlichen Einrichtungen ihrerseits nur mit einem Teil des ihnen zur Verfügung stehenden Vermögens haften.

Dass diese Situation insofern rechtspolitisch unbefriedigend ist, als der Staat durch die Gründung von Einrichtungen und staatlichen Organen als juristische Personen das diesen Rechtssubjekten zugewiesene Vermögen dem Zugriff seiner Gläubiger entziehen kann, wird auch in der russischen juristischen Literatur gesehen. Das russische System wird wegen der Vielzahl der Träger des staatlichen Vermögens als „pluralistisches Modell" der Beteiligung des Staates am vermögensrechtlichen Rechtsverkehr bezeichnet und dem als bürgerfreundlicher empfundenen „monistischen Modell" gegenübergestellt, in dem keine gesonderten, dem Zugriff der Gläubiger des Staates entzogenen Vermögensmassen der Organe, Einrichtungen und Unternehmen des Staates gebildet werden[58]. Dennoch ist *de lege lata* der gegebene Zustand hinzunehmen.

3. Einrichtung als Rechtsform für staatliche Organe?

In der Literatur wurde nach der ursprünglichen Fassung des ZGB die Rechtsform der Einrichtung als diejenige angesehen, die u.a. für staatliche Organe bzw. Organe der staatlichen Gewalt, die juristische Personen sind, zur Verfügung steht[59]. Dies entspricht auch der Verwaltungspraxis. Danach werden diejenigen Organe des Staates, die nach ihren Gründungsakten juristische Personen sein sollen, als Einrichtungen behandelt, wobei allerdings gewisse Besonderheiten gelten. Auch in der gerichtlichen Praxis scheint die Auffassung herrschend zu sein, dass staatliche Organe grundsätzlich zivilrechtlich wie Einrichtungen im Sinne des Art. 120 ZGB zu behandeln seien[60].

---

58 *Ivanov, A.A.*, in: Sergeev / Tolstoj (Fn. 21), S. 247.

59 *Suchanov E.A.*, in: ders. (Hrsg.): Naučno-praktičeskij kommentarij k časti pervoj Graždanskogo kodeksa Rossijskoj Federacii dlja predprinimatelej (Wissenschaftlich-praktischer Kommentar zum ersten Teil des Zivilgesetzbuchs der Russischen Föderation), 2. Aufl., Moskau 1999, S. 213; *Leonova, G.B.*, Učreždenie kak sub''ekt graždanskogo prava (Die Einrichtung als Subjekt des bürgerlichen Rechts), Vestnik MGU. Serija 11. Pravo (Mitteilungsblatt der Moskauer Staatlichen Universität. Serie 11. Recht), 1998, Nr. 1, S. 56; *Braginskij, M.I.*, in: Sadikov (Fn. 29), Art. 125 Anm. 8; *Komjagin, D.L.:* Pravovye mechanizmy nedopuščenija rosta zadolžennosti bjudžeta (Rechtliche Mechanismen zur Verhinderung des Anwachsens der Verschuldung des öffentlichen Haushalts), Pravo i ėkonomika 2000, Nr. 5 (zit. nach der Datenbank Consultant Plus).

60 So z.B. die amtliche Zusammenfassung der Gerichtspraxis des Arbitragegerichts der Republik Nordossetien-Alanija zur subsidiären Haftung vom 29. Dezember 2008, verfasst von der Richterin *Baskaeva, T.S.*, verfügbar unter: http://alania.arbitr.ru/pract/obobschenie_sudebnoj_praktiki_arbitrazhnogo_suda_respubliki_severnaja_osetija-alanija__o_primenenii_norm_o_subsidiarnoj_otvetstvennosti (abgerufen am 29. November 2010).

Gegen die Behandlung der staatlichen Organe als Einrichtungen im Sinne von Art. 120 ZGB wird in der Literatur vor allem von *Čirkin* angeführt, dass zwischen staatlichen Organen und Einrichtungen im Sinne des ZGB grundlegende Unterschiede bestehen[61]. Daraus sei zu folgern, dass solche staatlichen Organe als juristische Personen des öffentlichen Rechts, nicht als juristische Personen im Sinne von Art. 48 ff. ZGB anzusehen seien[62]. *De lege lata* scheint jedoch im Ergebnis auch *Čirkin* die herrschende Auffassung zu billigen, wenn er feststellt, sie habe in einigen Fällen Gerichten „die Lösung [ihres] Falles ermöglicht“[63].

In den vergangenen Jahren hat sich in Russland, wohl vor allem infolge der geschilderten offenen Fragen des Status der Organe des Staates und der Kommunen im Zivilrecht, eine umfangreiche Diskussion darum entsponnen, ob im russischen Rechtssystem die Figur der juristischen Person des öffentlichen Rechts eingeführt werden solle oder sogar bereits existiere[64].

Betrachtet man die Praxis, so ist wohl davon auszugehen, dass der Staat und die kommunalen Körperschaften in der Lage sind, durch den Erlass von Organisationsstatuten staatlichen Organen bürgerlich-rechtliche Rechtsfähigkeit zu verleihen, ohne sich der im ZGB geregelten oder zugelassenen Rechtsformen zu bedienen, obwohl das ZGB selbst ein abgeschlossenes System der Rechtssubjekte des Zivilrechts konzipiert und gemeinsame Regeln für alle juristischen Personen enthält. Dies ist ein ausgesprochen unbefriedigender Zustand, der ein erhebliches Maß an Rechtsunsicherheit schafft.

Mit Recht fordern daher viele Stimmen in der Literatur energisch eine Fortentwicklung der Gesetzgebung. Eine Verbesserung ließe sich bereits dadurch erreichen, dass der allgemeine Teil des Rechts der juristischen Personen in Art. 48-65 ZGB für die Schaffung juristischer Personen (öffentlichen Rechts) durch öffentlich-rechtliche Rechtsakte derart geöffnet würde, dass das ZGB solche öffentlich-rechtlichen juristischen Personen als Rechtssubjekte des Privatrechts anerkennen würde. Gleichzeitig würde diese gesetzliche Anerkennung der

---

61 *Čirkin, V.E.*, Juridičeskoe lico publičnogo prava (Die juristische Person des öffentlichen Rechts), Moskau 2007, S. 116 f.; Kritik an der herrschenden Praxis äußern auch *Minaškin, A.V.:* Osnovy administrativno-pravovogo statusa gosudarstvennych učreždenij (Grundlagen des zivilrechtlichen Status staatlicher Einrichtungen), Pravo i ėkonomika 2003, Nr. 1 (zit. nach der Datenbank Consultant Plus) und andere Autoren.

62 *Čirkin, V.E.* (Fn. 61), S. 221.

63 *Čirkin, V.E.* (Fn. 61), S. 221.

64 Dazu s. vor allem drei monographische Abhandlungen (in der Reihenfolge des Erscheinens): *Andreev, Ju.N.:* Učastie gosudarstva v graždansko-pravovych otnošenijach (Die Beteiligung des Staates an zivilrechtlichen Beziehungen), St. Petersburg 2005; *Kutafin, O.E.:* Sub''ekty konstitucionnogo prava Rossijskoj Federacii kak juridičeskie i priravnennye k nim lica (Subjekte des Verfassungsrechts der Russischen Föderation als juristische und ihnen gleichgestellte Personen), Moskau 2007; *Čirkin, V.E.* (Fn. 61). Ferner gibt es eine Vielzahl von Zeitschriftenartikeln zu dem Thema.

contra legem bereits praktizierten Lage es ermöglichen, an die existierenden und neu zu schaffenden juristischen Personen des öffentlichen Rechts Anforderungen im Sinne einer größeren Transparenz und demokratischen Kontrolle zu stellen und Rechtssicherheit zu schaffen. Dies betrifft schon die Begründung der Rechtsfähigkeit der staatlichen Organe. Während z.B. in Deutschland eine rechtsfähige Anstalt öffentlichen Rechts als selbständiger Verwaltungsträger nur durch Gesetz oder aufgrund Gesetzes geschaffen werden kann[65], wird die Rechtsfähigkeit staatlicher Organe in Russland oft ohne gesetzliche Ermächtigung durch untergesetzliche Rechtsakte verschiedener Art, vereinzelt sogar durch nicht veröffentlichte Akte, begründet.

Oft wird in der russischen Literatur gegen die Anerkennung der Figur der juristischen Person des öffentlichen Rechts eingewandt, durch öffentlich-rechtliche Akte geschaffene Personen müssten öffentlichen, nicht privatrechtlichen Zwecken dienen und seien daher nicht geeignet, als juristische Personen im Sinne des Privatrechts zu fungieren. Diese Überlegung geht wohl am Sinn der Unterscheidung zwischen Privatrecht und öffentlichem Recht vorbei: Vielfach knüpft das Privatrecht an Sachverhalte an, die unabhängig vom Privatrechts entstehen und bestehen. Man kann bereits an den Menschen (als „natürliche Person") denken, der Ausgangspunkt jeglichen rechtlichen Konstruierens und nicht dessen Produkt ist. Ebenso kann das Privatrecht durch öffentlich-rechtlichen Akt geschaffene juristische Personen anerkennen[66]. Eine juristische Person des öffentlichen Rechts bleibt dieselbe, ob sie nun öffentlich-rechtliche Befugnisse wahrnimmt oder am bürgerlichen Rechtsverkehr teilnimmt[67].

An dem Beispiel der juristischen Person des öffentlichen Rechts zeigt sich deutlich ein Nachteil der vom Gesetzgeber des ZGB ausgiebig eingesetzten Regelungstechnik, möglichst viele Regelungen in allgemeinen Teilen vor die Klammer zu ziehen (s. z.B. auch den allgemeinen Teil des Immaterialgüter-

65 Statt vieler *Maurer, Hartmut:* Allgemeines Verwaltungsrecht, 17. Auflage, 2009, § 23 Rn. 51 (S. 607).

66 Ausführlich *Čanturija, L.L.:* Juridičeskie lica publičnogo prava: ich mesto v graždanskom prave i osobennosti pravovogo regulirovanija (Juristische Personen des öffentlichen Rechts: ihr Platz im Zivilrecht und Besonderheiten ihrer rechtlichen Regelungen), Gosudarstvo i pravo 2008, S. 38-45, mit Hinweisen zum georgischen Recht, wo juristische Personen des öffentlichen Rechts anerkannt und gesetzlich geregelt sind. Dazu s. auch *Knieper, R. / Chanturia, L. / Schramm, H.-J.:* Das Privatrecht im Kaukasus und in Zentralasien. Bestandsaufnahme und Entwicklung, Berlin 2010, S. 108-111 und 119-122.

67 So zum sowjetischen Recht *Bratus':* Juridičeskaja ličnost' gosudarstva i bjudžetnych učreždenij (Die Rechtspersönlichkeit des Staates und der Haushaltseinrichtungen), in: VIJuN MJu SSSR. Učenye trudy. Vyp. IX, Moskau 1947, S. 11: „Der Fiskus und der Staat als Subjekt der öffentlichen Gewalt sind keine unterschiedlichen Subjekte: dies sind Seiten einer und derselben Erscheinung – des Staates.", zit. nach *Kantor, N.:* O gosudarstvennych organach kak juridičeskich licach publičnogo prava (Über staatliche Organe als juristische Personen des öffentlichen Rechts), ChiP 2005, Nr. 4, S. 53, 57.

rechts im siebten Abschnitt des ZGB): Wenn die Vorschriften des allgemeinen Teils nicht für alle von seinem Anwendungsbereich erfassten Beziehungen passen, dann führt dies entweder zur Einengung der Praxis oder, wenn die unangemessene gesetzliche Regelung ignoriert wird, zur Entwertung des Gesetzes.

IV. Konzeption der Fortentwicklung des Zivilrechts und das System der juristischen Personen

Gegenwärtig ist eine detaillierte Reform des Zivilgesetzbuchs der Russischen Föderation in Arbeit. Durch Ukaz von Juli 2008[68] hat Präsident *Dmitrij Medvedev* den Rat für Kodifikation und Vervollkommnung der Zivilgesetzgebung[69] und das 1991 geschaffene Forschungszentrum für Privatrecht beim Präsidenten der Russischen Föderation damit beauftragt, bis Juli 2009 eine Konzeption zur Fortentwicklung der Zivilgesetzgebung sowie bis Ende des Jahres 2010 Entwürfe für Änderungsgesetze vorzulegen (Pkt. 3 des Ukaz vom 18. Juli 2008). Der Rat bildete sieben thematische Arbeitsgruppen zur Vorbereitung der Konzeption. Nachdem diese Arbeitsgruppen im Frühjahr 2009 Konzeptionen zu Teilgebieten des Zivilrechts vorgelegt hatten, beschloss der Rat am 07. Oktober 2009 die auf dieser Grundlage erarbeitete Konzeption zur Fortentwicklung der Zivilgesetzgebung der Russischen Föderation[70]. Seit Ende des Jahres 2010 liegen auch konkrete Gesetzgebungsentwürfe zur Änderung des Zivilgesetzbuchs vor[71], so dass der im Ukaz von Juli 2008 vorgesehene Zeitplan bisher eingehalten ist.

Ziel der Überarbeitung des Zivilgesetzbuchs ist seine umfassende Bewertung und Anpassung an die Bedürfnisse des wirtschaftlichen und gesellschaftlichen Lebens (Pkt. 1 des Ukaz vom 18. Juli 2008). Dabei misst die Konzeption der Anpassung weiterhin vom sowjetischen Rechtssystem beeinflusster Rechts-

---

68 Ukaz des Präsidenten der Russischen Föderation vom 18. Juli 2008 Nr. 1108 „O soveršenstvovanii Graždanskogo kodeksa Rossijskoj Federacii“ (Über die Vervollkommnung des Zivilgesetzbuchs der Russischen Föderation), SZ RF 2008, Nr. 29 (Teilband 1), Pos. 3482.

69 Dieses Gremium war noch durch Präsident *Boris El'cin* ins Leben gerufen worden durch Ukaz vom 05. Oktober 1999 Nr. 1338 „O Sovete pri Prezidente Rossijskoj Federacii po kodifikacii i soveršenstvovaniju graždanskogo zakonodatel'stva“ (Über den Rat beim Präsidenten der Russischen Föderation für Kodifikation und Vervollkommnung der Zivilgesetzgebung), SZ RF 1999, Nr. 41, Pos. 4904. Seine Aufgabe war (und ist) es, die Zivilgesetzgebung in Übereinstimmung mit den Anforderungen des Wirtschaftslebens und des öffentlichen Lebens zu bringen und sie zu vervollkommnen (Einleitungssatz des genannten Ukaz).

70 Buchveröffentlichung: Makovskij, A.L. (Hrsg.): Koncepcija razvitija graždanskogo zakonodatel'stva Rossijskoj Federacii (Konzeption zur Fortentwicklung der Zivilgesetzgebung der Russischen Föderation), Moskau 2009.

71 Veröffentlicht auf der Internet-Seite des Forschungszentrums für Privatrecht beim Präsidenten der Russischen Föderation unter http://privlaw.ru/index.php?section_id=100 (abgerufen am 09. Januar 2011).

institute an die veränderten gesellschaftlichen Verhältnisse die größte Bedeutung bei. Das sowjetische Erbe zeigt sich im ZGB am deutlichsten am Sachenrecht und im Recht der juristischen Personen (s. Abschnitt I.3 der Konzeption). Die vorgeschlagenen Änderungen betreffen daher auch besonders diese beiden Rechtsgebiete[72]. Zu den Organen mit unbenannter Rechtsform enthält die Konzeption nur recht knappe Aussagen. Es sei nicht erforderlich, Regelungen zu juristischen Personen des öffentlichen Rechts in das Zivilgesetzbuch aufzunehmen, da dieses Konzept im Privatrecht anderer europäischer Länder nicht einheitlich behandelt werde[73].

Damit wird wohl eine Chance vergeben, die gesetzliche Regelung so zu gestalten, dass sich die Praxis darauf einrichten kann und dass sie gleichzeitig näher an die auf den Prinzipien des demokratischen Rechtsstaats beruhenden Anforderungen an die Handhabung öffentlichen Vermögens und an das Handeln der öffentlichen Hand im Privatrechtsverkehr herangeführt werden kann.

72 Dazu auch *Makovskij, A.L.*, Einführung, in: ders. (Hrsg.), Koncepcija razvitija graždanskogo zakonodatel'stva Rossijskoj Federacii (Konzeption der Fortentwicklung der Zivilgesetzgebung der Russischen Föderation), Moskau 2009, S. 6 ff.

73 Pkt. 7.2.4 der Konzeption von Oktober 2009. Dieser Punkt befindet sich im Abschnitt über „Einrichtungen" im Sinne von Art. 120 ZGB.

Corporate Litigation in Russia: Procedural Reform of 2009

Prof. Dr. Hiroshi Oda[*]

I. Introduction

It is common for foreign companies dealing with Russian companies to provide for international commercial arbitration in their dispute clauses. Such arbitration can be handled at institutions such as the ICC (Paris), the LCIA (London), or the SICA (Stockholm). It can even be at the ICCA (Moscow), or by *ad hoc* arbitration using UNCITRAL Rules. The conventional wisdom is that Russian courts should be avoided if possible.

However, there are instances where, regardless of the desire of foreign companies, Russian courts have jurisdiction. Disputes over taxes and customs tariff are such examples. Cases involving licences related to natural resources, as well as licences for investing in strategic sectors, also fall within the jurisdiction of Russian courts. Furthermore, even if the foreign company wins in arbitration, the award has to be enforced. If the respondent Russian company does not have assets outside Russia, the award has to be enforced in Russia. This will inevitably involve Russian court procedure. Although cases where the enforcement of arbitral awards is rejected by the Russian courts on grounds of broadly-interpreted public policy are not common anymore, a possibility remains that enforcement is rejected on grounds of lack of arbitrability[1]. Enforcement procedure still requires time and effort in Russian courts on the part of the foreign party.

The problem is how the Russian court system operates and to what extent it is reliable. In the following, the author intends to examine the current state of the Russian court system, and then review the reform of the system of corporate litigation which took place in July 2009.

---

* Sir Ernest Satow Professor of Japanese Law, Faculty of Laws, University College London, Professor, College d'Europe, LL.D (Tokyo).

1 *H. Oda*, "Enforcement of Arbitral Awards in Russia", ICC Bulletin 2005 No. 2, pp. 51 seq.

II. The Russian System of Courts

There are two parallel systems of courts in Russia: courts of general jurisdiction and commercial courts (*arbitrazhnyi sud*)[2]. Among other things, the procedural law is different in both court systems. The Code of Civil Procedure is applicable in the former, while the Code of Commercial Court Procedure is applicable in the latter.

Demarcation of jurisdiction of both courts was not always clear. There were categories of cases where the same kind of dispute could be heard by either court. The Code of Commercial Court Procedure provides that the court handles economic disputes and other entrepreneurial activities involving juridical persons and individuals licensed for entrepreneurial activity arising out of civil law or public/administrative law relations. Foreign and international organisations also qualify as a party (arts. 27 and 28). Thus, commercial courts handle disputes between entities involved in entrepreneurial activities. Decisions and rules of administrative agencies can also be contested in the commercial court, a majority of which involves tax. On the other hand, courts of general jurisdiction also handle civil and administrative cases. The criterion for the demarcation of jurisdiction of the commercial court and the court of general jurisdiction is whether or not the party is a juridical person or a licensed individual entrepreneur (subjective criteria). However, there have been a number of instances where it has not been clear which court has jurisdiction.

This problem was partly rectified when the 2002 Code of Commercial Court Procedure introduced a provision on the 'special jurisdiction' of the commercial court. This is a provision on the exclusive jurisdiction of this court regardless of the nature of the parties, i.e. whether they are juridical persons or entrepreneurs or not. Insolvency and tax cases were among such cases where the commercial court had an exclusive jurisdiction.

Nevertheless, the problem still persisted. In a case decided by the Supreme Commercial Court in 2010, a foreign party to a LCIA arbitration (an individual) applied for an interim measure at the commercial court. In fact, this party had applied for such a measure at the court of general jurisdiction, but the Supreme Court had dismissed the case on grounds of lack of jurisdiction. The commercial court at the cassation level rejected the application on grounds of lack of jurisdiction because the applicant was an individual. However, the Supreme Commercial Court quashed the decision and reverted the case to the lower court. In this particular case, the individual in question was an entrepreneur who effectively controlled a company in Cyprus[3].

---

2 Despite the name "arbitration", the *arbitrazhnyi sud* is a state court and has nothing to do with arbitration. The name comes from its predecessor in the socialist period, "*gosarbitrazh*".

3 Decision of the Supreme Commercial Court, 20. April 2010 (17095/09).

In 2006 the Russian government adopted the 'Development Plan of the Judicial System 2007-2011'. It began with the declaration that the independent and fair solution of disputes by court was one of the conditions for ensuring the attractiveness of Russia as a place of investment and the vitalisation of entrepreneurial activities. When President *Medvedev* assumed office in 2008, he put judicial reform as one of the priority tasks. He stressed the importance of the judicial system being effective (the right to have a fair and speedy trial realised); independent, competent, and transparent to society; and, above all, not corrupt[4]. A project team for judicial reform was set up within the President's Administration[5]. It is hard to say that the reform has made any major progress so far, but changes are indeed happening.

The Russians themselves do not seem to have much confidence in their judicial system. It is reported that the number of cases where they initiated proceedings at the European Court of Human Rights in Strasbourg, based upon the European Convention on Human Rights which Russia has ratified, is increasing. Senior members of the judiciary are apprehensive of this trend and the necessity of a fundamental reform, including the strengthening of independence of the courts, is being stressed as ever[6]. President *Medvedev* recently stressed the need to improve the judicial system, so that people do not need the service of international court at a meeting on judicial reform where the chief justices of the court of general jurisdiction, the commercial court, and the Constitutional Court attended[7].

In 2009 a report entitled 'Russian Court System: Its Problems' was published in Russia. This was commissioned by an institute in which *Medvedev* had been a director before becoming President[8]. The report is based upon hearings of over 100 judges, lawyers, legal journalists, and entrepreneurs. Although the samples are small in number, it still provides an important insight into the Russian judicial system.

Respondents in general observed that the independence of Russian courts was obviously at a low level. This is largely attributed to corruption. People with a legal background among the respondents pointed out that the lack of independence was caused by the subordination of the courts to the government. According to these people, 'the court[s], in many cases, do not take a neutral stance and stands by the state, defends or supports the interest of the government and do not defend the lawful interests of individuals' and 'the court is completely

---

4 http://www.president.kremlin.ru/news/6787.

5 Nezavisimaia gazeta, 11. August 2010.

6 Statement of *V. D. Zorkin*, the President of the Constitutional Court, in Rossiiskaia iustitsiia 2009 No. 1, pp. 8-9.

7 Supra note 4.

8 Tsentr politicheskykh tekhnologii, Sudebnaia sistema; sostoianie problemy, Moscow 2009. This report was commissioned by the Institut sovremennogo razvitiia.

integrated in the state system and is perceived by the people to be non-transparent'.

The Report specifically referred to the 'subordination of the court to the government' at all levels of the court. Decisions of the lower court, which are against the interest of higher administrative agencies, are reversed by the higher court with some certainty. The more often the lower court judge renders such a decision, the more the chance of him being dismissed. Judges watch each other, learn the rule of the game, and come to understand in which direction decisions should be made, regardless of legal grounds. In Russia, a strict time limit for procedure is set and judges who fail to comply are subject to disciplinary measures which may lead to dismissal. Such disciplinary measures are discretionary and are often imposed in a selective manner on judges who do not conform. Such a system exists from lower courts to the higher courts and 'there is no chance of survival for judges who defy the instruction from above'.

This is supported by a comment from a member of the board of Sverbank who pointed out that 'a judge may be independent at one level, but there are cases where the appellate or cassation instances bring your independence to nil'[9]. A survey of 1,200 large, medium, and small companies suggested that they did not have much chance in winning a dispute vis-à-vis local and regional administration, not to mention the central government agencies in court[10].

It should be noted that the Report does not imply that such a distortion exists in each and every case. On the contrary, the Report pointed out that in normal cases, where both parties are ordinary people or entities, judges will handle the cases fairly and objectively. It is those cases where a party to the dispute is a state or state related entity that the independence of the court comes to be an issue. In such cases 'there is no guarantee that the result would be fair'.

The observation of this Report seems to be compatible with what foreign observers have found in Russian court practice and also with the experience of foreign companies in Russian courts.

The fundamental problems with the Russian court system are the lack of independence as well as corruption. These may overlap, since political pressure may at the same time accompany economic and other benefits. The problems are even acknowledged by senior judges such as the president of the Supreme Commercial Court[11].

The problem of independence – political neutrality – can be divided into local or regional political pressure on lower courts and pressure exercised over higher courts. If the pressure is regional, to a certain extent, the problem can be rectified by appealing to higher instances. In contrast, in disputes where the in-

9 Nezavisimaia gazeta, 11. August 2010.

10 Vedomosti, 1. July 2010.

11 Speech of the President of the Supreme Commercial Court at the VIIth All-Russian Congress of Judges, http://www.arbitr.ru/press-centr/news/speeches/20242.html.

terest of the Russian state or a large company in which the State has a stake, or where one of the parties have close connections, independence of the court cannot always be expected. The celebrated Sidanco case, where the oil producing company Sidanco was dismantled and sold to a rival company, is one such example[12]. Numerous tax procedures involving Yukos which resulted in its dissection and transferral of its assets to companies close to the government, is another example. With or without political pressure, as a Russian practising lawyer pointed out, in cases where the interest of the state or a large company is involved, it is not difficult to foresee that every uncertainty or defect of law will be interpreted in favour of them[13].

Concerning the corruption of judges, according to the report of the chairman of the High Qualification Committee of Judges, between 2005 and 2008, 279 judges, including the presidents of the court, were dismissed. The Committee gave consent to the prosecution of 64 judges in the same period. In the first half of 2010, one judge was dismissed at the Federal level, while 35 lower court judges, including one from the commercial court, were dismissed and ten judges were prosecuted[14].

> A shareholder brought an action contesting the validity of the resolution of the shareholders' meeting of a large company. The owner of the company approached the judge, who was keen to meet. The judge himself declined the offer of a bribe, but instead asked the company to arrange shares of Gazprom to be given to his acquaintance. This was duly done, and the company won the case[15].

In order to address the problem of local influence on courts, a system whereby judges rotate among different regions has been proposed[16]. At present, judges are locally recruited and seldom move outside the region. However, this proposal does not seem to have gained much support.

As the campaign against corruption has progressed, it is now rare that bribery takes place as overtly as before. Also, corruption is rarer in the higher courts, so by appealing to the higher instances, the problem may be sorted out.

In the commercial court, there are four instances. The first instance court decision can be appealed to the appellate court (second instance). The third instance is the cassation instance. A limited number of cases are heard at the supervisory instance at the Presidium of the Supreme Commercial Court. According to the statistics of the commercial court (*arbitrazhnyi sud*), at the cassation instance heard by the Federal Commercial Court and the supervisory instance,

---

12 *H. Oda*, Russian Commercial Law, 2nd ed., Leiden 2007, pp. 208-211.

13 *A. Muranov*/D. *Davydenko*, "S chem. Mogut stolknut'sia inostrannye litsa v rossiiskykh arbitraznykh sudakh", Korporativnyi iurist 2009 No. 11, p. 34.

14 Report of the Committee at the 7th All Russian Conference of Judges, Rossiiskaia iustitsia 2009 No. 1, pp. 32-33.

15 *A. Molotnikov*, Sliianiia i pogloshcheniia, Moscow and St. Petersburg 2007, pp. 209 seq.

16 See also the speech of *A. Ivanov*, supra note 11.

judgments of the lower courts which had entered into force are contested. In 16.6% of the cases heard by the commercial court in the second half of 2009 and in 18.6% of cases heard in the first half of 2010, judgments are appealed to the appellate court, and in 8.9% and 9.1% of all cases, the case is heard at the cassation instance (it is possible to bypass the appellate instance). It is interesting to note that while 2.6% in 2009 II and 2.7% in 2010 I period of the decisions of the first instance court were quashed or modified at the appellate level, at the cassation level, the quash/modification rate was 8.9% and 9.1% of the first instance court decisions at the cassation level[17].

The rate of appeal is much higher in cases involving a foreign party. One may say that foreign companies tend to contest the case up to the higher level, and thus gain a higher rate of success. Concerning disputes involving a foreign party (parties), the commercial court has handled 740 case and 849 cases in the second half of 2009 and the first half of 2010 respectively. Of these cases, in 51.1% and 56.7%, the plaintiff won. At the appellate level and cassation level, 276 cases and 124 cases were heard in the second half of 2009 and 411 and 133 cases in the first half of 2010[18]. Incidentally, there is a substantial gap in the quality of judges between lower and higher court judges[19]. Therefore, it is worth appealing to a higher court to have one's case understood and correctly handled.

In tax cases, i.e. cases between the tax-payer contesting the decision of the tax agency, surprisingly, the plaintiff enjoys a high success rate. Court statistics show that the plaintiff won in 68% and 64.2% of cases in the second half of 2009 and the first half of 2010[20]. According to a survey conducted by Ernest & Young, of the 95 reported cases involving a foreign company, the success rate was 67% in 2009 as compared to 87% in 2008. These companies rated the independence, objectivity, and integrity of Russian courts average or slightly less than average. Some companies observed that courts lack independence and are influenced by political considerations[21].

It is not clear whether the ongoing judicial reform has produced any significant progress in strengthening the independence of the court and cleaning up of corruption, but certainly, in the last couple of years, the system has become much more open and transparent. This is largely due to the Law on the Ensurance of Public Access to the Activities of the Court[22]. Information on commercial court proceedings is now accessible by internet. For example, the procedure

---

17 http://www.arbitr.ru/_upimg/7B73A0DDEFB4E2917AAC3420A6E1A202_общая.pdf.

18 http://www.arbitr.ru/_upimg/0B7DF6E9D7079385908DDBE8FF159983_ин_лица.pdf.

19 *A. Muranov/D. Davydenko*, supra note 13, pp. 38 seq.

20 http://www.arbitr.ru/_upimg/3935FB81A2A1111010C254FA77D9B3F1_налоги.pdf.

21 Ernest & Young, Russian Tax Survey – Perception of the Tax Authority and the Court System 2010; http://www.ey.com/Publication/vwLUAssets/2010-Tax-Survey-EN/$FILE/2010-Tax-Survey-EN.pdf.

22 FZ-262, 2008, 28. December 2008.

at the Presidium of the Supreme Commercial Court is available online[23] and in some lower courts, the progress of the procedure can also be monitored by internet. The regular Presidium meetings at the Supreme Commercial Court are as well accessible on the internet.

There has also been an organisational change. The caseload of the commercial court has been in steady increase in recent years. In 2009, one and a half million cases reached the court. This was a 50% increase as compared to 2008[24]. The number of judges is around 3,500, and on average, a judge handles around 45 cases a month. The President of the Supreme Commercial Court has repeatedly warned that this situation would affect the quality of judgments[25]. As a measure to alleviate the burden on the courts, mandatory administrative procedures, i.e. an obligation to go through the complaint procedure to the superior administrative agency before taking an action in court, has been introduced in some areas of public-administrative law litigation. A new patent court, which is to handle intellectual property disputes (not limited to patent) is going to be set up in 2011.

Another major step of reform was the amendment to the Code of Commercial Court Procedure and other laws in relation to corporate disputes which took place in 2009[26]. This was part of the reform concerning corporate disputes, and therefore, amendments to the Code of Commercial Court Procedure was the core of the reform, but also involved the Joint Stock Company Law, Limited Liability Company Law, and the Law on the Securities Market. The procedural aspects of this reform will be discussed below.

III. The Procedural Reform of 2009

1. The background

The problem with the Russian court system is not only insufficient independence, but also that it is subject to abuse by the users in commercial disputes, namely in corporate disputes. The background to the 2009 reform was the increasing number of corporate disputes, i.e. disputes over the control of a company, where the existing laws and institutions were abused by corporate raiders. The phenomenon is called *reiderstvo* in Russian.

As the chairman of the Duma Committee on Property put it, in Russia there is no clear distinction between hostile takeover and takeover resorting to unlawful means.

---

23 http://www.arbitr.ru/vas/presidium/nadzor/32331.html.

24 http://www.arbitr.ru/_upimg/FA3FC94A074D0525F14625D4699C1ECE_осн_показатели.pdf.

25 See also *S. S. Zavriev*, "Aktual'nye problemy arbitrazhnogo sudoproizvodstva", Vestnik Vyshego Arbitrazhnogo Suda 2009 No. 12, pp. 67 seq.

26 FZ-205, 2009, 26. December 2008.

> Parties to corporate disputes resorted to seemingly lawful means, utilising imprecise provisions of the procedural law and company law, by means of abuse of rights or extortion, to take over companies that were most dynamically thriving with a bright future. Often in such cases, procedures such as interim measures are used, which make the operation of the company impossible[27].

Disputes over the control and reallocation of power within companies, and 'hostile takeovers', have been on the increase since 2004. The abuse of the unclear demarcation of competence between the commercial court and the court of general jurisdiction and the underdeveloped provisions on territorial jurisdiction have been major issues. According to the director of the department of corporate administration at the Ministry of Economic Development:

> 'Jurisdiction (particularly artificial change of jurisdiction) is actively utilised by the parties. Litigation is initiated not at the location of the company which is involved in the dispute, but in the courts in various locations or sometimes in the same court in different proceedings. In order to secure the action, mutually contradictory interim measures are granted, and in the end, there are mutually contradicting judgments. This led to the sad situation of the loss of credibility of the judicial power'[28].

Actions were brought to the court of general jurisdiction in order to block the procedure in the commercial court. There were problems regarding the territorial jurisdiction of courts. This was particularly true with courts of general jurisdiction. Relevant provisions were complex, and although the general rule was for the court of the place of the company to handle cases against the company, it was possible to initiate litigation elsewhere by 'manipulating' jurisdiction[29]. There were cases where those who were contesting control over a company took an action vis-à-vis the company in a court in a remote region in the absence of the representative of the defendant, obtained a judgement or an interim measure in the favour of the plaintiff and enforced it in the place of the company.

> At the general shareholders' meeting of one company, after the meeting began, a bailiff turned up and handed over the decision of a court in a remote region which prohibited the participation of a certain shareholder. Without his shares represented, the meeting failed to stand, due to the lack of quorum. Under the Law on Joint Stock Companies at that time, in such cases another shareholders' meeting was to be called and the quorum was reduced to one third of the votes present. This meant that with a small number of votes, a proposal could be endorsed by the shareholders' meeting[30].

Disputes often involved the registrar of shares.

---

27 *V. Pleskachevskii/A. Popova* in Korporativnyi iurist 2006 No. 2, pp. 10-11.

28 *Ibid.*

29 *A. Muranov/D. Davydenko*, supra note 13, p. 38.

30 *M. G. Iontsev*, Korporativnyi zakhvaty, 3rd ed., Moscow 2003, pp. 159-170; *G. Panov*, "Obespechitel'nye mery kak instrument v korporativnykh voinakh", Korporativnyi iurist 2007 No. 3, p. 33.

A bailiff turned up at the organisation managing the share register of a company located in the Far East and handed over a decision of the court ordering the company to switch share registration from this entity to another organisation, which was located in the city of Ivanovo in Central Russia. The ground for this decision was the protection of interests of shareholders of the company residing in Ivanovo. The company was unaware of such a court proceeding. A shareholders' meeting based upon the register administered by the new registrar in Ivanovo was convened. The incumbent general director who held 40% of the shares was also invited, but his share had been reduced to 4%. He flew to Ivanovo to take part in the shareholders' meeting, but there was no meeting there. He found from a local paper in the Far East that the shareholders' meeting had been held and new management had been appointed. It took substantial time and cost for the company to contest the decision of the court to change the registrar and to invalidate resolutions of this shareholders' meeting and restore the *status quo ante*[31].

It is not uncommon that shares are 'stolen' by manipulating the share register or false application for the transfer of shares, sometimes in collusion with the share registrar[32]. Also there are instances where the share is attached by an interim measure in order to prevent the shareholder from voting[33].

Thus, defects and loopholes in the court system were abused in disputes over the control of the company. A practising lawyer observed that while ideally, procedural forms should follow substantive-law relations and ensure that this or that claim is protected, in this case, it dominates over the substance of the norm[34].

In 2006 the draft 'Law on the Amendments to the Code of CCP and some related Laws for the Purpose of Improving the System of Settling Corporate Disputes' was submitted to the government by the Ministry of Economic Development and Economy. The reform proposal encompassed both procedural and substantive law. Concerning the procedural law, it was intended to ensure that:

- all corporate related disputes fall within the exclusive competence of the commercial court;
- the court of the place of the location of the company is given territorial jurisdiction on corporate disputes and interim measures related to them;
- a system of disclosure of information regarding corporate litigation by the company is introduced;
- the system of 'group action' is introduced.

---

31 *O. V. Osipienko*, Konfliktov v deiatel'nosti organov upravleniia aktsionernykh kompanii, 2nd ed., Moscow 2007, pp. 115-116.

32 *S. Egorov*, "Obespechenie aktsionerom sokhrannosti svoikh aktsii", Korporativnyi iurist 2006 No. 5, p. 23.

33 *O. V. Osipienko*, supra note 31, pp.120-121; *G. Panov*, supra note 30.

34 *D. Stepanov*, "Transformatsiia korporativnogo zakonodatel'stva: ot stimulirovaniia konfliktov k koordniatsii povedeniiia ikh uchastnikov", Korporativnyi iurist 2006 No. 2, p. 2.

However, the draft law was shelved for several years. It was only in July 2009 that it became law. Presumably, the financial crisis, which struck Russia in 2008, played a decisive role in the enactment of the Law: Russia was in need of soliciting foreign investors again and the curbing of abuse of the court system and the law was essential for that. In fact, this was not the only law which had been prepared some time ago, shelved, and finally enacted as part of 'anti-crisis measures'. Another example is the long-awaited reform of the law related to pledge, which was adopted in December 2008[35].

As a result of this amendment, the Code of Commercial Court Procedure was substantially amended. The Joint Stock Company Law was also substantially amended, but this will be covered in a separate article.

The amendment focuses on the procedural and substantive law concerning corporate disputes[36]. The amended Code introduced a separate chapter on corporate disputes which contains a non-exhaustive list of corporate disputes. Corporate disputes are those involving:

- setting up, reorganisation, and liquidation of companies;
- ownership of shares and quotas and pledging them;
- actions by shareholders/quota holders pursuing the liability of directors and executive officers, and actions contesting the validity of the acts of the company;
- appointment, suspension, and dismissal of directors and executives, as well as civil law disputes between the company and them;
- issuing of securities;
- acts of securities depositories;
- convocation of the general shareholders' meeting;
- resolutions and decisions of corporate bodies.

The gist of the amendment of the Code of CCP is as follows.

2. Exclusive Competence of the Commercial Court

Under the amended Code, the commercial court has exclusive competence over the following categories of cases:

- insolvency cases;
- corporate disputes;
- cases involving the rejection or omission of registration of juridical persons and individual entrepreneurs;
- cases involving the activities of share registration and administration organisations;

35 FZ-306, 2008, 30. December 2008.

36 For an overview of the changes, see "Izmeneniia v APK RF: Pliusy and minusy novogo regulirovaniia", Khozaiistvo i pravo 2009 No. 8, pp. 3 seq.

- cases involving the activities of government corporations;
- cases involving the protection of business reputation in the area of entrepreneurial activities.

A significant change brought by the 2009 amendment is that all corporate litigation has come to fall within the competence of the commercial court, regardless of whether the party is a juridical person or not. This had been proposed since 2006 in order to prevent abuses of jurisdiction in corporate litigation.

The subjective criterion, i.e. whether the party is a juridical person, a licensed entrepreneur, or a private individual, did not necessarily work. For instance, when a shareholder is contesting the validity of the resolution of the shareholders' meeting, the case could be heard either by the court of general jurisdiction or the commercial court, depending on the above subjective criterion. Disputes involving the ownership of shares could also be heard by either court. Such an arrangement could and did result in contradictory decisions.

By this amendment, the possibility of concurrent jurisdiction and contradictory decisions has been reduced. Those types of disputes, in which actions were brought to the court of general jurisdiction because the plaintiff was an individual, are now heard exclusively by the commercial court regardless of whether the party is an individual or not.

3. Territorial Jurisdiction

Before the amendment, actions were often brought against the company in the court in places other than the location of the company. In many cases, proceedings started usually in the court of general jurisdiction, remote from the location of the company by 'manipulation of jurisdiction' and without the knowledge of the company. The amended law now makes it a rule that in corporate litigation, the court of the location of the company has territorial jurisdiction. Thus, actions in corporate disputes are to be brought to the court of the location of the place of the juridical person involved (art. 38, para. 4.1).

The same applies to the territorial jurisdiction for interim measures. Application for interim measures shall be filed with the court of the place of the location of the juridical person in question, and if the dispute is with the registrar of securities, the location of the registrar (art. 99, para. 3.1).

4. Consolidation

In the past, there were often contradictory decisions of different courts on the same matter. As a result of the amendment, now, if the court of first instance establishes that there are several interrelated cases in relation to the claims or evidence, the court may, *ex officio* or upon the application of the participants to the procedure, consolidate the cases (art.130, para. 2.1).

5. Interim Measures

Interim measures were also often abused in corporate disputes. In one case, a bailiff turned up at the shareholders' meeting with a court order preventing the meeting from deciding on almost all the agenda items, including the payment of dividends and the approval of the annual account[37]. These are cases of contest of control over the company[38].

Even before the 2009 amendment, the Code required that interim measures should be proportional to the claim which it is intended to secure. However, there were cases where disproportionate interim measures were allowed in order to secure small claims:

> The governor of a province became interested in a successful precious metal company in the region. He negotiated for the purchase of shares with major shareholders but was unsuccessful. The governor arranged an intermediary to acquire a small number of shares of this company, who initiated various actions harassing the company and applied for an injunction. This was granted by a judge who prohibited the use of essential machinery needed for the refinement of metal. Suspension of the process would have caused substantial loss to the company. Shareholders were thus forced to give a controlling stake to the governor[39].

The guideline of the Supreme Commercial Court of 2003 provided that interim measures should not have the effect of making the operation of companies virtually impossible or extremely difficult or forcing companies to act against the law. However, in reality, this did not work[40]. The 2009 amendment accommodated this rule in the Code itself, in the section on corporate disputes (art. 225.6, para. 1).

The amended Code also expanded the system of compensation for loss as a result of infringement of rights or lawful interest by way of interim measures. The Code had a provision to the effect that those who suffered loss from an interim measure are entitled to claim damages after the judgment entered force vis-à-vis the party who applied for such a measure. By the amendment, a special provision for the loss arising from interim measures in corporate disputes was introduced. For such a loss 'in consideration of reason and justice' and in accordance with the nature of the loss, ten thousand to one million roubles of compensation can be claimed (art. 98, para. 2). Whether this is sufficient, and if a ceiling should be set in such cases, is questionable.

---

37 *A. Molotnikov*, supra note 15, pp. 91, 193-194; *O. V. Osipienko*, supra note 31, pp. 120-121, 164-167.

38 *G. Panov*, supra note 30.

39 *A. Molotnikov*, supra note 15, pp. 12-13.

40 *O. V. Osipineko*, supra note 31, pp. 120-121.

6. Disclosure of Information

The amendment has substantially expanded the system of disclosure of information regarding corporate disputes, both in the procedural Code and the Joint Stock Company Law. The amended Code has a provision on the ensurance of access to information regarding corporate disputes.

Before the amendment, no information was provided to shareholders and investors when the company was sued or the company sued someone else. It was not uncommon that the company itself was often not informed of the proceedings initiated against it, since such proceedings were initiated in the court of general jurisdiction remote from the place of location of the company. The amended law first provides for the duty of the commercial court to publish information on its website regarding the initiation of the proceeding, progress of the procedure, granted interim measures, and the conclusion of the case, including settlement (art. 225.6, para. 1). Secondly, while in the past, proceedings related to the company, but in which the company itself was not a party, such as actions against directors or actions between shareholders on the ownership of shares, proceeded without the knowledge of the company. The amended Code mandates the court to keep the company informed of the procedure. At the same time, the amended Joint Stock Company Law obligates companies to guarantee access of shareholders to the court decisions in corporate disputes at various stages within three days of application (art. 89, para. 3).

7. Group Actions

Another novelty of the 2009 amendment is the introduction of the system of group action (in Russia, it is also called 'class action'). A new chapter entitled 'the Defence of the Rights and Lawful Interests of Groups' was introduced in the Code. Participants of a dispute or legal relation which serves as a basis of a claim are entitled to bring an action to court for the benefit of others who are participants of the same legal relation in order to defend their infringed or contested rights and lawful interests (art. 225.10, para. 1).

Such group actions are available in corporate litigation as well as litigation vis-à-vis the professional participants of the securities market (art. 225.11). Actions by shareholders and investors, such as the shareholders' derivative action, are envisaged here. However, the resulting decision of the court is not binding on the members of the group who did not join the proceedings. On the other hand, facts established by a judgment in a group action which entered into force, do not need to be proved if another member of the same group is suing the same defendant (art. 225.17, para. 2).

8. Extension of the time limit for hearing the case

Before the amendment, judges were under statutory obligation to complete the hearing and render the judgment within one month of the case being referred to the hearing. However, as the number of cases handled by the commercial court substantially increased in recent years, it became difficult to keep this time limit. According to court statistics, 6-7% of the cases at the first instance are disposed of in excess of the time limit[41]. As the result of the amendment, the period is now three months from the time the action was brought to court (art. 152, para. 1).

IV. Concluding remarks

Russia is one of the very few industrialised countries in which the independence and integrity of the court is still being discussed at length. It is even pointed out that the judges themselves do not seem to aspire for independence and integrity. The government, particularly the present administration, has been making efforts to rectify the situation. The system, insofar as the commercial courts are concerned, has become much more transparent and information more accessible.

The problem with the judicial system was not only the lack of independence and corruption. The shortcomings in the procedural law were abused by obscure entrepreneurs in contests for taking control of a company. The very fact that the system enables such abuses has discredited the whole system. The long-awaited amendment of the Code of Commercial Law and of other laws in relation to corporate disputes has addressed the problem and has substantially improved the system. This should be valued as major progress.

On the other hand, the fact still remains that in some cases, where the interest of the state or quasi-state entities is involved, the court has not always acted impartially. Such preponderance of *Zweckmäßigkeit* over *Rechtmäßigkeit*, albeit occasional, sadly reduces the value of positive reforms in the eyes of foreign investors.

41 http://www.arbitr.ru/_upimg/667B035EB4C14ADF163720095AADBEF1_нарушение %20сроков.pdf.

Mediation in Litauen und Russland

Antje Himmelreich[*]

I. Einführung

Mit der Verabschiedung der Mediationsrichtlinie[1] haben einige Jahre währende Arbeiten auf der Ebene der Europäischen Union zur Schaffung eines gemeinsamen rechtlichen Rahmens für das Mediationsverfahren ihren vorläufigen Abschluss gefunden. Der verabschiedete Richtlinientext entspricht dem Gemeinsamen Standpunkt, auf den sich der Europäische Rat geeinigt hatte[2]. Vorausgegangen waren ein Grünbuch der Europäischen Kommission über alternative Verfahren zur Streitbeilegung aus dem Jahr 2002, der Vorschlag einer entsprechenden Richtlinie durch die Kommission im Jahr 2004 und deren erste Lesung im Europäischen Parlament im Jahr 2007[3].

Ziel der Mediationsrichtlinie ist die Etablierung und Förderung der Mediation als Alternative der außergerichtlichen Streitbeilegung, ohne dabei das Gerichtsverfahren gering zu schätzen[4]. Der Anwendungsbereich der Mediationsrichtlinie ist jedoch in dreifacher Hinsicht beschränkt. Erstens konzentriert sie sich auf Zivil- und Handelssachen; Straf- und Verwaltungssachen bleiben unberührt. Zweitens gilt die Richtlinie nur für grenzüberschreitende Streitigkeiten, wobei es den Mitgliedstaaten freisteht, die Regeln auch auf rein nationale Sachverhalte zu erstrecken. Drittens regelt sie die Sachprobleme des Mediationsverfahrens und seiner Beteiligten nicht umfassend und abschließend, sondern wählt nur einzelne Regelungsaspekte wie die Vollstreckbarkeit in der Mediation erzielter Vereinbarungen und die Auswirkung der Mediation auf Verjährungsfristen aus[5].

---

* Wissenschaftl. Referentin für russisches und ukrainisches Recht am IOR.

1 Richtlinie 2008/52/EG des Europäischen Parlaments und des Rates vom 21.05.2008 über bestimmte Aspekte der Mediation in Zivil- und Handelssachen, ABl. EU L 136 vom 24.05.2008, S. 3-8.

2 Gemeinsamer Standpunkt des Rates im Hinblick auf die Annahme einer Richtlinie des Europäischen Parlaments und des Rates über bestimmte Aspekte der Mediation in Zivil- und Handelssachen vom 28.02.2008, Interinstitutionelles Dossier 2004/0251 (COD) vom 29.02.2008, Dok.-Nr. 15003/07 (zitiert nach *Hopt/Steffek*, Mediation – Rechtsvergleich, Regelungsmodelle, Grundsatzprobleme, in: *Hopt/Steffek* (Hrsg.), Mediation. Rechtstatsachen, Rechtsvergleich, Regelungen, Tübingen 2008, S. 5-102 (5).

3 Zu den Vorarbeiten vgl. nur die Informationsseite der Europäischen Kommission unter http://ec.europa.eu/civiljustice/adr/adr_ec_en.htm (abgerufen am 30.04.2011).

4 *Hopt/Steffek*, a.a.O. (Fn. 2), S. 6.

5 Dazu insgesamt *Hopt/Steffek*, a.a.O. (Fn. 2), S. 6.

Die Mediationsrichtlinie ist von den Mitgliedstaaten der Europäischen Union bis zum 20.05.2011 in nationales Recht umzusetzen[6]. In Deutschland beschloss die Bundesregierung am 12.01.2011 einen Gesetzentwurf zur Förderung der Mediation und anderer Verfahren der außergerichtlichen Streitbeilegung[7]. Der Bundesrat nahm am 18.03.2011 positiv zu dem Regierungsentwurf Stellung[8]. Am 14.04.2011 wurde der von der Bundesregierung eingebrachte Gesetzentwurf (BT-Drs. 17/5335, BT-Drs. 17/5496) im Bundestag in erster Lesung behandelt und zur weiteren Beratung in den Rechtsausschuss überwiesen. Mit der Gesetzesnovelle soll erstmals die außergerichtliche und gerichtsinterne Mediation in Deutschland auf eine gesetzliche Grundlage gestellt werden. Der Gesetzentwurf beschränkt sich dabei nicht auf die Umsetzung der Mediationsrichtlinie, sondern bezieht vielmehr auch die von dieser aus Kompetenzgründen nicht erfasste innerstaatliche Konfliktbeilegung ein und will die Streitkultur in Deutschland weit über die Vorgaben der Richtlinie hinausgehend positiv beeinflussen[9]. Dabei sollen die Eigenständigkeit der Streitparteien gestärkt und gleichzeitig die Gerichte entlastet werden.

Anders als in Deutschland kann der litauische Gesetzgeber bei der Umsetzung der Mediationsrichtlinie auf eine bereits bestehende gesetzliche Grundlage zur Mediation in Zivilsachen aufbauen. Auch in den GUS-Staaten gibt es die Tendenz, gesetzliche Regelungen zur Etablierung und Förderung der Mediation zu schaffen. In Russland ist seit dem 01.01.2011 ein Gesetz über das Mediationsverfahren in Kraft. In der Ukraine gab es bereits mehrere Gesetzesinitiativen für eine stärkere Implementierung der Mediation in der Gesetzgebung[10].

Der vorliegende Beitrag will einen Überblick über die gesetzliche Regelung der Mediation in Litauen und Russland geben.

---

6 Ausgenommen ist Dänemark, das gemäß Art. 1 Abs. 3 der Mediationsrichtlinie nicht an der Annahme der Richtlinie beteiligt ist und nicht zum durch sie gebundenen Adressenkreis gehört.

7 Der Regierungsentwurf eines Mediationsgesetzes (Bearbeitungsstand: 08.12.2010) ist zugänglich unter http://gesetzgebung.beck.de/news/mediationsgesetz (abgerufen am 30.04.2011).

8 Die Stellungnahme des Bundesrats (BR-Drs. 60/1(B) und die Empfehlungen der Ausschüsse des Bundesrats (BR-Drs. 60/1/11) zum Gesetzentwurf sind zugänglich unter http://gesetzgebung.beck.de/node/1006518 (abgerufen am 30.04.2011).

9 *Greger*, Die Reglementierung der Selbstregulierung. Zum Referentenentwurf eines Mediationsgesetzes, ZRP 2010, S. 209-213 (209).

10 Ein entsprechender Gesetzentwurf wurde u.a. im Rahmen einer Konferenz in Regensburg zum Thema „Mediation als Verfahren konsensualer Streitbeilegung: die deutsche, polnische und ukrainische Perspektive" am 25./26.06.2010 vorgestellt. Am 21.02.2011 wurde ein durch den Abgeordneten *Tyščenko* in die Verchovna Rada der Ukraine eingebrachter Gesetzentwurf „Über die Mediation" unter Nr. 8137 registriert. Dieser ist zugänglich auf der Datenbank für Gesetzentwürfe der Verchovna Rada der Ukraine unter http://w1.c1.rada.gov.ua/pls/zweb_n/webproc4_1?id=&pf3511=39689 (abgerufen am 30.04.2011).

II. Gesetzliche Regelung der Mediation in Litauen

1. Gesetzgebungsverfahren

Nur wenige Wochen nach Verabschiedung der Mediationsrichtlinie erließ der Seimas (das Parlament) der Republik Litauen am 15.07.2008 das Gesetz der Republik Litauen über die aussöhnende Vermittlung[11] in zivilrechtlichen Streitigkeiten[12] (im Folgenden: „lt. MediationsG")[13]. Dieses am 31.07.2008 in Kraft getretene Gesetz berücksichtigt bereits die Mediationsrichtlinie, sodass es weitgehend dem Recht der Europäischen Union entspricht. Zur vollständigen Umsetzung der Mediationsrichtlinie muss jedoch auch das lt. MediationsG zum Teil geändert und ergänzt werden (siehe dazu näher unter II.3.).

2. Überblick über den Inhalt des lt. MediationsG in der Fassung vom 15.07.2008

Das lt. MediationsG bestimmt die wesentlichen Voraussetzungen für die Durchführung der Mediation in zivilrechtlichen Streitigkeiten und die rechtlichen Folgen ihrer Anwendung (Art. 1 Pkt. 1 lt. MediationsG). Gemäß Art. 2 Pkt. 3 lt. MediationsG ist die Mediation in zivilrechtlichen Streitigkeiten (im Folgenden: „Mediation") ein Verfahren zur Beilegung zivilrechtlicher Streitigkeiten, während dessen ein oder mehrere Mediatoren den Parteien der Streitigkeit helfen, diese friedlich beizulegen.

Nach Art. 1 Pkt. 2 lt. MediationsG findet das Gesetz auf die außergerichtliche und die gerichtsinterne Mediation in zivilrechtlichen Streitigkeiten Anwendung, d.h. auf Streitigkeiten, die in einem Zivilverfahren vor einem ordentlichen Gericht verhandelt werden oder werden können (vgl. Art. 2 Pkt. 2 lt. MediationsG). Davon sind jedoch Streitigkeiten über solche bürgerlichen Rechte und Pflichten ausgenommen, die nicht Regelungsgegenstand eines Vergleichs sein können. Keine Anwendung findet das lt. MediationsG auf die gerichtsinterne Aussöhnung durch den die Streitigkeit verhandelnden Richter (Art. 1 Pkt. 2

11 Die wörtliche Übersetzung aus dem Litauischen ist „aussöhnende Vermittlung" (*taikinamasis tarpininkavimas*). Der Einfachheit halber wird im Folgenden der Begriff „Mediation" (*mediacija*) verwendet, der vom litauischen Gesetzgeber in Art. 2 Pkt. 3 lt. MediationsG in einem Klammerzusatz als Synonym für den Begriff der aussöhnenden Vermittlung genannt wird.

12 Gesetz der Republik Litauen über die Mediation in zivilrechtlichen Streitigkeiten (*Lietuvos Respublikos civilinių ginčų taikinamojo tarpininkavimo įstatymas*) Nr. X-1702 vom 15.07.2008, Valstybės žinios (im Folgenden: „Vž") 2008, Nr. 87-3462, zugänglich (auch in amtlicher englischer Übersetzung) über die Datenbank des Seimas unter http://www3.lrs.lt/dokpaieska/forma_l.htm (abgerufen am 30.04.2011).

13 Zu einer Textübersetzung mit Einführung siehe *Himmelreich/Maršantas*, Republik Litauen: Gesetz über die Mediation in zivilrechtlichen Streitigkeiten, WiRO 2011 (in Vorbereitung).

Abs. 2 lt. MediationsG). Nach Art. 1 Pkt. 3 lt. MediationsG können andere Rechtsakte für einzelne Kategorien zivilrechtlicher Streitigkeiten über das lt. MediationsG hinausgehende besondere Bestimmungen für das Mediationsverfahren vorsehen.

Weitere Regelungen des insgesamt nur 11 Artikel umfassenden lt. MediationsG haben die Mediationsvereinbarung (Art. 3), die Ernennung und die Anforderungen an den Mediator (Art. 4), die Durchführung (Art. 5) und die Beendigung der Mediation (Art. 9), den in der Mediation durch die Parteien geschlossenen Vergleich (Art. 6), die Vertraulichkeit (Art. 7) und die Hemmung von Verjährungsfristen (Art. 8) sowie die staatliche Förderung der Entwicklung der Mediation (Art. 10) zum Gegenstand.

a) Verhältnis des Mediationsverfahrens zum streitigen Verfahren

Ebenso wie der deutsche Gesetzentwurf[14] behandelt das lt. MediationsG sowohl die außergerichtliche als auch die gerichtsinterne Mediation in zivilrechtlichen Streitigkeiten. Als Unterfall der außergerichtlichen Mediation ist auch die gerichtsnahe Mediation, bei der ein gerichtliches Verfahren mit einer außergerichtlichen Streitbeilegung kombiniert wird, von der gesetzlichen Regelung umfasst.

Ist eine zivilrechtliche Streitigkeit bereits vor einem Gericht anhängig, kann der Richter den Parteien nach Art. 3 Pkt. 3 lt. MediationsG eine Streitbeilegung im Mediationsverfahren vorschlagen. Sind die Parteien mit diesem Vorschlag des Richters einverstanden, wird das Gerichtsverfahren ausgesetzt und die Streitigkeit in die Mediation verlegt. Durch diese Regelung dürften sowohl die Verlegung in eine gerichtsinterne als auch in eine außergerichtliche Mediation gleichermaßen erfasst sein. Eine verbindliche Verweisungsmöglichkeit des Richters in das Mediationsverfahren bzw. Kostensanktionen für mediationsunwillige Parteien sind nicht vorgesehen[15].

Haben die Parteien eine Vereinbarung über die Streitbeilegung im Mediationsverfahren getroffen, müssen sie zunächst versuchen, die Streitigkeit auf diesem Weg beizulegen, bevor sie sich an ein Gericht oder Schiedsgericht wenden können (Art. 3 Pkt. 2 S. 1 lt. MediationsG). Sofern in einer Mediationsvereinbarung eine Frist für die Beendigung der Mediation bestimmt ist, können sich die Parteien erst nach Ablauf dieser Frist an ein Gericht oder Schiedsgericht wenden. Haben die Parteien keine Mediationsvereinbarung geschlossen, kann sich eine Partei, die der anderen Partei ein Angebot zur Streitbeilegung im Mediationsverfahren unterbreitet hat, erst nach Ablauf eines Monats nach Absendung ihres schriftlichen Angebots an die andere Partei an ein Gericht oder Schiedsgericht wenden. Ohne Einhaltung einer Frist kann sich eine Partei an ein Gericht bzw. Schiedsgericht wenden, wenn die Mediation aus einem anderen in Art. 9 lt. MediationsG geregelten Grund endet (vgl. Art. 3 Pkt. 2 S. 2-4 lt. MediationsG).

---

14 Siehe oben Fn. 7.

15 Zu Kostenanreizen und -sanktionen siehe *Hopt/Steffek*, a.a.O. (Fn. 2), S. 28 ff.

b) Durchführung der Mediation

Eine Mediation wird gemäß Art. 3 Pkt. 1 lt. MediationsG aufgrund einer schriftlichen Vereinbarung der Parteien durchgeführt. Die Parteien können sich über die Durchführung der Mediation sowohl bei einer bereits bestehenden Streitigkeit als auch vor Entstehung einer Streitigkeit, z.B. in einer Mediationsklausel eines größeren Vertragswerks, einigen. Über das Erfordernis der Schriftlichkeit der Mediationsvereinbarung hinaus sind keine weiteren Anforderungen an die Mediationsvereinbarung vorgesehen. Das lt. MediationsG überlässt damit den Parteien einen weiten Spielraum zur Ausgestaltung einer Mediationsvereinbarung.

Nach Art. 4 Pkt. 1 lt. MediationsG wird der Mediator aufgrund einer schriftlichen Vereinbarung der Parteien und mit seinem Einverständnis ernannt. Die Parteien können auch vereinbaren, dass ein Dritter oder ein sog. Verwalter von Mediationsdienstleistungen[16] einen Mediator empfiehlt oder ernennt (Art. 4 Pkt. 3 S. 1 lt. MediationsG).

Wenn die Parteien dies in der Mediationsvereinbarung vorsehen oder sich über die Ernennung eines Mediators nicht einigen können, kann das Amtsgericht nach Art. 4 Pkt. 3 S. 2 und 3 lt. MediationsG auf gemeinsamen Antrag der Parteien den Mediator in dem in Kapitel XXXIX der Zivilprozessordnung der Republik Litauen[17] (im Folgenden: „lt. ZPO“) bestimmten vereinfachten Verfahren ernennen. Voraussetzung ist das Vorliegen eines schriftlichen Einverständnisses des Mediators.

Das lt. MediationsG sieht vor, dass die Parteien die Verfahrensordnung der Mediation in der Mediationsvereinbarung selbst regeln, indem sie die Anwendung eines gewählten Regelwerks bestimmen oder im gemeinsamen Einvernehmen einzelne Regeln der Mediation festlegen (Art. 5 Pkt. 1 lt. MediationsG).

Können sich die Parteien über die Verfahrensordnung der Mediation nicht einigen oder haben sie in der Mediationsvereinbarung keine konkreten Handlungen des Mediators vorgesehen, hat der Mediator gemäß Art. 5 Pkt. 2 lt. MediationsG konkrete Handlungen angemessen durchzuführen. Dabei hat er nicht nur auf die Umstände der Streitigkeit, darunter das potenzielle Kräfteun-

---

16 Ein Verwalter von Mediationsdienstleistungen ist nach Art. 2 Pkt. 4 lt. MediationsG eine öffentliche oder private juristische Person, die Mediatoren empfiehlt oder ernennt, Mediationsregeln vorschlägt oder aufstellt, die Ausgaben der Mediation verwaltet, Räumlichkeiten für die Durchführung von Mediationsverfahren zur Verfügung stellt und andere mit der Mediation verbundene Dienstleistungen anbietet.

17 Gesetz über die Bestätigung, das Inkrafttreten und die Umsetzung der Zivilprozessordnung der Republik Litauen (*Lietuvos Respublikos civilinio proceso kodekso patvirtinimo, įsigaliojimo ir įgyvendinimo įstatymas*) Nr. IX-743 vom 28.02.2002, Vž 2002, Nr. 159-7203, in der Fassung des Gesetzes Nr. XI-1032 vom 23.09.2010, Vž 2010, Nr. 126-6457, zugänglich über die Datenbank des Seimas unter http://www3.lrs.lt/dokpaieska/forma_l.htm (abgerufen am 30.04.2011).

gleichgewicht zwischen den Parteien, die Wünsche der Parteien und das Bedürfnis einer zügigen Streitbeilegung, Rücksicht zu nehmen, sondern muss auch in Übereinstimmung mit den gesetzlichen Bestimmungen handeln. Anzumerken ist, dass das lt. MediationsG den Handlungsspielraum des Mediators nicht eindeutig regelt. Es wird z.B. nicht ausdrücklich bestimmt, ob der Mediator rechtliche Hinweise oder eigene Lösungsvorschläge zur Streitbeilegung unterbreiten darf. Zwar wird in Art. 4 Pkt. 4 S. 1 lt. MediationsG die neutrale Stellung des Mediators betont. Ob daraus auf eine Beschränkung des Mediators auf den Kommunikationsprozess zwischen den Parteien geschlossen werden kann, erscheint aber fraglich.

Nach Art. 4 Pkt. 7 S. 1 und 2 lt. MediationsG kann die Mediation sowohl entgeltlich als auch unentgeltlich angeboten werden. Wenn die Mediation entgeltlich angeboten wird, beginnt sie erst, nachdem der Mediator die Höhe der Vergütung und die Zahlungsmodalitäten mit den Parteien des Mediationsverfahrens schriftlich vereinbart hat.

Gelingt es den Parteien, ihre Streitigkeit im Mediationsverfahren friedlich beizulegen, wird ein sog. Vergleich (*taikos sutartis*) geschlossen. Für während der Mediation geschlossene Vergleiche gelten gemäß Art. 6 Pkt. 1 lt. MediationsG die im Zivilgesetzbuch der Republik Litauen[18] (im Folgenden: „lt. ZGB") und anderen Gesetzen bestimmten Anforderungen. Art. 6 Pkt. 2 lt. MediationsG bestimmt, dass solche Vergleiche für die Parteien des Mediationsverfahrens verbindlich sind. Mit dem Abschluss des Vergleichs endet die Mediation (Art. 9 Nr. 5 lt. MediationsG).

Nach Art. 5 Pkt. 5 lt. MediationsG kann jede Partei ohne Angabe von Gründen von der Mediation Abstand nehmen. In diesem Fall endet die Mediation, sobald die Partei dem Mediator und der anderen Partei eine schriftliche Erklärung über die Abstandnahme von der Mediation vorlegt (Art. 9 Nr. 3 lt. MediationsG). Die Mediation endet auch dann, wenn eine Partei die Streitbeilegung im Mediationsverfahren ablehnt oder innerhalb eines Monats nach Absendung des Angebots einer Streitbeilegung im Mediationsverfahren nicht schriftlich zustimmt, sowie dann, wenn der Mediator allen Parteien oder alle Parteien dem Mediator eine schriftliche Erklärung über die Beendigung der Mediation vorlegen (vgl. Art. 9 lt. MediationsG). Fristen, innerhalb derer ein Mediationsverfahren durchzuführen ist, sind nicht vorgesehen. Dementsprechend fehlt auch eine automatische Beendigung des Mediationsverfahrens nach Fristablauf[19].

---

18 Gesetz über die Bestätigung, das Inkrafttreten und die Umsetzung des Zivilgesetzbuchs der Republik Litauen (*Lietuvos Respublikos civilinio kodekso patvirtinimo, įsigaliojimo ir įgyvendinimo įstatymas*) Nr. VIII-1864 v. 18.07.2000, Vž 2000, Nr. 74-2262, in der Fassung des Gesetzes Nr. XI-1312 vom 12.04.2011, Vž 2011, Nr. 49-2367, zugänglich (auch in amtlicher englischer Übersetzung) über die Datenbank des Seimas unter http://www3.lrs.lt/dokpaieska/forma_l.htm (abgerufen am 30.04.2011).

19 Zu einer diesbezüglichen Regelung im russischen Recht siehe unter III.5.

c) Vertraulichkeitsschutz

Art. 7 lt. MediationsG enthält eine Regelung zum Vertraulichkeitsschutz als einem elementaren Grundsatz der Mediation. Danach müssen die Parteien des Mediationsverfahrens, die Mediatoren und die Verwalter von Mediationsdienstleistungen sämtliche während der Mediation erlangten und mit ihr im Zusammenhang stehenden Informationen geheim halten, sofern die Parteien nicht etwas anderes vereinbart haben. Davon ausgenommen sind nur solche Informationen, die zur Bestätigung oder Durchsetzung des während der Mediation geschlossenen Vergleichs erforderlich sind, sowie Informationen, deren Nichtoffenlegung dem öffentlichen Interesse widersprechen würde. Dies gilt insbesondere dann, wenn Kindesinteressen betroffen sind oder ein Schaden für die Gesundheit oder das Leben einer natürlichen Person abzuwenden ist.

Nach Art. 7 Pkt. 1 S. 2 lt. MediationsG gilt der Vertraulichkeitsschutz auch für streitige Verfahren vor einem Gericht oder Schiedsgericht sowie für andere Streitbeilegungsverfahren, und zwar unabhängig davon, ob sie mit dem Mediationsverfahren im Zusammenhang stehen oder nicht. Damit ist es den Parteien oder sonstigen am Mediationsverfahren Beteiligten verwehrt, sich in einem streitigen Verfahren oder einem anderen Streitbeilegungsverfahren auf während der Mediation erlangte oder mit ihr im Zusammenhang stehende Informationen zu berufen[20].

Art. 7 Pkt. 2 lt. MediationsG verbietet es dem Mediator, die ihm von einer Partei des Mediationsverfahrens anvertrauten vertraulichen Informationen der anderen Partei offenzulegen, sofern die Partei, die ihm die Informationen anvertraut hat, der Offenlegung nicht zugestimmt hat. Diese Bestimmung ist von besonderer Bedeutung, da der Mediator gemäß Art. 5 Pkt. 3 lt. MediationsG eine Beratung mit einer Partei in Abwesenheit der anderen Partei durchführen kann.

Die Mediatoren und die Verwalter von Mediationsdienstleistungen sind bei Nicht- oder Schlechterfüllung der in Art. 7 Pkt. 1 und 2 lt. MediationsG bestimmten Pflichten nach den allgemeinen gesetzlichen Bestimmungen verantwortlich (Art. 7 Pkt. 3 lt. MediationsG). Eine entsprechende Regelung für die Parteien des Mediationsverfahrens ist nicht vorgesehen.

d) Hemmung der verkürzten Verjährungsfristen

Mit dem Beginn der Mediation wird nach Art. 8 Pkt. 1 lt. MediationsG der Lauf der verkürzten Verjährungsfristen gehemmt, sodass die Parteien bei einem gescheiterten Versuch der friedlichen Streitbeilegung im Mediationsverfahren das Recht beibehalten, sich wegen ihrer verletzten Rechte an ein Gericht oder Schiedsgericht zu wenden. Sofern die Parteien keine Einigung im Mediationsverfahren erzielt haben, wird der Lauf der Verjährungsfrist nach Art. 8 Pkt. 3

20 Zur Unterscheidung zwischen Vortrags- und Beweismittelbeschränkung siehe *Hopt/Steffek*, a.a.O. (Fn. 2), S. 193.

S. 1 lt. MediationsG fortgesetzt. In diesem Fall wird die nach Ablauf der Verjährungshemmung verbliebene Verjährungsfrist gemäß Art. 8 Pkt. 1 S. 2 lt. MediationsG i.V.m. Art. 1.129 Pkt. 3 lt. ZGB um sechs Monate bzw., wenn die vorgesehene Verjährungsfrist kürzer als sechs Monate ist, um die volle Verjährungsfrist verlängert, sodass nach der Hemmung der Verjährung durch ein Mediationsverfahren eine Mindestfrist für die Verjährung verbleibt[21].

Die in Art. 8 lt. MediationsG vorgesehene Beschränkung auf die Hemmung des Laufs der verkürzten Verjährungsfristen dürfte Art. 8 der Mediationsrichtlinie widersprechen, wonach die Mitgliedstaaten sicherzustellen haben, dass die Parteien des Mediationsverfahrens durch das Ablaufen von Verjährungsfristen nicht daran gehindert werden, ein Gerichts- oder Schiedsgerichtsverfahren hinsichtlich derselben Streitigkeit einzuleiten. Um das litauische Recht an die Mediationsrichtlinie anzupassen, sollte Art. 8 lt. MediationsG – zumindest soweit grenzüberschreitende Sachverhalte betroffen sind – auf sämtliche Verjährungsfristen ausgedehnt werden (siehe dazu näher unter II.3.).

e) Vollstreckbarkeit des Vergleichs

Ist die sich im Mediationsverfahren befindende Streitigkeit bereits gerichtlich anhängig, wird der in der Mediation geschlossene Vergleich durch das Gericht, bei dem die Streitigkeit anhängig ist, durch Beschluss bestätigt, es sei denn, dass der Vergleich zwingenden Rechtsnormen oder öffentlichen Interessen widerspricht (vgl. Art. 42 Pkt. 2 lt. ZPO). Dem Gericht obliegt damit eine Prüfungspflicht hinsichtlich des Inhalts und des Zustandekommens des Vergleichs.

Wenn die sich im Mediationsverfahren befindende Streitigkeit nicht gleichzeitig gerichtlich anhängig ist, kann der Vergleich auf gemeinsamen Antrag der Parteien des Mediationsverfahrens einem Gericht zur Bestätigung gemäß dem in Kapitel XXXIX der lt. ZPO bestimmten vereinfachten Verfahren vorgelegt werden (Art. 6 Pkt. 3 S. 3 lt. MediationsG).

Ein Vergleich, der durch eine rechtskräftige gerichtliche Entscheidung bestätigt wird, hat nach Art. 6 Pkt. 3 S. 3 lt. MediationsG für die Parteien des Mediationsverfahrens die gleiche Rechtskraft wie eine endgültige gerichtliche Entscheidung (*res judicata*) und kann vollstreckt werden.

f) Rechtliche Stellung des Mediators

Der Mediator ist gemäß Art. 2 Pkt. 5 lt. MediationsG eine dritte unparteiische natürliche Person, die zur friedlichen Beilegung einer zivilrechtlichen Streitigkeit anderer Personen herangezogen wird. Die Parteien können grundsätzlich jede natürliche Person zum Mediator ernennen, wenn sie dieser vertrauen und

21 Sog. Ablaufhemmung, siehe u.a. auch § 203 S. 2 des deutschen BGB. . Allgemein zur Verjährung im litauischen Recht *Mizaras*, in: *Galginaitis/Himmelreich/Vrubliauskaitė*, Berlin 2010, § 7. Allgemeiner Teil, S. 77 f.

dies schriftlich vereinbaren. Nur Richter und Anwälte oder sonstige Vertreter der Parteien in derselben Streitigkeit sind davon ausgenommen. Allerdings kann der Mediator nach Art. 4 Pkt. 6 lt. MediationsG in derselben Streitigkeit zum Schiedsrichter ernannt werden, wenn die Parteien dies schriftlich vereinbaren und er dem nicht widerspricht.

Der Mediator kann das Angebot zur Aufnahme einer Mediation oder zur Fortsetzung einer begonnenen Mediation nur dann annehmen, wenn er die Parteien über die ihm bekannten Umstände, die Zweifel an seiner Unparteilichkeit hervorrufen können, informiert hat (Art. 4 Pkt. 4 S. 2 lt. MediationsG). Neben der Unparteilichkeit spielen die Regeln über die Vertraulichkeit des Mediators eine wichtige Rolle in der Mediation (siehe dazu oben unter II.2.c)).

Nach Art. 4 Pkt. 5 lt. MediationsG hat der Mediator die Parteien über seine Ausbildung und Erfahrung zu informieren. Keine Aussagen enthält das Gesetz über die Anforderungen an die berufliche und fachliche Qualifikation der Mediatoren und die erforderlichen Ausbildungsstandards. Der litauische Gesetzgeber scheint hier derzeit keinen Handlungsbedarf zu sehen und überlässt Fragen der beruflichen Qualifikation der Mediatoren der Regulierung durch die Marktteilnehmer, die Mediation anfragen und anbieten. Das Justizministerium plant jedoch, Fort- und Ausbildungskurse für Mediatoren anzubieten[22]. Ferner werden Lehrveranstaltungen zur Mediation an den juristischen Fakultäten der Universitäten angeboten.

3. Gesetzentwurf vom 25.11.2010 zur Änderung und Ergänzung des lt. MediationsG

Am 25.11.2010 hat die Regierung der Republik Litauen einen vom Justizministerium vorbereiteten Gesetzentwurf zur Änderung und Ergänzung des Gesetzes der Republik Litauen über die Mediation in zivilrechtlichen Streitigkeiten[23] (im Folgenden: „Gesetzentwurf") beschlossen. Nach den Erläuterungen des Justizministeriums zum Gesetzentwurf[24] werden mit dem Änderungsgesetz zwei Ziele verfolgt: erstens die vollständige Umsetzung der Mediationsrichtlinie und zweitens die Förderung der Entwicklung der Mediation in Litauen.

Der Gesetzentwurf sieht Änderungen in insgesamt sieben (Art. 1, 4, 5, 6, 8, 10, 11) der 11 Artikel des lt. MediationsG vor. Bei der im Gesetzentwurf vorgesehenen Ergänzung handelt es sich um einen Anhang mit einem expliziten Vermerk, dass mit dem lt. MediationsG die Mediationsrichtlinie umgesetzt werden soll. Art. 1 Pkt. 3 lt. MediationsG in der Fassung des Gesetzentwurfs vom

---

22 Beschluss des Justizministeriums der Republik Litauen Nr. 1R-256 vom 23.11.2010, Vž 2010, Nr. 139-7162, zugänglich über die Datenbank des Seimas unter http://www3.lrs.lt/dokpaieska/forma_l.htm (abgerufen am 30.04.2011).

23 Gesetzentwurf Nr. XIP-2708 vom 25.11.2010, zugänglich über die Datenbank des Seimas unter http://www3.lrs.lt/dokpaieska/forma_l.htm (abgerufen am 30.04.2011).

24 Ebenda.

25.11.2010 sieht ferner vor, dass das Gesetz auf die Beilegung von nationalen und internationalen zivilrechtlichen Streitigkeiten Anwendung findet. Der litauische Gesetzgeber beabsichtigt folglich, die Mediationsrichtlinie ähnlich wie der deutsche Gesetzgeber nicht nur in Bezug auf grenzüberschreitende Streitigkeiten umzusetzen, sondern die Geltung des lt. MediationsG auch auf rein nationale Sachverhalte zu erstrecken.

Darüber hinaus sieht der Gesetzentwurf vom 25.11.2010 folgende wesentliche Änderungen des lt. MediationsG vor:

1) *Staatlich gewährleistete Mediationsdienstleistungen*: Um die Entwicklung der Mediation in Litauen zu fördern, soll der Staat außergerichtliche und gerichtsinterne Mediationsdienstleistungen anbieten können. Das von der Nationalverwaltung der Gerichte (*Nacionalinė teismų administracija*) betreute Pilotprojekt gerichtsinterner Mediation läuft bereits seit mehreren Jahren an verschiedenen Gerichten (siehe dazu näher unter II.4.). Es sei deshalb notwendig, diese vom Staat kostenlos bereitgestellten Streitbeilegungsmechanismen auf gesetzlicher Ebene zu regeln und den Bürgern einen breiteren Zugang zu diesen Mechanismen zu ermöglichen. Ferner sollten die Anwendungsbereiche und die Verfahrensordnung der Gewährleistung kostenloser außergerichtlicher Mediationsdienstleistungen durch den Gesetzgeber in Spezialgesetzen bestimmt werden. Zwar werden solche Dienstleistungen bisher nicht angeboten, es könnte jedoch nach Beurteilung der Bedürfnisse und möglichen Kosten ein entsprechendes Regelungsmodell etabliert werden, z.B. im Gesetz der Republik Litauen über die staatlich garantierte Rechtshilfe[25].
2) *Plan zur Entwicklung der Mediation und Sicherstellung der Qualität von Mediationsdienstleistungen*: Um den Anforderungen der Mediationsrichtlinie gerecht zu werden, insbesondere um die Qualität von Mediationsdienstleistungen sicherzustellen und die Öffentlichkeit über dieses alternative Verfahren zur Streitbeilegung zu informieren, soll das Justizministerium einen Plan zur Entwicklung der Mediation und Sicherstellung der Qualität von Mediationsdienstleistungen vorbereiten und bestätigen. Dieser soll sowohl gesetzgeberische als auch organisatorische Maßnahmen zur Erreichung der jeweiligen Ziele enthalten.
3) *Einhaltung des Europäischen Verhaltenskodex für Mediatoren*: In der Mediationsrichtlinie wird die Bedeutung des Europäischen Verhaltenskodex für

25 Gesetz der Republik Litauen über die staatlich garantierte Rechtshilfe (*Lietuvos Respublikos valstybės garantuojamos teisinės pagalbos įstatymas*) Nr. VIII-1591 vom 28.03.2000, Vž 2000, Nr. 30-827, in der Fassung des Gesetzes Nr. XI-223 vom 16.04.2009, Vž 2009, Nr. 46-1801, zugänglich (auch in amtlicher englischer Übersetzung) über die Datenbank des Seimas unter http://www3.lrs.lt/dokpaieska/forma_l.htm (abgerufen am 30.04.2011).

Mediatoren[26] hervorgehoben. Um diesem zu entsprechen und um die Qualität von Mediationsdienstleistungen in Litauen sicherzustellen, soll bei der Ernennung eines Mediators im Regelfall die Pflicht zur Einhaltung des Europäischen Verhaltenskodex für Mediatoren vorgesehen werden.

4) *Einsatz moderner Technologien*: Wie in Erwägungsgrund Nr. 9 der Mediationsrichtlinie vorgesehen, sollen in näher festgelegten Fällen und nach einer bestimmten Verfahrensordnung im gemeinsamen Einvernehmen der Parteien des Mediationsverfahrens moderne Informations- und Kommunikationstechnologien im Mediationsverfahren angewandt werden können.
5) *Gerichtliche Bestätigung von Vergleichen und Verjährungshemmung*: Zur ordnungsgemäßen Umsetzung der Mediationsrichtlinie und zur Gewährleistung von Rechtssicherheit für die Parteien soll ein im Mediationsverfahren geschlossener Vergleich, falls die sich im Mediationsverfahren befindende Streitigkeit nicht gleichzeitig gerichtlich anhängig ist, nicht nur wie bisher auf gemeinsamen Antrag der Parteien (vgl. Art. 6 Pkt. 3 S. 1 lt. MediationsG in der Fassung vom 15.07.2008), sondern auch auf Antrag einer Partei mit schriftlicher Zustimmung der anderen Partei einem Gericht zur Bestätigung gemäß dem in Kapitel XXXIX der lt. ZPO bestimmten vereinfachten Verfahren vorgelegt werden können. Außerdem muss entsprechend Art. 8 der Mediationsrichtlinie mit Beginn der Mediation der Lauf sämtlicher Verjährungsfristen gehemmt werden, weshalb die bisherige Beschränkung im lt. MediationsG auf die Hemmung des Laufs der verkürzten Verjährungsfristen aufgehoben und eine Hemmung sämtlicher Verjährungsfristen eingeführt werden soll. Durch diese Regelung soll sichergestellt werden, dass die Parteien durch einen Versuch der Streitbeilegung im Mediationsverfahren nicht die Möglichkeit verlieren, ihre verletzten Rechte gerichtlich geltend zu machen, wenn sie im Mediationsverfahren keine friedliche Einigung durch den Abschluss eines Vergleichs erzielen können.

Der Gesetzentwurf sieht außerdem vor, dass die Bestimmung, wonach der Staat in einem von der Regierung bestimmten Verfahren die Entwicklung der Mediation fördert (Art. 10 lt. MediationsG in der Fassung vom 15.07.2008), gestrichen werden soll. Dies wird einerseits damit begründet, dass dadurch zusätzliche Haushaltsausgaben verursacht würden und diese derzeit, in Zeiten wirtschaftlicher Rezession, nicht vorhanden seien. Andererseits sei zu erwarten, dass die Entwicklung der Mediation durch andere Maßnahmen effektiv gefördert werden kann. Beispielhaft werden hierfür folgende alternative Maßnahmen genannt:

1) *Prozesskostenerleichterungen* für Personen, die vor Anrufung eines Gerichts oder während eines gerichtlichen Verfahrens einen Versuch der Streitbeile-

26 Europäischer Verhaltenskodex für Mediatoren vom 02.07.2004, zugänglich über das Europäische Justizielle Netz für Zivil- und Handelssachen in Englisch unter http://ec.europa.eu/civiljustice/adr/adr_ec_de.htm (abgerufen am 30.04.2011).

gung im Mediationsverfahren unternehmen. Ein entsprechender vom Justizministerium vorbereiteter Gesetzentwurf zur Änderung und Ergänzung der lt. ZPO[27] wurde durch die Regierung bereits am 11.11.2009[28] beschlossen und dem Seimas vorgelegt;

2) *Aus- und Fortbildung* im Bereich der Mediation für die am Pilotprojekt gerichtsinterner Mediation beteiligten Richter und andere Personen sowie Bekanntmachung der Öffentlichkeit mit diesem Projekt durch das Justizministerium. Außerdem wird der Nationalverwaltung der Gerichte vorgeschlagen, das Pilotprojekt gerichtsinterner Mediation durch die Aufnahme neuer Gerichte und die Einbeziehung weiterer Mediatoren, z.B. von Vertretern der akademischen Öffentlichkeit, auszuweiten;

3) *Vorschlag des Justizministeriums an den Richterrat* (*Teisėjų taryba*), in Zukunft bei der Beurteilung von Richtern darauf zu achten, wie viele Prozessvergleiche in den von ihnen geleiteten Gerichtsverhandlungen geschlossen worden sind und ob sie an dem Pilotprojekt gerichtsinterner Mediation teilgenommen haben. Darüber hinaus soll das Justizministerium dem Richterrat vorschlagen, an den Gerichten, an denen das Pilotprojekt gerichtsinterner Mediation durchgeführt wird, in familien- und arbeitsrechtlichen Streitigkeiten für die Parteien obligatorische Informationsveranstaltungen über die Möglichkeiten und Vorteile der Mediation zu organisieren.

Diese und andere Initiativen sind vom Justizministerium ausführlich im Plan zur Entwicklung der Mediation und Sicherstellung der Qualität von Mediationsdienstleistungen zu erläutern. Dabei soll vor allem darauf geachtet werden, dass die geplanten gesetzgeberischen und organisatorischen Maßnahmen keine zusätzlichen Haushaltsausgaben erfordern.

4. Bewertung der geplanten Änderungen im lt. MediationsG

Die rechtzeitige Umsetzung der Mediationsrichtlinie setzt voraus, dass der Seimas über den Gesetzentwurf zur Änderung und Ergänzung des lt. MediationsG im Frühjahr 2011 beschließt und das Änderungsgesetz bis zum 20.05.2011 in Kraft tritt. Auch der Plan zur Entwicklung der Mediation und Sicherstellung der Qualität von Mediationsdienstleistungen muss bis zum Ablauf der Umsetzungsfrist vom Justizministerium vorbereitet und bestätigt werden.

Nach den Angaben des Justizministeriums werden von der neuen Regelung positive Auswirkungen auf die Wirtschaftsbeziehungen und ihre Entwicklung in Litauen erwartet, da diese es den Wirtschaftssubjekten ermöglicht, alltägliche zivilrechtliche Streitigkeiten effizienter beizulegen. Der Gesetzentwurf und der

---

27 Gesetzentwurf Nr. XIP-1409 v. 16.11.2009, zugänglich über die Datenbank des Seimas unter http://www3.lrs.lt/dokpaieska/forma_l.htm (abgerufen am 30.04.2011).

28 Ebenda.

Plan zur Entwicklung der Mediation und Sicherstellung der Qualität von Mediationsdienstleistungen beinhalten wesentliche Maßnahmen zur Erleichterung und Verbesserung der friedlichen Streitbeilegung im Mediationsverfahren, sodass solche positiven Auswirkungen durchaus realistisch sind.

Fraglich erscheint jedoch, ob die neue Regelung die angestrebte Entwicklung der Mediation in Litauen effektiv fördern kann. Bisher entwickelt sich die friedliche Streitbeilegung im Mediationsverfahren in Litauen nur sehr zögerlich. Das bereits im Jahr 2006 begonnene Pilotprojekt gerichtsinterner Mediation ist zwar bis Ende 2010 auf fast 20 Gerichte und 43 Mediatoren ausgeweitet worden[29]. Es gibt jedoch bisher noch keine genauen Angaben darüber, wie viele Streitigkeiten tatsächlich im Mediationsverfahren friedlich beigelegt worden sind. Das Justizministerium verweist darauf, dass gerichtlich anhängige zivilrechtliche Streitigkeiten nur sehr selten durch einen Vergleich beendet werden[30]. Als Beispiel hierfür wird angegeben, dass von allen im Jahr 2009 in erster Instanz verhandelten Zivilsachen (insgesamt 229.221) weniger als 2% (4.601) durch einen Vergleich beendet worden sind. Obwohl die im Mediationsverfahren geschlossenen Vergleiche von dieser Statistik nicht gesondert erwähnt werden, sondern von ihr sämtliche gerichtlichen Vergleiche erfasst sind, kann daraus auf eine bisher nur sehr schwache Entwicklung der gerichtsinternen und gerichtsnahen Mediation in Litauen geschlossen werden.

Insgesamt ist festzuhalten, dass trotz guter Ansätze und der geplanten Änderungen des lt. MediationsG sowie anderer Rechtsakte weitere Regelungen und Maßnahmen notwendig sein werden, um eine friedliche Streitbeilegung im Mediationsverfahren in Litauen erfolgreich zu etablieren. Insbesondere sollte stärker als bisher in Informations- und Diskussionsveranstaltungen über die Möglichkeiten der Durchführung von Mediationsverfahren hingewiesen werden. Das Schaffen von Vertrauen der Parteien in das Mediationsverfahren ist eine wesentliche Voraussetzung für den Erfolg der Mediation. Auch in Aus- und Fortbildungskurse für Mediatoren sollte künftig mehr investiert werden. Darüber hinaus sollten zusätzliche Anreize für die Durchführung von Mediationsverfahren geschaffen werden. Die Einführung von Prozesskostenerleichterungen im Fall eines Versuchs der Streitbeilegung im Mediationsverfahren, wie dies im Gesetzentwurf zur Änderung und Ergänzung der lt. ZPO vorgesehen ist, wäre sicher ein Schritt in die richtige Richtung.

---

29 Vgl. die Benachrichtigung des Justizministeriums über die Zustimmung der Regierung zum Gesetzentwurf vom 24.11.2010, zugänglich unter http://www.tm.lt/naujienos/pranesimasspaudai/1588 (abgerufen am 30.04.2011).

30 Ebenda.

III. Gesetzliche Regelung der Mediation in Russland

1. Gesetzgebungsverfahren

In Russland ist am 01.01.2011 erstmalig eine gesetzliche Regelung der Mediation in Kraft getreten[31]. Sie wurde durch den Erlass zweier Gesetze verwirklicht: Neben dem föderalen Gesetz über das alternative Verfahren zur Streitbeilegung unter Beteiligung eines Vermittlers (Mediationsverfahren)[32] (im Folgenden: „russ. MediationsG") wurde ein weiteres föderales Gesetz verabschiedet[33], welches Änderungen im Zivilgesetzbuch (Erster Teil)[34] (im Folgenden: „russ. ZGB"), der Zivilprozessordnung[35] (im Folgenden: „russ. ZPO"), der Arbitrageprozessordnung[36] (im Folgenden: „russ. APO"), dem Gesetz über die Schiedsgerichte in der Russischen Föderation[37] und dem Gesetz über die Werbung[38] vornimmt.

Das Gesetzgebungsverfahren ging äußerst zügig vonstatten: der Präsident hat die Gesetzentwürfe am 11.03.2010 in die Staatsduma eingebracht[39]. Bereits am 27.07.2010 wurden die von der Staatsduma beschlossenen und vom Föderationsrat gebilligten Gesetze ausgefertigt und am 30.07.2010 bekanntgemacht. In den letzten Jahren gab es allerdings immer wieder Regelungsentwürfe im Bereich der Mediation[40]. Zu nennen sind das Regierungsprogramm „Entwicklung

---

31 Die Darstellung zu Russland basiert auf einer Textübersetzung mit Einführung von *Breig/Himmelreich*, Russische Föderation: Gesetz über alternative Verfahren zur Streitbeilegung unter Beteiligung eines Vermittlers (Mediationsverfahren), WiRO 2010, S. 369-373 (Teil 1), und 2011, S. 15-19 (Teil 2).

32 Föderales Gesetz Nr. 193-FZ vom 27.07.2010, Sobranie zakonodatel'stva Rossijskoj Federacii (im Folgenden: „SZ RF") 2010, Nr. 31, Pos. 4162.

33 Föderales Gesetz Nr. 194-FZ vom 27.07.2010, SZ RF 2010, Nr. 31, Pos. 4163.

34 Föderales Gesetz Nr. 51-FZ vom 30.11.1994, SZ RF 1994, Nr. 32, Pos. 3301, mit späteren Änderungen.

35 Föderales Gesetz Nr. 138-FZ vom 14.11.2002, SZ RF 2002, Nr. 46, Pos. 4532, mit späteren Änderungen.

36 Föderales Gesetz Nr. 95-FZ vom 24.07.2002, SZ RF 2002, Nr. 30, Pos. 3012, mit späteren Änderungen.

37 Föderales Gesetz Nr. 102-FZ vom 24.07.2002, SZ RF 2002, Nr. 30, Pos. 3019, mit späteren Änderungen.

38 Föderales Gesetz Nr. 38-FZ vom 13.03.2006, SZ RF 2006, Nr. 12, Pos. 1232, mit späteren Änderungen.

39 Zu diesen Gesetzentwürfen vgl. u.a. *Korsik*, Problemy i perspektivy primenenija procedur mediacii dlja uregulirovanija graždansko-pravovych sporov (Probleme und Perspektiven der Anwendung von Mediationsverfahren zur Beilegung zivilrechtlicher Streitigkeiten), Zakon 2010, Nr. 7, S. 143-149.

40 Zur Diskussion vgl. u.a. *Jarkov*, Mediation in Russland, in: *Trunk/Nuutila/Nekrošius* (Hrsg.), Schiedsgerichtsbarkeit und andere Formen alternativer Streitbeilegung. Erfahrungen und Tendenzen im Ostseeraum, Berlin 2006, S. 93 ff.

des Gerichtssystems in Russland in den Jahren 2007-2012"[41], in dem auf das Erfordernis hingewiesen wird, auf eine breitere Anwendung der Mediation hinzuwirken, und Gesetzentwürfe, die in den Jahren 2006[42], 2008[43] und 2009[44] in die Staatsduma eingebracht wurden.

Das neue Gesetz beruht seinem Aufbau nach auf den 2006 und 2008 eingebrachten Gesetzentwürfen und übernimmt von ihnen auch wesentliche Textteile. In den Gesetzesmaterialien finden sich ausdrückliche Hinweise auf die Mediationsrichtlinie der Europäischen Union.

2. Überblick über den Inhalt der Regelung

Unmittelbares Ziel des russ. MediationsG ist die Schaffung der Voraussetzungen für die Anwendung des Mediationsverfahrens; damit verbundene „Fernziele" sind die Förderung partnerschaftlicher Geschäftsbeziehungen, die Bildung einer Geschäftsethik und die Harmonisierung sozialer Beziehungen (Art. 1 Pkt. 1 russ. MediationsG).

Nach Art. 3 russ. MediationsG gelten im Mediationsverfahren die Grundsätze der Freiwilligkeit, der Vertraulichkeit, der Kooperation und der Gleichberechtigung der Parteien sowie der Unvoreingenommenheit und Unabhängigkeit der Mediatoren.

Art. 4 russ. MediationsG regelt Fragen des Verhältnisses zwischen gerichtlichem bzw. schiedsgerichtlichem Verfahren und der Mediation. Art. 5 und 6 russ. MediationsG enthalten Regelungen zur Sicherung der Vertraulichkeit des Mediationsverfahrens. Art. 7 bis 14 russ. MediationsG regeln die Voraussetzungen, die Einleitung und Durchführung des Mediationsverfahrens sowie die Me-

---

41 Bestätigt durch Verordnung der Regierung der Russischen Föderation Nr. 583 vom 21.09.2006, SZ RF 2006, Nr. 41, Pos. 4248, in der Fassung der Verordnung der Regierung der Russischen Föderation Nr. 271 vom 15.04.2011, SZ RF 2011, Nr. 17, Pos. 2406. Siehe dazu u.a. *Sevast'janov/Cyplenkova*, Tendencii razvitija institucional'nych načal al'ternativnogo razrešenija sporov (Tendenzen der Entwicklung institutioneller Ansätze der alternativen Streitbeilegung), Vestnik VAS RF 2007, Nr. 3, S. 32-43 (33 f.).

42 Gesetzentwurf Nr. 374014-4, eingebracht durch den Abgeordneten des Föderationsrats *Šarandin* und die Abgeordneten der Staatsduma *Pligin* und *Kraševinnikov*, zugänglich über die Datenbank für Gesetzentwürfe der Staatsduma der Russischen Föderation unter http://asozd.duma.gov.ru/ (abgerufen am 30.04.2011).

43 Gesetzentwurf Nr. 126244-5, eingebracht durch die Abgeordneten der Staatsduma *Kraševinnikov*, *Pligin* und *Gruzdev*, zugänglich über die Datenbank für Gesetzentwürfe der Staatsduma der Russischen Föderation unter http://asozd.duma.gov.ru/ (abgerufen am 30.04.2011). Siehe dazu *Kurzynsky-Singer*, Mediation in Russland, in: *Hopt/Steffek*, a.a.O. (Fn. 2), S. 837-851, sowie mit Übersetzung in: Mitteilungen der Vereinigung für deutsch-russisches Wirtschaftsrecht e.V., Nr. 40-41 (Jg. 20/2009), S. 4-27.

44 Gesetzentwurf Nr. 201888-5, eingebracht durch die Gesetzgebende Versammlung von St. Petersburg, zugänglich über die Datenbank für Gesetzentwürfe der Staatsduma der Russischen Föderation unter http://asozd.duma.gov.ru/ (abgerufen am 30.04.2011).

diationsvereinbarung, die als Ergebnis der Mediation angestrebt wird. Den Anforderungen an den Mediator, dessen rechtlicher Stellung und den Selbstregulierungsorganisationen der Mediatoren sind Art. 15 bis 19 russ. MediationsG gewidmet.

Art. 202 russ. ZGB wurde dahingehend ergänzt, dass während eines Mediationsverfahrens die Verjährung gehemmt ist. In der russ. ZPO und der russ. APO wurde ein Zeugnisverweigerungsrecht des Mediators eingeführt, das sich auf alle Umstände bezieht, die dem Mediator in Ausübung seiner Pflichten bekannt geworden sind. Nicht vorgesehen ist ein Zeugnisverweigerungsrecht des Mediators im Strafprozess.

Weitere Änderungen in den Prozessordnungen und im Gesetz über die Schiedsgerichte in der Russischen Föderation sollen die Möglichkeit sichern, das streitige Verfahren in Zivil- und Wirtschaftsstreitigkeiten jederzeit unterbrechen zu können, um einen Versuch der Streitbeilegung durch Mediation zu unternehmen.

Im Gesetz über die Werbung wurde eine Regelung eingefügt, nach der Mediatoren, die keine Schulung zum Mediator durch eine nichtkommerzielle Organisation nachweisen können, für ihre Mediationsdienstleistungen nicht werben dürfen. An danach noch zulässige Werbung für Mediationsdienstleistungen werden bestimmte Anforderungen gestellt (Art. 30.1 Gesetz über die Werbung).

3. Anwendungsbereich des russ. MediationsG

Das russ. MediationsG ist auf Streitigkeiten aus dem Bereich des Zivilrechts, darunter Rechtsverhältnisse im Zusammenhang mit der Ausübung unternehmerischer und anderer wirtschaftlicher Tätigkeit, des Arbeitsrechts und des Familienrechts anzuwenden (Art. 1 Pkt. 2 russ. MediationsG)[45]. Arbeits- und Familienrecht waren gesondert zu nennen, da sie nach der hergebrachten russischen Systematisierung als eigenständige Rechtsgebiete neben dem Zivilrecht gelten.

Ausgenommen sind nach Art. 1 Pkt. 5 russ. MediationsG Streitigkeiten des kollektiven Arbeitsrechts[46] sowie solche Streitigkeiten, die Rechte und Interes-

---

45 Zur Anwendung der Mediation im Strafrecht siehe u.a. *Golovko*, Institut ugolovno-pravovoj mediacii i ego perspektivy v Rossii (Das Institut der strafrechtlichen Mediation und seine Perspektiven in Russland), Zakon 2009, Nr. 4, S. 127-135; *Chidzeva*, Ponjatie mediacii v ugolovnom processe Rossijskoj Federacii (Der Begriff der Mediation im Strafprozess der Russischen Föderation), Rossijskoj sledovatel' 2008, Nr. 23 (zitiert nach der Datenbank Consultant Plus).

46 Für Streitigkeiten des kollektiven Arbeitsrechts sehen Art. 401 ff. Arbeitsgesetzbuch der Russischen Föderation die Durchführung eines Schlichtungsverfahrens vor, das unter Beteiligung eines Vermittlers durchgeführt werden kann. Siehe auch die Empfehlungen über die Organisation der Arbeit betreffend die Behandlung kollektiver Arbeitsstreitigkeiten unter Beteiligung eines Vermittlers, bestätigt durch Verordnung des Ministeriums der Russischen Föderation für Arbeit und soziale Fragen Nr. 58 vom 14.08.2002, Bulletin des Ministeriums der Russischen Föderation für Arbeit und soziale Fragen

sen nicht am Mediationsverfahren beteiligter Dritter oder öffentliche Interessen berühren oder berühren können. Damit kann nicht gemeint sein, dass keine Mediation durchgeführt werden darf, sondern dass Art. 1 Pkt. 5 ebenso wie Art. 1 Pkt. 2 russ. MediationsG allein den Anwendungsbereich des Gesetzes bestimmt. Auf der Tatbestandsseite ist unter anderem fraglich, in welchen Fällen eine Streitigkeit im Sinne der Vorschrift öffentliche Interessen berührt oder berühren kann. Öffentlich-rechtliche Streitigkeiten unterfallen dem russ. MediationsG ohnehin nicht. Es liegt nahe, anzunehmen, dass als *ratio legis* hinter Art. 1 Pkt. 5 russ. MediationsG der Gedanke steht, dass das Mediationsverfahren keine Anwendung findet, soweit der Streitgegenstand der Verfügung der Parteien entzogen ist. Der Wortlaut der Vorschrift lässt aber wohl Raum für eine extensive Auslegung der Vorschrift, die auch in anderen Fällen öffentliche Interessen berührt sieht, etwa dann, wenn an der Streitigkeit öffentlich-rechtlich verfasste Parteien oder staatliche oder staatsnahe Unternehmen beteiligt sind. In solchen Fällen lässt sich gegenwärtig nicht sicher voraussagen, ob die Rechtsfolgen des russ. MediationsG eingreifen. Es mag auch Fälle geben, in denen sich nicht leicht feststellen lässt, inwieweit ein Streit unverfügbare Rechte zum Gegenstand hat[47].

Außerhalb des Anwendungsbereichs des russ. MediationsG liegen ferner die Förderung der Einigung der Parteien durch einen Richter oder Schiedsrichter im Rahmen von Vergleichsverhandlungen während eines Gerichts- bzw. Schiedsgerichtsverfahrens (Art. 1 Pkt. 6 russ. MediationsG).

4. Verhältnis des Mediationsverfahrens zum streitigen Verfahren

Nach Art. 1 Pkt. 4 russ. MediationsG kann das Mediationsverfahren durchgeführt werden, nachdem eine Streitigkeit vor einem Gericht oder Schiedsgericht anhängig gemacht wurde. In Art. 7 Pkt. 2 russ. MediationsG wird klargestellt, dass das Mediationsverfahren sowohl vor Beginn eines streitigen Verfahrens als auch während eines solchen Verfahrens stattfinden kann. Während eines streitigen Verfahrens kann der Richter oder Schiedsrichter die Durchführung des Mediationsverfahrens vorschlagen. Eine verbindliche Verweisungsmöglichkeit des

---

2002, Nr. 8 (zitiert nach der Datenbank Consultant Plus); dazu *Begaeva,* Institut mediacii – al'ternativnyj sposob razrešenija korporativnych konfliktov (Das Institut der Mediation als alternatives Verfahren zur Beilegung gesellschaftsrechtlicher Konflikte), Predprinimatel'skoe pravo 2008, Nr. 3 (zitiert nach der Datenbank Consultant Plus).

47 Zur Auslegung des Begriffs der unverfügbaren Rechte im Sinne der Mediationsrichtlinie vgl. etwa *Eidenmüller/Prause*, Die europäische Mediationsrichtlinie – Perspektiven für eine gesetzliche Regelung der Mediation in Deutschland, NJW 2008, S. 2737-2743 (2740).

Richters in das Mediationsverfahren[48] bzw. Kostensanktionen für mediationsunwillige Parteien sind nicht vorgesehen.

Die neue Regelung des russ. MediationsG betrifft nur die außergerichtliche Mediation und als Unterfall davon die gerichtsnahe Mediation. Anders als in Deutschland, wo die Mediation auch innerhalb des Gerichts von einem nicht mit der Sache befassten Richter als Mediator bereits in vielen Bundesländern erfolgreich durchgeführt wird[49], behandelt das russ. MediationsG die richterliche bzw. gerichtsinterne Mediation nicht. Aus der deutschen Erfahrung kann dazu angemerkt werden, dass Parteien, die ihre Streitigkeit bereits bei Gericht anhängig gemacht haben, häufig nicht mehr bereit sind, das Verfahren noch einmal in den außergerichtlichen Bereich zu verlagern[50]. Zudem wird sich bei der außergerichtlichen Mediation einer bereits anhängigen Streitigkeit die Kostenproblematik stellen, da durch die Einschaltung einer außergerichtlichen Mediation in der Regel zusätzliche Kosten für die Parteien entstehen, was diese von der Inanspruchnahme des Mediationsverfahrens abschrecken könnte (zu möglichen Kostenerleichterungen siehe unter III.7.).

Gemäß Art. 4 Pkt. 1 russ. MediationsG haben die staatlichen Gerichte und die Schiedsgerichte eine Mediationsklausel der Parteien zu beachten. Die Klage ist ohne Behandlung in der Sache (als unzulässig) „zurückzugeben" (vgl. z.B. Art. 134 russ. ZPO) und kann erneut erhoben werden, wenn die Voraussetzungen der Mediationsklausel für eine Klageerhebung erfüllt sind. Allerdings kann jede Partei der Mediationsklausel nach Art. 4 Pkt. 1 a.E. russ. MediationsG jederzeit Klage erheben, wenn dies nach ihrer Ansicht zum Schutz ihrer Rechte erforderlich ist. Damit wird zwar dem Grundsatz der Freiwilligkeit des Mediationsverfahrens genüge getan, jedoch auch die zuvor aufgestellte Regel weitgehend entwertet, so dass sich die Frage stellt, welche Funktion Art. 4 Pkt. 1 russ. MediationsG zukommen soll. Art. 7 Pkt. 3 russ. MediationsG bekräftigt noch

---

48 Kritisch hierzu *Vasin*, Obzor izmenenij arbitražnogo processual'nogo zakonodatel'stva v 2010 g. (Überblick über die Änderungen der Arbitrageprozessgesetzgebung im Jahr 2010), Vestnik VAS RF 2011, Nr. 3, S. 103-116 (114 f.); *Lisicyn*, Mediacija – važnyj ėlement pravovoj kul'tury rossijskogo biznesa (Die Mediation als ein wichtiges Element der Rechtskultur der russischen Geschäftswelt), Vestnik Arbitražnogo suda goroda Moskvy 2009, Nr. 2 (zitiert nach der Datenbank Consultant Plus).

49 Für eine Übersicht der Modellprojekte und die Fundstellen der wissenschaftlichen Begleitprojekte siehe *Greger*, Justiz und Mediation – Entwicklungslinien nach Abschluss der Modellprojekte, NJW 2007, S. 3258-3262; *Seibert*, Mediation in der Verwaltungsgerichtsbarkeit. Erfahrungen und Überlegungen zu einer alternativen Streitbeilegung, NVwZ 2008, S. 365-370.

50 *Greger*, a.a.O. (Fn. 49), S. 3260.

einmal, dass die Parteien auch bei Vorliegen einer Mediationsklausel nicht daran gehindert sind, Klage zu erheben[51].

Art. 4 Pkt. 2 russ. MediationsG verweist für die Möglichkeit der Aussetzung eines streitigen Verfahrens auf die jeweilige Prozessordnung. Nach Art. 158 Pkt. 7 russ. APO und Art. 169 Pkt. 1 russ. ZPO jeweils in der ab 01.01.2011 geltenden Fassung kann das gerichtliche Verfahren für bis zu 60 Tage ausgesetzt werden, wenn die Parteien einen Vermittlungsversuch durch ein Mediationsverfahren unternehmen.

Nach der Änderung des Gesetzes über die Schiedsgerichte in der Russischen Föderation ist ein Schiedsverfahren unzulässig, wenn zwischen den Parteien eine Mediationsklausel vereinbart ist (Art. 5 Pkt. 5 des Föderalen Gesetzes über die Schiedsgerichte in der Russischen Föderation n.F.).

5. Durchführung des Mediationsverfahrens

Ein Mediationsverfahren wird nach Art. 7 Pkt. 1 russ. MediationsG auf der Grundlage einer schriftlichen „Vereinbarung über die Anwendung des Mediationsverfahrens" (*soglašenie o primenenii procedury mediacii*, vgl. Art. 2 Nr. 5 russ. MediationsG) durchgeführt, deren Inhalt die Übereinkunft der Parteien ist, in Bezug auf bestimmte Streitigkeiten das Mediationsverfahren anzuwenden.

Das Mediationsverfahren beginnt nach Art. 7 Pkt. 4 russ. MediationsG mit dem Abschluss einer schriftlichen „Vereinbarung über die Durchführung des Mediationsverfahrens" (*soglašenie o provedenii procedury mediacii*, vgl. Art. 2 Nr. 6 russ. MediationsG), die die in Art. 8 Pkt. 2 russ. MediationsG aufgezählten Mindestangaben enthält. Wenn die Parteien ohne eine solche Vereinbarung ein Mediationsverfahren beginnen, so finden nach dem Wortlaut des Gesetzes die Rechtsfolgen, die an ein Mediationsverfahren geknüpft sind, keine Anwendung. So läuft etwa die Verjährung weiter und die Regelungen zum Schutz der Vertraulichkeit greifen nicht ein.

Die Parteien können den Mediator selbst auswählen. Falls das Mediationsverfahren durch eine Organisation zur Gewährleistung der Durchführung des Mediationsverfahrens durchgeführt wird, kann diese auf Ersuchen der Parteien einen Mediator empfehlen oder ernennen (Art. 9 Pkt. 1, 2 russ. MediationsG).

Das russ. MediationsG sieht vor, dass die Parteien das Verfahren der Mediation selbst regeln können und dabei auch auf eine Verfahrensordnung, die von einer Organisation zur Gewährleistung der Durchführung des Mediationsverfahrens zur Verfügung gestellt wird[52], verweisen können (Art. 11 Pkt. 1 und 2 russ.

---

51 Zum Spannungsverhältnis zwischen der Freiwilligkeit des Mediationsverfahrens und der erzwungenen Durchsetzbarkeit von Mediationsabreden siehe *Hopt/Steffek*, a.a.O. (Fn. 2), S. 26 f.

52 Siehe u.a. die Verfahrensordnung des Kollegiums der Vermittler bei der Industrie- und Handelskammer der Russischen Föderation, bestätigt durch Erlass der Industrie- und Handelskammer der Russischen Föderation Nr. 32 vom 12.05.2006, zugänglich über die

MediationsG). Der Mediator ist vorbehaltlich einer anderen Bestimmung durch die Parteien nicht berechtigt, eigene Vorschläge zur Streitbeilegung zu unterbreiten (Art. 11 Pkt. 5 russ. MediationsG).

Gemäß Art. 13 russ. MediationsG sollen der Mediator und die Parteien sich bemühen, das Mediationsverfahren innerhalb von 60 Tagen zu beenden. Das Mediationsverfahren endet automatisch nach 180 Tagen bzw. – sofern das Mediationsverfahren durchgeführt wird, nachdem die Streitigkeit bei einem Gericht oder Schiedsgericht anhängig gemacht wurde – nach 60 Tagen (vgl. Art. 14 Nr. 5 russ. MediationsG). Die Rechtsfolgen einer solchen Beendigung des Mediationsverfahrens sind nicht ausdrücklich geregelt. Grundsätzlich werden die durch das Gesetz festgelegten Rechtsfolgen des Vorliegens des Mediationsverfahrens wegfallen. Einzelne Rechtsfolgen knüpfen dagegen nicht an das Fortbestehen des Mediationsverfahrens an. So wird sich das Zeugnisverweigerungsrecht des Mediators auch auf Tatsachen erstrecken, die dem Mediator nach Ablauf der Höchstdauer des Mediationsverfahrens bekannt geworden sind, wenn das Mediationsverfahren entgegen dem russ. MediationsG fortdauert. Das Gesetz stellt nur darauf ab, ob der Mediator von den Tatsachen in Ausübung seiner Pflichten Kenntnis erlangt hat.

Erzielen die Parteien im Mediationsverfahren eine Einigung, wird diese in einer schriftlichen „Mediationsvereinbarung" (*mediativnoe soglašenie*, vgl. Art. 2 Nr. 7 russ. MediationsG) festgehalten. Diese Vereinbarung muss nach Art. 12 Pkt. 1 russ. MediationsG Angaben über die Parteien, den Gegenstand der Streitigkeit, das durchgeführte Mediationsverfahren, den Mediator und die von den Parteien vereinbarten Verpflichtungen und Bedingungen sowie die Fristen für deren Erfüllung enthalten. Mit dem Abschluss der Mediationsvereinbarung endet das Mediationsverfahren (Art. 14 Nr. 1 russ. MediationsG). Weitere Beendigungsgründe sind in Art. 14 russ. MediationsG geregelt.

6. Vertraulichkeitsschutz, Verjährungshemmung, Vollstreckbarkeit

Das russ. MediationsG enthält Rahmenregelungen mit dem Ziel der Einbindung der Mediation in das Zivilverfahrens- und Verjährungsrecht. Es handelt sich um Vorschriften des Vertraulichkeitsschutzes, zur Hemmung der Verjährung und zur Vollstreckung von Mediationsvereinbarungen.

a) Vertraulichkeitsschutz

Art. 5 russ. MediationsG enthält Regelungen zur Sicherung der Vertraulichkeit des Mediationsverfahrens. Er verpflichtet den Mediator zur Verschwiegenheit über alle Informationen, die das Mediationsverfahren betreffen oder ihm bei der

Datenbank Consultant Plus unter www.consultant.ru/, in deutscher Übersetzung abgedruckt bei *Kurzynsky-Singer*, Mediation in Russland, in: Mitteilungen der Vereinigung für deutsch-russisches Wirtschaftsrecht e.V., Nr. 40-41 (Jg. 20/2009), S. 28-38.

Durchführung des Mediationsverfahrens bekannt geworden sind. Flankiert wird diese Regelung durch ein neu eingeführtes Zeugnisverweigerungsrecht des Mediators im Zivil- und Wirtschaftsprozess (Art. 69 Pkt. 3 Nr. 1 russ. ZGB, Art. 56 Pkt. 5.1 russ. APO, jeweils in der geänderten Fassung), das sich auf alle Tatsachen erstreckt, die dem Mediator in Erfüllung seiner Verpflichtungen bekannt geworden sind. Zusätzlich soll es nach Art. 5 Pkt. 4 russ. MediationsG vorbehaltlich anderweitiger gesetzlicher Regelungen unzulässig sein, von dem Mediator oder der Organisation zur Gewährleistung der Durchführung des Mediationsverfahrens Informationen über das Mediationsverfahren heraus zu verlangen. Dem Mediator ist es ferner untersagt, Informationen, die er von einer der Parteien erhalten hat, ohne deren Zustimmung an die andere Partei weiterzugeben (Art. 6 russ. MediationsG).

Den Parteien und sonstigen am Mediationsverfahren Beteiligten ist es nach Art. 5 Pkt. 3 russ. MediationsG verwehrt, sich in streitigen Verfahren vor einem Gericht oder Schiedsgericht auf bestimmte Tatsachen, die die Verhandlungs- oder Einigungsbereitschaft einer der Parteien im Mediationsverfahren betreffen, zu berufen. Damit wird klargestellt, dass die Vertraulichkeit als elementarer Grundsatz des Mediationsverfahrens grundsätzlich für alle Beteiligten gilt. Ein Zeugnisverweigerungsrecht der Rechtsberater und sonstiger beteiligter Dritter ist damit allerdings nicht verbunden[53].

b) Verjährungshemmung

Im Gesetzentwurf, der in die Staatsduma eingebracht wurde, war vorgesehen, dass die Verjährung durch das Mediationsverfahren unterbrochen wird und der Lauf der Verjährung danach neu beginnt. Diese Regelung wurde im weiteren Verlauf des Gesetzgebungsverfahrens geändert; die Mediation hemmt nun lediglich den Lauf der Verjährung. Dies entspricht dem Modell, das in der Konzeption zur Fortentwicklung der Zivilgesetzgebung[54] vorgeschlagen wird. Eine Regelung, nach der nach Hemmung der Verjährung durch ein Mediationsverfahren eine Mindestfrist für die Verjährung verbleibt[55], enthält das ZGB dagegen nicht.

c) Vollstreckbarkeit der Mediationsvereinbarung

Vollstreckbar ist eine Einigung in der Sache, die die Parteien als Ergebnis einer Mediation in einer Mediationsvereinbarung erzielt haben, nach Art. 12 Pkt. 3 russ. MediationsG nur, wenn die Streitigkeit bereits bei einem Gericht oder

53 Zum Adressenkreis der Vertraulichkeitspflichten siehe *Hopt/Steffek*, a.a.O. (Fn. 2), S. 39 ff.

54 Konzeption zur Fortentwicklung der Zivilgesetzgebung, angenommen durch Beschluss vom 07.10.2009 des Rats für Kodifikation und Vervollkommnung der Zivilgesetzgebung beim Präsidenten der Russischen Föderation, abrufbar unter http://www.privlaw.ru/vs_info8.html (abgerufen am 30.04.2011).

55 Sog. Ablaufhemmung wie sie etwa in § 203 S. 2 des deutschen BGB und in Art. 1.129 Pkt. 3 lt. ZGB vorgesehen ist.

Schiedsgericht anhängig war und die Mediationsvereinbarung als Prozessvergleich bestätigt wird. Anderenfalls ist die Einigung der Parteien lediglich ein zivilrechtlicher Vertrag, aus dem erneut geklagt werden muss, wenn er nicht erfüllt wird (Art. 12 Pkt. 4 russ. MediationsG). Diese Regelung trägt dem Umstand Rechnung, dass nur geringe Anforderungen an das Verfahren der Mediation und die materielle Ausgewogenheit der Mediationsvereinbarung vorgesehen sind. Eine im Gesetzentwurf noch enthaltene Regelung der notariellen Beglaubigung der Mediationsvereinbarung und die damit verbundene Vollstreckbarkeit wurde später gestrichen[56].

Die in Art. 12 Pkt. 3 russ. MediationsG vorgesehene gerichtliche Bestätigung der Mediationsvereinbarung als Prozessvergleich erfolgt durch das Gericht, bei dem die Streitigkeit anhängig ist. Das Gericht muss die Bestätigung verweigern, wenn durch sie das Gesetz oder Rechte oder gesetzmäßige Interessen anderer Personen verletzt würden (Art. 39 Pkt. 2 russ. ZPO; für den Wirtschaftsprozess etwas abweichend Art. 49 Pkt. 5 russ. APO). Dem Prozessgericht obliegt damit eine gewisse Prüfungspflicht hinsichtlich des Inhalts und des Zustandekommens der Mediationsvereinbarung[57]. Insbesondere im Hinblick darauf, dass auch Nichtjuristen als Mediatoren tätig sein können, scheint es erforderlich, dass das Gericht bzw. Schiedsgericht in dem Bestätigungsbeschluss bestimmt, in welchem Umfang der Gegenstand des anhängigen Verfahrens durch eine Mediationsvereinbarung tatsächlich erledigt ist.

7. Rechtliche Stellung des Mediators

Ausführliche Regelungen enthält das russ. MediationsG zur rechtlichen Stellung des Mediators. Nach dem Modell des russ. MediationsG können sog. Organisationen zur Gewährleistung der Durchführung des Mediationsverfahrens z.B. Verfahrensregelungen zur Verfügung stellen und Mediatoren empfehlen bzw. auf ein entsprechendes Ersuchen der Parteien ernennen. Anforderungen an diese Organisationen, wie z.B. eine Lizenzierung oder Akkreditierung oder das Erfordernis der Mitgliedschaft in einer Selbstregulierungsorganisation, sind nicht vorgesehen. Folglich besteht auch keinerlei Kontrolle durch staatliche Organe[58].

---

56 Siehe dazu den Bericht über die wissenschaftlich-praktische Tagung „Mediacija i ee vozmožnosti v rasrešenii korporativnych, mežkorporativnych i kommerčeskich sporov" (Die Mediation und ihre Möglichkeiten bei der Beilegung gesellschaftlicher, zwischengesellschaftlicher und kommerzieller Streitigkeiten), Vestnik Arbitražnogo suda goroda Moskvy 2007, Nr. 4 (zitiert nach der Datenbank Consultant Plus).

57 Dazu *Jarkov*, in: *Jarkov* (Hrsg.), Graždanskij process (Zivilprozess), 7. Aufl., Moskau 2009, Kapitel 14 § 5(6), S. 296 ff.; *Rogožin*, Primirenie storon v arbitražnom sudoproizvodstve: nekotorye praktičeskie aspekty (Aussöhnung der Parteien in der Arbitragegerichtsbarkeit: einige praktische Aspekte), Zakon 2003, Nr. 12, S. 47-55 (mit Rechtsprechungsnachweisen).

58 Eine solche staatliche Kontrolle wird gefordert von *Begaeva,* a.a.O. (Fn. 46).

Das russ. MediationsG sieht vor, dass die Tätigkeit des Mediators sowohl beruflich als auch nicht-beruflich ausgeübt werden kann (Art. 15 Pkt. 1 russ. MediationsG). Der Unterschied besteht vor allem in den Anforderungen an den Mediator und den gesetzlichen Beschränkungen für den Einsatz nicht-beruflicher Mediatoren. Ein nicht-beruflicher Mediator kann vor allem dann tätig werden, wenn die zwischen den Parteien erzielte Einigung nicht formalisiert werden muss, wie dies z.B. bei Nachbarschaftsstreitigkeiten oder Streitigkeiten im Arbeitskollektiv der Fall sein kann. Sofern eine Streitigkeit bereits vor einem Gericht oder Schiedsgericht anhängig ist, kann das Verfahren nur an einen beruflich tätigen Mediator abgegeben werden (Art. 16 Abs. 3 russ. MediationsG). Ein weiteres Privileg für beruflich tätige Mediatoren ist, dass nur für deren Dienstleistungen zur Durchführung des Mediationsverfahrens geworben werden kann (vgl. Art. 30.1 Pkt. 1 des Gesetzes über die Werbung).

Beruflich kann als Mediator nur tätig sein, wer ein berufsqualifizierendes Hochschulstudium abgeschlossen und einen Schulungskurs für Mediatoren besucht hat. Eine Lizenzierung oder Akkreditierung der Mediatoren ist nicht vorgesehen[59]. Keine Aussagen enthält das Gesetz über den Inhalt und die Dauer des Schulungskurses und damit zu den fachlichen Anforderungen an die Qualifikation von Mediatoren. Fragen der beruflichen Qualifikation bleiben den berufsständigen Organisationen überlassen, die entsprechende Standards der Ausbildung von Mediatoren erarbeiten (Art. 19 Nr. 8 russ. MediationsG). Das Schulungsprogramm wird nach einem von der Regierung der Russischen Föderation festgelegten Verfahren bestätigt (vgl. Art. 16 Pkt. 1 russ. MediationsG)[60]. Der dort vorgesehene Basiskurs für die Ausbildung von Mediatoren besteht aus 120 Unterrichtsstunden, einschließlich Seminaren und praktischen Übungen. Eine Organisation, die derzeit Schulungskurse für Mediatoren anbietet, ist z.B. das „Wissenschaftlich methodische Zentrum für Mediation und Recht“ in Moskau[61]. Darüber hinaus führt das Zentrum an drei Hochschulen in Moskau für Studierende ein Programm zur Einführung in die Mediation durch.

Nach Art. 15 Pkt. 5 russ. MediationsG können Personen nicht als Mediatoren tätig sein, die ein staatliches Amt der Russischen Föderation oder eines Subjekts der Russischen Föderation, ein Amt im zivilen Staatsdienst oder ein Amt im kommunalen Dienst innehaben. Damit sind auch Richter von der Tätigkeit als Mediatoren ausgeschlossen. Aus dem Gesetz über die Rechtsstellung der

59 Kritisch zu dieser „liberalen Regelung“ *Lisicyn*, a.a.O. (Fn. 48).

60 Siehe den Erlass des Ministeriums der Russischen Föderation für Wissenschaft und Bildung Nr. 187 vom 14.02.2011 über die Bestätigung des Schulungsprogramms der Mediatoren, Rossijskaja gazeta vom 23.03.2011, der aufgrund der Verordnung der Regierung der Russischen Föderation Nr. 969 vom 03.12.2010 über das Schulungsprogramm der Mediatoren, SZ RF 2010, Nr. 50, Pos. 6706, ergangen ist.

61 Internetseite des Zentrums: http://mediacia.com/ (abgerufen am 30.04.2011).

Richter[62] folgt ferner, dass auch Richter im Ruhestand jedenfalls keine entgeltlichen Mediationsdienstleistungen anbieten können (Art. 3 Pkt. 4 i.V.m. Pkt. 3 Nr. 5)[63].

Durch das russ. MediationsG werden ausführlich die Rechte und Pflichten der Mediatoren geregelt. Eine wichtige Rolle spielen die Regeln über die Vertraulichkeit, die Unabhängigkeit und die Unvoreingenommenheit des Mediators.

Im Unterschied zur Tätigkeit des Mediators, die entgeltlich oder unentgeltlich durchgeführt werden kann, ist die Tätigkeit von Organisationen zur Gewährleistung der Durchführung des Mediationsverfahrens entgeltlich. Die Vergütung erfolgt durch die Parteien mangels anderweitiger Vereinbarung zu gleichen Anteilen (Art. 10 Pkt. 1, 2 russ. MediationsG). Staatliche Zuschüsse für gering Verdienende sind nicht vorgesehen. Bei einer erfolgreichen Mediation kann jedoch dem Kläger die Hälfte der Gerichtsgebühren zurückerstattet werden (vgl. Art. 141 Pkt. 7 Nr. 3 APO)[64].

Nach Art. 17 russ. MediationsG richtet sich die Haftung der Mediatoren und Organisationen zur Gewährleistung der Durchführung des Mediationsverfahrens für ihre Tätigkeit nach den allgemeinen zivilrechtlichen Vorschriften.

Beruflich tätige Mediatoren sowie Organisationen zur Gewährleistung der Durchführung des Mediationsverfahrens können sich in Selbstregulierungsorganisationen zusammenschließen, die die Tätigkeit ihrer Mitglieder regulieren und die Einhaltung der aufgestellten Regeln kontrollieren (vgl. Art. 18 und 19 russ. MediationsG). Keine Regelung enthält das Gesetz über die Kontrolle der Tätigkeit der Mediatoren, die keiner Selbstregulierungsorganisation angehören.

8. Bewertung der gesetzlichen Regelung in Russland

Mit der neuen Regelung zur Mediation greift der Gesetzgeber wichtige Fragen der gesetzlichen Unterstützung privatautonomer statt hoheitlicher Streitbeilegung im Wege von Mediationsverfahren auf. Das Gesetz räumt in einem wichtigen Teilbereich der Streitbeilegung durch Verhandlungen zwischen den Parteien rechtliche Hindernisse für den Einsatz von Mediation aus und setzt gewisse Anreize für deren Einsatz. In welchem Maß dadurch die Zahl von Mediationsverfahren tatsächlich ansteigt und damit auch eine spürbare Entlastung für das Gerichtswesen eintritt, wird allerdings mehr als von der – begrüßenswerten – rechtlichen Regelung von tatsächlichen Umständen abhängen, insbesondere dem Vertrauen der Parteien in das Mediationsverfahren.

---

62 Gesetz der Russischen Föderation Nr. 3132-1 vom 26.06.1992, Vedomosti S''ezda narodnych deputatov i Verchovnogo Soveta Rossijskoj Federacii 1992, Nr. 30, Pos. 1792, mit späteren Änderungen.

63 Ebenso *Lukonkina* im Interview mit Zakon 2010, Nr. 8, S. 72-76 (74).

64 *Kurzynsky-Singer*, Mediation in Russland, in: *Hopt/Steffek*, a.a.O. (Fn. 43), S. 842.

Auch wenn die neue gesetzliche Regelung, mit deren Erlass eine der im Regierungsprogramm zur Entwicklung des Gerichtssystems in Russland[65] vorgesehenen Maßnahmen umgesetzt worden ist, nicht messbar dazu beitragen wird, bis 2012 das Vertrauen der Bevölkerung in das Gerichtssystem zu stärken[66], mag sie mittelfristig durchaus zu einer Änderung der Einstellung zum Gerichtssystem und zu dessen Entlastung beitragen.

IV. Schlussbemerkungen

Sowohl in Litauen als auch in Russland ist die Mediation in einem eigenständigen Gesetz geregelt. Während Litauen durch die Mediationsrichtlinie zur Etablierung und aktiven Förderung der Mediation verpflichtet ist, erfolgte die gesetzliche Verankerung der Mediation in Russland ohne vergleichbare Veranlassung von außen. Der russische Gesetzgeber erhofft sich vom Einsatz von Mediationsverfahren u.a. eine Entlastung der Gerichte und damit einhergehend einen effizienteren Einsatz finanzieller und personeller Ressourcen.

Bei der Auswahl des Regelungsmodells hat man sich in Russland für eine eher weitgehende Regulierung der Mediation entschieden, während Litauen einen zurückhaltenderen regulatorischen Ansatz gewählt hat, der in großen Teilen auf die selbstregulierenden Kräfte des Markts, also das Spiel von Angebot von und Nachfrage nach Mediationsdienstleistungen, baut[67]. Vom Regelungsbereich sind in beiden Ländern das Zivil- und das Handelsrecht umfasst. Das Arbeits- und das Familienrecht waren in Russland neben dem Zivilrecht gesondert zu nennen, da sie traditionell als eigenständige Rechtsgebiete gelten. In Litauen ist es dem Gesetzgeber vorbehalten, für einzelne Kategorien zivilrechtlicher Streitigkeiten besondere Bestimmungen für das Mediationsverfahren vorzusehen.

In Bezug auf das Verhältnis der Mediation zum Gerichtsverfahren sieht das lt. MediationsG wie der deutsche Gesetzentwurf[68] Regelungen zur gerichtsexternen, gerichtsnahen und gerichtsinternen Mediation vor, während das russ. MediationsG die außergerichtliche und als Unterfall die gerichtsnahe Mediation regelt. Eine gerichtsinterne Mediation ist von der russischen Regelung nicht erfasst. Mediationsabreden scheinen nach der litauischen Regelung eher als nach der entsprechenden russischen Regelung durchsetzbar zu sein. Zwar haben die russischen Gerichte eine Mediationsklausel der Parteien zu beachten. Allerdings sind die Parteien auch bei Vorliegen einer Mediationsabrede nicht daran gehindert, zum Schutz ihrer Rechte Klage zu erheben. Sowohl in Litauen als auch in Russland können die Richter den Parteien eine Streitbeilegung im Mediationsverfahren vorschlagen. Eine verbindliche Verweisungsmöglichkeit des Richters

65 Fundstelle siehe oben Fn. 41.

66 Zielvorgabe des Programms ist etwa eine Steigerung des Anteils der Bevölkerung, die den Organen der Rechtsprechung vertrauen, von 19% (2006) auf 50% (2011).

67 Zu den unterschiedlichen Regelungsmodellen siehe *Hopt/Steffek*, a.a.O. (Fn. 2), S. 18 ff.

68 Siehe oben Fn. 7.

in das Mediationsverfahren bzw. Kostensanktionen für mediationsunwillige Parteien sind nicht vorgesehen.

In beiden Ländern ist während eines Mediationsverfahrens die Verjährung gehemmt. In Litauen gilt dies bisher jedoch nur für die verkürzten Verjährungsfristen; eine Ausdehnung auf sämtliche Verjährungsfristen ist mit Blick auf die vollständige Umsetzung der Mediationsrichtlinie geplant. Im Unterschied zur russischen Regelung sieht das litauische Gesetz darüber hinaus eine sog. Ablaufhemmung vor.

Hinsichtlich der gesetzlichen Verankerung des Vertraulichkeitsschutzes sehen beide Gesetze materiell-rechtliche Verschwiegenheits- und sonstige Vertraulichkeitspflichten des Mediators, der Parteien und sonstiger am Mediationsverfahren Beteiligter vor. Darüber hinaus gelten für die Parteien und sonstige am Mediationsverfahren Beteiligte Vortrags- und Beweismittelbeschränkungen in Gerichts- und Schiedsgerichtsverfahren. In Russland wurde zudem ein Zeugnisverweigerungsrecht des Mediators im Zivil- und Wirtschaftsprozess eingeführt.

Das Mediationsverfahren wird durch das russ. MediationsG im Vergleich zum lt. MediationsG relativ umfangreich reguliert, u.a. stellt es Mindestanforderungen an die Vereinbarung über die Durchführung der Mediation sowie die Mediationsvereinbarung auf und enthält Regelungen über die Dauer des Mediationsverfahrens. Nach beiden Gesetzen können die Parteien sowohl den Mediator als auch die Verfahrensordnung selbst bestimmen. Die bei einer erfolgreichen Mediation getroffene Vereinbarung wird in Litauen in einem Vergleich, in Russland in einer Mediationsvereinbarung schriftlich festgehalten. War die Streitigkeit vor Durchführung der Mediation bereits gerichtlich anhängig, wird der Vergleich bzw. die Mediationsvereinbarung jeweils durch Gerichtsbeschluss bestätigt. In Litauen kann der in der Mediation geschlossene Vergleich auf Antrag der Parteien darüber hinaus auch bei einer nicht gleichzeitig gerichtlich anhängigen Streitigkeit durch Beschluss gerichtlich bestätigt werden. Dem Gericht obliegt dabei in beiden Ländern eine materielle Prüfungspflicht hinsichtlich des Inhalts und des Zustandekommens der Vereinbarung. Eine durch rechtskräftigen Gerichtsbeschluss bestätigte Vereinbarung ist sowohl in Litauen als auch in Russland vollstreckbar.

Während Litauen auf eine Regulierung des Berufsrechts der Mediatoren derzeit verzichtet und diese Aufgabe den Marktteilnehmern überlässt, unterscheidet das russ. MediationsG zwischen beruflich und nicht-beruflich tätigen Mediatoren. Gesetzliche Anforderungen an die Ausbildung der Mediatoren gelten nur für beruflich tätige Mediatoren, die mit Privilegien bei der gerichtsnahen Mediation und der Werbung für Mediationsdienstleistungen einhergehen. Ferner können sich nur beruflich tätige Mediatoren in Selbstregulierungsorganisationen zusammenschließen.

Das Gesetz über Gruppenklagen in Polen

Rechtsanwältin Tina de Vries[*]

I. Einleitung

Innerhalb der Europäischen Union findet seit Jahren eine Diskussion über die Verbesserung des Verbraucherschutzes durch die Effektivierung des Rechtsschutzsystems für Verbraucherklagen statt. Auch in der verbraucherpolitischen Strategie für die Jahre 2007 bis 2013 legte die EU-Kommission einen besonderen Schwerpunkt auf die Prüfung der Rechtsdurchsetzung. Neben anderen Verfahren der sog. *Alternative Dispute Resolution* (ADR) gilt die besondere Aufmerksamkeit den kollektiven Rechtsschutzverfahren. In Polen wurde Ende 2009 ein Gesetz über die Regelung von Gruppenklagen verabschiedet[1], das vor allem im Bereich des Verbraucherschutzes neue Rechtsschutzmöglichkeiten eröffnen soll.

II. Der Diskussionsstand über Gruppenklagen (Collective-Redress-Verfahren) auf EU-Ebene

Die Kommission befasst sich mit der Regelung der ADR-Verfahren im Bereich der Verbraucherstreitigkeiten schon seit längerem. In den 1990er Jahren wurde diese Thematik z.B. im Grünbuch Zugang der Verbraucher zum Recht und Beilegung von Rechtsstreitigkeiten der Verbraucher im Binnenmarkt[2], im Aktionsplan Zugang der Verbraucher zum Recht und die Beilegung von Rechtsstreitigkeiten im Binnenmarkt, in der Empfehlung der Kommission 98/257/EG vom 30. März 1998 betreffend die Grundsätze für Einrichtungen, die für die außergerichtliche Beilegung von Verbraucherrechtsstreitigkeiten zuständig sind[3], und weiteren Dokumenten behandelt. Eine Bestandsaufnahme über die vorhandenen alternativen Streitbeilegungsverfahren in den Mitgliedstaaten der EU, aber auch in einigen Staaten außerhalb der EU wurde ausführlich in dem sog. Leuven-Bericht[4] vorgelegt. Überprüft wurden dabei konkret die Regelungen bezüglich der direkten Verhandlungen, der Mediation, der Schlichtung, der Prozesse wegen kleinerer Ansprüche (*small claim procedures*), der Kollektivklagen

---

* Wissenschaftl. Referentin für polnisches Recht am IOR.

1 Eine Übersetzung der Autorin findet sich unter Punkt IV.

2 KOM/93/576 endgültig.

3 *ABl. Nr. L 115 vom 17.04.1998, S. 31–34.*

4 *J. Stuyck/E. Terryn*, An Analysis and Evaluation of Alternative Means of Consumer Redress Other than Redress through Ordinary Judicial Proceedings. Final Report, Leuven 2007.

(*collective redress*) wegen Schadensersatz und der Kollektivklagen wegen Unterlassung.

Dabei wurde festgestellt, dass im Bereich der Verfahren für kleinere Ansprüche in den Mitgliedstaaten bereits verschiedene Regelungen vorhanden sind, die allerdings nicht auf Verbraucherstreitigkeiten beschränkt sind, sonder für das gesamte Spektrum zivilrechtlicher Streitigkeiten zur Verfügung stehen. Die Kommission folgerte daraus, dass weitere Anstrengungen für die Etablierung von Rechtsschutzmöglichkeiten unternommen werden müssen.

Zuletzt legte die Kommission 2008 das Grünbuch über kollektive Rechtsdurchsetzungsverfahren für Verbraucher[5] vor. Dem folgte die Mitteilung der Kommission an das Europäische Parlament, den Rat, den Europäischen Wirtschafts- und Sozialausschuss und den Ausschuss der Regionen zum Stand der Durchsetzung des gemeinschaftlichen Besitzstands im Verbraucherschutz[6], in der erneut auf das Grünbuch Bezug genommen wurde. Als Diskussionsgrundlage für weitere Vorschläge innerhalb der EU dient gegenwärtig das „Consultation Paper for Discussion on the Follow-Up to the Green Paper on Consumer Collective Redress“[7], das die Diskussion über Gruppenklagen weiter anregen soll.

Das Grünbuch der Kommission über kollektive Rechtsdurchsetzungsverfahren für Verbraucher stellt verschiedene Optionen für zukünftige EU-Verbraucherschutzinstrumentarien vor, darunter – in einer vierten Option – auch die Schaffung der Möglichkeit von Gruppenklagen. Ein wichtiger Aspekt bei der Abwägung von kollektiven Rechtsschutzinstrumenten für Verbraucher ist die Entscheidung, ob ein Opt-in- oder ein Opt-out-Verfahren eingeführt werden soll[8]. Die Befragten äußerten sich zu den vorgestellten Optionen sehr unterschiedlich. Die Rückmeldungen wurden in der Zusammenfassung der Haupttrends der öffentlichen Anhörung zu Verbrauchergruppenklagen vom 29.05.2009[9] dargestellt.

---

5 KOM (2008) 794 endgültig.

6 KOM (2009) 330 endgültig.

7 Einzusehen unter http://ec.europa.eu/consumers/redress_cons/collective_redress_en.htm#Consultation, zuletzt aufgerufen am 26.03.2010.

8 Dazu das Grünbuch über kollektive Rechtsdurchsetzungsverfahren für Verbraucher, KOM (2008) 794 endgültig, Rn. 54.

9 Einzusehen unter http://ec.europa.eu/consumers/redress_cons/docs/overview_results_coll_redress_en.pdf, zuletzt aufgerufen am 12.04.2010.

III. Die Regelung von Gruppenklagen in Polen

1. Bisheriger Stand der Regelung

In Polen gab es vor der Verabschiedung des Gesetzes über Gruppenklagen für sog. „kleine Klagen" das vereinfachte Verfahren[10]. Dieses Verfahren ist nach der ausdrücklichen Bestimmung des Art. 505[1] Zivilverfahrensgesetzbuch[11] auch auf Verbraucherstreitigkeiten anzuwenden, wenn der Streitwert oder der Wert der Forderung 10.000,- PLN nicht übersteigt. Gruppenverfahren im eigentlichen Sinne existierten in der polnischen Rechtsordnung aber bislang nicht.

Im Juni 2008 legte das Justizministerium den Entwurf eines Gesetzes über Gruppenklagen vor. Nach der Unterrichtung und Abstimmung innerhalb der Ressorts wurde dieser Entwurf im April 2009 in den Sejm eingebracht. Im Laufe des Gesetzgebungsverfahrens wurden einige Regelungsvorschläge überarbeitet. So war im ursprünglichen Entwurf kein Katalog der Fallgruppen, in denen eine Gruppenklage zulässig ist, vorhanden. Ebenfalls erst im Laufe des Gesetzgebungsverfahrens wurden der Anwaltszwang für sämtliche im Katalog enthaltene Fallgruppen aufgenommen und die Höhe der Vergütung des Gruppenvertreters einer Begrenzung unterworfen. Einige weitere Vorschriften wurden ergänzt. Dennoch wurde der Entwurf insgesamt recht detailgetreu umgesetzt. Der Gesetzgeber wählte dabei den Weg der Verabschiedung in einem eigenständigen Gesetz und nicht die Novellierung des Zivilverfahrensgesetzbuchs, damit diese neue Verfahrensform besser erprobt werden kann[12].

2. Die Regelung des Gesetzes über Gruppenklagen im Einzelnen

a) Grundsätze des Regelungsmodells

Das Gesetz über Gruppenklagen setzt in seinem Bereich das sog. Opt-In-Modell um. Dieses Modell erfordert eine ausdrückliche Erklärung der Rechtssubjekte, die die Voraussetzungen für die Mitgliedschaft in der Gruppe erfüllen, dass sie der Gruppe beitreten wollen und dass die Klage auch ihren Fall umfassen soll.

b) Verfahrensabschnitte

Die Gruppenklage nach dem Gesetz gliedert sich in vier Verfahrensabschnitte. Im ersten Abschnitt wird geklärt, ob ein Gruppenverfahren zulässig ist. Kommt das Gericht zu der Schlussfolgerung, dass dies der Fall ist, so erlässt es einen Beschluss hierüber. Gegen diesen Beschluss ist die Beschwerde zulässig. Der

---

10 „Postępowanie uproszczone", das seit 2000 in den Art. 5051 ff. Zivilverfahrensgesetzbuch geregelt ist.

11 Nachfolgend abgekürzt: ZVerfGB.

12 Stellungnahme des Senats zum Gesetz über die Durchsetzung von Ansprüchen im Gruppenverfahren vom 19.10.2009, Senatsdrucksache Nr. 698.

Beschluss über die Einleitung des Gruppenverfahrens ist in der überregionalen Presse bekannt zu machen, in Ausnahmefällen kann dies auch in einer regionalen Zeitung geschehen. Die Bekanntmachung muss bestimmte Informationen enthalten, die in Art. 11 Abs. 2 geregelt sind. Insbesondere muss auch die Frist genannt werden, innerhalb derer weitere Mitglieder der Gruppe dem Verfahren beitreten können.

Dann wird in einem zweiten Schritt der subjektive und objektive Umfang der Rechtssache festgelegt. In dieser Phase können weitere Mitglieder der Gruppe beitreten. Mit dem Beitritt eines Mitglieds zur Gruppe entsteht zwischen ihm und dem Beklagten ein anhängiger Rechtsstreit. Die Gruppenmitglieder werden während des Prozesses als Partei vernommen. Nach Ablauf der Frist, die das Gericht genannt hat, kann man der Gruppe nicht mehr beitreten. Der Beklagte kann während dieser Phase Einwände gegen bestimmte Mitglieder der Gruppe erheben. Dieser Abschnitt des Verfahrens schließt mit einem Beschluss des Gerichts über die Zusammensetzung der Gruppe ab.

Danach wird in einem dritten Abschnitt über die Rechtssache entschieden. Für den Rechtsstreit gelten Besonderheiten bei einem Wechsel des Vertreters der Gruppe (Art. 18). Außerdem sind bestimmte Prozesshandlungen des Gruppenvertreters zustimmungsbedürftig (Art. 19). Die dritte Phase – der eigentliche Prozess – endet mit dem Urteil des Gerichts in der Rechtssache. Der Tenor des Urteils muss dabei gewissen Formerfordernissen genügen (Art. 21). Das Urteil im Gruppenverfahren kann mit den üblichen Rechtsmitteln angegriffen werden, wobei die Vorschriften des ZVerfGB entsprechende Anwendung finden.

Schließlich folgt als vierte Phase die Vollstreckung. Auf Antrag des Gruppenvertreters wird das Urteil vollstreckt. Das umfasst auch die Verfahrenskosten.

c) Anwendungsbereich von Gruppenklagen

Die Gruppenklagen können nur dann eingereicht werden, wenn auf Seiten der Kläger eine Gruppe von mindestens zehn Personen besteht, die Ansprüche derselben Art haben, weil sie auf demselben oder dem gleichen Sachverhalt basieren (Art. 1). Der Katalog der Ansprüche, in denen eine Gruppenklage statthaft ist, umfasst Ansprüche aus dem Verbraucherschutz, aufgrund Produkthaftung sowie Schadensersatzansprüche mit der Ausnahme, dass Ansprüche wegen der Verletzung von Persönlichkeitsrechten nicht umfasst werden. In Verfahren, in denen es um die Zahlung von Geld geht, muss die Höhe der Ansprüche vereinheitlicht werden. Dies kann auch innerhalb von Untergruppen erfolgen.

d) Repräsentant der Gruppe

Die Gruppe wird von einem Repräsentanten vertreten. Der Repräsentant kann entweder ein Mitglied der Gruppe oder der örtlich zuständige Verbraucherschutzbeauftragte sein. Er führt das Verfahren im eigenen Namen.

Für Gruppenverfahren herrscht Anwaltszwang. Nur wenn der Vertreter der Gruppe selbst Anwalt oder Rechtsberater ist, kann auf eine zusätzliche anwaltliche Vertretung verzichtet werden. Der Anwalt erhält eine Vergütung, die höchstens 20% der im Urteil zuerkannten Quote betragen darf.

e) Gerichtliche Zuständigkeit

Für Gruppenverfahren ist das nach allgemeinen Vorschriften zuständige Bezirksgericht zuständig, das in der Besetzung von drei Berufsrichtern entscheidet. Die Schriftsätze in einem Gruppenverfahren müssen den allgemeinen Anforderungen an gerichtliche Schriftsätze genügen.

3. Rechtspolitische Diskussion und Bewertung

Die Stimmen zu dem Gesetz über die Durchsetzung von Verfahren in Gruppenklagen sind unterschiedlich. Während die US-amerikanische Handelskammer in Polen schon während des Gesetzgebungsverfahrens vorschlug, die Anzahl der Gruppenmitglieder auf 40 zu erhöhen, wie es im amerikanischen Recht der Fall ist[13], warnten einige Arbeitgeberorganisationen, dass das Verfahren zu wenig in das polnische Rechtssystem passe. Es wurde auch vorgetragen, dass die Position des Gruppenvertreters zu weitgehend ausgestaltet sei, wenn er die Klage für alle übrigen Mitglieder der Gruppe, aber im eigenen Namen einbringt. Schließlich wurde die Fundamentalkritik angebracht, dass es eigentlich kein Bedürfnis für Gruppenklagen in Polen gebe[14].

Insgesamt wird man abwarten müssen, wie nach dem Inkrafttreten des Gesetzes von der Möglichkeit der Gruppenklage Gebrauch gemacht wird. Sollte sich das polnische Modell als erfolgreich erweisen, so wäre dies sicherlich ein weiterer Grund, auch auf europäischer Ebene die Arbeiten an einem Gruppenklagemodell weiter voran zu bringen.

IV. Textübersetzung

Gesetz über die Durchsetzung von Ansprüchen im Gruppenverfahren vom 17. Dezember 2009, Dz. U. 2010, Nr. 7, Pos. 44[15]

Art. 1 [Regelungsumfang]. (1) Das Gesetz normiert das Zivilverfahren in Angelegenheiten, in denen Ansprüche einer Art, die auf demselben oder dem gleichen Sachverhalt basieren, von wenigstens 10 Personen verfolgt werden (Gruppenverfahren).

(2) Das Gesetz findet Anwendung auf Rechtssachen wegen Ansprüchen aus dem Verbraucherschutz, aufgrund Produkthaftung sowie auf Schadensersatzan-

13 Propozycje amerykanskiej izby handlowej w Polsce w sprawie niebednych zmian do projektu ustawy o dochodzeniu roszczen w postepowaniu grupowym, einzusehen unter www.amcham.pl/file/pdf/class_action.pdf, zuletzt aufgerufen am 30.03.2010.

14 Rzeczpospolita vom 06.12.2008: „Pozew zbiorowy-ostrożnie z ogniem“.

15 Stand des Gesetzes 01.04.2010.

sprüche mit Ausnahme von Ansprüchen wegen der Verletzung von Persönlichkeitsrechten.

(3) Die Aufnahme eines Gruppenverfahrens schließt nicht die Möglichkeit aus, dass Personen, die dem Verfahren nicht beigetreten sind, bzw. die aus der Gruppe der Kläger im Gruppenverfahren ausgeschieden sind, ihre Ansprüche anderweitig durchsetzen.

Art. 2 [Geldschuld]. (1) Ein Gruppenverfahren, in dem es um Ansprüche auf Zahlung einer Geldschuld geht, ist nur dann zulässig, wenn die Höhe der Ansprüche jedes Mitglieds der Gruppe unter Berücksichtigung der gemeinsamen Umstände der Rechtssache vereinheitlicht wurde.

(2) Die Vereinheitlichung der Höhe der Ansprüche kann in Untergruppen erfolgen, die wenigstens zwei Personen umfassen.

(3) In Rechtssachen, in denen es um Ansprüche auf Zahlung einer Geldschuld geht, kann die Klage auf die Forderung der Feststellung der Verantwortlichkeit des Beklagten beschränkt werden. In diesem Fall ist der Kläger nicht verpflichtet, ein rechtliches Interesse an der Feststellung nachzuweisen.

Art. 3 [Zuständiges Gericht]. (1) Zuständig für Gruppenverfahren ist das zuständige Bezirksgericht.

(2) Das Gericht entscheidet in der Besetzung von drei Berufsrichtern über die Rechtssache.

Art. 4 [Gruppenvertreter, Anwaltszwang]. (1) Die Klage im Gruppenverfahren wird vom Vertreter der Gruppe eingeleitet.

(2) Vertreter der Gruppe kann ein Mitglied der Gruppe oder der Verbraucherschutzbeauftragte des Kreises oder des Ortes in dem Umfang, in dem er berechtigt ist, sein.

(3) Der Vertreter der Gruppe führt das Verfahren in eigenem Namen zugunsten aller Mitglieder der Gruppe.

(4) Im Gruppenverfahren ist die Vertretung des Klägers durch einen Anwalt oder einen Rechtsberater verbindlich, es sei denn, der Kläger ist Anwalt oder Rechtsberater.

Art. 5 [Höchstgrenze für die Vergütung des Bevollmächtigten]. Der Vertrag, der die Vergütung für den Bevollmächtigten regelt, darf als Vergütung höchstens 20% der Quote, die dem Kläger im Urteil zuerkannt wird, vorsehen.

Art. 6 [Formale Voraussetzungen der Klage]. (1) Die Klage muss den Bedingungen, die in dem Gesetz vom 17. November 1964 – Zivilverfahrensgesetzbuch (Dz. U. Nr. 43, Pos. 296, mit spät. Änd.) bestimmt sind, Genüge tun und darüber hinaus beinhalten:

1. den Antrag auf Untersuchung der Sache im Gruppenverfahren;

2. den Hinweis auf die Umstände nach Art. 1 Abs. 1 und bei Ansprüchen auf Zahlung einer Geldschuld auch auf die Regeln zur Vereinheitlichung der Höhe der Zahlungen für die Mitglieder der Gruppe oder der Untergruppen;
3. bei Ansprüchen auf Zahlung einer Geldschuld die Bestimmung der Höhe der Zahlung für jedes Mitglied der Gruppe oder der Untergruppen;
4. eine Erklärung des Klägers darüber, dass er als Repräsentant der Gruppe handelt.

(2) Der Klageschrift sind die Erklärungen der Mitglieder der Gruppe über den Beitritt zur Gruppe, über die Zustimmung zur Person des Repräsentanten der Gruppe und der Vertrag des Repräsentanten mit dem Bevollmächtigten über die Art seiner Entlohnung beizufügen.

Art. 7 [Verweis in die Mediation]. Das Gericht kann die Parteien zu jedem Zeitpunkt der Rechtssache in die Mediation verweisen.

Art. 8 [Kaution zur Sicherung der Kosten]. (1) Auf Forderung des Beklagten kann das Gericht den Kläger dazu verpflichten, eine Kaution zur Sicherung der Prozesskosten zu hinterlegen.

(2) Der Beklagte kann die Forderung der Sicherung der Prozesskosten spätestens bei der ersten Prozesshandlung stellen. Der Beklagte hat nicht das Recht, die Hinterlegung einer Kaution zu fordern, wenn ein von ihm anerkannter Teil der Forderung für die Absicherung der Kosten ausreicht.

(3) Das Gericht bestimmt eine Frist zur Hinterlegung der Kaution, die nicht kürzer als ein Monat sein darf sowie die Höhe der Kaution unter Berücksichtigung der wahrscheinlichen Höhe der Kosten, die von dem Beklagten zu tragen sein werden. Die Kaution wird bar hinterlegt. Die Kaution darf 20% des Wertes des Streitgegenstandes nicht übersteigen.

(4) Wenn im Laufe des Verfahrens festgestellt wird, dass die Kaution nicht zur Sicherung der Prozesskosten reichen wird, kann der Beklagte eine zusätzliche Sicherung verlangen.

(5) Nach dem unwirksamen Ablauf des vom Gericht festgesetzten Termins zur Hinterlegung der Kaution, weist das Gericht auf Antrag des Beklagten die Klage oder das Rechtsmittel ab und entscheidet über die Kosten sowie im Fall der Klagerücknahme.

(6) Der Beschluss über den Gegenstand der Kaution kann vom Gericht in einer nicht öffentlichen Sitzung erlassen werden. Gegen den Beschluss des Gerichts ist die Beschwerde zulässig.

Art. 9 [Verwertung der Kaution]. Das Gericht veranlasst auf Antrag des Beklagten die Befriedigung der ihm zugesprochenen Kosten aus der Kaution. Dieser Antrag ist innerhalb einer Frist von einem Monat ab dem Tag, an dem der Beschluss, der das Verfahren abschließt, rechtskräftig wird, bei Gericht zu stellen. Wurde kein Antrag gestellt, so beschließt das Gericht nach Ablauf der Frist auf Antrag des Klägers die Rückgabe der Kaution an den Kläger. Das Gericht beschließt die Rückgabe der Kaution an den Kläger unverzüglich, nachdem der Beschluss, der die Sache abschließt, rechtskräftig geworden ist, wenn dem Beklagten keine Kosten zugesprochen wurden.

Art. 10 [Verhandlung über die Zulässigkeit des Gruppenverfahrens]. (1) Das Gericht entscheidet während der Verhandlung über die Zulässigkeit eines Gruppenverfahrens und weist die Klage ab, wenn die Sache der Untersuchung im Gruppenverfahren nicht unterliegt. Anderenfalls erlässt das Gericht einen Beschluss über die Untersuchung der Sache im Gruppenverfahren.

(2) Gegen den Beschluss des Gerichts über die Untersuchung der Sache im Gruppeverfahren ist eine Beschwerde zulässig.

(3) Erhebt ein Mitglied der Gruppe innerhalb einer Frist von sechs Monaten seit dem Tag, an dem der Beschluss über die Abweisung der Klage rechtskräftig geworden ist, eine Klage über eine Forderung, die von der Klage des Gruppenverfahrens umfasst wurde, so bleiben in Bezug auf diesen Anspruch die Folgen der Einreichung der Klage im Gruppenverfahren bestehen.

Art. 11 [Bekanntmachung der Einleitung eines Gruppenverfahrens]. (1) Nachdem der Beschluss über die Untersuchung der Sache im Gruppenverfahren rechtskräftig geworden ist, gibt das Gericht die Einleitung des Gruppenverfahrens bekannt.

(2) Die Bekanntmachung über die Einleitung des Gruppenverfahrens muss enthalten:

1. die Nennung des Gerichts, vor dem das Gruppenverfahren geführt wird;
2. die Bestimmung der Verfahrensparteien und die Bestimmung des Verfahrensobjekts;
3. die Information an Personen, deren Forderungen in das Gruppenverfahren mit aufgenommen werden können, über die Möglichkeiten des Beitritts zu der Gruppe dadurch, dass dem Vertreter der Gruppe innerhalb einer festgelegten Frist, die nicht kürzer als ein und nicht länger als drei Monate seit dem Tag der Verkündung sein darf, eine schriftliche Erklärung über den Beitritt zur Gruppe vorgelegt wird;
4. die Grundsätze der Vergütung des Bevollmächtigten;
5. einen Hinweis auf die bindenden Folgen des Urteils für die Mitglieder der Gruppe.

(3) Die Verkündung über die Einleitung des Gruppenverfahrens wird in der auflagenstarken überregionalen Presse veröffentlicht. In besonderen Fällen kann das Gericht verfügen, dass die Verkündung in der regionalen Presse veröffentlicht wird.

(4) Die Verfügung über die Veröffentlichung der Verkündung der Einleitung des Gruppenverfahrens kann unterbleiben, wenn aus den Umständen der Sache hervorgeht, dass alle Mitglieder der Gruppe die Erklärung über den Beitritt zur Gruppe abgegeben haben.

(5) Der Beitritt zu der Gruppe nach dem Ablauf der vom Gericht genannten Frist ist unzulässig.

Art. 12 [Erklärung über den Beitritt zur Gruppe]. In der Erklärung über den Beitritt zur Gruppe hat der Berechtigte sowohl seine Forderung zu bezeichnen und die Umstände darzulegen, die seine Forderung und seine Mitgliedschaft in der Gruppe begründen als auch die Beweise vorzulegen. Die Liste der Personen, die der Gruppe beigetreten sind, wird von dem Kläger angefertigt und dem Gericht vorgelegt, die Beitrittserklärungen werden beigefügt. Das Gericht überreicht die Liste dem Beklagten.

Art. 13 [Anhängigkeit des Rechtsstreits]. (1) Im Zeitpunkt der Vorlage der Erklärung über den Beitritt zu der Gruppe bei Gericht entsteht zwischen dem Mitglied der Gruppe und dem Beklagten der Status eines anhängigen Rechtsstreits über die Forderung aus dem Gruppenverfahren.

(2) Eine Person, die vor dem Tag der Einleitung eines Gruppenverfahrens eine Klage gegen den Beklagten, die Gegenstand des Gruppenverfahrens sein kann, eingereicht hat, kann spätestens bis zum Tag der Beendigung des Verfahrens in erster Instanz die Erklärung über den Beitritt zur Gruppe abgeben. In diesem Fall stellt das Gericht das Verfahren durch Beschluss ein.

Art. 14 [Nebenintervention]. Die Nebenintervention eines Mitglieds der Gruppe an der Seite des Klägers ist unzulässig.

Art. 15 [Verteidigung gegen die Zusammensetzung der Gruppe]. Innerhalb einer vom Gericht festgelegten Frist, die nicht kürzer als ein Monat sein darf, kann der Beklagte Einwände gegen die Mitgliedschaft bestimmter Personen in der Gruppe oder in den Untergruppen erheben.

Art. 16 [Beweislast für die Gruppenzugehörigkeit]. (1) In Rechtssachen, in denen es um Ansprüche aus einer Geldschuld geht, liegt die Beweislast der Zugehörigkeit eines Mitglieds zu der Gruppe beim Kläger. In anderen Sachen reicht die Glaubhaftmachung zur Feststellung der Zugehörigkeit eines Mitglieds zur Gruppe aus.

(2) Der Kläger kann ein Mitglied der Gruppe dazu verpflichten, innerhalb einer gesetzten Frist zusätzliche Beweise vorzulegen und zusätzliche Erklärungen abzugeben.

Art. 17 [Beschluss über die Zusammensetzung der Gruppe]. (1) Nach dem Ablauf der vom Gericht gesetzten Frist, nicht kürzer als einen Monat seit dem Tag der Zustellung der Einwände gegen eine Mitgliedschaft an den Kläger, erlässt das Gericht einen Beschluss über die Zusammensetzung der Gruppe. Das Gericht kann diesen Beschluss in nichtöffentlicher Sitzung erlassen.

(2) Gegen den Beschluss nach Abs. 1 ist die Beschwerde zulässig.

(3) Nach Erlass des Beschlusses nach Abs. 1 ist eine Erklärung des Mitglieds der Gruppe über einen Austritt aus der Gruppe unwirksam.

(4) Im Fall der Einreichung einer Klage über Forderungen, die vom Gruppenverfahren umfasst sind, durch eine Person, die der Gruppe beigetreten war und die nicht in dem Beschluss des Gerichts über die Zusammensetzung der Gruppe aufgenommen wurde, wird innerhalb einer Frist von sechs Monaten seit dem Tag der Rechtskraft dieses Beschlusses Art. 10 Abs. 3 entsprechend angewandt.

Art. 18 [Wechsel des Vertreters der Gruppe]. (1) Auf Beschluss von mindestens der Hälfte der Mitglieder der Gruppe kann das Gericht einen Wechsel des Vertreters der Gruppe vornehmen. Dieser Beschluss muss den vorgeschlagenen Vertreter benennen und seine Einverständniserklärung enthalten, Gruppenvertreter zu werden. Das Gericht erlässt den Beschluss in nichtöffentlicher Sitzung.

(2) Der Wechsel des Vertreters der Gruppe bewirkt kein Erlöschen der im Verfahren erteilten Vollmacht.

(3) Im Fall eines Antrags auf den Wechsel des Vertreters der Gruppe nach Erlass des Urteils, darf die Frist zur Urteilsanfechtung nicht früher als zwei Wochen, seitdem der Beschluss nach Abs. 1 rechtskräftig geworden ist, ablaufen.

Art. 19 [Zustimmungspflichtige Prozesshandlungen]. (1) Die Klagerücknahme, die Begrenzung oder die Rücknahme des Anspruchs und der Abschluss eines Vergleichs erfordern die Zustimmung mindestens der Hälfte der Gruppenmitglieder.

(2) Das Gericht kann die Rücknahme der Klage, den Verzicht auf die Forderung, ihre Beschränkung sowie den Abschluss eines Vergleichs für unzulässig erklären, wenn die Umstände der Sache darauf hinweisen, dass die genannten Handlungen rechts- oder sittenwidrig sind, darauf abzielen, das Recht zu umgehen oder die Interessen der Mitglieder der Gruppe grob verletzen.

Art. 20 [Status der Gruppenmitglieder im Prozess]. Mitglieder der Gruppe oder einer Untergruppe werden als Partei vernommen.

Art. 21 [Tenor des Urteils im Gruppenverfahren]. (1) In dem Urteilstenor müssen alle Mitglieder der Gruppe oder der Untergruppe genannt werden.

(2) In dem Urteil, das die Zahlung einer Geldschuld zuerkennt, muss bestimmt werden, welche Summe jedem Mitglied der Gruppe oder der Untergruppe zugesprochen wird.

(3) Ein rechtskräftiges Urteil hat Auswirkung auf alle Mitglieder der Gruppe.

Art. 22 [Befreiung von den Gerichtskosten]. Die Befreiung von den Gerichtskosten, die der Partei durch das Gericht im Erkenntnisverfahren zuerkannt wurde oder die die Partei kraft Gesetzes genießt, erstreckt sich auch auf das Zwangsvollstreckungsverfahren.

Art. 23 [Einleitung der Vollstreckung]. (1) In Rechtssachen über eine nicht in Geld bestehende Leistung, wird die Vollstreckung der zugesprochenen Leistung auf Antrag des Vertreters der Gruppe eingeleitet.

(2) Wenn die zugesprochene Leistung, die nicht in Geld besteht, nicht innerhalb von sechs Monaten, berechnet seit der Rechtskraft des Urteils, erbracht wird und in dieser Zeit der Vertreter der Gruppe keinen Antrag auf die Einleitung der Vollstreckung stellt, kann der Antrag auf Erteilung der Vollstreckungsklausel und auf die Einleitung der Vollstreckung von jedem Mitglied der Gruppe gestellt werden.

Art. 24 [Entsprechende Anwendung des Zivilverfahrensgesetzbuchs]. (1) In den nicht durch dieses Gesetz geregelten Bereichen finden die Vorschriften des Gesetzes vom 17. November 1964 – Zivilverfahrensgesetzbuch – ausgenommen Art. 7, 8, 117-124, 194-196, 204, 205, Art. 207 § 3 sowie Art. 425-505 Anwendung.

(2) In den Rechtssachen, die im Gruppenverfahren untersucht werden, finden die Vorschriften der Art. 100 Abs. 2, Art. 101-103, 105, 107 und 109-112 des Gesetzes vom 28. Juli 2005 über die Gerichtskosten in Zivilsachen (Dz. U. Nr. 167, Pos. 1398, mit spät. Änd.) keine Anwendung.

Art. 25 [Änderungen in anderen Gesetzen]. Im Gesetz vom 28. Juli 2005 über die Gerichtskosten in Zivilsachen (Dz. U. Nr. 167, Pos. 1398, mit spät. Änd.) werden nachfolgende Änderungen vorgenommen:

1. In Art. 13 wird der bisherige Inhalt als Abs. 1 bezeichnet und es wird Abs. 2 eingefügt, der lautet: „(2) Die verhältnismäßige Gebühr in Vermögenssachen im Gruppenverfahren beträgt 2% des Streitwertes oder des Wertes, der der Anfechtung unterliegt, jedoch nicht weniger als 30,- PLN und nicht mehr als 100.000,- PLN.“;

2. In Art. 15 bekommt Abs. 2 den Inhalt: „(2) Die bisherige Gebühr wird in den Grenzen zwischen 30,- PLN und 1.000,- PLN und in den Sachen im Gruppenverfahren von 100,- PLN bis 10.000,- PLN festgesetzt.“;

3. In Art. 26 wird im Abs. 1 Nr. 6 der Punkt durch ein Semikolon ersetzt und es wird Nr. 7 angefügt, die lautet: „7. den Schutz der Rechte, die nicht Vermögensrechte darstellen, die im Gruppenverfahren geltend gemacht werden.“.

Art. 26 [Inkrafttreten]. Das Gesetz tritt sechs Monate nach seiner Verkündung in Kraft.

Umsetzung europarechtlicher Initiativen zur Gruppenklage im tschechischen Recht

Dr. Petr Bohata[*]

I. Einführung

Laut der Einleitung zum Weißbuch über Schadensersatzklagen wegen Verletzung des EG-Wettbewerbsrechts, müssen alle Bürger und Unternehmen, die aufgrund einer Zuwiderhandlung gegen die Wettbewerbsvorschriften[1] der Europäischen Union einen Schaden erleiden, das Recht haben, vom Rechtsverletzer Schadensersatz fordern zu können. Der Schadensersatzanspruch ist, wie der EuGH bereits 2001 feststellte und 2006 bekräftigte, im Gemeinschaftsrecht fest verankert[2]. Der Schutz eines funktionierenden Wettbewerbs ist einer der Pfeiler des Binnenmarkts, ohne den der Vertrag von Lissabon nicht konsequent umsetzbar ist.

In der Praxis erhalten jedoch Opfer von Verstößen gegen das EG-Wettbewerbsrecht gegenwärtig nur selten Schadensersatz zugesprochen. Der nicht zugesprochene Schadensersatz und insb. der durch die Geschädigten erst gar nicht geltend gemachte Schaden, beträgt mehreren Milliarden Euro jährlich[3].

Eine der aktuellen Fragen im Rahmen der wettbewerbsrechtlichen Schadensersatzklagen betrifft daher die zivilrechtliche Geltendmachung von Schadensersatzansprüchen direkt durch die geschädigten Subjekte und insb. durch die Verbraucher selbst. Die Fragestellung ist auch insoweit von Bedeutung, als dass sie einen radikalen Bruch mit der bestehenden Praxis herbeiführen würde. Die Durchsetzung der Regelungen gegen Monopole und Kartelle ist in den meisten Mitgliedsstaaten gegenwärtig in erster Linie den nationalen öffentlich-rechtlichen Organen vorbehalten.

Dieser Beitrag soll jedoch nicht die bestehenden Entwicklungstendenzen[4] der vergangenen Jahre aufzeigen, die wichtigsten Entscheidungen beispielsweise im Bereich der Bierlieferungsverträge, der Kfz-Haftpflichtversicherungen wie-

---

* Wissenschaftl. Referent für tschechisches und slowakisches Recht am IOR. Dieser Beitrag basiert auf *Šilhán/Bohata*, Neue Tendenzen des europäischen Wettbewerbsrechts und ihre Durchsetzung in der Tschechischen Republik, WiRO 2009, 334 ff.

1 Das betrifft insb. Art. 101 und 102 EGV (nach Lissaboner Zählung).

2 Soweit die Einleitung zum Weißbuch über Schadensersatzklagen wegen Verletzung des EG-Wettbewerbsrechts. Es ist einsehbar unter http://ec.europa.eu/competition/antitrust/actionsdamages/files_white_paper/whitepaper_de.pdf.

3 Näher dazu der Folgenabschätzungsbericht (Fn. 17), Abschn. 2.2.

4 Ausführlich dazu *Montag/v. Bonin*, Die Entwicklung des Europäischen Gemeinschaftsrechts bis Mitte 2007, NJW 2007, S. 3379 ff. (insb. 3402 f.).

dergeben[5] oder die amerikanischen Erfahrungen mit der Durchsetzung der Ansprüche der Verbraucher[6] oder die Motive[7] für die erforderliche Weiterentwicklung dieses Instruments zusammenfassen. Im Mittelpunkt der Abhandlung stehen die bestehenden Leitprinzipien und die legislativen Weiterentwicklungen, zu denen das Europäische Parlament die Kommission aufgefordert hat[8] sowie die zu erwartenden Umsetzungsprobleme innerhalb der tschechischen Rechtsordnung.

Die Frist für die Abgabe von Stellungnahmen zum Weißbuch ist bereits im Sommer 2008 abgelaufen[9]. Die Tschechische Republik erklärte zwar für den Zeitraum ihres Ratsvorsitzes[10] die Finalisierung des Verfahrens für eines der vordringlichsten Ziele, musste jedoch später sowohl erkennen, dass nicht nur andere dringende Fragen den Ratsvorsitz dominierten, sondern auch feststellen,

---

5 RS C-453/99, *Courage/Cregan*, Slg. 2001 Nr. 1-6297, EuZW 2006, S. 529 (Bierlieferverträge). Vergleichbar auch *Manfredi*, Slg. 2006 Nr. 1–6619 (Kfz-Haftpflichtversicherungen). Näher dazu EuZW 2006, S. 536 und *Emmerich*, JuS 2006, S. 1125 Nr. 3.

6 Diese kann sowieso kaum als Inspiration für die bevorstehende europäische Entwicklung herangezogen werden. Dazu auch das Weißbuch, S. 3, wo eindeutig auf „ausgewogene Maßnahmen" Bezug genommen wird, die sich auf die „europäische Rechtskultur und -tradition" stützen. In diesem Sinne auch *Mestmäcker/Schweitzer*, Europäisches Wettbewerbsrecht, 2. Aufl. 2004, Rn. 50 zu § 7, die insb. auf das bislang geltende Recht der VO (EG) Nr. 1/2003 und die unmittelbare Anwendbarkeit des Art. 81 Abs. 3 EG verweisen.

7 Zu der ausländischen Literatur siehe z.B. *Segal*, Public vs. Private Enforcement of Antitrust Law: A Survey, E.C.L.R. 2007, Nr. 5, S. 306–315; *Woods/Sinclair/Ashton*, Private Enforcement of Community Competition Law: Modernization and the Road Ahead, Competition Policy Newsletter 2004, Nr. 2, S. 31–37; *Holmes*, Public Enforcement or Private Enforcement? Enforcement of Competition Law in the EC and UK, E.C.L.R. 2004, Nr. 1, S. 25–36; *Komninos*, New Prospects for Private Enforcement of EC Competition Law: *Courage* v. *Crehan* and the Community Right to Damages, Common Market Law Review 2002, Nr. 39, S. 447–487, oder *Holmes/Lennon*, Causation – The Route to Damages, E.C.L.R. 2004, Nr. 8, S. 478–478.

8 Beschluss vom 25.04.2007 (2006/2007 INI). Zu der tschechischen Literatur siehe insb. *Neruda*, Schadensersatz wegen wettbewerbsverletzender Handlung als eine Form der privaten Durchsetzung der Antimonopolbestimmungen (tschechisch), Sborník příspěvků z konference „Odpovědnost za škodu" (Sammelband der Beiträge zur Konferenz: Die Schadenshaftung), Brünn 2005, S. 93–113.

9 Zu der deutschen Stellungnahme des Generalsekretärs der Deutschen Vereinigung für gewerblichen Rechtsschutz und Urheberrecht *Loschelder* siehe GRUR 2008, S. 976 ff. (weiterhin: „Stellungnahme *Loschelder*").

10 1. Halbjahr 2009. In diesem Zusammenhang wurde eine internationale Konferenz am 26. und 27.06.2009 in Prag durchgeführt, die ausschließlich der zivilrechtlichen Durchsetzung von Schadensersatzansprüchen wegen Wettbewerbsverletzungen gewidmet war.

dass die Umsetzung der Vorgaben in das eigene nationale Recht nicht einfach sein wird[11].

II. Entwicklungstendenzen und Ziele der Reform

Das Thema einer privatrechtlichen Durchsetzung von Schadensersatzansprüchen ist nicht ganz neu. Die Bemühungen um Verstärkung des sogenannten *private enforcement* bestehen schon länger und befinden sich spätestens seit der Herausgabe des Grünbuchs[12] im Bewusstsein der Rechtsöffentlichkeit.

Während in den USA im Bereich des Wettbewerbsrechts ca. 90% aller Fälle aufgrund der Geltendmachung privatrechtlicher Schadensersatzansprüche erledigt werden[13], erfolgt dies innerhalb der gesamten EU[14] nur in wenigen Fällen jährlich[15] und in der Tschechischen Republik praktisch überhaupt nicht. Einige neue Mitgliedsstaaten haben bereits konkrete Regelungen im Bereich der Gruppenklagen verabschiedet[16], in den meisten anderen Staaten wird die Frage des *private enforcement* jedoch bislang, falls überhaupt, nur zögerlich diskutiert.

Die aufgrund des Grünbuchs gewonnenen Erkenntnisse bewirkten jedoch weitere Aktivitäten. Diese spiegeln sich zunächst in dem sog. Weißbuch[17] wider, das bereits recht konkrete Entwürfe für eine zukünftige einheitliche Regelung in Europa enthält. Die bislang fehlenden oder sehr unterschiedlichen nationalen

---

11 Die private Durchsetzung von Schadensersatzansprüchen stand auch am 13. und 14.05.2009 im Mittelpunkt der internationalen Konferenz *European Competition Days* in Brünn, an der die Vertreter der nationalen Wettbewerbsbehörden, die zuständigen staatlichen Organe und Vertreter der Justiz teilgenommen haben.

12 Green paper – Damages actions for breach of the EC antitrust rules, in Deutsch: Grünbuch – Schadensersatzklagen wegen Verletzung des EU-Wettbewerbsrechts, SEK (2005) 1732 – KOM/2005/0672.

13 Allerdings ist eine Analogie zwischen Art. 101 Abs. 3 EGV und der *rule of reason* schon deswegen unzulässig, weil die US-amerikanischen wettbewerbsbeschränkenden Vereinbarungen nicht durch Vorzugswürdigkeit gegenüber dem Wettbewerb gerechtfertigt werden dürfen. Näher dazu *Mestmäcker/Schweitzer*, Europäisches Wettbewerbsrecht, 2. Aufl. 2004, Rn. 51.

14 Zu den Statistiken z.B. *Petr*, Weißbuch über die Schadensersatzklagen im Rahmen des Wettbewerbsrechts (tschechisch), Právní zpravodaj 2008, Heft 10, S. 6.

15 2005 waren es 43 Verfahren, 2006 sogar nur 30. Diese waren zudem nur auf wenige Mitgliedsstaaten der EU verteilt.

16 Zu den polnischen Regelungen siehe *Cierpial/Horwath*, Gruppenklagen im Zivilverfahren, WiRO 2010, S. 180 ff. und den Beitrag von *T. de Vries* in diesem Band.

17 Einzusehen unterhttp://ec.europa.eu/competition/antitrust/actionsdamages/files_white_paper/white_paper.cz. Siehe auch das *Staff Working Paper* unter http://ec.europa.eu/competition/antitrust/actionsdamages/files_white_paper/workinpaper.pdf sowie die Einschätzung der wirtschaftlichen Auswirkungen unter http://ec.europa.eu/competition/antitrust/actionsdamages/files_white_paper/impact_report.pdf.

Regelungen müssen daher entweder geschaffen oder an neue europäische[18] und/oder innerstaatliche Bestimmungen[19] so weit angepasst werden, dass eine zivilrechtliche Durchsetzung der Wettbewerbsbestimmungen europaweit effektiv gewährleistet ist.

III. Zielsetzung

Als generelle Zielsetzung gilt ein im Weißbuch formulierter umfassender Schutz aller Personen. Konkret bedeutet dies, dass jede Person, die aufgrund der Verletzung des europäischen Rechts im Bereich des Wettbewerbsrechts[20] einen Schaden erlitten hat, in voller Höhe entschädigt werden soll[21]. Die Entschädigung erfolgt durch Kompensation des Schadens. Die Regelung ist zwar nicht als Präventivmittel vorgesehen, allerdings kann erwartet werden, dass eine effektive Durchsetzung von Schadensersatzansprüchen auch Abschreckungswirkung entfalten wird.

Es darf jedoch nicht außer Acht gelassen werden, dass die privatrechtlichen Schadensersatzklagen lediglich ein ergänzender Teil des Schutzsystems sein und somit dessen öffentlich-rechtlichen Teil nicht ersetzen sollen. Grundsätzlich ist es daher unerheblich, ob die privatrechtlichen Klagen die Ergebnisse eines öffentlich-rechtlichen Verfahrens zur Durchsetzung der Art. 101 und 102 EGV ausnutzen oder unabhängig von diesen erhoben werden.

IV. Einzelne Eckpfeiler der geplanten Maßnahmen

1. Die Berechtigten

In erster Linie ist die Frage zu klären, wer zukünftig eine Schadensersatzklage erheben darf. Wie der EuGH in der Sache *Manfredi* bereits grundsätzlich ausgeführt hat, ist jede Person berechtigt, eine Klage vor einem innerstaatlichen Gericht zu erheben, die in Folge der Verletzung der wettbewerbsrechtlichen Bestimmungen einen Schaden erlitten hat. Die Maßnahmen betreffen daher alle Wirtschaftszweige und beziehen sich sowohl auf Einzelpersonen als auch auf

18 Zur unmittelbaren Anwendbarkeit der Art. 81 und 82 EGV siehe *Ritter* in *Immenga/Mestmäcker*, Wettbewerbsrecht, 4. Aufl. 2007, Rn. 1 zu Art. 83 EGV.

19 Der Einfluss des Gemeinschaftsrechts ist hier unverkennbar. Das Rangverhältnis ergibt sich aus den primärrechtlichen Wettbewerbsregeln. Soweit das Gemeinschaftsrecht ausschließliche Geltung in Anspruch nimmt, entfällt die nationale Gesetzgebungskompetenz. Entscheidend ist jedoch die Zwischenstaatlichkeitsklausel, die nach der Rechtsprechung des EuGH keine absolute Kompetenzsperre darstellt, sondern eine parallele Geltung zulässt, wobei bei Anwendungskonflikten das Gemeinschaftsrecht Vorrang genießt.

20 Unabhängig davon, ob es sich um Kartellabsprachen oder um Missbrauch einer beherrschenden Stellung handelt.

21 Die diesbezügliche deutsche Regelung findet sich in §§ 33–34a GWB.

Gruppen von Geschädigten und auf alle Formen von Verstößen gegen Art. 101 und 102 EGV.

Erfasst sein sollen daher auch die im zweiten oder einem weiteren Glied der Produktions- oder Vertriebskette stehenden Kunden, also auch die indirekten Abnehmer, auf die beispielsweise in einer Vertriebskette rechtswidrige Preisaufschläge abgewälzt wurden. Unabhängig von seiner Stellung muss aber der Kläger nach wie vor den eingetretenen Schaden, seine Höhe und die Kausalität zu der wettbewerbsverletzenden Handlung (Unterlassung) nachweisen.

In direktem Zusammenhang mit der Aktivlegitimation stellt sich vordergründig die Frage nach einem kollektiven Rechtsschutz. Dieser ist insb. wegen der oben erwähnten Beweislast, der komplizierten Prozessführung und der kaum kalkulierbaren Verfahrenskosten von zentraler Bedeutung[22] für die Effektivität des Schutzes.

Das Institut des kollektiven Rechtsschutzes (Gruppenklagen) ist dem tschechischen Wettbewerbsrecht[23] bislang vollkommen unbekannt. Es kennt in diesem Bereich weder Verbandsklagen[24] noch die sog. Opt-in- oder gar die Opt-out-Klagen[25]. Ohne einen kollektiven Rechtsschutz sind aber die Ziele der europäischen Vorgaben aus den oben aufgeführten Gründen nicht durchsetzbar. Nur wenn die Geschädigten die Möglichkeit eingeräumt bekommen, ihre Ansprüche zu bündeln, kann der beabsichtigte Effekt eintreten[26]. Dies gilt erst recht im Hinblick auf die gewünschte Präventivwirkung der neuen Regelungen.

Die Verbandsklagen werden von qualifizierten Einrichtungen[27] für eine Gruppe konkret bezeichneter oder (eher selten) noch näher zu identifizierenden

---

22 Auch die Tatsache, dass der Schaden häufig zwischen sehr vielen Personen mit einem relativ niedrigen individuellen Schadensbetrag gestreut ist, verhindert oft einen effektiven Rechtsschutz.

23 Zu den deutschen Regelungen siehe § 33 Abs. 2 GWB, der das Problem von Streu- und Bagatellschäden zu regeln versucht.

24 Dazu siehe § 13 UWG; grundsätzlich zu Verbandsklagen *Basedow/Hopt/Kötz/Baetge*, Die Bündelung gleichgerichteter Interessen im Prozess, Tübingen 1999 und *Schmidt*, Verbraucherschützende Verbandsklagen, NJW 2002, S. 25 ff.

25 Zur Kritik an den Opt-out-Klagen siehe die Stellungnahme *Loschelder*, Punkt II.1., S. 967.

26 Im Hinblick auf den kollektiven Rechtsschutz sieht die Kommission einen eindeutigen Bedarf nach Mechanismen, die eine Bündelung der individuellen Schadensersatzforderungen von Opfern von Wettbewerbsverstößen ermöglichen. Insb. bei relativ geringwertigen Streuschäden schrecken einzelne Verbraucher oder kleinere Unternehmen angesichts der mit einem Gerichtsverfahren verbundenen Kosten, Verzögerungen, Unwägbarkeiten, Risiken und Belastungen vor Individualklagen zurück.

27 Dies können entweder vorab oder *ad hoc* bestimmte berufsständische Kammern, staatliche Institutionen oder Verbraucherschutzverbände sein, die z.B. in einer Liste des Bundesamts der Justiz oder bei der Kommission registriert sind. Im Bereich des tschechischen Verbraucherschutzes sind Verbandsklagen inzwischen auch vorgesehen, allerdings nicht zur Durchsetzung von Schadensersatzansprüchen: § 25 des tschechischen

Personen erhoben. Praktische Erfahrungen zeigen, dass die qualifizierten Einrichtungen nicht immer bereit sind, eine Verbandsklage anzustreben[28]. Daher muss dieses Institut um die Zulassung der sogenannten Opt-in-Klagen[29] ergänzt werden. Bei diesen Verfahren schließen sich einzelne Geschädigte ausdrücklich und freiwillig[30] zusammen, um ihre Ansprüche in einer Klage zusammenzufassen.

Trotz der Erkenntnis der Wichtigkeit der Zulassung von bestimmten Formen der kollektiven Klagemöglichkeiten für die zivilrechtliche Durchsetzung von Schadensersatzansprüchen, ist die gegenwärtige Situation in der Tschechischen Republik unbefriedigend. Eine entsprechende Regelung fehlt. Lediglich die Durchsetzung von Ansprüchen auf Unterlassung rechtswidriger Handlungen im Rahmen der Regelungen des unlauteren Wettbewerbs bildet hier eine Ausnahme. Hier können neben den direkt Geschädigten auch juristische Personen klagen, die berechtigt sind, die Interessen von Verbrauchern zu schützen. Es handelt sich dabei aber um ein für diese Zwecke ungeeignetes Instrument, denn Schadensersatzansprüche können im Rahmen dieses Verfahrens nicht geltend gemacht werden.

Änderungen der tschechischen Rechtsordnung sind in diesem Bereich daher unumgänglich. Im Unterschied zu der Europäischen Kommission favorisiert das tschechische Amt zum Schutz des Wirtschaftswettbewerbs in Brünn die Opt-out-Variante, die für zivilrechtliche Klagen nach Auffassung des Amts besser geeignet sei.

Aber auch die deutschen Erfahrungen sind auf diesem Gebiet nicht sehr ermutigend. Obwohl den Verbraucherschutzverbänden inzwischen das Recht verliehen wurde, Forderungen der Verbraucher im Wege von Muster- oder Sammelklagen nach österreichischem Vorbild anzustrengen, wird die Einhaltung der gesetzlichen Voraussetzungen durch die Gerichte sehr restriktiv geprüft[31]. Ein

---

Verbraucherschutzgesetzes, in deutscher Übersetzung von *Bohata* in *Breidenbach* (Hrsg.), Handbuch Wirtschaft und Recht in Osteuropa, Loseblatt, München, Bd. 1, CS 290. Ausführlich zu Verbandsklagen und qualifizierten Einrichtungen *Philipp*, Schadensersatzklagen wegen Verletzung des EG-Wettbewerbsrechts, EuZW 2007, S. 654 ff. und *Micklitz/Rott* in *Dauses,* Handbuch des EU-Wirtschaftsrechts, 22. EL, 2008, Rn. 610 ff.

28 Oder den erstrittenen Schadensersatz in vollem Umfang an die Geschädigten auszuschütten.

29 Die Opt-out-Klagen wurden im Vorfeld ebenfalls erwogen, schließlich jedoch verworfen. Hier hätten zwar Klagen im Namen einer nicht näher spezifizierten Gruppe von Geschädigten erhoben werden können (die Geschädigten treten in diesem Fall nicht ausdrücklich dem Klageantrag bei, sondern müssen sich von ihm ausdrücklich distanzieren), die Gefahr von „amerikanischen Verhältnissen" bei Antitrustklagen wäre jedoch recht groß.

30 Noch ungeklärt ist die Frage, ob ein Beitritt weiterer Kläger zu einer bereits bestehenden Gruppe von Klägern deren Zustimmung bedarf oder nicht.

31 So z.B. OLG Düsseldorf, NJW 2004, S. 1532.

weiterer Nachteil dieser Regelung stellt der organisatorische Aufwand für die Ermittlung und Sammlung der Fälle sowie später für die Ausschüttung der erstrittenen Ausgleichszahlungen dar.

2. Beweislage

Verletzungen des Wettbewerbsrechts sind in Bezug auf die Sachverhaltsfeststellung ausgesprochen schwierig, da die für die Beweisführung und somit für die Durchsetzung der Ansprüche entscheidenden Beweismittel von den Unternehmen geheim gehalten werden. Hier gilt es daher, der strukturellen Informationsasymmetrie zwischen der Sphäre der Beklagten (Störer) und Dritter[32] wirksam zu begegnen. Andererseits darf jedoch die Gefahr des Missbrauchs nicht unterschätzt werden[33], denn zwischen dem Schutz der Rechte Dritter und der Gefahr von übermäßig weiten und belastenden Offenlegungspflichten auf Seiten der Beklagten ist nur ein kleiner Spielraum.

Aufgrund der bestehenden Problematik schlug daher die Kommission für Schadensersatzklagen wegen Verletzung des EG-Wettbewerbsrechts ein europaweit geltendes Mindestniveau für die Offenlegungspflicht vor. Unter Berücksichtigung der durch ein Gericht zu prüfenden Begründetheit und Verhältnismäßigkeit des Auskunftsersuchens des Klägers soll daher der Zugang zu den Informationen im Rahmen des Tatsachenvortrags[34] stattfinden.

Um der Missbrauchsgefahr möglichst wirksam zu begegnen, werden die nationalen Gerichte angehalten, die Beklagten nur unter bestimmten Voraussetzungen anzuweisen, konkrete Kategorien von relevanten Beweismitteln offenzulegen. Einem solchen Beweisbeschluss sollen zunächst bestimmte Prozesshandlungen des Klägers vorausgehen. Sie sollen verpflichtet sein,

- alle die für sie allgemein zugänglichen Tatsachen und Beweise darzulegen,
- um aus diesen die Wahrscheinlichkeit eines Verstoßes gegen die Regeln des EG-Wettbewerbs abzuleiten,

32 Häufig sind es kleinere Subjekte, in vielen Fällen sogar Endverbraucher, die ohne geeignete vorgeschaltete Maßnahmen keine Möglichkeit haben, den Sachverhalt zu erkennen, geschweige denn zu beweisen.

33 Die deutschen Regelungen sind in erster Linie in den §§ 142 und 144 ZPO enthalten. Die ZPO kennt jedoch in diesem Zusammenhang keinen unmittelbaren Zwang gegen den Verpflichteten wegen Nichtbeachtung einer Anordnung des Gerichts und lässt lediglich negative Schlussfolgerungen zu Lasten des sich weigernden Verpflichteten zu. *Loschelder* warnt in seiner Stellungnahme daher vor Ausforschungsbeweisen (S. 976) und schlägt erweiterte Beweismittelregelungen ausschließlich für die Feststellung der Schadenshöhe in den Fällen vor, in denen die Rechtsverletzung bereits durch eine behördliche Entscheidung festgestellt wurde.

34 Diese Regelung stützt sich auf die bereits in der Richtlinie 2004/48/EG des Europäischen Parlaments und des Rates vom 29. April 2004 zur Durchsetzung der Rechte des geistigen Eigentums enthaltenen Grundsätze, die einen Bereich mit vergleichbar schwer zugänglichen Beweisen betrifft.

- gegenüber dem Gericht glaubhaft darzulegen, dass sie auch unter Aufwendung der von ihnen gerechter Weise zu erwartenden vernünftigen Anstrengungen nicht in der Lage sind, die für die Begründetheit der Klage weiterhin erforderlichen Beweise zu beschaffen,
- die verschiedenen Kategorien der begehrten Beweismittel hinreichend genug zu konkretisieren, und schließlich
- das Gericht zu überzeugen, dass die begehrte Offenlegung von Geschäftsgeheimnissen oder geheimhaltungsbedürftigen Tatsachen für die Prozessführung seitens der Kläger erheblich, erforderlich und verhältnismäßig ist[35].

Auf der anderen Seite muss ab Klageeinreichung gewährleistet sein, dass solche Beweise nicht vorab vernichtet oder die gerichtlich angeordnete Offenlegung nicht durch vorgeschobene Behauptungen unterlaufen wird. Zu diesem Zweck sollen die nationalen Gerichte mit hinreichend abschreckenden Sanktionen ausgestattet werden. Gedacht ist daher auch eine radikale Regelung, wonach die nicht zur Verfügung gestellten Daten oder die vernichteten Beweise bei Vorliegen hinreichend glaubhafter Indizien grundsätzlich zum Nachteil des Beklagten ausgelegt werden dürfen.

Die betreffenden Regelungen der tschechischen ZPO sind für diese Zwecke nicht ausreichend und werden daher wohl umfangreichen Änderungen unterworfen werden müssen. Nach den gegenwärtigen Regelungen ist nämlich die Klagepartei verpflichtet, alle Beweise zu bezeichnen und individuell zu benennen. Das Gericht kann zwar gegenüber den Beklagten oder Dritten anordnen, dass sie die betreffenden Dokumente vorzulegen haben, wirksame Werkzeuge zur Durchsetzung dieses Anspruchs gegenüber dem Beklagten stehen jedoch weder dem Kläger noch dem Gericht zur Verfügung. Die tschechische ZPO ist gegenwärtig nicht in der Lage, die in solchen Fällen bestehende Asymmetrie zwischen den Klägern und Beklagten zu durchbrechen.

Die Beweislastumkehr ist zwar dem tschechischen Prozessrecht nicht vollkommen unbekannt[36], bei der zivilrechtlichen Durchsetzung von Schadensersatzansprüchen ist sie jedoch nicht anwendbar.

35 Hierbei müssen durch die nationalen Gerichte viele unbestimmte Rechtsbegriffe möglichst einheitlich ausgelegt werden. Damit bei einer entsprechend großzügigen Auslegung durch ein nationales Gericht den Beklagten kein unverhältnismäßiger Schaden entsteht, sollen weitere Schutzmechanismen greifen. Denkbar ist z.B. eine nicht öffentliche Sitzung, ein Verwertungsverbot der offengelegten Informationen für andere Zwecke, die Bereitstellung der Informationen nur gegenüber den Prozessvertretern der Kläger oder gar ausschließlich für den Bedarf der Sachverständigen und Wirtschaftsprüfer.

36 Im Recht gegen den unlauteren Wettbewerb bestehen Regelungen, die eine Beweislastumkehr zugunsten der Verbraucher zulassen.

3. Follow-on

Einen weiteren wichtigen Punkt der vorliegenden Problematik stellen die bereits rechtskräftigen Entscheidungen der nationalen Organe in den Verfahren wegen Verletzung der Art. 101 und 102 EGV und ihrer Bindungswirkung dar. Während sich die Opfer eines durch die Europäische Kommission festgestellten Verstoßes gegen diese Artikel gemäß Art. 16 Abs. 1 der Verordnung (EG) Nr. 1/2003[37] in zivilrechtlichen Schadensersatzprozessen auf die betreffende Entscheidung als verbindlichen Beweis berufen können, gelten in den meisten Mitgliedsstaaten[38] für die Entscheidungen der nationalen Organe solche Regeln bedauerlicher Weise nicht.

An dieser Stelle plant die EU einen weiteren Schritt zur Vereinfachung der Beweissituation der Kläger. Sie sieht zu Recht keinen Grund dafür, warum eine bestandskräftige Entscheidung[39] einer dem ECN[40] angehörenden nationalen Wettbewerbsbehörde in jedem Mitgliedsstaat[41] bei Folgeklagen auf Schadensersatz nicht als unwiderlegbarer Beweis für den bereits festgestellten Verstoß herangezogen werden sollte[42]. Dies hätte unter Umständen sogar für die Beklagten Vorteile, müssten sie doch keine weiteren Tatsachen im Rahmen eines Beweisverfahrens offenlegen.

Eine solche Vorgehensweise hätte neben einer höheren Rechtssicherheit auch eine deutlich höhere Prozesseffizienz aufzuweisen. Kann der Beklagte den eigenen, einmal bereits rechtskräftig festgestellten Verstoß gegen Art. 101 und 102 EGV in einem Folgeverfahren nicht mehr in Frage stellen, führt dies zu ei-

37 Verordnung (EG) Nr. 1/2003 des Rates vom 16. Dezember 2002 zur Durchführung der in den Art. 81 und 82 des Vertrags niedergelegten Wettbewerbsregeln.

38 Eine rechtspolitisch umstrittene Regelung enthält diesbezüglich § 33 Abs. 4 GWB.

39 Gemeint sind rechtskräftige Entscheidungen der Wettbewerbsbehörden oder rechtskräftige Urteile der Gerichte, die entweder selbst einen Verstoß festgestellt oder die Entscheidung der Wettbewerbsbehörde bestätigt haben.

40 ECN: *European Competition Network* (Europäisches Netz der nationalen Wettbewerbsbehörden).

41 Die nationalen Unterschiede sind derzeit noch groß. Während z.B. in Deutschland die Gerichte auch an die rechtskräftigen Entscheidungen der nationalen Behörden gebunden sind, sind sie in der Tschechischen Republik lediglich an die Entscheidungen des nationalen Amts für den Wettbewerbsschutz in Brünn gebunden. In einigen anderen Staaten besteht nicht einmal diese Bindung. Näher dazu *Petr*, Weißbuch über die Schadensersatzklagen im Rahmen des Wettbewerbsrechts (tschechisch), Právní zpravodaj 2008, Heft 10, S. 7.

42 Ausführlich dazu *Kless* in *Kilian/Heussen*, Computerrechts-Handbuch, 26. EL 2008, Grundlagen, Rn. 35 f. sowie die am 27.04.2004 in Kraft getretene Bekanntmachung über die Zusammenarbeit der Wettbewerbsbehörden selbst (Verkündungsstand 22.01.2009).

ner deutlichen Senkung der Verfahrenskosten, zu Zeitgewinn und es vermeidet zusätzliche Unwägbarkeiten für die Geschädigten[43].

Diese Bindungswirkung würde sich jedoch lediglich gegen die Beklagten entfalten, die vor den nationalen Behörden und/oder Gerichten alle gegebenen Rechtsmittel ausgeschöpft oder auf sie verzichtet haben. Allerdings würde eine konsequente Umsetzung dazu führen, dass die nationalen Gerichte einer bestandskräftigen Entscheidung einer nationalen ECN-Wettbewerbsbehörde nicht mehr widersprechen dürfen[44], was zumindest aus Sicht der Unabhängigkeit der Gerichte nicht unproblematisch sein dürfte.

Allerdings hätte eine europaweite Bindungswirkung gegenwärtig auch unübersehbare Nachteile und würde wohl schnell auf praktische Barrieren stoßen. Ungeklärt ist z.B. das weitere Vorgehen eines Gerichts, das einer bestandskräftigen Entscheidung einer nationalen ECN-Wettbewerbsbehörde nicht mehr widersprechen dürfte, wenn belastende oder entlastende Umstände in einem Mitgliedsstaat nicht vorliegen oder in dem Verfahren vor der ECN-Wettbewerbsbehörde keine Rolle spielten. Die Entscheidungen des tschechischen Amts zum Schutz des Wettbewerbs sind zwar für die tschechischen Gerichte inzwischen verbindlich, von ausländischen Entscheidungen kann dies jedoch nicht behauptet werden.

4. Verschuldenserfordernis

Die Regelungen über Verschulden sind europaweit noch vollkommen uneinheitlich. In einigen Staaten ist für die Zuerkennung eines Schadensersatzes ein Verschulden[45] beim Verstoß gegen Art. 101 und 102 EGV zwingend vorgesehen, was die Durchsetzung der Ansprüche in einigen Fällen zumindest wesentlich erschwert, in den meisten Fällen jedoch praktisch unmöglich macht. Aus der Sicht der EU-Kommission besteht in denjenigen Staaten der EU kein Handlungsbedarf, in denen kein Verschuldenserfordernis vorliegt oder bei nachgewiesenen Verstößen ein Verschulden unwiderlegbar vermutet wird, da eine solche Regelung für die Zwecke des *private enforcement* günstiger ist. Dieser

---

43 Allerdings kann auch die Gefahr des *forum shopping* nicht ganz übersehen werden. Da sich die Verletzungsschäden in vielen Fällen über das gesamte Gebiet der EU erstrecken, würden sich die Kläger zunächst an die Wettbewerbsbehörden und Gerichte wenden, deren Rechtsprechung für sie am günstigsten ist, um dann in anderen Gebieten der EU auf diese Entscheidungen verweisen zu können.

44 Davon unberührt bleibt das Recht und/oder die Pflicht der Gerichte, gegebenenfalls gemäß Art. 234 EGV um Erläuterung zur vorliegenden Auslegung der Art. 81 und 82 EGV zu ersuchen.

45 Die wenigen verschuldensunabhängigen Haftungstatbestände, die das deutsche Recht kennt, sind hier nicht einschlägig.

Grundsatz überwiegt inzwischen in Europa und ist auch in der Tschechischen Republik[46] verankert.

Das Verschulden als Voraussetzung für die Geltendmachung von Schadensersatzansprüchen im Rahmen von *private enforcement* spielt in der Tschechischen Republik keine Rolle. Das Verschulden ist, im Unterschied zur subjektiven Haftung im Zivil- oder Arbeitsrecht, keine Voraussetzung des Anspruchs und wird im Rahmen des Verfahrens auch nicht geprüft. Im Handels- und Wirtschaftsrecht[47] herrscht die objektive, verschuldensunabhängige Haftung vor, sodass im Hinblick auf die von der EU geplante Durchsetzung privater Schadensersatzansprüche wegen Verletzungen des Wettbewerbsrechts keine Eingriffe in die Rechtsordnung erforderlich sein sollten.

In anderen Staaten müsste dagegen eine Harmonisierung erfolgen. Diese wird sich wohl an den Grundsätzen der Rechtsprechung des EuGH zu den Voraussetzungen von zivilrechtlicher Haftung bei Verstößen gegen unmittelbar anwendbares Recht und an dem zu beachtenden Effektivitätsgrundsatz[48] orientieren. Eine Ausnahme wird der entschuldbare Irrtum (*genuinely excusable eror*) bilden müssen[49]. Die Exkulpationsmöglichkeit wird für die Situationen vorgesehen sein, in denen auch ein sorgfältiger Unternehmer nicht wissen konnte, dass sein Verhalten den Wettbewerb beeinträchtigt. Eine solche Aufweichung dürfte allerdings unproblematisch sein, da hier zwar die objektive zivilrechtliche Haftung durch subjektive Kriterien relativiert, die öffentlich-rechtliche Haftung jedoch davon unberührt bleiben wird.

5. Schadensersatz

Einer der problematischen Schlüsselbegriffe der angestrebten Regelungen ist der Schaden. Es handelt sich dabei nach Auffassung der EU-Kommission und des EuGH[50] eindeutig um den vollständigen Ersatz der real erlittenen Verluste des Geschädigten. Erfasst sind daher nicht nur die nominellen Verluste (*damnum emergens*), sondern auch der entgangene Gewinn wegen Umsatzeinbußen[51] und die Verzinsung dieser Verluste ab dem Zeitpunkt des Schadenseintritts (*lucrum cessans*). Der Ersatz der darüber hinausgehenden Ansprüche der Geschädigten

---

46 So in den Regelungen des § 757 HGB i.V.m. §§ 41 und 373 HGB, in deutscher Übersetzung von *Bohata* in *Breidenbach* (Hrsg.), Handbuch Wirtschaft und Recht in Osteuropa, Bd. 1, CS 300.

47 Hier kann das Ausmaß des Verschuldens beispielsweise im Kartellrecht bei der Strafzumessung durch das Kartellamt Berücksichtigung finden.

48 Näher dazu *Emmerich* in *Dauses*, Handbuch des EU-Wirtschaftsrechts, 21. EL 2008, Rn. 181.

49 Zu den Bedenken wegen eines schärferen Fahrlässigkeitsmaßstabs siehe die Stellungnahme *Loschelder,* S. 977.

50 Hier v.a. die Entscheidung *Manfredi* (Fn. 5), insb. die Rn. 95 und 97.

51 *Immenga/Mästmäcker*, Wettbewerbsrecht, 4. Aufl. 2007, Rn. 50.

wurde dagegen in den meisten nationalen Berichten genauso abgelehnt[52] wie der Ersatz des Schadens bei horizontalen Kartellen in doppelter Höhe und erst recht die bestehende amerikanische Regelung (*triple damages*).

Aber auch so bleibt die genaue Schadensberechnung mehr als problematisch. Sie würde gegenwärtig einen kaum zu leistenden Vergleich zwischen der tatsächlichen und der hypothetisch anzunehmenden ökonomischen Situation des Geschädigten[53] unter funktionierenden Marktbedingungen erforderlich machen. Um die Berechnungen zu erleichtern, beabsichtigt daher die Kommission, einen unverbindlichen Orientierungsrahmen[54] auszuarbeiten, der verschiedene Varianten umfasst und einen Rahmen für approximative Berechnungen sowie vereinfachte Regeln für Schätzungen dort enthalten soll, wo eine exakte Schadensberechnung nicht möglich ist.

Die Ermittlung der Schadenshöhe durch Schätzung des Gerichts ist in der Tschechischen Republik beispielsweise bei der Bestimmung des entgangenen Gewinns zwar theoretisch durchaus möglich, da die Rechtsordnung eine abstrakte Gewinnschätzung generell dort zulässt, wo eine exakte Berechnung nicht möglich ist, aber in der Praxis findet die Regelung kaum Anwendung.

6. Schadensabwälzung

Bei wettbewerblichen Verstößen tritt häufig die Situation auf, dass die rechtswidrigen wettbewerbsverletzenden Preisaufschläge durch den direkten Abnehmer (wenn er kein Endverbraucher ist) an seine Kunden weitergegeben werden. Die Verteidigung des Rechtsverletzers bestreitet dann zu Recht die Entstehung eines konkreten Schadens[55], da der erhöhte Preis per Preisaufschlag an den Endverbraucher weitergegeben wurde. Im Rahmen des anerkannten Kompensationsprinzips scheint diese Form der Verteidigung[56] legitim zu sein. Anderenfalls bestünde nämlich die Gefahr der ungerechtfertigten Bereicherung auf Seiten des Klägers, der, obwohl er keinen konkreten Schaden erlitten hat, den Rechtsverletzer erfolgreich auf Schadenersatz verklagen könnte.

In vielen anderen Fällen ist die Abnehmerkette jedoch vielgliedriger. Nach dem Schädiger kommen mehrere indirekte Abnehmer, deren Schaden umso grö-

---

52 In der Stellungnahme *Loschelder* wird darauf hingewiesen, dass auch die Nichtigkeitsfeststellung und die Folgenbeseitigung durchaus regelungsbedürftige Inhalte wären (S. 976).

53 Nach der deutschen, im unmittelbaren Zusammenhang mit der *passing-on-defence* stehenden Regelung des § 33 Abs. 3 GWB kann allerdings nur der direkte Abnehmer Schadensersatzansprüche geltend machen. Näheres siehe unter Punkt 6.

54 Die aus dem Wettbewerbsrecht bereits bekannten *guidelines*.

55 Näher dazu *Röhling*, Die passing-on-defence im deutschen Recht unter Berücksichtigung des europäischen, US-amerikanischen und britischen Rechts, in FS *Huber*, Tübingen 2006, S. 1117 ff.

56 Hinsichtlich der Beweislast dürften hier die gleichen Anforderungen gelten wie bei dem Nachweis des Schadens.

ßer ist, je näher sie am Ende der Vertriebskette stehen. Sie haben jedoch aufgrund der Entfernung zum Schädiger kaum eine Chance, die erforderlichen Beweismittel für die Abwälzung der rechtswidrigen Preisaufschläge zu beschaffen. Im Ergebnis soll die Beweiserleichterung dazu führen, dass die indirekten Abnehmer sich zunächst auf eine widerlegbare Vermutung stützen dürfen, dass der wettbewerbswidrige Preisaufschlag in voller Höhe an sie weitergegeben wurde.

Die Voraussage des Umgangs der tschechischen Gerichte mit dieser Problematik ist kaum möglich, einschlägige Urteile sind derzeit nicht bekannt. Rechtliche Hindernisse für *passing-on-defence* bestehen nicht, ein Bestreiten des Schadenseintritts ist jederzeit möglich. Anders verhält es sich bei der widerlegbaren Vermutung der Abwälzung von rechtswidrigen Preisaufschlägen. Dieses Institut ist dem tschechischen Prozessrecht vollkommen unbekannt und müsste erst entsprechend geregelt und durch die Praxis umgesetzt werden.

7. Verjährungsproblematik

Die Regelung der Verjährung spielt im Zusammenhang mit der Rechtssicherheit sicherlich eine wichtige Rolle, sie kann jedoch bei individuellen Klagen und erst recht bei Folgeklagen auf Schadensersatz auch als ein Hindernis empfunden werden. Zentraler Problembereich ist dabei der Zeitpunkt, ab dem bei dauernden oder fortgesetzten Zuwiderhandlungen der Lauf der Verjährung beginnen soll. Die Geschädigten wissen in der Regel nicht, dass eine Zuwiderhandlung gegen Art. 101 und 102 EGV überhaupt vorliegt.

Dieser Problematik soll künftig Rechnung getragen werden, indem der Beginn der Verjährungsfrist entweder auf das Ende der fortgesetzten Zuwiderhandlung oder auf den Zeitpunkt gelegt wird, in dem die Geschädigten von dem durch die Zuwiderhandlung verursachten Schaden erfahren oder wenigstens die Kenntnis des Schadens vernünftiger Weise erwartet werden kann (kennen und kennen müssen).

Ein besonderes Augenmerk verlangt die Regelung bei den *Follow-on*-Klagen[57]. Hier besteht die Gefahr, dass die Verjährung bereits während des Verfahrens vor den nationalen Wettbewerbsbehörden oder spätestens während der anschließenden Gerichtsverfahren eintritt. Hier wird man nicht um eine neue Verjährungsfrist von mindestens zwei Jahren umhinkommen, die nach der Rechtskraft der behördlichen oder gerichtlichen Entscheidung beginnt, auf die sich die Folgeklage bezieht.

8. Verfahrenskosten

Das mit zivilrechtlichen Schadensersatzklagen gegen wettbewerbsrechtliche Zuwiderhandlungen verbundene Prozesskostenrisiko ist für viele Geschädigte

57 Zu den *follow-on*-Klagen und der Problematik der *stand-alone*-Klagen siehe z.B. *Kless* in *Kilian/Heussen*, Computerrechts-Handbuch, 26. EL. 2008, Grundlagen Rn. 73.

einer der wichtigsten Gründe für einen Verzicht auf gerichtliche Überprüfung. Zur Beseitigung des hierfür verantwortlichen wirtschaftlichen Ungleichgewichts sind verschiedene Lösungswege denkbar. Sie betreffen die durch die Bestimmungen der einzelnen Staaten festgelegte Höhe der Gerichtsgebühren selbst, die Möglichkeit der Festlegung einer Obergrenze und den Weg über einen die Kosten des Verfahrens deutlich senkenden Vergleich[58].

Favorisiert wird gegenwärtig die prozessökonomische Lösung über einen möglichst schnell zu erzielenden gerichtlichen Vergleich. Hierzu müssten die Mitgliedsstaaten ihre Verfahrensregeln so weit ändern, als diese eine vergleichsweise Beilegung des Rechtsstreits deutlich begünstigen. Gleichzeitig könnten Regelungen eingeführt werden, die eine vom üblichen Kostenrecht abweichende Kostenentscheidung vorab ermöglichen.

Die Höhe der Prozesskosten spielt bei der Abschätzung des Prozessrisikos auch in der Tschechischen Republik eine negative Rolle und verhindert so im betreffenden Bereich die meisten privaten Schadensersatzklagen. Die Grundgebühr der Gerichte liegt gegenwärtig bei 4% des Streitwerts, eine teilweise oder vollständige Befreiung von Gerichtsgebühren wird in der Praxis kaum genutzt. Hinzu kommt, dass die tschechischen Gerichte grundsätzlich erst im Urteil über die Kosten entscheiden, sodass bis zum Abschluss des Verfahrens die genaue Kostenhöhe den Parteien nicht bekannt ist. Eine Verlagerung der Kostenentscheidung in eine frühere Phase des Verfahrens wäre für die Tschechische Republik in diesen Fällen sicherlich begrüßenswert.

V. Zusammenfassung

Der im Gemeinschaftsrecht verankerte Anspruch von Geschädigten auf Schadensersatz wird nach der Umsetzung der im Weißbuch angedachten Regelungsinhalte ein wenig realistischer. Allerdings enthalten die Vorschläge im Weißbuch für die Tschechische Republik auch einige Klippen und praktische Umsetzungsprobleme.

In erster Linie fehlt es im tschechischen Recht an kollektiven Rechtsschutzmöglichkeiten. Das Institut des kollektiven Rechtsschutzes ist dem tschechischen Wettbewerbsrecht bislang vollkommen unbekannt. Es kennt in diesem Bereich weder Verbandsklagen noch die sog. Opt-in- oder gar die Opt-out-Klagen. Für einen wirksamen kollektiven Rechtsschutz in der Tschechischen Republik sind die europäischen Vorgaben daher unverzichtbar. Im Unterschied zu der Europäischen Kommission favorisiert das tschechische Amt zum Schutz

58 Die Möglichkeit, die obsiegende Partei (in diesem Fall den Beklagten) zur Übernahme der Kosten zu verpflichten, könnte ohne jegliches Prozessrisiko für den Kläger zu ungerechtfertigten Klageandrohungen oder Vergleichen führen. Soweit sind die von *Loschelder* in der Stellungnahme (S. 977) geäußerten Bedenken nicht ganz von der Hand zu weisen. Hier allerdings von der erwünschten Erhaltung der „Waffengleichheit" zu sprechen, entbehrt im Verhältnis Unternehmen/Verbraucher jeglicher Realität.

des Wirtschaftswettbewerbs in Brünn die Opt-out-Variante, so wie sie derzeit beispielsweise in dem Verfahren der Schutzorganisationen für Autorenrechte (VG Wort u.a.) in den USA gegen Google geführt wird.

Änderungen bedarf es auch bei den Beweisregelungen, da dem Gericht gegenwärtig keine relevanten Durchsetzungswerkzeuge zur Verfügung stehen, die beklagte Partei zur Vorlage von nicht genau bestimmbaren Dokumenten zu zwingen oder bei der Beweisführung mit einer widerlegbaren Vermutung zu operieren. Die vorgesehenen Regelungen über Beweislastumkehr sind zwar der tschechischen Rechtsordnung im Bereich des Verbraucherschutzes bekannt, gegenwärtig jedoch bei der zivilrechtlichen Durchsetzung von Schadensersatzansprüchen bei Wettbewerbsverstößen nicht anwendbar.

Öffentliches Recht

Verfassungsidentität und Europäische Integration. Die Perspektive der mittel- und osteuropäischen Verfassungsgerichte

Prof. Dr. Rainer Arnold[*]

I. Die Verfassung ist der normative Kern einer staatlichen Rechtsordnung. Sie bestimmt die institutionelle Grundstruktur eines Staates in horizontaler und vertikaler Hinsicht, indem sie Staatsorgane einrichtet und ihnen Funktionen zuordnet und die territoriale Aufgliederung des Staates bewirkt. Sie gibt weiterhin die Grundorientierung des Staates an, indem sie Werte für verbindlich erklärt, die die Zielsetzung seines Handelns und insbesondere sein Verhältnis zum Individuum bestimmen. Diese beiden Funktionen der staatlichen Verfassung, die Institutionenbildung und die Werteorientierung, bewirken innere Einheit, interne Integration, die in ein Spannungsverhältnis zur externen Integration tritt, wie sie aus der Zugehörigkeit zur Europäischen Union resultiert.

Integrationsnormen einer staatlichen Verfassung ermächtigen zur externen Integration, ohne aber die interne preisgeben zu wollen. Beide Verfassungskörper, der staatliche und der supranationale[1], treten in Konkurrenz, sie schränken sich gegenseitig ein, doch bewahren sie ihre Identität. Die staatliche Identität ist aufgrund des Vorrangs des Unionsrechts, des Fundamentalprinzips der Supranationalität, gefährdet und bedarf der Sicherung. Schon der erste Vertrag über die EU von 1993 hat die Bedeutung des funktionellen Überlebens des integrierten Staates erkannt und in Art. 6 Abs. 3 dessen „nationale Identität" ausdrücklich garantiert. Wurde diese Klausel in Rechtsprechung und Literatur kaum thematisiert, so hat sie doch stetig an Bedeutung gewonnen und kehrt in erweiterter Form im neuen EU-Vertrag zurück: Art. 4 Abs. 2 fordert von der Union, die „jeweilige nationale Identität" der Mitgliedstaaten zu achten, und erklärt dies näher. Sie drücke sich aus „in ihren (der Mitgliedstaaten) grundlegenden politischen und verfassungsmäßigen Strukturen einschließlich der regionalen und lokalen Selbstverwaltung". „Strukturen" dürfte dabei nicht nur die institutionelle Festlegung einer Verfassung sein, sondern ihr funktioneller Grundgehalt, wie er insbesondere auch in den Wertorientierungen zum Ausdruck kommt.

---

* Inhaber des Jean-Monnet-Lehrstuhls für Europarecht und des Lehrstuhls für Öffentliches Recht, insbesondere Rechtsvergleichung, Recht der Europäischen Gemeinschaften, Wirtschaftsverwaltungsrecht und ausländisches öffentliches Recht der Universität Regensburg.

1 Zur Übertragung des Verfassungsbegriffs auf die supranationale Ebene vgl. *R. Arnold*, European constitutional law: its notion, scope and finalities, in: *Engelbrekt/Nergelius* (Hrsg.), New directions in Comparative Law, Cheltenham 2009, 99-107.

Diese Garantie der nationalen Identität im EU-Vertrag ist unionsrechtlicher Natur und nicht von vornherein kongruent mit der neu entdeckten Formel nationaler Verfassungsgerichte vom Kerngehalt einer Verfassung als „Verfassungsidentität“. Diese nimmt Bezug auf eine bestimmte nationale Verfassung und ist Resultat nationalen Verfassungsdenkens, jene bezieht die Verfassung des Mitgliedstaates allgemein aus unionsrechtlicher Perspektive ein, trifft also eine Aussage, die für alle Mitgliedstaaten und deren Verfassungen Geltung haben muss.

Das Primärrecht der neuen EU garantiert die nationale und auch die verfassungsrechtliche Identität, die exklusiven Unionskompetenzen nehmen nur einen geringen Umfang ein, das Austrittsrecht des Mitgliedstaates ist erstmals ausdrücklich verankert, die Stärkung der nationalen Parlamente wurde als wichtiges Ziel erkannt, die Rolle des Europäischen Rates, der Organcharakter erhält, wird gestärkt. Dies bedeutet, dass der Grundgedanke nicht Supranationalität in einer absoluten Form, sondern Integration im Sinne relativer Supranationalität, d.h. im Sinne eines Gleichgewichts von europäischer Zentralgewalt und dezentraler Macht der Mitgliedstaaten ist. Die mannigfache institutionelle Mitwirkung der Mitgliedstaaten in den zentralen Organen nach Art eines europäischen Beteiligungsföderalismus genügt dabei nicht, es muss auf beiden Seiten, zentral und dezentral, funktionelle Substanz bestehen, die alleine politische und normative Stabilität durch Gleichgewicht auch für die Zukunft sichern kann.

Um diese ausgleichende Funktionenbegrenzung auf beiden Seiten bemüht sich nicht nur die EU, sondern dies ist auch Ziel der nationalen Verfassungsgerichte. Diese verstehen sich seit jeher als rechtliche Garanten der nationalen Verfassung, wachen somit sorgsam über deren Bestand. Da die Verfassungen selbst die überstaatliche Integration zu einem ihrer Ziele erklären und die Integrationsnormen Integrationsermächtigungen sind, ist den Verfassungsgerichten auch der Schutz der Integration zugewachsen. Es kommt nicht von ungefähr, dass über die nationalen Verfassungsgerichte immer mehr auch das supranationale Recht – ist es ja von der nationalen Verfassung gewollt und geschaffen! – in seinem Bestand geschützt wird: Man denke an die Görgülü-Konzeption des Bundesverfassungsgerichts zur verfassungsgerichtlichen Sicherung der Europäischen Menschenrechtskonvention[2] oder an die Einbeziehung des EuGH in den Schutz des gesetzlichen Richters[3].

Trotz dieser integrativen Kooperation von nationalem Verfassungsgericht und supranationaler Gerichtsbarkeit ist es wesentlicher Streitpunkt, wem die Kompetenz zukommt, die Überschreitung der Grenzlinie zwischen nationaler und supranationaler Verfassungsordnung letztverbindlich festzustellen. Hier divergieren Bundesverfassungsgericht[4] und EuGH.

---

2 BVerfGE 111, 307, 323/324.

3 BVerfGE 73, 339; 82, 159, 192 ff.

4 BVerfGE 89, 155, 188 (Maastricht – ulra vires – Handlungen); BVerfG Lissabon-Entscheidung 30.06.2009, BVerfG, 2 BvE 2/08 v. 30.06.2009,

Verfassungsidentität aus nationaler Sicht ist aktuelles und zentrales Thema bei der verfassungsrechtlichen Beurteilung der neuen EU. Nicht nur das Bundesverfassungsgericht hat den Lissabon-Vertrag auf den Prüfstand gestellt, sondern auch und insbesondere die Verfassungsgerichte Mittel- und Osteuropas. Die Tschechische Republik[5], Ungarn[6] und Polen[7] haben wichtige Entscheidungen – vor und auch nach Inkrafttreten des Lissaboner Vertrags – hierzu gefällt. Kein Verfassungsgericht hat das Entstehen der neuen EU wegen Verfassungswidrigkeit gestoppt. Dennoch war es Anlass, über die Grenzen der Integrationsgewalt erneut nachzudenken und zu dem Gleichgewicht, von dem die Rede war, aus verfassungsrechtlicher Perspektive beizutragen.

Aber auch diejenigen Entscheidungen, die nicht den Lissaboner Vertrag, sondern grundsätzlich das Verhältnis zur EU betrafen, sind für das Gesamtverständnis von Bedeutung. Auf einige Grundlinien, die dieses Verhältnis charakterisieren, soll die folgende Analyse ihren Schwerpunkt legen: Der Begriff der Supranationalität, die Übertragung von Kompetenzen, die Konsequenzen für die staatliche Souveränität und insbesondere die Grenzen der Integrationsgewalt, ausgedrückt durch Verfassungsidentität oder Kerngehalt der Verfassung. Diese Punkte sollen im Folgenden in einer vergleichenden Rechtsprechungsanalyse überlegt werden, dabei können nur einige grundlegende Aspekte angesprochen werden.

II. Analysiert man die Entscheidungen der Verfassungsgerichte in Mittel- und Osteuropa, die die grundlegende Frage ihres Verhältnisses zur EU betreffen, so verdienen diejenigen Polens und der Tschechischen Republik wegen ihrer ausführlichen dogmatischen Betrachtung besondere Aufmerksamkeit. Auch das ungarische Verfassungsgericht, das eine vom äußeren Umfang her kürzere Entscheidung getroffen hat, hat die wesentlichen Punkte in Blick genommen.

Es fällt auf, dass der europäische Kontext der Entscheidungen in besonderer Weise zum „richterlichen Dialog" angeregt hat. So nimmt das Urteil des polnischen Verfassungsgerichts zum Lissaboner Vertrag vom November 2010 auf die europäische verfassungsgerichtliche Judikatur zu dieser Thematik Bezug und die Entscheidungen des deutschen Bundesverfassungsgerichts sind für die Perspektive des tschechischen Verfassungsgerichts und wohl auch für die polnische Entscheidung zur Mitgliedschaft in der EU aus dem Jahr 2005 von besonderem Einfluss.

---

http://www.bverfg.de/entscheidungen/es20090630_2bve000208.html, Abs. 218, 219, 239 ff., 332, 336, 343, 364 (Verfassungsidentität).

5 ÚS 19/08 Lissabon I (26.11.2008); ÚS 29/09 Lissabon 2 (03.11.2009); dazu *M. Hofmann*, Zum zweiten „Lissabon-Urteil" des Tschechischen Verfassungsgerichts, EuGRZ 2010, 153 ff.; deutschen Übersetzung des zweiten Urteils EuGRZ 2010, 209 ff. durch *M. Hofmann* und *L. Louzensky*.

6 Entscheidung 143/2010 (VII. 14.) AB (12.07.2010); dazu *Petr*.

7 K 32/09 Lissabon (24.11.2010); vgl. auch K 18/04 EU-Mitgliedschaft (11.05.2005).

Das lettische Verfassungsgericht hat sich hingegen auf die Frage konzentriert, ob die Zustimmung zum Lissaboner Vertrag durch Parlamentsgesetz oder durch Referendum zu erfolgen hatte, und musste nicht zu den materiellen Verfassungsproblemen vordringen[8].

Das litauische Verfassungsgericht hat sich nicht mit dem Lissaboner Vertrag befasst, doch 2006 mit der Grundfrage des Verhältnisses des litauischen Rechts mit dem EU-Recht auseinandergesetzt und dessen Vorrang vor dem Verfassungsrecht verneint[9].

III. Prüfungsmaßstab der Verfassungsgerichte ist nationales Verfassungsrecht, primär die jeweilige Integrationsnorm. Ihre Auslegung spielt eine zentrale Rolle, doch wird sie nur als Teil der Gesamtverfassung betrachtet; ihre funktionellen Grenzen werden aus denjenigen Bestimmungen abgeleitet, die den Kern der Verfassung bilden. Diese Verknüpfung der Integrationsnorm mit den übrigen Verfassungsbestimmungen, insbesondere solchen, die die „Identität der Verfassung" kennzeichnen, findet sich in der Rechtsprechung aller Verfassungsgerichte, aber auch ausdrücklich in der polnischen, tschechischen und ungarischen Rechtsprechung. Der Terminus „Verfassungsidentität", neuerdings verwendet vom französischen *Conseil constitutionnel*[10] und vom deutschen Bundesverfassungsgericht in seiner Lissabon-Entscheidung vom 30. Juni 2009, wurde nun auch vom polnischen Verfassungsgericht aufgegriffen und hat in diesem Urteil ausgiebig Erwähnung gefunden[11]. Doch auch die Rechtsprechung der Verfassungsgerichte, die diesen – an sich nicht neuen – Begriff verwenden, arbeitet einen unaufgebbaren Kern der Verfassungsordnung heraus, der die gleiche Funktion erfüllt. Noch weitergehend allerdings einige Verfassungsgerichte, wie das litauische[12], die die Verfassung als Ganzes als „EU-fest" betrachten.

Untersuchen wir den Text der Integrationsnormen in den mittel-, ost- und südosteuropäische Staaten, so fällt zunächst auf, dass nur ein Teil – wenn auch der überwiegende Teil – die Mitgliedschaft in der EU spezifisch nennt[13], während Polen, die Tschechische Republik und Slowenien jeweils nur von einer Übertragung von Kompetenzen auf „Internationale Organisationen" sprechen[14].

8 Entscheidung v. 07.04.2009, No. 2008-35-01.

9 Entscheidung v. 14.03.2006, http://www.lrkt.lt/dokumentai/2006/r060314.htm.

10 *M. R. Donnarumma*, Intégration européenne et sauvegarde de l'identité nationale dans la jurisprudence de la Cour de justice et des Cours constitutionnelles, RFDC 84 (2010), 719-750.

11 Entscheidung v. 24.11.2010, Ref. No. K 32/09.

12 Siehe Fn. 2.

13 So Art. 7 Abs. 1 Slowakische Verfassung, Art. 2a Ungarische Verfassung, Art. 148 Rumänische Verfassung, Art. 4 Abs. 3 Bulgarische Verfassung, Art. 68 Abs. 3 und 4 Lettische Verfassung, Litauisches EU Gesetz (13.07.2004) IX-2343, Estnisches Verfassungsgesetz 14.09.2003 RTI 2003, 64, 429.

14 Art. 90 Abs.1 Polnische Verfassung, Art. 10a Abs. 1 Tschechische Verfassung, Art. 3a Slowenische Verfassung.

Vermieden wird jeweils, den für die Besonderheit der EU immer häufiger verwendeten Begriff der „Supranationalität" zu verwenden, wohl aus dem Grund, hiermit nicht den – zumindest teilweisen – Verlust von Souveränität zu verbinden. So setzt sich das polnische Verfassungsgericht in seinem Urteil zur Mitgliedschaft in der EU von 2005 mit dieser Terminologie auseinander und lehnt eine andere Bezeichnung als die der Verfassung, nämlich „international", mit Entschiedenheit ab[15]. Dies hindert allerdings nicht, dass das Gericht die entscheidenden Merkmale der Supranationalität (mit Ausnahme des Vorrangs des EU-Rechts vor der nationalen Verfassung) ohne weiteres akzeptiert[16].

Auffallend ist weiterhin, dass i.d.R. nicht von der Übertragung von Hoheitsrechten wie in Art. 23 und 24 Abs. 1 des deutschen Grundgesetzes die Rede ist, sondern von Übertragung von Kompetenzen, teilweise sogar nur von Übertragung zur Ausübung von Kompetenzen, und dies nur von „einigen" Kompetenzen.

Während in der Rechtsprechung nur wenig Bezug zum Begriff der Übertragung und zum Begriff der Hoheitsrechte bzw. der Kompetenzen hergestellt wird[17], spielt die Eingrenzung auf „einige" Kompetenzen eine nicht unerhebliche Rolle. Davon wird noch die Rede sein.

Zentrales Thema ist die Begrenzung der Übertragungskompetenz, die argumentativ mit der Notwendigkeit begründet wird, die Integrationsnorm nur im Zusammenhang mit den übrigen Verfassungsbestimmungen zu interpretieren

---

15 K 32/09 III 2.1. „(...) modelem integracji europejskiej pozostaje forma organizacji międzynarodowej." Anders das Tschechische Verfassungsgericht ÚS 19/08 Lissabon I, Punkt 113 mit Bezug auf ÚS 50/04 Zuckerquoten (08.03.2006) „Přistoupením České republiky k EU došlo na základě čl. 10a Ústavy České republiky k přenosu pravomocí vnitrostátních orgánů na *orgány nadnárodní*"(Hervorh. d. Verf.). Siehe aber die Verwendung des Terminus „international" im Zuckerquotenurteil 2006 unter V B: „Ustanovení čl. 10a, který byl do Ústavy vložen ústavním zákonem č. 395/2001 Sb. (tzv. euronovelou Ústavy), totiž představuje ustanovení umožňující přenos některých pravomocí orgánů České republiky na *mezinárodní organizaci nebo instituci, tedy především EU a její orgány..*" (Hervorh. d. Verf.). Das BVerfG verwendet im Lissabon-Urteil den (früher vermiedenen) Begriff „supranational" ausgiebig, BVerfG, 2 BvE 2/08 v. 30.06.2009, Abs.-Nr. 1-421, http://www.bverfg.de/entscheidungen/es20090630_2bve000208.html, Abs.-Nr. 10, 59, 103, 143, 151, 227, 231, 237, 244, 246 f., 255 f. usw.

16 K 32/09 III 2.1. „Z punktu widzenia wpływu procesów integracyjnych na zakres suwerenności, porządek prawny Unii Europejskiej, na tle prawa stanowionego przez organizacje międzynarodowe, wyróżnia szerszy zakres kompetencji Unii w porównaniu z innymi organizacjami międzynarodowymi, wiążący charakter znacznej części prawa unijnego, bezpośredni skutek prawa unijnego w stosunkach wewnętrznych państw członkowskich."

17 Allerdings wird in der polnischen Rechtsprechung die Konsequenz der Übertragung als „Öffnung" der Rechtsordnung zugunsten des externen Rechts gesehen, so K 32/09 III 2.3 „(...) otwarcia porządku krajowego na prawo europejskie (...)"; ähnlich BVerfGE 37, 271, 280 Solange I.

und auf diese Weise den Kern der Verfassung, deren Identität, sicherzustellen. Teilweise wird diese Überlegung damit verknüpft, dass eben nur „einige“ Kompetenzen abgegeben werden dürfen, was niemals zu einer Aufgabe aller oder auch nur für einen speziellen Sachbereich relevanten Kompetenzen und damit auch nicht zur Preisgabe des Verfassungskerns führen dürfe[18]. Noch deutlicher wird allerdings betont, dass die Funktionalität der Integrationsnorm verfassungsgebunden sei, also die Grundstrukturen der Verfassung auch im Kontext der Integration zu erhalten seien.

IV. 1. Betrachten wir die Rechtsprechung mehr im Detail, so können wir zunächst feststellen, dass der besondere Charakter des supranationalen Rechts erkannt wird, auch wenn, wie erwähnt, dieser Terminus, der im Text der Verfassung nicht vorkommt, vermieden wird. Autonomie und Direktwirkung als wesentliche Attribute der Supranationalität werden als Charakteristika in der polnischen ebenso wie in der tschechischen Verfassungsrechtsprechung bestätigt, die *sui generis*-Natur, für die die traditionellen Schemata von Monismus und Dualismus nicht passen[19], wird anerkannt. Infolge der Wechselwirkung und gegenseitigen Verschränkung des Rechts der EU und der Mitgliedstaaten wird im polnischen Urteil zur EU-Mitgliedschaft auch lediglich von „relativer Autonomie[20]“ gesprochen. Das dritte Element der Supranationalität, der Vorrang des EU-Rechts vor dem nationalen Recht, wird dabei anerkannt, soweit es um einfaches Gesetzesrecht geht, für Verfassungsrecht von der Rechtsprechung in Polen und Litauen, in der Tschechischen Republik für das Verfassungsrecht nicht schlechthin, sondern nur für die Kernelemente der Verfassungsordnung, verneint.

2. Wie der Vorgang der Übertragung nationaler Kompetenzen auf die EU zu verstehen ist, wird in der Rechtsprechung dieser Gerichte kaum thematisiert. Mehr am Rande wird davon gesprochen, dass eine solche Übertragung eine „Öffnung“ der nationalen Rechtsordnung bedeutet und die Mitgliedstaaten darauf verzichten, auf den übertragenen Gebieten eine autonome Gesetzgebung vorzunehmen. Dieses Bild der Öffnung der vormals geschlossenen nationalen Rechtsordnung durch die Übertragung von Hoheitsrechten wird vom deutschen

---

18 K 32/09 2.1. „Konstytucja dopuszcza w art. 90 przekazanie kompetencji organów władzy państwowej jedynie w niektórych sprawach, co w świetle polskiego orzecznictwa konstytucyjnego oznacza zakaz przekazania ogółu kompetencji danego organu, przekazania kompetencji w całości spraw w danej dziedzinie i zakaz przekazania kompetencji co do istoty spraw określających gestie danego organu władzy państwowej (...).“

19 Entscheidung des polnischen Verfassungsgerichts K 18/04, These 12 (Kernthesen in *B. Banaszkiewicz*, Entscheidungen des Verfassungsgerichtshofes der Republik Polen seit dem Inkrafttreten der neuen Verfassung bis zum Urteil über die EU-Mitgliedschaft (1997-2005). Eine Übersicht, mit einem Nachwort von *R. Arnold*, Warschau 2006, in Deutsch, S. 315.

20 *Ibidem.*

Bundesverfassungsgericht bereits in den Solange-Entscheidungen vorgestellt; es erklärt den Übertragungsvorgang damit, dass die Bereitschaft erklärt wird, externes Recht in der eigenen Rechtsordnung zuzulassen und dadurch auf den Ausschließlichkeitsanspruch der Geltung nationalen Rechts auf eigenem Territorium zu verzichten[21]. Dies wird in der hier behandelten Rechtsprechung nicht in gleicher Weise ausführlich betrachtet, doch scheint der gleiche Grundgedanke, wie es durch das Bild der Öffnung ausgedrückt wird, der Rechtsprechung zugrunde zu liegen.

Die mit dem Übertragungsvorgang verbundene Argumentation konzentriert sich auf die Begrenzung der Übertragungsmöglichkeit durch die Einschränkung auf die Übertragung „bestimmter" Kompetenzen im Verfassungstext. Dies führt zur Aussage, dass nicht die Gesamtheit der Kompetenzen übertragen werden darf, aber auch nicht alle Aufgaben in einem bestimmten Sachbereich und nicht die wesentlichen Aufgaben, die zum Funktionsbereich eines bestimmten Staatsorgans gehören[22]. Eine zu weite Übertragung würde die Souveränität des Staates gefährden, diese verlange eine „Balance zwischen übertragenen und nicht übertragenen Kompetenzen[23]". *L. Garlicki* formuliert es einprägsam: Die Übertragung staatlicher Kompetenzen sei eine „Ausnahme vom Prinzip der Unabhängigkeit und Souveränität" und müsse daher eng ausgelegt werden[24]. Eine Übertragung von Kernkompetenzen, die die Souveränität des Staates beeinträchtigen, sei unzulässig (*L. Garlicki*)[25]; was für die Basis des politischen Systems fundamental sei, müsse bei den Staatsorganen verbleiben und sei Teil der Verfassungsidentität (*Działocha*)[26]. Dies wird besonders vom polnischen Verfassungsgericht hervorgehoben, doch auch das tschechische Verfassungsgericht stellt klar, dass keine Kompetenzen von „substanziellem Gewicht" übertragen werden dürften, was Souveränität und Demokratie beeinträchtigen würde[27].

---

21 BVerfGE 37, 271, 280.

22 Siehe Fn. 17.

23 K 32/09 III.2.2. „Zasada zachowania suwerenności w procesie integracji europejskiej wymaga respektowania w tym procesie konstytucyjnych granic przekazywania kompetencji, wyznaczonych przez zawężenie owego przekazania do niektórych spraw, a zatem zapewnienia właściwej równowagi pomiędzy kompetencjami przekazanymi a zachowanymi, polegającej na tym, że w przypadku kompetencji składających się na istotę suwerenności (w tym zwłaszcza stanowienie reguł konstytucyjnych i kontrola ich przestrzegania, wymiar sprawiedliwości, władza nad własnym terytorium państwa, armią i siłami zapewniającymi bezpieczeństwo oraz porządek publiczny) decydujące uprawnienia mają właściwe władze Rzeczypospolitej."

24 *Polskie prawo konstytucyjne*, Warszawa 2009, S. 57. t.

25 *L. Garlicki*, Fn. 21, S. 56. Auf beide Aussagen (Fn. 21 und 22) nimmt das Verfassungsgericht Bezug, K32/09 III 2.1.

26 Uwagi do art. 8 Konstytucji RP, in: *L. Garlicki* (Hrsg.), Konstytucja RP. Komentarz, Bd. 5, 2007, S. 14, K 32/09 III. 2.1.

27 ÚS 19/08 Lissabon I Pkt. 113 unter Bezug auf das Urteil Zuckerquoten III ÚS 50/04 „Česká republika propůjčila tyto pravomoci orgánům ES. Toto propůjčení části

3. Die Rechtsprechung in Polen, wohl unter dem Eindruck des Lissabon-Urteils des Bundesverfassungsgerichts, zieht in diesem Zusammenhang die Begriffe nationale Identität und Verfassungsidentität heran, ohne allerdings den Versuch zu unternehmen, sie genauer zu definieren[28]. Hierunter fasst man die „Grundwerte einer Verfassung", aber auch den historischen, traditionellen und kulturellen Kontext des Staates, wie er insbesondere – worauf besonders das Lissabon-Urteil des polnischen Verfassungsgerichtes hingewiesen hat – in der Verfassungspräambel Polens zum Ausdruck kommt[29]. Nach tschechischem Verfassungsrecht darf die Übertragung interner Kompetenzen nicht das „Wesen der Republik als souveräner und demokratischer Rechtsstaat" berühren[30].

4. Ob die Souveränität der Mitgliedstaaten angesichts der zahlreichen Kompetenzübertragungen noch gewahrt bleibt, ist eine weitere Frage, die von polnischen und tschechischen Verfassungsgerichten bejaht wird. Zentrales Argument ist die Freiwilligkeit der Mitgliedschaft in der EU, die dazu führe, dass Souveränität gemeinsam ausgeübt werde[31]. Hierin wird von der Rechtsprechung keine

---

pravomocí je propůjčením podmíněným; může trvat potud, pokud jsou tyto pravomoci vykonávány orgány ES způsobem slučitelným s uchováním základů státní suverenity České republiky a způsobem, jenž neohrožuje samu podstatu materiálního právního státu."

28 K 32/09 III 2.1. „Normatywnym wyrazem tej zasady jest Konstytucja, a w szczególności postanowienia preambuły, art. 2, art. 4, art. 5, art. 8, art. 90, art. 104 ust. 2 i art. 126 ust. 1, w świetle których suwerenność Rzeczypospolitej wyraża się w nieprzekazywalnych kompetencjach organów władzy państwowej, stanowiących o *tożsamości konstytucyjnej państwa.*" (Hervorh. d. Verf.); „Gwarancją zachowania *tożsamości konstytucyjnej Rzeczypospolitej* pozostaje art. 90 Konstytucji i określone w nim granice przekazywania kompetencji." (Hervorh. d. Verf.).

29 K 32/09 III 2.1. „Trybunał Konstytucyjny podziela wyrażony w doktrynie pogląd, że kompetencje objęte zakazem przekazania, *stanowią o tożsamości konstytucyjnej, a więc odzwierciedlają wartości, na których opiera się Konstytucja* (por. *L. Garlicki, Normy konstytucyjne relatywnie niezmienialne,* [w:] *Charakter i struktura norm Konstytucji,* red.: J. Trzciński, Warszawa 1997, S. 148)." (Hervorh. d. Verf.); siehe auch *ibidem,* „Tożsamość konstytucyjna pozostaje w ścisłym związku z pojęciem tożsamości narodowej, które *obejmuje także tradycję i kulturę.*" (Hervorh. d. Verf.).

30 Pl. ÚS 19/08 Punkt 97 „Z čl. 10a odst. 1 Ústavy plyne, že mezinárodní smlouvou lze přenést na mezinárodní organizace nikoli pravomoci všechny, nýbrž jen pravomoci některé. Uvedený článek je třeba interpretovat zejména v souvislosti s citovanými čl. 1 odst. 1 a čl. 9 odst. 2 Ústavy. Přenos pravomocí orgánů České republiky tedy *nemůže jít tak daleko, aby narušil samu podstatu republiky jako svrchovaného a demokratického právního státu založeného na úctě právům a svobodám člověka a občana a aby založil změnu podstatných náležitostí demokratického právního státu.*" (Hervorh. d. Verf.).

31 K 32/09 III.2.1. „Odróżnia się ograniczenia suwerenności, wynikające *z woli państwa,* zgodne z prawem międzynarodowym, o naruszeńsuwerenności następujących wbrew woli państwa i niezgodnych z prawem międzynarodowym." Vgl. auch das Tschechische Verfassungsgericht ÚS 19/08 „108. Z uvedených úvah lze tedy dovodit, že přenesení určitých kompetencí státu, které vyvěrá ze svobodné vůle suveréna a bude nadále

echte Einschränkung oder gar ein Verlust der Souveränität gesehen, sondern deren Bestätigung und Stärkung[32]. Dass durch die Mitgliedschaft in der EU Souveränität erhalten bleibt, wird aus verschiedenen Umständen gefolgert: dass keine widerrufbare Übertragung stattgefunden habe, dass die Mitgliedstaaten „Herren der Verträge“ bleiben und weiterhin „Subjekte des Integrationsprozesses“ sind, dass sie die Kompetenz-Kompetenz behalten und dass der Grundsatz der begrenzten Einzelermächtigung eine Kompetenzübernahme durch die EU gegen den Willen der Mitgliedstaaten ausschließe[33].

Ob bestimmte Bereiche von einer Übertragung auf die EU ausgeschlossen sind, wird von den Verfassungsgerichten nicht beantwortet. Insbesondere das ungarische Verfassungsgericht lässt diese Frage ausdrücklich offen, da sie vom Gesetzgeber und damit von der Politik zu bestimmen sei[34].

5. Die Verfassungsrechtsprechung zeigt deutlich, dass eine Tendenz besteht, sie entweder als Ganzes durch Verneinung des Vorrangs des EU-Rechts vor dem Verfassungsrecht überhaupt zu schützen oder bestimmte Teile für unantastbar zu erklären. Hier divergieren das polnische und litauische Verfassungsgericht einerseits und das tschechische und ungarische Verfassungsgericht andererseits. In Litauen ist das Argument wesentlich, dass die Verfassung nur den Vorrang vor den Gesetzen ausdrücklich vorsieht, während in Polen auf Art. 8 Abs. 1 der Verfassung rekurriert wird. Dieser bezeichnet die Verfassung als das oberste Recht im Staat, dem – so die Meinung des Verfassungsgerichts – auch nicht das EU-Recht übergeordnet sei.[35]Dass es hierbei nicht um ein Verhältnis der Normenhierarchie geht, sondern zwei autonome Rechtsordnungen nebeneinander stehen, deren Kollision im Wege des Anwendungsvorrangs des EU-

---

vykonáváno za jeho účasti předem dohodnutým, kontrolovaným způsobem, není pojmovým oslabením svrchovanosti, *ale může naopak ve svých důsledcích znamenat její posílení ve společném postupu integrovaného celku.* Integrační proces EU se neděje radikálním způsobem, který by obecně znamenal „ztrátu“ národní suverenity, nýbrž jde o proces evoluční, a – kromě jiného – i o reakci na postupující globalizaci ve světě.“ (Hervorh. d. Verf.).

32 K 32/09 III.2.1. „W przekonaniu Trybunału Konstytucyjnego zaciąganie zobowiązań międzynarodowych i ich wykonywanie nie prowadzi do utraty lub ograniczenia suwerenności państwa, ale jest *jej potwierdzeniem*, a przynależność do struktur europejskich nie stanowi w istocie ograniczenia suwerenności państwowej, *lecz jest jej wyrazem.*“ (Hervorh. d. Verf.).

33 K 32/09 III. 2.1. “(...) co jednak nie prowadzi do trwałego ograniczenia suwerennych praw tych państw, ponieważ przekazanie kompetencji *nie jest nieodwracalne*“; „Państwa te pozostają jednak podmiotami procesu integracji, *zachowują „kompetencję kompetencji”*, a modelem integracji europejskiej pozostaje forma organizacji międzynarodowej.“ (Hervorh. d. Verf.).

34 *P. Kovács*, Introduction à la jurisprudence de la Cour constitutionnelle de la République de Hongrie. Approche thématique, Entwicklungen im Europäischen Recht, *R. Arnold* (Hrsg.), Bd. 1, 2011, S. 118 ff.

35 So bereits K 18/04 und, dies bestätigend, K 32/09 III. 2.2. und 2.5.

Rechts gelöst wird, wird nicht erkannt. Es geht also nicht um einen Geltungsvorrang, wie dies das Argument der Normenhierarchie, das auf Art. 8 Abs. 1 der Verfassung gestützt wird, nahe legen würde. Das Verfassungsgericht verneint aber auch die Möglichkeit des Anwendungsvorrangs.

6. Ein Teil der Kollisionen zwischen dem Verfassungsrecht und dem EU-Recht kann dadurch vermieden werden, dass das nationale Verfassungsrecht „europarechtsfreundlich" ausgelegt wird. Diese Auslegungsmethode entspricht dem im Unionsrecht verankerten Grundsatz der gegenseitigen Loyalität (vgl. Art. 4 Abs. 3 des neuen EU-Vertrags). Schon früh hat sich die Verfassungsrechtsprechung Polens[36] und auch der Tschechischen Republik[37] dieser Methode bedient und manche schwierige Fragestellung, so z.B. zum Europawahlrecht von EU-Bürgern in Polen, ohne Konflikt mit dem Unionsrecht gelöst. Auch das deutsche Bundesverfassungsgericht anerkennt diese Möglichkeit der präventiven Kollisionslösung, auf die es im Lissabon-Urteil hinweist[38]. Diese vom Unionsrecht selbst gebotene Methode scheint nunmehr zum festen Bestandteil des europäischen Verfassungsdenkens geworden zu sein. Ihre Grenze findet sich jedoch dort, wo der Wortlaut des Verfassungstextes wegen seiner Eindeutigkeit nicht mehr auslegungsfähig ist.

V. Analysiert man die Verfassungsrechtsprechung in Mittel-, Ost- und Südosteuropa im Rahmen unserer Thematik, so kann man feststellen:

(1) Es besteht die Bereitschaft, auf der Grundlage der Integrationsnormen der Verfassung die Strukturmerkmale der supranationalen Organisationen, zumindest weitgehend, zu akzeptieren. Eine Ausnahme bildet der Anspruch, dass EU-Recht auch Vorrang vor dem nationalen Verfassungsrecht besitzt. Zum Teil wird der Verfassungsvorrang schlechthin verneint, zum Teil werden Grundelemente der Verfassungsordnung als „unionsfest" betrachtet.

(2) Die Verfassungsgerichte verteidigen die „Identität" der nationalen Verfassungsordnung. Dieser vom deutschen Bundesverfassungsgericht in seinem Lissabon-Urteil häufig gebrauchte Begriff hat Ausstrahlungswirkung auf die polnische Verfassungsrechtsprechung. Das tschechische Verfassungsgericht umschreibt den Inhalt dieses Begriffs mit dem Hinweis auf die Grundelemente der Verfassungsordnung. Auch wenn der Terminus „Verfassungsidentität" nicht gebraucht wird, so stellt der Schutz der Kerngehalte einer Verfassung funktionell das Gleiche dar.

(3) Was Verfassungsidentität und grundlegender Gehalt der Verfassungsordnung bedeuten, wird jeweils nur punktuell definiert. Eine umfassende Definition steht aus, wird aber, wie es scheint, von der Verfassungsrechtsprechung auch nicht angestrebt, um die Reaktion auf ein sich dynamisch entwickelndes

---

36 K 11/03 sowie K 18/04.

37 Z.B. die Entscheidung zum Europäischen Haftbefehl ÚS 66/04.

38 BVerfG, 2 BvE 2/08 v. 30.06.2009, http://www.bverfg.de/entscheidungen/es20090630_2bve000208.html, Abs.-Nr. 241.

Verfassungsverständnis und neu entstehende Souveränitätsanforderungen offen zu halten. Auch wird die Frage kaum berührt, ob Verfassungsidentität ganz oder teilweise nur substanziell oder auch funktionell zu begreifen ist. Dies ist die Frage, ob die Ablösung eines nationalen Verfassungsinstruments durch einen supranationalen, funktionell gleichwertigen Mechanismus die konkrete Verfassungsidentität wahrt oder beeinträchtigt. Dies ist im Grunde die Solange II-Konzeption des deutschen Bundesverfassungsgerichts, die es auch aus der nationalen Verfassungsperspektive erlaubt, dass der supranationale den nationalen Grundrechtsschutz ablöst. Verfassungsidentität wird also auf diese Weise funktionell gewahrt, ohne dass es auf die substanzielle Weiterexistenz des konkreten nationalen Verfassungsinstruments, also des nationalen Grundrechtsschutzes, ankommt. Sicherlich kann eine solche funktionelle Ablösung des nationalen durch das supranationale Instrument nur bei solchen Sachverhalten ohne Verletzung der nationalen Verfassungsidentität eingreifen, die ausreichenden Bezug zu beiden Rechtsordnungen – der nationalen und der supranationalen – besitzen und damit überhaupt die Frage der Konkurrenz des Grundrechtsschutzes aufwerfen.

(4) Der Schutz der nationalen Verfassungsidentität wird vom Unionsrecht akzeptiert, das in Art. 4 des neuen EU-Vertrags aus der Unionsperspektive die „nationale" Identität garantiert und – gleichfalls aus der Unionsperspektive – die Verfassungsidentität in diese Garantie einschließt. Wie weit es zu Divergenzen zwischen den beiden Perspektiven, derjenigen des Verfassungsgerichts und derjenigen des Gerichtshofs der EU kommen kann, wird in der Verfassungsrechtsprechung allerdings kaum thematisiert.

Insgesamt betrachtet kann man davon sprechen, dass die nationalen Verfassungsgerichte eine auf Gleichgewicht bedachte Koexistenz von nationalem Verfassungsrecht und supranationalem Unionsrecht mit Erfolg anstreben.

Neujustierung der Rolle zentraler Verfassungsorgane im politischen Prozess

Zur aktuellen Verfassungsrechtsentwicklung in der Ukraine, Kirgistan und Russland

Prof. Dr. Dr. hc Angelika Nußberger[*]

I. Von Originalen und Kopien

Nicht nur das Rad muss nicht immer wieder neu erfunden werden. Auch bei der Ausarbeitung von Verfassungstexten kann man auf Vorhandenes und Bewährtes zurückgreifen, kann das Wissen über Mechanismen zur Beschränkung und Regelung von Macht, das sich in anderen Kulturen und Zeitepochen angesammelt hat, verwenden. Allerdings ist es leichter, Texte zu kopieren, als Institutionen, die sich unter bestimmten Gegebenheiten bewährt haben, in anderem Kontext mit Leben zu erfüllen.

Es überrascht nicht, dass sich in den Transformationsstaaten Mittel- und Osteuropas, die nach der Wende neue Verfassungen ausgearbeitet haben, an vielen Stellen identische Formulierungen finden. Beispielsweise besteht große Einigkeit darin, den Staat als „Rechtsstaat“[1], als „Demokratie“[2] und als „sozialen Staat“[3] zu bezeichnen, Etiketten, die gerade in Gegenden wie Zentralasien, aber auch in anderen Teilen der ehemaligen Sowjetunion, nicht als traditionelle Konzepte einen lang in die Vergangenheit reichenden Rückhalt haben[4]. In der rechtsvergleichenden Forschung hat man – gerade auch mit Blick auf mögliche

---

* Direktorin des Instituts für Ostrecht der Universität zu Köln, Richterin am Europäischen Gerichtshof für Menschenrechte.

1 Im Russischen wird dabei i.d.R. die wörtliche Übersetzung des Wortes Rechtsstaat („*pravovoe gosudarstvo*“), verwendet, nicht aber die Übersetzung des englischen Begriffes „*rule of law*“. Die Konzepte sind nach historischer Herkunft und auch nach ihrer Schwerpunktsetzung unterschiedlich, da der Rechtsstaatsbegriff mehr als der Begriff „*rule of law*“ die Entwicklung des Rechts im staatlichen Rahmen betont; vgl. *K. Tuori*, The Rule of Law and the Rechtsstaat, in: Ratio and Voluntas, Kapitel 7, im Erscheinen.

2 Hier wird im Russischen wie auch in den westeuropäischen Sprachen der auf die griechische Sprache zurückgehende Begriff „demokratija“ verwendet.

3 Im Russischen lässt sich „Sozialstaat“ nur in der Form des „sozialen Staates“ (social'noe gosudarstvo) übersetzen; vgl. zu den Bedeutungsnuancen im Deutschen *H.F. Zacher*, § 28 Das soziale Staatsziel, in: Handbuch des Staatsrechts, *Isensee/Kirchhof* (Hrsg.), Band II, 3. Aufl., Heidelberg 2004.

4 Zu der sowjetischen Tradition anschaulich *F.-C. Schroeder*, 74 Jahre Sowjetrecht, München 1992.

Abstoßungsreaktionen – vielfach den Begriff der „Rechtstransplantation" bemüht[5]. Denn das, was man – manches Mal unbesehen und ungeprüft – übernimmt, findet oftmals nicht wirklich Eingang in anderen Rechtskreisen und Rechtskulturen. Der Transfer von Recht kann scheitern[6].

Für die Ostrechtsforschung war die Frage des Rechtstransfers, der Imitation und Adaption von Rechtsinstituten und Rechtskonzepten schon immer relevant[7]. An Beispielen ließ sich eine Vielzahl finden; die Tradition reicht von der Rezeption aufklärerischen Gedankenguts im „Bolšoj Nakaz" von Katharina II. bis zur Rezeption von EG-Richtlinien im modernen russischen Zivilrecht. In ganz besonderer Weise ist die Übernahme von Konzepten, Dogmen und Begründungsmustern auch im Bereich des Straf- und Strafprozessrechts zu beobachten, wie *Professor Dr. Dres. h.c. F.-C. Schroeder* in einer Vielzahl seiner Schriften, insbesondere mit Blick auf Russland, aufgezeigt hat. Dabei hat er auch deutlich gemacht, dass es in der Retrospektive, 20 Jahre nach dem juristischen Neubeginn, auch gute Gründe gibt, Rechtstransfer mit wenig Optimismus zu betrachten, haben sich doch trotz vieler Neuerungen oftmals wieder alte Stereotype durchgesetzt und damit die vorgezeichneten Spurrillen als dominante Richtungsgeber erwiesen.[8]

Dies soll im Folgenden an zwei Beispielen von Mutationen von aus dem Westen in den Osten, in die Nachfolgestaaten der ehemaligen Sowjetunion, transferierten Institutionen gezeigt werden, zum einen an der Veränderung der Funktion des Verfassungsgerichts im politischen Prozess in der Ukraine und in

---

5 Der Begriff stammt ursprünglich von *A. Watson* in seinem 1974 erschienenen Buch „Legal Transplants. An approach to Comparative Law" (2. Aufl. 1993). In der rechtsvergleichenden Wissenschaft löste die Metapher eine lang andauernde Theoriediskussion aus; vgl. dazu *C. Varga*, Transfers of Law. A conceptual analysis, in: Hungary's legal assistance. Experience in the age of globalization, Nagoya 2006; *A. Nußberger*, Verfassungsrechtstransfer von West nach Ost. Illusion, Desillusion, Neubeginn, Osteuropa 2010, S. 81-96.

6 Mit Blick auf die Rolle der Verfassungsgerichtsbarkeit *A. Nußberger*, Verfassungsgerichtsbarkeit als Krönung des Rechtsstaats oder als Feigenblatt autoritärer Regime?, JZ 2010, S. 533-540.

7 Zur traditionellen Ostrechtsforschung vgl. *F.-C. Schroeder*, Methodenprobleme der Ostrechtsforschung, in: *B. Meissner*, Grundsatzfragen der Ostrechtsforschung, Tübingen 1980, S. 79-102; *D.A. Loeber*, Rechtsvergleichung zwischen Ländern mit verschiedener Wirtschaftsordnung, RabelsZ Jg. 26, H. 2, S. 201-229; *K. Westen*, Die Rolle der Rechtsvergleichung im ost- und mitteleuropäischen Reformprozess, Recht in Ost und West 1991, S. 1-5; *A. Nußberger*, Die Frage nach dem tertium comparationis. Zu den Schwierigkeiten einer rechtsvergleichenden Analyse des russischen Rechts, Recht in Ost und West 1998, S. 81-88.

8 Zuletzt die umfassende Darstellung des russischen Straf- und Strafprozessrechts von *F.-C. Schroeder* in: *A. Nußberger*, Einführung ins russische Recht, München 2010, S. 313-344.

Kirgistan, zum anderen an der Neujustierung der Aufgaben des Föderationsrats in der Russischen Föderation.

II. Verfassungsgerichte als Katalysatoren in Verfassungsreformprozessen

1. Entscheidung des ukrainischen Verfassungsgerichts v. 30.09.2010

Am 30.09.2010 erließ das ukrainische Verfassungsgericht eine sehr überraschende Entscheidung: Mit sofortiger Wirkung erklärte es die Verfassung in der Version, die es durch das unmittelbar nach der orangen Revolution ausgearbeitete Verfassungsänderungsgesetz vom 08.12.2004 Nr. 2222-IV[9] bekommen hatte, für verfassungswidrig[10]. Damit wurde die Verfassung von 1996, die unter Präsident Kutschma gegolten hatte, wieder in Kraft gesetzt. Zur Begründung verwies das Gericht auf einen Formfehler bei der Verabschiedung der Verfassungsrevision, der schon damals nicht unbemerkt geblieben und vielfach kritisiert worden war[11]: Nach Art. 159 der Verfassung der Ukraine (VerfUkr) sind Verfassungsänderungen durch die Verchovna Rada nur möglich, wenn dazu ein Gutachten des Verfassungsgerichts vorliegt, das nach Art. 157 und 158 VerfUkr zu drei Fragen Stellung zu nehmen hat. Es muss prüfen, ob Menschen- oder Bürgerrechte abgeschafft oder eingeschränkt worden sind, ob die Verfassungsänderung die Unabhängigkeit oder territoriale Integrität der Ukraine gefährdet und ob die vorgeschlagenen Verfassungsänderungen schon einmal eingebracht worden sind. Ein entsprechendes Gutachten hatte im Jahr 2004 zu einem ersten Entwurf einer Verfassungsänderung, dem Gesetz Nr. 4180, vorgelegen, nicht aber zu dem nochmals überarbeiteten Gesetz Nr. 2222-IV. Aufgrund dieses Formfehlers hob das Verfassungsgericht im Jahr 2010 die aus dem Jahr 2004 stammenden Änderungen auf, ohne auf die materiell-rechtliche Frage einzugehen, ob ein entsprechendes Gutachten die Verfassungsänderung von 2004 überhaupt inhaltlich hätte beanstanden und den Verfassungsänderungsprozess damit hätte beeinflussen oder gar aufhalten können. Die Entscheidung wurde mit 17 gegen eine Stimme getroffen; nur der Richter *V. Šiškin* vertrat eine abweichende Auffassung.

9 Vidomosti Verchovnoï Rady Ukraïny 2005, Nr. 2, Pos. 44.

10 Entscheidung des ukrainischen Verfassungsgerichts v. 30.09.2010, Nr. 1-45/2010.

11 Siehe u.a. das Gutachten der Venedigkommission „Opinion on the amendments to the Constitution of Ukraine" (CDL-AD(2005)015).

2. Entscheidung des kirgisischen Verfassungsgerichts v. 14.09.2007

In der Geschichte der Verfassungsgerichtsbarkeit gibt es wohl kaum Entscheidungen, die mit derjenigen in der Ukraine vergleichbar wären, insbesondere, da die Nichtigerklärung aufgrund eines Formfehlers erst erfolgte, nachdem die entsprechenden Bestimmungen bereits fünf Jahre hindurch das politische Leben in der Ukraine bestimmt hatten und auch vom Verfassungsgericht in einer Vielzahl von Entscheidungen angewendet worden waren[12].

Ein wichtiger Präzedenzfall ist allerdings die Entscheidung des kirgisischen Verfassungsgerichts vom 14.09.2007, die nicht nur eine, sondern gleich zwei Verfassungsreformgesetze und damit die Verfassung in der Version vom 09.11.2006 und in der Version vom 30.12.2006 aus formellen Gründen für nichtig erklärte.[13] Auch hier war der Grund, dass, anders als in der Verfassung vorgesehen[14], dem Verfassungsgericht keine Möglichkeit gegeben worden war, zu den Verfassungsänderungen Stellung zu nehmen. Allerdings war der zeitliche Abstand zwischen dem Inkrafttreten der Verfassungsänderungen und der Entscheidung des Verfassungsgerichts nicht so lang wie in der Ukraine, sondern betrug nur ein knappes Jahr.

3. Die Problematik der Nichtigerklärung verfassungswidriger Verfassungsnormen durch ein Verfassungsgericht

a) Abgrenzung zwischen „Pouvoir constituant" und „Pouvoir constitué"

Nun ist die Aufgabe eines Verfassungsgerichts, so wie die Institution in der westeuropäischen Tradition entwickelt worden ist, primär, die Einhaltung der Verfassungsbestimmungen sicherzustellen. Dies findet im Gesetz „Über das ukrainische Verfassungsgericht"[15] explizit Ausdruck, wenn es in Art. 2 heißt, die Aufgabe des Verfassungsgerichts der Ukraine sei, „die Vorherrschaft der Verfassung der Ukraine als Grundgesetz des Staates auf dem Territorium der Ukraine zu garantieren". In ähnlicher Weise wurde dies auch im Verfassungsgerichts-

---

12 In der südamerikanischen Verfassungsrechtsgeschichte ist ein entsprechender Fall bekannt: Mit einer Entscheidung aus dem Jahr 1983 (Entscheidung des Obersten Gerichts von Kolumbien, Akt Nr. 51 de 03.11.1981 „Inexequibilidad de la reforma constitucional. Acto Legislativo Numero 1 de 1979) erklärte das Oberste Gericht von Kolumbien eine Verfassungsreform insgesamt aus formellen Gründen für ungültig.

13 Entscheidung des kirgisischen Verfassungsgerichts v. 14.09.2007.

14 Art. 96 Abs. 3 der Verfassung Kirgistans v. 05.05.1993 in der Fassung v. 18.02.2003, abrufbar unter http://www.ar-namys.org/read/526.html (letzter Zugriff 20.12.2010).

15 Gesetz v. 16.10.1996 mit nachfolgenden Änderungen von 2006, 2009 und 2010.

gesetz von Kirgistan formuliert[16]. Damit wird eine westeuropäische Denktradition rezipiert, die zum einen die Vorrangstellung der Verfassung als „Akt der Selbstbestimmung des Volkes resp. der Nation“[17] zum Ausdruck bringt, zum anderen aber auch dem Verfassungsgericht eine entsprechende Kontrollfunktion über die anderen Staatsgewalten zubilligt.

Grundlegend für das Verständnis der Verfassung als einem zu schützenden Gut und der Funktion des Verfassungsgerichts als eines Wächters dieses Guts, ist die Unterscheidung zwischen der verfassungsgebenden Gewalt (*Pouvoir constituant*) und den durch die Verfassungen geschaffenen und legitimierten Verfassungsorganen (*Pouvoirs constitués*). Letztere operieren in dem Rahmen, der ihnen durch die Verfassung gesetzt ist. Das bedeutet, dass es „begrenzte Gewalten“ sind, die die „Vorgaben der höheren Verfassungsordnung“ zu respektieren haben“[18]. Einer der zentralen Vordenker der modernen Verfassungsordnungen, *Abbé Sieyès*, hatte dies in seiner grundlegenden Schrift „Qu'est-ce que le tiers état?“ zum Ausdruck gebracht: „Eine an Verfassungsregeln gebundene Körperschaft kann nur nach ihrer Verfassung entscheiden. Eine andere Verfassung kann sie sich nicht geben.“[19] Dies muss grundsätzlich auch für ein Verfassungsgericht als „an Verfassungsregeln gebundene Körperschaft“ gelten, auch wenn dies für *Sieyès* noch nicht vorstellbar war.

b) Materiell-rechtliche Kontrolle von Verfassungsänderungen durch das Verfassungsgericht

Vor diesem Hintergrund ist es sehr problematisch, wenn ein Verfassungsgericht selbst die Grundlage, auf der es operiert, ändern oder gar außer Kraft setzen kann. Denkbar sind zwei Fälle: Zum einen kann die Nichtigerklärung von Verfassungsbestimmungen eine Sanktion für einen Verstoß gegen das für eine Verfassungsänderung vorgesehene Verfahren sein. Zum anderen kann es eine materiell-rechtliche Kontrolle geben, wenn die Verfassung selbst eine Hierarchisierung der Verfassungsbestimmungen vorsieht und einzelne Bestimmungen als unabänderbar, andere aber als änderbar ausweist.

Letzteres gilt beispielsweise für das Grundgesetz mit seinen in Art. 79 Abs. 3 GG zementierten „Ewigkeitsgarantien“. Damit wurde aufgrund der Erfahrungen in der Weimarer Zeit eine „Grenzmauer“ errichtet, die, wie

---

16 Art. 1 Abs. 2 Gesetz über das Verfassungsgericht v. 18.12.1993 (Nr. 1335-XII): „Das Verfassungsgericht wird mit dem Ziel gegründet, die Vorrangstellung der Verfassung der Republik Kirgistan auf dem Territorium der Kirgisischen Republik zu sichern, die verfassungsmäßige Ordnung sowie die Rechte und Freiheiten der Menschen zu schützen.“

17 *H. Dreier*, Gilt das Grundgesetz ewig? Fünf Kapitel zum modernen Verfassungsstaat, München 2008, S. 18.

18 *H. Dreier*, a.a.O. Fn. 17, S. 20.

19 *E.J. Sieyès*, Politische Schriften 1788-1790, übersetzt und herausgegeben von *E. Schmitt* und *R. Reichardt*, 2. Aufl., München, Wien 1981, S. 117-195 (172).

R. Thomas bereits 1948 erklärte, „nur um den Preis eines rücksichtslosen und offensichtlich rechtswidrigen Verfassungsbruchs überstiegen werden könnte". Nach seiner Meinung macht es die Ewigkeitsgarantie unmöglich, „die Revolution oder den Staatsstreich in den trügerischen Schafspelz scheinbarer Legalität zu hüllen"[20].

Allerdings bedeutet eine derartige Hierarchisierung der Verfassungsbestimmungen nicht unbedingt, dass sie auch einer justiziellen Kontrolle zugänglich wäre. Das deutsche Verfassungssystem ist eines der wenigen Beispiele, in dem das Verfassungsgericht die Verfassungswidrigkeit verfassungsändernder Gesetze überprüfen kann und in einer Vielzahl von Fällen auch tatsächlich überprüft hat[21]. Noch nie hat eine derartige Entscheidung allerdings zur Nichtigerklärung der entsprechenden Änderung geführt, anders als etwa in Österreich[22] und Bulgarien[23]. In den U.S.A. besteht zwar theoretisch eine entsprechende Überprüfungskompetenz, sie war aber in keinem der 27 Amendments seit 1787 von praktischer Bedeutung; dasselbe gilt für Norwegen[24]. Ein Gegenbeispiel ist allerdings die Türkei. Dort ist in Art. 4 der Verfassung geregelt, dass die in Art. 1, 2 und 3 normierten Grundprinzipien, wie etwa die Definition der Türkei als einheitlichen und säkularen Staat, nicht geändert werden dürfen. Verfassungsgerichtliche Überprüfung ist zugelassen, nach Art. 148 aber nur begrenzt auf die Kontrolle der Einhaltung bestimmter formeller und verfahrensrechtlicher Voraussetzungen. Die materiell-rechtliche Überprüfung und Nichtigerklärung einer Verfassungsänderung durch das türkische Verfassungsgericht[25], die das Tragen

---

20 *R. Thomas*, Über Wesen und Erscheinungsformen der modernen Demokratie (1948), in: *H. Dreier* (Hrsg.), Rechtsstaat – Demokratie – Grundrechte, Tübingen 2008, S. 406-442 (441).

21 BVerfGE 1, 14 (Südweststaat); 3, 225 (Gleichberechtigung); 4, 157 (Saarstatut); 30, 1 (Abhörurteil); 34, 9 (Besoldungsvereinheitlichung); 84, 90 (Bodenreform I); 87, 181 (7. Rundfunkentscheidung); 89, 155 (Maastricht); 94, 12 (Bodenreform II); 94, 49 (Sichere Drittstaaten); 95, 48 (Restitution und Vertragsanfechtung); 102, 370 (Körperschaftsstatus der Zeugen Jehovas); 109, 279 (Großer Lauschangriff); 113, 273 (Europäischer Haftbefehl); 123, 267 (Lissabon).

22 Entscheidung des österreichischen Verfassungsgerichts G 12/00-17 u.a. v. 11.10.2001, abrufbar unter http://www.vfgh.gv.at/cms/vfgh-site/entscheid.html?periode=old (letzter Zugriff 20.12.2010).

23 Entscheidung des bulgarischen Verfassungsgerichts 03/04 v. 05.07.2004 und Entscheidung 06/06 v. 13.09.2006.

24 In Norwegen beispielsweise dürfen nach Art. 112 der Verfassung Verfassungsänderungen nicht den Grundprinzipien der Verfassung widersprechen. Da es kein Verfassungsgericht gibt, haben grundsätzlich die allgemeinen Gerichte die Überprüfungskompetenz. Aber obwohl die Verfassung von 1814 mehr als 200 Mal geändert wurde, ist eine entsprechende Überprüfung bisher noch nicht vorgenommen worden.

25 Entscheidung des türkischen Verfassungsgerichts v. 05.06.2008, die das Gesetz Nr. 5735 für nichtig erklärte.

von Kopftüchern an Universitäten gestattete, wurde so als Kompetenzüberschreitung vehement kritisiert[26].

c) Formell-rechtliche Kontrolle von Verfassungsänderungen durch das Verfassungsgericht

Die Vorstellung, die Verfassung entstehe in einem „außerordentlichen Urakt der Rechtsschöpfung"[27], ist nur verfassungsrechtstheoretische Fiktion. Abgesichert wird der hierarchische Vorrang der Verfassung gegenüber dem einfachen Gesetzesrecht i.d.R. lediglich durch bestimmte Verfahrensbestimmungen, die besondere Mehrheiten, Fristen und Abstimmungsmodalitäten vorschreiben. Sicherzustellen, dass diese eingehalten werden, ist eine Aufgabe, die naheliegender Weise Verfassungsgerichten als den „Hütern der Verfassung" zugewiesen wird[28].

Damit scheinen sich die eingangs zitierten Entscheidungen des ukrainischen und des kirgisischen Verfassungsgerichts problemlos in die Tradition der Verfassungsrechtsprechung einzufügen, wurden doch in beiden Fällen, auch wenn die Verfassung selbst der Kontrolle unterzogen wurde, nur Verfahrensfehler gerügt und die Frage der inhaltlichen „Richtigkeit" der Bestimmungen bewusst ausgeblendet. Dieser Schein trügt allerdings, wirft man einen Blick auf den Kontext der verfassungsrechtlichen Entwicklung in den beiden Ländern.

4. Die Entscheidungen des ukrainischen und kirgisischen Verfassungsgerichts im politischen Kontext

Die Entwicklung sowohl in der Ukraine als auch in Kirgistan zeichnet sich im Vergleich zu der Mehrzahl der Nachfolgestaaten der Sowjetunion durch eine anhaltende Instabilität aus; in beiden Ländern gelingt es nicht, im Konsens eine allseits akzeptierte verfassungsrechtliche Basis für den politischen Prozess zu schaffen[29].

---

26 Dazu die Ausführungen in dem bereits zitierten Bericht der Venedigkommission zu Verfassungsänderungen (CDL-AD(2010)001, § 233).

27 *H. Dreier*, a.a.O. Fn. 17, S. 20.

28 Dazu die Stellungnahme der Venedigkommission (CDL-AD(2010)001, § 237): „Quite another matter is a purely *formal* control in order to check and ensure that the amendments have been adopted following the prescribed constitutional procedures. Here the Venice Commission would strongly support all systems that allow for effective and democratic supervision of the way in which the constitutional amendment procedures have been respected and followed. And if there is reason to believe that the amendments have been passed in breach of the constitutional requirements, then this is an issue which may suitably be tried before a court."

29 Zur Ukraine vgl. *O. Luchterhandt*, Der Kampf um das Regierungssystem der Ukraine – eine unendliche Geschichte, Ukraine-Analysen v. 12.10.2010 (Nr. 80), S. 2 ff., abrufbar unter http://www.laender-analysen.de/ukraine/pdf/UkraineAnalysen80.pdf (letzter Zugriff 20.12.2010); zu Kirgistan vgl. *T. Kunze*, Die Geschichte einer Verfassung: Machtsicherung für Präsident Akajew oder Stunde Null der Opposition in Kirgistan?, KAS/AI

In der Ukraine wurde nach langem Vorlauf erst 1996 eine neue Verfassung verabschiedet, die *de iure* eine vergleichsweise gut ausbalancierte Machtverteilung in einem gemischt präsidentiell-parlamentarischen System vorzugeben schien[30], eine zunehmend autoritäre Entwicklung unter Präsident *Kutschma* aber ebenso wenig wie eine andauernde Konfrontation zwischen Exekutive und Legislative verhindern konnte. Deutlich wurde die gegenseitige Blockade etwa an dem Gesetz „Über die Regierung der Ukraine", das Status und Kompetenzen der Regierung im Verhältnis zu Parlament und Präsident regeln sollte und das achtmal per Veto geblockt wurde, bevor es im Jahr 2007 in Kraft treten konnte. Die sogenannte „Orange Revolution" im Jahr 2004 war ein sichtbares Zeichen der Entfremdung zwischen politischer Elite und Volk. Unmittelbarer Auslöser der Massenproteste waren die Wahlfälschungen zugunsten des von Präsident *Kutschma* favorisierten Kandidaten *Janukowytsch*. Der Oppositionskandidat *Juschtschenko* setzte sich durch, musste aber mit der Verfassungsänderung von 2004 deutliche Einschränkungen seiner Befugnisse hinnehmen. Die Verfassungsänderung spiegelt einen in aller Eile ausgehandelten, handwerklich mehr als mangelhaften Kompromiss mit weitreichenden Folgen wider. Das politische System der Ukraine wurde von einem gemischten System in ein parlamentarisches System transformiert, allerdings mit einer Vielzahl von Bruchstellen und Widersprüchlichkeiten, die das Regieren auf Jahre hinaus nicht nur erschwerten, sondern aufgrund der personalpolitischen Konstellation nahezu unmöglich machten[31].

Im Grunde bestand bereits unmittelbar nach der Verabschiedung dieses Kompromisses Konsens, dass eine neue, grundlegende Reform notwendig wäre. Verschiedene Reformvorschläge wurden in den politischen Prozess eingebracht, allerdings allesamt ohne Erfolg, da sich die politischen Akteure gegenseitig blockierten.[32] Bei der Präsidentschaftswahl im Februar 2010[33] konnte *Janukowytsch* zwar eine Mehrheit erringen, jedoch keine Regierung bilden, da der von ihm geführten Koalition sieben Stimmen für eine Mehrheit von 226 Stimmen fehl-

---

2003, S. 46; *J. Beyer*, „Rhetoric of Transformation": The Case of the Kyrgyz Constitutional Reform, in: *A. Berg/A. Kreikemeyer* (Hrsg.), Realities of Transformation, Democratiazation. Policies in Central Asia Revisited, Hamburg 2006, S. 43.

30 Dazu *O. Luchterhandt*, a.a.O. Fn. 29, S. 2.

31 Dazu die Analyse der Venedigkommission „Opinion on the amendments to the Constitution of Ukraine" adopted on December 2004, (CDL_AD(2005)015); vgl. auch *E. Bos*, Stabile Instabilität, dynamische Blockade. Das politische System der Ukraine, in: *M. Sapper/V. Weichsel* (Hrsg.), Die Ukraine im Wandel. Stabile Instabilität in einem Zwischenland, Bonn 2010, S. 77-88.

32 *A. Nußberger/C. v. Gall*, Rechtsstaat ohne Masterplan. Recht und Gerichtswesen in der Ukraine, Osteuropa 2010, Heft 2-4, S. 89-104 (94).

33 *H. Dörrenbächer*, The Winner Takes It All. Die Präsidentschaftswahlen und die Folgen, in: *M. Sapper/V. Weichsel* (Hrsg.), Die Ukraine im Wandel. Stabile Instabilität in einem Zwischenland, Bonn 2010, S. 145-151.

ten. Daraufhin änderte die Verchovna Rada das Gesetz über die Verfahrensregelungen im Parlament dahingehend, dass eine Parlamentsmehrheit auch aus einzelnen Abgeordneten gebildet werden konnte, während zuvor einzelne Abgeordnete ausgeschlossen und nur Fraktionen zugelassen worden waren. Die Neuregelung aber widersprach dem 2004 eingefügten Art. 83 der Verfassung, der den Wechsel einzelner Abgeordneter zwischen den politischen Blöcken ausschließen wollte, um dem Verdacht von Korruption und Käuflichkeit vorzubeugen. Das ukrainische Verfassungsgericht hatte im Jahr 2008 festgestellt, dass es verfassungswidrig sei, wenn ein Abgeordneter die Fraktion der Partei, auf deren Wählerliste er in die Verchovna Rada gewählt worden ist, verlässt oder sich ihr nicht anschließt. Der Verbleib in der Fraktion der entsprechenden Partei wurde als „verfassungsrechtliche Pflicht" interpretiert[34]. Im Jahr 2010 dagegen urteilte das Gericht gegensätzlich und erklärte in einem abstrakten Auslegungsverfahren zu eben jenem Art. 83 der Verfassung, dass auch einzelne Abgeordnete eine parlamentarische Koalition bilden könnten[35].

Die eingangs erwähnte Entscheidung des ukrainischen Verfassungsgerichts ist nun in diesem politischen Kontext zu sehen. Sie ist nicht ein, sondern der wesentliche Baustein, um in einem seit mehr als einem Jahrzehnt andauernden Verfassungsreformprozess eine grundsätzlich neue Lage zu schaffen, indem zentrale Regelungen zur Machtverteilung zwischen Parlament und Präsident handstreichartig, nachdem sie mehr als fünf Jahre in Kraft waren und das verfassungsrechtliche System bestimmt hatten, für nichtig erklärt werden.

Aus juristischer Sicht ist dies aus einer Reihe von Gründen wohl kaum vertretbar, obwohl die Verfassungsänderung von 2004 formell in der Tat gegen die Verfassung verstieß. Zum einen wäre der Formverstoß vom Verfassungsgericht selbst unproblematisch zu heilen gewesen. Da die Verfassungsänderung auch bei Einhaltung des Verfahrens zu keinem anderen Ergebnis geführt hätte, lässt sich, wie *O. Luchterhandt* argumentiert, ein Verstoß gegen den Verhältnismäßigkeitsgrundsatz rügen; er spricht davon, dass „die rechtliche Bedeutung einer formellen Verfahrensverletzung in grotesker Verzerrung der Relationen verabsolutiert" worden sei[36]. Zu beachten ist zum anderen, dass das Verfassungsgericht bereits im Jahr 2008 mit derselben Frage der formellen Verfassungsmäßigkeit des Verfassungsreformgesetzes von 2004 konfrontiert gewesen war. Damals hatten 102 Abgeordnete – in derselben Weise, allerdings bei einer anderen parteipolitischen Konstellation wie 2010 – geltend gemacht, das Nicht-Vorliegen

---

34 Entscheidung des ukrainischen Verfassungsgerichts v. 25.06.2008, Nr. 12-rp/2008, Punkt 5.1.

35 Entscheidung des ukrainischen Verfassungsgerichts v. 06.04.2010, Nr. 11-rp/2010, Punkt 1; vgl. dazu auch *A. Nußberger*, Die Ukraine – ein streitbarer Rechtsstaat, Ukraine-Analysen Nr. 76 v. 08.06.2010, S. 2-5, abrufbar unter http://www.laender-analysen.de/ukraine/pdf/UkraineAnalysen76.pdf (letzter Zugriff 20.12.2010).

36 *O. Luchterhandt*, a.a.O. Fn. 29, S. 5.

des Gutachtens des Verfassungsgerichts bei der Verfassungsänderung sei ein Grund für ihre Nichtigkeit. Mit Entscheidung vom 05.02.2008 hatte das Verfassungsgericht erklärt, dass das Verfassungsänderungsgesetz mit Inkrafttreten seine Rechtskraft verloren habe und Teil der Verfassung geworden sei. Da aber eine Kontrolle von Verfassungsnormen an der Verfassung ausgeschlossen sei, sei der Antrag unzulässig[37].

Anzumerken ist, dass die ukrainische Verfassung die Kontrolle von verfassungsändernden Gesetzen an der Verfassung nicht ausdrücklich ausschließt. Explizit vorgesehen ist lediglich, wie bereits festgestellt, eine *ex ante*-Stellungnahme zu bestimmten Aspekten des verfassungsändernden Gesetzes. Auf einfachgesetzlicher Basis hatte der Gesetzgeber versucht, eine entsprechende Schranke für die Kompetenz des Verfassungsgerichts festzulegen und in das Gesetz über das Verfassungsgericht eine Änderung eingebracht, die „verfassungsändernde Gesetze, die bereits in Kraft getreten sind" von der Verfassungskontrolle ausschloss[38]. Dieses Gesetz erklärte das ukrainische Verfassungsgericht aber selbst für verfassungswidrig[39].

Auch wenn man davon ausgeht, dass Verfassungsgerichtsentscheidungen die Rechtslage nicht zementieren und einzelne Positionen aufgegeben oder geändert werden können, so scheint doch die Rechtsprechung des ukrainischen Verfassungsgerichts nicht nur inkonsistent, sondern willkürlich zu sein, insbesondere auch, da in der späteren Entscheidung aus dem Jahr 2010 die frühere – im Ergebnis entgegengesetzte – Entscheidung von 2008 noch nicht einmal zitiert wird[40].

Auch wenn man die Nichtigerklärung von formell verfassungswidrigen Verfassungsänderungen im Grundsatz anerkennt, so stellen sich doch besondere Probleme, wird diese Möglichkeit zeitlich nicht begrenzt. Erfolgt die Nichtigerklärung nicht unmittelbar nach Inkrafttreten, ergeben sich weitreichende Probleme mit Blick auf die Legitimität der auf der Grundlage der verfassungswidrigen Normen bestellten oder gewählten Machtorgane. Dies gilt in besonderer Weise dann, wenn in den für nichtig erklärten Normen andere Wahlverfahren, andere Wahlperioden und andere Kompetenzen vorgesehen sind. In der Ukraine ergibt sich in der Folge der Entscheidung des Verfassungsgerichts vom 30.09.2010 die paradoxe Situation, dass nach einem Rosinen-Pick-Verfahren mit Blick auf die Kompetenzen die – für den Präsidenten günstigeren – Bestimmungen der Verfassung von 1996 angewandt werden, man aber bei der Bestimmung der Wahlperioden auf die Bestimmungen der Verfassung von 2004

---

37 Entscheidung des ukrainischen Verfassungsgerichts v. 05.02.2008, Nr. 6-u/2008.

38 Abschnitt IV.3 des Verfassungsgerichtsgesetzes.

39 Entscheidung des ukrainischen Verfassungsgerichts v. 26.06.2008, Nr. 13-rp/2008.

40 Die Venedigkommission spricht in ihrer Stellungnahme „Opinion on the Constitutional Situation in Ukraine" (CDL(2010)126) von „a certain inconsistency in the case-law of the CCU" (§ 33).

zurückgreift. So hat die Verchovna Rada zwar eine Verfassungsänderung eingebracht, nach der die in der Verfassung von 1996 enthaltene Legislaturperiode von vier auf fünf Jahre, so wie es in der Fassung von 2004 vorgesehen war, erweitert werden soll, und damit implizit die Geltung der Regelung in der Verfassung von 1996 anerkannt. Dennoch wurden nicht, wie von der Verfassung von 1996 vorgeschrieben, die Vorbereitungen für die Parlamentswahlen eingeleitet; vielmehr blieb die Zentrale Wahlkommission untätig und rief das Verfassungsgericht mit der Frage an, wie die entsprechende Verfassungsbestimmung auszulegen sei. Aufgrund der zeitlichen Verzögerung war eine Durchführung der Wahl so, wie sie die Verfassung von 1996 vorgesehen hätte, ausgeschlossen[41]. Im Februar 2011 stimmte eine überwältigende Mehrheit der Abgeordneten der Verchovna Rada für eine Änderung der Verfassung von 1996, mit der die Präsidentschaftswahlen auf 2015 und die Parlamentswahlen auf 2012 festgelegt wurden.

Vor diesem Hintergrund wird deutlich, dass das Verfassungsgericht der Ukraine nicht die Funktion wahrnimmt, die vorgegebene Verfassungsordnung in ihrem Bestand zu wahren und damit den Willen des Volkes als „*Pouvoir constituant*" zu sichern. Vielmehr ist das Verfassungsgericht selbst ein zentraler politischer Akteur, der nicht nur auf eine bestehende Verfassung durch Auslegung gestaltenden Einfluss nimmt, sondern vielmehr in dem langjährig blockierten Verfassungsänderungsprozess gewissermaßen den gordischen Knoten durchschlägt und die Basis ändert, auf der die Diskussionen stattfinden.

Damit aber werden die demokratietheoretischen Grundlagen, auf denen das in Westeuropa in der Aufklärung ausgeformte Modell einer durch Verfassung begrenzten Machtausübung basiert, in Frage gestellt. Insbesondere greift das Modell der Volkssouveränität, das in den Eingangsklauseln zu den modernen Verfassungen pathetischen Ausdruck findet, nicht mehr. Es sind nicht mehr „*We the people*" wie in der amerikanischen Verfassung oder die „Verchovna Rada der Ukraine für das ukrainische Volk, die Bürger der Ukraine aller Nationalitäten, die den souveränen Willen des Volkes zum Ausdruck bringt", wie es in der Präambel zur ukrainischen Verfassung heißt, die über die Grundordnung des Staates entscheiden. Vielmehr vermag die Verchovna Rada gerade keinen Kompromiss über die Verfassungsordnung, insbesondere über die zentralen Fragen der Machtverteilung zu finden, sodass das Verfassungsgericht an ihre Stelle tritt und die Funktion eines Katalysators im Verfassungsgebungsprozess einnimmt.

In Kirgistan stellte sich die Situation in mancherlei Hinsicht vergleichbar, aber doch auch wieder sehr verschieden dar. Auch dort war es der politischen Elite – anders als in den zentralasiatischen Nachbarstaaten – nicht gelungen, langfristig stabile, autoritär geführte Systeme aufzubauen. Vielmehr erschütterten Machtwechsel und Revolutionen mehrfach das Land, wobei interessanter-

41 Zu den verfassungsrechtlichen Problemen die Stellungnahme der Venedigkommission siehe Fn. 40.

weise auch dort die Verfassungsgebung von entscheidender Bedeutung war. Die ursprünglich aus dem Jahr 1993 stammende Verfassung war unter Präsident *Akajev* mehrfach geändert worden, mit deutlichen Kompetenzverschiebungen zugunsten des Präsidenten, zuletzt 2003. Nach der sogenannten Tulpenrevolution im März 2005 war die Reform dieser autoritär-präsidentiellen Verfassung ein zentrales Petitum der Zivilgesellschaft. Diskutiert wurden verschiedene Varianten, die von einem klar präsidentiellen bis zu einem klar parlamentarischen System reichten, ohne dass eine Einigung zwischen den politischen Akteuren erreicht werden konnte. Insoweit glich die Situation der Entwicklung in der Ukraine. Anders als dort konnte aber im November 2006 eine neue Verfassung im Parlament verabschiedet werden, die ein parlamentarisches Regierungssystem vorsah. Allerdings gelang es den Anhängern des Präsidenten aufgrund angeblicher Widersprüchlichkeiten und Fehler bereits im Dezember, die Novemberverfassung grundlegend zu ändern und einen Teil der Reformen, die eine Schwächung der Stellung des Präsidenten bedeutet hatten, rückgängig zu machen. Die neue Version der Verfassung trat am 15.01.2007 in Kraft.

Anders als in der Ukraine durchschneidet damit die Entscheidung des Verfassungsgerichts, die beide neuen Versionen der Verfassung für nichtig erklärt, nicht einen gordischen Knoten in einem festgefahrenen Verfassungsgebungsprozess, sondern hebt den in der Jogorku Kenesch erreichten Kompromiss auf und macht den Weg frei für eine völlige Neubestimmung der verfassungsrechtlichen Grundlage der Machtverteilung. Mit der durch Referendum vom 21.10.2007 verabschiedeten Verfassung wird denn auch ein streng präsidentielles System installiert, das Zivilgesellschaft und Opposition für knappe zwei Jahre so gut wie keinen Entwicklungsraum mehr lässt[42], bevor mit einer weiteren Revolution im Frühjahr 2010 die Machtverhältnisse abermals umgekehrt werden. Die wiederum per Referendum am 27.06.2010 verabschiedete Verfassung sieht nunmehr ein im Wesentlichen parlamentarisches System vor[43]. Aufgrund der diffusen parteipolitischen Situation bleibt die Lage allerdings weiter instabil.

Auch in Kirgistan zeigt sich, dass das Verfassungsgericht auf der Ebene des „*Pouvoir constituant*“ zu agieren versucht. Allerdings scheitert es; in der Verfassung von 2010 ist die Institution „Verfassungsgerichtsbarkeit“ nicht mehr vorgesehen. Zu tief ist das Misstrauen gegenüber einer nicht nur offensichtlich nach politischen Zweckmäßigkeitserwägungen handelnden, sondern in ihrem Aktionsradius auch scheinbar nicht eingrenzbaren Institution.

---

42 Stellungnahme der Venedig-Kommission „Opinion on the constitutional situation in Kyrgyz Republic“ (CDL-AD(2007)045); vgl. auch *B. Pannier*, Kyrgyzstan: Court Ruling Restores 2003 Constitution, 2007; abrufbar unter http://www.globalsecurity.org/military/library/news/2007/09/mil-070917-rferl01.htm (letzter Zugriff 20.12.2010).

43 Stellungnahme der Venedigkommission „Opinion on the Draft Constitution of the Kyrgyz Republic“, (CDL-AD(2010)015).

Verfassungsgerichte haben mit den Grundfragen der Gestaltung des politischen Prozesses zu tun; sie sind ein „politischer Ort“[44]. So werden sie in den Staaten, die Verfassungsgerichten traditionell eine wichtige Funktion im Machtgefüge zuerkennen, wahrgenommen. Aus eben diesem Grund werden sie in anderen Demokratien, wie etwa in England und bis vor kurzem auch in Frankreich, grundsätzlich abgelehnt. Die Staaten Mittel- und Osteuropas haben nach der Wende Verfassungsgerichte als gewissermaßen selbstverständliches Zubehör zur Rechtsstaatlichkeit eingerichtet. Im postsowjetischen Raum haben es die Verfassungsgerichte in der Folge aber i.d.R. nicht geschafft, in gleicher Weise wie in Westeuropa zu wirken und rechtsstaatliche Grundsätze zu verankern[45]. Inwieweit sie aber den demokratischen Prozess sogar gefährden können und dies sogar dann, wenn sie „formell korrekte“ Entscheidungen treffen – sowohl in der Ukraine als auch in Kirgistan war die Beanstandung von Formfehlern im Verfassungsgebungsprozess richtig –, zeigen erst die Entwicklungen zwei Jahrzehnte nach dem Ende der kommunistischen Herrschaft. Der nicht auf den ersten, wohl aber auf den zweiten Blick erkennbare Missbrauch von Institutionen, die traditionell über ein hohes Ansehen verfügen und Sinnbilder von Rechtsstaatlichkeit sind, ist besonders problematisch, werden damit doch Versuche, dem Recht einen dominierenden Platz in der gesellschaftlich-politischen Auseinandersetzung einzuräumen, schnell in ein falsches Licht gerückt.

III. Neudefinition des Systems der Checks-and-Balances durch Kompetenzverschiebungen zulasten zentraler Machtorgane

Ein zweites Beispiel für eine Mutation einer aus dem Westen in den Osten, in die Nachfolgestaaten der ehemaligen Sowjetunion transferierten Institution, ist die Entmachtung des Föderationsrats im Verfassungsgefüge der Russischen Föderation.

1. Konzeption der Rolle des Föderationsrats nach der russischen Verfassung von 1993

Während Parlamente im Zentrum demokratischer Systeme stehen, sind nur in einer Minderzahl politischer Systeme auch zweite Kammern vorgesehen[46]. Ihnen können verschiedene Funktionen zukommen; zumeist sind sie in föderalistischen Systemen Repräsentationskammern der verschiedenen staatlichen Unter-

44 So *H. Prantl* in seinem Kommentar „Ab nach Karlsruhe“, SZ v. 18./19.12.2010, S. 4.

45 Dazu ausführlich *A. Nußberger*, a.a.O. Fn. 6, S. 533, 538.

46 Nach einer Studie der Venedigkommission gibt es weltweit in 70 Staaten Bikameralismus, wovon 17 Staaten in Europa gelegen sind; vgl. „Report on Second Chambers in Europe. Parliamentary Complexity or Democratic Necessity?“ (CDL(2005)059rev, § 1).

gliederungen. So haben alle sechs föderalen Staaten in Europa – Österreich, Belgien, Bosnien-Herzegowina, Deutschland, Russland und die Schweiz – auch zweite Kammern[47].

Die Einrichtung zweiter Kammern in den föderalen demokratischen Systemen Mittel- und Osteuropas ist nicht unbedingt Ergebnis eines Rechtstransfers. Vielmehr ließ sich – etwa am Beispiel von Russland – hier bereits auf Traditionen im Zarenreich zurückgreifen, auch wenn der Reichsrat eher als „Oberhaus" konzipiert war[48]. Ihm gehörten sowohl ernannte als auch gewählte Mitglieder an, wobei für letztere die Geistlichkeit, die Gouvernements-zemstva, die Adelsselbstverwaltung, die Akademie der Wissenschaften und die Organisationen des Handels und der Industrie wahlberechtigt waren.

Der Föderationsrat nach der russischen Verfassung von 1993 dagegen setzt sich aus Vertretern der Föderationssubjekte zusammen. Konkret wird in der Verfassung nur geregelt, dass im Föderationsrat je zwei Vertreter jedes Subjekts der Russischen Föderation, und zwar je ein Vertreter des repräsentativen sowie des exekutiven Organs der staatlichen Gewalt, sitzen (Art. 95 Abs. 2 RussVerf).

Nach der verfassungsrechtlichen Regelung ist der Föderationsrat ein sehr einflussreiches Gremium, da er Mitwirkungsrechte bei zentralen Entscheidungen wie der Verhängung des Kriegs- und Ausnahmezustands (Art. 102 Abs. 1 b), c) RussVerf), dem Amtsenthebungsverfahren (Art. 102 Abs. 1 f) RussVerf) sowie bei den zentralen Personalentscheidungen hat; so kann er beispielsweise bei der Berufung der Verfassungsrichter und des Generalstaatsanwalts mitbestimmen. Auch bei der Gesetzgebung spielt er eine wichtige Rolle, da er Gesetze blockieren und zur wiederholten Abstimmung in die Duma bringen kann, die dann mit einer Zweidrittelmehrheit entscheiden muss (Art. 105 Abs. 4 S. 2 RussVerf). Dabei wird zwischen einfachen Gesetzen und Gesetzen, die einer obligatorischen Erörterung im Föderationsrat bedürfen, beispielsweise dem Staatshaushalt oder Gesetzen über Finanz-, Währungs-, Kredit- und Zollregelungen, unterschieden (Art. 106 RussVerf). Zudem gibt es die besondere Kategorie der in der Verfassung vorgesehenen Föderationsverfassungsgesetze, die einer Dreiviertelmehrheit im Föderationsrat und einer Zweidrittelmehrheit in der Duma bedürfen (Art. 108 Abs. 2 S. 1 RussVerf).

Solange in den 1990er Jahren die vom Volk in den einzelnen Föderationssubjekten gewählten und damit unmittelbar demokratisch legitimierten Gouverneure selbst im Föderationsrat mitarbeiteten, konnten tatsächlich Belange der Föderationssubjekte eingebracht werden und der Föderationsrat als Gegenkraft das System der *Checks-and-Balances* unterstützen.

47 Ebenda.

48 *H. Küpper*, Einführung in die Rechtsgeschichte Osteuropas, Frankfurt 2005, S. 174.

2. Veränderungen der Funktion des Föderationsrats zu Beginn des 21. Jahrhunderts

Interessant ist nun zu beobachten, wie mit der Änderung der personellen Zusammensetzung des Föderationsrats erreicht wurde, seine Stellung im verfassungsrechtlichen Machtgefüge grundlegend zu verändern[49].

Der wichtigste Schritt war die Abschaffung der Volkswahl der Gouverneure im Jahr 2006.[50] *De facto* wurde das Recht, die Gouverneure einzusetzen, auf den Präsidenten übertragen, auch wenn *de iure* die jeweiligen Legislativorgane weiterhin ein „Wahlrecht" haben. Sie können nur den vom Präsidenten vorgeschlagenen Kandidaten wählen; widersetzen sie sich dem, können sie in letzter Konsequenz vom Präsidenten aufgelöst werden. Zudem reicht der „Verlust des Vertrauens des Präsidenten" nach dem neuen Gesetz bereits als ein Grund zur Abberufung der Gouverneure aus; eine auf einem derartig vagen, rein subjektiv zu bestimmenden Kriterium beruhende Entscheidung ist nicht justiziabel und führt damit letztlich zu einer Reduktion der politischen Eigenständigkeit der Regionen auf Null. Das Verfassungsgericht, das mit dieser Frage aufgrund einer Verfassungsbeschwerde einzelner Bürger befasst wurde, sah die Regelung als verfassungsgemäß an, obwohl sie in mehrfacher Hinsicht im Widerspruch zu zuvor in anderen Verfassungsgerichtsentscheidungen aufgestellten Prinzipien stand[51]. 2009 erfolgte erneut eine Reform dieses Systems. Nunmehr hat die aus der Wahl zu den Legislativorganen des jeweiligen Föderationssubjekts als Sieger hervorgegangene Partei das Recht, dem Präsidenten einen geeigneten Kandidaten für den Gouverneursposten vorzuschlagen. Allerdings ist der Präsident daran nicht gebunden[52].

---

49 Siehe hierzu *A. Heinemann-Grüder*, Putins Reform der föderalen Strukturen, Osteuropa 2000, S. 979-990; *O. Luchterhandt*, Der Ausbau der föderalen Vertikale unter Putin: Das Ende der Dezentralisierung?, in: *G. Brunner* (Hrsg.), Der russische Föderalismus. Bilanz eines Jahrzehnts, Münster 2004, S. 241-279.

50 Föderales Gesetz über die Änderung des föderalen Gesetzes „Über die allgemeinen Prinzipien der Organisation der gesetzgebenden (vertretenden) und ausführenden Organe der staatlichen Macht der Subjekte der Russischen Föderation" und des föderalen Gesetzes „Über die grundlegenden Garantien der Wahlrechte und des Rechts der Bürger der Russischen Föderation auf Teilnahme am Referendum", SZ RF 2004, Nr. 50, Pos. 4950.

51 Entscheidung des Russischen Verfassungsgerichts v. 21.12.2005, SZ RF 2006, Nr. 3, Pos. 336; deutsche Übersetzung abgedruckt in: *Nußberger/Schmidt/Morščakova* (Hrsg.), Verfassungsrechtsprechung in der Russischen Föderation. Dokumentation und Analyse der Entscheidungen des Russischen Verfassungsgerichts 1992-2007, 2009, S. 196 ff.; vgl. dazu im Einzelnen *Mommsen/Nußberger*, Das System Putin. Gelenkte Demokratie und politische Justiz in Russland, 2007, S. 117 ff.

52 Änderung des Gesetzes „Über die politischen Parteien" v. 05.04.2009, SZ RF 2009, Nr. 14, Pos. 1576.

Die Wirkung der Neuregelung zeigte sich öffentlichkeitswirksam bei der per Dekret erfolgten Entlassung des Moskauer Bürgermeisters *J. Luškov*, der das Amt von 1992 bis 2010 inne hatte. Als Begründung war der Hinweis auf den „Verlust des Vertrauens des Präsidenten“ ausreichend.

3. Selbstentmachtung des Föderationsrats durch freiwillige Aufgabe zentraler Kompetenzen

Mit Blick auf die Mutation von Institutionen und die dadurch bewirkte Verschiebung im verfassungsrechtlichen Machtgefüge ist, die jüngste Reform der Kompetenzen bei den zentralen Entscheidungen über Krieg und Frieden von besonderem Interesse. Bisher ist nach Art. 87 RussVerf der Präsident Oberbefehlshaber der Streitkräfte. Im Falle eines Angriffs gegen die Russische Föderation oder eines unmittelbar drohenden Angriffs kann der Präsident den Kriegszustand ausrufen. Dabei muss er Föderationsrat und Staatsduma unverzüglich benachrichtigen. Dagegen entscheidet der Föderationsrat nach Art. 102 Abs. 1 d) RussVerf über die Möglichkeit eines Einsatzes der Streitkräfte außerhalb des Territoriums der Russischen Föderation. Die Bedeutung dieser Kompetenz ist erst im russisch-georgischen Krieg im August 2008 deutlich geworden. Der Präsident ordnete den Einsatz der Truppen an, hatte dafür aber eigentlich nicht die verfassungsrechtliche Kompetenz, da kein Angriff auf die Russische Föderation vorlag; vielmehr spielten sich alle kriegerischen Handlungen ausschließlich auf georgischem Territorium ab. In den offiziellen Verlautbarungen wurde auf Art. 80 RussVerf verwiesen. Danach ist der Präsident „Garant der Verfassung … sowie der Rechte und Freiheiten des Menschen und Bürgers. Gemäß dem durch die Verfassung … festgelegten Verfahren ergreift er Maßnahmen zum Schutz der Souveränität der Russischen Föderation, ihrer Unabhängigkeit und staatlichen Integrität und gewährleistet das aufeinander abgestimmte Funktionieren und Zusammenwirken der Organe der Staatsgewalt“. Anknüpfungspunkt war der Schutz der russischen Staatsangehörigen, da auch den Bürgern von Südossetien und Abchasien die russische Staatsangehörigkeit erteilt worden war.

Trotzdem wurde das Fehlen einer Notfallkompetenz der Exekutive als Regelungslücke angesehen. Aufgrund der eindeutigen Regelung von Art. 102 Abs. 1 d) RussVerf wäre im Grunde eine Verfassungsänderung zu erwarten gewesen, die eine Ausnahmeregelung vorsieht. Anders das Vorgehen des russischen Gesetzgebers: Geändert wurde das „Gesetz über die Verteidigung“ von 1996[53]. Darin wurde eine neue Regelung eingefügt, nach der das russische Militär in bestimmten Situationen im Ausland eingesetzt werden kann und der Präsident das Recht hat, über den „operationellen Einsatz“ der Truppen auf der Grundlage einer Verordnung (Postanovlenie) des Föderationsrats zu entschei-

53 Gesetz Nr. 252-FZ v. 09.11.2009, SZ RF 2009, Nr. 45, Pos. 5270.

den. Auf dieser Grundlage erließ der Föderationsrat wenig später, am 16.12.2009, eine entsprechende Verordnung, in der er den Präsidenten allgemein ermächtigte, „Entscheidungen über den operationellen Einsatz der russischen Armee außerhalb des Territoriums der Russischen Föderation in Übereinstimmung mit den allgemein anerkannten Prinzipien und Normen des Völkerrechts, den völkerrechtlichen Verträgen der Russischen Föderation und dem Gesetz über die Verteidigung zu treffen." Ergänzend werden wortgleich wie in dem Gesetz die Fälle aufgezählt, in denen ein Auslandseinsatz möglich ist.

Damit gibt der Föderationsrat seine in der Verfassung normierte Kompetenz, über Auslandseinsätze des russischen Militärs zu entscheiden, mit einer „*Carte Blanche*" nicht nur in den Situationen, in denen ein unmittelbares Handeln geboten ist, sondern ganz allgemein auf. Er nimmt sich jede Möglichkeit der Einflussnahme, sowohl *ex ante* als auch *ex post*. Allenfalls könnte er auf Anfragen des Präsidenten reagieren, jedoch nicht mehr von sich aus tätig werden.

Auch dieses Beispiel zeigt, dass bestimmte Voraussetzungen, die für das Funktionieren verfassungsrechtlicher Institutionen als grundlegend angesehen werden, im postsowjetischen Rechtskreis nicht unbedingt gegeben sind. So liegt der verfassungsrechtlichen Kompetenzabgrenzung zwischen verschiedenen Verfassungsorganen die Annahme zugrunde, dass die jeweiligen Organe auch bestrebt seien, ihre Kompetenzen zu erhalten und in optimaler Weise auszufüllen. Freiwillige Kompetenzverzichte, die das verfassungsrechtliche Gefüge ins Ungleichgewicht bringen, sind nicht vorgesehen. Auch auf diese Weise kann ein grundlegendes verfassungsrechtliches Konzept, die Errichtung eines ausgeglichenen Machtgefüges auf der Grundlage von *Checks-and-Balances*, vollkommen verändert werden.

IV. Vom Wert der Kopien

Eine gute Kopie kann leicht mit einem Original verwechselt werden. Bei einer schlechten Kopie wird man sich nicht einmal mehr an das Original erinnern. Beides ist bei der Übernahme von aus anderen Rechtssystemen stammenden Konzeptionen und Institutionen möglich, vor allem im Verfassungsrecht, das in besonderer Weise in Geschichte und Tradition eines Landes verwurzelt ist. Die Beispiele von Verfassungsgerichten, die die Grundlage, auf der sie arbeiten sollen, für nichtig erklären, ebenso wie die Beispiele von Trägern staatlicher Macht, die ihre Machtbefugnisse freiwillig abgeben, sind Kopien, die mit den Originalen äußerlich noch verblüffende Ähnlichkeiten haben. Bei genauerer Betrachtung aber zeigt sich, dass es mehr Unterschiede als Gemeinsamkeiten gibt; mehr noch: Die Gemeinsamkeiten scheinen eher zufällig zu sein. Letztlich ist die Kopie nicht mehr Kopie, sondern Aliud.

Trial by Jury and the Russian Constitution

Distinguished Professor Stanislaw Pomorski[*]

In the Fall of 1999 and the Spring of 2000, I conducted an empirical investigation of the criminal justice administration in the Syberian city of Krasnoyarsk[1]. Of particular interest to me were questions of whether judicial independence is a reality, whether prosecutorial bias of judges, a grave legacy of the Soviet past, still persists, and how meaningful is lay participation in criminal proceedings[2]. At the time of my investigation, by far the most prevalent form of lay participation in criminal proceedings was a "mixed tribunal" composed of a presiding professional judge and two "people's assessors" (in Russian – *narodnyne zesedateli)*[3]. Trial judges whom I interviewed were nearly unanimous in their critical assessment of the impact of lay assessors. Almost all judges interviewed considered the assessors' input as close to non-existent and their participation as useless – a façade, lip service paid to the formal requirement of law. According to judges, assessors *never* influenced decisions on guilt and exceedingly rarely on sentencing decisions[4]. And yet, most judges were not against the very *idea* of lay participation in the administration of criminal justice. On the contrary, most of the interviewees were definitely positive, even enthusiastic, about the jury system at the time still absent from the Krasnoyarsk region as well as from most of Russia[5]. In order to test their real sentiments, I confronted them with the following hypothetical:

> "Suppose that someone close to you personally, for example a member of your family or a good friend, is bound for a trial on serious, contested charges. What kind of a tribunal would you prefer as giving the best hope for a fair result? In particular, would you prefer that the trial be held before a single judge, a panel of three judges, a mixed tribunal composed of one judge and two lay assessors, or before a jury?"[6]

---

* Rutgers School of Law, Camden.

1 For an extensive report based on this investigation see *S. Pomorski*, "Justice in Siberia: A Case Study of a Lower Criminal Court in the City of Krasnoyarsk", Communist and Post-Communist Studies, vol. 34 (2001), pp. 447-478. See also *S. Pomorski*, "In a Siberian Criminal Court", East European Constitutional Review, vol. 11, no. 1/2 (2002), pp. 111-116.

2 *S. Pomorski*, "Justice in Siberia", note 1, p. 449.

3 *Id.*, p. 469.

4 *Id.*, p. 470.

5 *V. Lebedev*, Nauchno-prakticheskii kommentarii k ugolovno-protsessulnomu kodeksu RSFSR, Moscow 1998 (Scientific-Practical Commentary to the Code of Criminal Procedure of the RSFSR), p. 682.

6 For this hypothetical, I have been indebted to the authors of a major Polish empirical study on the subject of lay participation in criminal cases. *S. Zawadski*, *L. Kubicki*

In response, the majority of judges expressed strong preference for a trial by jury. The principal reason offered in support of this preference was jurors' genuine independence and therefore their ability to render decisions consistent with the presumption of innocence and their conscience without fear of personally adverse consequences. Several judges juxtaposed and contrasted this quality of genuine independence and impartiality with their own situation of dependence and fear of consequences of rendering decisions displeasing the superior legal bureaucracy[7].

The developments of the last decade have fully vindicated the opinion of Krasnoyarsk judges whom I interviewed. Defendants tried by juries received much more favorable treatment than those who were tried by professional judges. Russian jurors demonstrated their genuine independence and impartiality, their ability to put the prosecution to its proof and to render verdicts consistent with the presumption of innocence. Regrettably, it would be impossible to attribute such qualities to professional judges as will be detailed below.

I. Russian judges, in theory and in law, are independent. The Constitution of the Russian Federation of 1993 (hereafter the Constitution), art. 120, sec. 1 reads, "Judges shall be independent and shall be subordinate only to Constitution and federal law. The Constitution, as well as other legislative enactments, includes several safeguards designed to protect judicial independence (The Constitution, arts. 121-122). Regrettably, reality presents quite a different picture. In the words of the former Russian Prime Minister *Fradkov*:

> "We will have to bring about qualitative changes in the existing situation in the next few years and make the judiciary truly independent not only de jure but also de facto"[8] (emph. added).

This goal has not been attained as of year 2010. Recently, *Fradkov's* statement was echoed by President *Medvedev*[9]. *Medvedev* was soon seconded by an architect of the first democratic changes in the USSR, known as *perestvoika* and *glasnost'*, *Gorbachev*, who complained that

> "... all major decisions are now taken by the executive branch, with the Parliament rubberstamping formal approval. *The independence of courts has been thrown into question*"[10] (emph. added).

The gulf between formal institutional façade and practical reality was aptly summarized by *S. Leutheusser-Schnarrenberger*, rapporteur for the Council of

---

(eds.), Udzial lawnikow w pastępowaniu karnym (Participation of Lay Assessors in Criminal Proceedings), Warsaw, 1970, p. 288.

7 *S. Pomorski*, "Justice in Siberia", note 1, p. 471.

8 "Remarks by PM Candidate Mikhail Fradkov", official Kremlin Int'l News Broadcast, March 5, 2004, available on Lexis-Nexis.

9 *E. Shishkunova*, "Sudebnoi sisteme ustoriat skaryi sud" ("The Judicial System Will Soon Face the Court"), Izvestia, May 2, 2008, p. 2.

10 *M. Gorbachev*, "Perestroika Lost", The New York Times, March 14, 2010, p. A9.

Europe's Parliamentary Assembly Committee on Legal Affairs and Human Rights:

> "The Russian Federation ... seems to have all the right legal structure in place, but my impression, based on the cases examined above, is that judges are still subject to fairly strong pressures compromising their independence in deciding individual cases and contributing to a work climate that could be compared to a permanent 'probation period'. Judges' careers and even their continued employment depend on their 'functioning as expected'. If criminal procedure *must almost always end in conviction, as is still the case in the Russian Federation, the power of prosecutors ... to put people behind bars is in reality almost unchecked*[11]" (emph. added).

There is an abundance of evidence supporting these opinions. Judges are *de facto* subordinated to and in many ways dependent upon government bureaucracy who creates and enforces its own standards of judicial behavior. In spite of solemn declarations to the contrary, Russian judges serve at the pleasure of court administrators who do the bidding of the powerful. Fragility of judicial tenure is reflected in high dismissal rates. In December 2008, "the Supreme Qualification Collegium of Judges reported that during the last four years, an average of 70 judges a year were removed from office"[12]. That number does not even include judges who resign "voluntarily" when confronted with the alternative of disciplinary action. Formal standards of disciplinary responsibility are broad and vague as stated and even broader as applied. As a practical matter, judges serve at the pleasure of the administration[13].

The lack of judicial independence has permitted operation of a policy of no-acquittals which has substantially tainted and compromised the integrity of the judicial process in criminal cases. In spite of the dismal quality of investigative and prosecutorial work, judgments of acquittal represent a minuscule, statistically remarkable fraction of the total number of judgments. In 2004, acquittals represented only 0.7 % of all judgments and less than half of these acquittals were rendered in cases brought by public prosecutors. In 2006, acquittals at the district court level represented only 0.5 % of all judgments[14]. In 2008, acquittals represented only 0.8 % of judgments on the merits, with only 35 % of them occurring in cases brought by public prosecutors. Thus, in cases of public prosecu-

---

11 Council of Europe Parliamentary Assembly, Committee on Legal Affairs and Human Rights, "Allegations of Politically Motivated Abuses of the Criminal Justice System in Council of Europe Member States", Explanatory Memorandum at § 135 (August 2009); hereafter Explanatory Memorandum 2009.

12 U.S. Department of State, 2009 Human Rights Report: Russia, p. 8.

13 Explanatory Memorandum 2009, note 11 at § 83.

14 *S. Pomorski*, "Modern Russian Criminal Procedure: The Adversarial Principle and Guilty Plea", The Criminal Law Forum, vol. 17 (2006), p. 146; *W. Burnham/J. Khan*, "Russia's Criminal Procedure Code Five Years Out", Review of Central and East European Law, vol. 33 (2008), p. 76.

tion, acquittals occurred in about 0.3% of cases[15]. In 2009, at the district court level less than 0.3 % of the defendants were acquitted[16].

As I observed on an earlier occasion, the no-acquittals doctrine left an unmistakable imprint on the substance and style of the trial. It is only natural that judges, who consider themselves duty bound to convict, cannot be open to contestation of guilt. Consequently, such judges are likely to attach greater weight to incriminating than to exculpatory evidence, to resolve doubts in favor of the prosecution, to play down the rights of the defendant or to treat them as mere formality[17].

Under the circumstances, "it is not surprising that Russian judges fail to rein in even egregious excesses of the law enforcement, but instead rather condone and rubberstamp them"[18].

Translated into normative language, the no-acquittals policy means that some fundamental rights of criminal defendants in theory guaranteed by the Constitution and international treaties binding upon the Russian Federation are routinely violated. The most prominent casualty is the presumption of innocence theoretically guaranteed by the Constitution, art. 49. It stands to reason that a judge who feels duty bound to convict acts rather on the presumption of guilt, which defendants in Russia manage to overcome only on very rare occasions. For the same reason, defendants are denied their right to an independent and impartial tribunal. In most cases the conviction is a foregone conclusion from the outset, instead courts function only as sentencing authorities. The right to defense, as a practical matter, rarely can rise to an effective contestation of guilt. It is rather limited to punishment.

The pattern of guilt determination by Russian juries has been consistently and dramatically different. Although the percentage of acquittals by juries has fluctuated from year to year, it has never fallen much below 15 % and quite often was substantially higher. And so, in his October 2004 paper, *V.P. Lukin*, Plenipotentiary for Human Rights in the Russian Federation, reported that in the past years the percentage of acquittals by juries oscillated around 21 % , acquittals by judges only around 0.5 %[19]. In 2008, it was reported that in the period of

---

15 *"Statisticheskaia spravka a rabate sudov obshchei iurisdiktsii za 2008 god"*, ("Statistical Information on Activities of the General Jurisdiction Courts in 2008"), Rossiiskaia Iustisiia, 2009, no. 3, p. 63.

16 *"Obzor federal'nykh sudov obshchei iurisdiktsii i mirovykh sudei v 2009 godu (Rassmotreniie ugolovnykh del)"*, ("Survey of Federal Courts of General Jurisdiction and Justices of the Peace (Criminal Cases)"), Rossiiskaia Iustitsiia, 2010, no. 8, p. 62; hereafter Survey 2009.

17 *S. Pomorski*, "Justice in Siberia", note 1, p. 458.

18 *S. Pomorski*, note 14, p. 147.

19 *V. Lukin*, Problemy sovershenstvovaniia deiatel'nosti suda prisiazhnykh v sovremennoi Rossii (Problems of Improvement of the Activity of the Jury Court in Contemporary Russia), Moscow, 2004, p. 16.

1994-2007, 17 % of the defendants were acquitted by the juries while "less than 1 %" by the judges[20]. In 2009, juries convicted 1066 individuals and acquitted 244 defendants[21]. Thus, the acquittals represented over 18 % of all jury verdicts.

This statistically remarkable phenomenon begs for explanation. It appears that year after year individuals tried by juries are about 30-40 times more likely to be exonerated in comparison with persons tried by professional judges. There is no reason to believe that the quality of investigation and prosecution in jury cases is inferior in comparison with cases handled by professional judges. Rather the opposite assumption seems to be justified[22] and the compelling conclusion is that Russian jury is the only judicial forum where guilt can be contested effectively, where the prosecution is put to its proof and where presumption of innocence is taken seriously. It is submitted that the jury is the only agency of the criminal justice giving defendants a fair chance of exoneration, the only agency willing and capable of checking the power of the prosecutor. Russian juries, year after year, have been saying "no" to the governmental policy of no-acquittals. It is, therefore, not surprising at all that "stubborn" and independent juries have not been in good graces with the increasingly authoritarian power system relying more than ever on police and security agencies and becoming increasingly intolerant toward activities which it is unable to control. Attacks on juries – the only existing form of direct democracy – have been a part of attacks on organized forms of civil society in general.

II. Governmental attacks on the power of the jury to determine guilt or innocence have been pursued along three distinct avenues.

First, jury acquittals under Russian law are not final, they are subject to review for legal errors by the Supreme Court. The Supreme Court has been using and abusing its considerable review power with respect to jury acquittals with particular zeal – in effect invading jury province in many cases by dubious or even perverse interpretation of statutory language[23]. In the period of 1994-2007, the Supreme Court reversed over 40 % of the jury acquittals[24], whereas in some

20 *Iu. Churilov*, "Prichiny otmeny opravdatel' nylkh prigovorov sudov s uchastiiem prisiazhnykh zasedatelei", ("Causes of Reversal of Judgments of Acquittals of Courts with Jury Participation"), Rossiiskaia Iustitsiia, 2008, no. 9, p. 59.

21 Survey 2009, note 16, p. 60.

22 Trials by jury have been from the inception available only at the level of courts of the higher order (regional and equal rank courts) and involve only cases of most serious crimes. Therefore, one can assume that jury cases have been, by and large, rather better investigated and prosecuted than more mundane cases most of which are processed by trial courts at the lower level of district courts or by justices of the peace.

23 For an extensive discussion of the Russian Supreme Court jurisprudence in this area see *S. Thaman*, "Nullification of the Russian Jury: Lessons for Jury-Inspired Reform in Eurasia and Beyond", Cornell International Law Journal, vol. 40 (2007), pp. 355-428.

24 *Churilov*, note 20, p. 59.

years, the percentage of such reversals was even higher[25]. This way, the Supreme Court enforces to a large extent the no-acquittals policy vetoed by juries.

In this connection, *S. Thaman*, a thorough student of the Russian jury, comments:

> "While the SCRF (Supreme Court of the Russian Federation – S.P.) insists that the jury must determine guilt, it has interpreted the prohibition against the jury determining 'other questions requiring juridical evaluation' as applying to some basic questions relating to guilt, thus effectively removing the guilt determination from the jury and arguably violating Articles 20 and 47 of the Russian Constitution"[26].

In support of this general statement, *S. Thaman* gives the following example:

> "Early in its jurisprudence, the SCRF began to treat mental elements of crimes as 'questions of law', and to place them solely within the competence of the professional judge to decide as 'questions requiring strictly juridical evaluations'. This jurisprudence has led to the reversal of a number of acquittals and judgment of convictions for lesser included crimes of homicide, *often when the jury has expressly found that the defendant did not harbor the intent to kill or killed in the heat of passion*"[27] (emph. added).

Moreover, in its authoritative 2005 decree, the Supreme Court ruled that the issue of insanity shall be decided by a trial judge rather than a jury[28]. It is difficult to imagine how the jury can pass upon the issue of guilt while being unable to reach the properly raised insanity question.

The second avenue of the attack on the legitimate jury power involves deliberate actions of various state agents trying either to evade jury trials or to undermine legal validity of the jury verdicts by "planting" reversible errors in the proceedings. The former include deliberate "undercharging", that is to say charging a defendant with an offense outside of jury jurisdiction contrary to the provable facts of the case, such as, for example, charging aggravated assault instead of murder[29]. The latter typically includes using violations of the victim's rights by the investigators or by the trial judge as a ground to raise a reversible error claim on appeal leading to the reversal of a not-guilty verdict[30].

More disturbing and brazenly unlawful are instances of government agents direct tampering with jurors in the midst of the trial. Two such occurrences involving a prominent, apparently politically motivated group prosecution were recently reported from Moscow: two jurors were approached by security agents

---

25 For example, in 1998, the Supreme Court reversed 66 % and in 2004 over 53 % of jury acquittals. *S. Thaman*, note 23, p. 407.

26 *Id.*, p. 391.

27 *Id.*, p. 397.

28 Postanovleniie Plenuma Verkhovnogo Suda Rossiiskoi Federatsii, no. 23 ot 22 noiabria, 2005 (Decree of the Plenum of the Supreme Court of the RF, no. 23, November 22, 2005), Official site of the Supreme Court of the Russian Federation at § 22.

29 *S. Thaman*, note 23, p. 367 and sources cited therein, note 66.

30 *Id.*, pp. 372-374, 410-411.

who pressed them to resign from the panel and thereby prevent the jury from reaching a verdict which was expected to be unfavorable for the government. One of the jurors duly reported the incident to the trial judge, without, however, any effect. When the jurors protested in public, the only reaction were thinly veiled insinuations "implying that they had been bribed by the defense." The threatening message was delivered by a powerful executive of the state controlled television station cum a politician of the ruling party[31]. Typically for contemporary Russia, the whistleblowers were censured rather than government agents whose unlawful conduct had been protested. The message for prospective jurors is rather clear: if tampered with by government agents – keep your mouth shut or else you can be smeared with accusations of corruption.

The third more direct and open tool of the governmental anti-jury policy is legislation further curbing already *ab initio* narrowly circumscribed, the right to trial by jury[32]. The balance of this paper will focus on this legislation and its constitutional status.

III. In December 2008, the Russian legislature hastily approved the law severely curtailing the right to trial by jury. The law eliminated trial by jury in cases of some 14 criminal offenses and instead mandated trials for these crimes before panels of three professional judges. Juries have been removed from practically all cases involving crimes against the state under a disguise of fighting terrorism[33]. In fact, several offenses covered by the law have nothing to do with

---

31 *E. Barry*, "In Russian Justice, the Jury is Something to Work Around", The New York Times, November 16, 2010, pp. A-1, A-6.

32 In the early 1990's the trial by jury figured prominently in the liberal blueprint of the judicial reform. According to some early proposals, trial by jury was to be afforded to all defendants charged with offenses punishable by imprisonment for a period longer than one year. Those proposals never materialized due to budgetary and organizational constraints in chaotic and impoverished Russia of the 1990's. Instead, beginning with the initial legislation of 1993, jury trials were instituted only at the level of regional and equal rank courts and limited to a relatively small group of most serious crimes. *S. Reynolds*, "Drawing Upon the Past: Jury Trials in Modern Russia" in *P. Solomon* (ed.), Reforming Justice in Russia 1864-1996. Amonk-London, 1997, pp. 345, 378-9. That restrictive legacy was taken over by the 2001 Code of Criminal Procedure (hereafter CCP) in its original version, the CCP, arts. 30, 31.

33 Federal law, December 30, 2009, O vnesenii izmenenii v otdel'nye zakonodatel'nye akty Rossiiskoi Federatsii po voprosam protivodeistviia terrorizmu (On amending several legislative enactments of the Russian Federation on the issues of fighting terrorism), Sabraniie Zakonodatel'stva Rossiiskoi Federatsii (hereafter SZRF), 2009, no. 1, item. 29. Art. 2 of the law amended art. 30 of the CCP to the effect that in cases involving charges under the Criminal Code, arts. 205, 206, parts 2-4, 208, part 1, 212, part 1, 276, 278, 279, and 281 shall be tried before panels of three professional judges rather than by juries.

terrorism as was pointed out by Deputy *E. Mizulina* during the heated parliamentary debate[34].

Deputy *E. Mizulina*, who happened also to be a well respected academic authority on criminal procedure, stated:

> "This draft law is not about fighting terrorism, but about limiting people's power, about supporting corruption in the law enforcement and justice system, about resistance to overcoming legal nihilism ..."[35].

The law was passed by the majority vote over strong dissent by the parliamentary opposition.

The legislation was denounced by extra-parliamentary opposition as well. A group of prominent citizens including academics, former judges, leaders of the bar, human rights activists, artists, journalists, and independent politicians, sent an open letter to President *Medvedev*, urging him to veto the anti-jury law. The opening paragraphs of the letter read:

> "The draft law passed by the State Duma removing from courts' jurisdiction trials by jury of crimes investigated by organs of FSB, along with its speed and lack of consideration for the opinions of the legal community and for civil society as a whole, has quite understandably alarmed us. *Trial by jury, one of civil society's few elements of control over judiciary, has been hijacked by deputies to the benefit of the special services*"[36] (emph. added).

President *Medvedev*, who paradoxically about that time spoke before the congress of judges about the need to strengthen independence of courts, ignored the protests and signed the anti-jury legislation into the law. Constitutional validity of the law was challenged soon thereafter, albeit unsuccessfully, as will be discussed below.

Five individuals, who had been charged under arts. 205 (terrorist act), 278 (violent seizure of power) and 279 (armed mutiny) of the Criminal Code, requested trial by jury. The trial court, applying the amended art. 30(2) of the CCP, denied the motion. The defendants turned to the Constitutional Court challenging validity of the new law as violating their constitutional right to trial by jury. The Court upheld the law as constitutionally firm over the dissent of two judges[37]. Technically speaking, the Court ruling is narrow in scope since it addresses validity of the legislative elimination of the jury trial only with respect to

---

34 *V. Khamraev*, "Deputaty spasaiut zhizn' prisiazhnym" ("Deputies Save Lives of Jurors"), Kommersant, December 8, 2008. See also *I. Rodin*, "Prisiazhnym otkazali' v doverii" ("They Refused to Trust Jurors"), Nezavismaia Gazeta, December 8, 2008.

35 *Khamraev*, note 34.

36 "Open Letter to Russian President", BBC Monitoring Former Soviet Union, December 17, 2008.

37 Decree of the Constitutional Court, April 19, 2010, no. 8-P, SZRF, 2010, no. 18, item 2276.

the three crimes with which the petitioners were charged[38]. Thus, constitutionality of the balance of the law is, at least theoretically, still an open question. However, the reasoning of the Court does not give much hope that other parts of the law would be treated any differently if challenged in the future.

While petitioners invoked at least nine articles of the Constitution in support of their claims, the Court's opinion focused primarily on two provisions: arts. 20(2) and 47(2). The former guarantees the right to trial by jury to individuals charged with capital crimes. The latter reads:

> "Any person accused of the commission of a crime shall have the right to have his case tried by the court with the participation of jurors in cases provided for by federal law."

The lengthy Court opinion boils down to the following essential points:

The constitutional guarantee of the right to trial by jury is explicitly limited to offenses punishable by death. The death penalty has been effectively banned in Russia by moratorium imposed by decisions of the Constitutional Court of February 2, 1999, no. N 3-P and November 19, 2009, no. 1344-0-P. Under these circumstances, art. 20, part 2 of the Constitution has become defunct or irrelevant. Beyond capital cases, trial by jury is not essential for the right to fair administration of justice guaranteed by art. 46 of the Constitution and art. 6 of the European Convention on Human Rights[39].

The Constitution, art. 47, part 2, delegated to the ordinary legislation the power to determine the scope of the trial by jury in non-capital cases. The legislator may therefore legitimately exercise its discretionary power as long as its decisions are neither arbitrary nor unreasonable[40].

The specific legislative decision to remove juries from terrorism related cases is not arbitrary, but rather based on sound policy judgments, opines the Court. In these types of cases jurors are likely to be intimidated as well as prejudiced by the extra-judicial sources of information on widely publicized terrorist acts and therefore likely to lose their capacity to make impartial and fair decisions. The Court also refers to complexity of terrorism related cases which, the opinion intimates, is beyond the intellectual capacity of an average juror[41].

In conclusion the Court states:

> "The federal laws granting the authority to try cases of terrorism and related crimes to a panel of three judges of a federal court of high level to the exclusion of such cases from the jurisdiction of a single judge and a panel of jurors under the circumstances cannot be considered unfounded, arbitrary or unreasonable"[42].

---

38 *Id.*, at § 1.4.
39 *Id.*, at § 2.2.
40 *Id.*, at § 3.
41 *Id.*, at § 4.1.
42 *Id.*, at § 4.2.

The decision of the Constitutional Court has some superficial appeal if one considers it within the four corners of the selected constitutional provisions. Indeed, the Constitution mandates that judges shall be independent and impartial. It is undeniable that the constitutional provision regarding the right to trial by jury in non-capital cases, taken in isolation, guarantees little. Art. 47, part 2 of the Basic Law apparently commits the pertinent decisions to the discretion of the federal legislature. That language made it easy for the legislative branch to curtail drastically the jurisdiction of the jury and for the Court to uphold this curtailment as valid. Therefore, if the issue is analyzed with the sole focus on art. 47, part 2, the Court was to some extent justified reviewing the December 2008 law under the abuse of discretion standard. However, even within such a narrow and formalistic approach, the Court appears too eager to credit government rationale of the law. The thesis that jurors sitting in terrorism related cases are easily intimidated or otherwise likely to be prejudiced was accepted without any supporting evidence. Moreover, the Court glided over several provisions of the CCP designed to deal with the problem of prejudice of individual jurors or the whole panel of jurors[43]. It was never explained why the legislature could not adopt, if needed, additional measures of enhanced protection of jurors' personal safety rather than simply exclude jury trials from politically most sensitive cases. It is also far from clear why the alleged prejudice should be less of a problem with respect to a three member panel of professional judges than with respect to a twelve member jury panel. After all, it seems common sense that it is easier to improperly influence (by intimidation or bribery) a small group of three than a larger group of twelve.

The basic flaw of the Court's opinion is, however, much deeper. In essence, the Court approaches the issue in a formalistic manner and focuses narrowly on the language of one constitutional provision in disregard of the Basic Law as a whole. In effect, the Court concludes that there is no constitutional right to trial by jury in Russia and that the legislature is free to determine its scope as long as its decisions are not arbitrary. One can fully expect, under this approach, that other parts of the amended art. 30(2) CCP, for example eliminating trial by jury in cases of espionage, treason or mass disorders, would be easily upheld as constitutionally firm.

Dissenting Judges *G.A. Gadzhiev* and *V.G. Yaroslavtsev* present in their opinions a refreshingly broader approach to the issue based on basic constitutional principles and facing up to realities of the administration of justice in Russia.[44] Judge *G.A. Gadzhiev* warns that the Court's approach inevitably leads to "deconstitutionalization" of the trial by jury contrary to the constitutional values,

---

43 The CCP, arts. 328, 330.

44 Dissenting opinions of Constitutional Court Judges *G.A. Gadzhiev* and *V.G. Yaroslavtsev*, available on the official site of the Constitutional Court, http://www.ksrf.ru.

the holistic reading of the interconnected constitutional provisions and clear preferences of the constitutional lawgiver[45]. Trial by jury has been considered by the Constitution as a superior form of the criminal justice administration, that is why the Basic Law guarantees that form of trial for most grievous offenses[46]. The right of the accused to trial by jury shall be considered as a "constitutionally protected value" anchored in the principles of democracy and the rule of law. This right of the accused is closely related to the right of Russian citizens to participate in the administration of justice, a form of direct democracy guaranteed by art. 32, parts 1 and 5 of the Constitution[47]. Since the right to trial by jury has its substantive constitutional content, it may not be encroached or limited by the legislature at its discretion as the Court opinion suggests. Instead, to be valid, the legislatively imposed limitations must meet the stricter standards specified by art. 55, parts 2 and 3 of the Constitution, that is to say must be "well founded, necessary and proportionate" to their purpose and function. According to Judge *G.A. Gadzhiev*, that standard was not met by the challenged amendment to art. 30(2) of the CCP[48]. "Constitutional value of the jury court consists first of all of jurors' full independence from the state"[49], asserts Judge *G.A. Gadzhiev*. That assertion resonates particularly loudly given the reality of judicial independence in Russia discussed earlier in this paper[50]. It dramatizes, if only in a muffled manner, what the Court's opinion completely, and no doubt deliberately, ignored. The Court remained oblivious to the crying fact that professional judges for years have followed bureaucratically imposed no-acquittals policy making mockery of the presumption of innocence in theory guaranteed by art. 49 of the Constitution. The Court elected to ignore the immense gap between the rates of acquittals rendered by the juries on the one hand and by professional judges on the other. That gap, no doubt, will be even greater in cases of high political sensitivity, where governmental interests are directly implicated[51]. This critical theme was more forcefully articulated in the dissenting opinion of Judge *V.G. Yaroslavtsev*, who does not mince words: he takes issue with the Court's majority view that the purpose of the challenged law was to assure an independent and impartial tribunal. The real purpose, unequivocally reflected by the legislative history, was the exclusion of juries because they render not guilty verdicts in a substantial number of cases to the great displeasure of the law enforcement agencies[52]. Those verdicts of acquittal demonstrate by no means that jurors are

---

45 Dissenting opinion of Judge *G.A. Gadzhiev* at §§ 1, 2.3.
46 *Id.*, at § 2.2.
47 *Id.*, at §§ 2.1, 2.2.
48 *Id.*, at § 2.3. Accord: Dissenting opinion of Judge *V.G. Yaroslavtsev* at § 3.1.
49 Dissenting opinion of Judge *G.A. Gadzhiev* at § 2.2.
50 See above, notes 8-22, and the accompanying text.
51 Dissenting opinion of Judge *G.A. Gadzhiev* at § 2.2.
52 Dissenting opinion of Judge *V.G. Yaroslavtsev*, note 44, at § 2. The opinion refers in particular to the explanatory memoranda of Duma's committee on security.

incompetent or prejudiced. On the contrary, asserts Judge *V.G. Yaroslavtsev*, juries render verdicts of acquittal, "when the prosecution was unable to prove the defendants' guilt ... consistent with the constitutionally mandated principle of the presumption of innocence"[53]. He concludes that the law is, therefore, infirm, as it arbitrarily interferes with the administration of justice in violation of the constitutional right to judicial protection[54].

As Russian commentators and legal experts have pointed out, the jury is the only agency capable and willing to check the power of the catastrophically incompetent and corrupt law enforcement and judiciary. Therefore, it is the only independent and impartial judicial forum putting the government to its proof and giving defendants a fair chance of exoneration[55].

Under the circumstances, the Constitutional Court's conclusion, that the legislature removed juries from cases involving crimes against the state in order to assure impartiality of the trial court, sounds disingenuous.

---

53 *Id.*

54 *Id.*

55 Editorial, "O eshche odnoi malenkoi vertikale" ("On One More Little Vertical"), Nezavisimaia Gazeta, October 26, 2009, p. 2; *E. Bilevskaia*, "Prisiazhnye ne dlia terroristov," Nezavisimaia Gazeta, April 20, 2010, p. 3; *Khamraev*, note 34; *I. Rodin*, note 34; *Id.*, "Duma potesnit prisiazhnykh" ("Duma Will Constrict Jurors"), Nezavisimaia Gazeta, December 3, 2008, p. 3. Contra: *V. Perekrest*, "Prisiazhnym ne doveriat shpionov i terroristov" (Spies and Terrorists Will Not Be Entrusted to Jurors"), Izvestia, April 20, 2010, p. 2.

Die Verfassung als Mittel der nationalen Identifikation in den Nachfolgestaaten der SFRJ

*Tomislav Pintarić**

Der Frage nach den Gründen für die Dismembration[1] der Sozialistischen Föderativen Republik Jugoslawien (nachfolgend: SFRJ) sind verschiedene Historiker und andere Publizisten nachgegangen[2]. Einig sind sich wohl alle darin, dass ein Zusammenwirken verschiedener historischer und gesellschaftlicher Gegebenheiten zu dem Untergang der SFRJ führte. Als einen der Gründe für die Auflösung kann man sicher die mangelnde Identifikation der Bevölkerung Jugoslawiens, bzw. großer Teile davon, mit ihrem damaligen Staat anführen. Ein Beleg dafür ist die hohe Zustimmung zu den Unabhängigkeitserklärungen bei entsprechenden Volksbefragungen in Kroatien, Slowenien, Bosnien und Herzegowina, Makedonien und Montenegro.

Jugoslawien war ein Bundes- und Vielvölkerstaat mit weitreichenden Kompetenzen der Teilrepubliken. Der nationalen Identität seiner Völker versuchten die Bundesverfassung sowie die Verfassungen der Teilrepubliken Rechnung zu tragen. Letztlich zogen es jedoch einige Völker Jugoslawiens vor, soweit die Bevölkerungsstruktur dies zuließ, nicht mehr in einem Vielvölkerstaat, sondern in einem Nationalstaat zu leben.

Nachfolgend soll ein Überblick darüber gegeben werden, in welcher Weise die Völker und Minderheiten nun in den neuen Verfassungen Berücksichtigung finden, um die Identifikation mit den neuen Staaten zu fördern und zum Ausdruck zu bringen.

I. Die Verfassung des jugoslawischen Bundes

Das ehemalige Jugoslawien nahm unter den sozialistischen Staaten in vielerlei Hinsicht eine Sonderstellung ein. Eine dieser Besonderheiten bestand in dem Stellenwert der Verfassung in Staat und Gesellschaft. Während man in den Staa-

---

* Wissenschaftl. Referent für das Recht der jugoslawischen Nachfolgestaaten am IOR.

1 Die von der EG-Friedenskonferenz zu Jugoslawien 1991 eingesetzte sogenannte Badinter-Kommission (*Arbitration Commission of the Peace Conference on the Former Yugoslavia*), deren Vorsitzender der französische Verfassungsrichter *R. Badinter* war, kam in einem Urteil vom 07.12.1991 zu dem Ergebnis, dass sich die Sozialistische Föderative Republik Jugoslawien im Prozess der Selbstauflösung befindet. Mit der Anerkennung der neu entstandenen Staaten war die SFR Jugoslawien aufgelöst.

2 Siehe dazu *H. Sundhaussen*, in: Aus Politik und Zeitgeschichte (APuZ) 32/2008, S. 9-18, m.w.N. der Literatur zu Krise und Zerfall Jugoslawiens.

ten des Ostblocks zwar Verfassungen hatte, die zum Teil auch etwa festschrieben, dass alle Staatsgewalt vom Volke ausgeht (Art. 3 Abs. 1 der Verfassung der DDR von 1949[3]), ohne dass die Regelungen der Verfassung aber in der gesellschaftlichen und staatlichen Praxis große Diskusionen auslösten oder gar zwingend Anwendung fanden, war die Verfassung im ehemaligen Jugoslawien ein Text, der verhältnismäßig ernst genommen und in der Gesellschaft auch diskutiert wurde[4].

Die jugoslawische Verfassung von 1974[5], die bis zum Untergang des Staates in Kraft blieb, sah für die einzelnen Republiken und autonomen Provinzen eine Fülle von Befugnissen vor, sodass die Teilrepubliken eine starke Position innerhalb der Föderation hatten.

Hintergrund dieser föderalen Ausgestaltung der Verfassung von 1974 waren die Studentenunruhen[6] in Kroatien vom November 1971, durch die eine Öffnung des Landes zu mehr Demokratie und zu einer größeren Autonomie der Teilrepubliken bewirkt werden sollte. Die Demonstrationen wurden von den Arbeitern und anderen gesellschaftlichen Gruppen, aber vor allem auch von der Kommunistischen Partei Kroatiens unterstützt. Der demokratische Aufbruch in Kroatien wurde durch die Regierung des Bundes in Belgrad gewaltsam beendet. Die Folge waren Verhaftungen der Protagonisten und zahlreicher Beteiligter. Die kommunistische Partei Kroatiens wurde von den abweichlerischen Mitgliedern gesäubert und an die Schlüsselpositionen des Staates und der Gesellschaft wurden linientreue Parteimitglieder gesetzt.

Gänzlich wirkungslos blieb der gescheiterte demokratische Aufbruch von 1971 jedoch nicht. In den folgenden Jahren kam es zu einer in der Gesellschaft breit angelegten Diskussion über eine Verfassungsänderung auf Bundesebene. Die daraus resultierenden Reformen nach 1971 betrafen sowohl das Wirtschafssystem als auch den Aufbau des Staates und die Freiheitsrechte des Einzelnen. Die Kompetenzen der Teilrepubliken und der autonomen Provinzen wurden gestärkt, sodass sich zwischen den Teilrepubliken auch eine gewisse Konkurrenz herausbilden konnte, die sich unter anderem in divergierenden Wirtschaftsergebnissen und gesellschaftlichen Freiheiten niederschlug.

---

3 Die Verfassung der Deutschen Demokratischen Republik vom 07.10.1949, Gesetzblatt der Deutschen Demokratischen Republik, 1949, S. 4.

4 Vgl. *G. Brunner*: Funktionen der Verfassung in den sozialistischen Staaten im Spiegel der neueren Verfassungen, in: *F.-C. Schroeder/B. Meisner* (Hrsg.): Verfassungs- und Verwaltungsreformen in den sozialistischen Staaten, Duncker & Humbold, Berlin, 1978, S. 11–42.

5 Ustav Socijalističke Federativne Republike Jugoslavije [Verfassung der Sozialistischen Föderativen Republik Jugoslawien], Sl.l. SFRJ (Gesetzblatt der SFRJ), Nr. 9/74.

6 Die Ereignisse von 1971 wurden auch „der kroatische Frühling" genannt. Siehe dazu etwa *L. Steindorf*: Der Kroatische Frühling. Eine soziale Bewegung in einer sozialistischen Gesellschaft, in: *J. Elvert* (Hrsg.): Der Balkan. Eine europäische Krisenregion in Geschichte und Gegenwart, Franz Steiner Verlag, Stuttgart, 1997, S. 197–210.

Die jugoslawische Verfassung von 1974 war das Ergebnis dieses von der kommunistischen Partei gesteuerten und überwachten gesellschaftlichen Diskurses. In ihren Formulierungen war sie sehr ausführlich und glich eher einem Parteiprogramm, denn einer Verfassung. Mit 406 Artikeln und einer Länge von weit über 100 Druckseiten war es eine der längsten Verfassungen der Welt[7].

Die Verfassung von 1974 hat in ihrem ersten Satz der Präambel eine Formulierung verwendet, die von den Völkern und Völkerschaften des Staates Jugoslawien spricht, die sich zu einem gemeinsamen Staat zusammengeschlossen haben. Die staatstragenden, konstitutiven Völker Jugoslawiens waren die Kroaten, Makedonier, Montenegriner, Muslime, Serben und Slowenen, wobei die Muslime erst 1971 als eigenes Volk deklariert wurden. Die restlichen in der SFRJ lebenden ethnischen Gruppen wurden nicht als Minderheiten, sondern als „Völkerschaften" (serb./kroat.: *narodnosti*) bezeichnet. Die Albaner hatten, obwohl sie nach der Volkszählung von 1981 einen Bevölkerungsanteil von 7,72% aufwiesen, ebenfalls den Status einer „Völkerschaft" (*narodnost*), also nicht den Status eines staatstragenden Volkes. Die übrigen Minderheiten wiesen, außer den Ungarn (1,9%), lediglich einen Bevölkerungsanteil von jeweils unter 0,7% auf.

Die entsprechende Formulierung in der Verfassung lautet:

> „Die Völker Jugoslawiens haben sich, ausgehend von dem Recht jedes Volkes auf Selbstbestimmung, das Recht auf Loslösung eingeschlossen, aufgrund des im gemeinsamen Kampf aller Völker und Völkerschaften im Volksbefreiungskrieg und in der sozialistischen Revolution frei geäußerten Willens [...] zu einer föderativen Republik freier und gleichberechtigter Völker und Völkerschaften vereint [...]."

Eine ähnliche Formulierung, die auch das Recht auf Loslösung umfasste, befand sich schon in der ersten Verfassung von Jugoslawien aus dem Jahr 1946. Diese Regelung sollte in der Krise des Jahres 1991 große Bedeutung erlangen, da sich die Initiatoren der Volksbefragungen zur Unabhängigkeit auf dieses verfassungsmäßig verbriefte Recht als Rechtsgrundlage berufen konnten.

Nach der Reform der Bundesverfassung von 1974 wurden im gleichen Jahr auch alle acht Verfassungen der Teilrepubliken und der zwei autonomen Provinzen reformiert und mit der Bundesverfassung in Einklang gebracht.

II. Kroatien

In den Jahren vor 1990 war aufgrund von verschiedenen Faktoren abzusehen, dass der Staat Jugoslawien ohne grundlegende Änderungen nicht fortbestehen kann. In Kroatien und Slowenien regte sich immer stärker der Wunsch nach Freiheit, Demokratie und nationaler Selbstbestimmung, während in Serbien an

---

7 Deutsche Übersetzung der Verfassung bei *H. Roggemann* (Hrsg.): Die Verfassung der Sozialistischen Föderativen Republik Jugoslawien, Berlin Verlag, Berlin, 1980.

der Idee eines unveränderten Staatssystems, jedoch mit einem verstärkten Zentralismus, festgehalten wurde[8].

Als Lösung der widerstreitenden Interessen wurde von slowenischer und kroatischer Seite die Bildung einer Konföderation vorgeschlagen, sodass der Staat Jugoslawien nach außen hin erhalten geblieben wäre, jedoch in den einzelnen Staaten der Konföderation verschiedene gesellschaftspolitische Wege hätten eingeschlagen werden können.

Nachdem alle Vorschläge einer Konföderation abgelehnt wurden, verließen auf dem letzten Parteitag der Kommunisten Jugoslawiens, am 21.01.1990, die slowenischen Kommunisten den Parteitag. Damit hatte die wichtigste Klammer der Gesellschaftsordnung nach der Verfassung von 1974, nämlich der „Bund der Kommunisten", faktisch aufgehört zu existieren.

Im April 1990 fanden dann in Slowenien und Kroatien freie Wahlen statt, bei denen die kommunistische Partei in beiden Ländern keine Mehrheit mehr erringen konnte. Die Abhaltung dieser Wahlen befand sich im Einklang mit den jeweiligen Verfassungen. Im Unterschied zu den früheren Wahlen waren jedoch auch andere Parteien als die Kommunisten zugelassen. Somit konstituierten sich zum ersten Mal frei gewählte Parlamente in Slowenien und Kroatien.

Im Juli 1990 nahm das kroatische Parlament (Sabor) die Verfassungs-Amandements Nr. 64–75 an, durch die sich Kroatien als souveräner Staat erklärte. Gleichzeitig gründete die serbische Bevölkerung in der Krajina[9] in Kroatien einen sogenannten Nationalrat und rief die „Souveränität und Autonomie des serbischen Volkes in Kroatien" aus. Es wurde damit die sogenannte Republik Krajina gegründet. Diese Aktion war jedoch verfassungsrechtlich nicht gedeckt, da ein entsprechendes Recht nicht bestand.

Im August begann dann die sogenannte „Baumstamm-Revolution". Serben in der Krajina errichten Straßen-Barrikaden (durch Baumstämme) und trennen so den südlichen Teil Kroatiens vom Nordteil ab und plündern Waffenlager der kroatischen Polizei. Damit begannen die gewaltsamen Auseinandersetzungen, die zum Krieg führten[10].

---

8 Zur gesellschaftspolitischen Entwicklung in Jugoslawien, die dann zum Krieg führte, siehe *D. Melčić* (Hrsg.): Der Jugoslawien-Krieg. Handbuch zu Vorgeschichte, Verlauf und Konsequenzen, 2. aktualisierte und erweiterte Aufl., VS Verlag für Sozialwissenschaften, Wiesbaden, 2007.

9 Landstrich an der Grenze zu Bosnien und Herzegowina.

10 Zu den verschiedenen Phasen des bzw. der Kriege auf dem Gebiet des ehemaligen Jugoslawien siehe *M. Križan*: Postkommunistische Wiedergeburt ethnischer Nationalismen und der Dritte Balkan-Krieg, in: Osteuropa, Zeitschrift für Gegenwartsforschung des Ostens, 45. Jahrgang, Heft 3/1995, S. 201–218.

Nach diesen und anderen dramatischen Ereignissen des Jahres 1990 gab sich Kroatien am 21. Dezember des gleichen Jahres eine neue demokratische Verfassung[11].

In der Präambel der kroatischen Verfassung wird auf die verschiedenen Phasen der Selbstständigkeit Kroatiens in der Geschichte seit dem 7. Jahrhundert Bezug genommen und festgestellt, dass das kroatische Volk den Willen hat, die Republik Kroatien als souveränen Staat zu errichten. Es wird ferner Bezug genommen auf das Selbstbestimmungsrecht der Völker und das Recht auf Abspaltung, welche auch die Bundesverfassung von 1974 garantierte, und laut Verfassung konstituiert sich die Republik Kroatien als Nationalstaat des kroatischen Volkes sowie als Staat der Angehörigen anderer Völker und Minderheiten, die seine Staatsbürger sind: Serben, Muslime, Slowenen, Tschechen, Slowaken, Italiener, Ungarn, Juden und andere.

In der kroatischen Verfassung von 1974[12] wurden noch die Serben als das Volk genannt, das mit dem kroatischen Volk eine Republik bildet. Der Umstand, dass das serbische Volk nicht mehr als ein „Volk" genannt wird, wurde von manchen als eine Degradierung des serbischen Volkes in Kroatien von einem „konstitutiven" Volk Kroatiens zu einer Minderheit gewertet. Diese Behauptung ist durch den Verfassungstext jedoch nicht begründet, da die Verfassungen der SFRJ weder den Begriff „konstitutiv" noch den Begriff der Minderheit kannten. Vielmehr wurden die größeren Völker als solche und die Minderheiten als „Völkerschaften" (*narodnosti*) bezeichnet. Dementsprechend wurde die Sozialistische Republik Kroatien in Artikel 1 Absatz 2 der Verfassung von 1974 als Nationalstaat des kroatischen Volkes, als Staat des serbischen Volkes in Kroatien und als Staat der in ihm lebenden Völkerschaften bezeichnet. Da die Serben in der SFRJ insgesamt den Status eines Volkes, und nicht einer „Völkerschaft" (Minderheit) hatten, wurde ihnen diese Bezeichnung auch in der kroatischen Verfassung von 1974 zuteil.

In der Präambel der Verfassung von 1990 wird Kroatien als Nationalstaat des kroatischen Volkes und als Staat anderer Völker und Minderheiten, die in ihm leben, bezeichnet, wobei in der folgenden Aufzählung die Serben an erster Stelle und dann die Moslems, Slowenen, Tschechen usw. genannt werden. Insoweit wird auch in der Verfassung von 1990 dem in Kroatien lebenden serbischen Volk der Status eines Volkes eingeräumt, wobei der Staat als solcher,

11 Ustav Republike Hrvatske [Verfassung der Republik Kroatien], Narodne novine (kroatisches Gesetzblatt) Nr. 56/90, 135/97, 8/98, 113/00, 124/00, 28/01, 41/20, 55/01, 76/10, 85/10 (bereinigte Fassung). Die deutsche Übersetzung der kroatischen Verfassung in der aktuellen Fassung von 2010 siehe unter: http://www.kas.de/wf/doc/kas_2764-1442-1-30.pdf?110114141431 (abgerufen am 02.02.2011).

12 Ustav Socijalističke Republike Hrvatske [Verfassung der Sozialistischen Republik Kroatien], Narodne novine (kroatisches Gesetzblatt), Nr. 8/1974.

ebenso wie schon in der sozialistischen Verfassung von 1974, als Nationalstaat des kroatischen Volkes bezeichnet wird.

Auch ist zu bedenken, dass die Formulierung, dass die Serben als Volk mit den Kroaten in Kroatien leben, erst in die kroatische Verfassung von 1974 eingeführt wurde. In der kroatischen Verfassung von 1963[13] war lediglich von der Gleichberechtigung des serbischen Volkes in Kroatien die Rede.

Die kroatische Verfassung und die Republik Kroatien werden heute von der Bevölkerung als identitätsstiftend angenommen. Auch die serbische Minderheit in Kroatien hat größtenteils diesen Staat als den eigenen angenommen, was auch durch die Beteiligung einer serbischen Partei an der derzeitigen Regierungskoalition zum Ausdruck kommt.

III. Slowenien

Die Teilrepublik Slowenien proklamierte zusammen mit Kroatien am 25.06.1991 ihre Unabhängigkeit. Die jugoslawische Bundesregierung und das Bundesparlament bezeichneten die Erklärungen für „null und nichtig". Zwischen der Jugoslawischen Volksarmee und der slowenischen Territorialverteidigung kam es daraufhin zu Gefechten und am 28.06.1991 besetzte die Jugoslawische Volksarmee die Grenzübergänge in Slowenien. Nachdem die KSZE die Streitparteien aufgefordert hatte, alle Kämpfe sofort einzustellen, zog die Jugoslawische Volksarmee im Juli aus Slowenien ab. Der kurze Krieg in Slowenien war dem Umstand zu verdanken, dass die Jugoslawische Volksarmee einen Krieg in Slowenien nicht durch den Vorwand des Schutzes von Minderheiten, namentlich der Serben, rechtfertigen konnte, da die Bevölkerung Sloweniens ethnisch homogen war.

Am 28.12.1991 trat die neue slowenische Verfassung[14] in Kraft. In der kurzen Präambel der Verfassung wird auf die Verfassungsurkunde über die Unabhängigkeit Sloweniens vom 25.06.1991, das Recht auf Selbstbestimmung und den jahrhundertelangen Kampf des slowenischen Volkes für seine nationale Unabhängigkeit und eigene Staatlichkeit Bezug genommen. In Art. 3 der Verfassung wird Slowenien dann als Staat, der auf dem dauerhaften und unveräußerlichen Recht des slowenischen Volkes auf Selbstbestimmung gründet und als Staat all seiner Staatsbürger bezeichnet. Obwohl Slowenien an keiner Stelle der Verfassung als Nationalstaat der Slowenen bezeichnet ist, ist er, aufgrund der Berufung auf die eigene Staatlichkeit und das Selbstbestimmungsrecht der Slo-

---

13 Ustav Socijalističke Republike Hrvatske [Verfassung der sozialistischen Republik Kroatien], Narodne novine (kroatisches Gesetzblatt) Nr. 15/63.

14 Ustava Republike Slovenije [Verfassung der Republik Slowenien], Uradni list RS (slowenisches Gesetzblatt), Nr. 33/91-I, 42/97, 66/00, 24/03, 69/04, 68/06. Deutsche Übersetzung der slowenischen Verfassung in der Fassung vom 25.06.1991 von *T. Longyka*, in: *G. Brunner* (Hrsg.), Verfassungs- und Verwaltungsrecht der Staaten Osteuropas, VSO, Band I 1, Teil Slowenien, Berlin Verlag Arno Spitz, Berlin, 1996.

wenen, als solcher anzusehen. Die slowenische Bevölkerung setzt sich zusammen aus 87% Slowenen, 2,8% Kroaten, 2,4% Serben und 1,4% Bosniaken.

Auch die slowenische Verfassung und die Republik Slowenien werden heute von der Bevölkerung als identitätsstiftend angenommen.

IV. Bosnien und Herzegowina

Das Bestreben die staatliche Unabhängigkeit zu erlangen, war in Bosnien und Herzegowina (nachfolgend: BuH) aufgrund des Vorhandenseins von drei konstitutiven Völkern zum Zeitpunkt des Niedergangs der SFRJ nicht ausgeprägt, da keines der drei Völker in dem unabhängigen Staat BuH über die absolute Mehrheit verfügt hätte und somit auch die Bildung eines Nationalstaates nicht möglich war. Nach der Verfassung von 1974[15] haben sich nämlich Serben, Muslime und Kroaten in einem gemeinsamen Staat vereinigt und bildeten gemeinsam das Volk von Bosnien und Herzegowina.

Nachdem Slowenien und Kroatien ihre Unabhängigkeit von Jugoslawien erklärt hatten, stand dennoch die Frage im Raum, wie sich Bosnien verhalten würde. *A. Izetbegović*, der damalige Staatspräsident, war zunächst für den Verbleib Bosnien-Herzegowinas bei Restjugoslawien und sprach sich für eine „gesunde Föderation“ aus. Doch bald entwickelte sich die politische Lage in eine Richtung, die es ihm als einzige Möglichkeit erscheinen ließ, die Unabhängigkeit anzustreben. Die jugoslawische Volksarmee unter dem Kommando des bereits im Kroatienkrieg hervorgetretenen Generals *Mladić* bereitete einen offenen Krieg für den Fall einer Unabhängigkeitserklärung Bosniens vor.

Am 15.01.1992 erkannte die EU Slowenien und Kroatien als souveräne Staaten an und stellte auch Bosnien-Herzegowina die Anerkennung unter der Bedingung in Aussicht, dass die Bevölkerung in einem fairen Referendum für die Unabhängigkeit votieren würde. Am 29.02.1992 fand das von der EU gewünschte Referendum über die Unabhängigkeit statt. Die Kroaten und Bosniaken in BuH stimmten mit über 90% für die Unabhängigkeit; die bosnischen Serben boykottierten die Abstimmung. Insgesamt sprach sich, trotz des Boykotts der Serben, die Mehrheit der Bevölkerung für eine Unabhängigkeit aus, worauf am 03.03.1992 die Ausrufung der Unabhängigkeit BuHs erfolgte.

Mit der Anerkennung BuHs durch die EU am 06.04.1992, wurde der bereits davor begonnene Krieg von *R. Karadžić*, dem damaligen Präsidenten der zuvor ausgerufenen Republika Srpska, gegen die Bosniaken (Muslime) und bosnischen Kroaten intensiviert und ausgeweitet.

Aufgrund der politischen Lage in BuH gab es vor dem Ausbruch des Krieges keine Initiativen zur Annahme einer neuen Verfassung, die unter den sich

---

15 Ustav Republike Bosne i Hercegovine [Verfassung der Republik Bosnien und Herzegowina], Službeni list RBiH (Gesetzbaltt von Bosnien und Herzegowina), Nr. 4/74, 21/76, 21/81, 10/84, 13/89, 2/90, 21/90, 34/90, 5/92, 9/92, 3/93, 5/93 (bereinigte Fassung).

wandelnden politischen Umständen als Basis für die Gesellschaft hätte dienen können. Während des Krieges galt also die Verfassung von BuH von 1974 fort.

Nach dem Ende des Krieges in BuH wurde auf einer Militärbasis in Dayton/USA 1995 in wochenlangen Verhandlungen das Dayton-Abkommen[16] ausgehandelt, welches einen Friedensvertrag darstellt und den die Präsidenten Izetbegović (für BuH), Tuđman (für Kroatien) und Milošević (für Serbien) unterzeichneten.

Der Vertrag, dessen Titel als „Allgemeines Rahmenabkommen" (*General Framework Agreement*) zu übersetzen wäre, beinhaltete in seinem Annex 4 auch die neue Verfassung von BuH[17].

In der Dayton-Verfassung wird in der Präambel davon gesprochen, dass die Bosniaken, die Kroaten und die Serben als konstitutive Völker die Verfassung annehmen. Ob diese Aussage so stimmt ist fraglich, da die Völker von BuH über die neue Verfassung nicht zu befinden hatten und die Vertreter dieser Völker starkem Druck von Seiten der USA ausgesetzt waren, den Dayton-Vertrag mitsamt der Verfassung anzunehmen.

In der Dayton-Verfassung wird nicht mehr von den Muslimen als Volk gesprochen, sondern von den Bosniaken. Die Muslime von BuH wurden erst 1971[18] von Seiten der Machthaber der ehemaligen SFRJ als eigenes Volk erklärt, und sollten als solches eines der drei konstitutiven Völker des sozialistischen BuHs sein.

BuH besteht seit der Dayton-Verfassung aus zwei „Entitäten", nämlich der Föderation BuH und der Republika Srpska.

Die Republika Srpska wurde am 09.01.1992 unter dem Namen „Srpska Republika Bosna i Hercegovina" (Serbische Republik Bosnien und Herzegowina) proklamiert und vollzog somit eine durch die Verfassung von BuH nicht legitimierte Sezession. Am 28.02.1992 wurde die Verfassung[19] dieser Republik vom Parlament der Republika Srpska angenommen und am 12.08.1992 nahm sie ihren heutigen Namen an. Die Verfassung der Republika Srpska wurde in der Folgezeit einige Male geändert. Eine der wichtigsten Änderungen[20] folgte aus dem Dayton-Vertrag, der vorsah, dass alle drei konstitutiven Völker Bosnien und Herzegowinas in beiden Entitäten ebenfalls konstitutiv zu sein haben. Bis

---

16 „*General Framework Agreement For Peace in Bosnia and Herzegovina*" (Dayton-Abkommen); den Text im englischen Original siehe bei *B. Bakotić* (Hrsg.), Daytonski sporazum [das Dayton-Abkommen], Manuskript der Juristischen Fakultät in Zagreb, Zagreb, 1998.

17 *B. Bakotić,* a.a.O., S. 64 ff.

18 Die Einführung der Muslime als konstitutives Volk der Sozialistischen Republik BuH erfolgte durch eine Änderung der Verfassung von BuH von 1971.

19 Ustav Republike Srpske [Verfassung der Republik Srpska], http://www.skupstinabd.ba/ustavi/rs/ustav_hrvatski.pdf (abgerufen am 02.02.2011).

20 Amendement LXVII zur Verfassung der Republik Srpska.

zum Vertrag von Dayton galt die Republika Srpska als Nationalstaat lediglich der Serben von BuH.

Die Föderation BuH nahm am 30.03.1994, als Folge des Abkommens von Washington[21], ihre Verfassung[22] durch die verfassungsgebende Versammlung an. Die Föderation war zunächst als staatliche Einheit der Bosniaken und Kroaten gemeinsam mit allen anderen Bürgern von BuH ausgestaltet. Um den bosniakisch-kroatischen Konflikt innerhalb des Bosnien-Krieges zu beenden, haben Kroatien, als Vertreter der bosnischen Kroaten und die Republik BuH, deren Regierung 1994 fast ausschließlich aus Moslems/Bosniaken bestand, auf Betreiben der USA das „Washingtoner Abkommen zur Gründung der Bosnisch-Kroatischen Föderation in Bosnien und Herzegowina" geschlossen. Damit kein Volk sich von einem anderen Volk dominiert fühlen würde, wurde die Föderation in zehn Kantone unterteilt. Nach der damaligen Idee sollte das Gebiet der Republika Srpska in die Föderation eingegliedert werden, sodass ein auf kantonaler Basis unterteiltes BuH entstehen sollte. Daher auch der Name „Föderation", obwohl es sich lediglich um eine von zwei „Entitäten" handelt.

Jeder Kanton hat auch eine eigene Verfassung, auf die hier aber nicht eingegangen werden soll, da die Zuständigkeiten der Kantone ohnehin sukzessive auf die Föderation übertragen werden, was allerdings dem Washingtoner Abkommen widerspricht.

Von der Unterteilung BuHs in die zwei „Entitäten" wurde ein Gebiet um die Stadt Brčko mit ca. 80.000 Einwohnern ausgenommen. Da sich die zwei „Entitäten" nicht einigen konnten, wem das Gebiet zufallen sollte, wurde nun das Gebiet als Kondominium ausgestaltet, das faktisch als dritte „Entität" anzusehen ist[23].

Insgesamt kann festgestellt werden, dass die Verfassungen, die in BuH in den letzten zwei Jahrzehnten angenommen wurden, ihre Aufgabe nicht erfüllt haben. Der Dayton-Vertrag hat zwar als Endpunkt für den Bosnien-Krieg eine Rolle gespielt, doch hat die darin aufoktroyierte Verfassung zu keinem wesentlichen Fortschritt im Zusammenleben der Bevölkerung geführt.

Als Beleg dafür gilt, dass der Hohe Repräsentant, der die internationale Gemeinschaft in Form der Vereinten Nationen in BuH repräsentiert, auch 2011 noch im Amt ist. Der Hohe Repräsentant für BuH, der 1995 durch Annex X des Dayton-Abkommens und die Resolution 1031 des UN-Sicherheitsrats mitsamt

---

21 Zum Washingtoner Abkommen siehe *Z. Ivanković/D. Melčić*: Der bosnisch-kroatische „Krieg im Kriege", in: *D. Melčić*, Fn. 8, S. 415 ff.

22 Ustav Federacije Bosne i Hercegovine [Verfassung der Föderation Bosnien und Herzegowina], http://skupstinabd.ba/ustavi/f/ustav_federacije_bosne_i_hercegovine.pdf (abgerufen am 02.02.2011).

23 Der Brčko-Distrikt verfügt nicht über eine Verfassung, sondern über ein Statut, das vor allem die Kompetenzen der Gewalten in dem Distrikt regelt. Der Text des Statuts ist abrufbar unter: http://www.skupstinabd.ba/statut/h/Statut%20Brcko%20distrikta%20BiH%20-%20precisceni%20tekst%202-10%20H.pdf (abgerufen am 02.02.2011).

dem ihm zugeordneten Büro des Hohen Repräsentanten (*Office of the High Representative – OHR*) installiert wurde, hat die Aufgabe, die Durchführung der zivilen Aspekte des Dayton-Abkommens zu überwachen[24]. Der Hohe Repräsentant hat geradezu uneingeschränkte Vollmachten, die ein demokratisches Staatswesen *ad absurdum* führen. Er wurde am 10.12.1997 auf dem „*Peace Implementation Council*" (Friedensimplementierungsrat), an dem Vertreter aus 55 Staaten und internationalen Organisationen teilnahmen, mit diesen Vollmachten, den sogenannten „*Bonn Powers*[25]", ausgestattet. Sie ermächtigen den Hohen Repräsentanten, Politiker und andere öffentlich Bedienstete zu entlassen, wenn sie „die rechtlichen Verpflichtungen, die im Rahmen des Friedensabkommens eingegangen wurden oder die Regeln für dessen Implementierung verletzen". Ferner ist der Hohe Repräsentant bevollmächtigt, Beschlüsse mit Gesetzeskraft zu erlassen, wenn die Legislative von BuH dazu nicht willens bzw. in der Lage ist, sowie jede Art von Gesetzen, Beschlüssen und Entscheidungen aufzuheben.

Gerade an Bosnien kann die Wichtigkeit einer Verfassung für den Beginn einer neuen Periode eines Staates bzw. für eine Staatsgründung studiert werden. Die Versuche, eine neue Verfassung in Kraft zu setzen, sind bislang an den widerstreitenden Interessen der drei Völker gescheitert.

V. Serbien

Nach der serbischen Verfassung[26] von 1974 hatten die territorial zu Serbien gehörenden Autonomen Provinzen Vojvodina und Kosovo so weitreichende Autonomierechte, dass sie sich von den übrigen Teilrepubliken der SFRJ kaum unterschieden. Durch die serbische Verfassung[27] vom 28.09.1990 wurde die Autonomie des Kosovo, nachdem sie bereits vorher ausgehöhlt wurde, endgültig aufgehoben. Die Provinz Kosovo wurde umbenannt in Kosovo und Metochien. Die Autonomie der Provinz Vojvodina wurde ebenfalls aufgehoben, was jedoch zu keiner offenen Auflehnung innerhalb der Bevölkerung führte, da in der Vojvo-

---

24 Siehe die Internet-Präsenz des *OHR* unter: http://www.ohr.int, m.w.N. Siehe auch: Kurzinformation des wissenschaftlichen Dienstes des Deutschen Bundestages, Nr. 06/06 vom 26.01.2006, http://www.bundestag.de/dokumente/analysen/2006/Der_Hohe_Bauftragte_fuer_Bosnien_und_Herzegowina.pdf (abgerufen am 02.02.2011).

25 Die „*Bonn Powers*" wurden nach dem Tagungsort des „*Peace Implementation Council*" auf dem Petersberg bei Bonn benannt. Zum Inhalt siehe unter: http://www.ohr.int/pic/default.asp?content_id=5182 (abgerufen am 02.02.2011).

26 Ustav Socijalističke Republike Srbije [Verfassung der Sozialistischen Republik Serbien], Službeni glasnik (serbisches Gesetzblatt), Nr. 8/74.

27 Ustav Republike Srbije [Verfassung der Republik Serbien], Službeni glasnik (serbisches Gesetzblatt), Nr. 1/90. Deutsche Übersetzung der Fassung von 1990, mit Einführung, von *U. Wiedemann*: Die neuen Verfassungen von 1990, in: Jahrbuch für Ostrecht, Band XXXII/2 (1991), S. 355–387.

dina der serbische Bevölkerungsanteil etwa 75% Prozent betrug. Nach der Verfassung von 1990 war Serbien ein demokratischer Staat aller Bürger, die in ihm leben. Serbien definierte sich hier also nicht als Nationalstaat der Serben.

Am 27.04.1992 wurde in Belgrad durch die Delegierten aus Serbien und Montenegro im ehemaligen Bundesparlament der SFRJ die Verfassung der Bundesrepublik Jugoslawien[28] (BRJ) angenommen. Den Bund bildeten die ehemaligen jugoslawischen Teilrepubliken Serbien und Montenegro. Die Verfassung sah auch die Möglichkeit für andere Republiken vor, dem Bund beizutreten. Um welche Republiken es sich dabei handeln könnte, wurde offen gelassen.

Auch in der BRJ kam es zu Zerwürfnissen zwischen Serbien und Montenegro. Ein Zerbrechen des Bundesstaates entlang der Republiksgrenze schien unaufhaltsam. Nur auf Drängen der EU kam es am 04.02.2003 noch einmal zur Bildung eines Staatenbundes zwischen Serbien und Montenegro unter dem Namen „Staatliche Gemeinschaft Serbien und Montenegro“[29]. Serbien und Montenegro waren nun schon souveräne Staaten, die sich zu einer Konföderation zusammengeschlossen haben. Eine tatsächliche Zusammenarbeit zwischen den beiden konföderierten Staaten gab es seit Beginn der Konföderation aber eigentlich nicht. Montenegro wartete lediglich die von der EU gesetzte Frist von drei Jahren ab, um sich für unabhängig zu erklären, was dann am 03.06.2006 auch geschah[30].

Nachdem nun auch der letzte Versuch eines Bundesstaates scheiterte, nahm das serbische Parlament am 30.09.2006 einstimmig eine neue Verfassung[31] an. Die neue Verfassung wurde am 28.10.2006 in einem Referendum dem Volk zur Abstimmung vorgelegt und mit 53% der abgegebenen Stimmen angenommen.

Die Republik Serbien wird nun als Staat des serbischen Volkes und all ihrer Bürger definiert. Da der Kosovo aufgrund des Kosovo-Krieges von 1999 bereits unter internationaler Verwaltung stand, Serbien den Kosovo allerdings weiterhin als integralen Bestandteil Serbiens betrachtet, wurde in der Präambel der Verfassung dezidiert festgeschrieben, dass die Provinz Kosovo und Metochien integraler Bestandteil der Republik Serbien ist.

---

28 Ustav Savezne Republike Jugoslavije [Verfassung der Bundesrepublik Jugoslawien], Službeni list SRJ (Gesetzblatt der Bundesrepublik Jugoslawien), Nr. 1/92.

29 Ustavna povelja državne zajednice Srbije i Crne Gore [Verfassungscharta der staatlichen Gemeinschaft von Serbien und Montenegro], Službeni list Srbije i Crne Gore (Gesetzblatt von Serbien und Montenegro), Nr. 1/2003.

30 Zu den bereits in der Verfassungscharta von 2003 angelegten Bestimmungen in Richtung Desintegration vgl. *A. Jakub*: Die Verfassungscharta von „Serbien und Montenegro“, Zeitschrift für ausländisches öffentliches Recht und Völkerrecht (ZaöRV), 63/3, 2003, S. 801–815.

31 Ustav Republike Srbije [Verfassung der Republik Serbien], Službeni Glasnik (serbisches Gesetzblatt), Nr. 98/06. Deutsche Übersetzung von *H. Küpper*, in: Jahrbuch für Ostrecht 2008/II, S. 489–537, mit Einführung: Die neue serbische Verfassung vom 10. November 2006, S. 249–296.

VI. Kosovo

Der Kosovo wird hauptsächlich von ethnischen Albanern bewohnt. Der Anteil der Serben an der Bevölkerung betrug 1948 noch etwa 24% und fiel kontinuierlich bis 1991 auf ca. 10%. Derzeit dürfte der Anteil der Serben im Kosovo bei ca. 4% liegen[32].

Am 17.02.2008 proklamierte das Parlament in Priština die Unabhängigkeit der Provinz von Serbien. Bisher erkennen 75 Staaten die Republik Kosovo als unabhängig an. Serbien betrachtet Kosovo unverändert als seine Autonome Provinz Kosovo und Metochien.

Kosovo wurde nach dem Kosovokrieg – bei formeller Wahrung der Zugehörigkeit zu Jugoslawien – durch die UN-Resolution 1244[33] unter die Verwaltung der Vereinten Nationen gestellt. Zudem wird die politische Entwicklung seit dem 09.12.2008 durch die Rechtsstaatlichkeitsmission der EU im Kosovo („EULEX Kosovo[34]") überwacht. Dies gilt auch für die hauptsächlich von Serben bewohnte Region Nordkosovo, die von der Regierung Kosovos derzeit nicht kontrolliert wird.

Im Zuge der Verfassungsänderungen in der SFRJ von 1974 hat auch der Kosovo am 27.02.1974 eine eigene Verfassung[35] angenommen, wodurch sein Status auch in dieser Hinsicht dem einer Teilrepublik der SFRJ angeglichen wurde.

Am 15.06.2008 hat sich der nunmehr unabhängige Kosovo die erste Verfassung[36] als souveräner Staat gegeben. Die Präambel der Verfassung spricht davon, dass das Volk des Kosovo bzw. die Bürger des Kosovo – die serbische und die albanische Version des Textes variieren an dieser Stelle – der Verfassung des Kosovo zustimmen. Der Kosovo definiert sich somit nicht als albanischer Nationalstaat, sondern als ein multiethnischer Staat.

Wenn man von den gesetzgebungstechnischen Mängeln des Verfassungstextes absieht[37], kann dieser als tragbare Grundlage für die Entwicklung und Befriedung des Staates dienen. Dies wird jedoch zum großen Teil davon abhängen, ob sich die wenigen im Kosovo verbliebenen Serben sowie das serbische Mut-

---

32 Zur Bevölkerungsstatistik siehe die Internet-Präsenz des Statistischen Amtes der Republik Kosovo unter: http://esk.rks-gov.net (abgerufen am 02.02.2011).

33 UN Security Council Resolution 1244 v. 10. Juni 1999, http://www.cfr.org/un/un-security-council-resolution-1244-kosovo/p12533 (abgerufen am 02.02.2011).

34 EULEX hat zur Aufgabe, im Kosovo die Verfassung unter Anwendung rechtsstaatlicher Mittel und Verfahrensweisen durchzusetzen. Die Mission im Kosovo ist die erste und derzeit einzige Rechtsstaatlichkeitsmission der EU.

35 Ustav SAP Kosova [Verfassung der Sozialistischen Autonomen Provinz Kosovo], Službeni list SAP Kosovo (Gesetzblatt der Sozialistischen Autonomen Provinz Kosovo), Nr. 14/74.

36 Deutsche Übersetzung von *H. Küpper*, in: Jahrbuch für Ostrecht 2008/II, S. 365–409, mit Einführung: Die kosovarische Verfassungsordnung, S. 297–350.

37 Siehe dazu *H. Küpper*, a.a.O.

terland für einen demokratischen Neubeginn des Kosovo als unabhängigem Staat gewinnen lassen.

VII. Montenegro

Montenegro teilte seit 1992 bis zu der Erklärung der Unabhängigkeit am 03.06.2006 weitgehend das Schicksal der ehemaligen jugoslawischen Teilrepublik Serbien.

Die Verfassung[38] von 1974, die von allen bisherigen montenegrinischen Verfassungen den längsten Bestand hatte, wurde durch die Verfassung[39] vom 27.04.1992 abgelöst. Nachdem sich bei dem Referendum von 1992 die Mehrheit für einen Verbleib Montenegros in einem gemeinsamen Staat mit Serbien ausgesprochen hat, war auch eine neue verfassungsmäßige Grundlage für den Teilstaat Montenegro notwendig geworden. Die Verfassung von 1992 war jedoch nicht in der Lage, die gegensätzlichen Interessen des großen serbischen Bevölkerungsanteils und der Montenegriner innerhalb Montenegros auf der einen Seite sowie der Republik Montenegro und der Republik Serbien auf der anderen Seite zu einem Ausgleich zu bringen. Die BRJ funktionierte als Föderation von zwei Teilrepubliken nur schlecht und es kam 1997 zu offenen Konfrontationen mit dem Belgrader Regime von *S. Milošević*, was in Montenegro zur Einführung und Ausarbeitung von selbstständigen staatlichen Institutionen, einer eigenen Währung und Zollschranken zu Serbien führte.

Das Intermezzo der Staatengemeinschaft Serbien und Montenegro hatte in Montenegro keine neue Verfassung zur Folge. Nach der Auflösung der Staatengemeinschaft mit Serbien nahm das montenegrinische Parlament am 19.10.2007 die aktuelle Verfassung[40] an, wodurch erstmals seit 1905 wieder eine Verfassung für einen unabhängigen montenegrinischen Staat beschlossen wurde.

Montenegro wird in Art. 1 Abs. 2 der Verfassung als ein bürgerlicher Rechtsstaat konzipiert. Das Konzept eines „Bürgerstaates" war naheliegend, da in Montenegro kein Volk, auch nicht die Montenegriner, über eine absolute Mehrheit verfügt, sodass die Erneuerung der Unabhängigkeit und Souveränität nicht auf den Prinzipien eines Nationalstaates eines Mehrheitsvolkes basieren kann. So wird auch in der Präambel – im Unterschied zu der Verfassung von 1992, in deren Präambel von Montenegro als einem Nationalstaat der Montenegriner gesprochen wird, den das montenegrinische Volk aufgrund seines in

38 Ustav Crne Gore [Verfassung von Montenegro], Službeni list SRCG (montenegrinisches Gesetzblatt), Nr. 8/74.

39 Ustav Republike Crne Gore [Verfassung der Republik Montenegro], Službeni list RCG (montenegrinisches Gesetzblatt), Nr. 48/92.

40 Ustav Crne Gore [Verfassung von Montenegro], Službeni list CG (montenegrinisches Gesetzblatt), Nr. 1/07. Deutsche Übersetzung von *T. Pintarić*, in: Jahrbuch für Ostrecht 2008/II, S. 459–487, mit Einführung: Die neue montenegrinische Verfassung vom 19.10.2007, S. 447–459.

jahrhundertelagen Kämpfen erworben historischen Rechts errichtet hat – lediglich von den freien und gleichberechtigten Bürgern Montenegros gesprochen.

VIII. Makedonien

Der Republik Makedonien ist es gelungen, sich aus den jugoslawischen Kriegen der 1990er Jahre weitgehend herauszuhalten, obwohl die ethnische Zusammensetzung des Landes nicht unbedingt darauf hätte schließen lassen. Nach der Volkszählung von 2002 sind von den Bürgern Makedoniens 64% Makedonier und 25% Albaner.

Bereits am 25.01.1991 hat das makedonische Parlament eine „Erklärung über die Souveränität der Sozialistischen Republik Makedonien[41]" beschlossen und darin auf die Aussagen der Verfassung der SFRJ über die Unabhängigkeit und das Recht auf Loslösung von der SFRJ im Rahmen des Selbstbestimmungsrechts Bezug genommen. Obwohl dadurch nicht explizit die Loslösung von der SFRJ erklärt wurde, hat das Parlament durch diese Erklärung doch die Geltung der jugoslawischen Bundesverfassung außer Kraft gesetzt. Durch diese vorsichtigen Formulierungen hat sich Makedonien verschiedene Optionen offen halten wollen, da nicht abzusehen war, wie sich die Dinge in den übrigen Teilrepubliken der SFRJ entwickeln würden. Bei dem Referendum vom 08.09.1991, nachdem Kroatien und Slowenien bereits ihr Unabhängigkeit erklärt hatten und die SFRJ aufgehört hatte zu existieren, sprachen sich 95% der an dem Referendum Beteiligten für eine Unabhängigkeit aus.

Am 17.11.1991 nahm Makedonien schließlich eine neue Verfassung[42] an, mit der die Unabhängigkeit des Landes proklamiert wurde. In ihrer Präambel nimmt die Verfassung Bezug auf die „Bürger der Republik Makedonien, das makedonische Volk sowie die Bürger, die [...] ein Teil des albanischen Volkes" sind. Makedonien versteht sich also einerseits nicht als reiner Nationalstaat der Makedonier, doch geht aus der Verfassung auch hervor, dass die Makedonier das eigentliche Staatsvolk sind, da etwa das Makedonische auf dem gesamten Territorium Amtssprache ist und eine andere Amtssprache daneben zwar möglich ist, dabei jedoch Albanisch nicht explizit genannt wird.

Die Verfassung, die federführend vom ehemaligen deutschen Bundespräsidenten *R. Herzog* und dem ehemaligen französischen Justizminister *G. Badinter*

---

41 Deklaracija za suverenost na Socijalistička Republika Makedonija [Deklaration über die Souveränitet der Republik Makedonien], Služben vesnik na RM (makedonisches Gesetzblatt) Nr. 5/91. Deutsche Übersetzung in: *Brunner, Georg* (Hrsg.): Verfassungs- und Verwaltungsrecht der Staaten Osteuropas, VSO, Länderteil Makedonien, Nr. 1.2a, Berlin, 1996-1999 (Loseblattsammlung).

42 Ustav na Republika Makedonija [Verfassung der Republik Makedonien], Služben vesnik na RM (makedonisches Gesetzblatt) Nr. 52/91. Deutsche Übersetzung von *K. Schrameyer*, in: Jahrbuch für Ostrecht, 2008/II, S. 417–446, mit Einführung: Die Verfassung der Republik Makedonien vom 17. November 1991, S. 411–417.

ausgearbeitet wurde, war lange Zeit nicht in der Lage, das Vertrauen der albanischen Bevölkerung zu gewinnen. Die Verfassungsänderungen[43] von 2001 stärkten jedoch die Stellung der Minderheiten mit dem Ziel, das Vertrauen in den gemeinsamen Staat der makedonischen und albanischen Bevölkerungsteile zu stärken.

43 Amandmani IV, V, VI, VII, VIII, IX, X, XI, XII, XIII, XIV, XV, XVI, XVII i XVIII na Ustavot na Republika Makedonija [Verfassungsänderungen [[…]] zur Verfassung der Republik Makedonien], Služben vesnik na RM (makedonischen Gesetzblatt) Nr. 91/01.

Arbeiterselbstverwaltung in Jugoslawien und Mitarbeiterbeteiligung in Europa – systemtranszendierende Aspekte eines sozialökonomischen Partizipationsgrundrechts auf dem Wege in eine neue Europäische Sozialordnung

Herwig Roggemann[*]

I. Über die Jahre

F.-C. Schroeder gehört zu den wenigen deutschen Rechtswissenschaftlern – oder sollte nicht nur anlässlich dieser, sondern auch seiner vorangegangenen Festschrift gesagt werden: er ist der einzige – dem es gelungen ist, sowohl in einem „klassischen" Fachgebiet, dem deutschen Straf- und Strafprozessrecht als auch in der Spezialdisziplin des Ostrechts und der Ost-West-Rechtsvergleichung über Jahrzehnte hinweg eine gleich gewichtige Rolle zu spielen. In Lehrbüchern, Kommentaren, Sammelbänden und Fachzeitschriften hat er als Autor ebenso wie als Universitätslehrer, Veranstalter nationaler und internationaler Tagungen und Konferenzen und nicht zuletzt als Institutsleiter und Organisator eines Schwerpunkts der deutschen Ostrechtswissenschaft in Regensburg und München Wesentliches und Prägendes, auch kontrovers Diskutiertes, zur Entwicklung auf beiden Wissenschaftsfeldern beigetragen.

Zu den reizvollen Herausforderungen der Ostrechtswissenschaft, die als funktionale und rechtspolitische Rechts- und Systemvergleichung über komparative Auslandsrechts- und Regionalwissenschaft hinausgeht, aber auch zu ihren spezifischen Schwierigkeiten gehört es seit je, dass die gemeinhin gepflegte Beschränkung und Selbstbeschränkung ausschließlich auf ein Rechtsgebiet der Suche nach Antworten auf fachübergreifende Fragen zu Problemen und Tendenzen der Rechtsentwicklung und deren Evaluierung in Mittel-, Ost- und Südosteuropa oft nicht gerecht werden kann, sondern grenzübergreifende Ansätze erfordert. So hat denn auch *F.-C. Schroeder* ein weites Feld der Rechtsentwicklung jenseits des Strafrechts in Osteuropa bearbeitet. Das schließt Fragen des Verfas-

* Bis zu seiner Emeritierung Professor für Recht am Osteuropa-Institut der FU Berlin, Leiter des Interuniversitären Zentrums für deutsches, kroatisches und europäisches Recht und Rechtsvergleichung.

sungsrechts[1], des Zivil- und Wirtschaftsrechts[2], der Gerichtsverfassung wie auch der Eigentums- und Wirtschaftsverfassung[3] ein. Und veranlasst den Verfasser dieser Zeilen, hier einige Reflexionen und Thesen zu einem, wie es scheint, zeitweise in den Hintergrund getretenen, wenn nicht gar verdrängten, Kernthema revolutionärer und postrevolutionärer, sozialistischer und postsozialistischer ebenso wie sozialstaatlicher Wirtschaftsverfassung zur Diskussion zu stellen: *Die angemessene materielle Beteiligung der Betriebs- und Unternehmensmitarbeiter am Wirtschaftsergebnis.*

Der Verfasser verbindet damit die Hoffnung, das über die Jahre gelegentlich auf Tagungen (u.a. der Deutschen Gesellschaft für Osteuropakunde), in Kommissionen (u.a. des Bundesministeriums für Gesamtdeutsche Fragen), in Bonn, München und anderswo, mündlich und schriftlich, bisweilen kontrovers geführte, immer aber anregende, von Erkenntnisneugier getragene, freundschaftliche, zeitweilig abgerissene und kürzlich am Kamin des 350 Jahre alten Bauernhäuschens der Galerie Wannsee in Berlin wieder angeknüpfte Rechtsgespräch mit *F.-C. Schroeder* fortzusetzen.

II. Thematischer Rahmen

1. Vom Ostrecht zum Recht der Sozialistischen Staaten zum Ostrecht

Die Ostrechtswissenschaft hat wie ihr Gegenstand tiefgreifende Wandlungen erfahren. Sie spiegelt politische und rechtliche Brüche und Umbrüche der neueren deutschen, mittel-, ost- und südosteuropäischen Rechtsgeschichte wider und ist selbst Teil derselben auf dem verlustreichen, nachgeholten Weg Deutschlands und der mittel-, ost- und südosteuropäischen Staaten zu friedensfähigen, freiheitlichen, demokratischen und sozialen Rechtsstaaten auf marktwirtschaftlicher Grundlage. Als „Ostrecht“ oder „Osteuropäisches Recht“ fanden sich dieser Gegenstand und die historischen, systemkritischen und vergleichenden Metho-

---

1 *F.-C. Schroeder* (Hrsg. zusammen mit *B. Meissner* und *K. Westen*), Kontinuität und Wandel in der kommunistischen Staatstheorie, 1985; *F.-C. Schroeder* (Hrsg. zusammen mit *B. Meissner*), Verfassungs- und Verwaltungsreformen in den sozialistischen Staaten, Berlin 1978.

2 *F.-C. Schroeder*, Das neue Bürgerliche Gesetzbuch der Russischen Sowjetrepublik, Teil I, ROW 1965, S. 1 ff.; Teil II, ROW 1965, S. 49 ff.; *F.-C. Schroeder* (Hrsg. zusammen mit *G. Brunner* und *K. Westen*), Sozialistisches Wirtschaftsrecht zwischen Wandel und Beharrung, 1997.

3 *F.-C. Schroeder*, Eigentumsrecht in der UdSSR, Marxismusstudien, Vierte Folge, 1962; Rechts- und Wirtschaftsprobleme bei der Kooperation von deutschen Unternehmen und jugoslawischen Organisationen assoziierter Arbeit (Hrsg. *F.-C. Schroeder*), Regensburg 1978; *ders.*, Grundbegriffe und Formen der Privatisierung in Osteuropa, OE 1995, S. 121 ff.

den seiner Erforschung[4] jahrzehntelang legitimiert durch die spezifische Entwicklungssituation und Problemlage des nicht nur geografisch, sondern seit den Anfängen des Sowjetsystems in der Russischen Föderation der RSFSR von 1917/1918 und als Folge der deutschen Aggression im Zweiten Weltkrieg seit 1945 in ganz Mittel-, Ost- und Südosteuropa auch inhaltlich definierten sozialistischen Rechtskreises des „Rechts der sozialistischen Staaten“[5] und der „Sozialistischen Staatengemeinschaft“.

Der ökonomische und politische Zusammenbruch der staatssozialistischen Regierungssysteme 1989/1990 markiert in diesen Staaten teils den überstürzten Beginn, teils die beschleunigte, nunmehr offene Fortsetzung einer bereits zuvor sich anbahnenden[6], tiefgreifenden Transformation der politischen, wirtschaftlichen und rechtlichen Ordnung.

Dieser rückschauend mit gewissem Recht ebenfalls als „Revolution“ charakterisierte Transformationsprozess Ost- und Südosteuropas in Richtung auf Demokratie, Rechtsstaat, Marktwirtschaft und Restitution des Privateigentums, ist auch nach zwei Jahrzehnten nicht abgeschlossen, sondern wird als Generationenprojekt weitere Jahrzehnte in Anspruch nehmen[7]. Er hat sich infolge seiner Rückwirkungen auf andere Staaten, wie insbesondere auf das nach dem Ende des Staatssozialismus in der DDR erneut vereinigte Deutschland, und auch auf den Verbund der seit 2000/2004 osterweiterten Europäischen Union zu einem gesamteuropäischen Transformationsprozess entwickelt. Ostrecht und Ostrechtswissenschaft sind damit auch ein wesentlicher Bestandteil der Transformationsforschung zum postsozialistischen (Ost-)Europa geworden. Gesteigertes wechselseitiges Informationsinteresse folgt nicht zuletzt aus der deutschen Rolle

---

4 Zu Aufgaben und Methoden der Ostrechtsforschung vgl. *Meissner/ Roggemann/Schroeder/Westen* (Hrsg.), Grundsatzfragen der Ostrechtsforschung (Studien des Instituts für Ostrecht, Bd. 28), München 1980; *Brunner/Schweisfurth* u.a. (Hrsg.), Sowjetsystem und Ostrecht (FS *Meissner)*, Berlin 1985; *F.-C. Schroeder*, 74 Jahre Sowjetrecht, München 1992.

5 Zum sozialistischen Rechtskreis vgl. *K. Westen* in: Einführung in die großen Rechtssysteme der Gegenwart, bearb. von *Grasmann/Klingmüller* u.a., München 1988; *H. Roggemann*, Die Gesetzgebung der Sozialistischen Staaten (Loseblattsammlung), Berlin 1971-1989.; *ders.*, Die Gesetzgebung der DDR, Berlin 1971 ff.; *G. Brunner*, Verfassungs- und Verwaltungsrecht der Staaten Osteuropas, Berlin 1995-1999.

6 Zu diesem Wandlungsprozess, der auch durch den grenzüberschreitenden Wissenschaftsaustausch mit Osteuropa nachhaltig gefördert worden ist, vgl. *F.-C. Schroeder*, Wandlungen der sowjetischen Staatstheorie, 1979; *ders.*, Wandel in Moskaus Rechtsdenken? FAZ v. 26.11.1986; *ders.*, Überlebenskampf der Staats- und Rechtstheorie in Russland, JZ 2008, S. 882 ff.

7 Umfassendes und aktuelles Material zum derzeitigen Entwicklungsstand bei *W. Ismar* (Hrsg.), Die politischen Systeme Osteuropas, 3. Aufl., Wiesbaden 2010; zum postsozialistischen Konstitutionalismus und seinen Entwicklungsproblemen *H. Roggemann* (Hrsg.), Die Verfassungen Mittel- und Osteuropas, Berlin 1999.

als wichtigster Wirtschaftspartner der Region, deren Rechtsreformen sich nach wie vor vielfach an deutschen Leitbildern orientieren.

Jenseits dieses Aktualitätsgewinns bildet Osteuropa für Deutschland mehr als für alle anderen europäischen Länder – mit Ausnahme Österreichs – in Geschichte und Gegenwart einen Bereich wechselseitiger politischer, wirtschaftlicher, wissenschaftlicher und persönlicher Beziehungen, Kooperationen aber auch Konflikte von besonderer Intensität. Hinzu kommt die deutsche Katastrophe des Zweiten Weltkriegs mit ihren einschneidenden Verlusten und Folgen für Osteuropa, ebenso wie für Deutschland. Grundlegende Fragen komparativer und retrospektiver Untersuchung verschiedenartiger politischer Systeme und Rechtsordnungen resultieren daraus als Forschungsaufgaben gemeinsam für die deutsche Ostrechtsforschung und die Rechtswissenschaft in den Staaten Ost- und Südosteuropas. In der Sozialismusfolgenforschung geht es ebenso wie in der Faschismusforschung um die rechtliche Aufarbeitung politischen Systemunrechts[8], Formen von Regierungskriminalität und Menschenrechtsverletzungen großen Umfangs, zuletzt beim Zerfall des Jugoslawischen Bundesstaates, sowie um ihre Aufklärung, Ursachenforschung und nachholende Kompensation[9]. Die Ostrechtswissenschaft sieht sich hier nach ihrem Beitrag zum internationalen Recht und insbesondere auch zum internationalen Strafrecht und vor den internationalen Strafgerichten, insbesondere dem Jugoslawientribunal der UN (ICTY) laufenden Kriegsverbrecherprozessen, gefragt[10].

Die Staaten Mittel-, Nordost- und Südosteuropas waren und sind einer dreifachen Transformation ausgesetzt: Während des Staatssozialismus durch dessen allumfassende, rigide Entwicklungsprogramme auf dem zentralplanwirtschaftlichen Weg in die gesuchte und nicht gefundene sozialistische und kommunistische Zukunftsgesellschaft, sodann nach dem Ende des Staatssozialismus durch dessen beschleunigte „Entsozialisierung" und Reprivatisierung auf dem Wege in einen bis heute ebenfalls nicht gefundenen postsozialistischen Sozialstaat und schließlich im Zuge des EU-Beitritts oder seiner Vorbereitung durch Übernahme der Normen und Standards des europäischen Rechts („*aquis communautaire*"). Dieser permanente Transformationsdruck hat das sozialökonomische und politi-

---

8 Auch diese Aufgabe ist noch keineswegs als erledigt zu betrachten, vgl. dazu Unrecht und Wiedergutmachung – NS-Zwangsarbeiter aus Ost- und Südosteuropa, in: Arbeitspapiere des Interuniversitären Zentrums, hrsg. von *H. Roggemann*, Heft 2, Berlin 2001.

9 Das internationale Strafrecht erfuhr entscheidende Anstöße durch den „neuen Balkankrieg" von 1991-1995, der zur Einrichtung des Internationalen UN-Tribunals für das ehemalige Jugoslawien (ICTY) in den Haag im Jahre 1993 führte, dazu *Lagodny*, Wirklichkeit und Perspektiven der Internationalen Strafgerichtsbarkeit, in: *D. Fischer* (Hrsg.), Transformation des Rechts in Ost und West, FS *Roggemann*, Berlin 2006, S. 453 ff.

10 Dazu *H. Roggemann*, Der Internationale Strafgerichtshof der Vereinten Nationen von 1993 und der Krieg auf dem Balkan, Berlin 1994; 2. Aufl., Die Internationalen Strafgerichtshöfe, Berlin 1998.

sche Konfliktpotenzial und die Zahl lösungsbedürftiger Probleme erhöht – und damit der Ostrechtsforschung weitere Tätigkeitsfelder in Rechtsvergleichung, Informationsaustausch und Rechtsberatung eröffnet.

2. Vom postrevolutionären Staatssozialismus zum postsozialistischen Sozialstaat

Diese aktuellen Aufgaben und Probleme der Rechtserneuerung, Reprivatisierung, Demokratisierung und Europäisierung einerseits und der Vergangenheitsverarbeitung von Systemunrecht ungeahnten Ausmaßes andererseits haben Fragen nach dem ideellen sozialökonomischen Hauptanliegen der von den ost- und südosteuropäischen Staaten ebenso wie von der DDR entwickelten sozialistischen Gesellschafts- und Wirtschaftsverfassungsmodelle von der gegenwärtigen politischen Tagesordnung weitgehend verdrängt. Dies geschah umso nachhaltiger, als die wegen ihrer offensichtlichen Demokratie- und Rechtsstaatsdefizite vielfach und jedenfalls in Bezug auf die DDR pauschal als „Unrechtsstaaten" (besser: „Nichtrechtsstaaten" oder „Vorrechtsstaaten") qualifizierten sozialistischen Staaten nach ihrem politischen und wirtschaftlichen Scheitern keine legitimen Anknüpfungspunkte für weiterführende Diskussionen sozialer, sozialdemokratischer oder sozialistischer Programme oder gar kommunistischer Ideen oder Alternativkonzepte mehr bieten konnten.

Zu den traumatischen Folgen spezifischer historischer Erfahrungen in Deutschland („Kulturbruch", Kriegs- und Menschlichkeitsverbrechen der NS-Zeit mit anschließender Besetzung und Teilung samt DDR-Gründung und Mauerbau) gehören auf der einen Seite die nach wie vor als unverzichtbar angesehene Kriminalisierung bestimmter (rechts-)radikaler Meinungsäußerungen[11] sowie auf der anderen Seite eine gewisse Tabuisierung und Ausgrenzung – während der Deutschen Teilung und des Ost-West-Gegensatzes bis hin zur Kriminalisierung – auch linksextremer Äußerungen. Ein anschauliches Beispiel für letzteren Sachverhalt – inzwischen allerdings jenseits der Reichweite eines insoweit zurückgenommenen politischen Strafrechts[12] – liefert die von der Vorsitzenden der Links-Partei Anfang des Jahres 2011 ausgelöste „Kommunismusdiskussion[13]".

---

11 *G. Foerstner*, Kollektivbeleidigung, Volksverhetzung und 'lex Tucholsky'. Eine Untersuchung zu Äußerungsdelikten und Meinungsfreiheit, Berlin 2002.

12 Zu Entwicklung und System umfassend *F.-C. Schroeder*, Der Schutz von Staat und Verfassung im Strafrecht, München 1970; ders., *Maurach/Schroeder/Maiwald*, Strafrecht Besonderer Teil, Teilband 2, Heidelberg 2005, S. 364 ff., 374 ff.; zum Problem der Eingrenzung *H. Roggemann*, Fragen des politischen Strafrechts im geteilten Deutschland, Berlin (West) 1965.

13 Mit ihrer Äußerung in einem Beitrag in der Zeitschrift „Junge Welt" v. Januar 2011: „Die Wege zum Kommunismus können wir nur finden, wenn wir uns auf den Weg machen und sie ausprobieren, ob in der Opposition oder in der Regierung" rief sie vielfältige Reaktionen, Widerspruch und Proteste hervor, was in Anbetracht des Scheiterns verschiedenster staatssozialistischer und kommunistischer Wege, wie auch des „Jugo-

Was also behaupteten Theorie und Ideologie der damaligen sozialistischen Staaten und sehen heutige sozialdemokratische, sozialistische oder kommunistische Theorien, Programme und politische Parteien – neben dem im Staatssozialismus des Einparteistaates zum beherrschenden Primärziel mutierten Sekundärziel des Gewinns und der unberührt von demokratischen Wahlen unbegrenzten Erhaltung der politischen Macht der „Avantgarde der Arbeiterklasse" – als ihr wesentliches *inhaltliches Ziel*? Verkürzt auf den sozialökonomischen Kern lässt sich die Antwort in Anlehnung an das frühe Gothaer Programm der Sozialdemokraten wie folgt zusammenfassen: Schaffung der ökonomischen und sozialen Bedingungen für die Sicherung menschenwürdiger Existenz und Chancengerechtigkeit für die lohnabhängig Arbeitenden durch *„gerechte Verteilung des Arbeitsertrags"*.

Dieses durch Überwindung ökonomischer Ungleichheit und sozialer Deklassierung infolge privaten Produktionsmitteleigentums durch dessen Beseitigung zu erreichende Ziel hat die jugoslawische „Selbstverwaltungs-Verfassung" von 1974[14] im Sinne eines hohen emanzipatorischen Anspruchs wie folgt beschrieben: *„Die durch diese Verfassung festgelegten Freiheiten, Rechte und Pflichten der Menschen und der Bürger stellen einen unabtrennbaren Teil und den Ausdruck sozialistischer, auf Selbstverwaltung beruhender, demokratischer Verhältnisse dar, in denen der Mensch von jeglicher Ausbeutung und Willkür befreit ist"*. Der DDR-Verfassungsgeber fasst diesen Anspruch ohne das jugoslawische Freiheits- und Selbstverwaltungspathos in Art. 2 Abs. 3 DDR-Verf. 1974 in die plakative Formel: *„Die Ausbeutung des Menschen durch den Menschen ist für immer beseitigt"*[15].

Doch diese ideologisch überhöhten Verfassungsaussagen entsprachen dem Problem sozialökonomischer Ungleichheit bis hin zu sozialer und politischer Deklassierung und Ausgrenzung, ja Eliminierung infolge differenzierter, leistungs- und erfolgsabhängiger Entlohnung und anderer systembedingt ungleicher politischer und sozialer Rahmenbedingungen undemokratischer (Ein-)Parteiherrschaften[16], weder in den vergangenen sozialistischen Staaten auf deren staatskapitalistischer Grundlage noch – und erst recht nicht entsprechen sie der sozialen Lage in den darauffolgenden postsozialistischen Sozialstaaten Mittel-,

---

slawischen Weges", verständlich erscheint. Vereinzelt wurde auch die – nicht mehr strafrechtsrelevante – Frage nach etwaiger Verfassungsfeindschaft der Autorin gestellt.

14 Verfassung der Sozialistischen Föderativen Republik Jugoslawien (SFRJ) v. 21.02.1974, Übers. *Höcker-Weyand/Verona*, in *H. Roggemann* (Hrsg.), Die Verfassung der SFR Jugoslawien, Berlin 1980, S. 105 ff., Einleitungsteil, Grundsätze V., S. 117.

15 *H. Roggemann,* Die DDR-Verfassungen, 4. Aufl., Berlin (West) 1989, S. 163 ff., 167.

16 Zu deren Wirken in der DDR aber auch im Jugoslawien *Titos*, ähnlich wie in anderen staatssozialistischen Systemen, Menschen- und Strafrechtsverletzungen durch Justiz-, Polizei-, Militär- und Geheimdienstorgane gehörten, deren Aufarbeitung die deutsche Strafjustiz auch zwei Jahrzehnte nach dem politischen Systemwechsel noch beschäftigt.

Ost- und Südosteuropas – auf privatkapitalistischer Grundlage mit ihren neuen, teilweise dramatischen sozialen Problemen[17]. Allerdings waren Egalisierungswirkungen und soziale Sicherheit im Rahmen sozialistischer Planwirtschaft und „sozialistischer Lebensweise" auf der Grundlage verstaatlichten Produktiveigentums ungleich größer als in der Wettbewerbsgesellschaft der alten und neuen Sozialstaaten auf der Grundlage von Marktwirtschaft und Privateigentum an Produktivkapital. Dieses größere Maß an Gleichheit und Sicherheit im sozialen Raum blieb in den sozialistischen Staaten, insbesondere auch in der DDR, jedoch erkauft mit Bedingungen und Einschränkungen der existenziellen politischen und persönlichen Freiräume und Rechtsschutzgarantien, die sich neben fehlender ökonomischer Wettbewerbsfähigkeit für einen zunehmenden Teil der Bevölkerung als zunehmend weniger erträglich darstellten. Die Reaktion der politischen Führungen beider Länder war signifikant verschieden. Während die DDR-Führung die destabilisierende Wirkung zunehmender „Republikflucht" fürchtete und darauf mit Schießbefehl und Mauerbau reagierte, öffnete die Sozialistische Föderative Republik (SFR) Jugoslawien für alle ausreisewilligen Staatsbürger, die als „Gastarbeiter" vor allem nach Deutschland, aber auch in andere Länder ausreisen wollten, ihre Grenzen, und förderte diese Emigration sogar zeitweise von Staats wegen.

Es gehört zu den Paradoxien der neueren deutschen Wirtschafts- und Sozialgeschichte, dass die der marktwirtschaftlichen Privateigentumsordnung immanenten „Ungleichfaktoren[18]" in den vergangenen zwanzig Jahren, eben seit dem Ende jener staatssozialistischen Systeme und der erneuten Vereinigung der beiden deutschen Staaten, ständig stärker geworden sind, inzwischen kritische Ausmaße erreicht haben und den sozialstaatlichen Grundkonsens in Frage stellen. Und dass die politische sich in einer wirtschaftlichen Ost-West-Migration innerhalb des vereinigten Deutschlands fortsetzt.

Die Frage nach Verteilungs- und Chancengerechtigkeit durch angemessene Teilhabe am Wirtschaftsergebnis stellt sich damit immer mehr auch als Existenzfrage des gegenwärtigen traditionellen wie postsozialistischen marktwirtschaftlichen Sozialstaats dar. Für die vereinigte Bundesrepublik Deutschland hat der Gesetzgeber diese ungelöste rechtspolitische Aufgabe wie folgt zusammengefasst: *„Es ist auch ein Gebot wirtschaftlicher Vernunft und sozialer Gerech-*

---

17 Zum Umbruch im Arbeitsrecht in der „dramatischen Wendezeit 1989/90" vgl. *Adomeit/Florek/Kollontay-Lehozky* (Hrsg.), Das Arbeitsrecht im Übergang vom Sozialismus zur Marktwirtschaft, Berlin 1996.

18 Zu diesen näher *Rosinus*, Vermögensdekonzentration und Mitarbeiterkapitalbeteiligung, Frankfurt/M, Berlin u.a. 2009, S. 23 f., 27, 32, 51, 63, 83.

tigkeit, dass Beschäftigte am Ertrag der Volkswirtschaft gerecht und ausgewogen teilhaben"[19].

Theorie und Staatsideologie, und vor allem die politische und wirtschaftliche Praxis der sozialistischen Staaten, suchte ihre Rechtfertigung im Marxismus-Leninismus als „wissenschaftlicher Weltanschauung"[20]. Dieser lag im Gegensatz zur politischen Position der Sozialdemokraten, die in ihrem Gothaer Programm auf mehr „*Verteilungsgerechtigkeit*" und die damit zu schaffende Verbesserung der Lebensbedingungen der Arbeitnehmer zielten, und in ihrem Erfurter Programm von 1891 einen „Staatssozialismus" durch Staatseigentum ausdrücklich ablehnten, die radikale Umwälzung der gesamten marktwirtschaftlichen privatkapitalistischen Wirtschaftsordnung durch Abschaffung des Privateigentums am Produktivkapital mit Ersetzung der Markt- durch eine Planwirtschaft zugrunde. Diese revolutionäre Alternative hatte *Marx* zuvor in seiner Grundsatzkritik an diesem Programm, in seinen Auseinandersetzungen mit *Proudhon* und *Stirner*, in seinen ökonomisch-philosophischen Schriften und im Kapital entwickelt und im Kommunistischen Manifest gemeinsam mit *Engels* zusammengefasst.

Nur auf diesem revolutionären Wege sahen *Marx* und die ihm folgende, von *Lenin* alsbald in eine langfristige, gewaltsame politische Praxis der „Diktatur des Proletariats" übersetzte kommunistische Doktrin die Voraussetzungen für die Schaffung einer zukünftig von den Ausbeutungs-, Unterdrückungs- und Entfremdungsmechanismen privatkapitalistischer Eigentums- und Wirtschaftsordnung freien Assoziation der sich selbst verwaltenden Werktätigen.

Während dieser emanzipatorische Ansatz in Russland bereits in den von den Bolschewiki unter Einsatz von Waffengewalt gesteuerten, anfangs durchaus noch offenen, kontroversen Beratungen der ersten Sowjetverfassung von 1918[21] verdrängt, im Leninismus bald gänzlich eliminiert[22] und im Stalinismus durch eine gewaltsame Entwicklungsdiktatur bislang ungekannten Ausmaßes ersetzt wurde, nahm die Theorie der Arbeiterselbstverwaltung in Jugoslawien nach dem

---

19 So die Regierungsbegründung zum Mitarbeiterkapitalbeteiligungsgesetz (MKBG) v. 07.03.2009, BGBl. I 2009, 451; Deutscher Bundestag, 16. WP, Drucks. 16/10531, Begr. A.

20 Zum Inhalt dieser Ideologie und ihrer Kritik näher *H. Roggemann,* Fn. 15, S. 104 ff., 129 ff.

21 Zum Verlauf dieser Beratungen und den dabei diskutierten und verworfenen revolutionären Alternativen vgl. näher *H. Roggemann,* Die Entstehung der ersten Sowjetverfassung von 1918, ROW 1985, S. 241 ff.

22 Dies geschah nicht nur durch die Abschaffung des Privateigentums und Grund und Boden und Wirtschafseigentum, sondern auch durch die Beseitigung der Vertragsautonomie und das Verbot vertraglicher Rechtsgeschäfte in der Wirtschaft, dazu näher *H. Roggemann,* Die Entwicklung des sowjetischen Betriebsrechts, JOR Bd. VIII/2 (1967), S. 59 ff.; ders., Entwicklung und allgemeine Grundlagen des sowjetischen Zivilrechts, JOR XII/1 (1971), S. 149 ff., 155 ff.

Bruch mit der Sowjetunion 1948 eben diesen emanzipatorischen Ansatz des Marx`schen Entwurfs (wieder) auf. Die jugoslawische Führung entwickelte daraus schrittweise das alternative Modell einer Arbeiterselbstverwaltung im Rahmen einer dezentralisierten, hochgradig föderalisierten Staatsverfassung. Und sie scheiterte mit diesem Selbstverwaltungskonzept nach zunächst bemerkenswerten wirtschaftlichen und auch politischen Aufbauerfolgen am Ende ebenso wie mit dem jahrzehntelang erfolgreichen Staatskonzept der SFR Jugoslawien.

Voraussetzungen, Grundzüge und Gründe für das Scheitern dieses sozialistischen Partizipationsmodells und die weitergehende, systemtranszendierende Suche nach Wegen zu mehr Verteilungsgerechtigkeit durch Formen immaterieller und materieller Partizipation (Mitbestimmung und Mitarbeiterbeteiligung) im Rahmen des marktwirtschaftlichen, auf Privateigentum gegründeten Sozialstaatsmodells in Deutschland und Europa, seien im folgenden unter Beschränkung auf einige grundlegende Aspekte erörtert.

III. Privateigentum, Vergesellschaftung, materielle Partizipation – Kernfragen des sozialistischen und des sozialstaatlichen Gesellschaftsentwurfs

1. Eigentum – Funktion und Funktionswandel

Eigentum strukturiert jede entwickelte Gesellschafts- und Wirtschaftsordnung und definiert damit insoweit auch die Stellung des Einzelnen als Wirtschaftsbürger in der (Markt-)Wirtschaftsgesellschaft[23]. Eigentumsrecht und Eigentumsord-

---

23 Zur ideengeschichtlichen Grundlage und zum Problem der Rechtfertigung von Eigentum *Holzhey* in: *Holzhey/Kohler* (Hrsg.), Eigentum und seine Gründe, Bern/Stuttgart 1983, S. 19 ff.; *R. Brandt,* Eigentumstheorien von Grothius bis Kant, Stuttgart 1974, S. 69, 151; *Hecker,* Eigentum als Sachherrschaft, Paderborn 1990, S. 165 ff.; *O. Gierke,* Der Entwurf eines bürgerlichen Gesetzbuchs und das deutsche Recht, Leipzig 1889, S. 342 ff.; *J. v. Gierke,* Bürgerliches Recht. SachenR, 4. Aufl., Berlin, Frankfurt/M 1959, S. 61; *Wolf/Wellenhofer,* SachenR, 24. Aufl., München 2008, S. 20, 122; *H. Roggemann,* Mitarbeiterbeteiligung und Eigentum, Berlin 2010, S. 91 ff.; zur Funktion des Eigentums bei der Ausdifferenzierung von Wirtschaft und Politik sowie bei der Strukturierung der Gesellschaft durch die Differenz von Eigentum und Nichteigentum siehe *Luhmann,* Die Wirtschaft der Gesellschaft, Frankfurt/M 1988, S. 150 ff., 189; kritisch zu den historischen Wandlungen seit dem 19. Jh. *Däubler/Sieling-Wendeling/Welkoborsky,* Eigentum und Recht, Darmstadt/Neuwied, 1976; für die Weimarer Republik siehe *M. Wolff,* Reichsverfassung und Eigentum, in: Festgabe für Wilhelm Kahl, Tübingen 1923, S. 2 ff.; zur ökonomischen Funktion näher *Heinsohn/Steiger* (1994: 337; 1996); *Hölscher* (1996: 97 ff.); zur Funktion von Sachzuordnung und Eigentum in der Wirtschaftsordnung vgl. *Wolf/Wellenhofer,* a.a.O., S. 12 ff., 20 ff.; umfassend *Leisner,* Eigentum, hrsg. von *Isensee,* Berlin 1996, dessen idealtypisierendes Eigentumsverständnis allerdings die sozialökonomische Relevanz und die sozialstaatliche Funktion

nung sind keine Konstanten, sondern historisch und sozialökonomisch abhängige Variablen[24]. Dies gilt für den gegenwärtigen Entstaatlichungs-, d.h. Privatisierungsprozess der postsozialistischen Länder in Mittel- und Osteuropa. Es gilt auch und erst recht für die marktwirtschaftlichen Reform- und Privatisierungsprozesse, in denen sich die bisherigen Modelle sozialer Marktwirtschaft in den alten Mitgliedsländern der EU befinden. Und es gilt insbesondere für Deutschland.

Im Laufe seines permanenten Wandlungsprozesses hat sich das heutige Privateigentum zu einem multifunktionalen Rechtsinstitut entwickelt. Dieser Funktionszusammenhang kann, in Gestalt von innen nach außen um die sachenrechtliche Kernfunktion gezogener konzentrischer Kreise, wie folgt vorgestellt werden:

→ Sachenrechtliche Zuordnungsfunktion
  → Zivilrechtliche Ausschließungs- und grundrechtliche Abwehrfunktion
    → Ökonomische Wertermittlungs- und Kreditsicherungsfunktion
      → Menschenrechtliche, freiheitssichernde Individualfunktion
        → Partizipationsfunktion im Arbeitsprozess
          → sozialstaatliche, Verteilungsgerechtigkeit schaffende Teilhabe und Sozialfunktion
            → Privatrechtliche, marktwirtschaftliche Bestandssicherungs funktion („Institutsgarantie“)
              → Politische Integrationsfunktion in der Zivilgesellschaft

Diese multifunktionelle Wirkung des Eigentums, insbesondere im Hinblick auf seine Sozialfunktion, formuliert das Bundesverfassungsgericht (BVerfG) als rechtspolitischen Auftrag an den inhaltsbestimmenden und schrankensetzenden Gesetzgeber wie folgt[25]:

---

des Eigentums nicht angemessen erfasst; zur Entwicklung in Osteuropa vgl. *Hiller,* Eigentumsgarantie und Eigentumsverständnis in der Rechtsprechung des ungarischen Verfassungsgerichts unter vergleichender Berücksichtigung der Rechtsprechung des Supreme Court der USA und des deutschen Bundesverfassungsgerichts, Diss. FU Berlin 2001; zum Wandel der Eigentumsordnung im Verlauf der deutschen Vereinigung vgl. *Will,* Eigentumstransformation unter dem Grundgesetz, Humboldt-Universität, Berlin 1996; *Tomuschat,* Eigentum im Umbruch, Berlin 1996.

24 „In jeder historischen Epoche hat sich das Eigentum anders und unter ganz verschiedenen gesellschaftlichen Verhältnissen entwickelt. Das bürgerliche Eigentum definieren heißt somit nichts anderes, als alle gesellschaftlichen Verhältnisse der bürgerlichen Produktion darstellen. Eine Definition des Eigentums als eines unabhängigen Verhältnisses, einer besonderen Kategorie, einer abstrakten und ewigen Idee geben wollen, kann nichts anderes sein als eine Illusion der Metaphysik oder der Jurisprudenz“, so *Marx,* Das Elend der Philosophie. Antwort auf Proudhons „Philosophie des Elends“, Marx/Engels Werke (MEW) Bd. 4, Berlin 1969, S.165.

25 In seinem Beschluss v. 22.02.2001 – 1 BvR 198/98. Vgl. auch BVerfGE 101, 54, 74.

> „Der Inhalt und Schranken des Eigentums bestimmende Gesetzgeber genießt keine unbeschränkte Gestaltungsfreiheit (vgl. BVerfGE 101, 239, 259). Er hat bei der Erfüllung des ihm in Art. 14 Abs. 1 Satz 2 GG erteilten Gestaltungsauftrags sowohl der verfassungsrechtlich garantierten Rechtsstellung des Eigentümers als auch dem aus Art. 14 Abs. 2 GG folgenden Gebot einer sozialgerechten Eigentumsordnung Rechnung zu tragen und muss deshalb die schutzwürdigen Interessen der Beteiligten in einen gerechten Ausgleich und ein ausgewogenes Verhältnis bringen."

Aus dieser für jedes marktwirtschaftliche System konstitutiven Bedeutung des Privateigentums ergeben sich weitere Begründungen für das unreformierbare strukturelle Defizit staatssozialistischer, auf dem Marx`schen Postulat der Eliminierung des Eigentums in seiner Funktion als Privateigentum an Produktionsmitteln beruhender Wirtschafts- und Rechtsordnungen. Dieser Zusammenhang liefert – neben dem in der politischen Wendezeit der neunziger Jahre schlagartig anwachsenden binnen- und außenwirtschaftlichen Anpassungs- und Wettbewerbsdruck – auch eine Erklärung für die schnelle, in einzelnen Breichen geradezu überstürzte und ohne Rücksicht auf soziale Brüche erfolgte Rückkehr der postsozialistischen Transformationsstaaten zum traditionellen Privateigentum als Grundlage der Wirtschaftsordnung.

Zugleich hat sich die Frage insbesondere nach Sozialfunktion und Funktionswandel des (Privat-)Eigentums und nach der offenbar unverzichtbaren Rolle des daseinsvorsorgenden Staates als Wirtschafts- und Eigentumssubjekt in unerwarteter Weise zugespitzt, durch die in ihren Ursachen wohl erst ansatzweise verstandene und in ihren Folgeproblemen insbesondere für die EU noch keineswegs beherrschte Systemkrise der Finanz- und Wirtschaftsordnung in den Jahren 2008/2009.

Die Analyse von Fehlentwicklungen der „eigentumssubjektlosen" staatssozialistischen Wirtschafts- und Eigentumssysteme aus der Sicht der Ostrechtswissenschaft könnte auch den Blick schärfen für neue Fehlentwicklungen eines durch mehrfache Vermittlung anonymisierten und damit „subjektlos" und dadurch „verantwortungslos" gewordenen Finanzprodukteigentums[26] im Rahmen einer auf Privateigentum gründenden, zunehmend Grenzen und Systeme transzendierenden, globalisierten Marktwirtschaft.

26 Zur Grundsatzkritik vgl. u.a. *H.-W. Sinn,* Kasinokapitalismus, Berlin 2010; zur Frage der Legitimation vielfach vermittelten Wirtschaftseigentums und seines problematischen verfassungsrechtlichen Schutzanspruchs s.u. Fn. 35; zu finanzrechtlichen Problemen des Anlegerschutzes im einzelnen vgl. *B. Breig,* Anlegerschutz und Wirtschaftskrise, in: *H. Roggemann* (Hrsg.), Wechselwirkungen zwischen europäischem und nationalem Recht – Beiträge zum Symposion des Interuniversitären Zentrums Berlin/Split 2010, Berlin 2011.

2. Eigentum – Partizipation – Verteilungsgerechtigkeit

a) Strukturprobleme und Asymmetrien des marktwirtschaftlichen Sozialstaats

Eigentum in Form des Privateigentums an Boden, Rohstoffen, Maschinen und Produktionsmitteln aller Art stellt als privates Produktiveigentum *Eigentum schaffendes Eigentum* dar. Als solches vermittelt es zu einem wesentlichen Teil jenseits des Arbeitsentgelts und über dieses hinaus Art und Umfang der materiellen Partizipation des Wirtschaftsbürgers am Wirtschaftsertrag. Dies gilt für den Besitzbürger als Wirtschafts- und Anteilseigentümer, nicht dagegen für den lohnabhängigen Arbeitnehmer ohne Beteiligungsvermögen. Die darin angelegten asymmetrischen Verteilungs- und Akkumulationseffekte führen offenbar unvermeidlich in allen bisherigen marktwirtschaftlichen Ordnungen auf der Grundlage von privatem Wirtschaftseigentum im Laufe der Entwicklung zu hochgradig ungleichen Einkommens- und Vermögensstrukturen. In diesem Befund wollen manche Betrachter eine Bestätigung der höchst kontroversen Marx`schen Kapitalismusanalyse und -kritik sehen[27].

In Deutschland hat die als *„Gerechtigkeitslücke"* kritisierte Ungleichheit der Einkommensentwicklung[28], verbunden mit außerordentlicher Konzentration von Eigentum und Vermögen, in den vergangenen zwei Jahrzehnten seit dem Zusammenbruch des Staatssozialismus in Osteuropa und der Vereinigung der beiden deutschen Staaten erheblich, wenn nicht gar bedrohlich, zugenommen[29]. In

---

27 So *Altvater,* Das Ende des Kapitalismus wie wir ihn kennen, Münster 2005; dagegen *Schirrmacher/Strobl,* Die Zukunft des Kapitalismus, Frankfurt/M 2010. Die Kritik von *H.-W. Sinn,* a.a.O., 108 ff., sieht die Ursachen für die schweren Funktionsstörungen der Finanzmärkte mit anschließender Wirtschaftskrise nicht als Systemkrise sondern (nur) im Fehlen angemessener und zwingender rechtlicher Rahmenbedingungen und greift damit wohl zu kurz.

28 Hierzu z.B. die Spiegel-Titel „Arm durch Arbeit", 2007/14 v. 02.04.2007 sowie „Die Gerechtigkeitslücke", 51/2007 v. 17.12.2007, S. 22.

29 Zusammenfassung der neueren Ergebnisse der Vermögensverteilungsforschung bei *Frick/Grabka/Hauser,* Die Verteilung der Vermögen in Deutschland, Berlin 2010; Statistisches Bundesamt, Volkswirtsch. Gesamtrechnungen. Inlandsproduktsberechnung., Wiesbaden 2009; *Grabka/Frick,* Deutsches Institut für Wirtschaftsforschung, DIW-Wochenberichte 2007/45, S. 665 ff.; 2009/4, S. 53 ff.; 2010/3, S. 2 ff. Ausführlich mit umfangreichem Zahlenmaterial aus wirtschaftswissenschaftlicher Sicht Rosinus, Fn. 18, S. 23 f., 27, 32, 51, 63, 83: Zwischen den Jahren 1991 und 2006 und darüber hinaus entspricht einem stetigen Rückgang der Einkünfte aus abhängiger Erwerbstätigkeit (von über 70% auf rund 59%) eine Zunahme der Vermögenseinkünfte aus selbstständiger Tätigkeit und Immobilienbesitz; dies ist verbunden mit dem Rückgang der Lohnquote (von 73% im Jahre 1993 auf 65% im Jahre 2007) bei gleichzeitig zunehmender steuerlicher Belastung der Arbeitseinkommen und Entlastung der Unternehmens- und Vermögenseinkommen (die im gleichen Zeitraum von 27% auf 35% stiegen). „Sämtliche Un-

der Begründung des Gesetzes zur steuerlichen Förderung der Mitarbeiterkapitalbeteiligung 2009[30] heißt es dazu für einen neueren Zeitabschnitt: „In den Jahren 2003 bis 2007 sind die Unternehmens- und Vermögenseinkommen um 37,6% gestiegen, während die Arbeitnehmereinkommen nur einen Zuwachs von 4,3% verzeichneten“[31]. Kurz: Einkommen aus Eigentum, vornehmlich auch aus Produktiveigentum, wuchsen in diesen wenigen Jahren rund neunmal so stark wie Einkommen aus Arbeit. Nach anderen Untersuchungen sind die um die Verbraucherpreissteigerungen bereinigten Nettorealeinkommen der Arbeitnehmer in den vergangenen zwei Jahrzehnten sogar gesunken[32].

Eigentumsstruktur, insbesondere die Konzentration von Privateigentum an Produktivkapital einerseits, und Einkommensstruktur, insbesondere stagnierende oder nur geringfügig steigende Einkommen der arbeitenden Nichteigentümer von Produktivkapital andererseits, stehen in einem wechselseitigen Abhängigkeitsverhältnis[33]. Dies erklärt die kontinuierlich zunehmenden Disproportionen der Eigentumsverteilung bei Geld-, Immobilien- und Unternehmensvermögen. Rund 10% der erwachsenen Deutschen besitzen nach neueren Untersuchungen[34] annähernd 60% des gesamten Nettovermögens in Höhe von 6,6 Billionen Euro. Die reichsten 20% der Bevölkerung kommen danach auf rund 80% des Vermögens. Oder umgekehrt: 80% der Bevölkerung teilen sich 20% des gemeinsam erwirtschafteten Vermögens. 25% der Bevölkerung besitzen kein Vermögen[35]. Mag auch in Erfassungsmethoden und Schlussfolgerungen manches kontrovers sein, so wird doch die Größenordnung dieser neuen systemischen Fehlentwicklung nach dem Ende des „Systemgegensatzes“ vor zwei Jahrzehnten durch die Angabe illustriert, dass die privaten Haushalte in Deutschland inzwischen ein Vermögen von brutto fast 11 Billionen Euro aufgebaut haben[36].

b) Ursachen und Folgen dauerhaft ungleicher Verteilungs- und Teilhabestrukturen

Dass dauerhaft derart gravierend ungleiche Verteilungsstrukturen des Privateigentums und fortgesetzte Konzentrationsprozesse am Ende zu einer latenten Infragestellung der Eigentumsinstitutsgarantie und darüber hinaus des sozialstaatlichen Grundkonsens führen können, ist offensichtlich und Gegenstand der

---

gleichheitsmaße deuten auf eine enorme Konzentration der Nettovermögen hin“, *Rosinus,* a.a.O., S. 32.

30 Mitarbeiterkapitalbeteiligungsgesetz v. 07.03.2009, BGBl. I 2009, 451, im Folgenden kurz: MKBG.

31 Deutscher Bundestag, 16. WP, Drucks. 16/10531.

32 Dazu m.w. *A. Bontrup,* Der Vorschlag der Bundesregierung für „Mehr Mitarbeiterkapitalbeteiligung in Deutschland“, BB-Spezial 1/2009, S. 2 ff.

33 Zur Verteilungssituation in Deutschland näher *Rosinus,* Fn. 18, S. 17 ff.

34 *Grabka/Frick,* Fn. 29, S. 665 ff.

35 Zum aktuellen Stand vgl. *Frick/Grabka/Hauser,* Fn. 29.

36 Bericht in Der Tagesspiegel (Tsp.) v. 08.03.2010.

Diskussion[37]. Aus ökonomischer Sicht hat auf diese Zusammenhänge und die dysfunktionalen Langzeitwirkungen ungleichgewichtiger Verteilungspolitik auf den Wirtschaftskreislauf, unter anderem durch Schwächung von Massenkaufkraft und sozialer Sicherheit, der amerikanische Ökonom L. O. Kelso bereits vor mehr als einem halben Jahrhundert hingewiesen. Die Grundgedanken dieser auf Privateigentum und Marktwirtschaft basierenden Beteiligungskonzeption publizierte L. O. Kelso zusammen mit M. Adler 1958 in bewusstem Gegensatz zum vor damals 110 Jahren erschienenen Kommunistischen Manifest unter dem Titel „The Capitalist Manifesto"[38]. Ausgehend von diesem Ansatz und unterstützt durch die US-Steuergesetzgebung hat sich in den USA ein erfolgreiches System der durch Bankkredite vorfinanzierten und vom Unternehmen besicherten Mitarbeiterbeteiligung in Form der ESOPs (Employee Share Ownership Plan) entwickelt[39].

---

37 So *J. Borchert,* ZRP 2010, 201, unter Hinweis auf die Warnungen von *G. Schwan* vor sozialen Konflikten. Zur Abwehr übermäßiger Konzentration von Privateigentum befürwortet *Papier,* in MDH (2008), Art. 14 GG, Rn. 16, eine staatliche Anti-Konzentrationsgesetzgebung gegen die übermäßige Konzentration von Wirtschaftseigentum sowie die aktive Förderung der Vermögensbildung. *Rittstieg,* Eigentum als Verfassungsproblem. Zur Geschichte und Gegenwart des bürgerlichen Verfassungsstaates, Darmstadt 1975, S. 182 ff., kritisiert die mangelnde Beachtung der realen Dimension der Eigentumsfrage für das politische System. Treffend dazu *F. Merz,* „Sozial ist, was Bürger zu Eigentümern macht" – Ein Ordnungsrahmen für eine breite Diversifizierung privaten Eigentums, in: *Depenheuer* (Hrsg.), Eigentumsverfassung und Finanzkrise, Heidelberg 2009, S. 19 ff., 23: „Die Eigentums- und Vermögensfrage und damit nicht zuletzt die Gerechtigkeitsfrage in den entwickelten Industrienationen entscheidet sich last but not least an der Beteiligung der Arbeitnehmer am wirtschaftlichen Erfolg der Unternehmen, in dem sie arbeiten". *Kirchhof,* Der Schaden der anderen, in: *Schirrmacher/Strobl* (Hrsg.), Die Zukunft des Kapitalismus, Berlin 2010, S. 44 ff., 47: „Je anonymer und je abstrakter das Eigentum und seine Berechtigten werden, desto mehr schwindet die innere Rechtfertigung des Privateigentums". Dies galt für die Anonymisierungstendenzen des „subjektlosen" sozialistischen Staatseigentums, es gilt in ählicher Weise für vergleichbare Tendenzen mehrfach vermittelten und nationale Rechtsgrenzen transzendierenden Wirtschafts- und Finanzeigentums multinationaler Rechtssubjekte der postsozialistischen Marktwirtschaft.

38 *Kelso/Hetter,* Two-Factor-Theory: The Economics of Reality, NY Vintage Books, Random House, 1967; *Kelso/Hetter-Kelso,* Democracy and Economic Power: Extending the ESOP-Revolution through Binary Economics, 2. ed., Lanham, MD: University Press of America; zur Entwicklung dieses Konzepts *Rosen/Case/Staubus,* Equity, Why Employee Ownership is Good for Business, Boston 2005, S. 45 ff.

39 Zu diesem ESOP-System (*Employee Stock Ownership Plan*) als auf einem Trust basierender Rechtsform des Belegschafts-buy-out) vgl. *K. R. Wagner*, Kapitalbeteiligung von Mitarbeitern und Führungskräften, 2. Aufl., Frankfurt/M 2008, S. 131 f.; näher *Menke/Hanisch* in: *Lowitzsch* u.a., Mitarbeiterbeteiligung für ein neues soziales Europa, Berlin 2008, S.53 ff.

Wenn die in der jüngsten Vergangenheit dramatisch zunehmenden Ungleichheiten in der Eigentums- und Vermögensstruktur kürzlich in einer Analyse des Präsidiums der Weltbank primär auf Fortschritte in den Informationstechnologien und den ungleichen Zugang zu ihnen zurückgeführt wurden, so übersieht eine solche Analyse ganz offenbar die zentrale Rolle des Eigentums und der daraus folgenden hochgradig asymmetrischen Güterzuordnung. Ursache unausgewogener Eigentumskonzentration, die das Gefüge des Sozialstaats ebenso destabilisiert wie die Funktionsfähigkeit der Märkte, ist nicht der technische Fortschritt und der fehlende Zugang zu den neuen Technologien, insbesondere den Informationstechnologien, sondern der fehlende Zugang zu Produktiveigentum und den aus solchem erwachsenden Chancen der Eigentumsschöpfung aus (Anteils-)Eigentum, kurz: der fehlende Zugang zu Eigentum schaffendem Wirtschaftseigentum[40].

Bei diesem Partizipationsdefizit handelt es sich nicht um ein partielles oder länderspezifisches, sondern um ein allgemeines Strukturproblem der postsozialistischen nationalen und europäischen Wirtschafts- und Sozialordnung. Die Finanz- und Wirtschaftskrise der Jahre 2008/2009 und der Folgezeit stellt sich aus dieser Sicht auch als Problem verfehlter Eigentumsverteilungsstruktur infolge fehlender Rahmenbedingungen und daher fehlender Beteiligung an Eigentumserwerbschancen dar. Es geht dabei weder um „Umverteilung" noch um „Abschaffung" des Privateigentums, auch nicht um sozialistische „Nivellierungsversuche" aus ungleichem persönlichen Leistungsaufwand resultierender ökonomischer und sozialer Unterschiede in der Gesellschaft, sondern um deren Öffnung durch Schaffung angemessener Eigentumserwerbschancen aufgrund persönlicher Leistung.

c) Freiheit - Gleichheit - Eigentum

Im Spannungsverhältnis zwischen Freiheit und Gleichheit wirken der zivilrechtliche Eigentumsschutz und die Verfassungsgarantie des Privateigentums zugunsten der Freiheit des Einzelnen als Privateigentümer und gegen die Gleichheit von Eigentümer und Nichteigentümer. Der Bestandschutz des Staatseigentums dagegen, wie ihn auch das geltende postsozialistische Verfassungs- und Zivilrecht noch kennt[41], sichert – formal – ein Mindestmaß an Gleichheit aller an dieser Rechtsposition als Staatsbürger teilhabenden Rechtssubjekte. Diese Korrelation lässt sich wie folgt darstellen:

---

40 Zur Finanz- und Wirtschaftskrise als Partizipationskrise vgl. *H. Roggemann*, Fn. 23, S. 33 ff.

41 So das Zivilgesetzbuch der Russischen Föderation (Erster Teil) von 1994, dazu *F.-C. Schroeder* in: *Roggemann/Bergmann* (Hrsg.), Zivilgesetzbuch der Russischen Föderation (Erster Teil) von 1994, Berlin 1997, 28 ff. zu den Grenzen und öffentlich-rechtlichen Vorbehalten im Russischen Zivilrecht und insbesondere im Eigentumsrecht.

Privateigentum
↓
Freiheit → ← Gleichheit
↑
Staatseigentum

Vermittelt durch die Eigentumsfunktionen, insbesondere durch die Zuordnungsfunktion des Privateigentums und die daraus folgende Freiheitssicherung setzt die Eigentumsordnung durch das Verhältnis von Eigentum privater Rechtsträger zum Eigentum des Staates und der Kommunen auch Rahmen und Maß individueller ökonomischer Entfaltungsfreiheit gegenüber der Staatsgewalt und dem von dieser zentralisierten und verwalteten (Staats-)Eigentum. Je weiter die Privatisierung von Staatseigentum voranschreitet, desto mehr verliert der Staat seine durch Eigentum vermittelte, originäre Interventions- und Kontrollkompetenzen, kurz: Entscheidungsmacht als Eigentümer und unmittelbarer Teilnehmer am Wirtschaftsprozess (Beispiel: „antizyklische Investitionspolitik[42]“).

Umgekehrt gilt aber auch, wie die staatssozialistische Erfahrung in Mittel- und Osteuropa gezeigt hat: je umfassender die Eigentumskonzentration in Staatshand, desto geringer die ökonomische und in deren Folge auch die persönliche Entfaltungsfreiheit des Einzelnen. Das optimale, d.h. zugleich wirtschaftlich effektive, sozial gerechte und personaler Entfaltungschance angemessene Gleichgewicht, in den Jahrzehnten des Staatssozialismus und des Systemgegensatzes blockiert[43], scheint auch zwei Jahrzehnte nach dem Ende des Ost-West-Gegensatzes, wie die Finanz- und Wirtschaftskrise der Jahre 2008/2009 zeigt, noch nicht gefunden und wird weiterhin Gegenstand ständiger Reformbemühungen sein.

d) Verteilungsgerechtigkeit = Chancengerechtigkeit

Zu fragen bleibt, ob und inwieweit die verschiedenen und verschieden weit reichenden Funktionen des Privateigentums im marktwirtschaftlichen Sozialstaat von heute auf angemessene Weise zum Ausgleich und damit zur Geltung gebracht werden können. Legt man die sinngemäß auch vom BVerfG formulierte Annahme zugrunde, dass in einer Marktgesellschaft wirtschaftliche und damit soziale Integration ebenso wie die Sicherung eines persönlichen Gestaltungsfrei-

---

42 Ein Beispiel für diesen Zusammenhang von Staatseigentum und wirtschaftlicher Entscheidungsmacht: Anlässlich der Vereinbarung einer strategischen Partnerschaft zwischen Daimler und Renault-Nissan erklärte der französische Industrieminister *Estrosi*, Frankreich begrüße diese Zusammenarbeit. Der französische Staat hält 15% des Aktienkapitals von Renault. „Die Politik will auf ihre Möglichkeiten der Einflussnahme auf die strategischen Entscheidungen des privatisierten Autokonzerns nicht verzichten“, dazu *H. Mortsiefer, H.-H. Bremer* in: Tsp. v. 07.04.2010.

43 Zu den strukturellen Defiziten staatssozialistischer Eigentumsordnung *H. Roggemann*, Fn. 7, S. 100 ff.

raums letztlich durch das Eigentum in seinen verschiedenen Formen vermittelt werden, so kann diese Frage angesichts der hochgradig ungleichen Eigentums- und vor allem auch der in die Zukunft weisenden Eigentumserwerbsstruktur in Deutschland[44] nur mit erheblichen Einschränkungen bejaht werden: Eine Gesellschaft mit so hochgradig ungleicher Teilhabe am existenz-, freiheits- und chancensichernden Privateigentum stellt keine materiell integrierte Zivilgesellschaft dar.

Einen systemkonformen Ausweg aus diesem seit langem bekannten Dilemma könnte eine wirksame finanzielle Partizipation durch Unternehmenskapitalbeteiligung möglichst vieler Unternehmensmitarbeiter eröffnen. Die Tatsache, dass in Deutschland nur rund 2% aller Unternehmen ihren Mitarbeitern diese Möglichkeit eröffnen, zeigt, wie weit der marktwirtschaftliche Sozialstaat noch von seiner Verwirklichung in eine *Zivilgesellschaft als (Mit-)Eigentümergesellschaft* entfernt ist.

Hierbei geht es nicht um grundlegende „Systemkritik" oder gar um die Wiederbelebung kommunistischer oder staatssozialistischer Alternativen und die Forderung nach „Umverteilung" gesellschaftlichen Reichtums. Ebenso wenig stehen das Leistungsprinzip oder die Freiheit zum wirtschaftlichen Erfolg zur Diskussion. Erst recht nicht geht es um die Wiederbelebung des durch die bisherige Entwicklung hinreichend widerlegten Marx`schen Theorems von der Abschaffung des Privateigentums[45] an Produktionsmitteln und Produktivkapital. Im Gegenteil: Es geht – unter Berücksichtigung der Erfahrungen aus vergangenen staatssozialistischen Eigentums- und Wirtschaftskonzeptionen – um die Eröffnung von Chancen in Gestalt geeigneter Rechtsformen zum Eintritt möglichst vieler Bürger als Wirtschaftsbürger in die vom BVerfG definierte Zivilgesellschaft als (Mit-)Eigentümergesellschaft der Marktwirtschaft auf der Grundlage eigener (Arbeits-)Leistungen. In diesem Sinne lässt sich die umstrittene Antwort auf die Frage nach der „Verteilungsgerechtigkeit" in der Leistungsgesellschaft daher auf die Kurzformel bringen: Verteilungsgerechtigkeit = Chancengerechtigkeit.

---

44 S.o. III. 2. a).

45 So die bekannte Formulierung im Kommunistischen Manifest, *Marx/Engels*, Fn. 24, S. 475: „Was den Kommunismus auszeichnet, ist nicht die Abschaffung des Eigentums überhaupt, sondern die Abschaffung des bürgerlichen Eigentums. Aber das moderne bürgerliche Privateigentum ist der letzte und vollendetste Ausdruck der Erzeugung und Aneignung der Produkte, die auf Klassengegensätzen, auf der Ausbeutung der einen durch die andern beruht. In diesem Sinn können die Kommunisten ihre Theorie in dem einen Ausdruck: Aufhebung des Privateigentums, zusammenfassen."

e) Eigentümergesellschaft und Nichteigentümergesellschaft

Der Eigentümergesellschaft entspricht eine Nichteigentümergesellschaft. Das Eigentum eines Eigentümers ist zugleich das Nichteigentum aller anderen (Nichteigentümer) in Bezug auf dieses Eigentumsobjekt[46].

Die höchstrichterliche Rechtsprechung zur Individualfunktion des Privateigentums liefert den theoretischen Hintergrund für eine Feststellung, die in Anbetracht der gesellschaftlichen Realsituation in Deutschland und anderen entwickelten Marktwirtschaften unabweisbar ist: Die fortwährend wachsende Vermögens- bzw. Eigentumskonzentration in den Händen einer prozentual kleinen Gruppe der Gesamtbevölkerung führt zu dem Schluss, dass die von der Rechtsprechung als essenziell hervorgehobene, freiheitssichernde Schutzwirkung des Eigentums, seine Individualfunktion[47], vorrangig den dieser Bevölkerungsgruppe zugehörigen Inhabern von Privateigentum zugute kommt. Das Institut des Privateigentums, insbesondere des Privateigentums an Produktivkapital, generiert mit seinen ungleichen Chancen zur rechtlichen, wirtschaftlichen und damit auch sozialen Partizipation eine zunehmend geteilte Gesellschaft. Für den größten Teil der Gesellschaft der Nichteigentümer, insbesondere solcher in Bezug auf das Produktivvermögen, bleibt die Eigentumstheorie des BVerfG samt ihren Rechtswohltaten daher weitgehend irrelevant.

Angesichts der Erfahrungen aus der ostrechtlichen Untersuchung der strukturellen Probleme und Defizite staatssozialistischer Eigentums- und Wirtschaftsrechtsordnungen, drängt sich die Frage auf, ob eine derartige Fehlentwicklung in eine langfristig überzeugende, marktwirtschaftliche sozialstaatliche Alternative zum gescheiterten staatssozialistischen Eigentumsmodell führen kann und weiter, welches rechtspolitische Programm des sozialstaatlichen Gesetzgebers erforderlich wäre, um dieses Ziel zu erreichen, ihm jedenfalls näher zu kommen.

---

46 Zum theoretischen Ausgangspunkt vgl. *Luhmann*, Fn. 23; zur Grundsatzkritik an dieser Ausschlussfunktion und der damit einhergehenden Differenzierungswirkung in der Gesellschaft schon *Rousseau*, dazu *R. Brandt*, Fn. 23.

47 Auf signifikante Weise gibt diesem verbreiteten gesellschaftlichen Wertungszusammenhang (Eigentum = Persönlichkeitsentfaltung = Freiheit) die Formulierung *Baurs* (*Baur/Stürner*, SachenR, 17. Aufl., München 1999) Ausdruck: Eigentum sei „der vermögensrechtliche Ausdruck der rechtlichen Persönlichkeitswertung“.

IV. Sozialistische Eigentumsrevolution und sozialstaatliche Eigentumsevolution

1. Marx versus Proudhon – zur Kritik des Privateigentums

Marx[48] ging mit seiner Grundsatzkritik am Privateigentum als Grundelement profitorientierter Marktwirtschaft über den sozialdemokratischen Ansatz des Gothaer Programms, der mehr Verteilungsgerechtigkeit nur als systemimmanente Forderung erhob, weit hinaus. Der Lösung des Entfremdungsproblems, der Beseitigung von Abhängigkeit, Unterdrückung und Ausbeutung des Lohnarbeiters und der Durchbrechung des Akkumulationskreislaufs, in dem sich die Negativfaktoren privatkapitalistischer Wirtschaft unaufhaltsam potenzierten, meinte er nur durch die Aufhebung der privaten Zuordnung der Produktionsmittel und ihrer dauerhaften, exklusiven, privaten Nutzung und Verfügung, d.h. durch Beseitigung des Rechtsinstituts Privateigentum insbesondere an den Produktionsmitteln, näher zu kommen. Kommunismus verstand sich in diesem Sinne „als positive Aufhebung des Privateigentums als menschlicher Selbstentfremdung und darum als wirkliche Aneignung des menschlichen Wesens durch und für den Menschen".

Im Kommunistischen Manifest brachten *Marx* und *Engels* diesen Ansatz auf die suggestive Kurzformel:

> „In diesem Sinne können die Kommunisten ihre Theorie in den einen Ausdruck: Aufhebung des Privateigentums, zusammenfassen[49]".

Rückschauend, und bestätigt auch durch Ergebnisse der Ostrechtsforschung aus jahrzehntelanger kritischer Begleitung und Untersuchung der (Wirtschafts-)Rechtsentwicklung in den sozialistischen Staaten, stellt sich diese Marx`sche These zusammen mit der Lehre von der transformatorischen Legitimation einer „Diktatur des Proletariats" auf dem Wege in eine selbstbestimmte kommunistische Zukunftsgesellschaft als eine der historisch folgenreichsten Fehlannahmen dar. Dies gilt sowohl für die zentralistische sowjetische Sozialismusvariante als auch für den dezentralisierten, föderalisierten „Jugoslawischen Weg". Beide Umsetzungsversuche vernachlässigen die konstitutive Funktion des Privateigentums für die Strukturierung jeder entwickelten Gesellschaft[50] und damit auch für jede Form von realer Demokratie und wettbewerbs-

---

48 Ökonomisch-philosophische Manuskripte, MEW Ergänzungsband, S. 536; Der Bürgerkrieg in Frankreich, MEW 17, S. 342 f.; *Marx/Engels*, Das Kommunistische Manifest, MEW 4, 461 ff., 475.

49 So im Kommunistischen Manifest, a.a.O.

50 Dazu grundlegend *Luhmann*, s.o. III. 1. In seiner Auseinandersetzung mit *M. Stirner*, vgl. Die deutsche Ideologie, MEW 3, S. 238 ff., lässt *Marx* immerhin die Frage offen, welche „fixen Begierden" „unter allen Verhältnissen existieren" und welche durch Veränderung der „gesellschaftlichen Verhältnisse" veränderbar seien. In diesem Sinne kann

fähiger sozialer Marktwirtschaft. Sie sind überdies, wie der Marx`sche Entwurf insgesamt, durch wesentliche anthropologische sowie demokratietheoretische und politische Defizite gekennzeichnet. Die spezifische Abwehr- und Integrationsfunktion des Eigentums in der Gesellschaft, die durch dezentrale Machtzuordnung zugleich zur Machtkontrolle und damit Demokratisierung beitragen kann – allerdings nur unter der Bedingung einer entsprechenden, wirtschaftsdemokratischen Eigentumsverteilung – hat *Proudhon*, der kongeniale Freund und spätere erbitterte Gegner von *Marx*, hellsichtiger als dieser erfasst[51].

Diese freiheitssichernde Abwehrfunktion des Privateigentums kann allerdings als konstitutives, wirtschaftsdemokratisches Element sozialstaatlicher Marktwirtschaft nur zum Zuge kommen, wenn und soweit allen Teilnehmern am Wirtschaftsprozess angemessene materielle Teilhabechancen als potentielle (Mit-)Eigentümer eröffnet werden. Ob diese Voraussetzung in einer Wirtschafts- und Eigentumsordnung mit so hochgradig asymmetrischen Verteilungsstrukturen wie im postsozialistischen Deutschland zwei Jahrzehnte nach dessen erneuter Vereinigung noch oder nicht mehr gegeben ist, wird zu einer offenen Frage.

2. Scheitern der Revolution als Eigentumsrevolution

Die Umwälzungen, die sich mit der Oktoberrevolution 1917 in Russland, dem Zusammenbruch des nationalsozialistischen Deutschland 1945 und der Ausweitung des zunächst stalinistischen staatssozialistischen Regierungssystems in Ost-, Mittel- und Südosteuropa sowie 1989/1990 mit dem Zusammenbruch dieses Systems und seiner „Entsozialisierung" vollzogen, können jenseits ihrer jeweiligen unterschiedlichen klassenkämpferischen, machtpolitischen sowie demokratisch-emanzipatorischen und rechtstaatlichen Aspekte in ihrem sozialökonomischen Kern als *Revolutionen durch Umwälzung der jeweils herrschenden Eigentumsverfassung* verstanden werden. Dies gilt mit einer Ausnahme: der Novemberrevolution 1918 in Deutschland. Diese ließ die herrschende Privateigentumsordnung weitgehend unangetastet[52]. In diesem Kernpunkt unterschieden sich die politischen Anläufe in Richtung auf das große Ziel *sozialer Gerechtigkeit durch mehr Verteilungsgerechtigkeit* seit jener Zeit wesentlich.

---

der fehlgeschlagene sozialistische Großversuch einer weitgehend (privat-)eigentumslosen Gesellschaft als Widerlegung dieses Marx´schen Ansatzes angesehen werden.

51 *Proudhon*, Theorie des Eigentums, in: ausgewählte Texte, hrsg. v. *Th. Ramm*, Stuttgart 1956, S. 194 ff., 277: „Die Staatsmacht ist eine Macht der Konzentration. Man lasse ihr freien Lauf – und jede Individualität wird bald verschwinden, von der Gesamtheit aufgesogen sein; die Gesellschaft verfällt in den Kommunismus. Das Eigentum ist nun im Gegensatz hierzu eine Macht der Dezentralisation; weil es selbst absolut ist, ist es antidespotisch und antiunitarisch. Deshalb ist es das Prinzip jeder Föderation".

52 Dazu die – in Anbetracht jahrzehntelanger staatssozialistischer Erfahrungen nicht begründete – Kritik von *S. Haffner* in: Die verratene Revolution, München 1993.

Erst mit dem Ende des Staatssozialismus in Osteuropa und mit dem Scheitern der Eigentumsrevolution als sozialer Utopie in dem ein halbes bis dreiviertel Jahrhundert dauernden Feldversuch des Staatssozialismus in Osteuropa, hat diese Suche wieder auf eine sozialstaatliche Linie im Rahmen der Privateigentumsordnung zurückgefunden. Nun im gesamteuropäischen Rechtsrahmen der MRK und ihrer Zusatzprotokolle sowie der Europäischen Grundrechtscharta und des Lissabonvertrags der EU von 2007. Privateigentum, Marktwirtschaft sowie deren wirksame immanente Sozialbindung gehören inzwischen zu den anerkannten Grundbausteinen des Europäischen Rechtsraums eines „Neuen Sozialen Europa" („*New Social Europe*")[53].

3. Vergesellschaftung und Arbeiterselbstverwaltung oder Mitbestimmung und Mitbeteiligung?

Vor und neben der revolutionären marxistischen Alternative entwickelten sich Konzepte materieller Mitarbeiterbeteiligung im Rahmen bestehender Privateigentumsordnung. Frühe Bestrebungen und auch erste Untersuchungen zur Mitarbeiterbeteiligung, zunächst vornehmlich in Form von Gewinnbeteiligung, gehen ins 19. Jahrhundert zurück[54]. In den bürgerkriegsähnlichen Konflikten nach der Novemberrevolution von 1918 setzte sich in Deutschland, anders als in Russland nach der Oktoberrevolution von 1917[55], die Konzeption einer parlamentarischen Präsidialdemokratie gegen Rätedemokratie und Sozialisierung der Wirtschaft samt Überführung der Produktionsmittel in Gemeineigentum durch. In diesem Zusammenhang gewann Mitarbeiterbeteiligung als systemstabilisierendes Programm zusätzliche legitimatorische Bedeutung: *Mitbeteiligung statt Vergesellschaftung*. Bereits 1919 wurde ein erster Gesetzentwurf hierzu ausgearbeitet, jedoch nicht verabschiedet[56]. Unterschiedliche Beteiligungskonzepte („Arbeitsaktie", „Volksaktie", „Arbeiteraktie") wurden erfolglos diskutiert. Ein Beteiligungsmodell „Krupp'sche Treuhand" scheiterte[57]. Zu einem relevanten oder gar prägenden Bestandteil der zunehmenden Zerreißproben bis hin zum Nationalsozialismus ausgesetzten Wirtschafts- und Rechtsordnung der Weimarer Republik konnte sich materielle Mitarbeiterbeteiligung nicht entwickeln.

53 Dazu *Lowitzsch* u.a., Fn. 39.

54 *V. Böhmert*, Die Gewinnbeteiligung. Untersuchungen über Arbeitslohn und Unternehmergewinn, Leipzig 1878; zur Entwicklung *B. Otto*, Mitarbeiterbeteiligung in Deutschland, Österreich und Großbritannien, Diss. FU- Berlin 2011, S. 42 ff.

55 *H. Roggemann*, Fn. 21.

56 *W. Homann*, Die Entwicklung der Sozialpartnerschaft dargestellt an den Wandlungen der Sozialpartnerschaft seit der Mitte des 19. Jahrhunderts, Berlin 1955, S. 98 ff.; dazu B. Otto, Fn. 54, S. 48.

57 Zur Entwicklung *Feilchenfeld*, Die Gewinnbeteiligung der Arbeiter und Angestellten in Deutschland, Berlin 1922; *B. Otto*, Fn. 54, S. 49 f.

Dies gelang dagegen mit dem ebenfalls aus dem überwundenen rätedemokratischen Ansatz hervorgegangenen Konzept der immateriellen Mitbestimmung durch Betriebsräte. Seit dem ersten Betriebsrätegesetz von 1920[58] hat sich das deutsche Mitbestimmungsmodell weitergehend als in einer Reihe anderer europäischer Länder entwickelt. Immaterielle, direktive Mitbestimmung ist auf der Grundlage des BetrVG und des MitbestimmungsG ungeachtet mancher Widerstände[59] zu einem Stabilitätsfaktor kommunikativer, konfliktfähiger Arbeitsverfassung und damit auch zur Voraussetzung für bisherige wirtschaftliche Erfolge Deutschlands geworden[60].

Auch nach dem Zusammenbruch und Neubeginn von 1945 wurde die Forderung nach Vergesellschaftung erhoben[61], trat jedoch in der Bundesrepublik Deutschland, anders als in der DDR und ähnlich wie in den Anfangsjahren der Weimarer Republik, bald hinter Konzepten zur Integration der abhängig Erwerbstätigen in die Soziale Marktwirtschaft mittels Sparförderung, Beteiligungsförderung und Mitarbeiterbeteiligung zurück. Parteiübergreifend wurden „Vermögensbildung in Arbeitnehmerhand“ und „Förderung der Eigentumsbildung bei den bisher Vermögenslosen“ zu sozial- und wirtschaftspolitischen Leitzielen erklärt. Hierzu sollte auch das Konzept der „Volksaktie“ beitragen und deren Erwerber in „Wirtschaftsbürger einer echten Wirtschaftsdemokratie“ verwan-

---

58 RGBl. 1920, S. 147; zur Geschichte *Gamillscheg*, Kollektives Arbeitsrecht I, München 1997, S. 111 ff., 120 ff.

59 Die das BVerfG in seinem grundlegenden Mitbestimmungs-Urt. v. 1979, BVerfGE 50, 290; NJW 1979, 699, ausgeräumt hat.

60 Zur gesellschaftspolitischen Bedeutung *Gamillscheg*, Kollektives Arbeitsrecht II, München 2008, S. 692 ff.: „Dass sich Deutschland 50 Jahre nach der größten Katastrophe seiner Geschichte als eine der drei Wirtschaftsmächte und als Motor der europäischen Einigung darstellt, wäre ohne die deutsche Arbeitsverfassung nicht zu erreichen gewesen“.

61 So noch im Ahlener Programm der CDU von 1947, das einen Sozialismus auf christlicher Grundlage unter Ablehnung des schon vom Erfurter Programm der Sozialdemokraten so bezeichneten „Staatssozialismus“ als Ziel formulierte. Sozialisierungsermächtigungen fanden ebenfalls Eingang in einzelne Landesverfassungen und Art. 15 GG. Die These *Leisners*, Eigentum, Berlin 1996, S. 233 ff., 248, die Sozialisierungsermächtigung des Art. 15 GG, in eine zusätzliche Eigentumsschutznorm umzudeuten, ist nicht, wie *Isensee* in seinem Vorwort dazu, a.a.O., S. X, meint, ein „erstaunlicher Nachweis“, sondern eine Verkehrung dieses historischen Hintergrunds und legislatorischen Zwecks der Vorschrift, Sozialisierung zumindest als rechtspolitische Ausnahmeoption im Verfassungssystem des GG offenzuhalten. Auf dem Höhepunkt der Finanzmarkt- und Wirtschaftskrise 2008/2009 gewann diese Option unvermutete Aktualität, als der Deutsche Bundestag aus zwingenden Gemeinwohlerwägungen erstmals in der Nachkriegsgeschichte eine gesetzliche Grundlage für die Enteignung (einer insolventen Privatbank) beschloss, vgl. das durch Finanzmarktstabilisierungsergänzungsgesetz (FMStErgG) eingeführte Rettungsübernahmegesetz – RettungsG, BGBl. I, 725.

deln[62]. Die Umsetzung dieses Gedankens einer Produktiveigentumsbeteiligung auf breiter Grundlage begann als Teil der Privatisierung von Staatsunternehmen 1959 mit der Preussag-Privatisierung.

Mit einer Reihe verschiedenartiger Förderinstrumente hat der Bundesgesetzgeber in den vergangenen Jahrzehnten versucht, diesem sozialstaatlichen Hauptziel näher zu kommen[63]. Diese Maßnahmen führten zunächst zu beachtlichen Erfolgen und einem Wohlstandsanstieg, in dem während der ersten Jahrzehnte nach 1945 das Durchschnittseinkommen (Pro-Kopf-Einkommen) in der Bundesrepublik um rund das Vierfache wuchs[64].

In der Folgezeit, insbesondere seit der Vereinigung der beiden deutschen Staaten 1990, begannen jedoch die Realeinkommen zu stagnieren und teilweise zu sinken, die Unterschiede in der Einkommens- und Eigentumsverteilung zu Lasten der abhängig Arbeitenden dagegen immer stärker zuzunehmen[65] und das sozialstaatliche Gleichgewicht in Frage zu stellen.

V. Das jugoslawische Modell der Arbeiterselbstverwaltung

1. Grundlagen und Entwicklung

a) Der politische Anspruch

Der jugoslawische Verfassungsgeber nahm für sich in Anspruch, mit dem in der „Selbstverwaltungs-Verfassung" von 1974 grundlegend neu und umfassend geregelten Modell der Arbeiterselbstverwaltung *„folgerichtiger und vollständiger als irgendeine bisherige Revolution in der Geschichte"* die Marx`sche Lehre vom Sinn und Ziel der Vergesellschaftung der Produktionsmittel und der allmählichen Überwindung des Gegensatzes von Kapital und Arbeit in neuen Formen wirtschaftlicher und politischer Selbstverwaltung zu verwirklichen[66]. In

62 So der damalige Bundesschatzminister *Lindrath*, vgl. dazu: Deutschen Volksaktien war kein großer Erfolg beschieden, FAZ v. 24.03.2009.

63 Hierzu zählen u.a.: Wohnungsbauprämiengesetz 1959, Sparprämiengesetz 1959, Vermögensbildungsgesetze 1961, 1965, 1970, Vermögensbeteiligungsgesetze 1982, 1986, 1998. Der Versuch der sozialliberalen Bundesregierung, ausgehend von 1974 formulierten Grundlinien eines VermögensbeteiligungsG betriebliche Mitbeteiligungsmodelle zu entwickeln und hierfür Unternehmen von einer bestimmten Größenordnung an generell in Pflicht zu nehmen, scheiterte am Widerstand der Gewerkschaften gegen jede Form unmittelbarer finanzieller Mitbeteiligung der Arbeitnehmer am arbeitgebenden Unternehmen. Erst nach dem Regierungswechsel konnte unter der Regierung *Kohl* 1984 das Erste VermögensbeteiligungsG in Kraft treten.

64 Zu dieser Erfolgsgeschichte vgl. *Erhard*, Wohlstand für Alle (1. Aufl. 1959), 8. Aufl. Düsseldorf 1964, S. 77 ff., 208 ff.

65 Dazu näher *Rosinus*, Fn.18, S. 27 ff.; *Bontrup*, BB-Special 1/2009, S. 3.

66 So *M. Todorović* vor dem Rat der Völker zum Verfassungsentwurf in: Verfassung der Sozialistischen Föderativen Republik Jugoslawien, Belgrad 1974, S. 17.

dem ausufernden, vielfach jeglicher juristischen Präzision entbehrenden und weitgehend eher an politisch-ökonomische Lehrbuchtexte als die Gesetzessprache eines Verfassungsgebers erinnernden Stil der SFRJ-Verfassung formuliert Art. 10:

> „Die sozialistische gesellschaftlich-wirtschaftliche Ordnung der Sozialistischen Föderativen Republik Jugoslawien beruht auf frei vereinter Arbeit mit den in gesellschaftlichem Eigentum befindlichen Produktionsmitteln, auf der Selbstverwaltung der Arbeiter in der Produktion und auf der Verteilung des Gesellschaftsprodukts in Grundorganisationen und anderen Organisationen vereinter Arbeit und auf der gesellschaftlichen Reproduktion als Gesamtheit".

b) Vergesellschaftetes Eigentum und seine strukturellen Defizite

Das jugoslawische Selbstverwaltungssystem ging von der Vergesellschaftung des Produktiveigentums aus[67]. Privateigentum wurde zur Ausnahme, soweit es um Handwerk, Gewerbe und Handel ging. Dieses sozialistische Eigentum wurde, anders als in der UdSSR („Staatseigentum") oder in der DDR („Volkseigentum") als „gesellschaftliches Eigentum" bezeichnet. Es handelte sich ungeachtet dieser begrifflichen Distanzierung jedoch nicht um betriebliches oder individuelles „Arbeitereigentum", sondern ein kollektiviertes, anonymisiertes und damit „subjektloses" Eigentumsrecht, dem die beiden Wesenselemente des Privateigentums fehlten: die individuelle oder zumindest individualisierbare Zuordnung von Besitz-, Nutzungs- und Verfügungsbefugnissen und der eigentumstypische Haftungskonnex, d.h. die Verbindung von Eigentümerbefugnissen und Eigentümer(verlust)risiko.

Damit setzte sich das „gesellschaftliche Eigentum" als Grundlage des „Jugoslawischen Modells" allen prinzipiellen Einwänden gegen die strukturellen Defizite und Funktionsmängel der verschiedenen Spielarten sozialistischen Eigentums als entprivatisierten Surrogateigentums aus[68]. Da die Mittel im gesellschaftlichen Eigentum „gleichzeitig jedermanns und niemandes" seien[69], so

---

67 Diese Voraussetzungen wurden von Partei und Regierung stalinistischem Vorbild folgend mit rigorosen Methoden entschädigungsloser oder weit unter Wert erfolgter, allenfalls symbolisch entschädigter Enteignungen sowie Zwangsmaßnahmen im ersten Jahrzehnt des „sozialistischen Aufbaus" geschaffen; hierzu und zur späteren rechtlichen Rehabilitierung und finanziellen Kompensation Betroffener in Kroatien vgl. *K. Mihaljevic*, Kroatiens langer Weg zur Restitution. Das Gesetzt zur Entschädigung des zur Zeit der kommunistischen Herrschaft entzogenen Vermögens, Diss. FU Berlin 2004, S. 8 ff. In Serbien kam nach zahlreichen Entwürfen und jahrelangen Diskussionen nur eine reduzierte Vorentwurfsfassung, in Bosnien und Herzegowina bis auf den heutigen Tag ebenfalls keine allgemeine Rechtsgrundlage für eine Kompensation derartigen Enteignungsunrechts zustande.

68 *H. Roggemann* (Hrsg.), Eigentum in Osteuropa, Berlin 1996, S. 26 ff.; *ders.*, Die Verfassungen Mittel- und Osteuropas, Berlin 1999, S. 98 ff.

69 So z.B. *V. Spaić*, Gradjansko pravo, I Opšti dio (ZivilR, Allgemeiner Teil), Sarajevo 1967, S. 311 ff.

wurde folgerichtig in der damaligen jugoslawischen Rechtslehre argumentiert, sei das gesellschaftliche Eigentum geradezu „die Negation des Eigentumsrechts".

Wie die Erfahrung in den sozialistischen Staaten und auch in Jugoslawien mit derartigen entindividualisierten Eigentumssurrogaten zeigte, waren diesem sozialistischen Eigentum wesentliche der (oben zu III. 1.) genannten Eigentumsfunktionen damit verloren gegangen, es war weitgehend strukturell funktionsunfähig geworden und konnte daher die Erwartungen als tragfähige Grundlage für eine selbstverwaltete Arbeits- und Wirtschaftsverfassung neuer Art zu dienen – Erwartungen, denen auch der Verfasser dieser Zeilen Sympathie entgegenbrachte – zu keiner Zeit einschränkungslos und mit zunehmendem Zeitablauf immer offensichtlicher immer weniger erfüllen[70].

- Es fehlte die individuelle oder *individualisierbare Zuordnung* von Eigentümerbefugnissen und Eigentümerverantwortung.
- Mit der Abwehrfunktion ging die *freiheitssichernde Individualfunktion* insoweit verloren, als es um Gestaltungsfreiheiten im Bereich der Wirtschaft geht.
- Von entscheidender Bedeutung wurde der Verlust der mit der individuellen Zuordnung verbundenen Risikotragung. Eigentum ohne *Eigentümer(verlust)risiko* ist ein Widerspruch in sich. Die Folge waren vielfältige Formen von Ressourcenverschwendung großen Umfangs in allen eigentumssubjektlosen staatssozialistischen Wirtschaftsordnungen.
- In Zusammenhang damit stand der Verlust der ökonomischen Funktion des Privateigentums als allgemeiner *Wertmaßstab*, der in der Marktwirtschaft und bis zu einem gewissen Grade auch in der damaligen „sozialistischen Marktwirtschaft" Jugoslawiens als unentbehrlicher Bezugspunkt und Grundlage für die Ermittlung von Marktwert, Zinskalkulation, Preis und Kreditsicherung zu dienen hatte[71].
- Eigentum verlor weitgehend oder völlig seine Funktion als *Kreditsicherungsmittel*. Dies galt in unterschiedlichem Maße auch für Rechtsformen wie Sicherungsübereignung, Eigentumsvorbehalt oder Grundpfandrechte.

---

70 *Jäger*, Arbeiterselbstverwaltung und gesellschaftliches Eigentum – Ein Beitrag zum Statusrecht jugoslawischer Unternehmen, Stuttgart 1969. Zu diesen im Jugoslawischen Modell angelegten Aporien vgl. *H. Roggemann*, Das Modell der Arbeiterselbstverwaltung in Jugoslawien, Frankfurt 1970, S. 106 ff.

71 Zu dieser ökonomischen Eigentumsfunktion vgl. näher *Heinsohn/Steiger*, Eigentum und Systemtransformation, in: *Hölscher* u.a. (Hrsg.): Bedingungen ökonomischer Entwicklung in Zentralosteuropa. Band 2: Wirtschaftliche Entwicklung und institutioneller Wandel, Marburg 1994, S. 337 ff.; Heinsohn/Steiger, Eigentum, Zins und Geld, Reinbek 1996, S. 97 ff. Zur Zuordnungsfunktion als „Grundlage für die Existenz marktfähiger Güter und damit für das Funktionieren des Marktes" vgl. zusammenfassend *Wolf/Wellenhofer*, Fn. 23, S. 21.

- Da bestimmte Eigentumsobjekte im staatlichen und gesellschaftlichen Eigentum rechtsgeschäftlicher Eigentumsübertragung ganz oder teilweise entzogen, also insoweit *res extra commercium* waren, bestand für diese Objekte kein (legaler) Markt und es konnte sich kein *Marktpreis* bilden.
- Anstelle eines funktionierenden Grundstücksmarktes als Austauschmechanismus, traten infolge übermäßiger staatlicher Reglementierung einerseits Umgehungsgeschäfte, andererseits Formen *ineffektiver Verwaltungsentscheidungen* (Genehmigungen, Höchstpreisfestsetzungen, Zuteilungsverfügungen).
- Anstelle des nicht übertragbaren (Staats-)Eigentums wurden *Eigentumssurrogate* („Recht der operativen Verwaltung", „Fondseigentum") geschaffen, um eine für den Wirtschaftsverkehr erforderliche, eigentumsähnliche Kompetenz- und Risikozuordnung zu bewirken.

c) Unternehmensorganisation

Auch der jugoslawische Gesetzgeber unterwarf das gesamte Unternehmensrecht in der Anfangsphase, ähnlich wie in den anderen sozialistischen Staaten der späten Stalinzeit, zunächst umfassenden staatlichen Vorgaben und Rahmenbedingungen bis hin zu ins Einzelne gehenden staatlichen Regelungen und setzte an die Stelle der traditionellen Vielfalt verschiedener kapital- und personalgesellschaftsrechtlicher oder einzelkaufmännischer Betätigungsformen eine einheitliche Rechtsgrundlage für unternehmerisches Handeln[72]. Anders als z.B. in der UdSSR und der DDR wurde der Handlungsspielraum für die jugoslawischen Unternehmen jedoch seit der Abkehr vom zentralistischen sowjetischen Modell seit 1948/1949 schrittweise ständig in Richtung auf eine halboffene „sozialistische Marktwirtschaft" erweitert und führte schließlich zu einem jugoslawischen „Managersozialismus", der zwar dem – vorrangig vom Bund der Kommunisten zu Funktionsträgern gemachten – Führungspersonal der Unternehmen wachsende Freiräume in einer „sozialistischen Marktwirtschaft" verschaffte, den unmittelbaren Einfluss der Arbeiterschaft in den Selbstverwaltungsorganen aber in gleichem Maße stagnieren ließ oder sogar wieder verringerte[73].

---

72 Als Beispiele seien hier aus der Phase einer gewissen vorübergehenden Konsolidierung des im permanenten Fluss befindlichen Selbstverwaltungssystems das Grundsatzgesetz über die Unternehmen v. 04.04.1968, SL SFRJ 1965 Nr. 17, Pos. 354 und das Gesetz über die Mittel der Wirtschaftsorganisationen v. 15.04.1961, SL SFRJ 1961, Nr. 17, Pos. 229, genannt, deutsche Übersetzung bei *H. Roggemann*, Grundlagen des jugoslawischen Betriebsverfassungs- und Unternehmensrecht, in: Berichte des Osteuropa-Instituts an der Freien Universität Berlin, Reihe Wirtschaft und Recht, Rechtswissenschaftliche Folge, hrsg. v. *W. Meder*, Berlin 1968.

73 Zu dieser Entwicklung auf der Basis umfangreicher – und im damaligen sozialistischen Wirtschafts- und Rechtsbereich einmaliger – empirischer Erhebungen in drei großen jugoslawischen Industriebetrieben kritisch *W. Soergel*, Arbeiterselbstverwaltung oder Managersozialismus, München 1979, S. 32 ff. Eine normative Bestandsaufnahme der

Das selbstverwaltete Unternehmen hatte als „Arbeitsorganisation" die Rechtsstellung einer juristischen Person, haftete für die Verbindlichkeiten mit seinen Betriebsmitteln, konnte im Rahmen weitmaschiger Wirtschaftsrahmenplanung seinen Geschäftsgegenstand ändern – in klassischen Planwirtschaften undenkbar – und im Falle erfolglosen Wirtschaftens auch Gegenstand eines Sanierungs- oder sogar Konkursverfahrens werden. Von dieser an sich folgerichtigen Möglichkeit – die das jugoslawische Wirtschaftsrecht als einzige sozialistische Rechtsordnung kannte[74] – wurde allerdings in der Praxis kein Gebrauch gemacht. Das eigentümerlose Wirtschaftsrisiko trugen im Falle von Managementfehlern, ebenso wie von Misswirtschaft und Absatz- und Finanzierungsproblemen infolge unvorhergesehener Marktentwicklungen, vielmehr in aller Regel die kommunalen oder andere gesellschaftliche Fonds der öffentlichen Hand. Gegen die selbstverwaltenden Stimmen der Unternehmensmitarbeiter die Durchführung eines Konkursverfahrens mit dem Ergebnis der Liquidation von Unternehmen und Arbeitsplätzen zu beschließen oder gar zu erzwingen, wäre im Selbstverwaltungssystem auch kaum durchsetzbar gewesen.

In der Folgezeit führte diese Konstellation zu einer stetig anwachsenden Verschuldung jugoslawischer Unternehmen und des jugoslawischen Staates in Gestalt des Föderations- und der Republikhaushalte mit am Ende ruinösen inflationären Folgen für den Finanzhaushalt. Das jugoslawische Selbstverwaltungs- und Industrialisierungsmodell wurde also zu einem nicht unerheblichen Teil mit außerordentlicher Auslandsverschuldung und zerrütteten Staatsfinanzen bezahlt.

An diesem Punkt und ebenso bei der Inkompatibilität des subjektlosen gesellschaftlichen Eigentums mit inländischem oder ausländischem unternehmerischen Privateigentum, zeigten sich die strukturellen Grenzen eines „eigentumslosen" Selbstverwaltungsmodells. Es fehlte nicht nur der Haftungskonnex, sondern der an Kooperation durch Einbringung eigener Mittel interessierte inländische Mitarbeiter oder ausländische Investor verlor mit der Einbringung automatisch sein Eigentumsrecht an der Investition und blieb auf in ihrer Wirkung zweifelhafte Mitwirkungsrechte unter Berücksichtigung der Selbstverwaltungsrechte der Unternehmensmitarbeiter verwiesen. Eine – im Übrigen systemwidrige – Ausnahmeregelung zugunsten ausländischer Investoren[75] konnte hier keine grundsätzliche Abhilfe schaffen. Eine schrittweise Öffnung führte zur Zulassung privater Unternehmensgründung, Beteiligung oder Auslandstätigkeit von Ar-

---

Rechtsentwicklung liefert *Ch. Höcker-Weyand*, Die Rechtsinstitute und Rechtsinstitutionen des jugoslawischen Selbstverwaltungssystems, Osteuropa-Institut der Freien Universität Berlin. Rechtswissenschaftliche Veröffentlichungen, hrsg. von *K. Westen* und *H. Roggemann*, Bd. 9, Berlin/Baden-Baden 1980, S. 67 ff., 291 ff.

74 Das Gesetz über Zwangsvergleich und Konkursverfahren v. 04.04.1965, SL SFRJ 1965, Nr. 15, Pos. 319; zur späteren Entwicklung *Beckmann-Petey*, Das neue jugoslawische Insolvenzrecht, RIW 1991, S. 206 ff.

75 Durch eine Novelle v. 12.07.1967 zum Gesetz über die Mittel der Wirtschaftsorganisationen.

beitsorganisationen durch die Wirtschaftsgesetzgebung auf der Grundlage der Verfassung von 1974[76].

d) Selbstverwaltungsorgane und Organisation

Arbeiterselbstverwaltung entwickelte sich im Jugoslawischen Modell in verschiedenen organisatorischen Ebenen und Verfahren:

- Im *Arbeitskollektiv* als allgemeiner, kollektiver Basis der Selbstverwaltung, der jeder Betriebsangehörige vom Mitarbeiter bis zum Management mit gleichem Stimmrecht angehörte, das Arbeiterrat und Verwaltungsausschuss sowie in einem mehrstufigen Wahlverfahren unter Beteiligung kommunaler und Republikvertretungskörperschaften auch den Direktor wählte; ein im Vergleich zu anderen sozialistischen Staaten und deren Nomenklaturpraktiken undenkbares Verfahren;
- in der *Grundorganisation vereinter Arbeit* als organisatorisch, technologisch und wirtschaftlich eigenständig definierbarer mikroökonomischer Basisorganisation in Gestalt von Abteilungen oder Arbeitsgruppen innerhalb eines Betriebes, in denen „die Arbeiter unmittelbar und gleichberechtigt ihre gesellschaftlich-wirtschaftlichen und sonstigen Selbstverwaltungsrechte[77]" durch ihre ebenfalls dort gebildeten Arbeiterräte am Arbeitsplatz mithilfe ihrer gewählten Organe wahrnehmen sollten;
- in *„Selbstverwaltungsabkommen"* zwischen diesen Grundorganisationen als den untersten, selbstständig organisierbaren Betriebseinheiten, um Selbstverwaltungsentscheidungen in rechtsgeschäftlicher Form (über Arbeitsteilung, Zusammenarbeit, Investitionsplanung, Einkommensverteilung, Zusammenschluss mit anderen Grundorganisationen) auf die betriebliche Basis zu verlagern;
- im *Arbeiterrat des gesamten Unternehmens* als dem zentralen Beratungs- und Entscheidungsorgan des Arbeitskollektivs, das alle wichtigen Entscheidungen und Richtlinien für die Unternehmenstätigkeit (insbesondere z.B. Unternehmensplanung in autonomer Ausfüllung staatlicher Rahmenrichtlinien, Produktionsprogramm, Unternehmensfinanzen, Investitionsplanung und -entscheidungen, Einkommensverteilung, Personalentscheidungen) zu erlassen, die Geschäftspolitik zu bestimmen und die Exekutivorgane einschließlich des Unternehmensdirektors (gemeinsam mit Vertretern) zu wählen hatte;
- im *Verwaltungsausschuss*, dessen fünf (vom Arbeiterrat auf Zeit gewählte) Mitgliedern als kollegialem Exekutivorgan die Leitung und Kontrolle der operativen Unternehmenstätigkeit und -verwaltung oblag;

---

76 Art. 35 und 44 SFRJ-Verf. 1974; zur späteren Reform und neueren Entwicklung des jugoslawischen Gesellschaftsrechts vgl. *Beckmann-Petey*, Neues Gesellschafts- und Investitionsrecht in Jugoslawien, RIW 1989, S. 271 ff.

77 So Art. 14 Abs. 2, 36 SFRJ-Verf. 1974.

- durch den (aufgrund Ausschreibung gemeinsam durch den Arbeiterrat und eine Wahlkommission aus Arbeiterrat, Gemeindeversammlung und Republiksrat gewählten) *Direktor*, der die Entscheidungen der kollektiven Entscheidungsorgane in der täglichen Geschäftstätigkeit umzusetzen und das Unternehmen im Geschäftsverkehr zu vertreten hatte;
- durch Wahl, Berichtspflicht und Abberufung der gewählten Organe sowie Beschlüsse und Anweisungen des Arbeiterrats gegenüber Direktor und Verwaltungsausschuss.

Mit diesem Konzept ging der jugoslawische Gesetzgeber in Richtung wirtschaftsdemokratischer Partizipation der Unternehmensmitarbeiter auf dem Wege von immaterieller, informationeller Mitbestimmung zu verantwortlicher, substanzieller Selbstentscheidung zeitweilig wesentlich weiter und schuf größere Freiräume für Diskussion, Kritik und Mitwirkung, als alle vergleichbaren staatssozialistischen Arbeits- und Wirtschaftsverfassungen in Ost- und Südosteuropa. Dieser Ansatz begann nicht nur in der Arbeitswelt, sondern darüber hinaus in den gesellschaftlichen und politischen Raum zu wirken[78]. Allerdings entsprach der normative Entwurf nur teilweise und nur mit erheblichen Einschränkungen der Rechtswirklichkeit. Rückschauend bestätigt sich angesichts der Verlagerung wirtschaftlicher Entscheidungskompetenzen auf die unterste Selbstverwaltungsebene und der damit verbundenen Dezentralisierung, „dass dabei die Bedeutung der Koordinationsproblematik offenbar unterschätzt“ wurde[79].

Die Diskrepanz zwischen Selbstverwaltungsmodell und -wirklichkeit entwickelte sich im weiteren Verlauf umgekehrt proportional zum legislatorischen Aufwand: Die Regelungen in Gestalt weiterer Verfassungsergänzungen und Gesetzesnovellen wurden immer komplexer, ihre regulative Wirkung immer schwächer.

„Die Resultate unserer Untersuchung erhärten die auch von anderer Seite gestellte Diagnose einer in vielen Bereichen ihres Inhalts beraubten Arbeiterselbstverwaltung. Die grundlegende Hypothese der Untersuchung, dass nämlich „die gegenwärtige Form der ASV mit den Interessen des Managements identisch ist, und im Widerspruch zu den Interessen der Arbeiter steht“, bestätigt sich in den Ergebnissen aller drei Betriebe“[80].

---

78 Beispiele bilden die Liberalisierung von Ein- und Ausreiseregelungen, die Einfuhr ausländischer, insbesondere westlicher Literatur und Presse (Ausnahme: Kritik an Tito und Grundsatzkritik am Jugoslawischen System), Spielräume für kritische Ideologie- und Reformdiskussion (die Grenzen markierten das Verbot der „Praxis-Gruppe“ und die bis hin zu Tötungsdelikten reichende geheimdienstliche Verfolgung nationalistischer Bestrebungen im In- und Ausland durch den Jugoslawischen Geheimdienst).

79 H. *Roggemann*, Fn. 14, S. 41.

80 So im Ergebnis der umfassendsten empirischen Studie zum Selbstverwaltungssystem aus deutscher Sicht von *W. Soergel*, Fn. 73, S. 291.

e) Entwicklung der Selbstverwaltung

Diesem hier nur in seinen Umrissen nachgezeichneten Modell[81] lag kein geschlossenes Konzept zugrunde. Es verdankt seine Entstehung der Suche der damaligen jugoslawischen Führung unter *Tito*, *Djilas*, *Kardelj* und anderen nach einem ideologischen, politischen und wirtschaftlichen Neubeginn in der für die junge jugoslawische Föderation existenzbedrohenden Krise, die sich aus dem Bruch *Titos* mit *Stalin*, dem Ausschluss Jugoslawiens aus dem Kominform 1948, dem Wegfall sowjetischer Unterstützung, sich verschärfender ideologischer und politischer Auseinandersetzung des in der Folgezeit „blockfreien" Jugoslawien mit der UdSSR und anderen Mitgliedern der „Sozialistischen Staatengemeinschaft" bis hin zur militärischen Aufrüstung und Vorbereitung auf einen erneuten Partisanenkampf zur Sicherung der Unabhängigkeit für den Fall militärischer Intervention durch die Sowjetunion ergeben hatte.

Seit der nicht nur im „Sozialistischen Lager", sondern in ganz Europa Aufsehen erregenden Rede, mit der *Tito* selbst am 27.06.1950 vor der jugoslawischen Volksversammlung die neue Rechtsgrundlage der Arbeiterselbstverwaltung[82] begründete, war das Selbstverwaltungsmodell in der Wirtschafts-, Unternehmens- und Arbeitsverfassung Jugoslawiens ebenso wie in der Staatsverfassung mit ihren zahlreichen, am Ende unlesbar ausufernden Verfassungsnovellen (*Amandmani*) bis zu ihrer Selbstauflösung ständigen Änderungen ausgesetzt.

Das Jugoslawische Modell stellte sich damit einerseits als ein einzigartiges sozialökonomisches Experimentierfeld von faszinierender Dynamik und mit beachtlichen Anfangserfolgen, andererseits als risikovoller politischer Integrationsversuch dar, zu dessen Scheitern neben vielen Ursachen am Ende auch ein dramatischer Akzeptanz- und Geltungsverlust der Rechtsordnung beitrug[83].

Nicht übersehen sollte die rückschauende Suche nach Gründen für das Scheitern jedoch, dass dieses Selbstverwaltungsmodell – nur entfernt vergleichbar dem im Rahmen von Privateigentumsordnung und Marktwirtschaft entwickelten deutschen Mitbestimmungsmodell während der „Wiederaufbaujahre" und des „Wirtschaftswunders" im Nachkriegsdeutschland – in seiner Anfangsphase in Jugoslawien zu einem erheblichen Motivationsschub der Arbeiterschaft

---

81 Näher dazu *Höcker-Weyand*, Die Rechtsinstitute, S. 65 ff.; *H. Roggemann*, Das Jugoslawische Modell der Arbeiterselbstverwaltung, S. 62 ff.

82 Durch das Gesetz über die Verwaltung der staatlichen Wirtschaftsunternehmen und der oberen Wirtschaftsvereinigungen durch die Arbeitskollektive, SLJ 1950, Nr. 43, Pos. 789.

83 „Heute, nach der Verabschiedung der neuen Verfassung, besteht die Gefahr, und sie war niemals größer, dass man den alten gesellschaftlichen Verhältnissen einfach einen neuen Namen verleiht. – Den technokratischen Tendenzen kommt die Kompliziertheit des Selbstverwaltungssystems sehr entgegen. Je mehr normative Organe, Organisationsstrukturen und Beschlüsse es gibt, umso leichter lässt es sich manipulieren". So *S. Šuvar*, Slobodna Dalmacija, Split, v. 25.04.1974, zit. nach *W. Soergel*, Fn. 73, S. 294.

während der Aufbruchsstimmung der Industrialisierung des Landes beitrug. Auch der mit dem Selbstverwaltungssystem nicht nur in politischer Rhetorik sondern auch in der Praxis des Arbeitslebens immer wieder und schließlich auch in einer zunehmenden Zahl von Arbeitskämpfen eingeforderte basisdemokratische Anspruch, schuf ein verändertes Selbstbewusstsein der großteils aus bäuerlichem Umfeld stammenden Arbeiterschaft wie auch in Teilen der jüngeren akademischen Elite.

Es darf durchaus gefragt werden, ob die außerordentlichen wirtschaftlichen Erfolge Jugoslawiens während der ersten Jahrzehnte der Industrialisierung und Modernisierung des Landes[84] ohne das Arbeiterselbstverwaltungssystem und seinen Motivationsschub möglich gewesen wären[85].

2. Funktionsprobleme der Arbeiterselbstverwaltung

a) Selbstverwaltungskompetenzen, Arbeitsorganisation und Qualifikationsprobleme

Die den Selbstverwaltungsorganen – und hier wiederum, dem emanzipatorischen Anspruch des Selbstverwaltungsmodells entsprechend, primär den Basisorganen, d.h. dem Arbeitskollektiv und vor allem dem Arbeiterrat – übertragenen Kompetenzen umfassten die gesamte betriebswirtschaftliche, rechtliche und soziale Bandbreite der Unternehmensführung: Unternehmensstatut und innerbetriebliche Rechtsvorschriften, Arbeitsplanung, Organisation und Produktionsprogramm, Absatz und Preisbildung, Nutzung der Unternehmensmittel, Finanzplanung, Abschlussrechnung, Investitionen und Gewinn- und Einkommensverteilung, Personalfragen (Einstellung, Entlassung, Qualifikation), Arbeitsschutz, Werkwohnungen. Mit der schrittweisen Entlassung der jugoslawischen Wirtschaftsbetriebe aus der sozialistischen Planwirtschaft und dem Übergang von imperativer Zentralplanung zu nur indikativer Rahmenplanung, wuchsen die Anforderungen an effektives Finanzmanagement. Hatte die sozialistische Zent-

84 So nahmen Volkseinkommen und Nettodurchschnitteinkommen in dem Jahrzehnt von 1956 bis 1966 um mehr als das Sechsfache zu. Zur Entwicklung *Leman*, Ungelöste Fragen im jugoslawischen System der Arbeiterselbstverwaltung, Köln 1969; zum Verhältnis von Selbstverwaltung und Wirtschaftsentwicklung *H. Roggemann,* Fn. 81, S. 148 ff.; zusammenfassender Überblick zur Entwicklung *Sundhaussen,* Geschichte Serbiens, 19.-21. Jahrhundert, Wien/Köln/Weimar 2007, S. 354 ff.

85 Dazu *W. Leonhard,* Eine Diskussion historischer und politischer Probleme, in: *Heuer/Mombauer* (Hrsg.), Jugoslawien – Sozialismus in Osteuropa, Bd. 2, Göttingen 1973, S. 1 ff., 7; nach *W. Soergel,* Fn. 73, S. 303: „Noch 1949 im Mai waren die Losungen so typische Sowjetlosungen wie: Arbeiter, erhöht die Produktion usw. – und dann lautete plötzlich überall die Losung, spontan und echt, es war praktisch der Prager Frühling vorweggenommen: „Fabrika radnicima!“ – die Fabriken den Arbeitern! Diese Losung wurde von der Bevölkerung sofort begeistert aufgegriffen, war wirklich echt populär und nicht wie bisher von oben verordnet“.

ralplanwirtschaft sowjetischen Typs ebenso wie in der DDR noch die Verplanung der gesellschaftlichen Reproduktion als sicherste Garantie gegen „anarchistisches Marktchaos" gesehen, so wurden in Jugoslawien mit der Wirtschaftsreform von 1965 die Investitionsfonds des Bundes, der Republiken und Kommunen abgeschafft und die neugeordneten und dezentralisierten Banken übernahmen die Investitionsfinanzierung. Das erhöhte die Anforderungen an eigenverantwortliches unternehmerisches Handeln der selbstverwalteten Unternehmen.

Wohl zu keiner Zeit in der europäischen Wirtschaftsgeschichte besaßen Unternehmensmitarbeiter in einem Land ein so weitgehendes, zudem verfassungsrechtlich gesichertes, normatives Maß an wirtschaftlicher Entscheidungskompetenz. Waren damit aus „Arbeitnehmern" in dieser Entwicklungsphase des jugoslawischen Selbstverwaltungssystems „Eigenunternehmer" geworden oder wenigstens Anfangsschritte auf dem Wege zur angestrebten „Befreiung der Arbeit" in einer gerechteren Wirtschafts- und Sozialordnung getan? Oder hatte dieser Weg sich in seinem weiteren Verlauf als nicht weiterführend herausgestellt?

Jedenfalls erwiesen sich die Arbeiter als Selbstverwalter bald überfordert, die damals viel zitierte, idealistische Marx`sche Sicht vom befreiten Menschen in einer befreiten Arbeitswelt als offensichtlich unrealistisch. Der volle Einsatz am Arbeitsplatz und die professionellen Anforderungen an eine parallele inhaltliche Mitwirkung an komplexen unternehmerischen Entscheidungen waren weitgehend unvereinbar:

> „Geschäfte, für die sie (die Manager) bezahlt werden, sind nicht unsere Geschäfte, wir haben keinen Einblick in die gesamte Produktionsabwicklung. Wenn wir unsere Arbeiten ausgeführt haben, haben wir deshalb ein Recht zu fordern, dass diese Arbeit im persönlichen Einkommen und im Einkommen unserer ökonomischen Einheit anerkannt wird[86]".

Hohe Anforderungen an Fachausbildung und arbeitsteilige Spezialisierung auch im Management führten daher bald zur Bildung zusätzlicher Fachkommissionen der Arbeiterräte, zur „Zurückdelegation" von Entscheidungsmacht vom Arbeitskollektiv und Arbeiterrat an Aufsichtsrat und Unternehmensdirektoren und auch zur Usurpation von alten und neuen Kompetenzen in einem „Managersozialismus". Die Folgen waren Vertrauensverlust, „Selbstverwaltungsapathie", erneute soziale Deklassierung[87] und Rechtsunsicherheit.

---

86 So die Äußerung eines Produktionsarbeiters, zit. nach *Leman,* Ungelöste Fragen im jugoslawischen System der Arbeiterselbstverwaltung, Köln 1969, S. 40 ff.

87 Hierzu die „Frage eines Arbeiters", bei *W. Soergel*, Fn. 73, S. 31: „Wie stellen Sie sich angesichts dieser sozialen Unterschiede unseren Sozialismus vor: man weiß ja, wer alles eine eigene Yacht, Wochenendhaus, Auto und sogar drei Wohnungen besitzt; aber der Arbeiter, der ehrlich schafft und arbeitet, hat nichts, nicht einmal genügend Geld zum Sattwerden…"

Neben Problemen mangelnder „Selbstverwaltungsqualifikation" einer vorwiegend aus der Landwirtschaft rekrutierten Arbeiterschaft der ersten Periode der jugoslawischen Industrialisierung sowie unentbehrlicher Arbeitsteilung und Spezialisierung, stellte sich die Praxis der Arbeiterselbstverwaltung als übermäßig kompliziert und zeitaufwendig heraus. Noch in den siebziger Jahren besaßen bis zu 50% der Betriebe in verschiedenen Branchen nicht die gesetzlich vorgesehene statutenmäßige Rechtsgrundlage[88] für die Anwendung des anspruchsvollen Selbstverwaltungsverfahrens.

Der Ausweg bestand für viele jugoslawische Unternehmen darin, die Partizipation der Arbeiterräte auf wichtige Grundsatzentscheidungen zu beschränken und die operative Betriebsführung im Übrigen dem professionellen Management zu überlassen. Eine solche pragmatische Lösung sollte nicht als enttäuschender Abschied vom Grundgedanken partizipatorischer Unternehmensverfassung kritisiert[89], sondern als realistische Beschränkung auf deren praktikables Maß angesehen werden. Dass gut ausgebildete, umfassend informierte und über die wirtschaftliche Situation des Unternehmens aufgeklärte Mitarbeiter durchaus in der Lage sind, klar formulierte Grundsatzfragen zu verstehen und notwendige Entscheidungen gegebenenfalls mitzutragen, haben erfolgreich praktizierte Mitarbeiterbeteiligungsmodelle in Deutschland und anderen EU-Ländern, vornehmlich in England und Frankreich, vielfach bewiesen[90]. Doch vergleichbare Voraussetzungen waren in der jugoslawischen Industriearbeiterschaft der ersten Generation kaum gegeben.

b) Systemimmanente Interessenkonflikte

Das eigentliche Strukturproblem aller Formen immaterieller und materieller Partizipation der Unternehmensmitarbeiter stellt die Einbeziehung in das jeweilige Eigentumssystem dar. Dieses Problem erfuhr im sozialistischen Jugoslawischen Modell eine eigenartige Zuspitzung. Mit dem „subjektlosen" Gesellschaftseigentum war der eigentumstypische Motivations- und Haftungszusammenhang – mit den bereits dargelegten negativen Folgen einschließlich fehlenden Eigentümerrisikos – verloren gegangen. Gleichzeitig aber wurde mit der nur teilweisen Ent-

---

88 Die im Gesetz über die Konstituierung und die Eintragung des Organisation vereinter Arbeit ins gerichtliche Register v. 13.05.1973, SLJ 1973, Nr. 22, Pos. 309 vorgesehen war, dazu *H. Roggemann*, Fn. 14, S. 42.

89 Zum Ziel, „die bürokratischen Deformationen des stalinistischen Entwicklungsmodells zu vermeiden", *W. Soergel*, Fn. 73, S. 20.

90 Bestandsaufnahme bei *Lowitzsch/Hashi/Woodward* (eds.), The PEPPER IV Report: Benchmarking of Employee Participation in Profits and Enterprise Results in the Member and Candidate Countries of the European Union, Berlin 2009, S. 216 ff.; zum bei der Aufbringung des Beteiligungskapitals sowie bei der Ausschüttung des Beteiligungsgewinns differenzierten und anspruchsvollen Pieroth-Beteiligungsmodell vgl. *Menrad*, Die soziale Offensive. Manifest für Vermögensbildung und Eigentum in Arbeitnehmerhand, Berlin/Schwäbisch Hall 2005, S. 15 ff.

lassung der Unternehmen in eine „sozialistische Marktwirtschaft" ein gewisser staatswirtschaftlicher Vorbehalt weiterhin aufrechterhalten (z.B. Finanzplanung, Außenwirtschaft, Finanzfondssystem, Nichtanwendung geltenden (Konkurs-)Rechts) und ein voll funktionsfähiger Markt mit der Möglichkeit der Bildung durchgängig marktkonformer Preise war nicht gegeben. Eine institutionell manifestierte Trennung der Interessenvertretung des zu bewirtschaftenden Gesellschaftseigentums in Gestalt des Unternehmens und seiner Mittel einerseits und der Arbeitnehmerinteressen andererseits, bestand nicht mehr. Vielmehr hatten Arbeitskollektiv und vor allem der Arbeiterrat als das zentrale Selbstverwaltungsorgan diesen Interessenkonflikt selbst in sich zu formulieren und auszutragen. Die leitenden Organe der Unternehmensführung (Direktor, Verwaltungsrat) waren nicht als rechtlich eigenständige Funktionsträger konzipiert, sondern als vom Arbeiterrat allein oder im Zusammenwirken mit kommunalen Vertretern gewählte, abhängige, (theoretisch) weisungsgebundene Ausführungsorgane. Dass dieses normative Konzept der Rechtswirklichkeit oft nicht entsprach, und sich die Management- und Führungsebene gegenüber der Arbeiterschaft bald wieder zu verselbstständigen begann, wurde bereits gesagt.

Während der am Unternehmenskapital beteiligte Mitarbeiter in einer auf Privateigentum basierenden Marktwirtschaft nach deutschem Modell zusammen mit dem Unternehmensträger und anderen Anteilseigentümern das partielle und eigentumsrechtlich konkretisierte Eigentümerrisiko (mit)trägt[91] und seine durch Eigentum und Mitarbeit vermittelten Rechte auf Partizipation am Prozess unternehmerischer Entscheidungsfindung sich grundsätzlich auf die limitierten gesellschaftsrechtlichen Mitwirkungsbefugnisse (Gesellschaftervertretung, Hauptversammlung) und im Übrigen auf die überwiegend immateriellen, gegebenenfalls kollektivvertraglich konkretisierten Mitwirkungs- und Mitbestimmungsrechte und das von den Gesellschaftsorganen definierte Dividendenrecht beschränken[92], war dies im Jugoslawischen Modell anders angelegt:

> „Der Arbeiter hat das Recht, aufgrund seines Arbeitsbeitrages und abhängig von den Arbeits- und Geschäftsergebnissen der Arbeitseinheit, bei der er arbeitet, und der

---

91 Vorausgesetzt es handelt sich um eine Beteiligung am Eigenkapital des arbeitgebenden Unternehmens. Fremdkapitalbeteiligungen z.B. in der Form von Mitarbeiterdarlehen oder Wandelschuldverschreibungen sind durch Bankbürgschaften oder Versicherungen gegen Insolvenzrisiko abzusichern, wenn die Steuervergünstigung in Anspruch genommen werden soll, vgl. § 2 Abs. 1 Ziff. 1 Buchst. k und l des Fünften Ges. z. Förderung der Vermögensbildung der Arbeitnehmer (5. VermBG), dazu *Bontrup*, Der Vorschlag der Bundesregierung für „Mehr Mitarbeiterkapitalbeteiligung in Deutschland", BB-Special 1/2009, S. 2 ff.; kritisch *K. R. Wagner*, Fn. 39 (Anm. 12), S. 129 f.

92 Soweit diese Mitentscheidungsrechte nicht reduziert oder sogar durch Vereinbarung ausgeschlossen sind, dazu *H. Roggemann*, Fn. 23, S. 120 ff.; *ders.*, ZRP 2011, S. 49 ff., 52.

> Arbeitsorganisation insgesamt, an der Verteilung der Mittel, die das Arbeitskollektiv für das persönliche Einkommen ausgibt, teilzunehmen[93]".

Diese Arbeitsrechtsnorm, die in späteren Bestimmungen des jugoslawischen Gesetz- und Verfassungsgebers wesentlich komplexer formuliert werden sollte, enthält den grundlegenden und, wie die weitere Entwicklung des Selbstverwaltungsmodells zeigt, offenbar unlösbaren Interessenkonflikt. Der Selbstverwalter selbst ist zugleich sein eigener und der Interessenwalter des von ihm verwalteten Unternehmens: Von „wahren Erdbeben" war die Rede, „wenn die Umschüttung des Einkommens von einer Arbeitseinheit in die andere und die Deckung der Verluste beginnt. Das sind ganze Dramen, die das große Kollektiv erregen[94]".

Insbesondere, soweit es um notwendige Investitionsentscheidungen- und Rationalisierungsmaßnahmen ging, um Modernisierung und künftige Wettbewerbsfähigkeit der Unternehmen zu sichern und gegen kurzfristige Einkommens- und Konsuminteressen durchzusetzen, erwies sich eine rationale Entscheidungsfindung als zunehmend schwierig oder gar unmöglich. Die Selbstverwalter gaben oft kurzfristigen Einkommensinteressen den Vorrang vor langfristigen Investitionsinteressen. Hinzu kam, dass – insoweit vergleichbar dem strukturellen Defizit anonymisierter Fondslösungen bei der Mitarbeiterbeteiligung in marktwirtschaftlichen Systemen – das subjektlose Gesellschaftseigentum des jugoslawischen Unternehmens und sein schwer kalkulierbarer Markterfolg keinen genügend konkreten Bezug zur individuellen Arbeitsleitung des einzelnen Mitarbeiters und dessen Entlohnung ermöglichte.

Substanzielle immaterielle und materielle Partizipationsrechte sind, wie sich hieran zeigt, ohne Rückbindung an Privateigentum mit seinen herkömmlichen Rechtsgarantien und ohne ein hinreichend differenziertes und durchsetzbares gesellschaftsrechtliches und arbeitsrechtliches Instrumentarium mit entsprechender Zuordnung von Dispositionsmacht, Verantwortung und Haftung, offenbar nicht erfolgversprechend organisierbar. Als ursächlich für bis heute nachwirkende mangelnde Wettbewerbsfähigkeit der Industrie in Jugoslawien und seinen Nachfolgestaaten seit 1990/1991 wird man daher nicht nur Spätfolgen von Krieg und Staatszerfall, sondern wohl auch im Selbstverwaltungssystem angelegte Modernisierungs- und Rationalisierungshemmnisse anzusehen haben.

c) Selbstverwaltungsdemokratie und Föderalismus versus Parteiherrschaft

Normative Ansätze wirtschaftlicher sowie politischer Demokratisierung, Dezentralisierung und Machtbegrenzung, die sowohl im jugoslawischen Selbstverwaltungssystem als auch im politischen Delegiertensystem und dem schließlich bis an die Grenze zur Unregierbarkeit fortentwickelten föderativen Staatsaufbau angelegt waren, konnten sich unter der Decke einer Einparteiherrschaft

---

93 Art. 78 Abs. I Grundsatzgesetz über die Arbeitsverhältnisse von 1965.

94 So *Borba* v. 25.02.1969, nach *Leman*, Fn. 84, S. 80.

nicht weiterentwickeln. An diesem Herrschaftsmodell versuchte der Bund der Kommunisten Jugoslawiens, insbesondere dessen Serbische Republiksorganisation, bis zum Ende des Bundesstaates mit allen Mitteln festzuhalten[95]. Forderungen nach demokratischer Öffnung des politischen Systems durch Einführung eines pluralistischen Wahlsystems stellten sich aus der Sicht des (noch) geltenden politischen Strafrechts der SFR Jugoslawien als Verstoß gegen Grundwerte der „Brüderlichkeit und Einheit" dar und wurden politisch als „Verrat am Titoismus" zurückgewiesen. Neben den oben dargestellten Strukturproblemen der Selbstverwaltung wird man in diesem Demokratiedefizit des auf den Staatsgründer zentrierten „Tito-Sozialismus" eine weitere wesentliche Ursache für das letztendliche Scheitern des faszinierenden Jugoslawischen Modells zu sehen haben[96].

Die Entschlossenheit der damaligen jugoslawischen Führung zu weitgehender Kompetenzverlagerung auf die unterste Ebene und die damit verbundene Dezentralisierung konnte einerseits Freiräume für eigenverantwortliche, d.h. selbstverwaltete Entscheidungen schaffen, führte aber andererseits zwangsläufig zum Verlust zentraler Steuerbarkeit. Traten an die Stelle imperativer Wirtschaftsverwaltungsvorschriften – wie sie in allen anderen staatssozialistischen Länder geläufig waren – noch rechtsgeschäftliche Selbstregulierungsmechanismen nach Art der „Selbstverwaltungsvereinbarungen", so musste dies zu weiterem normativem Regelungsverlust führen.

Dieser Weg hätte möglicherweise dann ohne verlustreiche Fehlentwicklungen beschritten werden können, wenn die essentielle Zuordnungsfunktion von Kompetenz und Haftung durch Privateigentum und der Interessenvermittlungs- und Austauschmechanismus eines funktionsfähigen Marktes und daneben ein demokratischer Entscheidungsfindung offenes, pluralistisches politisches Sys-

---

95 Dazu näher *O. Haberl*, Parteiorganisation und nationale Frage in Jugoslawien, Diss. FU Berlin 1974; *H. Roggemann*, Krieg und Frieden auf dem Balkan, 1993, S. 34 ff.; *ders.*, Zur Verfassungsdiskussion in der SFR Jugoslawien, ROW 1989, S. 273 ff.; zu der von *E. Pusić* bereits 1987 erhobenen Forderung nach Einführung eines Mehrparteiensystems vgl. *Kregar/Smerdel/Šimonović*: Die Verfassung der Republik Kroatien: Politische Rahmenbedingungen und grundlegende Probleme, in: *Marko/Borić* (Hrsg.), Slowenien – Kroatien – Serbien. Die neuen Verfassungen, Wien/Köln/Graz 1991, S. 205 ff., 208.

96 Ein anschauliches spätes Beispiel bietet die Schiffswerft in Split, einer der drei großen Industriebetriebe, der vor rund 30 Jahren auch Gegenstand der empirischen Untersuchung zur Situation des Selbstverwaltungssystems im damaligen Jugoslawien von *W. Soergel* war. In Anbetracht technologischen Rückstands, international allenfalls bedingt wettbewerbsfähiger Produktionsstandards und ineffektiver Arbeitsorganisation schlugen deutsche Werftsachverständige im Sommer 2010 tiefgreifende Restrukturierungsmaßnahmen durch massiven Personalabbau, Modernisierungsinvestitionen und Umstellung des gesamten Produktionsprogramms auf Spezialaufträge und „Nischenprodukte" vor, um dem Unternehmen eine „Überlebenschance" zu eröffnen. Der Vorschlag führte zu heftigen Diskussionen in und um diesen bis heute (Frühjahr 2011) noch nicht erfolgversprechend privatisierten und restrukturierten Staatsbetrieb.

tem gegeben gewesen wären. Diese Voraussetzungen waren aber in Jugoslawien aus einer Reihe von Gründen gar nicht (Eigentum) oder nur partiell (Marktwirtschaft), im politischen Raum ebenfalls nicht (Einparteiherrschaft des Bundes der Kommunisten) der Fall.

Wirtschaftsdemokratischer und politischer Machtkontrolle sollte ein weitgreifendes Wahl- und Rotationssystem mit Abberufungsrecht sowohl in Unternehmen als in Vertretungskörperschaften auf kommunaler, Republiks- und Föderationsebene dienen. Mitglieder des Arbeiterrats sollten sich alle zwei, Mitglieder der Geschäftsleitung alle vier Jahre Neuwahlen stellen, der Direktor war vom Rotationszwang, nicht dagegen vom Wahlverfahren ausgenommen. Diese Wahlregelungen waren in anderen sozialistischen Ländern ohne Beispiel. Sie wurden allerdings auch in Jugoslawien in zahlreichen Fällen nicht eingehalten.

Überdies gab ein abgestuftes Delegationssystem, in dem die Wahlbürgern als einfache Wähler und zusätzlich als Unternehmensangehörige in Industrie, Landwirtschaft und Gewerbe wahlberechtigt waren, zwar den als Werktätige, Wähler und Wahlmänner beteiligten Bürgern zusätzliche Partizipationsmöglichkeiten, zugleich aber auch dem sozialistischen Bund und dem Bund der Kommunisten Mittel und Wege, um in diesem unübersichtlichen Verfahren politisch maßgeblichen Einfluss auf Kandidatenaufstellung und Wahlablauf bei den Wahlen zu Gemeindevertretungen, Republiksversammlungen und Bundesversammlung mit ihren jeweiligen Mehrkammersystemen zu nehmen.

Das „verfassungspolitische und verfassungsrechtliche Wagnis des jugoslawischen Bundesstaates, auf dem schmalen Weg zwischen Föderation und Konföderation weiter voranzuschreiten[97]“, führte zu einem „kooperativen Föderalismus“ neuer Art und von fragiler Struktur. Dieser räumte den Gliedstaaten die Stellung „vollständiger staatsrechtlicher Rechtssubjekte“ ein[98] und verlieh ihnen über die obligatorischen Mitwirkungsrechte der Delegationen der Republiken im Rat der Republiken und Provinzen in der Bundesversammlung der SFRJ praktisch ein Vetorecht in allen wichtigen, republikszustimmungsbedürftigen Gesetzgebungsverfahren.

Ein Gegengewicht gegen diese auf der Ebene der Volksvertretungen sehr weit – aus kritischer Sicht bereits zu weit – fortgeschrittene Föderalisierung, die damit zugleich verfassungsrechtlich das Tor für eine Re-Nationalisierung innerhalb des jugoslawischen Bundesstaates geöffnet hatte, sollte neben dem Staatspräsidenten (*Tito* auf Lebenszeit) das neue Kollegialorgan des Präsidiums der SFRJ bilden. Um diese nationalitätenintegrierende Funktion ausfüllen zu kön-

---

97 Näher zum föderativen Staatsaufbau und zur Staatsqualität der Gliedstaaten *H. Roggemann*, Fn. 14, S. 48 ff.; *Beckmann-Petey*, Der jugoslawische Föderalismus, München 1990; *L. Schultz*, Die neue Verfassung der Sozialistischen Föderativen Republik Jugoslawien v. 21. Februar 1974, JOR Bd. XI/1 (1974), S. 7 ff.

98 So *Gerškovič/Djokič* u.a. (Hrsg.), Ustavi i ustavni zakoni (Verfassungen und Verfassungsgesetze), Zagreb 1974, S. 525 ff., 530.

nen, sah die Verfassung eine paritätische Zusammensetzung aus neun Mitgliedern, je einem Vertreter der sechs Gliedstaaten, der beiden Autonomen Provinzen Kosovo und Vojvodina und dem Präsidenten des Bundes der Kommunisten von Amts wegen vor.

Das bis in die Staatsspitze durchgeführte Rotationsprinzip sollte die politische Partizipation der Gliedstaaten und damit ihrer Nationalitäten durch den turnusmäßigen Wechsel des Präsidenten dieses Präsidiums mit nur einjähriger Amtszeit sicherstellen. Dieses Verfahren wurde jedoch zunächst und bis zu *Titos* Tod 1980 durch dessen Lebenszeitmandat als Staatspräsident überspielt und trat erst danach in Funktion. Nach dem Verfassungsstreich von 1989 und der Entziehung der wesentlichen Rechtsgrundlagen des Autonomiestatus der beiden Autonomen Provinzen durch den serbischen Verfassungsgeber, wurde dieses Integrationsinstrument jedoch funktionsunfähig und zu einem Instrument großserbischer Politik in den sich verschärfenden nationalen Konflikten, denen der auf grundsätzliche föderative Kooperationsbereitschaft zugeschnittene Rahmen der „Selbstverwaltungsverfassung“ und ihre rätedemokratischen Absicherungsversuche gegen politischen Machtmissbrauch nicht standhielten[99]. Auch ein letzter, von allen anderen Gliedstaaten getragener Versuch, die Jugoslawische Sozialistische Föderation in eine demokratische Konföderation umzuwandeln, scheiterte am serbischen Widerspruch.

3. Von der Selbstverwaltung zur Mitarbeiterbeteiligung im postsozialistischen Sozialstaat

Mit der Wiedereinsetzung des Privateigentums als Grundlage einer Privatrechts- und Marktwirtschaftsordnung im Zuge der Transformation in Ost- und Südosteuropa, stellte sich nunmehr die Frage nach immaterieller und materieller Partizipation des Arbeitnehmers erneut oder wieder im Rahmen postsozialistischer Sozialstaatsverfassung. Aus selbstverwaltenden Werktätigen sind lohnabhängige Arbeitnehmer im traditionellen Sinne des nationalen und europäischen Arbeitsrechts geworden. Die neuen Verfassungen der postjugoslawischen Staaten sind zur überkommenen Technik und Sprache der Verfassungsgesetzgebung mit entsprechendem Grundrechtsteil zurückgekehrt. Einzelne Verfassungen stellen die sozialökonomischen Grundrechte in den Rahmen allgemeiner Sozialstaatsgarantien[100]. Oder gewähren auch zusätzliche (fakultative) Mitwirkungsmöglichkeiten

---

99 Zur Wirkungsgrenze des jugoslawischen Föderalismus vgl. *B. Lukšić*, Die Erneuerung von Rechtsstaat und Rechtswissenschaft, in *Roggemann/Sundhaussen* (Hrsg.), Ost- und Südosteuropa zwischen Tradition und Aufbruch, Berlin und Wiesbaden 1996, S. 211 ff., 213.;

100 Art. 1 Verf. Serbien v. 28.09.1990 zählt „soziale Gerechtigkeit“ ausdrücklich zu den Fundamentalnormen der Verfassung, kennt in Art. 34 ein Recht auf Arbeit, im Übrigen aber keinerlei Mitwirkungs- oder Teilhaberechte. Auch Art. 1 Abs. 1 der Makedonischen Verf v. 17.11.1991 bezeichnet Makedonien als „Sozialstaat“, normiert aber keine

wie die Verf. Kroatien[101]: „*Die Beschäftigten können im Einklang mit dem Gesetz an den Entscheidungen im Unternehmen teilhaben*". „Sozialistische Überreste" können in dieser schwachen Erinnerung an die hohen programmatischen Ansprüche der jugoslawischen Selbstverwaltungsverfassung wohl kaum gefunden werden[102]. Weitergehende, grundrechtliche immaterielle Mitwirkungs- oder materielle Teilhaberechte kennen die geltenden Sozialstaatsverfassungen der postjugoslawischen Staaten nicht. Ob aus der verfassungsmäßigen Erwähnung eines fakultativen immateriellen „Mitentscheidungsrechts" der verfassungsmäßige Ausschluss eines darüber hinaus gehenden gesetzlichen materiellen Teilhaberechts zu schließen ist, erscheint fraglich und zu verneinen. Der kroatische Arbeitsgesetzgeber hat von der fakultativen Ermächtigung Gebrauch gemacht und in Art. 132-158 des kroatischen Arbeitsgesetzbuchs[103] die immaterielle Mitbestimmung ausführlich geregelt.

Die kroatische Verfassungslehre versteht die Vorschrift i.S.v. „Mitentscheidung und Aufsicht der Beschäftigten über die Unternehmenstätigkeit, nicht dagegen Selbstverwaltung, deren Grundlage die aufgegebene Konzeption des gesellschaftlichen Eigentums war[104]". Unter Bezugnahme auf die „deutsche Mitbestimmung" wird die Grundlage dieser Regelung treffend in der „Idee der Wirtschaftsdemokratie" und Partizipation „insbesondere in kapitalistischen Unternehmen" gesehen, wie sie die Entwicklung der gegenwärtigen demokratischen und sozialen Verfassungsstaaten begleite[105]. Damit hat die postsozialistische Rechtstheorie den Gedanken der Partizipation in den Argumentations- und Regelungszusammenhang einer marktwirtschaftlichen Sozialstaatsverfassung zurückgeführt. Ihn als Teil eines bereits vormarxistischen Programms sozialer Gerechtigkeit im Rahmen eines neuen europäischen Sozialstaatsmodells[106] auf der Grundlage von Privateigentum und Marktwirtschaft weiterzuentwickeln, ist Aufgabe des begonnenen europäischen Rechtsgesprächs.

Mitwirkungsrechte. Während die Verf. Kroatien v. 1990 i.d.F. v. 06.07.2010 , insoweit ähnlich Art. 20 Abs. 1 GG, Kroatien als „demokratischen und sozialen Staat" bezeichnet.

101 So Art. 56 Abs. 4 Verf. Kroatien.

102 Dazu *Küpper*, Sozialistische Überreste in den Verfassungen der neuen EU-Mitgliedsstaaten im Lichte des gemeinschaftsrechtlichen Homogenitätsgebots, JOR 2/2007, S. 203 ff.

103 Zakon o radu v. 1959, Narodne Novine (NN) 38/95 i.d.F. 17/2001.

104 So B. *Smerdel*, Grundzüge der Verfassungsordnung der Republik Kroatien. Zum zwanzigsten Jahrestag der "Weihnachtsverfassung", in: Verfassung der Republik Kroatien, bereinigter Text, Zagreb 2010, S. 85 ff., 129 f.

105 Dazu *A. Bačić*, Komentar. Ustava Republike Hrvatske, Split 2003, S. 161 f.

106 Näher *Lowitzsch* u.a., Fn. 39.

VI. Schlussbemerkung: Ost-, West- und Europäische Perspektiven

Neben und über den ebenfalls fakultativen europäischen Rechtsrahmen hinaus können sich aber substanzielle Teilhaberechte von Unternehmensmitarbeitern in den einzelnen ost- und südosteuropäischen Staaten aus deren Privatisierungsgesetzgebung ergeben[107].

Angesichts aktueller sozialstruktureller Entwicklungen und deren als „*Gerechtigkeitslücke*" kritisierten, oben des näheren dargelegten sozialen Verwerfungen in alten und neuen Wirtschaftsdemokratien Europas und EU-Mitglieds- oder Kandidatenländern, ist die Frage nach wirkungsvoller materieller Mitarbeiterbeteiligung zu einer aktuellen Aufgabe des Sozialstaatsgesetzgebers geworden: Es geht langfristig darum, immaterielle Mitbestimmung durch materielle Mitbeteiligung zu ergänzen und damit das bisherige strukturelle Defizit bei der Verwirklichung des sozialökonomischen Partizipationsgrundrechts im System des marktwirtschaftlichen, auf Privateigentum gründenden Rechtsstaats der Leistungsgesellschaft zu überwinden.

In Deutschland, wo Recht und Praxis materieller Mitarbeiterbeteiligung im Gegensatz zur immateriellen Mitbestimmung – im europäischen Vergleich – bislang unterentwickelt sind, hat der Bundesgesetzgeber kürzlich in Gestalt des Mitarbeiterkapitalbeteiligungsgesetzes (MKBG) von 2009 einen vielbeachteten neuen Anlauf in dieser Richtung unternommen. Dieser Versuch des Gesetzgebers stellt sich bei näherer Prüfung allerdings als unzureichend heraus[108]. Um dem dargelegten unabweisbaren sozial- und wirtschaftspolitischen Regelungsbedarf des Sozialstaatsgesetzgebers in Anbetracht vielfältiger Gründe für mehr und wirksamere finanzielle Mitarbeiterbeteiligung in der Leistungsgesellschaft gerecht zu werden, bedarf dieser Ansatz weiterer Reformschritte.

Auf europäischer Ebene sind hierzu durch den Europäischen Wirtschafts- und Sozialausschuss (EWSA) im Jahre 2010 neue Initiativen zur Mitarbeiterbeteiligung erarbeitet worden[109]. Diese in den alten und neuen Mitgliedsstaaten sowie den südosteuropäischen Kandidatenländern der EU auf breiter Grundlage zu entwickeln und wirksam umzusetzen, stellt eine gemeinsame Aufgabe der Rechtslehre und Gesetzgebung in West-, Ost- und Südosteuropa dar.

Und damit auch für die von *F.-C. Schroeder* so erfolgreich und nachhaltig geforderte, geförderte und weiterentwickelte Ostrechtswissenschaft in Regens-

107 Für Kroatien vgl. *S. Goić* in *Lowitzsch/Hashi/Woodward* (eds.), Fn. 90, S. 69 ff.; für Polen, Tschechien und die Slowakei vgl. *Lowitzsch*, Eigentum und Beteiligung – Am Beispiel des polnischen, tschechischen und slowakischen Modells, Berlin 2002.

108 Näher dazu *H. Roggemann*, Fn. 23, S. 131 ff.; *ders.*, Das Mitarbeiterkapitalbeteiligungsgesetz von 2009. Eine Rechtspolitische Kritik, ZRP 2011, S. 49 ff.

109 Initiativstellungnahme des EWSA SOC/371 (2010).

burg, München, Berlin, Köln, Kiel, Hamburg, Dresden, Frankfurt/Oder und andernorts in Deutschland.

Rechtswissenschaft in Ost und West

Beinahe 20 Jahre nach dem Ende der Sowjetunion – Was ist in der russischen Völkerrechtslehre von der sozialistischen Völkerrechtslehre übrig geblieben?

Ao. Prof. Dr. Michael Geistlinger[*]

I. Einleitende und grundlegende Bemerkungen

E. A. Korovin, einer derjenigen sowjetischen Völkerrechtsgelehrten, die als erste nach den Wirren der Oktoberrevolution zu einem System des Völkerrechts aus marxistisch-leninistischer Sicht fanden, wählte eine sehr plastische Darstellung, die es immer wieder wert ist, sich in Erinnerung zu rufen:

„Nachdem wir den Begriff des Völkerrechts der Übergangsperiode als eines örtlichen völkerrechtlichen Systems (vgl. z.B. das amerikanische Völkerrecht), entstanden durch den Eintritt in die internationale Gemeinschaft der bürgerlichen Staaten einer sozialistisch organisierten Gesellschaft, feststellten, die wichtigsten methodologischen Handgriffe, die dem gegebenen Zweig der Rechtswissenschaft eigen sind, herausarbeiteten, überblickten wir – unvermeidlich schematisch – die wichtigsten Probleme des modernen internationalen öffentlichen Rechts.

Die alten Rechtsnormen bekamen unter unseren Augen den Abglanz eines neuen Lebens. Bei der Berührung mit seinem lebendig machenden Atem stürzten und zerfielen einige Rechtsnormen, wie Haufen verfaulender Knochen, verwandelten sich andere, den dunklen Schimmel der Geschichte abwaschend, um die mächtigen Forderungen des laufenden Tages zu beantworten, erstanden dritte aus den Gräbern der tiefen Vergangenheit auf, die greisen Formen mit dem Inhalt der Neuheit erfüllend.

Aber in diesem Schmelzofen der rechtlichen Umschmelzung überragten zwei juristische Typen die übrigen: die Schaffung neuer und das lebendig Machen abgelebter Formen.[1]"

Drei Generationen von Ostrechtswissenschaftlern verfolgten den Gang dieser Lehre und fanden heraus, dass sie nicht statisch auf dem Boden *E. A. Korovins* verblieb, sondern sich fortentwickelte und sich Perioden bilden

---

* Ao. Professor am Fachbereich Öffentliches Recht, Universität Salzburg.

1 *E. A. Korovin*, Meždunarodnoe pravo perechodnogo vremeni. Moskva-Petrograd 1925[2] (Nachdruck: Berlin 1971), 135; dt: Das Völkerrecht der Übergangszeit. Berlin-Grunewald 1929 (Übersetzung der zweiten russischen Auflage: *I. Robinson-Kaunas*), 141.

ließen. Dabei zeigt die Zusammenschau der Werke von *B. Meissner*, *G. Brunner*, *O. Luchterhandt*, *Th. Schweisfurth*, *H.-J. Uibopuu*, *D. Frenzke* und anderen – jedenfalls auch – völkerrechtlich orientierten Spezialisten zum Sowjetrecht mit den staats- und rechtstheoretischen Schriften des Jubilars, dass die Periodenbildung, die für die sowjetische sozialistische Völkerrechtslehre – allen voran durch *B. Meissner* – herausgearbeitet wurde, Hand in Hand mit den generellen Entwicklungslinien verläuft, die *F.-C. Schroeder* für die sowjetische Rechtstheorie erhoben hat. Interessante Parallelen und Zusammenhänge ergeben sich so, wenn man *F.-C. Schroeders* wegweisenden Beitrag „Fünfzig Jahre sowjetische Rechtstheorie[2]" mit *B. Meissners* großer Arbeit „Die Entwicklungstendenzen in der sowjetischen außenpolitischen Theorie und Völkerrechtslehre 1962–1973[3]" vergleicht.

So fällt die Periode der sogenannten friedlichen Koexistenz, deren Beginn *B. Meissner* mit dem XX. Parteitag der KPdSU (Februar 1956) ansetzt[4], bemerkenswerter- und konsequenterweise mit dem Richtungswechsel zusammen, den *N. Chruščev* auf dem XXI. und XXII. Parteitag der KPdSU 1959 und 1961 hinsichtlich des Absterbens von Staat und Recht einleitete. *N. Chruščev* deutete, wie *F.-C. Schroeder* hervorhob, das Absterben des Staates um in die „Verwandlung der sozialistischen Staatlichkeit in die gesellschaftliche kommunistische Selbstverwaltung, in der einheitliche, allgemein anerkannte Regeln des kommunistischen Zusammenlebens bestehen …", parallel zur neuen Konzeption des Sowjetstaates als „Staat des gesamten Volkes"[5]. Ähnliche Parallelen könnten auch für die Perioden davor aufgezeigt werden[6].

Noch ein zweiter Gedanke ist *F.-C. Schroeders* rechtstheoretischen Schriften mit Gewinn für eine retrospektive Betrachtung des Völkerrechts im Übergang von der Sowjetzeit zur postsowjetischen Zeit unter besonderer Beachtung des Schicksals der sozialistischen Völkerrechtslehre zu entnehmen: Rechtstheo-

---

2 In: *R. Maurach*, *B. Meissner* (Hrsg.), 50 Jahre Sowjetrecht. Stuttgart, Berlin, Köln, Mainz 1969, 52–77.

3 In: *B. Meissner*, *D. Frenzke*, *E. Chilecki* (Hrsg.), Sowjetunion und Völkerrecht 1962-1973. Bibliographie und Analyse. Köln 1977, 9–58.

4 *B. Meissner* (Fn. 3), 25.

5 *F.-C. Schroeder* (Fn. 2), 67.

6 *K. Grzybowski*, Soviet Public International Law. Doctrines and Diplomatic Practice. Leyden, Durham 1970, 3, fasst die westliche völkerrechtliche Einschätzung zur Entwicklung der sowjetischen sozialistischen Völkerrechtslehre in folgende Perioden davor zusammen: Periode I: bis 1930 (endet in der sowjetischen Rechtstheorie gemeinsam mit dem sogenannten Tribunal über Pašukanis (dazu *F.-C. Schroeder* (Fn. 2), 59); Periode II: 1930–1938 (Das Ende dieser Periode bezeichnen die Thesen *A. J. Vyšinskijs*, und zwar, was sowohl die Rechtstheorie als auch die Völkerrechtslehre anbelangt (siehe dazu *F.-C. Schroeder* (Fn. 2), 60–62)); Periode III: 1938–1953 (Stalinistische Periode bestimmt durch die Dogmen von *A. J. Vyšinskij* (siehe dazu *F.-C. Schroeder* (Fn. 2), 62-64)).

rie wie Völkerrechtslehre standen vor der Aufgabe, „Recht“ und „Realität“ miteinander in Einklang zu bringen. Das Auseinanderfallen von „*Law in the books*“ und „*Law in action*“ stellte, wie *F.-C. Schroeder* zutreffend hervorhob, das Kernproblem für jede Analyse des sowjetischen Rechts dar[7]. Festzustellen, inwieweit Völkerrecht und seine dogmatische Behandlung für die Zwecke der sowjetischen Außenpolitik instrumentalisiert wurde und damit die Völkerrechtstheorie zur Verschleierung sowjetischer außenpolitischer Interessen herhalten musste, Recht so zur Fassade verkam, war zur gesamten Zeit der Existenz der Sowjetunion eine zentrale Aufgabe der westlichen Beobachtung der sowjetischen sozialistischen Völkerrechtslehre[8].

Bedenkt man, dass das zweite Charakteristikum der sowjetischen sozialistischen Völkerrechtslehre über alle ihre Perioden hinweg in ihrer Bindung an die marxistisch-leninistische Ideologie lag, so hatten innerstaatliche Rechtsreformen in Russland nach dem Ende der Sowjetunion die gleiche zentrale Aufgabe zu meistern wie ein neuer Zugang zur Betrachtung des Völkerrechts durch die russische Völkerrechtslehre: die Emanzipation von marxistisch-leninistischer Ideologie. Der Jubilar hat in seinem Beitrag über die Probleme der Gesetzgebung in Russland zu dem von ihm herausgegebenen Sammelband „Die neuen Kodifikationen in Russland“ die Wege aufgezeigt, wie diese Aufgabe im russischen Recht gelöst wurde, bzw. welche Schwierigkeiten sich auftaten[9]. Hinsichtlich der Völkerrechtslehre wäre diese Aufgabe erheblich einfacher zu meistern gewesen. Man hätte nicht einmal ausländische Experten heranziehen müssen[10], sondern es hätte genügt, sich dem Standpunkt der sogenannten klassischen oder westlichen Völkerrechtslehre einfach anzuschließen, hätte es nicht das Problem gegeben, dass Völkerrechtsgelehrte, die schon zur Zeit der Sowjetunion gelehrt haben, das Ende der Sowjetunion und den Neubeginn eines unabhängigen Russlands auf der Höhe ihrer Schaffenskraft und ihres Einflusses als Konsultanten der russischen Präsidenten, der russischen Regierung und des russischen Parlamentes oder in verantwortlichen Positionen auf internationaler Ebene miterlebten und -gestalteten.

Das wohl prominenteste völkerrechtliche Werk, das anhand seiner Herausgeber und Autoren dieses Schicksal widerspiegelt, stellt die siebenbändige Ge-

---

7 „True“ Law, „Façade“ Law, Shadow Law (Echtes Recht, Scheinrecht, Schattenrecht). In: *R. Clark, F. Feldbrugge, St. Pomorski* (eds.), International and National Law in Russia and Eastern Europe. Leyden 2001, 355–360 (358 f.).

8 So *B. Meissner* (Fn. 3), 11; *Th. Schweisfurth*, Sozialistisches Völkerrecht? Berlin, Heidelberg, New York 1979, 33–41.

9 *F.-C. Schroeder*, Probleme der Gesetzgebung in Russland. In: *Ders.* (Hrsg.), Die neuen Kodifikationen in Russland. Berlin 1997, 9–26 (10 f., 13 ff., 25).

10 Zu ihrer Rolle im russischen Kodifikationsprozess siehe z.B. *F.-C. Schroeder* (Fn. 9), 16–18.

samtdarstellung des Völkerrechts aus den Jahren 1989–1993 dar[11]. Das Werk war noch zu Sowjetzeiten geplant, organisiert und in Auftrag gegeben worden. Der erste Band erschien bezeichnenderweise unter der Ägide des Instituts für Staat und Recht der Akademie der Wissenschaften der UdSSR und verantwortliche Herausgeber waren niemand Geringere als *R. A. Müllerson* und *G. I. Tunkin*[12]. Für den zweiten und vierten Band, gleichfalls unter der Ägide der sowjetischen Akademie der Wissenschaften, zeichnete der ebenfalls als Größe der sowjetischen Völkerrechtslehre zu bezeichnende Wissenschaftler *I. I. Lukašuk*, für den dritten Band kein Geringerer als *N. A. Ušakov* verantwortlich. Die Bände 5–7 erschienen dann in den Jahren 1992 und 1993 unter der Ägide der Russischen Akademie der Wissenschaften und verantwortlich waren *V. S. Vereščetin*, der von 1995–2006 Richter am Internationalen Gerichtshof in Den Haag war (Band 5), *N. A. Ušakov* (Band 6) und *E. T. Usenko* (Band 7). Von keinem von ihnen konnte erwartet werden, dass sie während der Laufzeit dieses Akademieprojekts, oder auch später von einer Auflage ihres Lehrbuches zur nächsten oder mit der Veröffentlichung einer neuen Schrift, in das Lager des früheren ideologischen Gegners überwechseln würden, auch wenn hier in den individuellen Biographien doch auch bemerkenswerte Systemwechsel in der Folge festzustellen waren.

So wurde beispielsweise unlängst die dritte Auflage des vom 2007 verstorbenen *I. I. Lukašuk*, von 1995–2001 Mitglied der *International Law Commission* für die Russische Föderation, verfassten Lehrbuchs „Völkerrecht: Besonderer Teil“ vorgelegt[13], das sich von dem von ihm für die sowjetische Akademie der Wissenschaften zu verantwortenden Band 4, der den Zweigen des Völkerrechts, d.h. letztlich dem Besonderen Teil des Völkerrechts gewidmet war, sowohl vom

---

11 Kurs meždunarodnogo prava (Gesamtdarstellung des Völkerrechts). Moskva 1989-1993, t. 1-7.

12 *G. I. Tunkin* wartet im ersten Kapitel des ersten Bandes gleich auf der dritten Seite mit dem in Sowjetzeiten üblichen Zitat aus kommunistischen Parteidokumenten auf (S. 11) und legt den ideologischen Hintergrund offen, wenn er schreibt und zitiert: „Jedoch wächst die Stufe der Integration der Staaten im zwischenstaatlichen System, was unter den Bedingungen der Einheit und des Kampfes von Gegensätzen, vor allem der zwei sozial-ökonomischen Systeme stattfindet. „In der Verbindung des Wettkampfes und des Gegensatzes der zwei Systeme und der wachsenden Tendenz zur wechselseitigen Abhängigkeit der Staaten der universellen Gemeinschaft liegt die Dialektik der modernen Entwicklung – so hieß es im Politischen Vortrag des ZK der KPdSU auf dem XXVII. Kongress der KPdSU – (…)““.

13 *I. I. Lukašuk*, Meždunarodnoe pravo. Osobennaja čast‘. Moskva 20103. Die Auflage unterscheidet sich von der noch zu Lebzeiten von *I. I. Lukašuk* im Jahr 2000 erschienenen zweiten Auflage nicht wesentlich, aber doch in einigen Details, ohne dass angegeben wird, wer für diese Abweichungen verantwortlich ist, ob *I. I. Lukašuk* selbst vor seinem Tod oder jemand anderer. Was den allgemeinen Teil anbelangt, so ist hier noch Stand: *I. I. Lukašuk*, Meždunarodnoe pravo. Obščaja čast‘ (Völkerrecht. Allgemeiner Teil). Moskva 20002.

Inhalt als auch von der Darstellung her fundamental unterscheidet. *I. I. Lukašuk* hatte im Akademieband mit dem völkerrechtlichen Vertragsrecht begonnen, dann das Diplomaten- und Konsularrecht, das Recht der internationalen Sicherheit und das internationale Wirtschaftsrecht dargestellt. *N. A. Ušakov* steuerte in Band 6 des Akademiewerks das Recht internationaler Organisationen, das Recht internationaler Kooperation bei der Verbrechensbekämpfung und das internationale Konfliktrecht bei. *V. S. Vereščetin* nahm in Band 5 das internationale Seerecht, das internationale Luftrecht, das internationale Weltraumrecht, das internationale Atomrecht und das völkerrechtliche Umweltschutzrecht auf.

I. I. Lukašuk beginnt seinen Besonderen Teil in der jüngsten Lehrbuchauflage hingegen mit dem Kapitel „Völkerrechtlicher Menschenrechtsschutz" und bezieht sich dabei ausdrücklich auf das *„international law of human rights"* und nennt dieses Gebiet einen „neuen Zweig des Völkerrechts, der sich nach der Annahme der UN Satzung entwickelte"[14]. Das hätte freilich auch schon während der Zeit der Sowjetunion, vor allem aber bei Entstehung des Akademiewerkes, so gesehen werden können. Im Akademiewerk gibt es allerdings keinen Zweig „Völkerrechtlicher Menschenrechtsschutz". *Ju. A. Rešetov* behandelt im Kapitel 7 des sechsten Bandes die „Internationale Zusammenarbeit bei der Gewährleistung der Menschenrechte", zeigt offensichtliche Berührungsängste, nennt die Europäische Menschrechtskonvention die „Römer Konvention (*Rimskaja konvencija*)" und widmet dem Verfahren bei Individual- und Staatenbeschwerden, damals noch vor der Europäischen Menschenrechtskommission, ganze zwei Absätze[15]. *A. I. Movčan* behandelt in dem von *I. I. Lukašuk* selbst herausgegebenen Band 2 des Akademiewerkes („Grundprinzipien des Völkerrechts") dazu das Prinzip der allgemeinen Achtung der Menschenrechte und Grundfreiheiten[16].

Umso mehr überrascht *I. I. Lukašuk* mit einer nüchternen, vollkommen westlichen Lehrbüchern nachempfundenen Darstellung des völkerrechtlichen Menschenrechtsschutzes, bemüht um einen normativen Zugang, zeigt die Umsetzung der völkerrechtlichen Gewährleistungen in der russischen Verfassung auf, beginnt mit den bürgerlichen und politischen Rechten und begnügt sich mit einem kleinen Hinweis bei den wirtschaftlichen, sozialen und kulturellen Rechten, wonach diese im Völkerrecht durch die sozialistischen Staaten „entsprechend ihrer rechtlichen Konzeption" propagiert worden sind[17]. Keine Rede ist mehr von einer sozialistischen Grundrechtskonzeption, der zu Sowjetzeiten im Westen besondere Aufmerksamkeit gewidmet worden war und die die sowjeti-

---

14 *I. I. Lukašuk* (Fn. 13), 1.

15 Kurs meždunarodnogo prava. Moskva 1992, tom 6, 162–184 (179).

16 Kurs meždunarodnogo prava. Moskva 1989, tom 2, 148–167.

17 *I. I. Lukašuk* (Fn. 13), 7.

sche Antwort auf die sogenannte klassische (bürgerliche) Grundrechtslehre war[18].

I. I. Lukašuk bewies also gehöriges Anpassungsvermögen. Dasselbe gilt für den ganz Großen der sowjetischen sozialistischen Völkerrechtslehre, den 1993 verstorbenen *G. I. Tunkin*, der beispielsweise schon 1977 die Verantwortung dafür übernahm, dass die zweite Auflage von *J. Brownlie*, Principles of Public International Law. Oxford 1973, von *S. N. Andrianova* in zwei Bänden ins Russische übersetzt worden war. Die einleitenden Worte von *G. I. Tunkin* fielen schon damals bemerkenswert konziliant aus, ein Zeichen, dass eine verinnerlichte Bereitschaft zur Reflexion der Gegenseite schon deutlich vor dem Ende der sowjetischen (sozialistischen) Völkerrechtslehre vorhanden war[19]. Neben *I. I. Lukašuk, G. I. Tunkin* und anderen Völkerrechtswissenschaftlern der Übergangszeit von der Sowjetunion auf die Russische Föderation ist aber in der Zwischenzeit eine Reihe von Völkerrechtswissenschaftlern getreten, die an der Gestaltung des sowjetischen Erbes nicht beteiligt waren. Beinahe 20 Jahre nach dem Ende der Sowjetunion scheint daher ein geeigneter Zeitpunkt zu sein, um anhand einer Zusammenschau von sieben russischen Völkerrechtslehrbüchern aus dem Zeitraum 2008–2011 zu untersuchen, wie und mit welchen Kunstgriffen der Paradigmenwechsel von der sowjetischen sozialistischen zur russischen, und mit welchen wesentlichen heute erkennbaren unterschiedlichen Zügen gegenüber der klassischen Völkerrechtslehre erfolgt ist. Von sowjetischer sozialistischer Völkerrechtslehre wird deshalb einengend gesprochen, insofern es einer weiteren wesentlich größeren Arbeit bedürfte, um zu klären, wo die chinesische und mit ihr verbundene Doktrinen (z.B. nordkoreanische Völkerrechtslehre) heute in diesem Zusammenhang stehen. Erst daraus und ergänzt um eine detail-

18 Für viele: *G. Brunner*, Die Grundrechte im Sowjetsystem. Köln 1963; *O. Luchterhandt*, Entwicklung und Schwerpunkte der sowjetischen Grundrechtsdiskussion. In: Berichte des Bundesinstituts für Ostwissenschaftliche und Internationale Studien. Köln 1977, Bd.-54; *O. Luchterhandt*, UN – Menschenrechtskonventionen. Sowjetrecht – Sowjetwirklichkeit. Baden-Baden 1980; *W. A. Timmermans*, Human Rights in Socialist Constitutions: A Comparative Study. In: *F. J. M. Feldbrugge* (ed.), The Distinctiveness of Soviet Law. Dordrecht 1987, 35–59.

19 *Ja. Brounli*, Meždunarodnoe pravo (v dvuch knigach) (Völkerrecht (in zwei Büchern)). Moskva 1977. *G. I. Tunkins* Arbeiten werden auch lange Jahre nach seinem Tod immer noch neu aufgelegt. Siehe z.B. *G. I. Tunkin*, Teorija meždunarodnogo prava (Theorie des Völkerrechts). Moskva 2006, wobei der Herausgeber und gleichzeitig Schüler von *G. I. Tunkin, L. N. Šestakov*, einige „Kürzungen des Textes“ vorgenommen hat, und zwar dort, wo verschiedene Aussagen „unter den heutigen Bedingungen ihre politische Bedeutung verloren haben, aber die rechtlichen Aussagen des Autors nicht berühren.“ (so der Herausgeber auf Seite XVII). Beispielsweise wurde das Kapitel VII „Völkerrecht in den Beziehungen zwischen Staaten des universellen Systems des Sozialismus“ gegenüber der Originalausgabe entfernt. Von „sozialistischem Völkerrecht“, wie die Habilitationsschrift von *Th. Schweisfurth* lautet, wird also in den heute kursierenden Ausgaben der Theorie *G. I. Tunkins* nicht mehr gesprochen.

lierte Analyse völkerrechtlicher Institute und Norminhalte würde sich dann ergeben, was „sozialistische Völkerrechtslehre" heute noch bedeutet. Der Raum, der hier zur Verfügung steht, verbietet freilich auch für die Analyse der Reste der „sowjetischen sozialistischen Völkerrechtslehre" den Blick auf die Details. In den Blick werden nur die großen Linien der Lehre genommen.

II. Die russische Völkerrechtslehre im Dienst der russischen Außenpolitik

Folgende Lehrbücher wurden neben dem bereits genannten von *I. I. Lukašuk* für die Zwecke dieser Analyse ausgewählt:

- Die fünfte Auflage des Lehrbuchs von *G. V. Ignatenko* und *O. I. Tiunov* (2010)[20];
- Die umfangreiche Darstellung des Völkerrechts von *V. L. Tolstych* (2009)[21];
- Die fünfte Auflage des Lehrbuchs von *K. A. Bekjašev* (2011)[22];
- Das zum 50. Bestandsjubiläum der Russischen Universität für Völkerfreundschaft (Rossijskij Univerzitet Družby Narodov) vom Dekan ihrer Rechtswissenschaftlichen Fakultät *A. Ja. Kapustin* herausgegebene Lehrbuch (2008)[23];
- Die dritte Auflage des Lehrbuchs von *V. I. Kuznecov* (verstorben 2002) und weitergeführt von *B. R. Tuzmuchamedov* (2010)[24] und

20 *G. V. Ignatenko, O. I. Tiunov* (otv. red.), Meždunarodnoe pravo (Völkerrecht). Moskva 20105. Das Lehrbuch wurde von einem Autorenkollektiv verfasst, dem neben den schon in der Sowjetunion arrivierten Völkerrechtswissenschaftlern *G. V. Ignatenko, D. D. Ostapenko, P. I. Savickij, V. Ja. Sudorova* und *O. I. Tiunov* die postsowjetische Generation bestehend aus *M. V. Kučin, L. A. Lazutin, S. Ju. Maročkin, A. M. Teslenko* und *I. V. Fedorov* angehört.

21 *V. L. Tolstych*, Kurs meždunarodnogo prava (Gesamtdarstellung des Völkerrechts). Moskva 2009, 1032 Seiten.

22 *K. A. Bekjašev* (otv. red.), Meždunarodnoe publičnoe pravo (Völkerrecht) (durch den Hinweis „öffentliches" in deutlicher Abgrenzung von „internationalem Privatrecht"). Dem hier tätigen Autorenkollektiv gehören die schon in der Sowjetzeit bekannten Völkerrechtler *L. P. Anufrieva, K. A. Bekjašev, M. E. Volosov, L. I. Zacharova, E. L. Kuz'min* und *E. G. Moiseev* an. In postsowjetischer Zeit sind arriviert: *D. K. Bekjašev, Ja. S. Koževrov, I. N. Lebedinec, N. A. Sokolova, G. S. Starobudcev* (war wissenschaftlich mit dem Status eines Kandidaten der Wissenschaften allerdings schon in der Sowjetzeit tätig) und *V. V. Ustinov*.

23 *A. Ja. Kapustin* (red.), Meždunarodnoe pravo (Völkerrecht). Moskva 2008. Auch dieses Lehrbuch wurde von einem Generationen übergreifenden Autorenkollektiv verfasst, bestehend aus: *A. Ch. Abašidze, F. R. Ananidze, Ju. A. Arsent'ev, Ju. G. Barsegov, A. G. Bogatyrev, V. D. Bordunov, O. R. Gusejnov, G. P. Žukov, A. Ja. Kapustin, A. S. Agapeeva, P. A. Skamnickij, E. S. Alisievič, V. A. Kartaškin, R. A. Kalamkarjan, M. N. Kopylov, G. S. Starobudcev* und *V. M. Filippov*.

24 *V. I. Kuznecov*, B. *R. Tuzmuchamedov* (otv. red.), Meždunarodnoe pravo (Völkerrecht). Moskva 20103. Dem hier dahinterstehenden Autorenkollektiv gehören in erster Linie schon in der Sowjetzeit bedeutsame Völkerrechtswissenschaftler an, insbesondere

- Das von *A. N. Vylegžanin* herausgegebene Lehrbuch (2010)[25].

Allen aufgezählten völkerrechtlichen Darstellungen ist gemeinsam, dass sie eines der beiden Charakteristika, die *B. Meissner* seinerzeit für die sowjetische sozialistische Völkerrechtslehre ausgemacht hat, nämlich den Standpunkt eines Staates zu völkerrechtlichen Fragen als Teile seines außenpolitischen Standpunktes anzusehen[26], für ihre eigene Einschätzung in Bezug auf die Russische Föderation weiter fortführen. Am weitesten geht hier das Lehrbuch von *G. V. Ignatenko* und *O. I. Tiunov*, das in der Einleitung auf die Konzeption der Außenpolitik der Russischen Föderation ausdrücklich Bezug nimmt[27]. Ähnliches bietet das Lehrbuch von *A. Ja. Kapustin*, wo *A. Ch. Abašidze* beispielsweise im Anfangskapitel „Allgemeiner Teil: Die gegenwärtige Welt und das Völkerrecht" auf die Rede des russischen Präsidenten auf der Münchener Sicherheitskonferenz am 10.02.2007 Bezug nimmt und daraus wie folgt zitiert: „Es ist wichtig zu

---

A. Ch. Abašidze, V. V. Vereščetin, S. A. Egorov, V. S. Ivanenko, G. V. Ignatenko, A. Ja. Kapustin, V. A. Kartaškin, A. L. Kolodkin (von 1996–2007 Richter am Internationalen Seegerichtshof), *R. A. Kolodkin, M. N. Kopylov, V. I. Kuznecov* (zu Sowjetzeiten Mitglied der ILC), *I. I. Lukašuk, S. I. Markovič, S. M. Punžin, B. R. Tuzmuchamedov, V. N. Fedorov* und *V. M. Šumilov*. Nur die beiden Autoren *A. A. Podakov* und *J. S. Romašev* wurden erst in postsowjetischer Zeit bekannt.

25 *A. N. Vylegžanin* (red.), Meždunarodnoe pravo (Völkerrecht). Moskva 2010. Das dahinterstehende Autorenkollektiv versammelt aus anderen Lehrbüchern bereits bekannte Namen und viele zusätzliche, fast durchwegs ohne sowjetische Vergangenheit: *A. Ch. Abašidze, E. E. Andreeva, T. G. Anodin, D. K. Bekjašev, G. V. Bobylev, N. A. Voroncova, A. N. Vylegžanin, V. V. Golicyn, O. V. Glikman, D. V. Ivanov, E. I. Karkiščenko, Ju. M. Kolosov, I. I. Kotljarov, E. S. Krivčikova, A. V. Kukuškina, V. N. Kulebjakin, D. K. Labin, Ju. N. Maleev, A. V. Ovlaščenko, V. O. Petrov, M. A. Petčenko, A. A. Robinov, Ju. M. Rybakov, P. V. Savas'kov, L. V. Savel'eva, T. G. Saksina, A. Ju. Skuratova, I. Ju. Štodina, M. R. Juzbašjan* und *A. V. Jakovenko*. Das Lehrbuch ist in einem besonderen Naheverhältnis zum russischen Außenministerium zu sehen, steht dahinter doch letztlich das Moskauer staatliche Institut für internationale Beziehungen mit Universitätsstatus beim MID (Moskovskij gosudarstvennyj institut meždunarodnych otnošenij (univerzitet) MID Rossii).

26 *B. Meissner* (Fn. 3), 11.

27 *G. V. Ignatenko, O. I. Tiunov* (Fn. 20), 17: „Die Konzeption der Außenpolitik der Russischen Föderation, die am 12.07.2008 bestätigt wurde, geht davon aus, dass die allgemein anerkannten Normen des Völkerrechts zutiefst universell im Hinblick auf ihr Verständnis und ihre Anwendung in einer multipolaren Welt sind." (Übersetzung *M. Geistlinger*). Bei der Darstellung der Hauptcharakteristika des Völkerrechts schließt *G. V. Ignatenko* selbst an diese Formulierung an, wenn er auf Seite 26 schreibt: „Das moderne Völkerrecht ist allen Staaten gemeinsam in dem Sinn, dass insbesondere die allgemein anerkannten Prinzipien und Normen seinen Hauptinhalt und seinen sozialen und allgemeinmenschlichen Wert charakterisieren. Gleichzeitig hat es eine Bindung zu jedem einzelnen Staat, insofern auf der Grundlage der allgemein anerkannten Prinzipien und Normen und in Übereinstimmung mit ihnen jeder Staat auch seine völkerrechtliche Sphäre schafft, die aus den von ihm angenommenen lokalen Normen gebildet wird."

erreichen, „dass das Völkerrecht universellen Charakter, sowohl hinsichtlich des Verständnisses, als auch hinsichtlich der Anwendung seiner Normen hat“[28]. Wo immer in den Jahren seit dem Ende der Sowjetunion die Russische Föderation einen von den USA, der NATO und ihrer Mitgliedstaaten abweichenden Standpunkt bezogen hat, findet sich eine bemerkenswert einhellige Unterstützung dieses Standpunktes auf der Ebene der russischen Völkerrechtslehre. Dies ist nun freilich kein Spezifikum der russischen Völkerrechtslehre und findet sich in umgekehrter Richtung auch bei amerikanischen, deutschen, französischen oder österreichischen Völkerrechtlern in Hinblick auf die außenpolitischen Positionen, die ihr Staat bezogen hat. Auffällig ist indes, dass es nicht den Anflug irgendeiner Kritik oder abweichende Argumente von der Staatslinie gibt. Zuzugeben ist hier allerdings, dass alle internationalen Vorgänge, die in die aufgezeigte Kategorie fallen und sich zeitgleich zum Ende der Sowjetunion und in den ersten Jahren der Russischen Föderation ereignet haben, sich tatsächlich nicht oder nur mit großen Kunstgriffen mit dem geltenden Völkerrecht vereinbaren lassen.

So wird von *G. V. Ignatenko* die Anerkennung des Kosovo durch eine Reihe von Staaten, darunter einige NATO-Staaten, im Kapitel „Die Anerkennung von Staaten“, obwohl Kosovo Teil von Serbien ist, als unabhängiger Staat als rechtswidriger Akt qualifiziert, der politische Ziele verfolgt[29]. Dem wird man auf der Grundlage des Gutachtens des IGH zur Frage der Vereinbarkeit der einseitigen Erklärung der Unabhängigkeit in Bezug auf den Kosovo vom 20. Juli 2010[30] wenig entgegenhalten können. Die Bedingungen eines „hilfsweisen Sezessionsrechts“ (*„right to remedial secession*“), wozu der IGH in dem Gutachten keine Stellungnahme bezogen hat[31], und angenommen, es gäbe ein solches außerhalb des Dekolonialisierungsprozesses, würden einer näheren Prüfung im Falle des Kosovo wegen der aktuellen Letztverantwortung für die Ausübung der Staatsgewalt und Aufrechterhaltung des Status eines Waffenstillstandes beim Sicherheitsrat der Vereinten Nationen kaum standhalten können.

Nur einen Absatz weiter setzt sich *G. V. Ignatenko* mit der russischen Anerkennung der Republik Abchasien und der Republik Südossetien auseinander und schildert, dass die betreffenden *Ukaze* des Präsidenten der Russischen Föderation „von der Notwendigkeit der Realisierung des Rechts der Völker dieser Staaten auf Selbstbestimmung unter Beachtung der Prinzipien der Nichtanwendung von Gewalt und der Achtung der Menschenrechte ausgehen, die, wie auch eine Reihe anderer Prinzipien, von Georgien grob verletzt wurden, als es in Bezug auf diese Völker eine Politik der Aggression und des Völkermordes verwirklich-

28 *A. Ja. Kapustin* (Fn. 23), 10.

29 *G. V. Ignatenko, O. I. Tiunov* (Fn. 20), 87.

30 Text abrufbar unter http://www.icj-cij.org/docket/files/141/15987.pdf (abgerufen am 15.02.2011).

31 Siehe die Paragraphen 82 f. im Gutachten des IGH zur Unabhängigkeitserklärung des Kosovo (Fn. 30).

te[32]". *G. V. Ignatenko* belässt es bei dieser Schilderung ohne eigenen weitergehenden Kommentar, versteckt sich also letztlich hinter der offiziellen russischen Begründung und hält sie im gegebenen Kontext der Anerkennung von Staaten offensichtlich für ausreichend. Immerhin hätte er auch die Wahl gehabt, das Beispiel nicht zu erwähnen.

A. N. Vylegžanin und *Ju. M. Kolosov* erwähnen im Kapitel „Begriff des Völkerrechts und sein Gegenstand" ziemlich am Anfang ihres Lehrbuches die Fälle der Bombardements von Jugoslawien und dem Irak, wobei sie als Urheber ausschließlich die USA nennen, ohne diesbezügliche Ermächtigung des UN Sicherheitsrates als Beispiele, in denen die Rolle des Völkerrechts erniedrigt worden sei, was von den Gegnern der Verbindlichkeit völkerrechtlicher Normen als – von den beiden Autoren abgelehnte – Unterstützung der eigenen Position verwendet wurde[33].

In weniger exponierten Angelegenheiten finden sich aber dann doch eigene Standpunkte. So hat *V. L. Tolstych* kein Problem, die Entscheidung des Europäischen Gerichtshofs für Menschenrechte (EGMR) im Fall Isaev gegen die Russische Föderation vom 24. Februar 2005 anzuführen, und erwähnt in seiner Darstellung des internationalen Humanitätsrechts die Verurteilung der Russischen Föderation wegen Verletzung von Art. 2 Europäische Menschenrechtskonvention (EMRK) wegen Anwendung von Gewalt durch russische Soldaten im Tschetschenienkrieg durch den EGMR als Beispiel für die Geltung des Menschenrechtsschutzes, bzw. bestimmter Rechte (Recht auf Leben, Folterverbot usw.) in Konfliktzeiten[34]. *V. L. Tolstych* bezieht auch eine vorsichtig kritische Haltung zum Gutachten des IGH in der Frage der völkerrechtlichen Zulässigkeit der Androhung mit oder Anwendung von Nuklearwaffen vom 8.07.1996[35] und entfernt sich so von der offiziellen russischen Staatslinie. Er führt folgende Argumente für die Existenz eines rechtlichen Verbots der Anwendung von Nuklearwaffen an: „Unvereinbarkeit einer solchen Anwendung mit allgemeinen und auch einigen besonderen Verboten, die analog zur Anwendung gelangen; Unvereinbarkeit einer solchen Anwendung mit dem Recht der Neutralität und der Martens'schen Klausel; Vorhandensein von Gewohnheitsrecht, das eine solche Anwendung verbietet[36]."

In der Frage der Zugehörigkeit der Kurilischen Inseln zu Russland oder zu Japan schildert *V. L. Tolstych* sehr präzise die Genese und Vertragslage und bezeichnet die Problematik als ein „leuchtendes Beispiel" für die Probleme bei der Bestimmung eines Rechtstitels mit aktueller Bedeutung für die Russische Föde-

---

32 *G. V. Ignatenko, O. I. Tiunov* (Fn. 20), 87.

33 *A. N. Vylegžanin* (Fn. 25), 29.

34 *V. L. Tolstych* (Fn. 21), 765 (Kapitel 19.III, Randziffer (Rz.) 64).

35 Text des Gutachtens abrufbar unter: http://www.icj-cij.org/docket/files/95/7495.pdf (abgerufen am 15.02.2011).

36 *V. L. Tolstych* (Fn. 21), 788 (Kapitel 19.VII, Rz. 78).

ration, endet aber ohne weiteren Kommentar mit der Schilderung der gemeinsamen Erklärung der UdSSR und Japans von 1956. Gemäß Punkt 9 dieser Erklärung sichert die UdSSR Japan zu, dass die Inseln Habomai und Shikotan Japan übergeben werden. Die faktische Übergabe werde allerdings erst nach Abschluss eines Friedensvertrags zwischen Japan und der Sowjetunion erfolgen. Zum Abschluss eines solchen Friedensvertrags kam es bis heute nicht. 1960 habe sich die UdSSR geweigert, die Inseln zu übergeben, mit dem Argument, dass die Übergabe das Territorium vergrößere, das von den Streitkräften der USA genutzt werde[37]. *V. L. Tolstych* steht der aktuellen russischen Position in dieser Hinsicht eindeutig nahe, wenn er es auch vermeidet, sich festzulegen.

Andererseits distanziert er sich nicht von einem völkerrechtlich mehr als zweifelhaften Vorgehen, das die seinerzeitige Sowjetunion an den Tag gelegt hat. So lässt er beispielsweise gelten, dass Staatsgrenzen aus politischen Gründen gezogen werden können und führt als Beispiel den *casus belli* für den sowjetisch-finnischen Krieg 1939–1940 an. Finnland war damals den sowjetischen Forderungen nicht nachgekommen, die Grenze bei der Karelischen Landenge vom damaligen Leningrad hin in Richtung Finnlands zu verlegen, mehrere Inseln und einen Teil zweier Halbinseln an die Sowjetunion zu übertragen sowie einen Hafen zu verpachten. Im Gegenzug wären Finnland andere Gebiete übertragen worden. *V. L. Tolstych* kommentiert nicht weiter, dass die Begründung für die sowjetischen Forderungen durch die Notwendigkeit, die Sicherheit von Leningrad zu gewährleisten, begründet wurde und wie tauglich eine solche Begründung aus der Warte des Völkerrechts ist.[38]

Ebenso ambivalent schildert *I. I. Lukašuk* im Kapitel „Völkerrechtliches Luftrecht" die Frage eines von der EG mit Wirkung ab 01. April 2002 verhängten Verbots, mit Flugzeugen, die Fluglärm jenseits einer festgelegten Toleranzgrenze hervorrufen, Flughäfen innerhalb der EG anzufliegen. Er erwähnt, dass darunter zwei Drittel der Flüge der russischen Fluggesellschaft Pulkovo gefallen wären, die allein zwischen St. Petersburg und Berlin 672 Flüge pro Jahr abwickelte. Der Entfall dieser Flüge bedeutete für die Gesellschaft einen enormen Schaden. Das russische Transportministerium habe im Februar 2002 eine befristete Ausnahme für Flüge der Gesellschaft Pulkovo erbeten und davor gewarnt, dass ansonsten die Flüge der Gesellschaft Lufthansa nach Russland verboten würden. Das hätte für diese Gesellschaft eine Katastrophe bedeutet, zumal sie 72 Flüge pro Woche nach Russland und die GUS Staaten durchführte und über russischen Luftraum viele Flüge nach Asien abwickelte. *I. I. Lukašuk* erwähnt dieses Beispiel als „einigermaßen kompliziertes rechtliches, genauso wie wirtschaftliches und politisches Problem", zumal sich der Großteil der internationa-

37 *V. L. Tolstych* (Fn. 21), 865 (Kapitel 21.III, Rz. 51). Deutlich ausführlicher und fundierter bei *G. P. Žukov* in: *A. Ja. Kapustin* (Fn. 23), 209–212.

38 *V. L. Tolstych* (Fn. 21), 852 (Kapitel 21.II, Rz. 38).

len Flüge über dem Territorium von Staaten abspiele[39]. Er erwähnt aber nicht, wie dieses Problem gelöst wurde, noch bewertet er, welche der beiden Seiten sich im Recht befunden hat.

III. Die Geschichte des Völkerrechts und die Rolle der Sowjetunion und der sozialistischen Oktoberrevolution aus der Perspektive der russischen Völkerrechtslehre

Der Ansatz *E. A. Korovins*, wonach mit der sozialistischen Oktoberrevolution, die eine neue sozial-ökonomische Ordnung hervorbrachte, auch ein fundamental neues Völkerrecht entstand, blieb das Dogma der sowjetischen sozialistischen Völkerrechtslehre bis zum Ende der Sowjetunion. *G. I. Tunkin* hatte in seiner „Völkerrechtstheorie" (1970), die von *Th. Schweisfurth* im Jahr 1972 ins Deutsche übersetzt herausgegeben wurde, dies folgendermaßen auf den Punkt gebracht: „Die völkerrechtlichen Konzeptionen der Oktoberrevolution lassen sich hinsichtlich ihrer Wirkung auf das Völkerrecht und die internationalen Beziehungen in drei eng miteinander verbundene Hauptgruppen einteilen:

a) die Grundsätze des sozialistischen Internationalismus in den Beziehungen zwischen den sozialistischen Staaten;
b) die Grundsätze der Gleichberechtigung und Selbstbestimmung der Nationen und Völker, die sich gegen das Kolonialsystem und gegen jegliche nationale Unterdrückung und Ungleichheit wenden;
c) die Grundsätze der friedlichen Koexistenz, die die Beziehungen zwischen Staaten mit unterschiedlicher sozialer Ordnung bestimmen.

Auf der Basis dieser Ideen und Grundsätze der Oktoberrevolution entwickelte sich eine neue Art internationaler Beziehungen und ein neues Völkerrecht"[40].

In Konsequenz dieses Ansatzes nahm die sowjetische sozialistische Völkerrechtslehre am Beispiel der großen von *F. I. Koževnikov*, *V. M. Koreckij*, *D. B. Levin*, *G. I. Tunkin*, *N. A. Ušakov* und *V. M. Šuršalov* unter der Gesamtlei-

---

39 *I. I. Lukašuk* (Fn. 13), 163.

40 *Th. Schweisfurth* (Hrsg.), *G. I. Tunkin*, Völkerrechtstheorie (Aus dem Russischen von *H. Müller* und *V. Rathfelder*). Berlin 1972, 21. *Th. Schweisfurth* selbst hat in seinem englischen Summary seiner Habilitationsschrift folgende zusammenfassende Bewertung dieser Idee vorgenommen: "In the *conclusion* the question raised in the title of this study as to the existence of 'socialist' international law is answered in the negative. The complex of structural principles of international law governing the relations between socialist States cannot, with regard to its contents and coherence, be regarded as existing in the manner claimed by Soviet-Marxist theory. Although there are some new 'socialist' principles, it seems too pretentious to speak of a 'new type' of international law, because these new principles, being unable to outlaw the universal ones, only add to them." (Fn. 8), 584 (Hervorhebungen im Original).

tung von *V. M. Čchikvadze* verfassten sechsbändigen Gesamtdarstellung des Völkerrechts im Auftrag der Akademie der Wissenschaften der UdSSR folgende Periodenbildung in der Völkerrechtsgeschichte vor: Das Völkerrecht in der Periode der Sklavenhaltergesellschaft, das Völkerrecht in der Feudalgesellschaft, das Völkerrecht in der Epoche des Kapitalismus, das Völkerrecht in der Periode des zum Imperialismus mutierten Kapitalismus, das Völkerrecht in der Periode der aufkeimenden wissenschaftlichen Ideologie des Proletariats, das Völkerrecht seit der sozialistischen Oktoberrevolution[41].

Die letzte Periode, jene seit der sozialistischen Oktoberrevolution, wurde vereinzelt und auch unterschiedlich in der Spätphase der sowjetischen sozialistischen Völkerrechtslehre untergegliedert. Am Beispiel des von *L. A. Modžorjan* und *N. G. Blatova* im Jahr 1979 herausgegebenen Lehrbuchs waren das folgende Phasen:

a) Periode bis zum Zweiten Weltkrieg: Kampf des Sowjetstaates um die Integration neuer progressiver Prinzipien in das Völkerrecht, Bürgerliche völkerrechtliche Theorien nach dem Ende des Ersten Weltkrieges und parallel dazu die Entstehung einer sowjetischen Doktrin des Völkerrechts und Entwicklung bis zum Zweiten Weltkrieg;
b) Periode während und nach dem Zweiten Weltkrieg: Weitere Demokratisierung und progressive Entwicklung des modernen Völkerrechts, Kalter Krieg und reaktionäre völkerrechtliche Konzeptionen dieser Periode sowie sowjetische Antwort darauf, Sperre der internationalen Anspannung unter *L. Brežnev* und friedliche Koexistenz[42].

Knapp vor Ende der Sowjetunion wartete *V. Vasilenko* mit folgender Periodenbildung in der Völkerrechtsgeschichte auf, mit der die Sowjetunion dann auch zugrunde ging:

> „Das Voroktobervölkerrecht: 1) Das Völkerrecht der Sklavenhaltergesellschaft; 2) Das Völkerrecht der Übergangsperiode vom Sklavenhaltertum zum Feudalismus; 3) Das Völkerrecht der feudalen Gesellschaft; 4) Das Völkerrecht der Übergangsperiode vom Feudalismus zum Kapitalismus; 5) Das Völkerrecht der kapitalistischen Gesellschaft oder bürgerliche Völkerrecht (altes Völkerrecht).
>
> Das Nachoktobervölkerrecht: 6) Das Völkerrecht der Übergangsperiode vom Kapitalismus zum Sozialismus (heutiges Völkerrecht); 7) Das sozialistische Völkerrecht (Das Völkerrecht der Zukunft)[43]".

Dies war der letzte Versuch, zu retten, was nicht zu retten war, aber er bedeutete eine große Aufgabe für die nachsowjetische russische Völkerrechtslehre, bar

---

41 Kurs meždunarodnogo prava v šesti tomach (Gesamtdarstellung des Völkerrechts in sechs Bänden). Moskva 1967–1973, I (1967), 39–72.

42 *L. A. Modžorjan, N. T. Blatova* (otv. red.), Meždunarodnoe pravo (Völkerrecht). Moskva 1979, 27–43.

43 *V. A. Vasilenko*, Osnovy teorii meždunarodnogo prava (Grundlagen einer Theorie des Völkerrechts). Kiev 1988, 35.

jeden marxistisch-leninistischen Hintergrunds, die Völkerrechtsgeschichte neu zu periodisieren und dabei auch die Sowjetzeit einzuordnen und zu bewerten.

In diesem Zusammenhang zeigt sich doch eine gewisse Heterogenität der Ansätze in der heutigen russischen Völkerrechtslehre. Das Lehrbuch von *A. Ja. Kapustin* beispielsweise, in dem *G. S. Starobudcev* für das betreffende Kapitel 4 verantwortlich zeichnet, nennt folgenden Ablauf: Das Völkerrecht der Alten Welt (4. Jahrtausend v. Chr. bis 476 n. Chr.); das Völkerrecht des Mittelalters (476 bis einschließlich *H. Grotius* und seinem *De iure belli ac pacis* (1625)); das Völkerrecht der Neuzeit (Englische bürgerliche Revolution (1642–1649) und Westfälischer Frieden (24.10.1648) bis einschließlich *F. F. Martens*, der einen Entwurf für die Haager Konvention 1899 „Über die friedliche Beilegung von Streitigkeiten" verfasst hat, und hin zum Ersten Weltkrieg); das Völkerrecht an der Wende vom 2. zum 3. Jahrtausend (1919 bis zur Gegenwart)[44]. Zusätzlich widmet *G. S. Starobudcev* der Völkerrechtswissenschaft in Russland bis 1917, der russischen Völkerrechtswissenschaft in der Emigration in den Jahren 1918 bis 1939, der einheimischen Völkerrechtswissenschaft von 1917 bis 1991 und der postsowjetischen russischen Völkerrechtswissenschaft je einen eigenen Abschnitt im Anschluss an die geschilderten Völkerrechtsperioden[45].

Richtet man bei *G. S. Starobudcev* im von *A. Ja. Kapustin* herausgegebenen Lehrbuch das Hauptaugenmerk auf die Schilderung des Beitrags der Sowjetunion und der sowjetischen Völkerrechtswissenschaft zur Entwicklung des Völkerrechts und seiner Lehre, so fällt zunächst auf, dass die gesamte Periode bis zum Zweiten Weltkrieg mit der Bemerkung übergangen wird, dass es wenig Schriften gab und die, die es gab, ideologisch überfrachtet waren. *E. A. Korovins* „Geschichte des Völkerrechts" aus 1946, *F. I. Koževnikov*, die Autoren der 60er Jahre, *G. I. Tunkins* „Theorie des Völkerrechts", Schriften zum Recht der Vereinten Nationen und internationalen Organisationsrecht, aber vor allem der Beitrag der Sowjetunion und ihrer Lehre zur Weltraumnutzung und zum Weltraumrecht, zum internationalen Seerecht und das Sowjetische Jahrbuch des Völkerrechts[46] werden positiv hervorgehoben[47].

44 *A. Ja. Kapustin* (Fn. 23), 44–58. Da *G. S. Starobudcev* auch im Lehrbuch herausgegeben von *K. A. Bekjašev* (Fn. 22) für das zweite Kapitel („Geschichte des Völkerrechts") verantwortlich zeichnet, überrascht es wenig, dass auch dieses Lehrbuch eine übereinstimmende Periodisierung vorweist (71–86), mit einem Überblick auf Seite 72.

45 *A. Ja. Kapustin* (Fn. 23), 58–65. Damit übereinstimmend aber deutlich ausführlicher *G. S. Starobudcev* in: *K. A. Bekjašev* (Fn. 22), 87–104.

46 Russ.: Sovetskij ežegodnik meždunarodnogo prava.

47 *G. S. Starobudcev* in: *A. Ja. Kapustin* (Fn. 23), 63, resümiert folgendermaßen: „Ungeachtet des ideologischen Drucks und der Notwendigkeit, dass die wissenschaftlichen Ausarbeitungen im Rahmen der marxistisch-leninistischen Theorie erfolgten, standen viele Schöpfungen sowjetischer Gelehrter auf dem Niveau der besten Vorbilder der allgemeinen universellen Völkerrechtswissenschaft." (Übersetzung *M. Geistlinger*).

Deutlich differenzierter geht *G. S. Starobudcev* im von *K. A. Bekjašev* herausgegebenen Lehrbuch an diese, aber auch an die Perioden davor, heran. Er bietet da zunächst einen detaillierten Überblick über die russischen Völkerrechtswissenschaftler, die die Ideen der Oktoberrevolution von Anfang an mittrugen oder sich damit zurechtfanden. Erwähnt werden *V. E. Grabar'*, *N. N. Kravčenko*, *N. N. Golubev* und die jüngeren Völkerrechtler *E. A. Korovin*, *V. N. Durdenevskij* sowie *A. M. Ladyženskij* und einige andere[48]. *G. S. Starobudcev* schildert die Schwierigkeiten, denen die übrigen Völkerrechtswissenschaftler in den darauf folgenden Jahren ausgesetzt waren und denen viele nur durch die Flucht ins Exil entkamen, beispielsweise *B. E. Nol'de*, der 1919 nach Finnland floh und sich dann in Paris niederließ. Letztlich setzte sich in dieser Periode *E. A. Korovin* durch. Der Autor schildert, wie dessen „klassenhafte Methode" im westlichen Ausland, insbesondere von *B. S. Mirkin-Gecevič*, kritisiert wurde und anhand eines Zitates der Schlusspassagen des Werkes wie sich *E. A. Korovin* selbst Lügen strafte, was die Geschichte zu Ende des 20. Jahrhunderts zeigte[49].

Was die Nachkriegsperiode der sowjetischen sozialistischen Völkerrechtslehre anbelangt, so erwähnt *G. S. Starobudcev* in diesem Lehrbuch zusätzlich als deren Verdienste Beiträge zum völkerrechtlichen Umweltschutzrecht, zum Recht der friedlichen Nutzung der Kernenergie, zum Diplomaten- und Konfliktrecht sowie zum Recht der friedlichen Streitbeilegung[50].

Der Autor lässt keinen Zweifel aufkommen, dass das Ende der Sowjetunion für die russische Völkerrechtswissenschaft überraschend kam und sie sich noch geraume Zeit danach als Teil eines einheitlichen intellektuellen Raumes in den Grenzen der früheren Sowjetunion verstand, der sich erst allmählich in neue nationale Völkerrechtsdoktrinen aufzulösen begann. Er spricht auch offen an, dass der damit verbundene ideologische Wandel für die russische Völkerrechtswissenschaft und diejenigen in den anderen Staaten, die aus der früheren Sowjetunion hervorgingen, schwerwiegende Orientierungsprobleme hervorrief. Dazu kamen enorme finanzielle Schwierigkeiten, die zu einer Ausdünnung der Zahl der Völkerrechtler und zu einer Schrumpfung der Zahl völkerrechtlicher Monographien führte. Publikationen zur Völkerrechtstheorie versiegten gänzlich. Doch sieht *G. S. Starobudcev* diesen Niedergang als mittlerweile überwunden an und unterlegt dies mit zahlreichen Beispielen aus der jüngsten Zeit[51].

R. A. Kolodkin, der § 1 des ersten Kapitels im Lehrbuch von *V. I. Kuznecov* und *B. R. Tuzmuchamedov* („Entstehung und Entwicklung des Völkerrechts") behandelt, stellt sich dem Problem durch eine ganz kurze Gegenüberstellung, gewissermaßen im Vorbeigehen, der sowjetischen Periodisierung und der Perio-

48 *G. S. Starobudcev* in: *K. A. Bekjašev* (Fn. 22), 92.
49 *G. S. Starobudcev* in: *K. A. Bekjašev* (Fn. 22), 96 f.
50 *G. S. Starobudcev* in: *K. A. Bekjašev* (Fn. 22), 98 f.
51 *G. S. Starobudcev* in: *K. A. Bekjašev* (Fn. 22), 100–104.

denbildung, wie sie im Westen in der Enzyklopädie des Völkerrechts getroffen wird. Er sieht den Unterschied zwischen beiden Ansätzen im Abstellen des sowjetischen Zugangs auf die gesellschaftlich-wirtschaftlichen Formationen, die den zwischenstaatlichen Beziehungen zugrunde liegen, und demgegenüber auf Unterscheidungsmerkmale der einzelnen Perioden im westlichen Ansatz. Weiterhin betont er das Gemeinsame zwischen beiden Ansätzen, das zeige, dass die Entwicklung des Völkerrechts untrennbar mit der Entwicklung der zwischenstaatlichen Beziehungen verbunden sei[52].

R. A. Kolodkin, der sich in seinen Ausführungen ausdrücklich auf den im Jahr 2002 verstorbenen *V. I. Kuznecov* bezieht, bewertet die Rolle der sozialistischen Oktoberrevolution 1917 deutlich positiver als *G. S. Starobudcev*. Sie habe nicht nur Russland fundamental verändert, sondern habe sich als zusätzlicher Stimulus im Kampf um soziale, wirtschaftliche und politische Veränderungen in anderen Staaten erwiesen. Er hebt das Selbstbestimmungsrecht der Völker und die friedliche Koexistenz, den Einfluss der Sowjetunion als Führerin des sozialistischen Lagers verstärkt durch ihre Stellung als ständiges Mitglied des UN Sicherheitsrates, die Arbeiten *G. I. Tunkins*, den Einfluss der Sowjetunion auf Resolutionen der Generalversammlung der Vereinten Nationen (z.B. die Aggressionsdefinition) und auf verschiedene multilaterale völkerrechtliche Verträge hervor. Auch preist er die sechsbändige Gesamtdarstellung des Völkerrechts der Akademie der Wissenschaften aus den 60er Jahren, betont aber auch, dass „die im Land damals herrschenden politischen und ideologischen Konzeptionen keineswegs immer und in allem für das Völkerrecht nützlich waren, das eine objektive Realität widerspiegelte – die Koexistenz und den gegenseitigen Kampf des kapitalistischen und des sozialistischen Systems, die sich voneinander durch einen breiten Kreis von Parametern stark unterschieden: ökonomische, politische und wertbezogene[53]“. Die Reformen der Außenpolitik der Sowjetunion zu Ende der 1980er Jahre haben sich vor allem in der Einstellung zu den Menschenrechten und in der Unterwerfung der Sowjetunion unter die Zuständigkeit des IGH völkerrechtlich niedergeschlagen. Der Übergang zu Russland als Fortsetzerstaat der UdSSR habe sich positiv auf die Rolle des Völkerrechts im innerstaatlichen russischen Recht, auf die Öffnung Russlands für grenzüberschreitenden Personen-, Güter- und Geldverkehr sowie auf die Anerkennung relativer und funktioneller statt absoluter Immunität des Staates ausgewirkt. Die Teilung des Völkerrechts in ein sozialistisches und ein kapitalistisches sei weggefallen. Russland habe im Gegensatz zur Sowjetunion zu einer undogmatischen und pragmatischen Außenpolitik gefunden und die Rolle der Vereinten Nationen und speziell des UN Sicherheitsrates gestärkt. Die heutige russische Völkerrechtswissenschaft sei vom Staat unabhängig und profitiere von der sowjetischen Völker-

---

52 *V. I. Kuznecov, B. R. Tuzmuchamedov* (Fn. 24), 37–39.

53 *V. I. Kuznecov, B. R. Tuzmuchamedov* (Fn. 24), 49–54 (51) (Übersetzung *M. Geistlinger*).

rechtslehre, was den systemhaften Zugang zum Völkerrecht betreffe, unterscheide sich von ihr aber durch Meinungsvielfalt[54].

O. I. Tiunov, der das zweite Kapitel „Entstehung und Entwicklung des Völkerrechts“ in dem von ihm gemeinsam mit *G. V. Ignatenko* herausgegebenen Lehrbuch verfasst hat, gliedert die Geschichte des Völkerrechts in folgende Perioden: 1) Alte Welt; 2) Vom Fall des Römischen Reiches bis zum Westfälischen Frieden; 3) Vom Westfälischen Frieden bis zu den Haager Friedenskonferenzen und 4) Von den Haager Friedenskonferenzen bis zur Gründung der Vereinten Nationen und der Schaffung des modernen Völkerrechts[55]. Im Wege dieser Periodenbildung, aber auch deren von der Sowjetunion und der sozialistischen Völkerrechtslehre vollkommen gelösten Darstellung im Einzelnen, gelingt es *O. I. Tiunov* in diesem Kapitel, den Eindruck zu vermitteln, als habe es eine Periode sowjetischer sozialistischer Völkerrechtslehre nie gegeben. Von der Oktoberrevolution bleibt bei ihm das Dekret über den Frieden und dessen Rolle für einen gerechten und demokratischen Friedensschluss ohne Annexionen und Kontributionen sowie für das Verbot des Aggressionskrieges. Für den Autor ist es die Anti-Hitler-Koalition, wobei die Sowjetunion nur am Rande erwähnt wird, die für die Gründung der Vereinten Nationen und das moderne Völkerrecht auf der Grundlage der UN Satzung ausschlaggebend war[56].

P. V. Savas'kov, der im von *A. N. Vylegžanin* herausgegebenen Lehrbuch das zweite Kapitel „Geschichte des Völkerrechts und seiner Wissenschaft“ verfasst hat, vertritt im Wesentlichen dieselbe Periodenbildung, gliedert allerdings die Zeit seit dem Westfälischen Frieden in eine Periode von 1648 bis 1815 und damit dem Wiener Kongress und eine Weitere, die von 1815 bis zum Ende des Ersten Weltkrieges gedauert hat[57]. Die nächste Zäsur bedeutet die Gründung der Vereinten Nationen, deren Statut die Zeit ab da und in der Gegenwart markiert[58]. Auch *P. V. Savas'kov* sieht den Haupteinfluss der Sowjetunion und ihrer Völkerrechtswissenschaft im Verbot von Aggressions- und Kolonialkriegen, im Verbot von Annexionen und Kontributionen, im Selbstbestimmungsrecht der Völker und bei der Propagierung sozialer Grundrechte[59].

V. L. Tolstych schließlich wählt einen anderen Zugang. Er setzt sich ausführlich mit der Entstehung des Völkerrechts und den Phasen seiner Geschichte anhand der klassischen westlichen und heutigen russischen Autoren auseinander, bezieht keine ausgeprägte Position und beschränkt die Rolle der Oktoberrevolution in diesem universell angelegten Abschnitt auf den Einfluss des Dekrets über

---

54 *V. I. Kuznecov, B. R. Tuzmuchamedov* (Fn. 24), 53 f.
55 *G. V. Ignatenko, O. I. Tiunov* (Fn. 20), 48–68.
56 *G. V. Ignatenko, O. I. Tiunov* (Fn. 20), 63 f.
57 *A. N. Vylegžanin* (Fn. 25), 62–66 und 67–71.
58 *A. N. Vylegžanin* (Fn. 25), 71–76 und 76–78.
59 *A. N. Vylegžanin* (Fn. 25), 72, 73 f.

den Frieden[60]. Davon getrennt behandelt er die Geschichte der (universellen) Völkerrechtswissenschaft, in der als russischer Autor nur *N. M. Korkunov* in einer Kritik von *A. W. Heffter* vorkommt[61]. Daneben schildert *V. L. Tolstych* die Geschichte der internationalen Beziehungen Russlands von der Kiewer Rus‘ an bis einschließlich die sowjetische Phase, wobei er die Zwischenkriegszeit als isolationistische Phase der sowjetischen Außenpolitik charakterisiert und für die Phase nach dem Zweiten Weltkrieg nur den Aspekt des Kalten Krieges für erwähnenswert findet[62]. Der Autor schließt den historischen Abschnitt mit der Geschichte der russischen Völkerrechtswissenschaft und erkennt dort an, dass zwar die Arbeiten sowjetischer Völkerrechtler ideologisch verbrämt waren, dass sie aber dennoch tiefschürfend waren und ihre Aktualität nicht verloren haben. Als ideologische Standpunkte identifiziert er die Teilung der Welt in ein kapitalistisches und ein sozialistisches System, die Qualifikation des sozialistischen Staates als eines besonderen Völkerrechtssubjekts, die Qualifikation von Völkergewohnheitsrecht als *pactum tacitum*, eine überzogene Bewertung der Rolle der Prinzipien des Völkerrechts, das Prinzip der friedlichen Koexistenz, das sozialistische Völkerrecht zwischen sozialistischen Staaten und die mangelnde Akzeptanz einer internationalen Gerichtsbarkeit. Einige dieser Prinzipien haben ihre Anwendbarkeit verloren, andere wieder – *V. L. Tolstych* nennt die Konzeption der Willensübereinstimmung als Beispiel – haben ihre Bedeutung beibehalten.

IV. Einige abschließende Bemerkungen zur Neubewertung völkerrechtlicher Institute und Inhalte

In der Tat wäre die hier geleistete Darstellung des globalen Umgangs der heutigen russischen Völkerrechtslehre mit einer gar nicht so lange zurückliegenden Periode ihrer Geschichte und ihres Staates als einem der Hauptgestalter dieser Geschichte nun mit einer Analyse der Sicht der völkerrechtlichen Institute und Norminhalte zu verbinden, um aufzuspüren, was von den von *V. L. Tolstych* genannten Elementen, darüber hinaus aber auch von sonstigen Besonderheiten der sowjetischen sozialistischen Völkerrechtslehre in den einzelnen Instituten und Normen des modernen Völkerrechts übrig geblieben ist, die nicht notwendigerweise als ideologisch gesteuert zu bewerten sind. Ideologisch wie nicht-ideologisch motivierte und argumentierte Feinheiten zogen sich durch alle Aspekte des Völkerrechts in der Sicht der sowjetischen sozialistischen Lehre. Sie betrafen die Quellenlehre (z.B. Rolle und Verständnis der allgemeinen Rechts-

60 *V. L. Tolstych* (Fn. 21), 22–52 (51).
61 *V. L. Tolstych* (Fn. 21), 53–78 (62 f.).
62 *V. L. Tolstych* (Fn. 21), 79–88 (88).

grundsätze, Konzept der „ungleichen Verträge")[63], die Subjektslehre (z.B. Völker im Kampf um ihre Unabhängigkeit, Internationale Organisationen), das Verhältnis von Völkerrecht zu innerstaatlichem Recht (z.B. die Rolle einer sozialistischen Revolution und von Revolution schlechthin)[64] und viele andere Aspekte mehr. Sich mit ihnen auseinander zu setzen und so das Bild abzurunden, könnte dem nächsten runden Geburtstag des Jubilars vorbehalten werden.

---

63 Siehe zur Quellenfrage einen globalen Überblick z.B. bei *G. Brunner*, Die Quellen des Völkerrechts. In: *R. Maurach, B. Meissner* (Fn. 2), 39–70.

64 Zur sogenannten sozialistischen Revolutionsregel siehe z.B. *M. Geistlinger*, Revolution und Völkerrecht. Wien u.a. 1991, 151–354.

Der „rote“ Osten ist tot. Muss deshalb auch die Ostrechtswissenschaft sterben?

Rechtsanwalt Dr. Stefan Pürner[*]

I. Einleitung

Dieser Beitrag geht der Frage nach, ob die Ostrechtswissenschaft und somit das Forschungsgebiet, auf dem der Jubilar, dem diese Festschrift gewidmet ist, sein Leben lang gearbeitet hat, nach dem Umbruch im Osten überhaupt noch eine Existenzberechtigung als gesonderte wissenschaftliche Disziplin[1] besitzt. Eine unangenehme Frage. Aber eine Frage, die sich jede überwiegend steuerfinanzierte Betätigung nun einmal gefallen lassen muss. Und eine Frage, die von manchen, die *nicht* im Bereich des Ostrechts tätig sind, in Gesprächen durchaus ab und an einmal gestellt wird. Tatsächlich gibt es eine Reihe von Gründen, über diese Frage nachzudenken. Schließlich war Forschungsgegenstand der Ostrechtswissenschaft das Recht der (vom Standpunkt eines westlichen Betrachters aus gesehen) östlich gelegenen, sozialistischen Staaten. Diese Staaten liegen zwar nach wie vor im Osten, sozialistisch sind sie jedoch nicht mehr. Der Osten ist schließlich schon lange nicht mehr „rot“, weite Teile davon sind sogar schon Mitglied der Europäischen Union; dort gilt also der gemeinschaftliche rechtliche Besitzstand. Auch andere früher sozialistische Staaten haben schon Assoziierungs- und Stabilisierungsabkommen unterzeichnet, beziehungsweise arbeiten darauf hin. Dort ist die Rechtsharmonisierung schon im vollen Gange. Dadurch, so könnte man argumentieren, sei der wesentliche Unterschied zum eigenen Recht, der bei der Erforschung anderer Rechtsgebiete ein „ungeschriebenes Tatbestandsmerkmal“ darstellt, weggefallen. Demzufolge, so könnte man weiter folgern, sei auch die Berechtigung für eine eigene Ostrechtswissenschaft weggefallen. Da es „den Osten“ (lies: die osteuropäischen kommunistischen Systeme)

---

* Der Verfasser ist Rechtsanwalt und Leiter der Projektbereiche Bosnien und Herzegowina, Kosovo, Mazedonien und Montenegro bei der Deutschen Stiftung für internationale rechtliche Zusammenarbeit e.V. (IRZ-Stiftung) in Bonn. Außerdem war er selbst als Lang- und Kurzzeitexperte in zahlreichen Projekten der IRZ-Stiftung und anderer Organisationen in den verschiedenen Staaten des ehemaligen Jugoslawiens tätig. Der vorliegende Beitrag gibt die persönlichen Auffassungen des Verfassers wieder.

1 Darunter wird hier die „klassische“ forschende und lehrende Ostrechtswissenschaft verstanden. Daneben ist seit fast zwei Jahrzehnten die „angewandte Ostrechtswissenschaft“ getreten, die insbesondere durch Organisationen wie die Deutsche Stiftung für internationale rechtliche Zusammenarbeit e.V. (IRZ-Stiftung), im Rahmen von ausgeschriebenen Projekten z.B. der EU oder der Weltbank aber auch durch Privatunternehmen Unterstützung bei der Rechtstransformation leistet.

nicht mehr gibt, sei eine eigene Ostrechtswissenschaft schließlich nicht mehr nötig. Diese Überlegung soll nachfolgend, vornehmlich anhand von Beispielen aus dem Arbeitsbereich des Verfassers, aber auch mit Blick auf einige andere Transformationsstaaten, überprüft werden

II. „Sozialistisches" Erbe und Wiedergänger im Recht von Transformationsstaaten

1. Vorbemerkung

Die eben dargelegten Überlegungen klingen jedoch nur auf den ersten Blick schlüssig. Eine solche Argumentation unterstellt nämlich, dass mit dem Systemwechsel in diesen Staaten nicht nur der Sozialismus als Staatsform aufgehört hat zu bestehen, sondern dass auch jede Besonderheit, die mit dem Sozialismus zu tun hat sowie jedes sonstige rechtliche Erbe aus dieser Zeit aus dem Rechtssystem verschwunden ist. Und zwar sowohl aus dem geschriebenen, als auch aus dem gelebten Recht. In Anbetracht der Resistenzen sonstiger sozialistischer Hinterlassenschaften in den Gesellschaften dieser Staaten würde dies jedoch der allgemeinen Lebenserfahrung widersprechen. Und tatsächlich trifft man in diesen Staaten auch heute noch auf Schritt und Tritt auf Regelungen und Verhaltensweisen, die genauso gut auch aus der Vorwendezeit stammen könnten. Wie nachfolgend an einigen Beispielen dargelegt wird, durchzieht das sozialistische Erbe die Rechtssysteme einiger Transformationsstaaten auch heute noch bis ins Detail. Hierbei wird der Begriff „sozialistisch" nicht als politischer Begriff verstanden. In diesem Beitrag werden darunter Vorschriften, aber auch Auslegungs- und Verhaltensweisen gefasst, die vielleicht nicht spezifisch sozialistisch sind, in sozialistischen Systemen aber besonders gut gedeihen konnten[2]. Hierzu gehören zum einen „auch sozialistische" Erscheinungen wie übertriebener Formalismus und „Scheren im Kopf". Zum anderen zählt dazu die Angst vor der Übernahme von Verantwortung durch zuständige Stellen, einschließlich der Richter auf der einen, aber auch die Anmaßung von Kompetenzen und das Erfinden zusätzlicher Hürden für die Aufnahme einer unternehmerischen Tätigkeit durch Private auf der anderen Seite. Außerdem zählen hierzu Vorschriften und Verhaltensweisen, die Denkweisen entspringen, die noch aus sozialistischer Zeit stammen, etwa, weil sie noch planwirtschaftliche und dirigistische Ansätze verfolgen, also „klassische sozialistische" Regelungen und Verhaltensweisen.

2 Oder unter den Systemen, die vor dem Sozialismus in den betreffenden Ländern herrschten. Schließlich ist manches, was wir am Anfang des 21. Jahrhunderts als typisch sozialistisch ansehen mögen, etwas, das bereits von den sozialistischen Systemen von deren Vorläufern übernommen wurde.

2. Beispiele für „Sozialistisches" im Recht von Transformationsstaaten aus dem Arbeitsbereich des Verfassers

Einige nachfolgende Beispiele und Beobachtungen aus dem Arbeitsbereich des Verfassers sollen verdeutlichen, um welche Arten von Vorschriften und Verhaltensweisen es geht.

a) Beispiele aus dem geschriebenen Recht

In der Föderation Bosnien-Herzegowina besteht die „Verordnung über die Bedingungen, die ein Unternehmen, bzw. eine andere juristische Person, zur Ausübung der registrierten Tätigkeit hinsichtlich der Zahl der beschäftigten Arbeiter verpflichtet ist zu erfüllen"[3]. Danach sind Unternehmen zum einen verpflichtet, den „Direktor" (Geschäftsführer oder Vorstand) in einem sozialversicherungspflichtigen Verhältnis anzustellen[4]. Außerdem sind danach – abhängig von der registrierten Tätigkeit, aber unabhängig von dem Umfang, in dem dieser nachgegangen wird – eine bestimmte Anzahl von Arbeitnehmern einzustellen[5]. Wie viele Arbeitnehmer mindestens eingestellt werden, kann also nicht der Arbeitgeber, dessen finanzielle Leistungsfähigkeit und seine, unter Beachtung der zwingenden Arbeitsschutznormen vorgenommene Arbeitsorganisation bestimmen, sondern wird durch diese Verordnung festgelegt. Dies zudem einzig und allein auf der Basis der Tätigkeiten, die das Unternehmen durchführt. Diese Vorschrift soll wohl die Einstellung von Arbeitnehmern anregen. Tatsächlich verhindert sie jedoch die Gründung neuer Unternehmen und offenbart, dass die Urheber noch tief im dirigistischen Denken verhaftet sind. Eine ähnliche gründungserschwerende und -verhindernde Wirkung haben Vorschriften, die es auch in Nachbarstaaten des genannten Landes gibt, durch die „minimale technische Voraussetzungen und die Art der Erbringung" bestimmter Dienstleistungen auch für nicht eben gefahrenträchtige unternehmerische Tätigkeiten vorgeschrieben werden. Hierzu gehört beispielsweise die Quadratmeterzahl der Geschäftsräume für den

---

3 Službene novine Federacije Bosne i Hercegovine (Gesetzblatt der Föderation Bosnien und Herzegowina) Nr. 15/98.

4 Soweit es die Anstellung des Direktors angeht, gab es dergleichen auch in Kroatien; vgl. den früherer Art. 34 Abs. 4 des Gesetzes über die Handelsgesellschaften (Zakon o trgovačkim društvima), eingeführt durch Gesetz zur Änderung und zur Ergänzung des Gesetzes über die Handelsgesellschaften, Narodne Novine Republike Hrvatske (NN RH: Gesetzblatt der Republik Kroatien) Nr. 34/99, außer Kraft gesetzt durch Beschluss des kroatischen Verfassungsgerichts v. 10.05.2000 (NN RH 52/00).

5 Zu näherem vgl. S. Pürner, Rahmenbedingungen für ausländische Investitionen, BiH SYST 01, Rn. 102 f., in Breidenbach u.a. (Hrsg.), Handbuch Wirtschaft und Recht in Osteuropa, München, EL 31.

Betrieb eines Reisebüros[6]. In diesen Vorschriften offenbart sich eine Denkweise, die noch tief von den Schemata aus den angeblich sozialistischen Zeiten geprägt ist. Das „Unternehmen" ist hier immer ein großer und leistungsfähiger Komplex, der solche Anforderungen unabhängig von ihrer tatsächlichen Berechtigung erfüllen kann. Der mittelständische und nebenberufliche Gründer ist in solchen Vorschriften nicht vorgesehen. Gerade solche Gründungen sind es jedoch, die, insbesondere wenn es um neue Technologien geht, oft den Grundstein zu einem erfolgreichen Unternehmen legen[7]. Weitere Vorschriften[8] werden so ausgelegt, dass man den Gegenstand einer Gesellschaft in den Gründungsdokumenten nicht frei und relativ kurz formulieren, sondern anhand einer einheitlichen Klassifikation von Tätigkeiten aufschlüsseln muss. Dabei fordert die Praxis, dass man nicht nur die Tätigkeit angibt, die den Hauptgegenstand der Gesellschaft bildet, sondern alle Tätigkeiten, die im Rahmen der Geschäftstätigkeit anfallen könnten[9]. Da oftmals befürchtet wird, dass man Tätigkeiten vergessen könnte, die die Gesellschaft später möglicherweise einmal ausüben könnte, neigen viele in der Praxis dazu, möglichst viele dieser Tätigkeiten zu nennen. Schwerpunkt der Ausarbeitung von Gesellschaftsverträgen ist demnach nicht das kreative Gestalten der Beziehungen zwischen den Gesellschaftern, sondern das „Erbsenzählen" bezüglich der Tätigkeiten. Oft besteht deshalb der überwiegende Teil des Gründungsvertrags aus der Aufzählung der Tätigkeiten. Wenn an einer Gründung Ausländer mitbeteiligt sind, führt dieses Vorgehen dazu, dass die erforderlichen Übersetzungskosten steigen. Allgemein verliert man aus dem Blick, welche Tätigkeit die Gesellschaft eigentlich wirklich ausüben möchte. Begründet wird das Erfordernis der Aufzählung der einzelnen Tätigkeit nicht selten mit sta-

---

6 So z.B. in Montenegro die „Regelung über die minimalen technischen Bedingungen hinsichtlich der Ausstattung der Geschäftsräume von Reisebüros" (Pravilnik o minimalno-tehničkim uslovima u pogledu opremanja poslovnih prostorija turističkih agencija), Službeni list Republike Crne Gore (SL RCG: Gesetzblatt der Republik Montenegro) Nr. 9/03, die u.a. vorschreibt, dass die Toilette eines Reisebüro bis in 1,5m Höhe gefliest sein muss und einen gesonderten Vorraum, in dem sich das Waschbecken befinden muss, zu haben hat (Art. 11 der genannten Vorschrift). Dies ist kein Einzelfall. Wer „pravilnik o minimalno-tehničkim uslovima" (Regelung über minimale technische Bedingungen) „googelt", erhält nicht weniger als 16.100 Treffer, die auf zahlreiche ähnliche Vorschriften in verschiedenen Staaten verweisen.

7 Über die Ursachen solcher Vorschriften kann man lange sinnieren. Ein bosnischer Kollege nahm in einem Gespräch mit dem Verfasser an, dass die Ursache nicht Blauäugigkeit und Weltferne der Verfasser wäre, sondern der Versuch, es potentiellen Konkurrenten der bestehenden Unternehmen bewusst schwer zu machen. Womit diese Vorschriften in einem weiteren Sinne sozialistisch wären, da sie so gezielt den fairen Marktwettbewerb verhindern würden.

8 Art. 6 des Gesetzes über die Klassifikation der Tätigkeiten in Bosnien und Herzegowina (Zakon o klasifikaciji djelatnosti u Bosni i Hercegovini), Službeni glasnik Bosne i Hercegovine (SG BiH: Gesetzblatt des Staates Bosnien und Herzegowina) Nr. 76/06.

9 S. Pürner, Rahmenbedingungen, EL 24, Rn. 41.

tistischen Gründen; wobei dieses Ziel gerade durch die Häufung der genannten Tätigkeiten eher vereitelt wird. Völlig sinnentleert stellt sich einem das seitenweise Aufzählen verschiedener Tätigkeiten im Gründungsvertrag dar, wenn man dann erfährt, dass für die statistische Anmeldung wiederum aus diesen vielen Tätigkeiten nur diejenige ausgewählt wird, die man tatsächlich als Haupttätigkeit betreibt. Letztlich ergibt sich in der Praxis also ein erheblicher Aufwand wegen einer Kombination von Relikten aus der sozialistischen Zeit mit denen der inzwischen aufgegebenen *ultra-vires*-Lehre, obwohl eigentlich kaum Fälle denkbar sind, in denen es noch praktische Auswirkungen haben könnte, wenn eine Gesellschaft außerhalb des im Gesellschaftsvertrag festgelegten Rahmens tätig wird. Die wenigen Fälle, die auftreten könnten, ließen sich wohl auch zivilrechtlich durch die Anwendung der Regelungen über kollusives Zusammenwirken oder im Innenverhältnis zwischen den Gesellschaftern und dem handelnden Vertreter der Gesellschaft durch die Regeln über eine Verletzung vertraglicher Pflichten lösen. Andere Gesetze dieser Staaten betonten auch mehr als ein Jahrzehnt nach dem Systemwechsel marktwirtschaftliche und rechtsstaatliche Selbstverständlichkeiten, beispielsweise, dass Handelsgesellschaften „von den Kapitaleigentümern verwaltet werden", oder „bei der Ausübung der wirtschaftlichen Tätigkeit gleichberechtigt sind" und dass Mittel von Handelsgesellschaften „im Rechtsverkehr sein können"[10]. Verständlich werden solche eigentlich überflüssigen Vorschriften nur, wenn man ihre Vorgeschichte kennt. Ein weiteres sozialistisches Erbe ist die Neigung, die Nichtbeachtung von gesetzlichen Vorschriften (auch solchen, die primär schuldrechtlichen Charakter haben) als Ordnungswidrigkeit mit Geldstrafe zu belegen[11]. Hier wird man sicher vorsichtig sein müssen, da man westliche Überlegungen nicht allzu schnell auf Transformationsstaaten übertragen kann, in denen immer ein gewisses Maß an Rechtsnihilismus präsent ist. Dort herrscht teilweise auch Manchesterkapitalismus, sodass es beispielsweise durchaus diskutabel erscheint, die Nichterteilung eines schriftlichen Nachweises über den Inhalt eines abgeschlossenen Arbeitsvertrags mit Geldstrafe zu bedrohen[12]. Ebenfalls stellt auch die Korruption ein großes Problem in diesen Staaten dar. Somit kann jede Vorschrift, die mit einer Strafe verbunden ist und von einer entsprechenden „Inspektion" überwacht wird, der Korruption Vorschub leisten. Wer die Verhältnisse und die Mentalität vor Ort kennt, wird bestätigen können, dass es nicht unwahrscheinlich ist, dass wenn

---

10 S. Pürner, a.a.O., SYT 01, EL 24, Rn. 36.

11 Beispiele hierfür finden sich in Art. 630 des kroatischen Gesetzes über die Handelsgesellschaften, in deutscher Übersetzung vom Autor dieses Beitrags in Breidenbach u.a. (Hrsg.), KRO 300, der nicht weniger als 88 solcher Fälle regelt und im Arbeitsgesetzbuch der Föderation Bosnien und Herzegowina, Art. 140, in deutscher Übersetzung vom Verfasser dieses Beitrags, a.a.O., BiH 600.

12 Wie dies z.B. Art. 140 Ziff. 3 des Arbeitsgesetzes der Föderation Bosnien und Herzegowina tut, vgl. dazu bereits die vorstehende Fn.

ein entsprechender Verstoß festgestellt wird, der Kontrollierte nachfragt, ob man die Situation nicht „auf andere Weise" lösen könne. Oder aber der Kontrollierende selbst weist darauf hin, dass diese Möglichkeit durchaus besteht. Mit anderen Worten: Solche Strafdrohungen leisten, auch dort, wo sie vielleicht der Sache nach gerechtfertigt wären, potentiell der Korruption – die ja an anderen Stellen gerade vehement bekämpft wird – Vorschub.

Wie hartnäckig sich der sozialistische „Stallgeruch" auch nach dem politischen Wandel hin zu einem konservativen, national geprägten Staat halten kann, zeigt das kroatische Gesetz über die Arbeit[13]. In dessen ursprünglicher Version war, nach langen diesbezüglichen Diskussionen, der zu sozialistischen Zeiten gebrauchte Begriff „Arbeiter" (*radnik*) durch „Beschäftigter" (*zaposlenik*) ersetzt worden. Bei einer späteren Novellierung dieses Gesetzes[14] führte man dann jedoch den ursprünglichen Begriff „Arbeiter" wieder ein. Auch – oder weil – es hier „nur" um eine terminologische Frage geht, lässt dieser Vorgang erahnen, wie präsent „das Sozialistische" noch im kroatischen Recht(sdenken) ist. Dass man wesentliche Grundprinzipien eines „westlichen" Arbeitsrechts noch nicht verstanden hat, zeigt Art. 250 des jetzigen, erst im Jahre 2009 erlassenen kroatischen Arbeitsgesetzes[15], in dem festgelegt wird, dass die Gewerkschaftsbeiträge der in einem Betrieb beschäftigten Arbeitnehmer vom Arbeitgeber eingezogen und an die Gewerkschaft weitergeleitet werden. Dies ist eine Regelung, die wohl mit dem Grundsatz der Gegnerfreiheit kaum vereinbar sein dürfte[16].

b) Beispiele aus der Rechtsanwendung und -auslegung

„Sozialistisches" im hier unterstellten Sinne findet sich jedoch nicht nur im geschriebenen Recht. Viel schwerwiegender als das *„law in the books"* prägt sich das frühere Recht, bzw. das frühere Rechtsverständnis, in der täglichen Rechtspraxis aus[17]. Diese geht teils am geschriebenen Recht vorbei, teils stellt sie aber

13 Zakon o radu (Arbeitsgesetz), NN RH Nr. 38/95.

14 Art. 1 des entsprechenden Änderungsgesetzes zum Gesetz über die Arbeit, NN RH Nr. 17/01.

15 Zakon o radu (Arbeitsgesetz), NN RH Nr. 149/09.

16 Im Übrigen erscheint die „Gegnerförderungspflicht", die dem Arbeitgeber dadurch auferlegt wird, auch anderweitig zweifelhaft.

17 Deshalb ist es ein Irrtum, dass mit dem Erlass neuer Vorschriften die „mission" der Transformation des Rechtssystems im jeweiligen Land bereits „accomplished" sei. Die Praxis zeigt, dass dann die Arbeit erst beginnt. Programme und Projekte, die dies nicht genügend berücksichtigen, bzw. dem, was man neudeutsch „Implementierung" nennt, zu wenig Zeit einräumen, sind von vorneherein zum Scheitern verurteilt. Vgl. zur Bedeutung der Rechtsanwendung auch S. Hülshörster, Recht im Umbruch (Diss.), Frankfurt a.M., 2008, S. 203. Nach Ansicht des Verfassers belaufen sich die hierfür erforderlichen Zeiträume nicht auf Jahre, sondern auf Jahrzehnte. Auch weil es in vielen Transformationsstaaten, anders als in der ehemaligen DDR, nicht darum geht, einen gerade einmal einige Jahrzehnte dauernden Irrweg zu korrigieren, sondern darum, Fundamente zu legen, die aufgrund ihrer vorsozialistischen Geschichte noch nie bestanden haben.

auch Erfordernisse auf, die im geschriebenen Recht auch bei gehöriger Anstrengung nicht zu finden sind. Zur letzteren Kategorie gehören Auffassungen von Registergerichten in Bosnien und Herzegowina, nach denen zum satzungsgemäßen Sitz einer Handelsgesellschaft auch die genaue Adresse gehört. Dies hat in der Praxis zur Folge, dass jeder Umzug, auch am Sitz der Gesellschaft selbst, eine Sitzverlegung darstellt und entsprechend aufwändig ist[18]. Ähnliche überflüssige Hürden stellt die Praxis der Registergerichte desselben Landes dar, bei jeder Mitteilung einer Änderung eintragungspflichtiger Tatsachen sämtliche Unterlagen zu verlangen[19], die auch bei der Gründung erforderlich sind. Hierzu gehören u.a. Bescheinigungen darüber, dass die Gesellschafter keine unbeglichenen Steuerschulden haben und dass alle etwaigen Ordnungswidrigkeitsstrafen beglichen sind. Dies wird verlang, obwohl gemäß Art. 80 des Gesetzes über die Registrierung der Geschäftssubjekte „die verantwortliche Person bei Gericht", die von Antragstellern Unterlagen verlangt, die von Gesetzes wegen gar nicht erforderlich sind, mit einer Geldstrafe bestraft werden kann[20]. Ein weiterer kritischer Punkt ist die Ermessens(nicht)ausübung durch Verwaltungsbehörden[21]. Hier werden nicht selten Kann-Vorschriften zu Lasten der Bürger und Unternehmen als Muss-Vorschriften ausgelegt. Ein diesbezügliches praktisches Beispiel, das der Verfasser in Sarajevo beobachten konnte, war die sofortige Schließung eines gastronomischen Betriebes, der bei einer Stichprobe keine Einkaufsquittungen für bestimmte, zum Verkauf angebotene Waren vorgelegen konnte. Die staatliche Verwaltung agiert insoweit nicht viel anders, als sie es zu sozialistischen Zeiten getan hätte[22,23]. Schwierigkeiten haben auch die neu ge-

---

18 So schon S. Pürner, Rahmenbedingungen, in Breidenbach u.a. (Hrsg.), EL 66, Rn. 91; vgl. nun auch V. Softić, Problemi pri registraciji privrednih društava u Bosni i Hercegovini (Probleme bei der Registrierung von Wirtschaftsgesellschaften in Bosnien und Herzegowina), unveröffentlichtes Manuskript, S. 11.

19 V. Softić, a.a.O., S. 10.

20 V. Softić, a.a.O., S. 10, Anm. 12.

21 S. Pürner, Rahmenbedingungen, in Breidenbach u.a. (Hrsg.), EL 66, Rn. 92.

22 Hier liegt in Bosnien und Herzegowina eine der ganz großen Aufgaben, die erst noch angegangen werden müssen. Während nämlich bereits verschiedene Versuche zur Reform der Justiz unternommen wurden, ist man die Reform der Verwaltung bislang noch nicht einmal ansatzweise angegangen.

23 Von dem Ideal „Öffentliche Verwaltung im Rechtsstaat: Serviceeinrichtung für den Bürger", das *U. Karpen* in *H. J. v. Oertzen* (Hrsg.), Rechtsstaatliche Verwaltung im Aufbau I – Kreisreform und Ämterverfassung, Baden-Baden, 1992, S. 23 ff., beschreibt, ist man in diesen Staaten auch heute noch sehr weit entfernt. Insgesamt sollte man sich bewusst sein, dass Deutschland wegen der „Transformation im eigenen Land" zwar ein Stück weit bessere Voraussetzungen hat, Transformationsstaaten zu unterstützen, als andere Staaten, für die Transformation immer nur ein „externes" Thema war. Jedoch sollte man sich hüten, die deutschen Erfahrungen zu sehr auf die sonstigen Transformationsstaaten zu übertragen. Schließlich muss Rechtsberatung in selbstständigen Transformationsstaaten immer auch bis zu einem gewissen Grad ergebnisoffen sein und auf

gründeten Verwaltungsgerichte (falls es solche in den betreffenden Staaten überhaupt gibt) bzw. die für Verwaltungssachen zuständigen Richter, in ihre Rolle zu finden. Hier hat man nicht selten den Eindruck, diese Richter sähen ihre Aufgabe weniger darin, den Bürger vor staatlichem Fehlverhalten zu schützen, sondern primär darin, den staatlichen Behörden Unbedenklichkeitsbescheinigungen zu erteilen[24]. Hinzu kommt eine weit verbreitete Ablehnung öffentlicher Verhandlungen durch diese Richter und von Maßnahmen des einstweiligen Rechtsschutzes im Verwaltungsrecht. Außerdem wird von etlichen für Verwaltungsstreitsachen in diesen Ländern zuständigen Gerichten so gut wie gar nicht in der Sache selbst entschieden[25].

Wenn man von Rechtsanwendung spricht, dann nimmt die Rechtsanwaltschaft eine zentrale Rolle ein. Auch hier steht nicht alles zum Besten[26]. Häufig verstehen sich die Anwälte in diesen Ländern, die beispielsweise Unternehmensmandanten bei Gründungen unterstützen, primär als Führer durch den Verwaltungsdschungel, während interessenorientierte und kreative Kautelarjurisprudenz nicht ihre Sache ist. Auch wer in den Transformationsstaaten Gerichtsverhandlungen besucht oder den kollegialen Gedankenaustausch mit Anwälten und Richtern aus diesen Staaten pflegt, wird feststellen, dass die Anwaltschaft sich nur schwer in die Rolle eines Interessenvertreters in dem Sinne, wie sie in westlichen Staaten verstanden wird, einfindet. Deshalb ist festzuhalten, dass auch in diesem Feld noch eine ständige Unterstützung und Begleitung erforderlich ist, bevor wirklich davon die Rede sein könnte, dass der Sozialismus und sein Erbe tatsächlich überwunden sind.

---

die Gegebenheiten vor Ort Rücksicht nehmen. Einen „Masterplan" wie ihn der Einigungsvertrag darstellte, gibt es dabei nicht. Dafür aber ein vielstimmiges Konzert internationaler „*player*", die teilweise auch mit sehr materiellen Verlockungen (*per diems* für Teilnahme an Workshops, *study visits* zu anderen Kontinenten) um die Gunst der Beratenden buhlen. Dies macht, abgesehen von Sprachproblemen, einen gewaltigen Unterschied zur Transformation im Beitrittsgebiet und stellt auch an die Berater zusätzliche Anforderungen, die im Zusammenhang mit der deutschen Wiedervereinigung nicht erforderlich waren.

24 Zur Rolle der Richter allgemein noch unter II 2.

25 Dazu z.B. *O. Luchterhand* (Hrsg.), Verwaltung und Verwaltungsrecht im Erneuerungsprozess Osteuropas, Berlin, 2001. Es sind Umstände wie die oben geschilderten, die dazu geführt haben, dass die IRZ-Stiftung einen Schwerpunkt ihrer Tätigkeit auf die Unterstützung der Verwaltungsgerichtsbarkeit in den verschiedensten Ländern legt. Die diesbezüglichen Maßnahmen sind zu zahlreich um sie hier alle aufzuzählen. Für die Ukraine vgl. ausführlich *S. Hülshörster*, a.a.O. Im Übrigen wird auf den Tagungsband zur Dubrovnik-Konferenz 2009, Deutsche Stiftung für internationale rechtliche Zusammenarbeit (Hrsg.), Der Staat vor Gericht – Die Rolle von Verwaltungsrecht und Verwaltungsgerichtsbarkeit für die Entwicklung des Rechtsstaats, Bonn, 2010, sowie auf die verschiedenen Jahres- und Länderberichte unter http://www.irz.de verwiesen.

26 Vgl. *S. Pürner*, Rahmenbedingungen, in *Breidenbach* u.a. (Hrsg.), EL 66, Rn. 89 f.

3. Hat die „Dritte Rechtstradition" überlebt?

Diese Beobachtungen zeigen, dass das kommunistische Erbe im Recht der Transformationsstaaten nach wie vor präsent ist und sowohl Bürgern als auch Unternehmen das Alltagsleben schwer macht. Nun könnte man einwenden, dass es sich dabei bis jetzt um Erfahrungen aus einem begrenzten Kreis von Ländern und ausschließlichen Beobachtungen des Verfassers handelt. Dieser steht damit jedoch nicht alleine auf weitem Feld, auch Autoren aus den betroffenen Staaten sehen den bisherigen Erfolg der ausländischen Unterstützung der Rechtsreformen mitunter kritisch[27]. Der Slowene *A. Galič* beispielsweise ist bezüglich der erfolgten Reform der slowenischen ZPO der Auffassung, dass auch die frühere slowenische ZPO einem guten Richter genügend Möglichkeiten geboten hätte, für ein effektives Zivilverfahren zu sorgen. Deshalb habe man letztlich nicht wegen der schlechten Qualität des früheren Gesetzes, sondern wegen dessen schlechter Auslegung ein neues Gesetz erlassen. Was wiederum die Frage aufwirft, woraus sich eigentlich die Hoffnung nährt, dass dieses neue Gesetz nun besser ausgelegt wird. Tatsächlich scheint es auch so zu sein, dass das neue Gesetz in der Anwendung/Auslegung zu keinem anderen Verhalten führte als das frühere[28]. Letztlich belegen Befunde wie dieser, dass der Ansatz, das gelebte Recht vor allem durch den Erlass neuer Gesetze zu verbessern, häufig unzutreffend ist, da es primär die Fähigkeiten der Rechtsanwender sind, die über die Qualität des Rechts entscheiden[29]. Maßnahmen zur Unterstützung dieser Fähigkeiten erfordern jedoch nicht nur eine größere Nachhaltigkeit als reine Gesetzgebungsprojekte, sondern auch mehr Vorkenntnisse – nicht nur im geschriebenen Recht des jeweiligen Partnerlandes, sondern auch in dessen tatsächlicher Rechtspraxis. Dass der Unterschied zwischen beidem oft größer ist als in westlichen Staaten, dürfte ein weiterer Beleg dafür sein, dass es nach wie vor sozialistische Erscheinungen in diesen Rechten gibt. Kritisch sieht das durch Gesetzesreformen Erreichte auch *F. Zoll*[30], der für Polen berichtet, dass der gesetzliche Abschied vom Prinzip der materiellen Wahrheit[31] nur ein unvollständiger war,

---

27 Zudem meist kritischer als die ausländischen Berater.

28 *P. Oberhammer*, Richterbild im Zivilprozess: Zwischenbilanz eines Jahrzehnts der Reformen in Mitteleuropa, S. 138, in *P. Oberhammer* (Hrsg.), Richterbild und Rechtsreform in Mitteleuropa, Wien, 2011.

29 Folgende Überlegung mag dies verdeutlichen: Sicher würde jeder gerne in einem Land mit guten Gesetzen und guten Juristen leben. Wenn beides jedoch nicht gleichzeitig zu bekommen wäre, dann wäre wohl ein Staat mit schlechten Gesetzen aber guten Juristen näher an einem Rechtsstaat als einer, bei dem zwar die Gesetze gut, aber die Juristen schlecht sind.

30 *F. Zoll*, Die Stellung des Richters in Polen, in *P. Oberhammer* (Hrsg.), Richterbild, S. 69 ff.

31 Das freilich nicht schon *per se* sozialistisch ist, vgl. dazu *P. Oberhammer*, a.a.O., S. 137 ff., insbes. S. 141 oben.

da Teile der Lehre und der richterlichen Praxis diesem gesetzgeberischen Auftrag nicht folgten und es über auslegungstechnische Hilfskonstruktionen wieder in das Gesetz „hineinlasen". Kritische Stimmen zum Erfolg der Reformen im Bereich des Zivilprozessrechtes gibt es auch zur Slowakei und zu Tschechien[32], wobei sich die letzten Ausführungen auch auf die Slowakei, Tschechien und Polen beziehen, die samt und sonders bereits Mitgliedstaaten der EU sind. Damit zeichnet sich ab, dass sich das sozialistische Erbe nicht nur in Staaten wiederfindet, die zeitlich verzögert in die Transformation gestartet sind.

Den wohl pointiertesten Standpunkt zur Frage der „sozialistischen Restbestände" im Recht der Transformationsstaaten (und zur Rolle der ausländischen Beratung in diesen) nimmt der kroatische Autor *A. Uzelac* ein, der sich jüngst zu der Feststellung veranlasst sah, dass das kommunistische Rechtssystem als „*Third Legal Tradition*" überlebt habe[33]. Er stellt fest, dass die Ansicht, etwaige sozialistische Überbleibsel im Recht der Transformationsstaaten seien lediglich Schwachstellen im immer noch nicht vollständig beendeten Transformationsprozess, eine unzulässige Simplifizierung darstellen würde. Auch zwei Jahrzehnte nach Beginn des Transformationsprozesses würden sich einige Merkmale der alten Tradition überraschend resistent und trotz des gesellschaftlichen Wandels unverändert zeigen[34]. Als Beleg führt er mehrere Teilbereiche an, in denen sich seiner Ansicht nach trotz des Systemwechsels im Grunde nichts geändert hat. Dies sind – und das sollte all jenen zu denken geben, die als Hauptaktionsgebiet der Transformation im Rechtsbereich die Schaffung neuer Gesetze ansehen – allesamt Bereiche, die nicht das „*law in the books*", sondern mentalitätsbedingte Umstände und „*soft skills*" betreffen. Neben dem Umstand, dass das Recht nach wie vor als Instrument zum Schutz der Interessen der politischen Eliten angesehen wird[35], nennt er insbesondere die Angst davor, Entscheidungen zu fällen und die Vermeidung der Übernahme von Verantwortung bei den Richtern[36,37]. Den letztgenannten zentralen Punkt führt *A. Uzelac* näher aus. Dabei

---

32 *P. Bohata*, Tschechische und Slowakische Republik, in Center of Legal Competence, Beschleunigung des zivilgerichtlichen Verfahrens in Mittel- und Osteuropa, Wien, Graz, 2004, S. 219 ff., dort insbes. S. 267 ff.

33 *A. Uzelac*, Survival of the Third Legal Tradition, Supreme Court Review (201), 49 S.C.L. (2d), S. 377-396, im Internet von der Homepage des Autors als Pdf-Dokument herunterladbar unter http://alanuzelac/from/hr/pubs/B843-Third_SupremeCourtCanada.pdf. Lediglich auf Kroatien bezogen, aber mit ähnlichen Ergebnissen, *ders.* in Center of Legal Competence, Beschleunigung des zivilgerichtlichen Verfahrens in Mittel- und Osteuropa, Wien, Graz, 2004, S. 121.

34 Wörtlich führt *A. Uzelac* aus: "Now, two decades after the beginning of the 'transition', some features of the 'old' tradition have proven to be surprisingly resilient and unaffected by change.", a.a.O., S. 378 f.

35 *A. Uzelac*, a.a.O., S. 382 f.

36 *A. Uzelac*, a.a.O., S. 383 ff.

findet er nicht weniger als neun noch aus sozialistischer Zeit überkommene Merkmale, die nach seiner Meinung[38] auch heute noch den Zivilprozess zumindest in den südosteuropäischen Transformationsstaaten prägen. Diese sind[39]:

1) ein nicht konzentriertes Verfahren und der Mangel an einer Verhandlung im tatsächlichen Wortsinne,
2) Mündlichkeit als bloße Formalität,
3) exzessiver Formalismus,
4) das Streben nach materieller Wahrheit,
5) fehlende Planung und fehlende prozessuale Disziplin,
6) Kontrolle durch Rechtsmittelverfahren als unpersönlicher und anonymer Prozess,
7) Vielfalt an Rechtsmitteln, die die Vollstreckung hinauszögern können,
8) endloser Kreislauf von Zurückweisungen,
9) unzureichende Bemühungen [der Richter][40], die zu kurzfristigen und sozial unangemessenen Ergebnissen führen.

In diesem Zusammenhang weist *A. Uzelac,* ähnlich wie *A. Galič*, darauf hin, dass zumindest im ehemaligen Jugoslawien die Zivilprozessordnung bereits früher ein mündliches, unmittelbares und konzentriertes Verfahren vorgesehen hat, das jedoch nicht in die Praxis umgesetzt wurde[41]. Auch dies ist ein Punkt, der belegt, dass es mit reinen Gesetzesreformen nicht getan ist. Genauer betrachtet kann man aus dieser Feststellung auch folgern, dass es teilweise gar nicht notwendig ist, das bestehende Recht zu ändern, da die problematischen Verhältnisse in der Rechtswirklichkeit nicht durch die Gesetze als solche verursacht werden, sondern durch die Art der Rechtsanwendung. Dies wiederum bedeutet, dass vor jedem Schritt in Richtung einer neuen Gesetzgebung die gründliche Analyse der bestehenden Gesetze und vor allem auch der diesbezüglichen Anwendungspraxis stehen sollte. Das mag durchaus als Selbstverständlichkeit erscheinen[42]. Wenn man jedoch die Gesetzgebungspraxis der Transformationsstaaten be-

---

37 Womit sich eine paradoxe Situation ergibt: Während Richter in diesen Staaten in streitigen Gerichtsverfahren häufig die ihnen vom Gesetz übertragenen Möglichkeiten zur Entscheidung nicht wahrnehmen, maßen sie sich im Bereich der Freiwilligen Gerichtsbarkeit Entscheidungen an, die ihnen von Gesetzes wegen gar nicht zustehen (siehe das oben zu der Praxis verschiedener Registergerichte in Bosnien und Herzegowina Gesagte).

38 Und zumindest der Autor dieses Beitrags würde ihm hier nicht widersprechen.

39 *A. Uzelac*, a.a.O., S. 390.

40 Ergänzung durch den Verfasser.

41 *A. Uzelac*, a.a.O., S. 390 f., meint dort u.a.: "The law that was in actual practice, however, was never interpreted or applied in this way".

42 Wobei zuzugeben ist, dass auch in unserem eigenen Rechtssystem nicht jedem Gesetzgebungsvorhaben eine solche Analyse vorausgeht.

obachtet, auch soweit sie von ausländischen Organisationen beraten, begleitet und oft initiiert wird, beobachtet, stellt man fest, dass dem leider nicht so ist.

III. Kritik der ausländischen Unterstützung der Rechtstransformation

1. Beispiele für von Ausländern initiierte überflüssige und/oder wenig in die vorhandene Rechtstradition passende Gesetze

a) UNMIK-Kosovo

Oft werden in den Transformationsländern in Ermangelung entsprechenden Sachverstands seitens der ausländischen Berater überflüssige und/oder wenig in die vorhandene Rechtstradition passende Gesetze erlassen und sogar von Ausländern initiiert. Hierzu einige Beobachtungen. Die ersten Beispiele sind bewusst dem Recht des Kosovo entnommen. Dieses weist zwar einige Besonderheiten, wie insbesondere die jahrelange direkte internationale Verwaltung auf, die in anderen Transformationsstaaten nicht zu finden sind, gerade dadurch eignet sich das Kosovo jedoch dazu, die Verhaltens- und Vorgehensweisen ausländischer Berater „in Reinkultur" zu studieren.

aa) Neue Gesetze trotz fehlenden Regelungsbedarfs

Die UNMIK-Verwaltung erließ für das Kosovo im Dezember 2001 ein neues Warenkaufrecht[43]. Offensichtlich war man der Meinung, dass es im Kosovo kein entwickeltes Kaufrecht gäbe. Wenn dem wirklich so war, dann war dem *Office of Legal Adviser* nicht bekannt, dass im Kosovo als Teil des ehemaligen Jugoslawiens das Gesetz über die Schuldverhältnisse galt, das 1978 nach Schweizer Vorbild geschaffen wurde und allgemein als sehr gutes Gesetz angesehen wird, und das durchaus passable – und vor allem den einheimischen Juristen bekannte und in der dortigen Rechtspraxis erprobte – Vorschriften über den Kaufvertrag enthielt. Diese Annahme wird auch dadurch gestützt, dass in Sektion 1.2 dieser UNMIK-Regulation die bisherigen kaufrechtlichen Vorschriften aufgehoben werden, ohne dass man sie beim Namen nennen konnte. Die betreffende Sektion lautet: „*Laws inconsistent with the provisions of the present regulation are repealed*". Ähnliche pauschale Formulierungen, durch die Vorschriften aufgeho-

43 Regulation No. 2000/68 UNMIK/REG/68 on Contracts for the sale of good, englische Version unter http://www.unmikonline.org/regulations/unmikgazette/02english/E2000regs/RE2000_68.htm; die albanische und serbische Version dieser UNMIK-Regulation sind dagegen nicht mehr auf der UNMIK-Homepage erhältlich, da die entsprechende Verweise unter http://www.unmikonline.org/regulations/unmikgazette/03albanian/Acontents.htm bzw. http://www.unmikonline.org/regulations/unmikgazette/04serbian/Scontents.htm ins Leere führen.

ben werden, die nicht im Mindesten bezeichnet werden, finden sich in vielen weiteren von der UNMIK erlassenen Vorschriften. Solche weiten Formulierungen sind nicht nur aus rechtsstaatlichen Grundsätzen bedenklich. Sie legen darüber hinaus auch den Schluss nahe, dass die Juristen des *Office of Legal Adviser* das anwendbare Recht im Kosovo, das sie durch ihre Tätigkeit in vielfacher Weise änderten, gar nicht kannten. Natürlich konnte man in der kurzen Zeit vom Beginn der UNMIK-Verwaltung bis zum Erlass dieser Vorschrift kein neues, konsistentes Warenkaufrecht für das Kosovo ausarbeiten. Deshalb „copypastete" man mehr oder weniger das Wiener UN-Kaufrecht, das eigentlich für grenzüberschreitende Sachverhalte gedacht ist. Dabei schrieb man fest, dass das neue Kosovo-Warenkaufrecht in Übereinstimmung mit den bekannten Entscheidungen, die zum UN-Kaufrecht ergangen sind, ausgelegt werden soll. In Sektion 1.1 heißt es hierzu: „*The present regulation ... shall be interpreted consistently with the reported decisions on that Convention.*" Dadurch wollten die Autoren wohl ein generelles Problem lösen, das sich beim Erlass neuen Rechts in den Transformationsstaaten stellte. Die Rede ist davon, dass zu solchen Vorschriften meist noch keine Literatur und insbesondere auch keine Rechtsprechung besteht, was wiederum zu Problemen bei der Lösung gesetzlich nicht explizit geregelter Fragen und zu Rechtsunsicherheit führt. Man kann allerdings mit gutem Grund bezweifeln, dass kosovarischen Juristen viel damit geholfen ist, wenn sie auf die für sie meist gar nicht zugängliche und sprachlich auch nicht verständliche Rechtsprechung zum UN-Kaufrecht verwiesen werden. Die Rechtsprechung und vorhandene Literatur[44] zum ehemals gesamtjugoslawischen Schuldrechtsgesetz können diese Kolleginnen und Kollegen jedoch meist ohne weiteres verstehen. Wohlgemerkt auch dann, wenn es sich dabei, wie meist, um Literatur und Rechtsprechung handelt, die in einer der Varianten der serbokroatischen Sprache verfasst sind, da diese nämlich von den meisten im Kosovo tätigen Juristen verstanden werden. Nicht wenige haben sogar in der entsprechenden Sprache außerhalb der damaligen Autonomen Provinz Kosovo studiert oder ein Postgraduiertenstudium absolviert. Der Erlass eines neuen Warenkaufrechts durch die UNMIK-Verwaltung war deshalb vermutlich ein gesetzgeberischer Schildbürgerstreich. Insbesondere hat man dadurch den Juristen, die dieses Recht anwenden sollten, die einzige Literatur zu diesem Rechtsgebiet, die sie

---

44 An erster Stelle ist hier der zweibändige „Komentar Zakona o obligacionim odnosima" (Kommentar des Gesetzes über die Schuldverhältnisse) von *B. T. Blagojević*, *V. Krulj* (Hrsg.), der in mehreren Auflagen in Belgrad erschien, zu nennen, zudem der mehr als 1000-seitige Kommentar „Zakon o obveznim odnosima sa komentarom" (Gesetz über die Schuldverhältnisse mit Kommentar) von *V. Gorenc*, Zagreb, 1998. Darüber hinaus gibt es zahlreiche einführende Lehrbücher auf der Basis dieses Gesetzes und Einzelwerke zu bestimmten Unterthemen wie *V. Kapor/S. Carić*, Ugovori robnog prometa (Verträge des Warenhandels), ebenfalls in Belgrad in verschiedenen Auflagen erschienen.

nutzen hätten können, weggenommen[45]. Die Gründe, wie es dazu kommen konnte, dürften u.a. in mangelnden Kenntnissen des lokalen Rechts liegen. Anders ausgedrückt: in fehlenden *ostrechtlichen* Kenntnissen[46].

bb) Neue Gesetze bei bestehendem Regelungsbedarf, aber mit unzutreffendem Ansatz

Manchmal mögen neue gesetzliche Regelungen tatsächlich erforderlich sein, jedoch raten ausländische Institutionen – wiederum in Unkenntnis der örtlichen Verhältnisse – nicht selten zu Lösungen, die wenig zum Rechtssystem und zur Gesellschaft des betreffenden Transformationsstaates passen. Hier könnte man als Beispiel, wiederum für das Kosovo, die dortige *Regulation on Legal Aid*, die Mitte des Jahrzehnts von der UNMIK-Verwaltung verabschiedet und vom *Office of Legal Adviser* ausgearbeitet wurde, nennen[47]. Diese enthält ein nach kanadischem Vorbild geschaffenes *Legal Aid*-System, in dem Beratungs-, Prozesskosten- und Verfahrenskostenhilfe unter Aufsicht einer von staatlichen Behörden unabhängigen *Legal Aid Commission* geleistet wird, wobei u.a. sogenannte *„students legal aid services“* und *„legal clinics“* die bedürftigen Rechtssuchenden beraten sollen. Hier lässt sich sicher trefflich darüber streiten, ob derlei wirklich in das Kosovo als balkanisches Postkonfliktgebiet mit ungezählten finanziellen und sozialen Problemen, zu denen insbesondere auch erhebliche Defizite bei der Juristenausbildung gehören, passt. Weiß man darüber hinaus, dass der Sachbearbeiter im *Office of Legal Adviser*, der die diesbezügliche Regulation ausgearbeitet hat, Kanadier war[48], dann wird einem klar, dass hier wiederum

45 Die Situation stellt sich also so dar, dass die UNMIK-Juristen ein Recht einführten, auf dessen Literatur zwar sie selbst, nicht aber die eigentlichen Rechtsanwender Zugriff hatten.

46 Möglicherweise traten auch noch weitere Gründe hinzu. Schließlich liest sich die Mitwirkung an der Ausarbeitung eines neuen Gesetzes in den CVs der beteiligten westlichen Juristen besser, als wenn dort zu lesen wäre, dass die Betreffenden durch ihre Tätigkeit und Kenntnisse im lokalen Recht ein eigentlich überflüssiges gesetzgeberisches Projekt vermieden haben, weil sie erkannten, dass das bisherige Recht, möglicherweise unter Modifikationen, durchaus beibehalten werden kann. Insoweit verhält es sich wie mit der Anerkennung des Chefs eines Autohauses einerseits für einen Mechaniker, der ein Auto repariert, und andererseits für einen Mechaniker, der den Kunden statt zu einer Reparatur zum Kauf eines Neuwagens überredet. Nicht immer also erntet das richtige und ressourcenschonende Verhalten die Anerkennung, die es verdient. Das mag man zu Recht bedauern, überrascht davon sollte man jedoch nicht sein. Schließlich wäre es erstaunlich, wenn der bekannte Ausspruch von Bismarck über die Ähnlichkeiten der „Herstellung“ von Gesetzen und Würsten ausgerechnet beim Aufeinandertreffen von Balkan und internationaler Verwaltung weniger Geltung hätte als anderweitig.

47 Regulation No. 2006/36 on Legal Aid v. 07.06.2006, englische Version im Internet unter http://www.unmikonline.org/regulations/unmikgazette/02english/E2006regs/RE2006_36.pdf; zu den albanischen und serbischen Sprachversionen vgl. bereits Fn. 43.

48 Honi soit qui mal y pense.

nicht die Erforschung der vor Ort gegebenen Verhältnisse am Beginn der Ausarbeitung der entsprechenden Vorschrift stand, sondern die in einer ganz anderen Kultur und Lebensumgebung erworbenen Kenntnisse des betreffenden ausländischen „Beraters".

b) Der Strafprozess als weiteres Beispiel (*Plea Bargaining* und die Illusion vom „*best of both worlds*")

Die bisherigen Beispiele stammten überwiegend aus dem Bereich des Zivilrechts. Dass bei der Rechtsberatung von Transformationsstaaten häufig nicht von den rechtlichen und sozialen Gegebenheiten vor Ort ausgegangen wird (wie das ostrechtlich ausgebildete Berater tun würden), sondern von den eigenen Erfahrungswelten, lässt sich jedoch auch an anderen Rechtsgebieten[49] belegen. Ebenso, dass ein solcher Ansatz nicht selten zu Ergebnissen führt, die kontraproduktiv sind. Ein Beispiel hierfür ist die Propagierung des *Plea Bargainings* als Mittel zu einem effektiven Strafprozess. Wie die Erfahrungen in Georgien sowie Bosnien und Herzegowina zeigen[50], hat das *Plea Bargaining* teilweise sehr negative Auswirkungen auf die öffentliche Wahrnehmung der Justiz. Gerade diese ist für die Durchführung und Akzeptanz rechtsstaatlicher Reformen jedoch von zentraler Bedeutung. In Kulturen, in denen dieses Rechtsinstitut nicht bekannt ist (und es wohl auch an den Voraussetzungen fehlt, die andernorts zu dessen Herausbildung geführt haben), wird ein solcher „*deal*" nämlich häufig als „*just another form of Corruption*"[51] oder als „*institutionalized form of bribery*"[52] angesehen. Ein Umstand, der insbesondere in Staaten wie Georgien, in denen zahlreiche politische Entscheidungsträger unter Korruptionsverdacht stehen und das *Plea Bargaining* zudem noch vor allem in Korruptionsfällen Anwendung findet[53], das ohnehin kaum vorhandene öffentliche Vertrauen in die Justiz erheblich erschüttern kann. Bezüglich Bosnien und Herzegowina kommt darüber hinaus noch erschwerend hinzu, dass das *Plea Bargaining* dort auch in Verfahren wegen Kriegsverbrechen angewendet werden soll. Hierdurch wird die Funktion

---

49 Aber auch an anderen Staaten; auch solchen, die nicht zu den Transformationsstaaten gehören. Vgl. zur Rezeption US-amerikanischen Gesellschaftsrechts in Japan T. Uemura, Japan als Land des Rechtsvergleichs – Die Problemstellung der Forschungsgruppe „Creating a New Corproate Legal Framewirk for a Mature Civil Society", in H. Küpper/W. Brenn (Hrsg.), Rechtstransfer und internationale rechtliche Zusammenarbeit, Bd. 64, der u.a. vom Jubilar herausgegebenen Studien des Instituts für Ostrecht, Frankfurt a.M., 2010, S. 19 ff., insbes. S. 25 und S. 27.

50 Vgl. hierzu C. Alkon, Plea Bargaining as a Legal Transplant: A Good Idea for Troubled Criminal Justice Systems?, 2009; der Beitrag kann kostenlos heruntergeladen werden unter http://works.bepress.com/cynthia_alkon/3/.

51 C. Alkon, a.a.O., S. 365.

52 J. D. Reichelt, A Hobson's Experiment: Plea Bargaining in the Republic of Georgia, 11 J. E. EUR. L. 159-160 (2004), zitiert nach C. Alkon, a.a.O., S. 366.

53 C. Alkon, a.a.O., S. 366.

solcher Strafverfahren, bestimmte Sachverhalte auch gerichtsförmig festzustellen, um sie für die zu erwartenden zukünftigen politischen Diskussion – soweit dies unter den dort herrschenden gesellschaftlichen Verhältnissen überhaupt möglich ist – möglichst unstreitig zu stellen, konterkariert. Außerdem erfährt ein Kriegsverbrecher, der sich einen Handel mit dem Gericht erlauben kann, in den Augen der Opfer und ihrer Hinterbliebenen eine Behandlung, die sich mit dem berechtigten Verlangen der Allgemeinheit nach Aufklärung und Sühne – gerade bei Delikten dieser Art – in keinster Weise verträgt. Aus rein technisch-juristischer Sicht kommt hinzu, dass das *Plea Bargaining* in Bosnien und Herzegowina als Teil eines hybriden Systems eingeführt wurde[54]. Solche hybriden Ansätze finden sich nicht selten in den Überlegungen zu neuen Gesetzen in den Transformationsstaaten. Nicht nur die Verantwortlichen in den Staaten selbst, auch ausländische Berater vertreten gelegentlich die Auffassung, dass man die einmalige historische Situation in diesen Staaten nutzen könnte, um „*the best of both worlds*" zu einem neuen und besseren Ganzen zu kombinieren. Einmal abgesehen davon, dass sich die Transformationsstaaten aufgrund ihrer anderweitigen Probleme erfolglose Experimente in der Gesetzgebung noch weniger erlauben können als Staaten allgemein, übersieht ein solcher Ansatz die Funktion, aber auch den Wert der Einheit der Rechtsordnung. Nur wer ein homogenes Rechtssystem besitzt, kann in Zweifelsfällen, wie sie gerade in Transformationsstaaten gehäuft auftreten, als ergänzende Erkenntnisquelle auf grundlegende Gedanken, die die ganzen Kodifikationen durchziehen, zurückgreifen. Bei „Legogesetzen" ist dies jedoch nicht möglich[55]. Äußerst fragwürdig ist es deshalb, wenn bei der Vorstellung neuer Gesetze die Anzahl der an der Entstehung beteiligten Berater als Qualitätsmerkmal genannt wird[56].

c) Ausländische Beratung, die sozialistische Erscheinungen perpetuiert?

Zurück zu den oben bereits angesprochenen Ausführungen von *A. Uzelac*, die den bisherigen Reformbemühungen in den Transformationsstaaten im Rechtsbereich (und damit zumindest mittelbar auch der westlichen Unterstützung hierbei)

54 C. Alkon, a.a.O., S. 370 f.

55 Man kann es auch mit einem Vergleich zur EDV deutlich machen. Gesetze, vor allem Verfahrensordnungen, sind letztendlich nichts anderes als Betriebssysteme, auf deren Basis andere „Programme" ablaufen. Unter EDV-Fachleuten würde jedoch niemand versuchen wollen, „the best of both worlds" zur kombinieren. Jedem wäre klar, dass die Hälfte von Windows, angereichert um die Hälfte von Linux (auch wenn es sich um die jeweils „besseren Hälften" handelt), nicht funktionieren, sondern zum sofortigen Systemabsturz führen würde.

56 Wie dies bei der neuen mazedonischen StPO der Fall ist, die ebenfalls versucht, Elemente aus mehreren Rechten zu vereinen. Laut „Skopje diem" vom 18.11.2010, S. 7, wurde dabei betont, dass am Zustandekommen des Gesetzes „ca. 50 in- und ausländische Experten" beteiligt gewesen wären.

kein gutes Zeugnis ausstellen. *A. Uzelac* geht sogar noch weiter und kommt zu dem Ergebnis, dass die Versuche ausländischer Berater, das Justizsystem in diesen Staaten näher an westliche rechtsstaatliche Standards zu bringen, den *status quo* sogar noch verstärkt hätten[57]. Ein Grund sei die Verstärkung der richterlichen Unabhängigkeit, die auch dazu missbraucht werden kann, alte Verhaltensweisen und Praxen nun noch ungehinderter zu pflegen[58]. Diese Feststellung muss man nicht teilen. Man sollte sich aber bewusst sein, dass Vorschriften und Rechtsinstitutionen nicht beliebig verpflanz- oder exportierbar sind und dass sie in anderen Umgebungen aufgrund von mentalitätsbedingten Auslegungsunterschieden nicht selten ganz anders funktionieren als von den Urhebern gedacht. Als Beispiele hierfür wurden bereits die korruptionsfördernde Wirkung allzu ausufernder Ordnungswidrigkeitsvorschriften, die Auslegung von Kann-Vorschriften als Muss-Vorschriften und die Probleme bei der Reformierung des Zivilprozessrechts in verschiedenen Staaten genannt. Jeder, der Erfahrungen mit der Unterstützung der Transformation im Rechtsbereich gesammelt hat, wird aus seiner eigenen Tätigkeit weitere Beispiele kennen, in denen westliches Gedankengut, bzw. insbesondere Gesetzesvorschriften, die nach Inhalt und Formulierung westlichen Vorbildern nachgebildet sind, in der praktischen Anwendung in diesen Ländern entweder keine Änderungen der Praxis mit sich brachten[59] oder aber, was noch schlimmer ist, zu ganz anderen, häufig unerwünschten Ergebnissen führten. Folglich bewahrheitet sich in diesen Fällen das Sprichwort, nachdem „gut gemeint" häufig einer der Gründe dafür ist, warum etwas „schlecht gemacht" wurde. Die Ursache für solche Fehlschläge liegt häufig auch darin, dass westliche Berater, denen mangels spezifischer ostrechtlicher Ausbildung die erforderlichen Vorkenntnisse fehlen, oftmals davon ausgehen, dass in den Transformationsstaaten „nach denselben Spielregeln gespielt" wird, wie im eigenen Heimatland. Dem ist jedoch gerade nicht so. Insbesondere hat das geschriebene Gesetzesrecht in diesen Ländern häufig eine andere, nämlich weitaus geringere Bedeutung, als beispielsweise in der Bundesrepublik Deutschland. Die Ursache hierfür liegt wiederum – zumindest u.a. – im ehemals kommunistischen System. Dieses System hat nicht nur die zur damaligen Zeit ausgebildeten und praktizierenden Juristen sozialisiert, sondern auch eine Tradition geprägt, die

---

57 A. Uzelac, a.a.O., S. 394, wörtlich: "An interesting paradox could be noted here – the fact that the very attempts to bring the justice system closer to the Western rule of law standards have actually strengthened the status quo."

58 A. Uzelac, a.a.O., S. 394 f., wiederum wörtlich: "... it [the organizational autonomy and self-management of the judicial branch (Ergänzung durch den Autor)] was also a magic wand that could assist in the continuation of the old attitudes and practices by creating a protective veil against any public criticism (even legitimate ones). Thus, the judiciaries of the third legal tradition – often with the generous help of the Western partners – have formed impenetrable barriers to substantial changes."

59 Beispielsweise bei den entsprechenden Vorschriften, die schlichtweg nicht angewendet werden, weil sie entweder überhaupt nicht gelesen oder nicht verstanden werden.

sich als solche auch noch auf Juristen auswirkt, die erst nach dem Fall des Systems ausgebildet wurden. Zum einen deshalb, weil es für Traditionen gerade kennzeichnend ist, dass sie eine über die Lebzeiten ihrer Begründer hinausgehende Wirkkraft entfalten. Zum anderen aber auch, weil es – auch darauf weist *A. Uzelac* hin[60] – die Vertreter der alten juristischen Eliten sind, die die jungen Juristen auch in den Jahren danach (und teilweise noch heute) ausbildeten (bzw. noch ausbilden) und sozialisierten (bzw. noch sozialisieren).

IV. Fazit und Ausblick

Zusammenfassend lässt sich feststellen, dass die obigen Beispiele gezeigt haben, dass das Recht der Transformationsstaaten auch heute noch zahlreiches sozialistisches Erbe enthält. Manches von diesen alten Relikten ist nur dann erkennbar, einordbar und bekämpfbar, wenn man das früher geltende Recht kennt. Hier besteht die Notwendigkeit, das Ausmaß dieser Erscheinung wissenschaftlich begründet festzustellen, auch um herauszufinden, ob es sich bei den genannten Fällen nur um Ausnahmen oder aber die Spitze eines Eisberges handelt. Dafür bedarf es jeweils entsprechend ausgebildeter Juristen. Hier besteht also ein reiches Betätigungsfeld für die Ostrechtswissenschaft als „bestandsaufnehmende“, aber auch als ausbildende Wissenschaft. Wie die Beispiele weiter zeigen, fehlt der Rechtstransformation, und auch der ausländischen Beratung hierbei, häufig der erforderliche theoretische „Unterbau“, insbesondere hinsichtlich der bestehenden rechtlichen, aber auch gesellschaftlichen Voraussetzungen sowie des mentalitätsbedingten Umfelds. Auch hier eröffnet sich ein reiches Betätigungsfeld für die Ostrechtswissenschaft. Es liegt zwar eine ganze Reihe von Arbeiten vor, die die Transformation in einzelnen Rechtsgebieten und Staaten begleitet haben, auch der Jubilar war und ist diesbezüglich tätig[61]. Die Anzahl der entsprechenden Arbeiten ist sogar beachtlich[62]. Bedenkt man jedoch, dass es sich bei der Rechtstransformation um einen Prozess handelt, der nicht nur etliche Jahre in Anspruch nimmt, sondern sich auch auf zahlreiche Rechtsgebiete (und vor allem Länder, die einen beträchtlichen Teil der beiden Kontinente Europa und Asien einnehmen) erstreckt, dann dürfte in Anbetracht der schieren Masse, sowie der gesellschaftlichen und politischen Bedeutung dieses Prozesses offensichtlich sein, dass tatsächlich noch zu wenige diesbezügliche Arbeiten vorliegen[63] – insbesondere, wenn man sich die große Anzahl der Fragestellungen, die der wissenschaftlichen Aufarbeitung bedürfen, vor Augen hält.

---

60 A. Uzelac, a.a.O., S. 395.

61 F.-C. Schroeder (Hrsg.), Justizreform in Osteuropa, Frankfurt a.M., 2004.

62 Zum Beispiel die zahlreichen, bei A. Fodor, Rechtsreform durch Normentransplantation in Osteuropa, Berlin, 2009, S. 8 f., in Fn. 24 genannten Werke.

63 Auch deshalb, weil es mit einer einmaligen Bewertung nicht getan ist. Schließlich lässt sich der Erfolg von Rechtsreformen kaum unmittelbar nach Erlass eines neuen Gesetzes – gerade auf diesen Zeitpunkt bezogen werden jedoch die meisten diesbezüglichen Ar-

Solche Fragen stellen sich bereits bezüglich des grundsätzlichen Vorgehens bei der Rechtstransformation. Von diesen sollen hier nur einige genannt werden. Die Weltbank und die EU unterstützen die Rechtstransformation durch Ausschreibungen[64] und es kommen Ausschreibungsregeln zur Anwendung, die auf denselben Verfahrensarten basieren, wie sie auch für große Bauprojekte gelten. Hier ließe sich in Kenntnis der unterschiedlichen Rechtstraditionen, die in den Transformationsstaaten präsent sind, fragen, ob diese Vorgehensweise, die ja mehr oder weniger unterstellt, dass jeder Transformationsstaat auch im Rechtsbereich von Organisationen aus allen EU-Staaten in gleicher Weise unterstützt werden kann, tatsächlich sachgerecht ist. Gerade im Hinblick auf die Nachhaltigkeit wäre hier wissenschaftlich fundiert auch der Frage nachzugehen, ob solche Projekte, oder aber die jahrelange bilaterale Unterstützung durch Einzelorganisationen aus Ländern mit einer Rechtstradition, die derjenigen des jeweiligen Partnerlandes nahe steht, das Mittel der Wahl sind[65]. Bei den soeben angesprochenen Fragen geht es primär um die Methode bei der Unterstützung des Transformationsprozesses in den verschiedenen Staaten. Ein zweiter grundsätzlicher Fragenkomplex betrifft die (Zwischen-)Ziele der Transformation und der einschlägigen Unterstützung. Hier wäre zum einen zu klären, ob angebotsorientierte oder bedarfsorientierte ausländische Rechtsberatung für die Partnerstaaten zu den besten Ergebnissen führt. Antworten sollten jedoch auch im Hinblick auf die Schwerpunkte einer solchen Unterstützung gesucht werden und ob diese, gerade in Zeiten knapper Mittel, bei der Gesetzgebungsberatung oder aber bei der Aus- und Weiterbildung der Juristen in diesen Staaten liegen sollten. Soweit es die Gesetzgebungsberatung angeht, sollte ebenfalls untersucht werden, ob es im Hinblick auf die bestehende Rechtstradition, aber auch die zum bisherigen Recht vorhandene Literatur, wirklich sinnvoll ist, in den Transformationsstaaten bereits zum jetzigen Zeitpunkt umfassende Kodifikationen des bürgerlichen Rechts nach Art des BGB vorzubereiten[66].

---

beiten geschrieben – beurteilen, sondern erst nach kontinuierlicher Beobachtung der Anwendungspraxis, der dabei auftauchenden Probleme und auch der Widerstände seitens der Rechtsanwender.

64 Zu Einzelheiten bzgl. des IPA-Programms (Instrument for Peraccession Assistance) der EU vgl. http://europa.eu/legislation_summaries/agriculture/enlargement/e50020_en.htm.

65 Ähnliche Fragen könnte man auch bezüglich des TAIEX-Programms der EU (http://ec.europa.eu/enlargement/taiex/index_de.htm) überprüfen.

66 Zweifelnd hierzu S. Pürner, Einleitende Anmerkungen zum Plan eines mazedonischen Zivilgesetzbuches, in Makedonska akademija na naukite i umetnoste (Hrsg.), Kodifikacija na makedonckoto gradjancko i trgovcko pravo, S. 35 ff. Eines der vielen Argumente, das gegen ein solches Vorgehen spricht, ergibt sich bereits aus dem Umstand, dass solche Neukodifikationen inhaltlich dennoch meist nur bisherige Regelungen wiederholen. Wer jedoch solchen alten Wein in neuen Schläuchen produziert, macht mit einem (unnötigen) Federstrich des Gesetzgebers (unnötigerweise) das wenige an Litera-

Dies alles sind Aufgaben, die von den derzeit bestehenden ostrechtlichen Institutionen schon aus Kapazitätsgründen nicht umfassend bearbeitet werden können. Dies ist umso bedauerlicher, als ostrechtliche Kenntnisse bei der Unterstützung der Transformationsstaaten Irrwege vermeiden können, die nicht nur für die Partnerstaaten lästig, sondern auch für die Unterstützerstaaten teuer sind, da diese Projekte durchwegs aus Steuermitteln finanziert werden[67].

Die gerade angesprochenen sind beileibe noch nicht alle Aufgaben, die sich der „Ostrechtswissenschaft 2.0" stellen. Außer in der Forschung besteht für die Ostrechtswissenschaft auch ein erheblicher, derzeit nicht gedeckter Bedarf hinsichtlich der Ostrechts*lehre*. Dieser liegt in der Ausbildung westlicher Juristen, die in Transformationsprojekten tätig werden und solcher, die anderweitig in Bezug auf diese Länder arbeiten, hier insbesondere Anwälte und Unternehmensjuristen. Der Bedarf besteht deshalb, da man die Wirkung von Reformgesetzen in einem spezifischen Rechtssystem nur dann voraussehen können wird, wenn man die Vorläuferregelungen sowie die Praxis und die Literatur hierzu – also das gesamte Umfeld bzw. die tatsächliche Rechtswirklichkeit – kennt. Für den anwaltlichen Bereich kommt hinzu, dass man beispielsweise bei Verhandlungen über geplante Joint Venture bestimmte Meinungen und Wünsche der Partnerseite nur vor diesem Hintergrund tatsächlich nachvollziehen kann. Aber auch in den Transformationsstaaten selbst gäbe es Erfordernisse für die lehrende Ostrechtsforschung, insbesondere wegen der oben beschriebenen sozialistischen Relikten und Wiedergänger im Recht dieser Staaten, die von den Lehrenden selbst aus Gründen der eigenen Biographie häufig nicht adäquat beschrieben und angesprochen werden. Deshalb besteht durchaus ein Bedarf an „Ostrecht für Ostler". Soweit es um die wissenschaftliche Begleitung der Rechtstransformation in den betreffenden Ländern geht, wird es auch erforderlich sein, dass die im Bereich des Ostrechts tätigen Institutionen und ihre Mitarbeiter praktische Er-

---

tur, das zu den bestehenden Gesetzen in dem jeweiligen Transformationsstaat überhaupt besteht, zunichte. Oder er bewirkt zumindest, dass diese Literatur in Zukunft erst nach einer aufwendigen Kompatibilitätsüberprüfung, die für jede Vorschrift und die Kommentierung hierzu gesondert durchzuführen ist, genutzt werden kann. Die Hoffnung aber, dass sich angesichts der Kleinheit vieler Transformationsstaaten zukünftig eine eigenständige, auch wirtschaftlich selbsttragende juristische Literatur abseits dessen entwickelt, was üblicherweise im Rahmen von klar umrissenen und zeitlich begrenzten Projekten mit ausländischen Geldern subventioniert wird, dürfte kaum eine praktische Grundlage haben. Gerade eine solche Literatur sollte es jedoch geben, wenn man die Forderung nach mehr „ownership" (im Sinne von Selbstverantwortung) ernst nimmt. Deshalb konterkariert die Forderung nach mehr „ownership", wer ein Rechtssystem durch überflüssige, aber auch durch vorschnelle Rechtsimplantate von seiner bisherigen eigenen Literatur „abschneidet". Siehe dazu im Übrigen bereits Fn. 45-47.

67 Bezüglich der oben angesprochenen hybriden Lösungen dürfte es so sein, dass es ostrechtlich ausgebildeten Juristen, die um die Rechtstraditionen der Partnerstaaten in Transformation wissen, wohl kaum in den Sinn kommen würde, solchen Gesetzen vorschnell das Wort zu reden.

fahrungen in diesbezüglich unterstützenden Projekten sammeln. Dies führt notgedrungen dazu, dass die Ostrechtswissenschaft Teil ihres eigenen Forschungsgegenstands wird, und bringt es mit sich, dass sie in Zukunft den Spagat zwischen wissenschaftlicher Objektivität und Eigeninteressen bewältigen muss. Ein wichtiges Argument für den Fortbestand, ja sogar die Ausweitung der Ostrechtswissenschaft in allen ihren Teilbereichen, insbesondere aber in denjenigen der lehrenden und der angewandten Wissenschaft, ist die Gleichbehandlung von unseren östlichen Partnern und den westlichen. Hier sollten von deutscher Seite an die handelnden Akteure weitgehend dieselben Anforderungen gestellt werden wie an diejenigen, die in der rechtlichen Zusammenarbeit mit westlichen Staaten tätig sind. Dazu müssen deutsche Institutionen mit entsprechend ausgebildeten Fachleuten aufwarten können[68]. „Entsprechend" heißt hier mit spezifischen Rechts-, aber auch Sprachkenntnissen bezüglich eines jeden einzelnen Landes. Da diese Länder zahlreicher geworden sind[69], besteht hier also ein immenser Bedarf.

In dem vorliegenden Beitrag war es schon aus Platzgründen nicht möglich, der Ausgangsfrage umfassend nachzugehen. Sowohl die angeführten Beispiele aus dem Recht verschiedener Transformationsstaaten, wie auch die daraus abgeleiteten Überlegungen sind deshalb nur Ausschnitte eines viel größeren Ganzen. Gerade dieser Umstand belegt jedoch, dass der Bedarf für eine eigenständige Ostrechtswissenschaft mit dem Systemwechsel in den östlichen Transformationsstaaten keinesfalls weggefallen ist. Er ist, im Gegenteil, sogar größer geworden. Dies bringt ebenso einige Änderungen für die Ostrechtswissenschaft mit sich. An aktuellen ostrechtlichen Themen für weitere Festschriften für den Jubilar dürfte deshalb auch in Zukunft kein Mangel bestehen.

---

68 Hier könnte Deutschland mit verhältnismäßig geringem Aufwand durch entsprechende Anstrengungen gegenüber dem Rechtsexport aus dem US-amerikanischen Raum auch einen Wettbewerbsvorteil für die deutsch-rechtlich geprägte, partnerschaftliche Unterstützung bei der Rechtstransformation aufbauen. Da dieser Wettbewerb aus deutscher Sicht quantitativ wohl kaum zu gewinnen ist, sollte hier vor allem auf Qualität gesetzt werden. Dies darf sich jedoch nicht in dem Hinweis auf die Qualität des deutschen Rechts (das zugegeben in diesen Staaten einen guten Ruf genießt und häufig auch das bisherige Recht mitgeprägt hat) erschöpfen. Vielmehr muss Deutschland seinen Standortvorteil, den es u.a. aufgrund seiner traditionellen historischen und personellen Verbindungen zu den meisten Transformationsstaaten besitzt, durch vermehrte Anstrengungen in allen Bereich der Ostrechtswissenschaft, einschließlich der angewandten, zielgerichtet ausbauen.

69 O. Luchterhand spricht in seinem Vorwort zu „Verwaltung und Verwaltungsrecht" (siehe Fn. 25) noch davon, dass sich – damals – die Zahl der Staaten in der östlichen Hemisphäre des Kontinents von 8 auf 23 erhöht hätte. Inzwischen sind auf dem Gebiet des ehemaligen Jugoslawiens noch zwei weitere dazu gekommen.

Der Beitrag des Instituts für Ostrecht München und des Instituts für Gesetzgebung der Verchovna Rada der Ukraine zur Entwicklung der Gesetzgebung

Einige Aspekte der deutsch-ukrainischen Zusammenarbeit auf dem Gebiet des Rechts

*Prof. Dr. Oleksandr Kopylenko**, *Prof. Dr. Oleg Zaichuk***

Die Frage der Rechtsentwicklung in der Ukraine ist in erster Linie mit der Tätigkeit von wissenschaftlichen Forschungsinstitutionen verbunden, die mit der Aufgabe betraut sind, Rechtsnormen in Europa und der ganzen Welt zu erforschen, neue Ideen auf dem Gebiet des Rechts zu entwickeln sowie Konzepte und Empfehlungen zur Übernahme dieser Normen in das ukrainische Recht und die ukrainische Gesetzgebung zu erarbeiten. Diese wissenschaftlichen Institutionen sind für Regierungsorgane tätig und sind bevollmächtigt, Entscheidungen auf nationaler Ebene zu treffen.

Eine dieser Institutionen im ukrainischen Staat ist das Institut für Gesetzgebung der Verchovna Rada der Ukraine. Das Institut ist einzigartig hinsichtlich der Kompetenzen und es bildet eine Basiseinrichtung der rechtswissenschaftlichen Fundierung der gesetzgeberischen Tätigkeit der Verchovna Rada.

Die Richtlinien des Parlaments stellen das Institut vor verantwortungsvolle und komplexe Aufgaben, da Gesetzesbeschlüsse vom rechtlichen, sozialen und ökonomischen Standpunkt aus begründet sein müssen, üben sie doch Einfluss auf die Lebensqualität der Gesellschaft und die Position des Staates in der internationalen Arena aus. Die Erfüllung dieser Aufgaben obliegt den verschiedenen Abteilungen des Instituts:

- für europäisches Recht und internationale Integration;
- für die Entwicklung der nationalen Gesetzgebung;
- für Theorie und Praxis der Gesetzgebungstätigkeit;
- für die Überwachung einer effektiven Gesetzgebung.

* Direktor des Instituts für Gesetzgebung der Verchovna Rada der Ukraine, Mitglied der Nationalen Akademie der Wissenschaften der Ukraine.

** Erster stellvertretender Direktor des Instituts für Gesetzgebung der Verchovna Rada der Ukraine, Mitglied der Nationalen Akademie der Rechtswissenschaften der Ukraine.

In allen diesen Abteilungen sind hochqualifizierte Experten tätig, die Mehrzahl von ihnen hat einen akademischen Grad auf den Gebieten Recht, Staatsverwaltung, Ökonomie oder Philosophie.

Das Institut entwickelt beständig neue Formen und Methoden seiner Tätigkeit, die in bedeutendem Maße durch die Bedürfnisse der gesetzgebenden Organe bedingt sind. In den letzten Jahren wurde eine neue Methodik der Analyse von Gesetzentwürfen eingeführt, deren Ziel darin liegt, solche Entwürfe zu erforschen, die auf die Regelung wichtiger Bereiche des gesellschaftlichen Lebens zielen. Beobachtet werden nicht nur Inhalte der eingetragenen Gesetzesvorlagen, sondern auch programmatische und regulative Materialien, die Geschichte der gesetzgebenden Regelung und die Sachlage der Gesetzgebung in diesem Bereich, internationale Standards, Empfehlungen internationaler Organisationen sowie ausländische Erfahrungen bei der Regelung entsprechender Bereiche der gesellschaftlichen Beziehungen. Diese Materialien werden an das Parlament übergeben, wo sie im Prozess der rechtsetzenden Tätigkeit verwertet und danach zwecks Verbreitung in Fachkreisen in zusammengefasster Form in der Sammlung „Probleme der legislativen Sicherung in wichtigen Bereichen der gesellschaftlichen Beziehungen" veröffentlicht werden.

Eine derart systematische Herangehensweise vereinfacht in bedeutendem Maße die Tätigkeit der gesetzgebenden Organe und findet breite Anwendung bei der Ausarbeitung der Entwürfe von Legislativakten. Experten des Instituts für Gesetzgebung werden von speziellen Kommissionen und Arbeitsgruppen hinzugezogen, deren Aufgabe es ist, Gesetzesvorlagen hinsichtlich der Rechte und Freiheiten der Bürger in den Bereichen Politik, Wirtschaft und Sozialwesen zu erarbeiten. In diesem Kontext sollen auch Anmerkungen zu Gesetzen über Wahlen, zum Gerichtssystem, der Staatsbürgerschaft sowie gegen Korruption ausgearbeitet werden.

Zu den weiteren Aufgaben des Instituts gehört unter anderem die Vorbereitung wissenschaftlicher Expertisen bezüglich Fragen, die vom Verfassungsgericht der Ukraine entschieden werden. Insbesondere hat das Institut für Gesetzgebung eine Expertise bezüglich der Verfassungsmäßigkeit einer Reihe von Gesetzesbestimmungen vorbereitet, z.B. über die Reduzierung der Auswirkungen der Finanzkrise auf den Beschäftigungsgrad der Bevölkerung, die Vorbeugung von Korruption, die Privatisierung des staatlichen Immobilienbestands oder über Änderungen im Bodengesetzbuch der Ukraine. Diese Expertisen haben einen wissenschaftlich-rechtlichen Charakter.

Eine besonders wichtige Aufgabe des Instituts für Gesetzgebung ist die Überwachung der effektiven Anwendung von Gesetzen und anderen Normativakten mit Relevanz für Staat, Wirtschaft, Beschäftigung und Sozialsystem, was die Entwicklung des Rechts begünstigt. Mit Hilfe eines solchen „Monitorings" kann man Probleme der Gesetzgebung sowie Möglichkeiten ihrer Reform schneller erkennen. Diese Arbeit trägt zur Verwirklichung der Kontrollfunktion des Parlaments bei. Das Institut hat eine Reihe von Untersuchungen durchgeführt, um Wege und Mechanismen zur Steigerung der Qualität der ukrainischen Gesetzgebung zu finden. Aufgrund der Resultate dieser Untersuchungen wurde eine Reihe von Änderungen und Ergänzungen in der geltenden Gesetzgebung erarbeitet sowie der Sammelband „Monitoring der Effektivität der Gesetzgebung: Ziele, Kriterien, Durchführbarkeit" veröffentlicht.

Von nicht geringerer Bedeutung ist die Hilfeleistung des Instituts für Gesetzgebung bei der Steigerung des Wissensniveaus von Parlament, Exekutive und örtlichen Selbstverwaltungen im Bereich der Normsetzung. Innerhalb des Instituts besteht seit mehr als sechs Jahren eine Ukrainische Schule für Rechtsetzung, die über eine Lizenz des Ministeriums für Bildung und Wissenschaft verfügt und sich als Einzige mit methodischen Ausbildungsstrukturen im Bereich Rechtsetzung beschäftigt. Das Institut entwickelt Programme und Pläne für den Eingangskurs „Rechtsetzung" und gibt wissenschaftliche und methodische Lehrbücher, Fachwörterbücher und Informationsmaterial heraus. Besonderer Beliebtheit erfreut sich die Bibliothek für Rechtsetzung. Eine interessante und wichtige Neuerung ist die Herausgabe des Werkes „Gesetzeskenntnis". In Kürze werden die Lehrbücher „Gesetzentwürfe" und „Rechtsetzung" veröffentlicht.

Ihre Grundlage bilden Arbeiten aus nationalen Wissenschaftskreisen, Ergebnisse der rechtsetzenden und der rechtsanwendenden Praxis sowie Schlussfolgerungen ausländischer Legislativorgane. Die Vorlesungen an der Schule werden von renommierten Wissenschaftlern, Volksdeputierten, Vertretern der Organe der Staatsmacht sowie von führenden europäischen Fachleuten abgehalten. In diesem Jahr hat die Schule sieben Kurse durchgeführt und zählte fünfhundert Absolventen, deren Kompetenz die Grundlage für die Professionalität der Arbeit des Parlaments hinsichtlich der Entwicklung der Gesetzgebung bildet.

Somit ist das Institut für Gesetzgebung auch Basis für die Entwicklung der Rechtswissenschaft, der staatlichen Verwaltung und Wirtschaft. Am Institut arbeiten Wissenschaftler zwecks der Verteidigung ihrer Dissertationen, die Recherchen für die Dissertationen sind auf die angewandten Wissenschaften ausgerichtet und tragen im Wesentlichen nicht nur zur Entwicklung theoretischer Grundlagen, sondern auch zur Lösung praktischer Aufgabenstellungen der Organe der Staatsmacht bei. Das Institut erarbeitet Analysen der Dissertationen, erfasst ihr wissenschaftliches Potenzial und spricht Empfehlungen zu ihrer Verwendung bei der Arbeit im Parlament und bei sonstigen Machtorganen aus. Eine derartige Analyse des Zeitraums von 2002 bis 2009 ist z.B. in der Ausgabe „Rechtswissenschaft und gesetzgeberische Praxis: Analyse von Dissertationen" veröffentlicht worden.

Eine der wichtigsten Aufgaben des Instituts für Gesetzgebung ist es, die Gesetzgebung der Ukraine aufgrund der Erforschung von Tendenzen des internationalen Rechts sowie der ausländischen Gesetzgebung im Kontext der Integration politisch-ökonomischer Prozesse in Europa und der ganzen Welt zu vervollkommnen. Besondere Beachtung verdient die Einhaltung der internationalen Verpflichtungen unseres Staates im Wege der Gesetzgebung, die infolge seiner Mitgliedschaft in zahlreichen internationalen Organisationen und der Entwicklung seiner Beziehung zur Europäischen Union entstanden sind.

Entsprechend studiert das Institut, wie der Gesetzgeber die Umsetzung von Normen des internationalen und europäischen Rechts gewährleisten kann. Die Abteilung für europäisches Recht und internationale Integration unterstützt die Tätigkeit der Verchovna Rada. Zu diesem Zweck wird die Entwicklung des Rechts in EU und Europarat ständig beobachtet (Dokumente des EU-Ministerrats, des Europäischen Parlaments und der Kommission, Entscheidungen des Europäischen Gerichtshofs für Menschenrechte in Beschwerden gegen die Ukraine). Ergebnisse dieser analytischen Arbeit werden vierteljährlich in der Reihe „Umschau des europäischen Rechts" veröffentlicht. Mittlerweile besteht diese Reihe aus 18 Ausgaben mit Beschlüssen der Regierungsberatungen zu Fragen der europäischen Integration aus dem Jahr 2008, welche regelmäßig an die Parlamentsausschüsse und alle Organe der Exekutive versandt werden.

Ferner erfolgt im Rahmen des Themenschwerpunkts „Rechtliche Mechanismen der Anpassung der ukrainischen Gesetzgebung an die Gesetzgebung der Europäischen Union" rechtsvergleichende und analytische Forschung, deren Ergebnisse sowohl in Publikationen des Instituts als auch in speziellen Sammlungen erscheinen, darunter „Vergleichende Rechtskenntnis (rechtstheoretische Forschungen)", „Vergleichende Rechtskenntnis (Rechtssysteme der Welt)", „Ukraine: europäische und internationale Normen im Bereich der sozialen Versorgung. Vergleichende Analyse", „Politik in der Arbeitsmigration. Nationale Gesetzgebung und internationale Standards, Praxis anderer Länder", „Rechtliche Regelung bioethischer Fragen im Kontext der Anwendung internationaler und europäischer Standards", „Menschenrechte in der politischen Gesellschaft", „Rahmenkonvention über den Schutz nationaler Minderheiten. Ukraine: der heutige Stand", „Europäische Rechtsstandards als Orientierung für die Entwicklung der ukrainischen Gesetzgebung", „Dialog zwischen Gesellschaft und Machtorganen: europäische Standards und Erfahrung" u.a.

Die Abteilung für methodische Nachschlagewerke, zu welcher das Zentrum für Übersetzungen der Akte des europäischen Rechts gehört, bereitet thematische Sammelwerke vor und veröffentlicht sie. Dazu zählen insbesondere „Europäische Rechtsakte: kurze Übersicht", „Europäische Rechtsakte bezüglich sozialer Fragen", „Europäische Rechtsakte zu Fragen der Regionalpolitik" und „International-rechtliche Akte aus dem Bereich Sport".

Eine wichtige Quelle der Kenntnisse über die Besonderheiten der Entwicklung des Rechts und der Gesetzgebung europäischer Staaten und ebenso eine Plattform zur Erprobung von Ideen sind die Realisierung gemeinsamer wissenschaftlicher Arbeiten, der Austausch von Erfahrungen und wissenschaftlicher Literatur und die Durchführung von Konferenzen und Seminaren im Rahmen internationaler Projekte. Diese Arbeitsweise des Instituts für Gesetzgebung hat sich bei der Zusammenarbeit mit dem Europarat, der EU, der Vertretung der UNO in der Ukraine, dem Kinderhilfswerk UNICEF, der ILO, des UNHCR sowie bei internationalen Programmen und Fonds sehr bewährt.

Besonders wertvoll ist die Entwicklung der Kooperation zwischen dem Institut für Gesetzgebung und wissenschaftlichen Einrichtungen in Deutschland. Als sehr wichtig hat sich die gemeinsame Arbeit des Instituts für Gesetzgebung und des Instituts für Ostrecht München erwiesen, die im Jahre 2006 durch einen Vertrag über wissenschaftliche Zusammenarbeit beschlossen wurde; initiiert wurde der Vertrag durch die Leiter des Instituts für Ostrecht, Prof. Schroeder und Prof. Küpper. Im Laufe der letzten Jahre hat diese Kooperation stark an Bedeutung gewonnen. Gefördert wurde dies vom Deutschen Akademischen Austauschdienst und der Deutschen Stiftung für internationale rechtliche Zusammenarbeit im Rahmen des Programms „Unterstützung der Demokratie in der Ukraine“.

Das hohe wissenschaftliche Niveau der Zusammenarbeit wird durch Forschungen auf ausgesuchten Einzel- und Gesamtgebieten gewährleistet. Hierfür werden das Wissen und die Erfahrungen der ukrainischen und deutschen Spezialisten genutzt, gemeinsame Konferenzen durchgeführt, auf welchen die Resultate dieser Forschungen vorgestellt und Erfahrungen ausgetauscht werden. Ferner werden Perspektiven zur Vervollkommnung der nationalen Gesetzgebung, die an der Entwicklung des europäischen Rechts ausgerichtet ist, erörtert.

Die Ergebnisse der vorgestellten Forschungen und die Vorträge in den Konferenzen werden in speziellen Sammelwerken in ukrainischer und deutscher Sprache veröffentlicht, um sie dem Parlament der Ukraine, verschiedenen Bibliotheken sowie einem breiten Fachpublikum zugänglich zu machen. Diese Forschungen sind anwendungsorientiert und dienen der Arbeit von ukrainischen und deutschen Gesetzgebern, Exekutivorganen, Rechtspraktikern sowie der Ausbildung von Berufsanfängern.

Forschungsgegenstand eines Kooperationsprojektes im Jahre 2009 war das Thema „Auslandsinvestitionsrecht in der Ukraine: Rechtliche Rahmenbedingungen und Beilegung von Investitionsstreitigkeiten“. Die Wahl des Themas war dadurch begründet, dass in der heutigen Lage der Wirtschaft in Ukraine, Europa sowie der ganzen Welt derart wesentliche und zusammenhängende Probleme wie der Ausweg aus der Krise und der Übergang zu Marktreformen gelöst werden müssen. Eine wichtige Frage war auch die Vorbereitung des Entwurfs der neu getroffenen Kooperationsvereinbarung zwischen der EU und der Ukraine, welche die Gründung einer Freihandelszone vorsieht.

Es ist bekannt, dass die Kapitalschwäche in der Ukraine das Hinzuziehen ausländischer Investitionen notwendig macht. Eine erfolgreiche Durchführung von Marktreformen in unserem Staat ist nicht möglich ohne eine effektive strukturelle Investitionspolitik einschließlich der Umgestaltung des Wirtschaftssektors mit dem Ziel, ein günstiges Investitionsklima zu schaffen. Als Perspektive für die Beendigung der Krise kann in der Ukraine die Errichtung eines starken Produktionssektors mit Beteiligung von Investitionskapital sein. Die Grundlage müssen neueste Technologien, modernes Know-how sowie neue Formen der Organisation von Arbeit bilden.

In diesem Kontext ist Deutschland ein gutes Beispiel, ein leistungsstarker und erfahrener Partner. Besonderes Augenmerk verdient die Tatsache, dass unsere Länder nicht nur gemeinsame historische Wurzeln in der fernen Vergangenheit haben, sondern seit der Erlangung der Unabhängigkeit auch eine lange Tradition der wirtschaftlichen Zusammenarbeit, was sich in hohen Investitionen im Banken-, Versicherungs- und Handelssektor sowie in Wissenschaft und Forschung ausdrückt. Verglichen mit sonstigen Staaten der EU ist Deutschland der größte Investor in die Wirtschaft der Ukraine.

So haben zwei wissenschaftliche Konferenzen, die 2009 in Kiew und Regensburg unter der Leitung von Prof. Schroeder und Prof. Küpper, Leiter des Instituts für Ostrecht München, sowie Prof. Kopylenko, Direktor der Instituts für Gesetzgebung, und Prof. Zaichuk, Erster stellvertretender Direktor des Instituts für Gesetzgebung, stattgefunden, die große Beachtung bei bedeutenden ukrainischen und deutschen Forschern und Spezialisten aus den Bereichen Recht und Wirtschaft gefunden haben. Vorträge der beiden Konferenzen sind in diesem Jahr in dem Sammelband „Zusammenarbeit zwischen der Ukraine und Deutschland im Bereich Investitionen: Probleme der rechtlichen Regelung und Praxis der wirtschaftlichen Integration“ in ukrainischer Sprache veröffentlicht.

Das Thema des Projekts der wissenschaftlichen Zusammenarbeit unserer Einrichtungen im Jahr 2010 war „Mediation als Verfahren konsensualer Streitbeilegung“. Es wird in den heutigen Kontext der Reform der ukrainischen Gesetzgebung auf den Gebieten Verwaltung, Korruptionsvorbeugung und Gewährleistung von Rechtshilfe integriert.

Die großen rechtsstaatlichen Reformen machen es notwendig, nach innovativen Wegen zur Lösung von verschiedenen Fragen, die sowohl für den privaten als auch den öffentlichen Bereich der Lebensgestaltung einer Gesellschaft bedeutend sind, zu suchen. Die effektive Regelung bei der Lösung von Streitigkeiten und Konflikten ist eine dieser Fragen. Ungeachtet der Tatsache, dass sich Gerichte mit der Lösung solcher Probleme beschäftigen, halten es ukrainische Wissenschaftler für wichtig, alternative Methoden zur Streitbeilegung zu finden.

Das Projekt des Jahres 2010 konnte dank der Heranziehung von Spezialisten aus Polen drei Perspektiven ausleuchten. Im Hinblick darauf, dass die Thematik relativ neu ist, lag das Gewicht auf der Erforschung der rechtstheoretischen und praktischen Grundlagen der Mediation in zivilen, Familien- und staatsrechtlichen sowie staatlichen Angelegenheiten. Die Ergebnisse der Forschung wurden auf der deutsch-ukrainisch-polnischen Konferenz in Regensburg vorgestellt, die mehr als 50 Teilnehmer zu verzeichnen hatte. Die Teilnehmer haben eine Reihe wichtiger Themen bezüglich der Perspektiven der Mediationsregelungen in Deutschland, Polen und in der Ukraine erörtert. Besprochen wurde die Rolle der Mediation als Form der Rechtsprechung in Wirtschaftsfragen und in Bereichen des öffentlichen, Arbeits- und Familienrechts sowie die Bedeutung der Mediation im Prozess der Demokratisierung der Gesellschaft.

Diese Vorträge waren von Grundsatzdiskussionen begleitet, deren Ergebnisse besagen, dass die Mediation nicht nur eine sehr effektive Methode der Unterstützung des Gerichtssystems ist, sondern auch zur Kostensenkung des Staatsetats beiträgt. Die Materialien der Konferenz werden einem Publikum gleich in drei Ländern zugänglich gemacht.

Der nachfolgende Schritt wird der Eingangskurs „Mediation: Rechtliche Grundlagen, Methoden und Praxis“ sein, welcher in der Ukrainischen Schule für Rechtsetzung des Instituts für Gesetzgebung mit Unterstützung von ukrainischen und deutschen Fachleuten durchgeführt wird. Den Hörern des Kurses werden spezielle ukrainisch-deutsche Zertifikate verliehen.

Wichtig zu erwähnen ist auch die Sitzung des Runden Tisches „Mediation als Methode zur Entwicklung einer bürgerlichen Gesellschaft: die ukrainische und deutsche Perspektive“, die in der Botschaft der Bundesrepublik stattgefunden hat. Mitglieder der Sitzung waren ukrainische und ausländische Experten: Diplomaten, Wissenschaftler, Richter, Rechtsanwälte, Spezialisten aus dem Bereich Mediation, junge Juristen sowie Vertreter der Presse. Nahezu 100 Personen haben daran teilgenommen.

Ein wichtiger Fakt ist der vorhandene Gesetzesentwurf der Ukraine „Über die Mediation“, der vom Justizministerium der Ukraine erarbeitet wird. Dabei wird er von Experten des Europarats, der Deutschen Stiftung für internationale rechtliche Zusammenarbeit sowie weiteren internationalen Organisationen unterstützt. An der Entwicklung des Gesetzentwurfs haben sich auch Vertreter der Öffentlichkeit beteiligt, die Mediation in der Ukraine im Rahmen von Pilotprojekten bereits praktizieren. Die vorliegende Fassung des Gesetzes wird gerade zur Vorlage im Ministerkabinett vorbereitet und nach Genehmigung an das Parlament zur Ausarbeitung übergeben. Im offiziellen „Bulletin des Justizministeriums der Ukraine“ wurde zwecks Unterstützung des Gesetzgebers in diesem Jahr eine spezielle Rubrik eingeführt, die dem Thema Mediation gewidmet ist; zahlreiche einheimische und ausländische, aber in erster Linie deutsche Fachleute sind eingeladen, dort zu veröffentlichen.

Trotz allem stellen Wissenschaftler fest, dass die Gesetzesnovellen zur Einführung der Mediation nur begrenzt in die Gesamtreform der Gesetzgebung hinsichtlich des Rechtsprechungssystems, der Strafprozessordnung sowie der Rechtsanwalts- und Staatsanwaltsordnung einfließen. Diese Reformen haben einen komplexen und perspektivischen Charakter und für das Parlament gilt es, den Nutzen der Einführung eines Mediations-Rechtsinstituts abzuwägen.

Zusammenfassend ist zu betonen, dass die Tätigkeit des Instituts für Gesetzgebung der Verchovna Rada und des Instituts für Ostrecht München ein gutes Beispiel für eine partnerschaftliche Zusammenarbeit zum Zweck der gegenseitigen Erforschung von innovativen Rechtsnormen ist, was eine effektive Arbeit im sich zunehmend integrierenden Rechts-, Wirtschafts- und Politikraum Europa ermöglicht.

Aus dem Ukrainischen übersetzt von Irina Adam, Institut für Ostrecht

Juristische Wissenschaft unter dem Blickwinkel naturwissenschaftlicher Erkenntnissuche – Versuch eines unwissenschaftlichen Vergleichs

Prof. Dr. jur. Andreas Steininger, Dipl.-Ing. (Mechanik)[*]

Nicht erst seit dem Tage, an dem ein Bundesminister eine zweifelhafte Dissertation vorlegte, stellt sich auch die Frage nach der Glaubwürdigkeit der juristischen Wissenschaft als solcher. Wie konnte es passieren, dass die Dissertation zunächst mit *summa cum laude* bewertet wurde? Zitate fehlten, Plagiate wurden aufgedeckt. Nur: Läge bei korrekter Zitierweise eine wissenschaftliche Leistung vor? Worin besteht überhaupt juristische Wissenschaft?

Wer als Jurist interdisziplinär mit Kollegen aus den Naturwissenschaften wissenschaftlich zusammenarbeitet, der wird wissen, wie schwer es ist, von diesen überhaupt als Wissenschaftler ernst genommen zu werden. Naturwissenschaftlern, die versuchen, in langen und ermüdenden Testreihen, in Laboren, vor dem Computer oder in Versuchshallen der Natur und ihrer Funktionsweise Geheimnisse zu entlocken, ist kaum vermittelbar, worum es sich bei juristischer Wissenschaft überhaupt handelt und wie eine solche Art der Kopie wie die eingangs erwähnte überhaupt möglich ist. Worin liegt die tiefe Erkenntnis juristischer Wissenschaft? In der Interpretation von durch Menschen geschaffenen Regelungen, die sich von heute auf morgen ändern? In der Analyse gerichtlicher Entscheidungen, die sich bisweilen nach dem „*common sense*" oder gar nach dem im jeweiligen Land herrschenden Regime richten? Wie wirkt juristische Wissenschaft in der Praxis? Hilft sie zu heilen, eine Brücke zu bauen oder Äcker zu bestellen?

Es ist keine neue Feststellung, dass Zweifel an der juristischen Wissenschaft auch von Juristen selbst geäußert werden. Bereits 1848 sprach *Julius von Kirchmann* vor der Deutschen Juristischen Gesellschaft das geflügelte Wort „Ein Federstrich des Gesetzgebers, und ganze Bibliotheken werden zu Makulatur"[1].

Der Ausspruch *Kirchmanns* lässt sich in diesem Sinne weiterspinnen, dass juristische Wissenschaft wie eine Art Mode erscheint, ähnlich einer Strömung wie dem Minirock oder einer Dauerwellenfrisur. Der einzige Unterschied bestünde darin, dass diese Mode der Rechtswissenschaft durch den Gesetzgeber bestimmt ist, der sich wiederum nach der gesellschaftlichen Anschauung und

* Professor für Wirtschaftsrecht an der Hochschule Wismar.

1 *J. v. Kirchmann*, Von der Werthlosigkeit der Jurisprudenz als Wissenschaft, Berlin 1848.

Akzeptanz richtet. Jedoch: Gesellschaftliche Einstellungen ändern sich und soziale Konflikte ergeben sich, auf welche der Gesetzgeber reagiert. Kann aber eine Modeströmung oder die daraus erwachsende Regelungsstruktur Gegenstand einer wissenschaftlichen Betrachtung sein?

Es existiert bereits eine Vielzahl von Darstellungen, Analysen und Kommentaren zur Philosophie, zum Hintergrund, zum Selbstverständnis und auch zur Existenzlegitimation juristischer Wissenschaft[2]. Allerdings entspringen die neueren Betrachtungen i.d.R. dem Blickwinkel der Jurisprudenz selber. Man könnte dies als eine Art autonome Auslegung juristischer Wissenschaft bezeichnen – oder mit anderen Worten: Eine Wissenschaft legt Rechenschaft über sich selbst ab. Das Ergebnis ist vorhersehbar, niemand wird ernsthaft sein eigenes Bild, seine eigene Existenzberechtigung in Frage stellen. Eine Beurteilung nicht von einem philosophischen oder gar juristischen Standpunkt her könnte hier hilfreich sein, um ein etwas alternatives Bild zu erhalten.

I. Postulat der Vergleichbarkeit der Vorgehensweise

Daher sei im Folgenden der Versuch unternommen, die juristische Wissenschaft einmal unter dem Blickwinkel eines Naturwissenschaftlers zu betrachten. Dabei soll es nicht um eine Subsumtion unter den Begriff der Wissenschaft selber gehen, denn diese lässt sich verstehen als das Grundbedürfnis, Ordnung in die Mannigfaltigkeit von Ereignissen und Erscheinungen zu bringen und nach Erkenntnis zu streben, also nach gesicherten Erklärungen und Vorhersagen natürlicher, soziologischer und gesellschaftlicher Prozesse[3]. Im Rahmen dieses Begriffes wird ausdrücklich mit umschlossen, dass Wissenschaft nicht nur eine theoretische Funktion hat, sondern vielmehr auch eine ganz praktische und soziale, nämlich die Existenz- und Entwicklungsbedingungen der Gesellschaft zu erhalten und fortzuentwickeln[4]. Geht man allerdings von diesen Begriffsdefinitionen aus, so fällt es nun schwer, eine neue Perspektive im Hinblick auf die juristische Wissenschaft zu gewinnen. Denn jede Wissenschaft wird sich unter diese Begriffe subsumieren lassen.

---

2 Das Thema der Existenzlegitimation von Recht zieht sich wie ein roter Faden durch die juristische Wissenschaft und auch durch die Philosophie; hier seien nur beispielhaft *Montesquieu*, De l'esprit des lois, 1748 (deutsche Edition von Forsthoff 1951) und *Kant*, Die Metaphysik der Sitten, 1. Teil, Rechtslehre, 1797, erwähnt. Einen guten Überblick bietet *Zippelius*, Rechtsphilosophie, 5. Aufl., München 2007; mit einer interessanten historischen Herleitung *Mahlmann*, Rechtsphilosophie und Rechtstheorie, Baden-Baden 2010, insbesondere S. 62 ff.

3 Siehe m.w.N. Europäische Enzyklopädie zu Philosophie und Wissenschaft, *Sandkühler* (Hrsg.), Bearbeiter *U. Jensen*, Hamburg 1990, Band 4, Begriff „Wissenschaft"; Historisches Wörterbuch der Philosophie, *Ritter*, *Gründer*, *Gabriel* (Hrsg.), Basel 2004, Begriff „Wissenschaft", siehe insbesondere S. 911.

4 *U. Jensen*, a.a.O., Begriff „Wissenschaftstheorie", S. 952.

Daher sei zum Versuch des Vergleichs ein anderer Ansatz gewählt: Es sollen einige Grundprinzipien der Vorgehensweisen zum Erkenntnisgewinn aus der täglichen wissenschaftlichen Arbeit von Jurisprudenz und Naturwissenschaft miteinander verglichen werden.

Nun sind Naturwissenschaften nicht gleich Naturwissenschaften. Eine Eingrenzung ist unabdingbar, um konkrete Ergebnisse zu erhalten. Bereits der Begriff der Naturwissenschaft ist kompliziert und schwer abzugrenzen. Herkömmlich wird als Naturwissenschaft die Erforschung der unbelebten und der belebten Natur verstanden, verbunden mit dem Versuch, diese zu beschreiben, zu messen und zu erklären. Als ein typischer Protagonist der Naturwissenschaft gilt die Physik[5], die hier deswegen für den Vergleich herangezogen sei.

Ist die Hinwendung zur Physik als Vergleichsmaßstab zur Jurisprudenz willkürlich? Vergleicht man nicht Äpfel mit Birnen, wenn man solch unterschiedliche Wissenschaften über ihre Untersuchungsschritte miteinander in Beziehung setzt?

Hierzu sei zum einen noch einmal hervorgehoben, dass nicht Physik mit Rechtswissenschaft direkt verglichen werden soll, sondern nur die Methodik der Erkenntniserarbeitung. Zum anderen existiert noch ein anderes Argument der Vergleichbarkeit der Vorgehensweise: Rechtswissenschaft ist ein axiomatisches Fach und Physik bedient sich eines axiomatischen Fachs, nämlich der Mathematik.

Mit anderen Worten: Die Mathematik ist eine von Menschen erdachte und definierte Methode zur Beschreibung von natürlichen Ereignissen. Sie gehört daher auch nicht zu den Naturwissenschaften, sondern zu den sogenannten Strukturwissenschaften[6]. Sicherlich könnte man auch numerisch definieren, dass 2=3 ist und somit 1+2=4 ist – alles eine Frage der Definition. Allerdings muss die Gesamtheit der Definitionen ein System bilden, in das sich die einzelne Definition ohne Widerspruch einfügt.

Hier besteht ein Zusammenhang mit der Rechtswissenschaft. Nach dem herkömmlichen Verständnis bedeutet Rechtswissenschaft die Auslegung und Systematisierung gegenwärtiger und geschichtlicher juristischer Texte und sonstiger rechtlicher Quellen. Dies umfasst auch eine Beschäftigung mit der Entstehung und der Anwendung von Rechtsquellen und Normen[7]. Die Auslegung muss zur Schaffung und Erhaltung eines Gesamtsystems, des Rechtssystems, führen und

---

5 Philosophie Lexikon, *Prechtl/Burkhard* (Hrsg.), Bearbeiter *Metzler*, Stuttgart 1996, Begriff „Naturwissenschaft".

6 Aufschlussreich *Küppers*, Die Strukturwissenschaften als Bindeglied zwischen Natur- und Geisteswissenschaften, http://www.personal.uni-jena.de/~x7kube/download/pdf/Strukturwissenschaften.pdf; vgl. auch *Bourbaki*, The Architecture of Mathematics, Amer. Math. Monthly 67(1950), S. 221-232 sowie *Fowler*, Mathematical Modelling in the Applied Sciences, Cambridge 1997, S. 3 ff.

7 Hierzu siehe *Neumann*, Einführung in Rechtphilosophie und Rechtstheorie der Gegenwart, *Kaufmann/Hassemer/Neumann* (Hrsg.), 7. Aufl., Heidelberg 2007, S. 385 ff.

sich diesem anpassen. Mit anderen Worten: Genauso wie man 2 mit 3 gleichsetzen kann, lassen sich juristische Begriffe im Rahmen einer weiten wissenschaftlichen Auslegung umdefinieren oder mit einer gänzlich anderen Bedeutung belegen. Beispiele hierfür sind etwa die „gewöhnliche Verwendung" in § 434 BGB oder der im Gaststättenrecht häufig verwendete Begriff der „Zuverlässigkeit". Hier tritt der axiomatische Anteil der Rechtswissenschaft zu Tage.

Auf dieser Grundlage ist das Postulat der Vergleichbarkeit der Vorgehensweise zwischen Physik, soweit sie auf ihrer Struktur- und Hilfswissenschaft Mathematik beruht, und Rechtwissenschaft zu rechtfertigen.

II. Der naturwissenschaftliche Ansatz

Erkenntnisgewinn in der Physik verläuft i.d.R. in den folgenden Schritten. Als Beispiel sei hier eine fallende Metallkugel aus der Experimentalphysik gewählt, da diese sich leichter illustrieren lässt als Vorgänge der Quantenmechanik.

1. Schritt: Beobachtung und Beschreibung eines Vorgangs – Erkenntnis-Ebene 1

Zunächst wird ein Vorgang in der Natur beobachtet und beschrieben, also ein Vorgang, dessen Ursache nicht vom Einfluss des Menschen abhängig ist. Beispiel: Eine Metallkugel fällt aus einem Meter Höhe auf den Boden.

Dieser Schritt ist noch vollständig deskriptiv. Er beruht allein auf der exakten wissenschaftlichen Erfassung der Bewegung der Kugel.

Allerdings liegt bereits in dieser Beobachtung eine Erkenntnistätigkeit begründet, nämlich in der Bewusstwerdung über einen bestimmten Vorgang und in der deskriptiven Darstellung. Dieser Schritt sei Erkenntnis-Ebene 1 genannt.

2. Schritt: Analyse und Modellbildung – Erkenntnis-Ebene 2

Im zweiten Schritt wird der Versuch unternommen, diesen Vorgang zu analysieren, so z.B. in der Physik mit den Regeln der Mathematik. Man schließt also von einem beobachteten speziellen Zustand auf eine allgemeingültige Beschreibung des Vorgangs. Diese Beschreibung soll für alle vergleichbaren Fälle gelten, also nicht nur für die eine, auf Erkenntnis-Ebene 1 genannte Metallkugel, sondern für alle Kugeln oder sonstigen körperlichen Gegenstände, die auf diesem Planeten fallen.

Dieser zweite Schritt ist der eigentlich entscheidende Erkenntnisschritt; er sei Erkenntnis-Ebene 2 genannt. Hier wird die allgemeine Formel für die physikalische Bewegung, für das chemische Produkt, für die Maschine, für die Anlage etc. erstellt. Es wird ein allgemeines Modell gebildet, mit dem man Vorhersagen treffen kann[8]. Dies ist die Basis, auf deren Grundlage wieder Rückschlüsse im konkreten Fall gezogen werden können.

Aus diesem Schritt speist sich auch ein wesentlicher Teil der Existenzlegitimation der Naturwissenschaft, hier der Physik. Denn durch die allgemeine Formel entsteht erst die Möglichkeit industrieller Vervielfältigung und Produktion, was weiterführend ist für die Gesamtgesellschaft.

3. Schritt: Empirischer Abgleich der allgemeingültigen Formel an der Praxis – Erkenntnis-Ebene 3

Im dritten Schritt schließlich wird wieder von der allgemeinen Formel auf die speziellen Fälle geschlossen. Diese allgemeine Formel, die aus Spezialfällen entwickelt wurde, wird nun wiederum auf Spezialfälle angewandt. Dieser Schritt sei Erkenntnis-Ebene 3 genannt.

Auch wenn diese Erkenntnis-Ebene 3 anmutet, als würde sie lediglich die Früchte der Erkenntnisse der ersten beiden Schritte ernten, so liegt hierin auch noch ein gewichtiger Erkenntnisgewinn. Mit diesem Schritt wird nämlich die Tauglichkeit der ersten beiden Schritte auf Erkenntnis-Ebenen 1 und 2 verifiziert. Man könnte diesen Schritt auch als eine Art Selbstüberprüfung der wissenschaftlichen Ergebnisse aus den ersten beiden Schritten betrachten. Damit wird die vorläufige Erkenntnis zu einer gesicherten Erkenntnis.

Insgesamt bilden diese drei Schritte naturwissenschaftlicher Erkenntnisgewinnung einen Zyklus: Vom Besonderen zum Allgemeinen und damit zu einem Modell, vom Modell wieder zurück zum Besonderen. Es handelt sich um ein in sich geschlossenes System, das – je länger es sich dreht – an Festigkeit gewinnt.

III. Zum Vorgehen juristischer Wissenschaft

Zum Vergleich sei das unter Ziffer II. skizzierte Schema naturwissenschaftlichen Erkenntnisgewinns als Grundlage für die Betrachtung der Vorgehensweise in der Jurisprudenz herangezogen:

1. Schritt: Beobachtung und Beschreibung eines Vorganges?

Sicherlich hinkt hier bereits der Vergleich mit der Experimentalphysik. Was soll die juristische Wissenschaft denn beobachten? Es gibt keine Kugeln oder sonstige Gegenstände, die fallen.

Dennoch: Es gibt eine Mehrheit von Menschen, von Individuen, eine Gesellschaft, ein gesellschaftliches System eben, das beobachtbar wäre; es ergeben sich soziale Konflikte in dieser Gesellschaft, die zu beschreiben wären, um auf dieser Grundlage im 2. Schritt Regelungen zu schaffen, welche diese sozialen

---

8 Exemplarisch und mit einer systematischen Beschreibung *Fowler*, Mathematical Modelling in the Applied Sciences, Cambridge 1997, S. 3 ff.

Konflikte beseitigen. Diese sozialen Konflikte sind durchaus vergleichbar mit der Dynamik chaotischer Systeme, z.B. nichtlinearer Reaktions-Diffusionsgleichungen, mit denen die Mischung zweier Flüssigkeiten genauso wie die Entwicklung einer Population beschrieben werden können[9]. Ein weiteres aufschlussreiches Beispiel zur besseren Illustration sind etwa Untersuchungen über die Entwicklung und Ausbreitung von Bauerngehöften in Zentraleuropa während des Mittelalters. Die Entwicklung ihrer Verbreitung entspricht einem Tropfen einer hochviskosen Flüssigkeit, die mit einer anderen Flüssigkeit vermischt wird[10]. Insofern verhält sich also ein gesellschaftlicher Prozess vergleichbar mit einem rein naturwissenschaftlichen. In diesem Zusammenhang ist nun die Mathematik als „Hilfswissenschaft" dazu berufen, den naturwissenschaftlichen Prozess zu beschreiben und die Rahmenbedingungen für ein Modell zu bieten, auf dessen Grundlage auch zukünftige Mischungen im Voraus berechnet werden können. Hieraus ergibt sich auch der Bezug zur Rechtswissenschaft. So legt das geltende Recht die Rahmenbedingungen fest, innerhalb derer die Ausbreitung der Bauerngehöfte stattfindet und kanalisiert werden kann.

In der Konsequenz sei dem sozialen Konflikt, der zu einer gesetzgeberischen Handlung Anlass gibt, der Stellenwert zugebilligt, welcher die fallende Kugel in der Physik einnimmt. Die Flüssigkeitsmischung findet statt, und die Mathematik beschreibt und determiniert den Vorgang; die Bauerngehöfte breiten sich aus, und Recht determiniert diesen Vorgang und reagiert auf ihn.

Beobachtet und beschreibt nun die juristische Wissenschaft diese sozialen Konflikte, beschreibt sie die Gesellschaft, um eine Basis für Regelungsmechanismen zu schaffen?

Nein, die juristische Wissenschaft widmet sich vornehmlich der Beschreibung, wie der Gesetzgeber die Gesellschaft sieht und ihr Regelungen verabreicht. Juristische Wissenschaft befasst sich – von Ausnahmefällen (etwa bei der Schaffung der *cic* oder der Figur des „Täters hinter dem Täter", siehe folgende Ziffer 2) abgesehen – nicht mit dem sozialen Konflikt und den Lösungsmöglichkeiten selber, sondern in der Mehrheit der Fälle damit, wie der Gesetzgeber diesen Konflikt behandelt hat, um ihn entweder gar nicht erst entstehen zu lassen oder – soweit er bereits entstanden ist – zu entschärfen.

Auf dieser rein deskriptiven Stufe beschreibt die juristische Wissenschaft also nicht die von der Natur gesetzten Regeln an der Wurzel, also nicht den vorab definierten sozialen Konflikt, sondern nur die vom Gesetzgeber, von Menschen, verabschiedete Norm. Insofern findet ein wissenschaftlicher Erkenntnisgewinn auf dieser Erkenntnis-Ebene 1 vom Standpunkt eines Physikers her gar nicht statt.

---

9 *J. D. Murray*, Mathematical Biology, 3. Aufl., Berlin, Heidelberg, S. 400 f.

10 *A. J. Ammermann/L.L. Cavalli-Sforza*, Measuring the rate of spread of early farming, Man, 6:674-688, 1971; siehe auch *J. D. Murray*, a.a.O, S. 444.

Allerdings lässt sich hiergegen argumentieren, dass wissenschaftliche Betrachtung nicht vom zu beobachtenden Objekt abhängen darf. Juristische Wissenschaft beobachtet eben nicht den „natürlichen" sozialen Konflikt, sondern die Tätigkeit des Gesetzgebers und setzt somit eine Stufe später an. Das kann ihr bei der Beurteilung der Wissenschaftlichkeit nicht zum Nachteil gereichen.

2. Schritt: Analyse und Modellbildung

Nun zum Vergleich mit dem für die Naturwissenschaft zentralen Schritt, nämlich der Analyse und der Modellbildung; zu dem Schluss vom speziellen Fall, der beobachtet wurde, zur allgemeinen Formel und zum allgemeinen Modell, von dem wieder Rückschlüsse auf den Spezialtatbestand möglich sein sollten.

Hier spätestens laufen Rechtswissenschaft und Physik methodisch auseinander. Wer schafft in der juristischen Wissenschaft allgemeingültige Modelle?

Ein positives Beispiel hierfür ist die *culpa in contrahendo*. Der Gesetzgeber des BGB hatte dem – nennen wir ihn gemäß obiger Definition – sozialen Konflikt der Haftung bei Vertragsanbahnung nicht ausreichend Beachtung geschenkt. Die Wissenschaft entwickelte die Rechtsfigur der *cic*[11], die Rechtsprechung nahm diese Anregung auf und verfolgte sie über Jahrzehnte hinweg[12] und schließlich schloss sich auch der Gesetzgeber dieser wissenschaftlichen Erkenntnis in § 311 Abs. 2 BGB an[13]. Dies ist ein Beispiel für eine wissenschaftliche Modellbildung, die derjenigen in der Physik nahekommt.

Der soziale Konflikt der planwidrigen Lücke in der Strafbarkeit eines sich im Hintergrund haltenden Täters wurde zunächst von der juristischen Wissenschaft aufgedeckt: Der Jubilar entwickelte die Figur des „Täters hinter dem Täter"[14], die in der Folge Eingang nicht nur in die deutsche Rechtsprechung gefunden hat, sondern sich sogar zu einem „Exportschlager" der deutschen Strafrechtslehre entwickelte und von etlichen Staaten vor allem bei der Aufarbeitung der Verbrechen vorangegangener Diktaturen rezipiert wurde. Allerdings ist anders als bei der *cic* der deutsche Gesetzgeber nicht tätig geworden, um diese dogmatische Figur zu kodifizieren – da sie sich unproblematisch mit dem hergebrachten Gesetzeswortlaut vereinbaren lässt, besteht hierzu auch kein Anlass. Durch die Akzeptanz der Rechtsprechung ist der „Täter hinter dem Täter" jedoch genauso normative Realität, wie er es bei einer gesetzgeberischen Verankerung wäre.

---

11 Ursprünglich geht die *culpa in contrahendo* auf eine Überlegung von *R. v. Jhering* zurück: *R. v. Jhering*, Culpa in contrahendo, in: Jahrbücher für die Dogmatik des heutigen römischen und deutschen Rechts (Jhering-Jahrbuch), 4. Bd., 1861, 1 ff.

12 Siehe vor allem BGH NJW 79, 1983.

13 Für alle *Palandt/Heinrichs* (Hrsg.), § 311, Rn. 5, 69. Aufl., München 2009.

14 *F.-C. Schroeder*, Der Täter hinter dem Täter. Ein Beitrag zur Lehre von der mittelbaren Täterschaft, 1965.

Allerdings darf man nicht die Augen davor verschließen, dass solche Modellierungen in der Rechtswissenschaft von der Erfassung des Problems über die Modellbildung bis zur Implementierung durch den Gesetzgeber eher die Ausnahme darstellen.

Jedoch ließe sich wie folgt argumentieren: Jeder Meinungsstreit, jede von der Wissenschaft geäußerte Ansicht oder Interpretationshilfe, Strukturbeschreibung oder Analyse, kann als ein Modell zur Auslegung einer bestimmten Vorschrift oder eines Vorschriftenkomplexes verstanden werden. Ein Modell, wie in einem bestimmten Fall, unter einer bestimmten Konstellation, mit einer Vorschrift umzugehen ist und das im Zusammenhang mit einer auslegungsbedürftigen Vorschrift im konkreten Fall einen Anhaltspunkt bietet. Auch die Beschreibung einer bestimmten Systematik des Zusammenspiels von Vorschriften mag man als Modell bezeichnen.

Selbst wenn man dies als Modellbildung ausreichen lässt, so stellt sich die Frage, ob dies qualitativ an die naturwissenschaftliche heranreicht. Ist sie überhaupt vergleichbar mit naturwissenschaftlicher Modellierung?

Die naturwissenschaftliche Modellierung setzt unmittelbar bei der Beobachtung des natürlichen Prozesses an, z.B. bei der fallenden Kugel. Der Prozess bzw. das Problem wird beschrieben (Erkenntnis-Ebene 1) und in eine allgemeine Formel (Erkenntnis-Ebene 2) gefasst. Hieraus resultiert dann die Gesamterkenntnis, wie also die spezielle Kugel fällt und wie alle Kugeln fallen.

Wie bereits im Hinblick auf Erkenntnis-Ebene 1 festgestellt, greift die juristische Wissenschaft nicht bei dem ursprünglichen Problem, dem sozialen Konflikt, den es zu regeln gilt, direkt an, sondern überlässt dies in aller Regel dem Gesetzgeber. Er muss selber die Erkenntnis haben, dass ein sozialer Konflikt besteht und einen Vorschlag zur gesetzlichen Regulierung dieses Konflikts unterbreiten. Auch schafft der Gesetzgeber das Modell zur Problemlösung und wirkt damit auf Erkenntnis-Ebene 2. Ob gut oder schlecht, sei dahingestellt. Dabei ist die juristische Wissenschaft i.d.R. nur mittelbar an der Modellbildung beteiligt und steuert Strukturüberlegungen und Argumente bei. Nicht unerheblicher Einfluss kommt allerdings auch von Interessenverbänden, aus der Politik und aus den Ministerien, die nicht nur nach wissenschaftlichen Maßstäben arbeiten[15].

---

15 Als Beispiel aufschlussreich ist hierfür das Zustandekommen des Schuldrechtsmodernisierungsgesetzes aus dem Jahre 2001 (BGBl. 2002 I S. 42). Zwar haben an der Schuldrechtsreform auch Wissenschaftler mitgewirkt (Schuldrechtskommission), allerdings waren entscheidende Passagen durch EG-Richtlinien und auch durch die (nicht wissenschaftliche) Kommission des Bundesjustizministeriums bestimmt. Hierzu im Überblick MüKo/*Ernst*, 5. Aufl., München 2007, vor § 275 Rn. 3 ff.; *Canaris*, Schuldrechtsmodernisierung, München 2002, S. 349 mit Hinweisen auf die sogenannte „konsolidierte Fassung des Schuldrechtsmodernisierungsgesetzes; *Palandt/Heinrichs* (Hrsg.), Einleitung Rn. 10a ff., 69. Aufl., München 2009.

Was der Rechtswissenschaft auf der Erkenntnis-Ebene 2 bleibt, ist also nicht die alleinige Modellbildung am sozialen Konflikt, sondern die Mithilfe bei der Konzeption einer Regelung, wobei die letzte Entscheidung dem Gesetzgeber vorbehalten bleibt. Ferner steht die Untersuchung und Interpretation von Vorschriften, die zur Lösung eines sozialen Konfliktes vom Gesetzgeber geschaffen wurden, im Mittelpunkt der Untersuchung, so etwa ob diese Vorschriften in sich konsistent und praktisch anwendbar sind und vor allem, ob diese Vorschriften sich in das Gesamtsystem des Rechts einpassen.

Dies mag seine Berechtigung insbesondere in der Praxis der Rechtsanwendung haben. Der in den Naturwissenschaften übliche Schritt vom Besonderen zum allgemeinen Modell auf Erkenntnis-Ebene 2 findet jedoch bei Vergleich der Vorgehensweisen weniger nachhaltig statt, wenn man nicht gerade vor einem Ausnahmephänomen wie der Schöpfung einer Rechtsfigur wie der *cic* oder des Täters hinter dem Täter steht.

Auch das zuvor genannte Argument, die Wissenschaft schaffe mit ihrer Meinungsvielfalt Modelle zur Auslegung gesetzgeberischer Normen, kann diesen Unterschied kaum wettmachen. Denn die naturwissenschaftliche Modellbildung schafft ihre Normen selbst. Die juristisch-wissenschaftliche Modellbildung schafft nur hilfsweise Normen, Argumente und Strukturen, wenn die gesetzgeberischen nicht mehr ausreichen oder diese im Rahmen des Gesamtsystems auszulegen sind.

3. Schritt: Empirischer Abgleich der allgemeingültigen Formel an der Praxis

Wie bereits dargestellt, haben naturwissenschaftliche, in Formeln oder allgemeine Modelle gegossene Erkenntnisse i.d.R. den Vorteil, dass man sie durch die Praxis verifizieren kann: das Medikament wirkt, die Brücke hält, der Strom fließt. Von naturwissenschaftlichen Erkenntnissen, die nicht der Verifikation unterliegen, so z.B. in der Kosmologie, sei hier abgesehen.

Angenommen, man betrachtet eine wissenschaftlich-juristische Interpretation als Modell, so stellt sich die Frage, wo und wie diese verifiziert werden kann. Hypothetisch könnte man davon ausgehen, dass eine Verifikation dann stattfindet, wenn Gerichte die wissenschaftliche Erkenntnis umsetzen und wenn der Gesetzgeber einen Vorschlag der Wissenschaft aufnimmt. Hierbei ist aber zu berücksichtigen, dass juristische wissenschaftliche Erkenntnisse gewissen Modifikationen unterliegen; i.d.R. werden diese nicht eins zu eins umgesetzt. Ob hingegen ein Modell aus der Physik Bestand hat, lässt sich an der Praxis leicht verifizieren (z.B. die Statik einer Brücke hält, wenn ein LKW die Brücke passiert).

Die Rückkopplung im Hinblick auf ein abstraktes juristisches Auslegungsmodell und die Erkenntnis, ob sich dieses in der Praxis bewährt, erfolgt durch die Rechtsprechung oder durch die Nutzung eines Auslegungsmodells durch sonstige Anwender, z.B. Anwälte. Es wäre eine durch empirische Studien zu untersuchende Frage, wie oft und in welcher Weise juristische wissenschaftliche Theorien und Modelle sich in der Anwendungspraxis wiederfinden. Ohne einer solchen Studie, die sich im Hinblick auf die Existenzlegitimation juristischer Wissenschaft wirklich lohnen würde, vorzugreifen, ist es wohl nicht übertrieben zu sagen, dass kaum ein Anwalt sich in einem Prozess allein auf die wissenschaftliche Auslegung eines Professors stützen würde, es sei denn, es existierten keine einschlägigen Entscheidungen; kaum ein Unternehmensjurist würde einen Vertrag auf der Grundlage eines Modells entwerfen, das alleine auf juristischen wissenschaftlichen Erkenntnissen begründet ist.

IV. Ergebnis

Im Ergebnis dieses Schlaglichts naturwissenschaftlicher Betrachtungsweise soll ganz bewusst keine Wertung erfolgen. Eines lässt sich jedoch sicherlich konstatieren: Der in Naturwissenschaften wie der Physik bekannte wissenschaftliche Zyklus vom Besonderen zum allgemeinen Modell und anschließend vom allgemeinen Modell zum Besonderen zurück, wird in der Rechtswissenschaft bei Weitem nicht so kontinuierlich nachzuvollziehen sein. Dies liegt zum einen daran, dass die Rechtswissenschaft mit ihrer Modellbildung häufig erst in einem Moment ansetzt, in dem ein anderer, nämlich der Gesetzgeber, bereits das Grundmodell bestimmt hat. Insofern liefert die juristische Modellbildung, so sie denn überhaupt stattfindet und nicht allein in der Darstellung von Vorschriftenkomplexen endet, in der Hauptsache Erkenntnisse im Hinblick darauf, inwieweit eine gesetzgeberische Regelung sich in das Gesamtsystem einpasst. Systemeingriffe von Seiten der Rechtswissenschaft wie im Falle der *cic* oder des „Täters hinter dem Täter", die nachher von der Rechtsprechung und dann ggf. auch vom Gesetzgeber akzeptiert wurden, bilden hier wohl eher die Ausnahme.

Insofern bleibt der Sinn juristischer Wissenschaft vor allem in einem begründet: der Interpretationshilfe, der Argumentationshilfe und dem Versuch der Systematisierung und Strukturschaffung temporär geltender gesetzgeberischer Normen. Letzteres ist vor allem aufgrund der Menge der existierenden Vorschriften sicherlich in der Praxis unabdingbar. Ein wie in der Physik bekannter Erkenntnisgewinn ist damit jedoch nur im Einzelfall (siehe *cic* oder „Täter hinter dem Täter") zu erzeugen. Betrachtet man Wissenschaft allein vom in den Naturwissenschaften vorherrschenden Blickwinkel der belastbaren Modellbildung und Hypothese aus, so dürfte sich Rechtswissenschaft nur dann Wissenschaft nennen, wenn sie Rechtsfiguren wie die *cic* oder den „Täter hinter dem Täter" hervorbringt.

All dies mag banal und schon bekannt klingen. Aber in einer Welt stetig wachsender Verteilungskämpfe, so auch um finanzielle Ressourcen in der Wissenschaft, sind die genannten Überlegungen nicht gerade zuträglich für eine Förderung der juristischen Wissenschaft. Und genau dies lässt sich ja auch in der Praxis ablesen. Das beste Beispiel sind die Kürzungen der Mittel für juristische Institute. Wenn es hart auf hart kommt, steht die juristische – wie im Übrigen auch andere Geisteswissenschaften – im Vergleich mit naturwissenschaftlicher Wissenschaft bei der Förderung hinten an.

Dies mag beklagenswert sein. Aber vielleicht wäre sinnvoll darüber nachzudenken, ob die juristische Wissenschaft die schon ausgetrampelten Wege der Dissertationen, Habilitationen, Aufsätze und sonstigen Beiträge, die sich vor allem in der Darstellung und ggf. in der Auslegung von Vorschriften und im Wiederstreit verschiedener juristischer Glaubensrichtungen ergehen, wirklich in der Weise weiterverfolgen möchte, oder ob auch alternative Forschungsmöglichkeiten bestehen. Sicherlich ist dies kein Plädoyer dafür, der traditionellen juristischen Wissenschaft abzuschwören, sondern vielmehr dafür, auch alternative Wege wissenschaftlicher Arbeit ins Auge zu fassen.

Die Welt wird immer komplizierter, durch Bevölkerungswachstum, Kommunikation und Globalisierung, um nur einige Punkte zu nennen. Der Bedarf an Regelungen und Regelungsmechanismen, nach gut durchdachten Vorschlägen, wie soziale Probleme gesetzgeberisch in den Griff zu bekommen sind, wird immer größer. Hier könnte sich die Rechtswissenschaft viel stärker einbringen. Bei vernünftigen, mit den Wirtschaftswissenschaften kongruenten Regelungen und Modellen hätte vielleicht eine Finanzkrise wie im Jahre 2008 verhindert werden können. Hier könnte eine neue juristische Forschung durch das Angebot von Alternativen und Lösungen ansetzen. Allerdings setzt dies auch eine Öffnung gegenüber anderen Wissenschaften wie der Informatik, den Wirtschaftswissenschaften, der Soziologie oder sogar der Psychologie voraus. Interdisziplinarität und Modellbildung könnten auf die Dauer zukunftsweisende Pfeiler juristischer Wissenschaft sein.

Prof. Dr. Dres. h.c. Friedrich-Christian Schroeder Verzeichnis der ostrechtlichen Publikationen

A. Ostrecht

I. Monographien

Das Strafrecht der UdSSR de lege ferenda, 1958

Die Grundsätze der Strafgesetzgebung der UdSSR und der Unionsrepubliken (Übersetzung und Kommentar), 1960

Die Entwicklung rechtsstaatlicher Elemente in der UdSSR, 1960, Referat, gehalten am 11.3.1960 vor der Marxismus-Kommission der Evangelischen Studiengemeinschaft in Heidelberg (Privatdruck)

Grundsätze der Strafgesetzgebung, Staatsschutz- und Militärstrafrecht der UdSSR (Übersetzung und Einleitung), 1975

Wandlungen der sowjetischen Staatstheorie, 1979

Das Oberste Gericht der UdSSR (Recht und Staat, Bd. 105), 1983

74 Jahre Sowjetrecht (Schriftenreihe der Juristischen Studiengesellschaft Regensburg e.V., H. 9), 1992; Übersetzung ins Tschechische unter dem Titel "Hlavní etapy vyvoje sovetského práva" in: "Tri studie z novodobych dejin ruskeho práva" Edicní Stredisko pf uk praha, 1994, S. 5-56

Die Rechtsordnung Rußlands und die Anforderungen der Europäischen Menschenrechtskonvention (Vorträge, Reden und Berichte aus dem Europa-Institut der Universität des Saarlandes, hrsg. von G. Ress und T. Stein, Nr. 347), 1996

Strafgesetzbuch der Russischen Föderation, Einführung, Dtsch. Übersetzung (zus. mit T. Bednarz) (Sammlung ausländischer Strafgesetzbücher in deutscher Übersetzung, Bd. 108, 1998). Freiburg i.Br.; auszugsweise (Wirtschaftsdelikte) in: Wirtschaftsrecht der Osteuropäischen Staaten WOS, Abtlg. Russische Föderation, VI. Gerichtsbarkeit, 6 a, 1997, S. 1-58, 2. Aufl, 2007

Die neue russische Strafprozeßordnung – Durchbruch zum fairen Strafverfahren? (forost - Forschungsverbund Ost- und Südosteuropa, Arbeitspapier Nr. 10), 2002

Das Institut für Ostrecht München. Tätigkeit – Entwicklung – Perspektiven, o. J. (2010)

II. Editionen

Bundesstaat und Nationalitätenrecht in der Sowjetunion (zusammen mit Boris Meissner im Auftrag der Deutschen Gesellschaft für Osteuropakunde, Berlin), 1974

Verfassungs- und Verwaltungsreformen in den sozialistischen Staaten (zusammen mit Boris Meissner im Auftrag der Deutschen Gesellschaft für Osteuropakunde), 1978

Der Schutz individueller Rechte und Interessen im Recht sozialistischer Staaten (zusammen mit K. Westen und B. Meissner), 1980

Kontinuität und Wandel in der kommunistischen Staatstheorie (Osteuropaforschung, Schriftenreihe der Deutschen Gesellschaft für Osteuropakunde, Bd. 15; zusammen mit B. Meissner und K. Westen), 1985

Sozialistisches Wirtschaftsrecht zwischen Wandel und Beharrung (Osteuropaforschung, Schriftenreihe der Deutschen Gesellschaft für Osteuropakunde, Bd. 22; zusammen mit K. Westen und G. Brunner), 1988

Die neuen Kodifikationen in Rußland (Osteuropaforschung, Schriftenreihe der Deutschen Gesellschaft für Osteuropakunde, Bd. 38), 1997, 2. Aufl. 1999

Justizreform in Osteuropa (Studien des Instituts für Ostrecht München, Bd. 51), 2004

Die rechtliche Aufarbeitung der kommunistischen Vergangenheit in Osteuropa (Studien des Instituts für Ostrecht München, Bd. 63, zus. mit H. Küpper), 2010

III. Aufsätze in Zeitschriften und Sammelwerken

Täterschaft und Teilnahme im sowjetischen Strafrecht, Recht in Ost und West 1960, S. 5-10

Der Allgemeine Teil des Strafgesetzbuchs der RSFSR, Jahrbuch für Ostrecht, Bd. III/2, 1961, S. 57-75

Inhalt und Entwicklung von Staat und Recht nach dem neuen Parteiprogramm der Kommunistischen Partei der Sowjetunion, Jahrbuch für Ostrecht Bd. III/1, 1962, 45-68; II/2, 1962, S. 49-71

Das Eigentumsrecht in der UdSSR, Marxismusstudien, Vierte Folge, 1962, S. 219-258

Gesellschaftsgerichte und Administrativjustiz im vorrevolutionären Rußland. Ein Beitrag zum Problem der Kontinuität des russischen Rechts, Osteuropa Recht 1962, S. 292-305

Das Sowjetrecht, Aus Politik und Zeitgeschehen, Beilage zur Wochenzeitung "Das Parlament", B 32/62, 1962, S. 413-431

Der strafrechtliche Staatsschutz in der Sowjetunion, in Der strafrechtliche Staatsschutz in der Sowjetunion, der Tschechoslowakei, Ungarn und Polen, 1963, S. 19-112

Die neuere Entwicklung der sowjetischen Kriminalpolitik, Jahrbuch für Ostrecht Bd. IV/2 (1963), S. 69-90

Das Notariatswesen in der Sowjetunion, Deutsche Notar-Zeitschrift 1964, S. 654-671

Das neue Bürgerliche Gesetzbuch der Russischen Sowjetrepublik, Recht in Ost und West 1965, 1-9, S. 49-58

Die ideologischen Grundlagen des Völkerrechts und der innerstaatlichen Ordnung im Streit zwischen Moskau und Peking, Jahrbuch für Ostrecht Bd. VI/1 (1965), S. 221-250

Art. "Sowjetunion (Rechtssystem)" im Evangelischen Staatslexikon, 1966, Sp. 2026-2035, 2. Aufl. 1975, Sp. 2330-2343, 3. Aufl. 1987, Sp. 3169-3182

Der Kampf der Sowjetunion gegen das Rowdytum, Jahrbuch für Ostrecht Bd. VII/2 (1966), S. 87-132

Die Abschaffung der Gesellschaftsgerichte in der Sowjetunion und die Periodisierung der sowjetischen Rechtsentwicklung, Osteuropa Recht 1967, S. 89-96

Krieg und Koexistenz im Streit zwischen Moskau und Peking, Marxismusstudien, Fünfte Folge, 1968, S. 164-196

Die Hydra der Fragen. Ein Sowjetrichter vor Münchner Studenten, Frankfurter Allgemeine Zeitung vom 2.3.1968

Systematische Stellung und Gegenstand des Gerichtsverfassungsrechts in der Sowjetunion, Jahrbuch für Ostrecht IX/1 (1968), S. 99-122

Die zentralen juristischen Forschungsinstitute der Sowjetunion. Entwicklung und gegenwärtige Organisation, Osteuropa Recht 1969, S. 42-57

Fünfzig Jahre sowjetische Rechtstheorie, 50 Jahre Sowjetrecht, 1969, S. 52-77

Neues Strafvollzugsrecht in der UdSSR, Wort und Wahrheit 1969, S. 561-564

Die sog. Grundprinzipien des Sowjetrechts, insbesondere der Humanismus, Jahrbuch für Ostrecht X/2 (1969), S. 44-56

Eine Gesetzessammlung zum Ostrecht, Recht in Ost und West, 1971, S. 139-142

Versagen der gesellschaftlichen Rechtspflege in der UdSSR, Recht in Ost und West 1972, S. 265-267

"Rechtsphilosophie" in der Sowjetunion, Juristenzeitung 1973, S. 417

The Politics of Criminal Law Reform: Eastern Europe, The American Journal of Comparative Law, Vol. XXI, 1973, Nr. 2, S. 304-317

Die nationale Emanzipation in Südosteuropa, dargestellt an der Entwicklung des Strafrechts. Ethnogenese und Staatsbildung in Südosteuropa (Beiträge des Südosteuropa-Arbeitskreises der Deutschen Forschungsgemeinschaft zum III. Internationalen Südosteuropa-Kongreß der Association Internationale d'Etudes du Sud-Est-Europeen, Bukarest, 10.9.1974), hrsg. von Klaus-Detlef Grothusen, 1974, S. 304-310

Integration und Rechtsvereinheitlichung im RGW auf dem Gebiet des Strafrechts, Deutschland Archiv 1974, S. 1271-1280; auch in: Rechtsfragen der Integration und Kooperation in Ost und West, hrsg. von O. Wolff von Amerongen, 1976, S. 195-211

Fünfzehn Jahre Jahrbuch für Ostrecht, Jahrbuch für Ostrecht Bd. XV (1974), S. 7-12

Straftatbestände und Kriminalität in den sozialistischen Staaten, Der Kriminalist 1976, S. 43-49; und: Kriminalität (Forschung und Information, hrsg. von Ruprecht Kurzrock, Bd. 20), 1976, S. 37-45

Verschärfung der "Parasitenbekämpfung" in der DDR. Vergleich zu den übrigen sozialistischen Staaten, Deutschland Archiv 1976, S. 834-843

Wandel der strafrechtlichen Behandlung der privatunternehmerischen Tätigkeit in der Sowjetunion, Recht in Ost und West 1977, S. 1-5

Strafbares Privatunternehmertum in der Sowjetunion - Praktische Fälle, Recht in Ost und West 1977, S. 206-207

Entschärfung des Prinzips der Parteilichkeit der sozialistischen Rechtswissenschaft?, Deutschland Archiv 1977, S. 462-465

Renaissance der "Kriminalpolitik" in den sozialistischen Staaten. Kultur. Kriminalität. Strafrecht. Festschrift für Thomas Würtenberger zum 70. Geburtstag am 7.10.1977, hrsg. von R. Herren, D. Kienapfel und H. Müller-Dietz, 1977, S. 283-296

Einführung zu: Strafgesetz der Sozialistischen Föderativen Republik Jugoslawien vom 28. Juli 1976 Jahrbuch für Ostrecht Bd. XVIII (1977), S. 297-301

Die Planerfüllungsfälschung als Form der kommunistischen Wirtschaftskriminalität, Monatsschrift für Kriminologie und Strafrechtsreform 1979, S. 140-148; Kurzfassung in: Wirtschaftskriminalität - kommunistisch, Frankfurter Allgemeine Zeitung vom 13.6.1978 (auszugsweise unter dem Titel "Wirtschaftskriminalität in der Sowjetunion" im St. Galler Tagblatt vom 13.7.1978)

Zum Problem des "sozialistischen Strafrechts", Zbornik pravnog fakulteta u Zagrebu, god. XXVIII-broj 3-4. Spomenica prof. Bogdan Zlataric, Zagreb 1978, S. 479-485

Falsche Übersetzungen russischer rechts- und politikwissenschaftlicher Bücher in der DDR, Deutschland Archiv 1979, S. 174-177

Das Strafrecht der DDR und der Sowjetunion. Ein Beitrag zur Meso-Rechtsvergleichung, Zeitschrift für die gesamte Strafrechtswissenschaft, Bd. 91 (1979), S. 1065-1095; Kurzfassung unter dem Titel: Das Strafrecht der DDR und der Sowjetunion - ein Vergleich, in: Gesellschaft für Deutschlandforschung, Jahrbuch 1979: Die DDR - Parnter oder Satellit der Sowjetunion? Hrsg. von S. Mampel und K.C. Thalheim, 1980, S. 186-201

Der "Mechanismus der rechtlichen Regulierung" als Kategorie der sowjetischen Rechtstheorie, Rechtstheorie 1979, S. 187-198

Kommentar zu Li Bangning: Mit dem Ausdruck "Sozialgefährlichkeit" allein kann man die wesentlichen Merkmale der Straftat nicht erklären, H.-D. Schwind - K. Wegmann - H. Legarth, Studien zum chinesischen Recht, Bd. I, 1979, S. 223-226

Systemtheoretische Ansätze in der sowjetischen Staats- und Rechtstheorie, Jahrbuch für Ostrecht, Bd. XX (1979), 1. Halbbd., S. 7-31

Einführung zum Strafgesetzbuch der Sozialistischen Volksrepublik Albanien vom 15. Juni 1977, Jahrbuch für Ostrecht, Bd. XX (1979), 1. Halbbd., S. 223-229

Further Trends in Soviet Criminal Justice, Soviet Law After Stalin, Part. III: Soviet Institutions and the Administration of Law, ed. by D.B. Barry,F.J.M. Feldbrugge, G. Ginsburgs, P.B. Maggs, 1979, S. 89-92

Einführung zum ungarischen Strafgesetzbuch vom 22. Dezember 1978, Jahrbuch für Ostrecht, Bd. XXI (1980), S. 183-194

Kreditaufnahme als Verrat - Zum neuen albanischen Strafrecht, Frankfurter Allgemeine Zeitung vom 28.5.1980, S. 10

Rückwirkungsprobleme im sowjetischen Strafrecht, Juristenzeitung 1981, S. 336-337

Zwiebelwährung unter Zwiebeltürmen - Systemwidriges aus der sowjetischen Landwirtschaft, Frankfurter Allgemeine Zeitung vom 7.12.1981, S. 10

Towarischtsch Jennerwein - Wilddieberei in der Sowjetunion weit verbreitet 25, Frankfurter Allgemeine Zeitung vom 15.3.1982, S. 7

Ab in die Kolchose! - Vor einem Moskauer Kollegen-Gericht, Frankfurter Allgemeine Zeitung vom 11.8.1982, S. 8; engl. Fassung unter dem Titel "Send her to a Kolkhoz!", Soviet Union, vol. 11, part 3, 1984, S. 290-293

Einführung zum kroatischen Strafgesetz vom 20. Juni 1977, Jahrbuch für Ostrecht, Bd. XXII/2 (1981), S. 391-398

25 Jahre Institut für Ostrecht München, Jahrbuch für Ostrecht, Bd. XXIV (1983), 1. Halbbd., S. 9-13

Kontinuität und Wandel in der sowjetischen Staatstheorie, Osteuropa Recht 1983, S. 52-57

Fahrlässige Vermögensdelikte im Strafrecht des realen Sozialismus, Zeitschrift für die gesamte Strafrechtswissenschaft, Bd. 95 (1983), S. 483-498

Handbuch der Sowjetverfassung, red. von M. Fincke, Bd. I und II, 1983: Einleitung II 3 (Staatstheorie); Art. 4 (Sozialistische Gesetzlichkeit); Art. 54 (Unverletzlichkeit der Person); Art. 55 (Unverletzlichkeit der Wohnung); Art. 56 (Schutz der Privatsphäre); Art. 61 (Pflicht zur Achtung des sozialistischen Eigentums); Art. 62 (Pflicht zur Staatstreue); Vorbemerkung zu Abschn. VII (Rechtsprechung, Arbitrage und staatsanwaltschaftliche Aufsicht); Vorbemerkung zu Kap. 20 (Gericht und Arbitrage); Art. 153 (Oberstes Gericht der UdSSR); Art. 159 (Gerichtssprache; Recht auf Dolmetscher)

Mühlen der Sowjetjustiz - Das Rechtsmittel "Aufsichtsprotest", Frankfurter Allgemeine Zeitung vom 17.12.1983, S. 10

Die Strafbarkeit der Republikflucht in Ungarn, Jahrbuch für Ostrecht, Bd. XXIV (1983), 2. Halbbd., S. 389-395

Desintegration des Strafrechts, Jugoslawien. Integrationsprobleme in Geschichte und Gegenwart, 1984, S. 292-298

Die Gliederung der Straftat in der Sowjetunion und in der DDR, Festschrift für Hans-Heinrich Jescheck zum 70. Geb., hrsg. von T. Vogler, 1985, S. 1249-1264

Neubestimmung des Notwehrrechts in der Sowjetunion, Festschrift für Dietrich Oehler zum 70. Geb., hrsg. von Rolf Dietrich Herzberg, 1985, S. 581-588

Strafrechtliche und kriminologische Dissertationen in der Sowjetunion, Monatsschrift für Kriminologie und Strafrechtsreform 1985, S. 251-255

Wandelt sich Moskaus Rechtsdenken?, Vorschläge eines hohen Juristen, Frankfurter Allgemeine Zeitung vom 26.11.1986, S. 12

In Scheinwahlen bestimmt. Die willfährigen sowjetischen Richter, Frankfurter Allgemeine Zeitung vom 18.5.1987, S. 16

Statistik als Rechtshemmnis. Warum gibt es so wenige Freisprüche in der Sowjetunion? Frankfurter Allgemeine Zeitung vom 20.7.1987, S. 8

Mängel der Juristenausbildung in der Sowjetunion, Recht in Ost und West 1987, S. 256-257

Zweimal "sozialistischer Humanismus". Die Abschaffung der Todesstrafe in der DDR ist ein Affront gegen Moskau, Frankfurter Allgemeine Zeitung vom 29.7.1987, S. 10

Menschenrechte im Strafverfahren und Strafvollzug. Unterrichtung durch die Bundesregierung, Menschenrechte in den Staaten des Warschauer Paktes - Bericht der unabhängigen Wissenschaftlerkommission, Deutscher Bundestag, 11. Wahlperiode, Drucksache 11/1344, S. 195-208; veröffentlicht auch als: Menschenrechte in den Staaten des Warschauer Paktes - Bericht der unabhängigen Wissenschaftlerkommission, 1988, S. 342-366; und: Human Rights in Criminal Proceedings and in the Enforcement of Prison Sentences, Georg Brunner et al., Before Reforms, Human Rights in the Warsaw Pact States 1971-1988, 1990, S. 403-432

Moskau entdeckt den Rechtsstaat. Neubeginn nach einer Zeit der Begriffsverdrehung, Frankfurter Allgemeine Zeitung vom 19.7.1988, S. 10

Zu wenig Richter in elenden Gerichtsgebäuden. Woran die sowjetische Justiz auch leidet, Frankfurter Allgemeine Zeitung vom 7.12.1988, S. 12

Schattenwirtschaft, Schattenrechtsordnung. Die organisierte Kriminalität in der Sowjetunion, Frankfurter Allgemeine Zeitung vom 26.1.1989, S. 12

Die "Perestrojka" im sowjetischen Strafprozeß, Jahrbuch für Ostrecht, Bd. XXIX (1988), 1. u. 2. Halbbd., 23-37

Von der Besserungsarbeit zur Heilarbeit, Sowjetische Arbeitslager werden zu "Heilanstalten", Frankfurter Allgemeine Zeitung vom 27.7.1989, S. 10

Rybinsk - für wie lange?, Frankfurter Allgemeine Zeitung vom 5.8.1989, S. 2

Wandlungen und Konstanten der "sozialistischen Gesetzlichkeit", Recht in Ost und West 1989, S. 358-362; auszugsweise in: "Wieviele hast Du erschießen lassen?", Einzelheiten vom "guten Lenin", Frankfurter Allgemeine Zeitung vom 24.1.1990, S. 12

Gesetzgebungskonflikt um das politische Strafrecht in der Sowjetunion, Jahrbuch für Ostrecht, Bd. XXX (1989), 2. Halbbd., S. 291-304

Wissenschaftliche Ausarbeitung von: Milderung - zum Teil und zum Schein. Neues politisches Strafrecht in der Sowjetunion, Frankfurter Allgemeine Zeitung vom 16.5.1989, S. 12

Die Volksdeputierten greifen ein. Gesetzgebungskonflikt in der Sowjetunion, Frankfurter Allgemeine Zeitung vom 5.8.1989, S. 8

Ein seltsamer deutsch-sowjetischer Erbrechtsfall, Osteuropa 1990, S. 64-67

Eine neue Form der Zwangsarbeit. Wozu man in der Sowjetunion die "Chemiker" braucht, Frankfurter Allgemeine Zeitung vom 3.3.1990, S. 12

1,7 Millionen "Klassenfeinde" erschossen. Bereits Lenin legte die Grundlage für die Entartung des Kommunistischen Systems, WELT am SONNTAG vom 25.3.1990, S. 27

Das neue Gesetz der Sowjetunion gegen die Mißachtung des Gerichts, Juristenzeitung 1990, S. 479-481; Kurzfassung unter dem Titel: Gesetz und Telefonhörer. Richterliche Unabhängigkeit in der Sowjetunion, Frankfurter Allgemeine Zeitung vom 22.2.1990, S. 14

Rechtsstreit um den Nachlaß der Anna Achmatowa, Osteuropa 1990, S. 646-650; Kurzfassung unter dem Titel: Querelen, Frankfurter Allgemeine Zeitung vom 22.9.1989, S. 36

Zum Begriff "Diebe im Gesetz", Osteuropa 1990, S. 768

The Reform of Legal Consultation in the Soviet Union, Review of Socialist Law 1990, S. 127-133; Kurzfassung unter dem Titel Rechtberatung in der Sowjetunion. Der Kampf zwischen Rechtanwälten und Rechtsberatungsgenossenschaften, Frankfurter Allgemeine Zeitung vom 11.12.1989, S. 16

Schutz der Amtsehre in der Sowjetunion. Staatspolitisches Bedürfnis oder persönlicher Ehrgeiz?, Frankfurter Allgemeine Zeitung vom 9.10.1990, S. 14

Das Kollektiv schützt vor Erpressung. Neue Entwicklungen in der sowjetischen Rechtsanwaltschaft, Frankfurter Allgemeine Zeitung vom 23.4.1991, S. 12

Das Komitee für Verfassungsaufsicht in der Sowjetunion, Jahrbuch für Ostrecht, Bd. XXXI (1990), 2. Halbbd., S. 285-297; Kurzfassung unter dem Titel: Vor einer sowjetischen Rechtsstaatlichkeit? Die ersten Entscheidungen des Komitees für Verfassungsaufsicht, Frankfurter Allgemeine Zeitung vom 7.1.1991, S. 8

Wie Moskau die Pornographie bekämpft. Schutz der Menschenwürde und der religiösen Gefühle, Frankfurter Allgemeine Zeitung vom 11.6.1991, S. 10; russ. Übersetzung in: Zschr. "Za rubezom", Nr. 28 (1617), 5.-11.7.1991, S. 7

Die strafrechtliche Regelung des Handels in der Sowjetunion, Zeitschrift für vergleichende Rechtswissenschaft, 1991, S. 444-465

Perestroika and Developments in Soviet Criminal Law, F.J.M. Feldbrugge (ed.), The Emancipation of Soviet Law, 1992, S. 185-197

Wie kann Rußland gegliedert werden? Das Haupthindernis für die Verfassungsreform, Frankfurter Allgemeine Zeitung vom 30.10.1992, S. 14

Viel Lametta auf der Brust. Eine ungebrochene Tradition in Rußland, Frankfurter Allgemeine Zeitung vom 26.3.1993, S. 12

Sturz in eine neue Rechtsordnung. Osteuropa braucht Hilfe bei der Gesetzgebung, Frankfurter Allgemeine Zeitung vom 2.7.1993, S. 14

Das Recht als Waffe. Wirklichkeit und Wahn des "Realen Sozialismus". Zur Aufarbeitung der SED-Diktatur durch eine Enquete-Kommission des Deutschen Bundestages, Zeitthemen, Schriftenreihe der CDU/CSU-Bundestagsfraktion Nr. 3, 1993, S. 108-115, leicht veränderte Fassung unter dem Titel: Die Übernahme der sozialistischen Rechtsauffassung in ihrer Stalinschen Ausprägung in der SBZ/DDR, Recht und Politik, 1993, S. 201-206

Richter mit gebrochenem Rückgrat. Schwierigkeiten des Justizaufbaus in Kasachstan, Frankfurter Allgemeine Zeitung vom 14.12.1993, S. 16

Gesetz über die Staatsanwaltschaft Rußlands von 1992. Übersetzung und Einführung, Jahrbuch für Ostrecht, Bd. XXXIV (1993), S. 159-182

Ehrenkodex der russischen Richter, Wirtschaft und Recht in Osteuropa, 1994, S. 101

Die russische Staatsanwaltschaft kämpft um ihren Besitzstand, Wirtschaft und Recht in Osteuropa, 1994, S. 290-291

Neue Rechtssysteme in Osteuropa. Die Bedeutung der Ostrechtswissenschaft heute, Blick in die Wissenschaft (Forschungsmagazin der Universität Regensburg), H. 5, 1994, S. 60-65; Nachdruck in: WGO - Monatshefte für Osteuropäisches Recht, H. 1-2, 1995, S. 91-97

Grundbegriffe und -formen der Privatisierung in Osteuropa, Wirtschaft und Recht in Osteuropa, 1995, S. 121-125

Die außerstrafprozessuale Tätigkeit der Staatsanwaltschaft in Rußland, Wirtschaft und Recht in Osteuropa, 1995, S. 155-156

Gesetz der Russischen Föderation "Über die operative Ermittlungstätigkeit" (Übersetzung, zus. mit T.J. Brendel), Jahrbuch für Ostrecht, Bd. XXXV/2 (1994), S. 308-316

Erster Verjährungsbeschluß des Ungarischen Verfassungsgerichts vom 3. März 1992 (Einführung), Jahrbuch für Ostrecht, Bd. XXXV/2 (1994), S. 391-393

Die Mafia wird dreister. Wie Rußland seine Richter schützt, Frankfurter Allgemeine Zeitung vom 7.8.1995, S. 8

Die Bestellung der Richter in Rußland, Recht in Ost und West, 1995, S. 165-169

Wie Rußland Wohnungen privatisiert. Manipulationen, Verbrechen, Rechtsverweigerung, Frankfurter Allgemeine Zeitung vom 16.10.1995, S. 16

Recht und Rechtspflege in Rußland nach dem Sozialismus, Jahrbuch für Ostrecht, Bd. XXXVI/1 (1995), S. 9-28

Streit um ein Kombinat. Schwieriger Föderalismus in Rußland, Frankfurter Allgemeine Zeitung vom 30.12.1995, S. 10

Wie in Rußland Gesetze entstehen. Der Präsident und alte Genossen, Frankfurter Allgemeine Zeitung vom 9.3.1996, S. 12

Gerichte und Richter in Rußland. Wirtschaft und Recht in Osteuropa, 1996, S. 161-163

Die Zukunft der russischen Militärgerichtsbarkeit, Osteuropa Recht, 1996, S. 156-159

Abkehr vom übertriebenen Staatsschutz. Neues Strafrecht für Rußland, Frankfurter Allgemeine Zeitung vom 20.8.1996, S. 10

Expertise on Russian Laws and Bills (zus. mit H. Lesage), Council of Europe, Parliamentary Assembly, Doc. AS/Jur (1996) 17 vom 11. März 1996, S. 9-15

Das neue russische Strafgesetzbuch, Juristenzeitung, 1997, S. 19-21; Überarbeiteter Nachdruck in F.-C. Schroeder (Hrsg.), Die neuen Kodifikationen in Rußland, 2. Aufl. 1999, S. 221-229

Ein Notruf der russischen Justiz. Für alles fehlt das Geld, Frankfurter Allgemeine Zeitung vom 25.3.1997, S. 14

Probleme der Gesetzgebung in Rußland. F.-C. Schroeder (Hrsg.), Die neuen Kodifikationen in Rußland, 1997, S. 9-26; 2. Aufl. 1999, S. 9-27

Etwas für entlassene Geheimpolizisten. Auftragsmorde in St. Petersburg, Frankfurter Allgemeine Zeitung vom 12.8.1997, S. 12

Die russische Verfassungsgerichtsbarkeit in der Praxis, Juristenzeitung, 1998, S. 132-134

Das neue russische Strafgesetzbuch im Lichte der Menschenrechte, Albin Eser (Hrsg.), Festschrift für Haruro Nishihara zum 70. Geburtstag, 1998, S. 486-495

Hohe Kriminalität und leere Kassen. Unerfüllte Programme in Rußland, Frankfurter Allgemeine Zeitung vom 9.3.1998, S. 16

„Verräter und räudige Hunde" - Die Justiz im Stalinismus, Der Rechtsstaat hat die Pflicht zur Wiederherstellung der Gerechtigkeit, Weber/Piazolo (Hrsg.), Justiz im Zwielicht. Ihre Rolle in Diktaturen und die Antwort des Rechtsstaates, München, 1998, S. 151-159, S. 321-324

Das Notariatswesen in Rußland, Jahrbuch für Ostrecht, Bd. XXXIX (1998), S. 13-21

Vom Gulag zum Guin. Die Neuordnung des Strafvollzugs in Rußland, Frankfurter Allgemeine Zeitung vom 24.2.1999, S. 16

Am Rande der Katastrophe. Alkoholmißbrauch in Rußland, Frankfurter Allgemeine Zeitung vom 23.7.1999, S. 12

Wie hoch ist die Kriminalität in Rußland? Beschönigung der Kriminalstatistik, Frankfurter Allgemeine Zeitung vom 22.11.1999, S. 16

Das neue Strafgesetzbuch von Belarus im Vergleich zum russischen und dem GUS-Modellstrafgesetzbuch, M. Hofmann/H. Küpper (Hrsg.), Kontinuität und Neubeginn. Staat und Recht in Europa zu Beginn des 21. Jahrhunderts. Festschr. für Georg Brunner aus Anlaß seines 65. Geburtstags, 2001, S. 324-335

„True" Law, „Façade" Law, Shadow Law, R. Clark/F. Feldbrugge/St. Pomorski (eds.), International and National Law in Russia and Eastern Europe. Essays in honour of George Ginsburgs, 2001, S. 355-360

Das Sowjetrecht als Grundlage der Prozesse gegen deutsche Kriegsgefangene, A. Hilger, U. Schmidt, G. Wagenlehner (Hrsg.), Sowjetische Militärtribunale. Bd. 1. Die Verurteilung deutscher Kriegsgefangener 1941-1953, 2001, S. 69-92

Das Ende der Dekoriertenamnestie. Entscheidung des russischen Verfassungsgerichts, Frankfurter Allgemeine Zeitung vom 20.11.2001, S. 16

Schutz des Grundeigentums in Rußland. Verfassungsgericht desavouiert Moskauer Stadtparlament, Frankfurter Allgemeine Zeitung vom 20.4.2002, S. 12

Das neue russische Wirtschaftsstrafrecht, Zeitschrift für die gesamte Strafrechtswissenschaft, 114. Band (2002), S. 215-235

Rußland und seine „gastarbajtery". Der Zustrom schafft Probleme, Frankfurter Allgemeine Zeitung vom 17.6.2002, S. 12

Kasernen zu Gefängnissen. Die Notlage des Strafvollzugs in Rußland, Frankfurter Allgemeine Zeitung vom 5.9.2002, S. 10

Fabrizierte Anklagen in Rußland. Jahrbuch für Ostrecht, Band 43 (2002), 1. Halbbd., S. 59-67

Raffgier oder vorsorgende Rechtspflege. Zehn Jahre freies Notariat in Rußland, Frankfurter Allgemeine Zeitung vom 20.8.2003, S. 10

Rechtsgrundlagen der Verfolgung deutscher Zivilisten durch Sowjetische Militärtribunale, A. Hilger, M. Schmeitzner, U. Schmidt (Hrsg.), Sowjetische Militärtribunale. Bd. 2: Die Verurteilung deutscher Zivilisten 1945-1955, 2003, S. 37-58; Kurzfassung unter dem Titel: Terrorjustiz in der Sowjetischen Besatzungszone. Militärtribunale urteilten ohne Rechtsgrundlage, Frankfurter Allgemeine Zeitung vom 8.4.2004, S. 14

Der Transplantationsskandal in Moskau. Streit um den „biologischen Tod", Frankfurter Allgemeine Zeitung vom 15.1.2004, S. 10

Ein Hohelied auf das Strafrecht, Juristenzeitung 2004, S. 347-348

Strafverfolgung in Rußland. Verwechslungen und Täuschungen, Frankfurter Allgemeine Zeitung vom 3.7.2004, S. 10

Die Änderungen des russischen Strafgesetzbuchs seit 1996, Osteuropa Recht 2004, S. 256-260

Grundrechtsschutz durch das russische Verfassungsgericht, Juristenzeitung 2005, S. 139-141

Abgenötigtes Sponsoring. Hilflosigkeit der russischen Strafverfolger, Frankfurter Allgemeine Zeitung vom 19.7.2006, S. 10

Die Sprache des russischen Strafgesetzbuches, D. Fischer (Hrsg.), Transformation des Rechts in Ost und West. Festschrift für Herwig Roggemann zum 70. Geburtstag, 2006, S. 199-202

Der Gleichheitsgrundsatz im Recht Osteuropas im 20. Jahrhundert, B Beck/R. Lühr (Hrsg.), Normen und Wertbegriffe in der Verständigung zwischen Ost- und Westeuropa, 2007, S. 197-202

Die scheinbare Wiedereinführung der Vermögenskonfiskation in Russland, Zeitschrift für die gesamte Strafrechtswissenschaft 119. Bd (2007), S. 450-458

Die russischen Strafvorschriften gegen Extremismus, Rußlandanalysen Nr. 149 (16.11.2007), S. 14-16

Grundsätze der Gerichtsverfassung der Union der Sozialistischen Sowjetrepubliken vom 29.10.1924, 1000 Schlüsseldokumente zur russischen und sowjetischen Geschichte (1917-1991) im Internet http://mdzx.bib-bvb.de/1000dok/start.html

Das Gesetz über die Gerichtsverfassung der UdSSR, der Unions- und der Autonomen Republiken vom 16.08.1938, 1000 Schlüsseldokumente zur russischen und sowjetischen Geschichte (1917-1991) im Internet http://mdzx.bib-bvb.de/1000dok/start.html

50 Jahre Institut für Ostrecht München, Jahrbuch für Ostrecht, Bd. 48 (2007), 2. Halbbd., S. 199-200

Etablierung der Rechtsstaatlichkeit in der Ukraine, B. Rill (Hrsg.), Die Ukraine – Partner der EU, 2008, S. 13-18

Antiwestliche Feindbilder. Angriffe auf Stipendiaten europäischer Stiftungen, Frankfurter Allgemeine Zeitung vom 29.07.2008, S. 10

Überlebenskampf der „Staats- und Rechtstheorie“ in Russland, Juristenzeitung 2008, S. 882-884

Russlands Richter unter Druck. Eingriffe in die Unabhängigkeit, Frankfurter Allgemeine Zeitung vom 29.12.2009, S. 8

B. Allgemeine Ostforschung

Die Erforschung der östlichen Westforschung in der Bundesrepublik Deutschland, Deutschland Archiv 1978, S. 34-35

Hundert Jahre Unabhängigkeit Rumäniens 1877-1977, Schriftenreihe des Regensburger Osteuropainstituts, Bd. 4 (Hrsg.), 1978

Die Westforschung des Ostens, Frankfurter Allgemeine Zeitung vom 18.9.1978

"Kommunistische" oder "sozialistische" Staaten? - Hintergründe der Begriffsbildung, Frankfurter Allgemeine Zeitung vom 19.10.1982, S. 12

Cliquenwirtschaft und Protektionswesen - Neue Schlagworte in der sowjetischen Publizistik, Frankfurter Allgemeine Zeitung vom 3.12.1982, S. 12

Erziehung zum Haß, Frankfurter Allgemeine Zeitung vom 13.6.1983, S. 10

Die Mauer als Schutz vor Störung - Der 13. August 1961 in der westdeutschen Publizistik, Frankfurter Allgemeine Zeitung vom 13.8.1983, S. 10

Lenin und der Terrorismus - Geschichtsfälschung in der DDR, Frankfurter Allgemeine Zeitung vom 21.1.1984, S. 10

C. Innerdeutsche Rechtsvergleichung und Rechtsprobleme der Wiedervereinigung

Die Strafgesetzgebung in Deutschland. Eine synoptische Darstellung der Strafgesetzbücher der Bundesrepublik Deutschland und der Deutschen Demokratischen Republik, 1972

Materialien zum Bericht zur Lage der Nation 1972 (Mitverfasser), Gutachten zum Stand der DDR- und vergleichenden Deutschlandforschung (Mitverfasser), 1978

Das Strafrecht des realen Sozialismus. Eine Einführung am Beispiel der DDR, 1983

Die strafrechtliche Entwicklung in Deutschland - Divergenz oder Konvergenz -, 1988 (Hrsg., zusammen mit Gottfried Zieger)

Bericht der Enquete-Kommission "Aufarbeitung von Geschichte und Folgen der SED-Diktatur in Deutschland", Deutscher Bundestage, Drucksache 12/7820, 1994 (Mitverfasser)

R. Eppelmann/H. Möller/G. Nooke/D. Wilms (Hrsg.), Lexikon des DDR-Sozialismus, 1996 (wiss. Betreuung der Artikel zu Recht und Polizei), 2. Aufl. 1997

Art. "Sowjetische Besatzungszone/Deutsche Demokratische Republik" (Rechtsentwicklung) im Evangelischen Staatslexikon, 1966, Sp. 1968-1994, 2. Aufl. 1975, Sp. 378-383, 3. Aufl. 1987, Sp. 482-491

Die neuere Entwicklung der Strafgesetzgebung in Deutschland, Juristenzeitung 1970, S. 393-396

Arbeitsscheu und Asozialität im Strafrecht der DDR. Zum Beschluß des Präsidiums des Obersten Gerichts vom 7. Januar 1971, Jahrbuch für Ostrecht, Bd. XII (1971)/1, S. 103 - 109

Gibt es noch ein deutsches Strafrecht? Ein Vergleich der Strafrechtsreform in beiden Teilen Deutschlands, Königsteiner Kreis 1971, 1-8 und Regensburger Universitätszeitung 1971, H. 4, S. 2-7

Kriegsverbrechen, Verbrechen gegen Frieden und Menschlichkeit im Recht beider deutscher Staaten, Deutschland Archiv 1973, S. 845-851

Ernüchterung in der Strafrechtpflege der DDR, Juristenzeitung 1973, S. 656-659

Schuld als Entscheidung. Zur Regelung der "Schuld" im Strafgesetzbuch der DDR, Jahrbuch für Ostrecht XIV/2 (1973), S. 9-35

Die Strafrechts- und Strafprozeßreform der DDR von 1974/75, Neue Juristische Wochenschrift 1977, S. 169-177; Kurzfassung in: Politik und Kultur 1977, H. 2, S. 15-25

Jugendstrafrecht und Jugendkriminalität der DDR im westdeutschen Schrifttum, Deutschland Archiv 1978, S. 497-500

Die neue Strafrechtsreform der DDR, Deutschland Archiv 1979, S. 1064-1076

Humanität mit Hintergründen - Die Geburtstags-Amnestie der DDR, Frankfurter Allgemeine Zeitung vom 7.11. 1979, S. 12

Aufwertung des Strafverteidigers in der DDR? Deutschland Archiv 1980, S. 130-132

Zunahme der Gewaltkriminalität in der DDR, Deutschland Archiv 1980, S. 282-284

Die Entwicklung der Kriminalität in der DDR 1979, Deutschland Archiv 1981, S. 845-849; Kurzfassung in: Frankfurter Allgemeine Zeitung vom 30.7.1981, S. 8

Probleme der DDR-Rechts-Forschung, in: Clemens Burrichter (Hrsg.), Deutschlandpolitik und Systemauseinandersetzung, 1982, S. 98-119

Der Kausalzusammenhang im Strafrecht der DDR. Sowjetsystem und Ostrecht (Festschrift für Boris Meissner zum 70. Geburtstag), hrsg. von G. Brunner, T. Schweisfurth, A. Uschakow, K. Westen, 1985, S. 499-514

Das Rechtssystem in der DDR - Strafrecht, Deutschland - Portrait einer Nation, Bd. 2: Gesellschaft - Staat - Recht, 1985, S. 427-431

Tendenzen in der Strafzumessung der DDR, Recht in Ost und West 1986, S. 338-340

Umdefinierung der Rechtssicherheit in der DDR, Recht in Ost und West 1987, S. 23-24; Kurzfassung unter dem Titel: "Die neue Rechtssicherheit der DDR", in: Frankfurter Allgemeine Zeitung vom 20.9.1986, S. 12

Widersprüche im Sozialismus? In der DDR wird über die Ursachen der Kriminalität gestritten, Frankfurter Allgemeine Zeitung vom 6.1.1987, S. 8

Eine Panne bei der Amnestie. Die DDR zwei Monate ohne Strafverfahren?, Frankfurter Allgemeine Zeitung vom 5.8.1987, S. 10

Geheime Rechtsprechungsanweisungen in der DDR (zusammen mit Dieter Gräf), Recht in Ost und West 1987, S. 291-294

Zweifel an der Asozialenkriminalisierung in der DDR, Juristenzeitung 1987, S. 1004-1008

Amnestie und Kriminalstatistik. Die Strafverfolgungslücke in der DDR, Frankfurter Allgemeine Zeitung vom 30. Dezember 1987, S. 10

Die "gesellschaftlichen Kräfte" im Strafverfahren der DDR, Recht in Ost und West 1988, S. 1-8

Die neuere Entwicklung des Strafrechts in beiden Staaten in Deutschland, in: G. Zieger/F.-C. Schroeder (Hrsg.), Die strafrechtliche Entwicklung in Deutschland - Divergenz oder Konvergenz -, 1988, S. 5-22; aktualisierte Fassung: Die neuere Entwicklung des Strafrechts in beiden deutschen Staaten, Aus Politik und Zeitgeschichte, Beilage zur Wochenzeitung "Das Parlament", B 4-5/88, S. 18-28

Zweideutige Betreuung. Strafentlassene in der DDR, Frankfurter Allgemeine Zeitung vom 10.5.1989, S. 14

Das 5. Strafrechtsänderungsgesetz der DDR, Recht in Ost und West 1989, S. 201-209; Kurzfassung unter dem Titel: Diplomatennötigung und Glücksspiel. Neue Strafvorschriften in der DDR, Frankfurter Allgemeine Zeitung vom 11.3.1989, S. 12

Menschenrechte im Strafverfahren und Strafvollzug, in: G. Brunner (Hrsg.), Menschenrechte in der DDR, 1989, S. 257-273

Was Juristen aus der DDR können. Nach-Ausbildung, eine zweite Prüfung?, Frankfurter Allgemeine Zeitung vom 22.12.1989, S. 16

Die Reaktion der DDR auf die "Perestrojka" auf dem Gebiet von Recht und Rechtsstaatlichkeit, in: K. Löw (Hrsg.), Beharrung und Wandel - Die DDR und die Reformen des Michail Gorbatschow, 1990, S. 19-29

Die Strafrechtsdogmatik in der DDR, Juristische Rundschau 1990, S. 89-93

Übernahme oder Rechtsangleichung? Der erste Juristentag der DDR, Frankfurter Allgemeine Zeitung vom 28.4.1990, S. 12

Die Strafgewalt des Staates, in: Bundesministerium für innerdeutsche Beziehungen (Hrsg.), Bürger und Staat (Materialien zur Lage der Nation), 1990, S. 251-282

Vorbeugen durch Teilnahme am Rechtswesen. Abschaffung eines modernen Prangers oder Verlust einer Konfliktregelung?, Frankfurter Allgemeine Zeitung vom 3.7.1990, S. 14

Ein Schritt zur Strafrechtseinheit. Neue Vorschriften in der DDR, Frankfurter Allgemeine Zeitung vom 31.7.1990, S. 8

Minderung um ein Drittel. Überhöhte und politisch motivierte Strafen in der DDR, Frankfurter Allgemeine Zeitung vom 29.9.1990, S. 12

Revolution mit Schonfristen. Versäumnisse bei Veränderungen in der DDR, Frankfurter Allgemeine Zeitung vom 9.10.1990, S. 10

The Rise and Fall of the Criminal Law of the German Democratic Republic, Criminal Law Forum, 1991, S. 217-233

Reformdruck aus dem Osten, Die politische Meinung 1991, 43-46

Der sexuelle Mißbrauch von Jugendlichen nach § 149 DDR-StGB, Deutsch-Deutsche Rechts-Zeitschrift 1991, S. 240-241

Antwort auf eine Umfrage zur Bewahrenswürdigkeit von DDR-Recht, Staat und Recht 1991, S. 137-138

Schadensersatzpflicht der PdS. Verantwortung für Tötung, Freiheitsberaubung und Umweltverseuchung, Frankfurter Allgemeine Zeitung vom 21.5.1991, S. 12

Fühlen Sie sich schuldig? Zum Umgang der Mächtigen in der einstigen DDR mit sich selbst, Frankfurter Allgemeine Zeitung vom 3.8.1991, S. 8

Unrechts-Altlasten des SED-Regimes. Strafrechtliche Probleme ihrer Beseitigung, Politische Studien, Sonderheft 1/1991, S. 37-43

Urteilsanmerkung (zum "mildesten" Gesetz im Verhältnis zur DDR), Juristische Rundschau 1991, S. 335-337

Urteilsanmerkung (zur Bedeutung der Strafzumessung bei der Ermittlung des "mildesten" Gesetzes), Juristische Rundschau 1991, S. 469-470

"Rehabilitierung" von SED-Opfern? Kritische Bemerkungen zum Gesetzentwurf der Bundesregierung, Zeitschrift für Rechtspolitik 1992, S. 41-42; Kurzfassung unter dem Titel: "Rehabilitierung" - ein Begriff, der in die Irre führt. Wann nimmt Bonn Abschied von einer belasteten Vokabel?, DIE WELT vom 15.11.1991, S. 2

Von "Siegerjustiz" gegen Honecker kann keine Rede sein. Ablenkungsmanöver bei der Verfolgung von Regierungskriminalität der Ex-DDR, DIE WELT vom 3.1.1992, S. 2

Urteilsanmerkung (zur Strafbarkeit von DDR-Spionen gegen in der Bundesrepublik stationierte USTruppen), Juristische Rundschau 1992, S. 205-206

Die Enquetekommission des Deutschen Bundestages "Aufarbeitung von Geschichte und von Folgen der SED-Diktatur in Deutschland", Politische Studien 1992, S. 23-27

War das DDR-Grenzgesetz Unrecht? Unterschiedliche Gerichtsurteile, Frankfurter Allgemeine Zeitung vom 24.12.1992, S. 12

Die Rechtswidrigkeit der Flüchtlingserschießungen zwischen Transzendenz und Immanenz, Juristische Rundschau 1993, S. 45-51

Juristische Schützenhilfe für das SED-Regime aus der Bundesrepublik, Deutschland Archiv 1993, S. 442-453; Kurzfassung unter dem Titel: Als es den roten Teppich für Honecker gab. Wie das SED-Regime juristische Unterstützung aus der Bundesrepublik bekam, Frankfurter Allgemeine Zeitung vom 9.11.92, S. 12, 13

Rückwirkung milderen Rechts und Wiedervereinigung, - Zugleich zum DDR-Wahlfälschungsurteil des BGH, NStZ 1993, S. 216-218; Kurzfassung unter dem Titel: Funktionärs-Kriminalität in der DDR. Zur fortwirkenden Strafbarkeit von Verstößen gegen vergangenes Recht, Frankfurter Allgemeine Zeitung vom 26.5.1993, S. 12

Strafrechtliche Verantwortlichkeit für die Ausübung politischer Strafjustiz in der ehemaligen DDR, Deutsche Wiedervereinigung. Die Rechtseinheit. Arbeitskreis Strafrecht. Bd. II. Die Verfolgung von Regierungskriminalität nach der Wiedervereinigung, hrsg. von E.-J. Lampe, 1993, S. 109-121

Haftung der PDS für Justizunrecht?, Deutsch-Deutsche Rechts-Zeitschrift, 1993, S. 203-204

Zur Verjährung von SED-Unrechtstaten, Zeitschrift für Rechtspolitik, 1993, S. 244-246; Nachdruck in C. Varga (ed.), Coming to Terms with the Past under the Rule of Law.The German and the Czech Models, Budapest 1994, S. 59-61

Rechtliche Aspekte der Aufarbeitung der DDR-Geschichte und SED-Herrschaft, Eisenmann/Hirscher (Hrsg.), Bilanz der zweiten deutschen Diktatur, 1993, S. 37-54

Wann war es Rechtsbeugung? Die Justiz aus DDR-Zeiten - eine Altlast, Frankfurter Allgemeine Zeitung vom 17.3.1994, S. 14

Der Generalbundesanwalt bleibt untätig. Als die DDR einen Angriffskrieg vorbereitete, Frankfurter Allgemeine Zeitung vom 2.5.1994, S. 14

Ein Haus an der Ostsee. Aus dem Korruptionsalltag der SED, Frankfurter Allgemeine Zeitung vom 30.5.1994, S. 14

Unrecht und Normalität im Recht der DDR, Rainer Eppelmann/Hartmut Koschyk / Peter Maser/Friedrich-Christian Schroeder / Dorothee Wilms / Roswitha Wisniewski, Die Diktatur der SED - Geschichte und Folgen (Aktuelle Fragen der Politik, hrsg. von der Konrad-Adenauer-Stiftung, H. 18), 1994, S. 21-28

Als die Stasi Postsendungen plünderte. DDR-Unrecht vor Gericht, Frankfurter Allgemeine Zeitung vom 7.1.1995, S. 8

Seltsames Urteil aus Rostock. Abermals: Ungeahndetes DDR-Unrecht, Frankfurter Allgemeine Zeitung vom 3.7.1995, S. 10

Die strafrechtliche Verfolgung von Unrechtstaten des SED-Regimes, G. Brunner (Hrsg.), Juristische Bewältigung des kommunistischen Unrechts in Osteuropa und Deutschland (Osteuropaforschung - Schriftenreihe der Deutschen Gesellschaft für Osteuropakunde, Bd. 34), 1995, S. 211-227

Die Ahndung des SED-Unrechts durch den Rechtsstaat, Aus Politik und Zeitgeschichte (Beilage zur Wochenzeitung Das Parlament), B 38/95, S. 17-29

Zuviel der Nachsicht. Unbefriedigende Entscheidungen des Bundesgerichtshofs zum Justizunrecht der DDR, Frankfurter Allgemeine Zeitung vom 31.10.1995, S. 16

Urteilsanmerkung (Rechtsbeugung durch DDR-Richter), NStZ 1995, S. 546

Die Strafbarkeit der Ausforschung der Bundesrepublik durch die DDR, Juristische Rundschau 1995, S. 441-445

Spitzfindig bis zum Grotesken. Der Bundesgerichtshof und das Justizunrecht der DDR, Frankfurter Allgemeine Zeitung vom 1.2.1996, S. 8

Geschichtsbewältigung durch Strafrecht?, Deutsche Richterzeitung 1996, S. 81-88

Das Recht als Herrschaftsinstrument der SED-Diktatur, E. Kuhrt (Hrsg.), Am Ende des realen Sozialismus. Bd. 1. Die SED-Herrschaft und ihr Zusammenbruch, 1996, S. 83-89

Die Rechtsprechung der DDR aus der Sicht des Bundesgerichtshofs, Heiner Timmermann (Hrsg.), Diktaturen in Europa im 20. Jahrhundert - der Fall DDR, 1996, S. 63-70

Stichwörter: Amnestie, Aufenthaltsbeschränkung, Kriminalität, Rechtsverständnis, sozialistische Gesetzlichkeit, Strafrecht, Todesstrafe, Verwaltungsrechtsschutz, wiss. Betreuung der Artikel zu Recht und Polizei, R. Eppelmann/H. Möller/G. Nooke/D. Wilms (Hrsg.), Lexikon des DDR-Sozialismus, 1996, 2. Aufl. 1997

Urteilsanmerkung (politische Verdächtigung in der DDR), NStZ 1997, S. 436-437

Volksvertreter in der Diktatur. Die Verantwortlichkeit der Volkskammer für das Unrecht in der DDR, Frankfurter Allgemeine Zeitung vom 23.9.1997, S. 16

Vom Unrechtssystem zum Systemunrecht. Wissenschaftliche Begriffswechsel und ihre Funktion, Frankfurter Allgemeine Zeitung vom 10.11.1997, S. 16

Die Verfolgung der DDR-Staatsverbrechen nach der Wiedervereinigung, K. Eckart/J. Hacker/S. Mampel (Hrsg.), Wiedervereinigung Deutschlands. Festschrift zum 20jährigen Bestehen der Gesellschaft für Deutschlandforschung (Schriftenreihe der Gesellschaft für Deutschlandforschung, Bd. 56), 1998, S. 399-416

Urteilsanmerkung („Rettung" von DDR-Flüchtlingen), Juristenzeitung 1998, S. 368; Populärwiss. Fassung: Gerettet für den Kerker. Noch ein Freispruch nach DDR-Unrecht, Frankfurter Allgemeine Zeitung vom 5.2.1998, S. 16

Urteilsanmerkung (zur Rechtsbeugung durch Überdehnung von Strafvorschriften), Juristenzeitung 1998, S. 911-912; Kurzfassung unter dem Titel: Adenauer als faschistische Provokation. Der Bundesgerichtshof und die DDR-Justiz, Frankfurter Allgemeine Zeitung vom 15.7.1998, S. 12

Fünfzig Jahre Königsteiner Kreis, Deutschland Archiv 1998, S. 709-711

Urteilsanmerkung (Aufnahme von Terroristen in der DDR), Juristische Rundschau 1998, S. 428-429

Die Ahndung des SED-Unrechts durch den Rechtsstaat, P.G. Klussmann/F. Hoffmann (Hrsg.), Die Opfer der SED-Diktatur: Ohnmacht und Protest (Kleine Schriften aus dem Institut für Deutschlandforschung, Reihe B, Nr. 1), 1999, S. 55-62

Die westdeutsche Wahrnehmung der DDR-Justiz in den siebziger und achtziger Jahren, in: Roger Engelmann/Clemens Vollnhals (Hrsg.), Justiz im Dienste der Parteiherrschaft. Rechtspraxis und Staatssicherheit in der DDR, 1999, 43-58, 2. Aufl. 2000, S. 43-58

Urteilsanmerkung (Rechtsbeugung in der DDR durch Verfahrens-„Drehbuch"), NStZ 1999, S. 620-621

Zehn Jahre strafrechtliche Aufarbeitung des DDR-Unrechts, Neue Juristische Wochenschrift 2000, S. 3017-3022

Die rechtliche Aufarbeitung der kommunistischen Vergangenheit in Deutschland (zus. m. H. Küpper), Schroeder/Küpper (Hrsg.), Die rechtliche Aufarbeitung der kommunistischen Vergangenheit in Osteuropa (Studien des Instituts für Ostrecht München, Bd. 63), 2010, 61-97

D. Überregionale Rechtsvergleichung, Völkerrecht und internationales bzw. interlokales Strafrecht

Der Schutz von Staat und Verfassung im Strafrecht. Eine systematische Darstellung, entwickelt aus Rechtsgeschichte und Rechtsvergleichung, 1970

Schroeder/Yenisey, Dürüst Yargilanma Hakki (Fair Trail), Istanbul 1997

Schroeder/Yenisey/Peukert, Ceza Muhakemesinde 'Fair Trial' ilkesi (Der Grundsatz des "fair trial" im Strafverfahren), Istanbul 1999

Schroeder/Yenisey, Ceza Muhakemesinde Adil Yargılanma Hakkı/Der Grundsatz des "fair trial" im Strafverfahren

Avrupa Birliği Sürecinde, Ceza Hukukunun Güncel Kaynaklari (Contemporary Sources of European

Criminal Law in the Way Leading to EC), Istanbul 2002, C VI.1

Art. "Völkermord" im Evangelischen Staatslexikon, 1966, Sp. 2425-2426, 2. Aufl. 1975, Sp. 2809-2811, 3. Aufl. 1987, Sp. 3872-2875

§ 92 StGB und die Vermittlung von Reisen in die SBZ, Recht in Ost und West 1967, S. 68-70

Die Rechtmäßigkeit des Krieges nach westlicher und sowjetischer Völkerrechtsauffassung, Völkerrecht in Ost und West, 1967, S. 178-218

Der "räumliche Geltungsbereich" der Strafgesetze, Goltdammer's Archiv für Strafrecht, 1968, S. 353-356

Der Schutz des äußeren Friedens im Strafrecht, Juristenzeitung 1969, S. 41-48

Schranken für den räumlichen Geltungsbereich des Strafrechts, Neue Juristische Wochenschrift 1969, S. 81-85

Die sowjetische Westforschung, Osteuropa Recht 1969, S. 357-362

Politische Delikte. Sowjetsystem und demokratische Gesellschaft. Eine vergleichende Enzyklopädie, Bd. V, 1972, S. 137-140

Die Notwehr als Indikator politischer Grundanschauungen, Festschrift für Reinhart Maurach zum 70. Geburtstag, 1972, S. 127-142

Zur Strafbarkeit der Fluchthilfe. Unter besonderer Berücksichtigung der Notwehrprobleme, Juristenzeitung 1974, S. 113-117; Kurzfassung in: Ist Fluchthilfe strafbar?, Frankfurter Allgemeine Zeitung vom 23.11.1973

Literaturbericht Rechtsvergleichung, Zeitschrift für die gesamte Strafrechtswissenschaft, Bd. 86, 1974, S. 917-942

Urteilsanmerkung (Ost-Berliner Grenztafeln als zum öffentlichen Nutzen dienende Gegenstände nach § 304 StGB), Juristenzeitung 1976, S. 100-101; Kurzfassung in: Seltsames von der West-Berliner Justiz, Frankfurter Allgemeine Zeitung vom 3.2.1976, S. 6

Die Kriminalisierung der Fluchthilfe ist unzulässig, Zeitschrift für Rechtspolitik, 1976, S. 32-34

Urteilsanmerkung (Begehungsort einer Straftat), Neue Juristische Wochenschrift 1976, S. 490

Der Rhein-Main-Donau-Kanal und die Sowjets, Frankfurter Allgemeine Zeitung vom 30.6.1977, S. 10; abgedruckt auch in: Die Bundesbahn 1977, S. 590-591, Der bayerische Steuerzahler 1977, Nr. 8, S. XI, St. Galler Tagblatt vom 4.10.1977, S. 9

Das Grundgesetz im Rücken. Die Bundesregierung und die kommerzielle Fluchthilfe, Frankfurter Allgemeine Zeitung vom 1.3.1978, S. 12; auszugsweise unter dem Titel "Umstrittene Fluchthilfe" im St. Galler Tagblatt vom 3.5.1978

Das interdeutsche Strafrecht vor und nach Roggemann, Deutschland Archiv 1978, S. 708-710

Strafrechtliche Probleme im Verhältnis zwischen der Bundesrepublik Deutschland und der DDR, Deutschland Archiv 1978, S. 854-864

Die Westforschung des Ostens, Frankfurter Allgemeine Zeitung vom 18.9.1978

Notwehr bei Flucht aus der DDR, Neue Juristische Wochenschrift 1978, S. 2577-2579

Rechts- und Wirtschaftsprobleme bei der Kooperation von deutschen Unternehmen und jugoslawischen Organisationen assoziierter Arbeit, Schriftenreihe des Regensburger Osteuropainstituts, Bd. 5, 1978 (Hrsg.)

Die Donauhoheit für ein Linsengericht?, Frankfurter Allgemeine Zeitung vom 28.9.1979, S. 12

Rechtsstaat und "sozialistische Gesetzlichkeit", Aus Politik und Zeitgeschichte, Beilage zur Wochenzeitung "Das Parlament", B 3/80, S. 3-15

Methodenprobleme der Ostrechtsforschung, B. Meissner/H. Roggemann/K. Westen/F.-C. Schroeder Grundsatzfragen der Ostrechtsforschung (Studien des Instituts für Ostrecht, München, Bd. 28), 1980, 79-102

Gefahren der rechtsvergleichenden Methode in der Ostrechtswissenschaft, K. Westen - B. Meissner - F.-C. Schroeder (Hrsg.), Der Schutz der individuellen Rechte und Interessen im Recht sozialistischer Staaten, 1980, S. 235-238

Urteilsanmerkung (Geltung des StGB für Taten in der DDR), Neue Zeitschrift für Strafrecht 1981, S. 179-181

Strafen zum Heimattarif? - Probleme der Strafzumessung bei Ausländern, Frankfurter Allgemeine Zeitung vom 13.10.1983, S. 12

Literaturbericht Rechtsvergleichung, Zeitschrift für die gesamte Strafrechtswissenschaft, Bd. 96, 1984, S. 917-942

Bestrafung hier - oder im Heimatstaat? - Neue Rechtsinstitute im Widerstreit, Frankfurter Allgemeine Zeitung vom 16.2.1985, S. 10

The Two Legal Levels of East-West Trade 20, Journal of East and West Studies, Vol. XV, No. 1, 1986, 165-179 = New Directions in East-West Relations - German and Korean Perspectives - (East and West Studies Series 2), ed. by D. Kim and W. Gumpel, 1987, S. 109-123

Die Übertragung der Strafvollstreckung, Zeitschrift für die gesamte Strafrechtswissenschaft Bd. 98, 1986, S. 457-485

Rechtfertigung und Entschuldigung im deutschen Strafrecht im Vergleich zum sowjetischen, A. Eser/G. Fletcher, Rechtfertigung und Entschuldigung - Rechtsvergleichende Perspektiven, Bd. I, 1987, S. 523-547

Methoden und Probleme der Vergleichung zwischen westlichen und östlichen Rechtssystemen, Law in East and West/Recht in Ost und West, Festschrift zum 30-jährigen Jubiläum des Instituts für Rechtsvergleichung der Waseda Universität, Tokio, 1988, S. 213-230; in japanischer Sprache in: Comparative Law Review, Vol. 22, Nr. 1, 1988

Urkundenfälschung mit Auslandsberührung, Neue Juristische Wochenschrift 1990, S. 1406-1407

Der Geltungsbereich der Menschenrechte in den Stadien des Strafverfahrens, 140 Goltdammer's Archiv für Strafrecht, hrsg. von J. Wolter, 1993, S. 205-213

Die Prozesse aus rechtlicher Sicht, G. Wagenlehner (Hrsg.), Stalins Willkürjustiz gegen die deutschen Kriegsgefangenen, 1993, S. 48-51

Der XVI. Internationale Strafrechtskongreß der Association Internationale de Droit Pénal, Bericht über die Verhandlungen der III. Sektion: Strafrecht Prozessualer Teil, ZStW Band 112 (2000), S. 716-717

Entschließungen des XVI. Internationalen Strafrechtskongresses in Budapest 1999 Sektion III Strafrecht, Prozessualer Teil, Empfehlungen (Übersetzung), ZStW Band 112 (2000), S. 731-733

Die Gesamtprüfung der Verfahrensfairness durch den EGMR, Goltdammer's Archiv für Strafrecht, 2003, S. 293-298

Faires Strafverfahren in Europa. Das Grünbuch der Europäischen Kommission, Frankfurter Allgemeine Zeitung vom 15.12.2003, S. 10

Probleme der Übersetzung von Gesetzestexten, Zeitschrift für die gesamte Strafrechtswissenschaft, 117. Bd. (2005), S. 236-244

Chodorkowskij und die Menschenrechte. Ein Fall für den Europäischen Gerichtshof, Frankfurter Allgemeine Zeitung vom 15.6.2005, S. 8

Urteilsanmerkung (Auslieferung an Rußland), StV 2005, S. 401-402

Gefahren des europäischen Strafrechts. Besteht ein Demokratiedefizit?, Frankfurter Allgemeine Zeitung vom 01.08.2006, S. 10

Ein merkwürdiger Tag des Sieges. Der Partisanenkrieg vor dem Gerichtshof für Menschenrechte, Frankfurter Allgemeine Zeitung vom 10.09.2008, S. 10

Erweiterte Fassung in: Der EGMR und die Bestrafung stalinistischer Verbrechen (zus. m. H. Küpper), Jahrbuch für Ostrecht, Bd. 50 (2009), 1. Halbbd., S. 213-266

Schranken für das europäische Strafrecht. Ein „Manifest zur Europäischen Kriminalpolitik“, Frankfurter Allgemeine Zeitung vom 5.3.2010, S. 10

Streit um die Geschichte. Partisanenverbrechen vor dem Menschenrechtegerichtshof, Frankfurter Allgemeine Zeitung vom 30.6.2010, S. 8

E. Herausgeberschaft und ständige Mitarbeit an Zeitschriften und Reihen

Herausgeber der „Strafrechtlichen Abhandlungen, neue Folge“ (Bd. 62-143 zus. m. E. Schmidhäuser, ab Bd. 198 zus. m. A. Hoyer))

Herausgeber des "Jahrbuchs für Ostrecht"

Mitherausgeber der Zeitschrift "Osteuropa Recht"

Mitherausgeber der Zeitschrift „Politik und Kultur“ (1974-1990)

Mitwirkung bei der Herausgabe der "Juristenzeitung", "Juristische Rundschau", "Jura - Juristische Ausbildung" und von "Recht in Ost und West" (bis 1998)

Ständiger Mitarbeiter von "Goltdammer's Archiv für Strafrecht"

Ständiger Mitarbeiter der "Frankfurter Allgemeine Zeitung"